SURVEY OF LONDON
VOLUME XLV

All Saints' Church, Ennismore Gardens. From a watercolour by R. L. Roumieu of *c*.1860 showing the original west front and Roumieu's own unexecuted design for the campanile. On the right are Nos 64–65 Ennismore Gardens, and to the left the backs of Nos 1–11 Princes Gate

SURVEY OF LONDON

GENERAL EDITOR: JOHN GREENACOMBE

VOLUME XLV

Knightsbridge

THE ATHLONE PRESS
Published for English Heritage
2000

First published 2000 by
THE ATHLONE PRESS
1, Park Drive, London NW11 7SG,
and New Brunswick, New Jersey

for

ENGLISH HERITAGE

© Crown copyright 2000

British Library Cataloguing in Publication Data
Survey of London
    Volume XLV: Knightsbridge
    I. Architecture — England —London
    I. Greenacombe, John   II. English Heritage

    ISBN 0 485 48245 2

Library of Congress Cataloging-in-Publication Data
Knightsbridge/general editor, John Greenacombe.
    p.   cm.   — (Survey of London; v. 45)
    "Published for English Heritage."
    Includes bibliographical references and index.
    ISBN 0-485-48245-2 (cloth)
    1. Knightsbridge (London, England)—Buildings, structures, etc.
    2. Historic Buildings — England — London. I. Greenacombe,
    John, 1941–. II. English Heritage.   III. Series.
    DA675.J6   vol. 45
    [DA685.K58]
    942.1—dc21

                                   98–49246
                                      CIP

Distributed in the United States, Canada and South America by
Transactions Publishers
390 Campus Drive
Somerset, New Jersey 08873

Designed by Wolfgang Klär
Typeset, printed and bound in Great Britain by
BAS Printers, Over Wallop, Hampshire

Preface

Knightsbridge, the forty-fifth volume of the Survey of London, is the first of the series to be published under the aegis of English Heritage, which took over responsibility for the work of the Survey on its amalgamation with the Royal Commission on the Historical Monuments of England in 1999. English Heritage is proud to have been entrusted with a project which its idealistic founder, the architect C. R. Ashbee, conceived of in terms far broader than mere antiquarianism and architectural history. His aim for the Survey was:

> to make nobler and more humanly enjoyable the life of the great city ... and to stimulate among her citizens that historic and social conscience which to all great communities is their most sacred possession.

Poised between the West End and Kensington, the subject of the present volume is a district without precise boundaries yet is clearly established in the popular imagination. 'Knightsbridge' has long since become a byword for exclusive shops and smart homes for the rich. In some respects no greater contrast can be imagined between this area and that last studied by the Survey – Poplar, Blackwall and the Isle of Dogs. The one, huge in extent, an old dockland and industrial area with a high proportion of public housing, which since the mid-1980s has seen urban regeneration on an unprecedented scale; the other small and up-market, consisting largely of private residences – nineteenth-century terraces, Edwardian mansion blocks, twentieth-century flats and desirable mews houses – interspersed with shops, hotels and restaurants. But as this volume shows, Knightsbridge has a more richly varied past than its present face may suggest – a largely forgotten world of music-halls and dubious boarding-houses, of exhibition rooms and skating-rinks, and the famous Tattersalls' horse-mart on Knightsbridge Green. Among its more remarkable landmarks were a towering factory for making floorcloth and a brightly coloured Chinese pagoda which ended its days in a public park in Hackney in the 1950s.

Many local people have helped in the preparation of this book, and English Heritage is grateful to them all, and particularly to those residents who very kindly gave the staff access to their homes, and allowed photographs to be taken and drawings made.

This volume has been prepared under the direction of the General Editor, John Greenacombe, who with Philip Temple edited all the material. It was researched and written by Alan Cox, John Greenacombe, Harriet Richardson, Ann Robey, Philip Temple, Colin Thom and Rosalind Woodhouse. Additional material was provided by Tara Draper, Michael Goldman, Paul Hutchings and Sonia Larsen. The drawing programme was carried out by Michael F. Clements and Malcolm Dickson, and the photography by Sid Barker and Derek Kendall.

NEIL COSSONS
Chairman
English Heritage

Acknowledgements

English Heritage thanks Her Majesty Queen Elizabeth II for gracious permission to use material from the Royal Archives. Grateful acknowledgement is also made to the numerous individuals and institutions who have assisted in the preparation of this book, particularly the following:

Malcolm Airs; Francis Baden-Powell; Victor Belcher; Neil Bingham; Nicholas Black; Anthony Blee; Frank E. Boswell; Simon Bradley; Sarah Brown; Diana Burfield; Bridget Cherry; Pamela Clark; Rafe Clutton; Mary Cosh; George Crabb; Dr A. E. L. Davis; Jeffrey Davis; W. T. S. Digby-Seymour; James Douet; the late Marie Draper; Rev. Dr R. W. D. Fenn; Fr Alexander Fostiropoulos; Brian Girling; Lord Gladwyn; Nicholas Guttridge; John Harris; Richard Hewlings; Hermione Hobhouse; Michael Howarth; David C. Humphreys; Derek Keene; Nick Kimber; Giulia King; Fr Lawrence King; Hon. C. Lennox-Boyd; Rosa Maria Letts; Thomas Lloyd; Nancy McKay; M. P. Mandrigin; Martin Meade; Linda Merrill; Lady (Isabella) Naylor-Leyland; Louis P. Nelson; Jeanette Parsons; Anne Riches; John Martin Robinson; Lucy Roe; Julie Ronald; Countess of Rosebery; Vernon Russell-Smith; late Duke of Rutland; Andrew Saint; Charles Sebag-Montefiore; Carol Seymour-Newton; Betty C. Slaven; Dan Smith; Peter Smith; Geoffrey P. Stell; Adam Tihany; Jackie Turner; Kathleen Villiers-Tuthill; the late Clive Wainwright; Isobel Watson; Lady Willoughby de Eresby; Diana Willson; Joan Winterkorn; Mrs P. S. Wolfston; Giles Worsley; Laetitia Yeandle.

Aerofilms Ltd; ASK Planning; BBC; British Library; Buckinghamshire Record Office; Centre for Global Energy Studies; Church of England Record Centre; Cluttons; Cluttons Daniel Smith (Alan Flint); Conway Library; Corporation of London Record Office; *Country Life* Picture Library; Danish Club; Denbighshire Record Office; (West) Devon Record Office; Deutsche Evangelische Christuskirche; W. A. Ellis (Michael Duncan); Family History Centre; Farrer & Company; Fine Art Society; Flintshire Record Office; Free Library of Philadelphia; Freer Gallery, Washington, DC; Friends House Library; Guildhall Library, Corporation of London; Guardian Media Group; Gwent Record Office; Hammersmith Archives and Local History Centre; Harrods Ltd; Harvey Nichols; Heber-Percy & Parker Architects; Hobart Slater; Household Cavalry (Lieut. Julian Barnard); Household Cavalry Museum; Hulton Getty Picture Collection; Hunter & Partners; Imperial College of Science, Technology and Medicine, Archives (Ann Barrett), Estates Division (Stuart Murray) and Management School (Professor David Norburn); Institute of Historical Research; Iranian Embassy; Kensington & Chelsea Libraries (Local Studies); Knightsbridge Association; Kylemore Abbey; Lincolnshire Archives; London Library; London Metropolitan Archives (Tim Harris, Harriet Jones, Louise Falcini); London Transport Museum; Mandarin Oriental Hyde Park; Montessori St Nicholas Centre; Mouchel & Partners; National Archives of Canada; National Art Library (V & A); National Farmers' Union; National Library of Wales; Pierpont Morgan Library, New York; Public Record Office; Quaritchs; RCAHM Scotland; RIBA (British Architectural Library); RoSPA; Royal Academy of Arts; Royal Academy of Dancing; Royal Archives (Pamela Clark); Royal College of General Practitioners; Royal Engineers Library, Brompton Barracks; Royal Parks Agency; Russian Orthodox Cathedral of the Dormition of the Mother of God and All Saints; St George's Hospital Archives; Schlesinger Library, Radcliffe College, Cambridge, Mass.; Ann Scott Associates; Sheraton Park Tower Hotel; Tattersalls; Theatre Museum; Trevor Estate Ltd; University of Nottingham, Department of Manuscripts & Special Collections; Victoria & Albert Museum, Print Room & Picture Library; Watney Mann; Wellcome Institute Library; Westminster Abbey Library (Tony Trowles); City of Westminster, Archives Centre (Elizabeth Cory, Alison Kenney, John Sargent), Building Control (Colin French), and Planning Department.

In addition, the help and co-operation of all those owners, occupiers and agents who have allowed access to properties for inspection and recording is gratefully acknowledged.

Owners of photographs and other illustrations reproduced in these volumes are acknowledged in the List of Plates.

Contents

Plates *at end*

List of Figures

BAL   British Architectural Library, Royal Institute of British Architects
LMA London Metropolitan Archives
NMR National Monuments Record
OS   Ordnance Survey
PRO Public Record Office
WBC Westminster City Council Building Control Department
WCA Westminster City Archives

All the figures were drawn by Michael F. Clements, unless otherwise indicated

Select list of abbreviations used in the figures

a	area	L	lift
B	bedroom	Lav	lavatory
Bth	bathroom	LR	living-room
cpd	cupboard	MR	morning room
dr	dressing-room	PH	public house
DR	dining-room	SB	servant's bedroom
DrR	drawing-room	Sh	shower
H	hall	sc	scullery
Htg	heating	st	store
K	kitchen	wc	water-closet

List of Plates

BAL   British Architectural Library, Royal Institute of British Architects
GL   Guildhall Library, Corporation of London
KLS   Royal Borough of Kensington & Chelsea, Education and Libraries, Kensington Local Studies
LMA   London Metropolitan Archives
NMR   National Monuments Record
RCHME Royal Commission on the Historical Monuments of England
V&A   Victoria and Albert Museum
WCA   Westminster City Archives

Frontispiece. All Saints' Church, Ennismore Gardens, c.1860. *Watercolour by R. L. Roumieu in BAL (Drawings Collection, W15/41)*

Black and white

1. Knightsbridge, c.1905. *NMR photograph (DD87/00033)*

2–3. (a) *Extracts from Joshua Rhodes's* Topographical Survey of the Parish of Kensington ..., *1766; photographs by courtesy of KLS (L/5902, 5904)*
(b) *Extracts from* A Representation of ... a sham engagement in Hyde Park, *1799;* © *The British Museum (Crace Collection, 9/89)*

4. *Extracts from a watercolour of 1811 by Joseph Salway, reproduced by permission of the British Library (Add. MS 31325)*

5. (a), (b) *Extracts from a watercolour of 1811 by Joseph Salway, reproduced by permission of the British Library (Add. MS 31325)*
(c) *Extract from R. Horwood,* A Plan of the Cities of London & Westminster ..., *1813 edition*

6. (a) *Detail from a watercolour by G. R. Vawser, senior, c.1846, in GL (Pr W2/KNI)*
(b) *Detail from* Aeronautical View of the Palace of Industry for All Nations, *lithograph by C. Burton, published by Ackerman & Company, 1851; V&A (H.174)*

7. *Detail from* A Trihedral View of the Palace for the Exhibition of the Industrial Products of Mankind, *lithograph by C. P. B. Shelley and H. H. Treppass, published by Ackerman & Company, 1851; V&A (Museum No. 106.A.26 (103); photo BW45315)*

8. Knightsbridge in 1963. *Aerofilms photograph (A121362)*

9. (a) Old houses east of Old Barrack Yard in 1854. *Watercolour by T. H. Shepherd,* © *The British Museum (Crace Collection, 10/28)*
(b) St George's Place in the 1830s. *Engraving by R. Osborn, reproduced from a St George's Hospital House Committee dinner menu, 1934 (Wellcome Institute Library photograph)*
(c) Nos 1–11 Knightsbridge in 1939. *Photograph courtesy of Anthony Blee*

10. (a) Knightsbridge, c.1910. *Hulton Getty Picture Collection photograph (T51235)*
(b) Nos 11–13 Knightsbridge, c.1914. *London Transport Museum photograph (25706)*
(c) Nos 33–45 Knightsbridge in 1963. *NMR photograph (AA63/06633)*

11. (a) Entrance to the Chinese Collection exhibition hall, St George's Place. *From W. B. Langdon,* A Descriptive Catalogue of the Chinese Collection ..., *1842, frontispiece*
(b) Nos 19–23 Knightsbridge, c.1946. *NMR photograph (BB95/04833)*
(c) Interior of the Chinese Collection exhibition hall, c.1842. *Engraving by J. Shury, in GL (W2/HYD/COR)*

12–13. No. 15 Knightsbridge, c.1897. *Baden-Powell family photographs reproduced by kind permission of Francis Baden-Powell*

14. Woollands
(a) Perspective view. *From* The Building News, *23 February 1900, p.279*
(b) Showrooms in 1899. *Bedford Lemere photograph in the NMR (BL 15362c)*

15. Harvey Nichols. *RCHME photographs (NMR BB96/00859, BB99/00525, BB96/00858)*

16. Knightsbridge, south side in 1996. *RCHME photographs (NMR BB96/00849, 00846, 00850)*

17. (a) Berkeley Hotel, Knightsbridge front in 1996. *RCHME photograph (NMR BB96/00852)*
(b) No. 60 Knightsbridge in 1993. *RCHME photograph (NMR BB93/23495)*
(c) Sheraton Park Tower Hotel, c.1973. *Photograph by courtesy of the Sheraton Park Tower Hotel*

Introduction

A name without a town

In the social hierarchy of London place-names, Knightsbridge ranks among the highest. Few others, whether of streets or districts – Knightsbridge is both – can match its power to evoke glamorous images of affluence and exclusivity. But for all its *réclame* (which is of fairly recent origin), Knightsbridge can present something of a puzzle to the visitor expecting a particular spirit of place. The district shades almost imperceptibly into the neighbouring areas of South Kensington, Chelsea, and Belgravia. And despite Knightsbridge's fame as a shopping centre, the thoroughfare itself, for much of its length, is conspicuously not a shopping street at all.

In broad terms, Knightsbridge describes the area immediately south of Hyde Park, stretching from Hyde Park Corner to the museums area of South Kensington, but its southern extent is indeterminate, and always has been. Modern-day Knightsbridge, as defined by popular usage and estate-agents' particulars, takes in substantial portions of northern Chelsea and eastern South Kensington, including Lowndes Square and areas formerly thought of as parts of Brompton and Hans Town. The present volume is restricted to a relatively small part of this 'greater Knightsbridge' (see figure 1 on page 18).

The vagueness of Knightsbridge's southern limits is partly accounted for by a lack of defining topographical features; unlike districts such as Mayfair, Soho and Fitzrovia, it is not confined within a more or less continuous perimeter of streets. Nor has it ever been an administrative entity. As far back as 1857, when bricks and mortar were spreading fast over the remaining unbuilt ground in the vicinity, a local inhabitant (apropos a reported 'town without a name') dubbed Knightsbridge a 'name without a town' on the grounds that, deserving parish status itself, it was split between no fewer than four parishes. This circumstance he believed (incorrectly) to be the result of 'encroachments' on an anciently independent community.[1] In his *Memorials of the Hamlet of Knightsbridge*, completed at this same time, Henry George Davis also made the point that the district was 'absurdly divided' and should have become a separate parish, but attempted no exact definition of its extent. If anything he contributed to the uncertainty by adding much of the 'immediate neighbourhood' to his area of study, including the district parish of St Paul's, Wilton Place, and thus a portion of Pimlico extending as far as the Thames.[2] Knightsbridge, however, never did achieve administrative independence, nor did it emerge from its Victorian expansion with a clear sense of its own identity.[a]

Reginald Colby, writing in the mid-1960s, pointed out that 'Knightsbridge has become larger as it has become more fashionable', and that many 'Knightsbridge' residents and shops are really in Brompton.[3] The process of expansion continues today. Between Knightsbridge and Brompton in particular, however, there has long been a confusion. The sensational authoress Harriette Wilson, living in Trevor Square in the 1820s, seems to have used the names interchangeably in her address.[4] Knightsbridge was not then a name to conjure with, and it was not really until after the Second World War that it took on much of its contemporary lustre. At the eastern end of Knightsbridge, for instance, the Alexandra Hotel, destroyed in the Second World War, gave its location as Hyde Park Corner, not Knightsbridge, in its advertisements.

The identification of Knightsbridge as a district rather than merely a street was doubtless helped in the twentieth century by the use of the single word to describe the road west of Hyde Park Corner,

---

[a] The 'parish' assigned in 1849 to the new church of All Saints, Ennismore Gardens, took in most of the historic hamlet of Knightsbridge, as well as parts of Kensington, but had no civil administrative function.

and, in consequence, the underground station at the top of Sloane Street and Brompton Road. Until 1903, present-day Knightsbridge, often loosely known as Knightsbridge Road, was officially divided into no fewer than eight components: St George's Place, Lowndes Terrace, Middle Row, High Road, Trevor Terrace and South Place on the south side, Park Side and Albert Gate on the north, all of which had distinct connotations of status. Two further names, High Row and Albert Terrace, had been abolished in 1877. Knightsbridge Road might well have seemed the obvious choice for the consolidated name, and had in fact been suggested years earlier,[5] but plain 'Knightsbridge' was chosen instead, and this became the name of one of the new Piccadilly Line stations, opened in December 1906. (The adjacent stations on the line were Hyde Park Corner, with a surface building at Nos 11–13 Knightsbridge, now the Pizza on the Park, and Brompton Road, long since closed.) The influence of tube stations in redefining the names of various parts of London is, of course, an irresistible one. In recent years, the association of Harrods with Knightsbridge, assiduously promoted by the Brompton Road store, and Harrods' international fame, has done much to further the public perception of Knightsbridge as a district, and added to its desirability as an address.

The area shown in figure 1 has no real claim to integrality as a district of modern London. It does, however, correspond to all intents and purposes with the historic hamlet of Knightsbridge as it existed by the early nineteenth century, when the first new streets and squares south of the Knightsbridge–Kensington road were laid out. Exhibition Road, a creation of the 1850s, is taken as the westernmost limit. Apsley House and the Lanesborough Hotel (formerly St George's Hospital) are both excluded, as more properly belonging to Hyde Park Corner than Knightsbridge. The Knightsbridge or Hyde Park Barracks, on the other hand, is included, although actually built on part of Hyde Park itself, generally considered quite distinct from Knightsbridge. It carries on the line of building adjoining the park along most of the north side of Knightsbridge.

The greater part of the area belonged to a detached portion of the ancient parish of St Margaret, Westminster, which extended westwards of Exhibition Road and also covered part of Hyde Park. On the north side of Knightsbridge the buildings east of the entrance to Albert Gate, and on the south side those east of William Street, belong historically to the parish of St George, Hanover Square, itself formed in the early eighteenth century out of the much older parish of St Martin-in-the-Fields. The line of the Westbourne river, which passes beneath Albert Gate, marks the boundary between the two parishes here. The short stretch of frontage between William Street and Sloane Street also belongs to the old parish of St Margaret, but the ground immediately south is part of St Luke, Chelsea.

On the north side of Brompton Road, the boundary between St Margaret's parish and St Mary Abbots, Kensington, runs through individual properties and has never been of significance in building-development terms. The developments fronting Brompton Road on its north side, including the V & A, Brompton Oratory and Brompton Square, are described in volumes XXXVIII and XLI of the *Survey*; some slight overlap between these volumes and the present work occurs north-east of Lancelot Place, and in Exhibition Road immediately north of the V & A. With very minor exceptions, the entire area described is today part of the City of Westminster.

Not only was Knightsbridge split administratively from an early date, but there was little in the way of other defining limits, topographical or proprietorial, to encourage the eventual suburb towards a particularly distinct identity. Inevitably, the various portions took on much of the character of the adjacent areas as they developed. Nowhere is this more obvious today than in western Knightsbridge, between Rutland Gate and Exhibition Road, an area scarcely distinguishable in architectural character from much of neighbouring South Kensington (of which it is often assumed to be a continuation). There is a close affinity, too, between the area of Trevor and Montpelier Squares and the adjoining parts of Brompton, and at the eastern end of the area the pull exerted by Belgravia was considerable, though only apparent today at Albert Gate, where mansions of a distinctly Belgravian character flank the park entrance. To some extent, stylistic similarities may simply reflect the involvement of the same developers – James Bonnin and John Gooch in Brompton and in Trevor and Montpelier Squares, C. J. Freake in South Kensington and western Knightsbridge, and Thomas Cubitt in Belgravia and at Albert Gate.

Old Knightsbridge

Several factors contributed to Knightsbridge's potential for development as a fashionable suburb. In the first place, it was situated on one of the most important approach roads to the capital, 'scarcely more remote from the houses of parliament, & the places of gay resort, than several of the fashionable squares of London'.[6] There were natural and scenic advantages to the situation, too, less obvious today. The ground, sloping gently down towards the south, was sheltered and well-drained, giving rise to a reputation for salubrity. This was one of the reasons for the choice of Lanesborough House as the new St George's Hospital in 1733, giving patients 'the Benefit of a Country Air'.[7] As well as Hyde Park, there were splendid views to the south over the Thames Valley and the Downs, a strong likely selling-point for building ground, as an advertisement of 1764 for a site adjoining Kingston House makes clear:

The beautiful Situation and Prospect of this Ground are beyond all Description; and therefore whoever has a Mind to treat for it and take it, may have opportunity of judging for themselves, if they will take the Trouble to go to the Ground, and see it from a Stage erected upon it for that purpose.[8]

But set against these general attractions were negative factors. In the first place, other than at the western end of Knightsbridge, land for building was confined to narrow roadside strips, formerly manorial 'waste', which offered limited scope for formal and large-scale urban planning. Moreover, by the late eighteenth century, when pressure for the expansion of the West End was growing intense, most of this roadside ground had already been built up, much of it in the 1720s and '30s. The western part of the hamlet, west of the Green, between the Kensington and Brompton roads, consisted of comparatively broad acres, but a good deal of this area was occupied as the gardens and grounds of a series of large private houses. Though the remainder was only nursery ground and pasturage or market gardens, Knightsbridge as a whole offered limited virgin territory to the prospective developer, and much of the new building in Knightsbridge from the early nineteenth century therefore involved some measure of redevelopment. Hardly a trace remains of the old Knightsbridge today, and then only in the pattern of development here and there, but as recently as the 1930s several eighteenth-century buildings survived.

Our picture of the old hamlet is essentially that drawn up by H. G. Davis in the mid-nineteenth century, its more vivid features endlessly repeated by later writers with little or no attempt at modification. The terrible state of the road, the dangers of footpads and highwaymen, the bad reputation of the inns, secret or runaway marriages at the local chapel, all feature prominently.

The road had long been notorious for its badness and the risk of assault. In 1736 Lord Hervey, writing to his mother from Kensington, made the remark, quoted by Davis, that 'the road between this place and London is grown so infamously bad, that we live here in the same solitude as we should do if cast on a rock in the middle of the ocean, and all the Londoners tell us there is between them and us a great gulf of mud'.[9] Legislation was sought in 1724 for improving the paving; more than sixty years later representations were made to the architect and builder Henry Holland about obtaining a Knightsbridge paving Act, to prevent so many ladies 'from being lamed and crippled by the excessive pickedness and asperity of the stones and pebbles between Hyde Park Corner and Sloane Street'.[10] In the early nineteenth century, 'modern paving' was only laid at Knightsbridge Terrace, a short row of houses on the south side of the road.[11] In 1826 an Act of Parliament placed the roadway itself under the control of a board of metropolitan turnpike commissioners.[12]

While the conniving nature of Knightsbridge innkeepers may to some extent be a matter of legend rather than fact, wayfarers were often in real danger. The nineteenth-century writer Thomas Allen quotes an annotation, probably Elizabethan, to Norden's *Speculum Britanniae* on the perils of Knightsbridge, 'where I wish no good man to walk too late, unless he can make his pathe good'.[13] There are many accounts of highway robberies in the Knightsbridge area throughout the eighteenth century. As late as 1799, it was necessary to have a light-horse patrol between Hyde Park Corner and Kensington every night, and Davis recorded that 'it is within the memory of many when pedestrians walked to and from Kensington in bands sufficient to ensure mutual protection, starting at known intervals, of which a bell gave warning'.[14] However, the 'Wild West' character of old Knightsbridge can perhaps easily be over-emphasized. If it was dangerous at night for travellers, that was equally the case with other parts of London and its fringe. Long before this period, most of Knightsbridge was lined with buildings on both sides of the road, from inns, shops and other business premises to substantial terraces with gardens, and detached villas and mansions in ornamentally-planted grounds. There was a foot-guards barracks towards Hyde Park Corner, and the newer cavalry barracks lay at the other end of the hamlet. Shops proliferated in the 1820s and '30s as the district grew.

The nucleus of old Knightsbridge, from which the hamlet took its name, was the bridge carrying the road over the river Westbourne at present-day Albert Gate. This bridge was known originally as the King's bridge, later corrupted to Knightsbridge. It is as Kyngesbyrig that the locale first appears in the written record, a charter of Edward the Confessor. The oldest buildings to survive into comparatively recent times were gathered here, and by the 'village' green at the apex of the Kensington and Brompton roads. Situated beside the Westbourne on the north side of the road was the hamlet's principal establishment, a lazar-house, which was in operation from the Middle Ages until early in the eighteenth century. The chapel attached to this hospital, in effect a chapel-of-ease for the local people, continued to flourish after the hospital's closure. The small complex of buildings comprising the lazar-house, some of which dated from the sixteenth and seventeenth centuries, was still standing in the early 1840s, when the site was cleared as part of the Albert Gate development. In addition to these buildings, there were several old houses and long-established inns dotted along the main road. Probably the greater number of existing buildings by Queen Victoria's reign, however, were not ancient, but of eighteenth-century date.

The character of Knightsbridge as it had evolved by the late eighteenth century was not only socially mixed but becoming suburban in tone; it was emphatically not an agricultural community. Consequently, much of the existing building of old Knightsbridge was absorbed seamlessly into the denser fabric of Victorian and later times, and was only gradually removed in the course of various redevelopments. But there were acknowledged eyesores from village days, targeted for destruction by developers and residents: the lazar-house buildings, demolished by Cubitt; the Halfway House tavern, demolished by John Elger; houses in the High Road and near the Green, demolished piecemeal in late Victorian times; Park Side, mostly rebuilt in the early 1900s; and above all the original cavalry barracks, the subject of much condemnation from the 1850s.

Knightsbridge Green still exists in a residual state, the present enclosure and narrow passage preserving part of the layout as it had evolved by the mid-nineteenth century. Lancelot Place maintains the line of a driftway which once led to the Rose and Crown inn on Knightsbridge. Another relic of the hamlet is Park Close, laid out in the 1720s as a court of houses. The entrance to Old Barrack Yard, too, is of some antiquity, originally giving access to a field behind the roadside waste where the foot-guards barracks was built around 1760. Elsewhere, a few field boundaries may still be traced in the shape of developments: Rutland Gate, for example. One of the old village inns survives, though long rebuilt, as the Paxton's Head public house.

Progress of development

Knightsbridge, like so much of London outside the control of the 'great estates', is to a large extent the creation of speculative builders working within the haphazard framework of comparatively small landholdings, made available for development from time to time. Though much of central and western Knightsbridge had formed a single estate, belonging to a Huguenot family, the Moreaus, this was dispersed in the late 1750s. The largest landowner was Westminster Abbey, whose manor of Knightsbridge and Westbourne Green included the strips of roadside waste in east and central Knightsbridge, and larger tracts of copyhold ground to the west, among them much of the Kingston House property and Brompton Park Nursery. With the limitations imposed by the landholding pattern, and the inevitable fluctuations in building activity governed by trade cycles and local circumstances affecting demand for houses, the progress of development was sporadic and untidy. Lowndes Terrace, Trevor Square, Montpelier Square, Raphael Street, Albert Gate, Rutland Gate and Rutland Gardens were each marked by failures or delays in their development. In some cases – particularly Montpelier Square and Rutland Gate – the architectural record of these fits and starts can still readily be traced. Elsewhere – in Lowndes Terrace and Raphael Street – the original buildings have been completely erased by redevelopment.

While H. G. Davis was compiling his local *Memorials* in the 1840s and '50s, Knightsbridge was experiencing the most important of several distinct phases in its transition from semi-rural hamlet to built-up suburb. The 1820s had seen a wave of reconstruction and new development sweep across the eastern part of the district, but without making a radical change to its character, which remained essentially that of a ribbon development, albeit a ribbon of heterogeneous pattern, formed over several centuries. Such inroads as had been made into the hinterland were fairly modest in aspiration – the most ambitious, Montpelier Square, foundered temporarily in the depression years of the late 1820s. When local development again gathered pace, from the late 1830s, the scale was greater, and there was a corresponding emphasis on architectural grandeur, seen in the Italianate terraces of Rutland Gate and Princes Gate, and the mansions of Albert Gate.

The abolition in 1825 of the century-old turnpike across the east end of Knightsbridge at Hyde Park Corner removed a psychological as well as physical barrier between the hamlet and the metropolis. By the early 1840s Knightsbridge was said to be 'now as much London as Tottenham Court Road'.[15] But, as in neighbouring South Kensington, it was not until after the Great Exhibition of 1851, and the scramble for land south-west of the exhibition site, that high-class building well away from the immediate main-road frontage (where both a view and some tenuous relationship with the park itself could be claimed) became viable. Thus the builder John Elger, initially attracted to the area in the 1840s by the roadside ground on either side of Kingston House, felt confident enough by 1853 to take on the entire southern half of Rutland Gate, where building had run into the sand some years earlier. Following the success of Elger and his associates in establishing Princes Gate and some of the backland (now Ennismore Gardens) as a fashionable locale, the developer C. J. Freake undertook much further building near by in the 1850s and '60s, pushing the frontier westwards and southwards, and nearly meeting up with his other housing developments in South Kensington.

By the time of Davis's death, in 1857, Knightsbridge could fairly lay claim to some of the most prestigious and sought-after addresses in London. But to think that the name Knightsbridge bestowed any automatic cachet at this time is almost certainly incorrect. Much of the old heterogeneity remained, and had given rise to parallel developments of an altogether more popular character than the new upper-class enclaves of Rutland Gate and Princes Gate. As western Knightsbridge increasingly took on the character of an exclusive suburb, central Knightsbridge became denser, busier, and seedier: in modern terms distinctly 'inner-city'. The population, estimated at 5,000 in 1848 and to a great extent working-class, was concentrated in crowded conditions near the barracks.[16] Music-halls opened in the High Road, and at Knightsbridge Green the large old houses were redeveloped – one as a showy pub – and their gardens built over, with low-class houses in Raphael Street and Tattersalls' new horse-auction rooms. For many years there remained a sharp contrast between central and western Knightsbridge, but by the late nineteenth century the music-halls had been closed down, and the tone of the High Road seems to have been improved.

A sign of the growing intolerance of rowdy behaviour was the refusal of local people in 1872 to allow a covered cab-stand in Knightsbridge, near Sloane Street, on the grounds that it would attract loafers. Construction of the experimental shelter, to have been 'roofed in with glass in a horticultural fashion', was proposed by the police with Home Office support. It would have provided a coffee- and news-paper-stand in addition to shelter for cabmen and bus-queues.[17]

By the 1880s, as in Kensington and other suburbs, the large family terrace-house was becoming an obsolete vehicle for speculative development, as the builder William Radford found to his cost in northern Ennismore Gardens. Blocks of mansion flats were the coming thing, and a series of them was built in Knightsbridge between the 1880s and the early years of the next century, mostly in place of houses of various classes. On the main road, the turn of the century saw shops and houses replaced by mixed commercial and residential blocks.

Not only were the old houses going out of fashion, but they were increasingly unsuited to the busier, noisier environment of the major roads and losing their appeal as residences for that reason. In the early twentieth century traffic vibration – whether from underground trains or motor-buses – afflicted one of the best houses near Hyde Park Corner, No. 23 Knightsbridge, the effects being felt throughout the building.[18]

Redevelopment with blocks of flats resumed in the 1930s, though not on such a scale as to alter greatly the local character. One regrettable victim of flat-building was Kingston House, built when Knightsbridge was still a country hamlet. Without undergoing any sudden, radical redevelopment, the most desirable parts of Knightsbridge began to take on an urban rather than suburban air. In the early 1930s, Harold P. Clunn, with his characteristic enthusiasm for modernization, felt that Knightsbridge's transformation since the 1880s 'almost invites comparison with that of some great city in the United States or South America'. At the time, it looked as if the older, small-scale developments so prized today, including the 'shabby relic' Trevor Square and the 'rather depressing' Montpelier Square, might soon be swept away and replaced by up-market flats.[19]

By the end of the Second World War, Knightsbridge was poised on the brink of what might have been drastic reconstruction. In parts, the redevelopment in the post-war property boom was indeed drastic, especially along the main road and around Knightsbridge Green. So much of the building stock – the large family houses in particular – was not only socially and economically obsolete but had suffered as a result of wartime requisitioning. However, flat-conversions and institutional use, particularly by embassies, saved several fine terraces from demolition.

Knightsbridge and Hyde Park

Of all the influences on the growth and character of Knightsbridge one of the most important has been Hyde Park. In the eighteenth century its influence was initially slight, though it was presumably a factor behind the choice of location of Kingston House and other large houses in Knightsbridge and Kensington Road. The creation of the South Carriage Drive in the 1730s to replace Rotten Row as the royal road through the park coincided with extensive building along the north side of Knightsbridge, where a long terrace of houses was built in High Row, on the site of present-day Bowater House. But the design of these houses showed no special interest in proceedings over the park wall: they faced Knightsbridge and the backs were conventionally treated with closet wings and landing windows. Forty years later, however, when the adjoining Park Row was built, the new houses took full advantage of the park view, with large bows facing north; and in 1793 *The World*, in a review of 'Fine situations long neglected', censured the planning of the earlier houses as an 'error'.[20]

In 1791 the same paper had reported that 'some Opulent builders' were proposing a scheme for building houses, presumably for the rich, all along the park wall from Hyde Park Corner to Kensington – an idea which would have greatly accelerated the rise of Knightsbridge as a fashionable location.[21] In the event, no such houses were erected on the park side of Knightsbridge until Nos 1 and 2 Albert Gate and Hyde Park House were built there in the early 1840s and the 1850s.

Albert Gate occupies a prominent place in the story of the development of Knightsbridge. It was a speculation, but more importantly it was an improvement – sweeping away objectionable industrial premises and decrepit tenements, tackling head-on the problem of how to integrate the evolving suburb with one of its greatest assets, the park. What its developer, Thomas Cubitt, and the park authorities, really had in mind for the long term remains unclear, but there is evidence that something much more extensive than the eventual gateway and trio of houses was seriously considered. As it was, it must soon have become apparent that Albert Gate occupied the wrong place for the main local entrance to the park; one critic even suggested its demotion to pedestrian use only, and the transfer of the name to something distinctly grander directly opposite Sloane Street.[22] The idea of a Sloane Street extension into the park was new, and efforts were subsequently made, on private and public initiatives, to open a new park gate in this position, a much more suitable one, both visually and practically, than Albert Gate. Nothing towards this end took place on the ground, however, until the creation of Edinburgh Gate in the 1950s (in a development which fails to make of the gateway anything more than a traffic-chute).

By the time of the Albert Gate development, Hyde Park itself had seen great improvements, including the replacement of most of the old perimeter wall with iron railings and the building of new lodges, and was rapidly gaining in status as a fashionable rendezvous. Riding in Hyde Park, and especially parading in Rotten Row and the South Carriage Drive, was firmly established as a social routine, and the extraordinary process of ritualization and elaboration which eventually came to characterize this activity was well under way.

The growing social importance of the park, however, was never to be officially acknowledged by any large-scale public improvement to bring the adjoining highways up to a suitably impressive standard (at least until the Park Lane widening in the early 1960s), something particularly desirable on the Knightsbridge side, where the landownership pattern made the existing development so messy.

Knightsbridge differs from its northern counterpart the Bayswater Road, and for that matter from Park Lane, in being built-up on the park side for a good part of its length. The difference is a fundamental one. Bayswater Road, though narrow, has a boulevard-like appearance. Knightsbridge, starting out promisingly spacious at Hyde Park Corner, with the park on one side and well-set-back frontages on the other, is soon squeezed between tall buildings looming up from narrow pavements.

The historic pattern of landownership is the explanation for what has proved an intractable planning problem over the past two centuries. Separately owned from the land behind, the roadside strips along much of the way from Hyde Park Corner to the Knightsbridge Barracks have been too narrow to allow the building line to be set back enough for major road-widening, while at the same time the properties have been too valuable to make their complete obliteration viable. The problem was compounded in the late eighteenth century when the barracks was built, right on the edge of the park, continuing the line of built-up ground along the roadside.

The meanness of the road through Knightsbridge and of the roadside buildings was a subject repeatedly aired as the district rose in status through the Victorian period. The entire road from Piccadilly Circus to Kensington, thought one anonymous writer in 1871,

may be denominated London's Western Boulevard. The importance of buildings in its course, the new Royal Academy, and especially the stupendous Hall of Arts [the Royal Albert Hall], bestow upon it an increased importance; and since the sinuosities in the Royal town of Kensington have been opened and improved, the remaining straits on the line become more obvious.

There were two major bottlenecks, one in the vicinity of Albert Gate, where for 150ft the road was only about 46ft wide, the other at the barracks, 'which obtrudes upon the main thoroughfare fully half its width'.[23]

Not only was the route constricted, but its character was badly marred by some of the buildings along the way – the 'huddled, shapeless, and crazy tenements' in Park Side and eastern High Row, and the barracks, 'presenting a stable and a barrack-wall with windows where first-class mansions ought to stand'.[24]

Piecemeal improvements have been made. When the barracks was rebuilt in the 1870s the site was reduced slightly to allow the bottleneck at that point to be removed. In the 1890s and 1900s the London County Council worked in co-operation with the Ecclesiastical Commissioners (successors to the Dean and Chapter of Westminster Abbey as freeholders here), to broaden the road between Wilton Place and William Street as part of a complete redevelopment. (The inadequacy of the widening here was, however, apparent by the 1930s, and probably much earlier.[25]) Other widenings have occurred from time to time, as rebuilding permitted, and in the late 1950s the easternmost of the shops on the north side of the road were removed to allow the narrow 'gore' on which they stood to be partly added to the highway. But the road through Knightsbridge remains rather constricted, both as regards traffic flow and architectural effect.

There has never been any consensus of opinion as to how the roadside sites bordering Hyde Park should be regarded. In the eighteenth century the question did not arise, Knightsbridge being a fairly unimportant out-of-town location. Since then, some have argued for complete clearance on the grounds that the various buildings disrupted the scenery, and this view gained ground before the Victorian rebuilding of the barracks, there being some hope that a new and more appropriate site would be found. When the government ultimately decided to rebuild on the existing site, the architect James Fergusson suggested that the government should buy up all the property between the barracks and the three mansions at Albert Gate, using the combined sites to straighten and widen the road into the 'finest and most noble' entrance to the metropolis, and still accommodate a new barracks with space to spare:

and if the barrack were made a handsome building, which it might easily be, it would be a far more pleasing object from the Drive in the park than the backs of the houses in [Albert Terrace], and the rubbishy summer-houses that now disfigure the locality.[26]

In the absence of the large-scale planning initiatives necessary to deal effectively with the problem of the roadway, the successive developers of Knightsbridge were obliged to exploit their ground as best they could. Clearly, any site with a good view of Hyde Park had great potential for house-building, while convenient access to the park, on foot or horseback, or by carriage, made particular sites even more desirable than others. The result was a series of 'Gates': Albert Gate, Rutland Gate and Princes Gate (and further west in Kensington, Queen's Gate, Hyde Park Gate and Palace Gate). H. G. Davis denounced the term as absurd, 'a modern stupidity for a square or terrace'.[27] But, of course, the name implied nearby and privileged access to the park, and aspirations to membership of the beau monde. Obtaining a new gate to the park for the benefit of the inhabitants of a new development was difficult and expensive, as both Cubitt and Elger found, but the benefit to property values was immeasurable.

First of the Knightsbridge 'Gates' was Rutland Gate, a development begun in the late 1830s under the name Serpentine Terrace (another reference to Hyde Park) and renamed about 1840. Though the developers had hoped to obtain permission for a park gate opposite, the only gates at Rutland Gate were to close it off from the main road at night. They were eventually removed as an inconvenience.[28] Albert Gate, on the other hand, really was a gate into the park. The building of Elger's Princes Gate began in 1845, the year that Albert Gate opened, though the scheme had been broached much earlier, certainly by early 1840. An important part of the plan there was the creation of a new entrance to the park, called Prince of Wales Gate. Princes Gate gained such status as an address that C. J. Freake retained the name for his adjoining development, thus carrying Princes Gate nearly all the way down Exhibition Road, and associating his other houses close by with it under the name Princes Gardens. In a similar way, Rutland Gate was followed years later by Rutland Gardens, laid out on ground with no historic connection to Rutland Gate or the former house on its site, Rutland House.

Albert Gate was much too prestigious a name to be restricted to just two or three houses as an address, which was at first the case. Having soon given rise to the renaming of some old houses near by as Albert Terrace, it was eventually adopted, in the 1870s (at the inhabitants' request), as the address of all the houses fronting the main road between Park Side and the barracks.[29] Albert Gate became widely used as a loose description for much of central Knightsbridge; Tattersalls, situated well away at Knightsbridge Green, liked to use it as their address, and the name was taken for new flats (Albert Gate Mansions) built on the south side of the road in the 1880s. In the late 1890s, the Park Mansions development at the junction of Knightsbridge and Brompton Road was promoted as being in Albert Gate.[30]

The question of gates was something which raised issues of social status and *amour-propre* over and above mere access to the park. In the late 1850s, the inhabitants of Rutland Gate managed to get a new wicket-gate made for their convenience just west of the barracks. There was already a wicket-gate for the general public near by, but it was on the east side of the barracks in a rough, crowded part of Knightsbridge and the approach was of a character to put its use out of the question for the residents of addresses such as Rutland Gate. As well as having several low-class shops selling refreshments, it was lined by street-vendors' tables and benches. The passage was reduced to a crowded gangway, while 'the stall-holders now threaten violence to any wayfarer who passes on the public pavement'.[31]

Proximity to the park encouraged builders to erect their largest and most stylish houses. This is noticeable even in the modest Trevor Square area development of the Regency period, where Trevor Terrace, facing the park (or at any rate the barracks, then quite new) was on a larger scale than the terraces comprising the square itself. In later developments, size and architectural display were much more pronounced, but it took time for the level to be pitched just right. Cubitt, at Albert Gate, built on rather too large a scale, and early drawings for Princes Gate by H. L. Elmes display an extravagance that had to be toned down when the houses came to be built. The flamboyance of the terrace designed by F. R. Beeston senior at St George's Place in the 1850s was almost certainly a response to its fine position facing the park, and carried an echo of Nash's Regent's Park terraces of thirty years before. In general, the *palazzo*-style terrace which had become usual for the sides of squares was successfully adapted for park-view sites (where detached or semi-detached villas, for example, might have been a feasible alternative for the speculative builder to venture).

The arrival on the sylvan scene of such a vast edifice as the Crystal Palace was naturally a cause for some consternation among inhabitants and developers. The builders of eastern Princes Gate, John Elger and John Kelk, both blamed the Crystal Palace for discouraging prospective purchasers of their new houses immediately opposite. 'It is not a popular subject at Knightsbridge', wrote Sir George Cornewall Lewis of Kent House, 'particularly at this moment [December 1850], when we are over-run with workmen who stream along the road at meal-times as if a manufactory was breaking up.' Even before the opening of the exhibition, Lord Campbell, living next door at Stratheden House, was complaining that 'the neighbourhood is already infested by mobs, day and night'. Sir George, in particular, had harboured doubts about the value of the Great Exhibition, but when it opened was completely won over both by the building itself and the exhibition in general.[32]

On the north side of Knightsbridge, the relation of the buildings with the park could prove problematic, and this has continued to be so in comparatively recent times. The construction of the Hyde Park Hotel provoked great controversy in the 1880s on account of its height, and in the twentieth century the building of Bowater House and the second rebuilding of Knightsbridge Barracks again led to much debate about the effect of the proposed tall structures on the view across Hyde Park. At other times, friction with the park authorities has arisen in connection with right to light, gutters and summer-houses, and in the case of the Hyde Park Hotel over the commercial vulgarity of prominent lettering on the park side of the building.

Social divisions

The gentrification of smaller houses and mews properties, and the institutionalization or conversion to flats of the bigger houses, have, as elsewhere in London, tended to level out old social divisions within Knightsbridge, formerly strongly marked. Writing in 1854, the Knightsbridge architect W. W. Pocock drew attention to the disparity between the aristocratic character of the new terraces along or adjoining Knightsbridge and the character of the highway itself. At the time, inhabitants of Brompton were up in arms at the builder John Elger's refusal to allow a road connecting Brompton Square with his developments to the north, and thus to Knightsbridge and Kensington Road, a stance apparently supported by many of the occupants of the houses he had built. Should these rich citizens ever have occasion to extend their walks in the direction of Belgravia and Buckingham Palace, suggested Pocock,

they would find a shorter and far more respectable route through Brompton-square, etc. than through Knightsbridge, which, thanks to the military and the present tenure of church property, is never very enticing; and after a very early hour in the day is literally impassable for ladies or families, unless in carriages or under the protection of powerful escorts.[33]

With Elger's developments in Rutland Gate, Princes Gate and Ennismore Gardens, western Knightsbridge was indeed taking on an aristocratic (and plutocratic) character. Smaller houses further east, including those in Pocock's own development, Trevor Square, meanwhile languished in a state of dingy multi-occupancy as boarding-houses and tenements. The entire triangle east of Rutland Gardens to the apex of Brompton Road and Knightsbridge was at best unfashionable, and much of it was solidly working-class. There was a smaller pocket of predominantly low-class housing in Park Place and Mills's Buildings near the barracks. The juxtaposition of different social types in a small compass was common enough in London, but the contrast was given a particular emphasis by Knightsbridge's growing reputation as a place of popular entertainment. In the middle decades of the nineteenth century night-time Knightsbridge was riotous with noisy, drunken crowds, soldiers and prostitutes prominent among them. Music-halls, pubs, eating-houses and other attractions occupied premises in the High Road between Knightsbridge Green and Trevor Street. Time and again the barracks was held up as *fons et origo* of the problem, and it was a bitter blow to local feeling when the campaign to get the barracks relocated met with failure. Whether or not the barracks was the chief cause, the area of Knightsbridge Green remained a dubious locality certainly up to the Second World War. (In the early 1990s it was alleged that the Pakenham Tavern, demolished in the 1950s, had been a haunt of high-society homosexuals, who picked up young guardsmen there.[34])

To some extent social divisions account for the lack of coherent planning in the district, seen, for instance, in the complete separation of the Montpelier estate development (laid out in the 1820s) from Rutland Gardens, a cul-de-sac, created fifty years later and aimed at a higher class of resident than Montpelier Square. There was no incentive here to link the two developments. As the dispute over the proposed road from Brompton Square shows, John Elger, building in the 1840s and '50s for the upper end of the house market, saw every reason to keep his streets cut off from slightly earlier, less aspiring, houses, and to prevent through-traffic between Brompton Road and Knightsbridge crossing his developments – producing, in Rutland Gate and (in its original form) Ennismore Gardens, two very large culs-de-sac. The same consideration was still current half a century later, when the complete rebuilding of the Trevor Square area was in contemplation by its new owner:

The property lies in such a neighbourhood as would, if properly developed, permit of the erection of good class houses commanding high rents; but immediately adjoining it in Raphael-street is a lower class of property, which if brought into direct relationship to the estate would tend to lower its value.

From the point of view of the estate the tendency would be to shut out this neighbouring low-class property, screen it off, and ignore it altogether; so preserving for the estate an exclusiveness for which a certain class of well-to-do people would be willing to pay high rents. From the public point of view, general intercommunication between all parts of the town is a necessity, and the general democratic spirit of the age which is, after all, at the bottom of all such co-operative movements as town planning is a tendency in opposition to social exclusiveness.[35]

Nothing came of this scheme, perhaps because the First World War intervened. Subsequently, the unredeveloped Trevor estate achieved a thoroughly well-to-do character through a natural process of gentrification, which, but for bombing in the Second World War, might have spread to Raphael Street.

Equally unpredictable was the fate of the stately terraces of western Knightsbridge. In the 1920s Princes Gate and Ennismore Gardens were said by the freeholder Lord Listowel's agent to 'occupy an unique position in these days of turmoil and traffic':

They are byeways of quietude yet so near to the Park and the centre of fashion that the position is one which should always command tenants of the class that have occupied them in the past and are occupying them today.[36]

Already, however, such large houses were becoming uneconomic to run and were beginning to be converted into flats or taken over by institutions, greatly altering the old residential character of the area. After the Second World War hardly any of the properties here were occupied as family houses, a situation showing signs of change in recent years, as buildings are reconverted from flats back into single dwellings.

THE FABRIC

Knightsbridge is chiefly a private residential district, but shops, hotels, offices and other commercial or institutional buildings have a strong presence too. Some of the main building types and development themes are discussed below. Conspicuously absent are any municipal buildings, excepting the former All Saints' School at Knightsbridge Green, and public housing, a consequence of Knightsbridge's position at the periphery of other districts, small extent, and lack of administrative independence.

Less surprising is the absence of industrial premises, yet as recently as the early 1970s the west side of Trevor Place was still dominated by a former factory. Dating from the 1820s, this was built for the manufacture of ornamental floorcloth, an industry associated with Knightsbridge from the mid-eighteenth century. Another (long vanished) industrial structure on a large scale was the early-nineteenth-century Cannon Brewhouse, demolished for the making of Albert Gate. Both these premises were designed by capable architects – W. F. Pocock and George Byfield – and were of some architectural distinction.

One unusual complex that may be mentioned here is Tattersalls' horse and carriage mart on Knightsbridge Green, bombed in the Second World War and later demolished. Built in the 1860s to replace the famous 'Corner' behind St George's Hospital, it combined up-to-date engineering techniques with classical architectural formality.

The mansions of old Knightsbridge

West of Knightsbridge Green on the south side of the Kensington road, the narrow strips of waste on which so much of old Knightsbridge grew up gave way to sizeable fields and meadows. On this land, clear of the hamlet proper, a series of large houses in spacious gardens was built from the late seventeenth century until the beginning of the nineteenth. There were six: from the east, Powis House (c.1689); Kent House (1793, enlarged 1801); Stratheden House (1770–2); Rutland House (1752–3); Kingston House (1757–8); Park House (1753). Further west, along Kensington Gore, lay Eden Lodge (c.1745); Gore House (1750s); Grove House (late 1740s); Noel House (1804); Madeley House (c.1802); Kensington House (c.1690); Colby House (c.1713). In the opposite direction, the sequence continued with Lanesborough House (c.1718) and Apsley House (1771–8), and so to the mansions of Piccadilly and Mayfair.

Of the Knightsbridge houses, only Kingston House, which survived into comparatively recent times, was reasonably well recorded before its demolition, and knowledge of the others is fairly limited, but most seem to have been architect-designed and expensively constructed and fitted. Sir William Chambers and (probably) John Vardy were among the architects involved. Two at least, Kingston House and Kent House, were exquisitely furnished and decorated. Although several had aristocratic connections, none of the houses approached the scale of stately homes; they were in effect early examples (if on rather a grand scale) of suburban villas. In this sense, they relate to some of the detached houses built in Knightsbridge in the Victorian period, especially Alford House, which stood next door to Kingston House. An interesting common feature of three of the houses is that they were built to accommodate mistresses of the aristocracy: Kent House was enlarged for the Duke of Kent and Madame de St Laurent; Rutland House was built for the 3rd Duke of Rutland and Mrs Drake and their son; Kingston House was built for the Duke of Kingston's mistress Elizabeth Chudleigh. Possibly a similar purpose was behind the building of Stratheden House for John Calcraft, a 'free liver' who had several children by two actresses.[37]

The presence of these detached houses in grounds preserved for this part of Knightsbridge a country character which must long have been missing from the densely built-up eastern part of the hamlet. All six houses existed together for no more than a few years, however, and from the 1790s the view across the park from the easternmost four was spoiled by the presence of Knightsbridge Barracks.

Terrace-houses

From the early eighteenth century until the 1880s, development in Knightsbridge, conventionally enough, mostly took the form of terraces of houses in streets and squares, or ranged along parts of the main road. The earliest examples to survive are those in and around Trevor Square, begun in the second decade of the nineteenth century. Fully stuccoed façades were introduced to Knightsbridge in the mid-1820s on the south side of Montpelier Square. The architecture here was fairly unsophisticated. An altogether different order of architectural ambition was shown a few years later at Rutland Gate, where the two park-facing terraces – one at least probably the work of (Sir) Matthew Wyatt –

were given elaborate and accomplished Italianate treatments. This formula was to be used on a bigger scale and with greater architectural verve (supplied by H. L. Elmes) at Princes Gate in the 1840s, and the new grandeur was carried on over the next two decades by C. J. Freake in Princes Gate and Princes Gardens. Though on private land, these new terraces were clearly conceived as forming backdrops to the views from Hyde Park, in the manner of the Nash terraces at Regent's Park.

The scale of these terrace-houses was such that some modification of the conventional side-passage plan became desirable, a third main room being introduced on the principal floors, behind the usual two. In Princes Gate, John Elger placed a top-lit staircase between the front and back rooms. More radical departure from the standard plan was generally restricted to end-of-terrace houses, which gave scope for centralized planning if entered on the long side of the building.

Externally, various permutations of stuccoed Italianate decoration were tried in the 1850s and '60s, but without producing anything superior to the best work designed in the '40s, seen at Nos 13–25 Princes Gate. The vista of stuccoed or half-stuccoed terrace-houses with pillared porticoes, one of the most characteristic and evocative images of Victorian London, is still well represented in Knightsbridge. In Ennismore Gardens, however, the area has the distinction (rare for London) of having terraces in the same Italianate style faced in ashlar: the choice of freestone over stucco here was, it turns out, a matter of opportunity rather than architectural purism. From the same period is the pair of houses at Nos 15–17 Knightsbridge, also Italianate but constructed in white brick with stone dressings.

Artistic houses and interiors

Though Knightsbridge was never an artistic colony, and in fact attracted relatively few professional artists as residents, it did become something of a centre for wealthy collectors and connoisseurs of art, including notable patrons of painters and architects. While suitable building land remained available locally, a number of these artistic figures commissioned large houses for themselves and their collections, which are considered below. Others adapted the work of speculative builders, or existing individual houses, to their requirements.

Among the major art collectors and connoisseurs with houses in Knightsbridge were John Sheepshanks and William Jones in Rutland Gate in the 1840s; John Harris at Princes Gate from the 1850s; F. R. Leyland at No. 49 Princes Gate, and Thomas Eustace Smith and his wife 'Eustacia' at No. 52, in the 1870s; John Pierpont Morgan at Princes Gate from the 1890s; and, in more recent times, Count Seilern at No. 56 Princes Gate after the Second World War.

While a few are well-documented and recorded in photographs, tantalizingly little is known of some of these houses in their heyday, and many of the buildings have been destroyed, or their interiors stripped and altered.

In some cases, as at No. 14 Princes Gate and the now-demolished South Lodge, period-style schemes of interior decoration were naturally selected as appropriate back-drops for collections of paintings, tapestries and *objets d'art*, often incorporating antique panelling or other authentic elements. Of greater interest are decorative schemes of high artistic value in themselves. Among these, James McNeill Whistler's Peacock Room at No. 49 Princes Gate is the supreme example here, though the entire creation has long been in the USA. Only a freak of chance in the way it was constructed made it possible for the Peacock Room to be uprooted. The building, however, still contains some relics of Whistler's patron F. R. Leyland and later occupants, including Thomas Cundy's virtuoso staircase-balustrade of the 1820s, salvaged from Northumberland House.

Probably the most remarkable Victorian decorative work still surviving in a Knightsbridge house is only a few doors away at No. 52 Princes Gate, where substantial parts of George Aitchison's Aesthetic-style schemes for several rooms, including much inlaid woodwork, remain intact. Other interesting Victorian and later interiors are known, from descriptions or photographs, but most of the surviving grand houses in Knightsbridge have suffered too badly at various times from neglect and institutional use or wholesale redecoration for much to have escaped destruction.

Individually commissioned houses

Although the great majority of houses built in Knightsbridge during Queen Victoria's reign were speculative, a number were individually commissioned – and from architects of the first rank. In each case (with the exception of South Lodge, a curious house, which grew in stages from small beginnings), these one-offs were erected on plots portioned out of estates where speculative building was proceeding or had already taken place. There is a noticeable correlation between the building of these individual houses and problems with the speculative side of development.

In the early 1840s, the erection of Clytha House and Park House on the Rutland House estate coincided with a loss of impetus in the building of the terraces which had been planned for the whole of Rutland Gate. Some years later Thomas Cubitt, having experienced difficulties in disposing of Nos 1 and 2 Albert Gate, decided not to proceed with speculative building on the rest of his ground adjoining but to wait for a private commission for a big house there (Hyde Park House).

On the Kingston House estate, the circumstances of the building of Alford House are not quite clear, but it seems that the allocation of the site for a single house resulted from a direct approach to the owner, Lord Listowel, by Lady Alford herself. Later, neighbouring Bolney House was built on a site previously designated for terrace-houses. Near by, Gustav Natorp acquired the plot for his house at No. 70 Ennismore Gardens from the builder William Radford, whose speculative development of large houses here was working out badly.

One obvious likelihood is that most estate owners preferred relatively high-density terraces to one-off houses, however magnificent they might be. If so, the reason was perhaps long-term considerations rather than any difference in ground-rents: big, maybe unconventionally planned, houses are likely to prove difficult to let on reversion, or command relatively poor rents. And this appears to be borne out by the fate of the individually commissioned houses compared with their terraced neighbours. Hyde Park House, Clytha, Alford, Bolney and Moncorvo Houses, Natorp's house, and South Lodge, have all disappeared. Of these, Hyde Park House was for many years a clubhouse, while South Lodge would have become a dancing academy but for financial difficulties. Of the two survivors, Kent House has long been a synagogue, while Park House, after periods of institutional occupation since 1945, has recently been reinstated as a private residence.

It was also the case that demand was too unpredictable for custom-built houses to be a reliable basis for estate development, whether built on lease or on plots sold off freehold. Thomas Cubitt had to wait years before finding a client to commission a house on his vacant site west of Albert Gate, while on the Kent House estate the owner, Mitchell Henry, was only able to dispose of one of the three large plots for mansions facing Hyde Park for the intended purpose. This was the site of the present Kent House, built for Lady Ashburton.

Now nearly all pulled down, Knightsbridge's individual mansions were among its most remarkable architectural works. The majority were commissioned by men or women with small families (or no family living with them at all) and a strong involvement in the arts, usually as collectors or patrons. The art collector John Sheepshanks, of No. 24 Rutland Gate (Park House), was a bachelor, as was Natorp, a dilettantish figure who fancied himself as a painter; Lady Ashburton and Lady Marian Alford were both widows with small families; William Jones of Clytha House had only a small family, and A. H. Huth of Bolney House was married but had no children. None of the first owners were significant artists in their own right, and only one house, Natorp's, incorporated a working studio.

The planning of these houses was dictated to a large extent either by the owner's collection or the requirements of large-scale entertaining (or both, as at Captain Leyland's Hyde Park House), rather than accommodating a large household. Both Clytha House and Sheepshanks' house incorporated galleries for pictures, and Bolney House a large wing for Huth's important book collection. At Alford House an entire room was created to display the fountain commissioned by Lady Marian Alford (long before Alford House was thought of) from her sculptress friend Harriet Hosmer.

At Rutland Gate, the exterior style of No. 24 Rutland Gate and Clytha House was conventional and suited to the neighbouring houses; Hyde Park House followed the exterior style of Nos 1 and 2 Albert Gate adjoining more or less exactly. The later individual houses, built from the late 1860s to the mid-

'80s, were varied in style. One, Bolney House, was a close imitation of Queen Anne or early Georgian. Three – Kent, Alford and Moncorvo Houses – were French-influenced. France also provided not merely the inspiration but the architect (Henri Parent) for a house which had it been built would have eclipsed any in Knightsbridge – Lord Rosebery's projected mansion on the site now occupied by the former Hyde Park Hotel.

In the twentieth century, a Beaux-Arts refronting at No. 14 Princes Gate, by the New York architect Thomas Hastings, marked the culmination of successive remodellings of the building for American clients. Hastings cited certain Italian Renaissance buildings as the chief sources of his design, which as executed was fancifully ornamented with carved heads of American Indians.

Mansion flats

Knightsbridge has several examples of the genre, large and small: Albert Gate Court (1887); Hyde Park Court (1888–91); Park Lodge (1890–2); Wellington Court (1893–5); Park Mansions (1897–1902); Rutland Court (1901–3); Parkside (1906–7). Albert Gate Mansions, built in 1883–4 and subsequently extended, has been demolished; Hyde Park Court became the Hyde Park Hotel in 1902. Stylistically, these new flats adopted the eclecticism that had already largely displaced the convention of Italianate classicism in the design of houses in the 1870s, but the new freedom was seldom used with great panache, Hyde Park Court being a notable exception. Planning was occasionally labyrinthine, and much of the appeal of the buildings to tenants was the freedom from maintaining a large household staff, or any staff at all, and the technological wizardry the blocks offered, in the form of the latest plumbing and heating systems, lifts, electric lighting, and telephones. Several of the new mansion blocks also offered views over Hyde Park; at Parkside the shallowness of the building allowed apartments to have views both over the park and on to Knightsbridge.

Places of entertainment

While it is almost certainly misleading to speak of Knightsbridge as having a 'tradition' of providing places of public entertainment, its proximity to Hyde Park made it an ideal location for exhibitions and other attractions during Victorian times.

Earlier, in the seventeenth and eighteenth centuries, there had been the Spring Gardens resort (roughly on the site of Lowndes Square), as well as sundry taverns along both sides of the main road. Not much is known for certain of the character of these latter establishments, which were perhaps as much necessary refreshment-places for travellers and their horses as destinations for pleasure-seekers (or hideouts for highwaymen).

There is some evidence, too, of theatrical entertainment locally during the Civil War: in 1647 it was reported that 'Stage-Playes are still acted at *Knightsbridge*'. As no theatre in the area is known to have existed, it seems likely that these plays were staged at a private house or inn-yard, or perhaps on the village green.[38] Much later, in the 1780s, Sheridan and others planned to build a theatre or opera house in the area, apparently on part of the Spring Gardens property east of Sloane Street.

What persuaded the American Sinophile Nathan Dunn to choose Knightsbridge for showing his collection of Chinese art and artefacts in the 1840s is not known. Very likely the inducement was simply the availability of a suitably inexpensive site for erecting the large exhibition hall needed. With transatlantic pizzazz, Dunn set up a colourful and eye-catching pagoda at the entrance to the exhibition (the hall itself being placed back from the road behind houses). But an attempt to replicate the spectacular success of the exhibition in a so-called 'Celestial Palace' at Albert Gate in 1851 flopped, in spite of being well positioned to pull in some of the visitors flocking to see the Crystal Palace.

Though the Great Exhibition was effectively in Knightsbridge (the way in from the road being through Prince of Wales Gate), it was neighbouring South Kensington on which the Commissioners for the Exhibition of 1851 focused as they began putting together their great estate for cultural and scientific institutions with the proceeds from the exhibition. Too much of Knightsbridge was already built up or spoken for.

Meanwhile, the original Chinese Collection hall continued in use as a gallery for a variety of artistic and cultural shows. During this same, early Victorian, period, Knightsbridge became something of a centre for the less respectable entertainments offered by pub-based 'free and easies' and music-halls. Knightsbridge never boasted anything to compare with the great London music-halls and palaces of variety, but did have several smaller establishments, whose boards were trod by a number of famous performers. Victorian Knightsbridge's noisy night-life, concentrated near the barracks, the Green and the High Road (as the road immediately west of present-day Scotch Corner was called) was loathed by better-class inhabitants. Property development and local opposition to the granting of music and dancing licences seem progressively to have killed off this popular-entertainment side of Knightsbridge by the 1890s. However, traces of the seediness associated with this phase of Knightsbridge's history remained for many years, especially in the Raphael Street area.

Respectable entertainment was provided by one important venue, Humphreys' Hall in the High Road, a capacious iron-and-glass structure which housed several major exhibitions during the 1880s. These culminated in the long-running and influential Japanese Village exhibition, from which W. S. Gilbert derived some authentic detail for the staging of *The Mikado*, and which may have helped inspire the opera itself. Bazaars and private functions were also held here, and in the 2nd Duke of Wellington's private riding-school, which stood across the road near the cavalry barracks. Knightsbridge's last important exhibition hall was the former floorcloth factory in Trevor Place, where several exhibitions of social and cultural interest were held before the First World War. These included 'What To Do With Our Girls' (1909), an exposition of activities deemed suitable for young gentlewomen, such as ju-jitsu, fly-tying, beekeeping, photography and target-shooting.

Indoor sports were associated with Knightsbridge at two principal venues from the late nineteenth century – ice-skating at the old floorcloth factory, and racquets and real tennis at Prince's Club, a splendid facility converted from Humphreys' Hall. Both establishments were of the highest class, and their existence marked a high-point in Knightsbridge's social status, not to say snobbishness.

Of all these Victorian and Edwardian places of entertainment not a trace is still standing today. Since the Second World War several foreign cultural institutions, such as the Accademia Italiana at No. 24 Rutland Gate and the Goethe Institute at No. 50 Princes Gate, have held exhibitions, lectures, film-showings and other events. The Polish Institute at No. 20 Princes Gate includes a museum relating to General Wladyslaw Sikorski. A commercial cinema, the Minema, opened in Knightsbridge in the 1960s.

Shops

From Victorian times until well after the Second World War, Knightsbridge was particularly associated with three stores, two of which began as humble draper's shops, the other as a grocery. Of this great triumvirate, one, Woollands, closed in the 1960s and was demolished, while the most famous, Harrods, lies outside the area covered by the present study. (Harrods is described in volume XLI of the *Survey*; included here, however, is the firm's former depot occupying the south side of Trevor Square and connected to the store by a subway beneath Brompton Road.) The third, Harvey Nichols, has come through many vicissitudes to become one of the world's most fashionable shops. Architecturally it is not in the front rank, though a respectably monumental pile in the tradition of the West End and large provincial city centres.

Knightsbridge has a long tradition as a shopping centre, though many of the best shops have always been in Brompton Road and Sloane Street rather than along Knightsbridge itself. Shops supplying and servicing local households, and catering to visiting pleasure-seekers, were well established by the early years of Queen Victoria's reign. 'Forty years since,' wrote Davis in the late 1850s, 'there was neither draper's nor butcher's shop between Hyde Park Corner and Sloane Street, and only one in the whole locality where a newspaper could be had, or writing paper purchased'.[39] Forty years after Davis was writing, Knightsbridge had two of the finest drapery stores in the country, and a butcher patronized by the Royal Household. The shops were concentrated on the south side of Knightsbridge west of Old Barrack Yard, and further west along the old High Road as far as Trevor Street. On the north side of the road, they extended east of Albert Gate, with a further cluster towards the barracks in Knightsbridge and Park Place (present-day Park Close).

With the exception of Harvey Nichols (1889–94 and later), the oldest shop premises along Knightsbridge are units in large mixed developments: at Albert Gate Court in Park Close (1887); Park Mansions at Scotch Corner (1897–1902); Nos 55–93 Knightsbridge (1902–3), and Parkside (1906–7). Owing to various redevelopments, such as the obliteration of the buildings east of Parkside in the 1950s, there are far fewer shops along Knightsbridge today than in former times. Closure and redevelopment has also greatly reduced the number of small shops off the main road. In Montpelier Square, for instance, there were once a grocer's, a newsagent's and a dairy, as well as a public house; all have been converted to private residences or replaced by houses.

Hotels

Several of Knightsbridge's most prominent buildings are (and were) hotels. The Alexandra, destroyed in the Second World War, derived ultimately from one of the old local hostelries. Its premises, facing Hyde Park, were originally built in the 1850s as a small hotel and a row of houses, all united in a grand classical design (by Beeston) topped by statues. The most famous Knightsbridge hotel, the Hyde Park (now the Mandarin Oriental Hyde Park), was built as apartments and a club in the late 1880s, and is an impressive example of the High Victorian style. Inside, the original richly marbled entrance hall survives substantially intact and has recently been restored.

The early twentieth century saw the opening of several smaller and less architecturally flamboyant hotels in Knightsbridge. The first was built over the new Hyde Park Corner tube station (now the Pizza on the Park) in 1908–9. It has long been closed. The Knightsbridge Palace Hotel, latterly the Normandie, followed in 1910–11, on the west side of Knightsbridge Green; it is also long defunct. Another hotel deriving from a long-established Knightsbridge inn was the Royal Park Hotel, opened during the First World War in a former temperance hotel or coffee-palace, and demolished after the Second World War. Two large hotels were built in the 1960s and '70s. The Sheraton Park Tower, on the site of Woollands' department store, is cylindrical and belongs to the 'glass stump' genre of architecture. The new Berkeley, built to replace the hotel of that name in Piccadilly and only partly impinging on the present area of study, is much less assertive.

Churches

Just two churches stand within the area covered by this volume.[b] A very few others have been demolished. Holy Trinity Church, a modest mid-Victorian edifice in the Gothic style, replacing an earlier chapel, was pulled down in the early 1900s; the former Trevor Congregational Church was demolished after the Second World War. Both existing churches share the distinction of serving foreign congregations few of whose members have ever resided in the locality. They are the Russian Orthodox Cathedral in Ennismore Gardens and the German Evangelical Church, the Christuskirche, in Montpelier Place. The cathedral, however, was built as an Anglican church and was an integral and necessary part of the new residential district centring on Princes Gate and Ennismore Gardens. This was not the case with the German church, which was erected early in the twentieth century by German Lutherans evicted from the Chapel Royal at St James's Palace. The choice of site, one already developed with houses of fairly low class, was slightly odd, given the obscurity of the locale and the absence of a nearby German community on any scale. The cathedral, built in the 1840s and enhanced by a later refronting, is of particular interest as an example of the adoption, comparatively unusual, of the Lombardic style in English nineteenth-century architecture, and for its extensive Arts and Crafts decorations in sgraffito by the artist Heywood Sumner. The Christuskirche is the only extant building in Knightsbridge belonging to the Gothic Revival.

---

[b] St Paul's, Knightsbridge, in Wilton Place, lies just outside the area and is not included. The Mormon church in Exhibition Road, on the former Freake estate, is described in volume XXXVIII of the *Survey*.

Modern architecture

The Modern Movement in architecture is fairly well represented in Knightsbridge, though sometimes by works of less interest than those they replace (buildings of this period being invariably on previously occupied sites). Michael Rosenauer's Kingston House estate development is the prime example, replacing not only old Kingston House but a whole series of late-Victorian houses commissioned from leading architects by the most discerning clients. In other cases, Modern buildings interrupt stereotypical Victorian terraces in a manner no longer acceptable to planners and conservationists: Walter and Eva Segal's flats in Rutland Gate, for instance. Elsewhere, as at Bowater House, Modern buildings were simply constructed on too large a scale for the immediate surroundings.

Among the most interesting Modern buildings in the area are de luxe apartment blocks of the 1930s: Adie, Button & Partners' elegant white building at Nos 59–63 Princes Gate, in Exhibition Road, and T. P. Bennett & Son's much less rigorously Modern-style Eresby House in Rutland Gate. (Inside, however, the ocean-liner finish of Eresby House contrasts with the unexpectedly 'safe' neo-Georgian treatment accorded to the Princes Gate building.) Septimus Warwick's flats in Princes Gate, facing Hyde Park, illustrate the architecturally disastrous consequence of the developer's failure to obtain the whole intended site. Nearer Hyde Park Corner, Mitchell & Bridgwater's stylish block of flats and shops at Nos 37–39 Knightsbridge show how vulnerable architectural style is to various forms of refurbishment, in this case replacement windows.

None of these pre-war Modern, or more loosely 'moderne', buildings was on a very much larger scale (although generally rather taller) than the earlier buildings on their sites; nor was the group of now-demolished Modern-style houses at Nos 4–8A Rutland Gate, another park-facing site, designed by Francis Lorne in the 1930s. During the post-war property-development boom, however, several extremely large-scale redevelopments took place, destroying the established character of parts of the district, or at the least, as with the Sheraton Park Tower hotel, establishing an assertive and alien-seeming presence. Perhaps the most ill-conceived was the redevelopment in the 1950s and '60s of much of the area of Knightsbridge Green and the old High Road west of Scotch Corner, with the building of office blocks such as Mercury House and Bowater House. An even more far-reaching proposed scheme, for a super-roundabout at Scotch Corner, with attendant slab blocks and underground shopping mall, was eventually aborted after years of planning dialogue between the developers and the London County Council.

Greater architectural interest attaches to two institutional undertakings of the same period, one of them only partially carried out and leaving a legacy of planning problems not yet resolved. These were the complete rebuilding of Knightsbridge Barracks, and the Princes Gardens redevelopment by Imperial College. Both projects showed the influence of the later work of Le Corbusier. At Knightsbridge Barracks, a major problem was posed by the shape and size of the site, which was too small and narrow for the accommodation required without building further upwards than appropriate for such a location. In Princes Gardens the site was ideal for the purpose, but the original architectural conception was ultimately abandoned in the face of financial cuts and changing circumstances.

Most recent architecture is concentrated on the south side of Knightsbridge towards Hyde Park Corner, but nothing there is really worthy of the exceptional sites facing across the road to the park. The redevelopment of South Lodge and the old floorcloth factory site, carried out in the 1970s, now appears rather dated. Among contemporary interiors, Eva Jiricna's work at No. 14 Rutland Gate is outstanding.

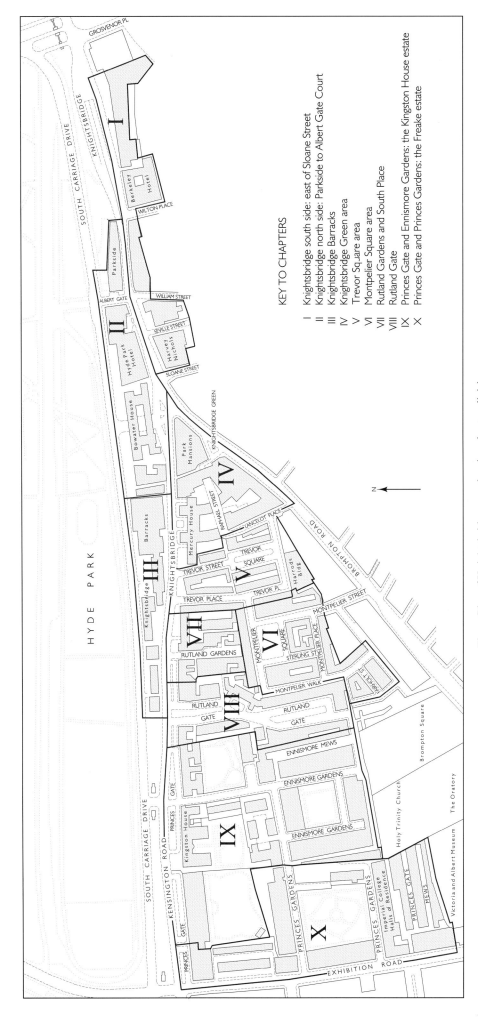

KEY TO CHAPTERS

I   Knightsbridge south side: east of Sloane Street
II   Knightsbridge north side: Parkside to Albert Gate Court
III   Knightsbridge Barracks
IV   Knightsbridge Green area
V   Trevor Square area
VI   Montpelier Square area
VII   Rutland Gardens and South Place
VIII   Rutland Gate
IX   Princes Gate and Ennismore Gardens: the Kingston House estate
X   Princes Gate and Princes Gardens: the Freake estate

Fig. 1. Plan of Knightsbridge area showing chapter divisions

CHAPTER I

Knightsbridge South Side:
East of Sloane Street

This chapter describes the strip of development between the Lanesborough Hotel (the former St George's Hospital) and Harvey Nichols store at the corner of Sloane Street. The Lanesborough itself, part of Hyde Park Corner, is excluded. Two demolished buildings of historic interest have been dealt with which did not strictly speaking front the road: the Knightsbridge foot-guards barracks and the Chinese Collection exhibition hall on part of the barracks site. Old Barrack Yard generally, however, is not included in this account.

Before 1903 the buildings along this side of Knightsbridge (then generally called Knightsbridge Road) were numbered under the names St George's Place and Lowndes Terrace. St George's Place extended from St George's Hospital as far as William Street, Lowndes Terrace occupying the remainder of the frontage up to Sloane Street. (A small part of St George's Place at its west end was known until 1860 as Knightsbridge Terrace.) In 1903 both these names were abolished and the buildings renumbered as part of Knightsbridge.

Summary of development

There was very little building here before the end of the seventeenth century. At that time a narrow roadside belt of manorial 'waste' belonging to Westminster Abbey extended, unbroken by any turning and almost entirely unbuilt upon, from Hyde Park Corner to the site of present-day William Street. By the late 1660s almost all of this ground – the future St George's Place – had come into the hands of one man, Sir William Poultney. The only part of the road frontage not held by him was an enclosure immediately to the east of William Street – later occupied by Knightsbridge Terrace – which had for very many years been let by the Abbey with a hospital or lazar-house on the north side of the road (where the French Embassy now stands). Poultney was also the lessee of two fields – the Great and Little Spittlefields – eastwards of the line of present-day Sloane Street; the northern field fronted the Knightsbridge road, where Lowndes Terrace was later built. These fields, their name suggesting that they once belonged to the lazar-house, had become separated from the rest of the Abbey estate and passed into the ownership of the Crown. A house and pleasure ground called Spring Gardens was established here in or soon after 1670.[1]

After Poultney's death his estate was broken up. The

Crown land was assigned in 1692 to William Lowndes, whose family subsequently obtained the freehold. The strip of waste was surrendered by Poultney's son in 1699, and was leased successively by the Dean and Chapter to Henry Guy, esquire, of Tring, and Joseph Shayle, gentleman, of St James's. A small portion at the east end was leased in 1718 to John Clark(e) of St James's, baker, who soon afterwards acquired much of the frontage on the north side of the road (roughly the area now occupied by Bowater House and the properties eastwards as far as Albert Gate).[2]

These changes in ownership were accompanied or soon followed by changes on the ground. In 1691 there had been only two houses on the Poultneys' Abbey land (both near Hyde Park Corner), but within thirty years it had been more or less completely built up. William Penn is said to have lived in a house here (later No. 8 St George's Place) for a time until 1706.[3] Lanesborough House was built about 1718, and houses and a brewhouse were built on the enclosure belonging to the lazar-house at about the same time.[4] The ribbon of new building eventually acquired the name St George's Place, presumably after St George's Hospital, founded in 1733 at Lanesborough House (but also reflecting the fact that it lay in the parish of St George, Hanover Square). Further building and some rebuilding occurred throughout the rest of the eighteenth century, and continued in the nineteenth.

The buildings between St George's Hospital and the entrance to Old Barrack Yard were rebuilt in the late 1820s with substantial houses, which attracted high-class residents. The road was at its widest here, the houses were set well back, and there were no buildings opposite, where the park wall ran along the roadside with no intervening verge or waste. This redevelopment followed further changes in landownership, with the sale by the Dean and Chapter in 1800 of the freeholds of the small estate leased by Clark in 1718 (to the then lessee, John Warner), and of much of the adjoining ground (to the lessee, Francis Burton).[5] In the early years of Queen Victoria's reign the occupants of the houses here included several noblemen and MPs, and this part of the road remained a good residential address well into the twentieth century.

West of the entrance to Old Barrack Yard, by contrast, the street developed a commercial character. The building of the Knightsbridge foot-guards barracks c.1760, on ground belonging to the Grosvenor family immediately south of the former waste, may have been a factor, perhaps reducing the desirability of the houses there as residences. Further along, the road narrowed sharply and there was continuous building on both sides of the road as the centre of Knightsbridge 'town' was reached, a situation perhaps conducive to a lower class of development than that nearer Hyde Park Corner.

When the brewhouse on the lazar-house property here was pulled down and redeveloped by John Mayor, in 1773–4, the new houses attracted just two 'esquires', and, for a short time only, the Countess of Salisbury in the largest house, at the west end of the row of eight. Her house was subsequently occupied as a 'College for the Deaf and Dumb' run by James Telfair (d.1796) and his son Cortez (d.1816). By 1830 all but two houses in Knightsbridge Terrace, as 'Mayor's Row' became known, were being used as shops or other business premises, and the countess's former house had been divided into two by 1841. In 1860 Knightsbridge Terrace was subsumed in St George's Place (Nos 45–53).[6]

Immediately east of Wilton Place, a row of houses with shops, Nos 28–32 St George's Place, was probably built for Francis Burton in the mid-1820s.[7]

Also in the 1820s, pressure from development on the estates to the south led to the creation of streets opening into the main road: Wilton Place, running north from Wilton Crescent on the Grosvenor estate, and William Street and Charles (now Seville) Street on the Lowndes estate (the Spring Gardens site), as the northern approaches to Lowndes Square. Even so, there was a general disjunction between the development of the ground alongside the main road and that of the backland, which remains obvious today, notably in the way Kinnerton Street stops short where it joins Duplex Ride, and in the absence of any street turnings (other than Old Barrack Yard) between Hyde Park Corner and Wilton Place (figs 4, 6).

With the building up of the Lowndes estate Spring Gardens finally disappeared; with them, too, went the floorcloth factory established here in the middle of the eighteenth century by the wallpaper makers Crompton and Spinnage. The new buildings on the estate fronting Knightsbridge, comprising Lowndes Terrace, were again all shops.

The closure in the mid-1830s of the foot-guards barracks (latterly a depot only) did not lead immediately to any great redevelopment, largely, no doubt, because the site had no frontage to the main road. It did, however, provide an opportunity for the erection of a gallery for displaying the celebrated Chinese Collection. This was the first of several exhibition venues in Knightsbridge (among which may be included the Crystal Palace itself).

More shops were built on Burton's property (by then in the ownership of O. B. Cole) in the later 1840s and '50s, and the White Horse inn, on the corner of the entrance to Old Barrack Yard, was rebuilt as an up-market hotel.

The businesses in this part of Knightsbridge included hatters, tailors, dressmakers, upholsterers and jewellers.

Drapery emerged as the predominant trade. Many, perhaps most, of these shops were of good class, and between William Street and Sloane Street there ultimately grew up two of the great London emporia, Woollands and Harvey Nichols, both originally small drapery shops.

No. 32 St George's Place (later No. 53 Knightsbridge), with a columned shop-front on the corner of Wilton Place, was a chemist's throughout its existence; the business itself dated back to the 1830s. Another long-lasting business was the English and Foreign Library, run here from 1849 by Charles Westerton, previously of Park Side, at No. 20 (later renumbered 27) St George's Place. This was set up to supply 'all classes of Readers . . . and at such a Low Subscription as to make it thoroughly a popular Establishment'. The annual fee was one guinea and by the late 1850s some 125,000 volumes were available. Later Bolton's Library was established further west at Nos 39–40 St George's Place. Both businesses survived well into the twentieth century, Bolton's latterly at No. 81 Knightsbridge.[8]

None of the houses built along the south side in the early nineteenth century was of special architectural interest. Nos 7–13 Knightsbridge (formerly Nos 4–7 St George's Place), built by William Cubitt in 1828–9 for Matthew Kinsey of Oxford Street, calico-printer, were much taller than their neighbours but of conventional design, with stuccoed ground-floor fronts and Doric porches (Plates 9b–c, 12a).[9] Lowndes Terrace, again of the 1820s, was also unexceptional. The most ambitious redevelopment architecturally took place in the 1850s, on the Cole estate (at the site now largely occupied by No. 27 Knightsbridge). This was a terrace with a splendid palace façade, designed by Frederick Robert Beeston senior (described below).

None of this, or any earlier building fabric, remains. Most of the old buildings which survived the piecemeal redevelopment of the nineteenth century were destroyed early in the twentieth, when all the houses and shops between Wilton Place and William Street were pulled down for road-widening (and replaced by the present shops, offices and flats). Beeston's terrace was wrecked by bombing in the Second World War. Since the war many houses have been pulled down for redevelopment: the last of the 1820s houses near St George's Hospital was demolished in 1991. A pair of large houses erected in 1870–1, Nos 15 and 17 Knightsbridge, are the oldest surviving buildings.

The decline of this part of Knightsbridge as a residential street did not begin until the First World War, but the arrival of the underground railway in the 1900s and the growth of heavy motor traffic were already undermining its desirability. By the late 1920s several houses had passed into institutional or commercial use, and some were divided into flats and offices. Adams, Holden & Pearson, architects to St George's Hospital, had offices at No. 9 Knightsbridge in the 1920s and '30s, while No. 25 became a foreign legation and then the premises of the furniture makers Betty Joel Ltd. No. 1 Knightsbridge had always been in the occupation of the hospital, having been built about 1828 for the accommodation of the chaplain and

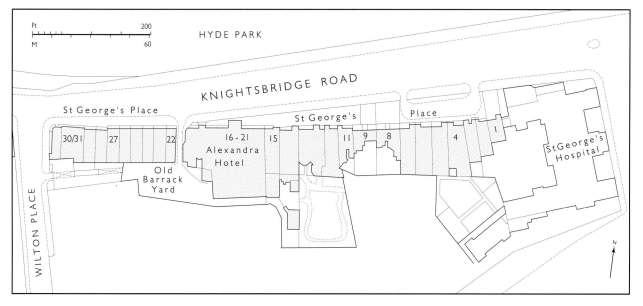

Fig. 2. Knightsbridge, south side, Hyde Park Corner to Wilton Place in 1869: Nos 1–32 St George's Place

other staff, and rebuilt on a much larger scale in the 1860s. In time Nos 3–9 were all occupied by departments of the hospital, and by the end of the Second World War only one house between the hospital and Old Barrack Yard remained a private residence: No. 19, occupied by Brig.-Gen. Sir George Cockerill.[10]

Today, the south side of Knightsbridge as far west as Wilton Place is dominated by commercial blocks built since the Second World War, few of them of more than passing architectural interest. With the exception of the 1930s block at Nos 37–39 Knightsbridge, all the buildings between Old Barrack Yard and Wilton Place were cleared for redevelopment in the 1960s. Further west, Knightsbridge retains much of its early-twentieth-century character, both architecturally and as a high-class shopping street.

Hyde Park Corner to Wilton Place

Before the Second World War the buildings along this part of Knightsbridge were predominantly of nineteenth-century date, the exceptions being the original Hyde Park Corner underground station at Nos 11–13 and the 1930s flats at Nos 37–39, both of which survive. In the main they belonged to two phases of building: late 1820s at the east end, on the former Warner estate, and early to mid-Victorian on the former Cole estate. Nothing now remains of the first phase, and of the second the only vestige is the pair of early 1870s houses at Nos 15 and 17.

The Cole Estate

Part freehold and part leasehold, the Cole estate extended from the site of No. 15 Knightsbridge nearly as far west as William Street. The leasehold of this entire strip was acquired in 1793 by Francis Burton, a distinguished lawyer and MP, partly as trustee for his mother and sister. Burton himself lived in a house near the entrance to the footguards barracks, and his mother a few doors away. In 1800 he had the opportunity to purchase the freehold from the Dean and Chapter of Westminster Abbey. Challenging their valuation, he argued that most of the existing houses were too old to last more than a few decades, that the ground was insufficiently drained, and that the plots were too shallow to allow rebuilding 'to much advantage'.[11]

In the event, because of a troublesome undertenant whose consent to the arrangement was required, Burton bought only part of the freehold (as far west as the site of Wilton Place), and he continued to lease the remaining property further west, where his underlessee was the brewer Thomas Goding. At the same time, Goding acquired from Burton the freehold of two of the houses towards the east end (the site of the present No. 25 Knightsbridge), which he had also been holding as Burton's tenant, thus splitting the estate in two. Two of Burton's leasehold houses were pulled down in 1827 for the creation of Wilton Place (another house, on the east corner of Wilton Place, went in the mid-1840s to widen the junction).[12]

After his death in 1832, Burton's estate passed in quick succession to his nephews Francis Burton Cole and Owen Blayney Cole.[a] The Coles were a well-connected Anglo-

___

[a] The Cole brothers were friends and Oxford contemporaries of W. E. Gladstone, who became technically involved in the administration of the estate as a trustee under O. B. Cole's marriage settlement in 1834.[13]

Irish family, with property in Meath and Monaghan; they also owned the Cole Brewery in Twickenham, which had public houses in various parts of London. Whether or not as a consequence of the Cole property interests here, St George's Place as far west as Old Barrack Yard attracted a large number of well-off residents with Irish connections during the nineteenth century.[14]

O. B. Cole's mental state made it impossible for him to handle business matters, and it was left to his family and advisers to manage the property.[15] The remaining leasehold houses were given up in 1834,[16] and the estate was further reduced in size in 1846 by the sale of the freehold of two houses at the east end (on the sites of Nos 15 and 17 Knightsbridge). But from 1847 a fairly systematic redevelopment was carried out, and by the early 1860s most of the houses on the estate had been rebuilt. The architect for all this rebuilding was F. R. Beeston senior, who at the beginning of this period had his office very near that of O. B. Cole's friend and solicitor, Gilbert Stephens, in Northumberland Street.[17]

Redevelopment on the Cole Estate, 1847–61

The improvement of the estate began following the closure of the Chinese Collection in 1846. During the next couple of years, a terrace of six houses with shops – the easternmost occupying the site of the pagoda forming the entrance to the exhibition – was built immediately west of the turning into the old barracks (Old Barrack Yard). The lessees of this row (originally Nos 22–27 St George's Place, later Nos 33–43 Knightsbridge) included William Dear, a local upholsterer and auctioneer, his partner George Rogers, and John Phillips, lessee of the old barracks. Beeston's design was Italianate in style. The terrace was brick-faced with stucco or stone dressings, the end houses emphasized by the addition of an attic storey (Plate 10a, c).[18]

Dear then proceeded to redevelop the row of houses belonging to Cole just east of Old Barrack Yard (Plate 9a). The first of these – the easternmost (No. 15 St George's Place, later No. 27 Knightsbridge) – was rebuilt in 1849–50, but it was not until 1856–8 that the reconstruction of the rest, including the White Horse inn on the corner of the entrance to Old Barrack Yard, was undertaken. The completed range consisted of six houses, all leased to Dear, and a hotel, replacing the White Horse and leased to its last landlord, Martin Wallace.[19] The first house was probably built by H. W. Cooper, whose tender, the lowest received, was £2,879; the five following, on somewhat narrower frontages, were built by S. S. Wilson on a tender of £10,745. The hotel, tendered for at £7,189, was erected by Isaac Wilkinson & Son. Beeston's son supervised the construction.[20]

For these buildings, occupying a frontage of nearly 166ft, Beeston designed a unified palace façade, executed in cement stucco and Portland stone, with a centrepiece surmounted by a pediment and statues and urns on the skyline (Plate 10a). In the tympanum of the pediment was a sculptural group of St George and the Dragon, flanked by cornucopias of fruit and flowers, 'modelled expressly' by Dominico Brucciani of Covent Garden, who also supplied figures and urns for the parapet. There was a railed-off private carriageway along the front of the buildings. The *Building News* found the ensemble 'one of the most successful examples of street architecture that has been produced in London'.[21]

Prospective tenants, however, do not seem to have been so impressed. Most of the houses did not attract long-term residents, and two stood empty for some years. The easternmost house remained a private dwelling (it was used as a club-house before the Second World War), but in time the others became part of the Alexandra Hotel, as Wallace's hotel became in the 1860s (see below).

While building was in progress, F. R. Beeston senior installed himself a few doors away at No. 11 (later No. 12) St George's Place – his son is listed in the directories at the same address from 1859. Moving from there to one of the new houses, Beeston rebuilt the old place on a 99-year lease in 1860–1.[22] No. 21 Knightsbridge, as it later became, was a tall, French-looking house, stucco-fronted with shallow bows and fancy ironwork (Plate 11b). The house was a private residence until the 1930s, when it was made into service flats; it was used as offices from the 1940s.[23]

Next door, No. 19 Knightsbridge, designed by Beeston in the late 1840s or '50s, and later raised in height, was demolished in the early 1960s (Plates 11b, 12a).

The only buildings on the estate left untouched by the redevelopments overseen by the Beestons were the houses and shops immediately eastwards of Wilton Place, Nos 45–53 Knightsbridge, which were pulled down in the 1960s for the Berkeley Hotel development.

Nos 23 and 25 Knightsbridge (demolished)

The freehold of the sites of these two houses (Plate 11b) was bought in 1800 by the brewer Thomas Goding from Francis Burton (see page 21). Much the grander of the two, No. 23 (formerly No. 13 and originally No. 12 St George's Place) was rebuilt for Goding to the designs of Francis Edwards in 1837, replacing the double-fronted house indicated on Salway's plan of 1811. The house was occupied by the Godings until the mid-1880s; its large garden was mostly obliterated in the late nineteenth century by the creation of Grosvenor Crescent Mews. Later, it was the town residence of successive Earls of Lovelace, the Dowager Countess of Lovelace having moved there from the present No. 17 Knightsbridge in the 1890s. In its latter years the house was used commercially for receptions and banqueting.[24] It was demolished in the early 1960s, along with the two houses to the east, when the present No. 21 Knightsbridge was built.

No. 25, a plainer three-bay house, of uncertain date, was from 1928 until 1939 the London showroom of the furniture manufacturers Betty and David Joel. The architect H. S. Goodhart-Rendel, who regularly employed Betty

Joel Ltd to make up furniture, designed a Modernistic shopfront for the building in plate glass and coursed slate. This, together with metal 'shiprails' to the first-floor windows, was installed by Pollards of Clerkenwell in 1937.[25] That same year the Joels divorced, and the business was subsequently wound up.[26]

At the rear of the shop was a gallery for exhibitions of paintings, drawings and carpets. Badly damaged in the Second World War, the house was demolished in the 1950s for the building of Agriculture House.

Alexandra Hotel (demolished)

The Wallace Hotel, opened in 1858 on the site of the White Horse inn, at the eastern corner of the entrance to Old Barrack Yard, soon established itself as a first-class residential hotel, patronized by the nobility. The accommodation comprised a ground-floor apartment, 30ft by 20ft and almost 20ft high, a 'splendid bar', and a first-floor coffee-room 30ft square and 15ft high; the upper floors were divided into bedrooms with *en suite* dressing-rooms. Wallace soon found it necessary to expand the premises, taking over the house next door and the house on the opposite corner of Old Barrack Yard.[27]

In 1863 the hotel was acquired by the specially formed Alexandra Hotel Company Limited, with which Wallace himself seems to have had no connection. The original board, drawn entirely from Establishment ranks and rewarded with salaries of £1,500 a year, included the diplomatist Sir William Gore Ouseley, Vice-Admiral Sir George Lambert, and Lieut.-Col. Sir Charles Du Plat, a former equerry to Prince Albert. Shares in the new company were subscribed for, however, by a much wider range of people, including local and other tradesmen, and even servants, many, presumably, having business or employment links with the hotel. As well as the original Wallace Hotel, the company acquired the leases of the five houses adjoining to the east, and stabling at the rear.[28]

After initial alterations, probably designed by the architect Francis E. H. Fowler, the vastly enlarged establishment re-opened in the spring of 1864 as the Alexandra Hotel (Plate 10a).[b] That August it was reported that since the commencement of the London season every room had been occupied, and the manager 'overwhelmed' with applications for apartments. Further improvements, costing £20,000, were put in hand, to Fowler's designs. They included a new entrance portico with banded columns (Plate 22). It was probably at this time that a passenger-lift or 'ascending room' to all floors was installed.[30]

With its 'magnificent' premises and excellent location – 'one of the most cheerful, healthy, and pleasant' in London – the Alexandra achieved a high reputation.[31] In 1883 it acquired the services of a new manager, Joseph Gams, who

had worked at Delmonico's in New York, and had managed the Imperial Hotel in his native Vienna before running his own hotel in Marienbad.[32]

But despite the arrival of Gams, with his cosmopolitan sophistication, the real control of the Alexandra remained in the hands of George Bolton, who had, briefly, been the first manager, and later became company secretary and eventually managing director. Bolton's reign ended in 1897 when he was revealed as a fraudster. The scandal came to light following the discovery of a systematic overcharging racket at the Grosvenor Hotel in Victoria, organized by Richard Collins Drew, a butcher in St George's Place (whose customers included the Queen and other members of the royal family). The Grosvenor revelations, which led to a Board of Trade inquiry, caused questions to be asked about Drew's role as 'principal purveyor' to the Alexandra. Drew and Bolton turned out to have been working in collusion for years to defraud the hotel, and other serious malpractices by Bolton were discovered. The entire board of management was ultimately forced to resign, and effective control of the hotel passed into the hands of (Sir) Henry Kimber MP, who had exposed the Grosvenor scandal, and a fellow Grosvenor Hotel shareholder, Russell Spokes, an accountant.[33]

The hotel's finances were perhaps never fully restored, though its high reputation was undimmed. It was said in 1907 that almost every European royal house was represented in its guest lists, together with innumerable statesmen, diplomats and celebrities. Although it was taken over by a chain, the North Hotels, in the late 1920s, it seems to have retained its old ambience. Writing in the late 1940s, the journalist James Bone recalled 'that prim hotel of suites in Knightsbridge with its stiff, frail Ouidaesque air . . . probably the last hotel where country people still came up "for the season"'.[34] By then the Alexandra Hotel was largely a blitzed shell. It was finally demolished in the early 1950s, along with No. 27 Knightsbridge, to make way for Agriculture House.

Knightsbridge Foot-Guards Barracks (demolished)

The northern portion of Old Barrack Yard is all that remains of a large, irregularly shaped enclosure which was once the outer parade ground of an infantry barracks for some 500 men.[35] The barracks itself stood to the south of the yard, its inner courtyard being aligned more or less along what is now the eastern arm of Wilton Place (fig. 3). Immediately south of the buildings was a garden for the soldiers' use (see Plate 5c).

This establishment, though said to date from as early as 1758, seems to have originated with stabling erected here under a lease of 1760 from Sir Richard Grosvenor, the ground landlord, to Samuel Thresher and Thomas Fisher.

[b] The choice of name was obviously prompted by the marriage in March 1863 of the Prince of Wales and Princess Alexandra of Denmark. More specifically, it was later claimed that the preliminaries for the marriage were arranged in the (Wallace) hotel by Baron Blixea Finicke, the Danish Envoy, and the Duke of Cambridge.[29]

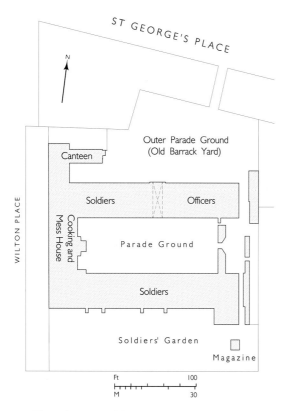

Fig. 3. Foot-guards barracks behind St George's Place;
plan in 1830. *Demolished*

These stables had been completed by November 1762, when they were in the occupation of the 2nd Troop of Horse Grenadier Guards (later reformed as the 2nd Life Guards), on a sub-tenancy.[36]

By October 1789 the buildings had been converted and newly fitted out for use by foot soldiers, and were in the occupation of the Coldstream Guards. So good was the revamped barracks – 'a treat to any military man' – that it was to have been used as a model in a proposed country-wide barrack-building campaign.[37] (Though no such scheme was implemented at this time, the principal building at Knightsbridge cavalry barracks near by, erected in 1792–3 for the Life Guards, may well have been designed with the foot-guards barracks in mind.)

The driving force behind this model establishment was probably George III's son Frederick Augustus, Duke of York and Albany, who had been colonel of the 2nd Horse Grenadier Guards since 1782 and colonel of the Cold-stream Guards since 1784. The duke, who showed throughout his career a particular interest in the well-being of his men, is known to have been responsible for two works connected with the barracks put forward early in 1790. These were the opening of a new gateway immediately opposite the barracks, for the soldiers to march into Hyde Park, and the acquisition and demolition of buildings adjoining the barrack-yard to improve ventilation.[38]

The barracks was given up by the military in the mid-1830s, and the old buildings let as tenements.[39] They were largely demolished in the early 1840s, when St Paul's Church was built on the site of the southern range and the soldiers' garden, and a hall for exhibiting the Chinese Collection was erected on the northern part of the barracks site, just behind the houses in St George's Place (see below). Any remains of the barracks were doubtless swept away when the site was redeveloped in 1857–9, with houses and a school fronting the eastern arm of Wilton Place.[40] The five houses (Nos 32–36 Wilton Place) were all built by Thomas Phillips, son of John Phillips, the long-time lessee of the barracks site. They, and the school to the east built in 1859 in connection with St Paul's Church, were pulled down for the construction of the new Berkeley Hotel, opened in 1972.

A plausibly military-looking building in the south-east corner of Old Barrack Yard has been assumed to be part of the old barracks, but is of later date. It was probably erected as livery stables, and belonged formerly to the Alexandra Hotel.[41]

The Chinese Collection and St George's Gallery (demolished)

In the summer of 1842 the *Illustrated London News* reported that

towards the extremity of St George's-place, a grotesque erection has lately sprung up with all the rapidity which distinguishes building operations of the present day. As work proceeded, many were the guesses at the purpose for which it was intended; and, to feed the suspense, the work was covered with canvass until just completed.[42]

The mysterious structure which had attracted such curiosity was a replica of a Chinese summer-house or 'pagoda' at the corner of the way in to Old Barrack Yard (Plate 6a). This arresting object was the entrance to an exhibition of Chinese art and artefacts known as the Chinese Collection, which had opened to the public on 23 June.[43] The exhibition itself was in a new building back from the main road, and the pagoda, designed after a model in the collection, served both as a ticket-office and way in to the exhibition hall, which was reached up steps and through a vestibule or covered walk at the rear (Plate 11a).

The Chinese Collection had been amassed by an American merchant, Nathan Dunn (1782–1844), during his twelve years in Canton, and exhibited by him from 1838 at the Philadelphia Museum. In 1842 – 'at the suggestion of many of the most influential, scientific, and learned persons of the British metropolis and kingdom'[44] – Dunn brought the collection to England and opened it to the public in the specially constructed hall in Knightsbridge, which occupied part of the site of the former foot-guards barracks. With Dunn came William B. Langdon, the London-born curator of the collection and the author of a descriptive catalogue, who had known him in China.[45]

Both the hall and the pagoda were erected by the public-works contractors Grissell & Peto, the pagoda at a cost of £800.[46] The pagoda stood about 19ft square, a 'somewhat squatly proportioned' wooden building with a single room to each of its two storeys. It was decorated in gold and bright colours – green roofs, and vermilion pillars with white capitals – and ornamented with brackets in the form of dragons. Over the doorway was a Chinese inscription signifying 'Ten Thousand Chinese Things'.[47] The hall, 225ft long and 50ft wide, was a plain affair externally (Plate 6a). Inside, it was largely taken up by a single lofty 'saloon', top lit and lined with pillars: 'a sort of Brighton Pavilion with permanent fittings'.[48] In Langdon's words:

The rich screen-work, elaborately carved and gilt, at either end . . . the many-shaped and varied-colored lanterns suspended throughout the entire ceiling; the native paintings which cover the walls; the Chinese maxims adorning the columns and entablatures; the embroidered silks, gay with a hundred colours, and tastefully displayed above the cases containing the figures, and the multitude of smaller cases crowded with rare and interesting objects, form a *tout ensemble*, possessing a beauty entirely its own.[49]

The 'figures' were life-size mannequins, made of fine clay and said to be portrayals of actual individuals drawn from many different classes of Chinese society, set in 'scenes and furnished dwellings'. Among the exhibits were a two-storey house from Canton and various shops from the city's streets.[50]

The Collection was well timed to capture the public imagination, opening just weeks before Britain's peace treaty with the Chinese at Nanking brought the first Opium War to a triumphant close. For a few years it was something which 'every one went to see as one of the duties of the London season' – a peak of success which its revival at Albert Gate in 1851 signally failed to regain.[51] The Duke of Wellington assured Dunn of its 'stature and real importance', and Queen Victoria, who with the Prince Consort was given a private view, felt that 'one could have almost fancied oneself in China'.[52]

A contributory factor in the exhibition's success may have been that it was, ostensibly at any rate, run for cultural and educational and not merely commercial reasons. Dunn was reported as wishing only 'to cover the current expenses', and the Queen was given to understand that any profits would go to charity. (A Quaker, and unmarried, Dunn made generous provision in his will for charitable and educational purposes in America and Britain.)[53]

At half-a-crown, the price of admission was much higher than at most London exhibitions, and drew some criticism. Dunn said he had fixed the charge after consulting his royal and noble visitors. In 1843 it was cut to the usual shilling. To maintain public interest, gaslighting was laid on, the better to bring out 'the splendour of the gilding and decorations of the gallery', and new attractions were introduced, including two Chinese youths as live exhibits, and a 'Fête of the Dragon', when an enormous illuminated dragon was suspended from the roof.[54]

After Dunn's death in 1844, an attempt was made to sell the collection to the British Museum. This was unsuccessful and the exhibition, now under Langdon's direction, continued in Knightsbridge until 1846. It subsequently toured Britain,[55] returning briefly to America before re-opening at a new site in Knightsbridge in 1851 (see page 52).

With the departure of the Chinese Collection, John Phillips, the lessee of the old barracks property, put the pagoda up for sale as a garden building, 'well worthy the attention of noblemen & gentlemen for country seats'. In 1847 it caught the eye of James Pennethorne, architect to the Commissioners of Woods and Forests, who purchased it for 100 guineas to ornament a lake island in Victoria Park, Hackney, which he was then laying out, and where it survived until demolished in 1956.[56]

The main building, which eventually became known as St George's Gallery, housed various exhibitions until the mid-1850s. They included the second and third annual shows of the Institution for the Free Exhibition of Modern Art (later the National Institution of Fine Arts), held in 1848 and 1849. Among the works shown in 1849 was Rossetti's *The Girlhood of Mary Virgin*, the first painting with the PRB monogram to be displayed in public. Another exhibitor in 1849 was Ford Madox Brown with *The Young Mother* and *Lear and Cordelia*.[57]

In 1850–2 a South African show was held by the Eton-educated lion-hunter Roualeyn George Gordon-Cumming, whom Livingstone described as 'a mad sort of Scotsman'. His collection of trophies made the gallery look like 'a combination of a baronial hall and a furrier's shop'. A 'Hottentot boy' was on hand to explain the exhibits: he spoke good English, but an American visitor detected the 'odor of gin about him'.[58]

Dioramas, running in tandem with the other shows, though presumably in another part of the building, were popular in the early 1850s. Queen Victoria's visit to Ireland was the subject of a 'moving diorama' painted by Philip Phillips in 1850, and a diorama of Jerusalem and the Holy Land (claimed to be the largest yet on this popular theme) was displayed in 1851–3. Based on sketches by W. H. Bartlett, author of *Walks about Jerusalem*, the latter was 'cleverly painted' under the direction of William Roxby Beverley of the Lyceum and Princess's Theatres, with life-size figures and 'objects of corresponding magnitude and grandeur'. There was a spoken commentary and an accompaniment of sacred music.[59]

In 1853 a display of 'Kaffir' life was held, with a native group from Natal to enact scenes such as a wedding, a hunt and an inter-tribal fight, against a moving panorama painted by Charles Marshall. After seeing the show, Charles Dickens was moved to conclude that 'if we have anything to learn from the Noble Savage, it is what to avoid. His virtues are a fable; his happiness is a delusion; his nobility, nonsense'.[60] The Kaffirs were followed in 1854 by a diorama of the Duke of Wellington's funeral and a Turkish exhibition of wax figures arranged in tableaux showing, as well as more prosaic scenes of middle-eastern life, a slave market and a sultan's harem. In 1855 this exhibition – the

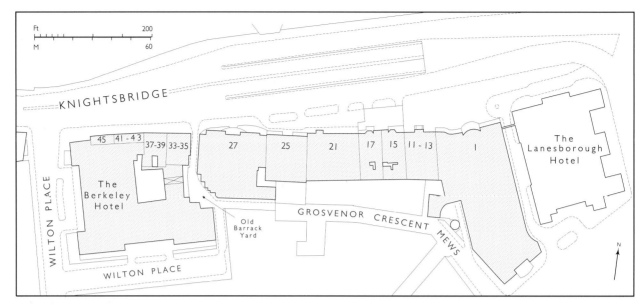

Fig. 4. Knightsbridge, south side, Hyde Park Corner to Wilton Place in 1991

final show at the St George's Gallery – transferred to the Great Globe in Leicester Square.[61]

The exhibition hall, rated a 'Museum', lingered on in the ratebooks until the early 1860s,[62] though the bulk, if not all of the building, must by then have been pulled down for the redevelopment along the eastern arm of Wilton Place in the late 1850s. If anything of the hall survived, as part of the commercial premises between the houses in St George's Place and Wilton Place, it would have succumbed to the Berkeley Hotel development in 1966–72.

Present-day buildings

No. 1 Knightsbridge. This office block, completed in 1991, was designed by the Fitzroy Robinson Partnership and built by Bovis for the Abu Dhabi Investment Authority (Plate 16b). Its outstanding features are the undulating Post-Modernist façade, faced in Williamson Cliff's Stamfordstone brick and Indiana buff limestone, and a 'spectacular' atrium extending the full depth of the building. The interior is finished in Comblanchian limestone and polished black (*nero assoluto*) marble.[63]

Nos 11–13 Knightsbridge. The Pizza on the Park restaurant at Nos 11–13 occupies the former Hyde Park Corner underground station, opened in 1906. The upper storeys, now offices, were opened a few years later as a hotel (Plate 10b).

In the late 1890s and early 1900s there was a flurry of schemes to build an electric tube railway through Knightsbridge to the West End, all with plans for a Hyde Park Corner station at the east end of St George's Place. The one to come to fruition was the earliest, the Brompton & Piccadilly Circus (later Great Northern, Piccadilly & Bromp-

ton) Railway, financed by the Underground Electric Railways Company of London Ltd. Terms for the compulsory purchase of the two houses on the station site, then numbered 6 and 7 St George's Place, were agreed in January 1903,[64] and in December 1906 the new railway, the core of the present-day Piccadilly Line, opened.

Hyde Park Corner Station was designed by Underground Electric's architect Leslie Green, and follows the pattern devised by him for the company's stations throughout London, on what are now the Piccadilly, Northern and Bakerloo Lines: a steel-framed structure clad in ox-blood faience, with large round-arched openings, intended as the podium for a multi-storeyed building. Inside, the walls of the ground floor were tiled in cream with a green dado. From the ticket-hall a corridor led to a staircase and lifts to the platforms, where the original brown, green and yellow tiling can still be seen today.

The central opening, which initially housed a branch of W. H. Smith & Son,[65] soon became the entrance to the new Hyde Park Corner Hotel. This comprised most of the first floor of the Leslie Green building, together with five storeys added in 1908–9. The developer was F. J. Coxhead, builder, of Leytonstone. Delissa Joseph, who had already designed several buildings above London underground stations, and who worked elsewhere for Coxhead, was the architect. He gave the building a strong French flavour, with an ornate façade of Portland stone and a high mansard roof.[66]

The Hyde Park Corner Hotel was soon renamed Sartori's Park View Hotel, after its new proprietor Felix Roneo Sartori, who moved there from the Hotel André in Jermyn Street, and was later known simply as the Park View Hotel. It closed in the 1950s.[67]

By that time the rest of the building had long ceased to be a station. The ticket-hall and lifts were closed in 1932, when a new below-ground ticket-hall and escalators, approached by pedestrian subways, were opened nearer Hyde Park Corner.[68] In March 1935 the old station re-opened as a Lyons teashop. The interior of this 258th Lyons had some novel features. As well as air-conditioning, it had a modernistic décor with tinted mirrors and coloured Vitrolite, a scheme which was used generally in new Lyons teashops between then and the Second World War, in place of the usual marble.[69]

At the time of writing a statue of the jazz musician 'Duke' Ellington, by the sculptor Nicholas Dimbleby, stands in the forecourt, erected in connection with the 1999 Soho Jazz and Heritage Festival.

Nos 15 and 17 Knightsbridge. These are the only survivors from the nineteenth-century rebuilding of St George's Place.[70] They were erected in 1870–1 for Mrs Helen Blake, widow of General Robert Blake, who had bought the freeholds of the old houses on the site from O. B. Cole's trustees in 1846.[71] The Blakes were then occupying the eastern of the two houses, No. 8 St George's Place; the other (No. 9) was occupied by James Goding, of the brewing family. The old houses – dismissed by the *Builder* as 'the disfigurement of one of the finest spots of the locality'[72] – were double-fronted (Plate 9b) and wide enough to allow rebuilding on a fairly large scale, each house having a frontage of 39ft.

The new Italianate-style houses (Plate 12a) were designed by George Legg, the Belgravia and Pimlico District Surveyor, and erected by Hill & Sons for something above £14,000.[73] They are built of white brick with stone dressings and red-granite columns to the porches. The original railings, with a gateway at each end to the shared carriage-drive, no longer exist.

The first occupant of No. 17 was Byron's son-in-law, the 1st Earl of Lovelace. It was later occupied by members of the Sassoon and Ezra families, and from 1948 until 1971 was used by the Royal Society for the Prevention of Accidents as an exhibition and training centre.[74]

No. 15 remained untenanted until 1876, shortly before Mrs Blake's death, when it was let to Henrietta Baden-Powell, widow of the Reverend Baden Powell, Savilian professor of geometry at Oxford. Five of her six children lived here with her: Warington, sailor and barrister; George, diplomat and MP; Frank, painter and sculptor; Baden, soldier and inventor; and Agnes, who became the first president of the Girl Guides. Robert, hero of Mafeking and founder of the scouting movement, stayed here when on leave from overseas service. When news of the relief of Mafeking reached London on 18 May 1900, Mrs Baden-Powell came out on to the balcony to acknowledge a cheering crowd.[75] Plates 12–13 show the house during the Baden-Powells' occupation: the internal finishing and decorating was all carried out for them. Frank designed the Gothic-style fireplace in the inner hall bearing the family monogram and crest. The pipe-organ in the double drawing-room was installed for Agnes.[76]

After Mrs Blake's death, intestate and without known heirs, her property passed by escheat to the Crown. Both Lord Lovelace and Mrs Baden-Powell subsequently tried, without success, to obtain the freeholds of their houses. In the late 1890s proposals for a tube railway with a station in the vicinity, which at one time threatened the houses with demolition, reduced the desirability of the location for Mrs Baden-Powell and she left in 1902. From 1906 until 1936 No. 15 was occupied by Robert Sauber, painter and newspaper illustrator; it was later used in connection with St George's Hospital.[77]

The interior today retains its original staircase, with a balustrade of a pattern very similar to one also found in C. J. Freake's houses in Princes Gate (see fig. 90 on page 197): there is an identical balustrade at No. 17. Very little of the Baden-Powells' decorative scheme is left, the main rooms having been redone in a Baroque classical style, with much ornamental plasterwork. In the back room on the ground floor is a painted ceiling in a pastiche eighteenth-century allegorical manner.

No. 21 Knightsbridge. Designed by Julian Keable and Partners for the Knightsbridge Comprehensive Property Investment Company, this block of offices and flats was built in 1962–3 by Firmin & Collins. It is faced in Britts Blue granite and dark, heat-absorbing glass (Plate 16a).[78]

Nos 25 and 27 Knightsbridge. These replace **Agriculture House**, which was built in 1954–63 on the site of the Alexandra Hotel and the two adjoining properties to the east as a headquarters for the National Farmers' Union (Plate 10c). Designed by Ronald Ward & Partners and built by Trollope & Colls, Agriculture House was a double-mansarded block with a 'Bankers' Georgian' façade given some distinction by a centrepiece of four recessed columns in Lutyens's New Delhi order. It was demolished in 1993.[79]

The present buildings are Post-Modernist office blocks of unequal size, designed by Hunter & Partners and built by Trollope & Colls in 1993–5 (Plate 16a, c). The smaller building, No. 25, faced in brick and Portland stone, was intended as the NFU's new headquarters, and originally had two bronzes, *The Sower* and *The Reaper*, by Mark Richardson, on its forecourt; these were removed when the NFU let the building to Carlton Television. No. 27, the headquarters of Dunhill International, is faced in Portland stone and pale grey granite, and has a bowed front and central atrium.[80]

The Berkeley Hotel development. The whole block between Old Barrack Yard and Wilton Place was acquired in the 1960s by the Savoy Hotels Group as the new site for the Berkeley Hotel, which had outgrown its premises in Piccadilly. It was almost entirely rebuilt in 1966–72, to designs by Brian O'Rorke. The main contractors were Beaufort Construction Ltd and Harry Neal Ltd.[81]

Of the old buildings on the site only **Nos 37–39** were retained. This block of flats and shops, designed by

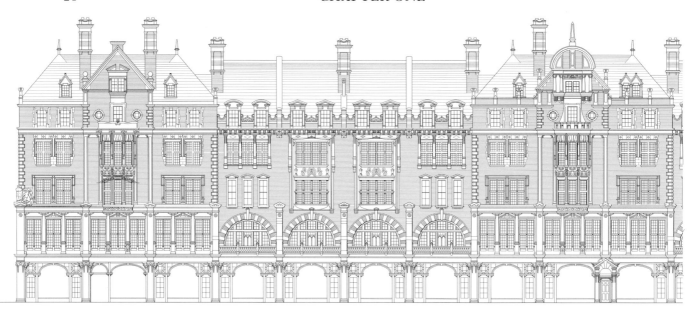

Mitchell & Bridgwater for Robert Heath Ltd, hatters (long established at No. 37), was erected in 1935–6. It is faced in greyish-brown bricks supplied by the Yorkshire Brick Company, with Portland-stone 'cornices'. But the stylish façade (Plate 10c) has been much disfigured by the replacement of the 1930s metal-framed glazing, and the original Travertine shopfronts have been re-faced.[82]

The new buildings fronting Knightsbridge – a block of flats at **Nos 33–35**, completed in 1967, and the flank of the new Berkeley (Plate 17a) – to some extent take their cue from the 1930s building, with projecting windows and similar facing materials (Stamfordstone buff bricks and Portland stone). They are of reinforced-concrete construction. Commercial premises on the ground floor of the hotel block include a cinema, the 68-seat 'Minema', at No. 45.

The hotel itself, opened in 1972, fronts Wilton Place, a rather plain neo-Georgian block, faced in Clipsham limestone, which the *Architectural Review* found 'a lugubrious and puddingy pile'. The conservatism and craftsmanship evident in the exterior were carried on inside, where a team of interior designers, including O'Rorke, Michael Inchbald, and Bridget D'Oyly Carte re-used panelling, fireplaces and other fittings from the old Berkeley, including the Grill Room designed by Lutyens in 1913, and materials from the houses demolished to make way for the hotel.

Wilton Place to William Street

The whole of this stretch of the road is occupied by a range of shops and flats, **Nos 55–93 Knightsbridge**, built in the early 1900s. This redevelopment, to allow the road to be widened, was one of the first major street improvements proposed by the new London County Council in 1889. Statutory powers were initially obtained in 1891, but, to avoid the expense of buying out the lessees, the work had to wait until the last leases expired in 1902 and the freeholders, the Ecclesiastical Commissioners (successors to the Dean and Chapter of Westminster Abbey), could hand over the strip of land required for the road with vacant possession.[83]

By this time the Ecclesiastical Commissioners were taking the line that the 'gradual extinction' of the renewable lease system (customary on church-owned properties) was one of the objects for which they had been appointed. New leases would be offered in the first place to occupiers only. Dismayed, head lessees saw their leases extinguished and premises on which they and their predecessors had spent heavily, often over many generations, destroyed.[84]

The old houses were demolished in the late summer of 1902, and redevelopment (nearly all of it completed during 1903) was carried out by making building agreements with the occupiers. By these agreements, leading to 80-year leases for themselves or their nominees, occupiers undertook to rebuild on approved but evidently variable plans, 'adapting' the fronts to a master elevation (which included the flank wall of No. 55, in Wilton Place) prepared by the Commissioners' architect, W. D. Caröe. Nos 83–91 were rebuilt by (Sir) William Houghton-Gastrell, occupier of one of the old houses, on a similar agreement to the rest, but he was somehow able to secure a 999-year lease, which he apparently wanted because such a long lease from the Commissioners did not require assignments to be approved. The new buildings consisted of shops with flats or maisonettes above, Gastrell's section including Wilton House, No. 87 Knightsbridge, a group of private apartments.[85]

Also affected by the road-widening was a small wedge of the Lowndes estate at the top of William Street, where the northernmost house had to be cut back. A turret was added on the corner, at No. 93, originally blending with the Caröe range but now painted over (Plate 17c).

W. D. Caröe's façade (fig. 5), perhaps the most success-

Fig. 5. Nos 55–91 Knightsbridge. W. D. Caröe, architect, 1902. *Shop fronts restored to presumed original appearance*

ful treatment of any of the late Victorian and Edwardian blocks along both sides of Knightsbridge, is carried out in two-inch brick with stone dressings. The rich and often quirky detail includes six busts, set in pediments over the first-floor windows: they portray Edward VII, Queen Alexandra, Field Marshal Lord Roberts, his second-in-command in the Boer War, Lord Kitchener, the Archbishop of Canterbury, Frederick Temple, and the Prime Minister, Lord Salisbury (Plate 38b–i). A plaque records the year of building as that of Edward's coronation, 1902.

Caröe's design, however, was made without much regard for the views and requirements of the occupants of the new block, one of whom, a butcher, complained that

The whole of the tenants have, either personally or through their architects and solicitors, strenuously resisted the unheard-of and unprecedented pretensions of the architect, who, not content with having a free hand (which he has used unsparingly in erecting these ornate and costly edifices at the expense of the tenants . . .) desires to dictate and impose upon them shop-fronts totally unsuited for their trades.[86]

Businesses in the newly built block included the Byzan-otype Portrait Company, art dealers, Robersons Ltd, the period-interiors specialists, a newspaper advertising agency, a theatre-ticket office, a bridge club, and one of Hamley Brothers' toy-shops.[87]

The redevelopment proved far from beneficial for some of the lessees, whose small businesses did not require large premises but who had to pay ground-rent on their buildings regardless of whether tenants could be found for their spare rooms. The problem became acute during the First World War, and by 1917 all along the new row businesses had closed; tenants decamped owing rent, and shops and flats remained empty, in some cases for several years, or were occupied at nominal rents.[88]

The Albert Café and Restaurant, an Italian-owned business founded here in the 1880s, was re-established at No.

77, but here there was a different problem: the lack of a spirits licence. In the past if diners wanted spirits a boy would run over the road to one of the public houses beside Holy Trinity Church for them, but after the pubs were demolished the Ecclesiastical Commissioners refused to allow a licence to be taken out. This became a serious hindrance to the restaurant, which passed through several hands before coming to an end during the First World War. Its last proprietor was 'Sunny Jim' Califano, who had made something of a name for himself at Romano's and the Savoy and Cecil Hotels.[89]

Within a few years of the end of the war things seem to have picked up and the block was again fully occupied. From this time the upper floors were increasingly used as offices.[90]

Since the Second World War the shops in the block have been largely occupied by clothing and footwear retailers. In the 1940s one firm, Margaret Marks Ltd, costumiers, occupied four adjacent shops, Nos 71–79, and for part of the '50s and '60s Harvey Nichols had its 'Little Shop' at Nos 73–79.[91]

In September 1975 the attempted armed robbery of the Spaghetti House restaurant at Nos 77–79 led to a six-day siege of the building, where the robbers, who were linked to the black rights movement, held hostages in the basement.

William Street to Sloane Street

The history of the short stretch of Knightsbridge between William Street and Sloane Street is dominated by two celebrated department stores, Woollands and Harvey Nichols. Both developed in the way of most such large stores, expanding in stages from shop to shop until a whole row had been taken over, when the establishment could be rebuilt on a grand scale.

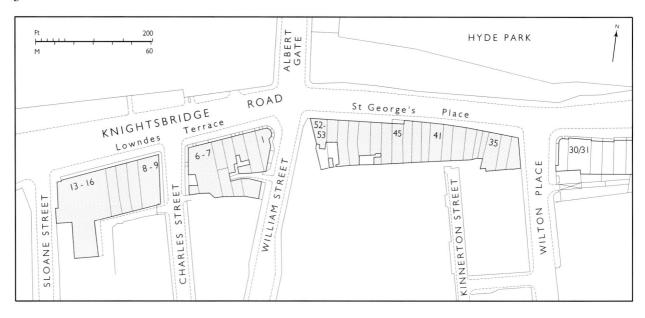

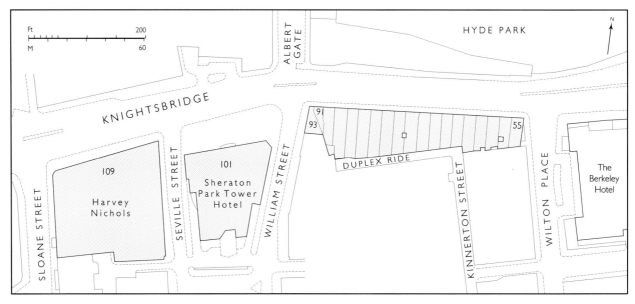

Fig. 6. Knightsbridge, south side, Wilton Place to Sloane Street in 1869 (top) and 1991. Buildings in 1869 are numbered in St George's Place and Lowndes Terrace

The exterior of Harvey Nichols is a mixture of somewhat lacklustre late Victorian and inter-war styles. Woollands, a much livelier turn-of-the-century building, has been replaced by the Sheraton Park Tower hotel, which, while sometimes likened to a gasometer, has a certain space-age verve.

Spring Gardens

In the seventeenth century the area now occupied by the Sheraton Park Tower and Harvey Nichols was the north-

ernmost part of the Spittlefields, then belonging to the Crown but before the Reformation part of the estate of Westminster Abbey. In 1668 these fields were leased to Sir William Poultney (who also held, as lessee of the Dean and Chapter, most of the ground fronting the south side of the road between here and Hyde Park Corner). The development of the northern end was begun in or soon after 1670 by Poultney's tenant Henry Swindell, who built a house there with extensive pleasure grounds.[92]

This well-known place of resort, originally called Spring Gardens,[93] survived in one form or another until the early nineteenth century. Horwood's map of 1794 shows a large building on the site, then called the Rural Retreat or Rural Castle and later Knightsbridge Grove or Grove House (see Plate 5c). It was here that Theresa Cornelys, the German-born singer whose balls and masques at Carlisle House in Soho Square had once attracted the cream of fashionable society, made a last attempt to restore her fortunes after her fall from grace. In 1795 she surfaced in Knightsbridge as Mrs Smith, retailer of asses' milk, and opened a suite of breakfast rooms, but the business failed and she died in the Fleet Prison in 1797. Her successor was William Ick, or Hicks, a 'sporting character', who had an archery ground at the rear and attracted the custom of the Prince Regent. The gunmaker Durs Egg, who lived at Knightsbridge Green, is said to have carried out balloon experiments in the grounds.[94]

In the mid-eighteenth century a floorcloth factory was set up on part of Spring Gardens, where Harvey Nichols now is (see Plate 5c). Following the creation of Sloane Street in the 1770s, terrace-houses were erected along the west side of Spring Gardens, and a row of six houses was also built at the north end, with gardens fronting Knightsbridge, on the site of the Sheraton Park Tower hotel. In 1815 shops were built over the front gardens and named Waterloo Market: they did not survive many years. A development scheme was already in hand for the Spittle-fields, or, as they had become, the Lowndes estate, and in 1823 the shops and houses, together with the floorcloth factory, were pulled down for the building of Lowndes Terrace.[95]

Downing's Floorcloth Factory (demolished)

In 1761 Richard Rolt wrote in his *New Dictionary of Trade*, 'There is a considerable manufactory of floor-cloths at Knightsbridge'. The factory Rolt was referring to stood close to the road just north-west of Grove House, on the site now occupied by Harvey Nichols. Established more than ten years earlier by William Spinnage, a painter-stain-er, it was the first of two important floorcloth factories set up in Knightsbridge during the eighteenth century (for the other see page 105). Spinnage took a lease of the site, where there was already a house, in 1748; ratebooks record a workshop there by 1750, and a warehouse by the 1760s.[96] From the early 1750s Spinnage was in partnership with Benjamin Crompton, working from premises in Charles Street off St James's Square, and near Charing Cross. Crompton and Spinnage were primarily wallpaper makers, becoming 'paper hanging manufacturers' to George III, but they also supplied all manner of decorations and furn-ishings, from papier mâché ceiling ornaments to spec-ially woven Axminster carpets. Floorcloth manufacture involved coating canvas in thick layers of paint, and their trade-card shows that this was seasonal work, advertising 'Painted Floor Cloths of all Sorts & Sizes Painted in the Summer at their Manufactory at Knightsbridge, dry and fit for immediate use'.[97]

After the dissolution of their partnership and Spin-nage's retirement, Crompton carried on in business in the West End with his son, James, but seems to have given up floorcloth manufacture in order to concentrate on wall-paper.[98] The Knightsbridge factory was let, in 1782–3, to John Harrison and Company, and then to Thomas Morley, both floorcloth manufacturers.[99] Morley acquired the head lease of the premises in 1791, and in 1794 opened a second factory, on the site of Wellington Square, Chelsea. In addition to floorcloth, he manufactured awnings and 'temporary rooms'.[100]

Morley's business was taken over in 1799 by Thomas Downing, who went into partnership at about this time with James Baber at the other Knightsbridge floorcloth factory. Downing carried on making floorcloth for many years at Morley's old premises, as well as awnings and 'all kinds of Temporary Erections, put up in any part of the kingdom, and Pack'd for Exportation'. The Knightsbridge factory (the original lease of which had expired several years earlier) was pulled down in 1823 for the building of Lowndes Terrace, in which Downing had showrooms. The business seems to have closed about 1873, when the Chelsea factory (by then rebuilt on the north side of King's Road) was destroyed by fire.[101]

Almost nothing of detail is known about the appearance of the Knightsbridge factory. When Crompton sublet it to Harrison the buildings included two brick-and-timber warehouses, one with 'offices communicating'. There is some suggestion that Morley rebuilt the factory. According to a description of 1813 the buildings, which included stables and a lean-to weaving shed, were mainly of timber. Some thirty years after the factory had been demolished, H. G. Davis, the Knightsbridge historian, wrote of it as 'a pleasant detached house, with a clean white front, and con-spicuous green verandahs'.[102]

Lowndes Terrace (demolished)

Along the frontage to Knightsbridge now occupied by the Sheraton Park Tower hotel and Harvey Nichols were formerly two rows of houses and shops, together called Lowndes Terrace but each originally independently num-bered. Built in the 1820s, these buildings were the first stage in the comprehensive development of the Spring Gardens site and the rest of the two Spittlefields.

In 1692 the Spittlefields (see page 19) had been assigned to William Lowndes (1652–1724), a Treasury official, who in 1723 obtained the right of reversion from the Crown.[103] When development of the Lowndes estate began, the property was in the hands of trustees for Lowndes' great-grandson William Lowndes, whose debts had brought him to the point of bankruptcy a few years before his father's death in 1808. The estate worked in with the much bigger Grosvenor estate adjoining: initial plans were formulated by the Lowndes surveyor, Henry Rhodes (a former pupil of the Grosvenor surveyor, William Porden), and negotia-tions between the two parties for co-ordinated develop-

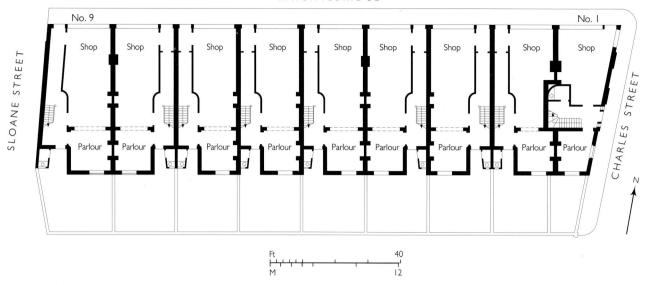

Fig. 7. Nos 1–9 (later Nos 8–16) Lowndes Terrace, ground-floor plan as proposed in 1824. Thomas Goodall, builder, for Benjamin Brecknell and Samuel Turner, 1824–6. *Demolished*

ment were in progress by 1810. An Act of Parliament was obtained in 1813 to expedite the improvement of the Lowndes estate by allowing parts to be sold or let on long lease, but it was not until 1819 that the development process was set under way, with a joint application by the two estates for permission to lay drains.[104]

Lowndes Terrace and the two roadways connecting the rest of the estate to Knightsbridge, William and Charles (now Seville) Streets, were the only parts of the plan to be carried out by 1826, when the development was taken over by Thomas Cubitt under a building agreement with the Lowndes trustees. Most of Cubitt's building activities here were left until the 1830s and '40s, when he built up much of Lowndes Square and the rest of the estate to the southeast.[105]

The construction of Lowndes Terrace began with the eastern range, where six of the seven houses and shops were erected in 1823–4: the nine-house western range followed in 1824–6. The eastern terrace was completed in 1828–9 by the building of No. 1 at the William Street corner. Erected under the general supervision of Henry Rhodes, who as estate surveyor approved the plans and elevations and may have been their author, the two halves of Lowndes Terrace presented two nearly symmetrical and unified façades to Knightsbridge (Plate 30c). The fronts were very plain, with hip-roofed pavilions at each end and attics set back behind balustrading. For the most prominent parts of the exterior, the building agreements specified 'best picked second Malm facing stocks laid with a very close joint', and York, Bath and Portland stone for the dressings. There were iron balconies at first-floor level on the fronts, and the roofs were slated.[106]

A single developer was responsible for the western terrace, where plans dated August 1824 were submitted by

Thomas Goodall, builder, on behalf of Benjamin Brecknell and Samuel Turner, tallow chandlers to members of the royal family, for whose Haymarket premises Rhodes had designed a shop-front in 1821. The whole range was leased to Brecknell, but Turner later inherited some of his partner's properties here and in other parts of London.[107] By contrast the eastern range was the work of several different builders and developers, among them James Howard and William Thomas Nixon, builders and carpenters of St Martin's Lane, and Thomas Cubitt, who built No. 1, giving its return to William Street a prominent bow.[108]

The shops in the western range (and probably also those in the eastern) were all similarly planned, each with a back parlour and basement store room (fig. 7), but in both halves of the terrace shop premises were customized to suit individual business requirements. In the eastern terrace Nos 6 and 7 were built as showrooms for George Downing, whose floorcloth factory west of Charles Street was pulled down about this time. Downing employed the services of the local architect W. F. Pocock for this work. A covenant in the lease barred him from carrying out there any of his manufacturing processes, which he thereafter concentrated at his works in Chelsea.[109] In the western terrace the shops at Nos 1 and 2 (later Nos 8 and 9) were thrown together by a firm of linen drapers, to make one big ground-floor shop, and at No. 4 (later 11) Brecknell installed for a haberdasher a shopfront with a single door in the middle, instead of the approved pattern which had doors at either side. Later, in 1837, an 'expensive' shopfront of mahogany, brass and plate glass was fitted at No. 3 (later No. 10), another draper's shop.[110]

The business character of the shops was originally quite mixed, but from early on there were harbingers of future specialization. By the 1840s four linen drapers and a firm of silk mercers together occupied a total of seven shops, and this trend continued until just two drapers occupied all sixteen shop premises. Both halves of Lowndes Terrace were pulled down in the late nineteenth century for the rebuilding of Woollands and Harvey Nichols, the two stores which by then had taken them over in their entirety.

Woollands (demolished)

The firm of Woolland Brothers began modestly in 1869, when Samuel and William Woolland, from Bridford in Devon, took over a draper's shop at No. 2 Lowndes Terrace. Though the shop was apparently aimed chiefly at the needs of servants,[111] it soon attracted notice in the trade press for its 'exceptionally good' window display:

The fancy window was dressed close up to the pane, and divided into tiers, with a long ticket right across the width, dividing the several classes of goods – piles of ribbons at the bottom, then a long stretch of flowers, scarves next, two or three rows of gloves, and rows of broad striped linen cuffs in conclusion; in the next window a bottom of blocked dress goods, with a row of light grenadines looped up along the front, cambrics at the back and side, the lobby being occupied in one pane with cuffs and lace goods and in the other with hosiery.[112]

Over the years the shop expanded into the neighbouring houses, until by 1892 it had taken over the entire eastern half of Lowndes Terrace (from 1903 Nos 95–107 Knightsbridge). The Woollands – three bachelor brothers, Samuel, William, and Moses, and their spinster sister Mary – were then living round the corner at No. 17 William Street.[113]

By this time the original drapery business had diversified to encompass household linens, soft furnishings, outfitting, haberdashery and accessories; and its clientele had become high-class, even aristocratic. The Duchess of Portland was spotted there in 1893, 'patronising the after-season sale'.[114]

In 1896 began the first phase of a programme of complete rebuilding, which continued into 1900–01, the final phase, covering the sites of houses at the rear of Lowndes Terrace in William Street (including No. 17). The new store was designed by Henry L. Florence and erected by W. Cubitt & Company. Of fireproof construction throughout, it was built on a steel frame and faced in Portland stone, with a profusion of carved baroque ornamentation and copper-covered domes at the corners. Other than on the ground floor, where there was a continuous run of plate-glass display window, it had all the appearance of a traditional masonry building, with a conventional pattern of fenestration (Plate 14a).[115]

The interior was elegantly ornamented and furnished, with panelling, decorative plasterwork and wall-mirrors, tall glazed display cabinets and upholstered chairs for customers' use. Following the conventional design of such stores, there was a top-lit showroom area at the head of the rather grand main stair (Plate 14b). As originally laid out, the ground floor was arranged as 'shop' space, with display rooms and fitting-rooms on the first and second floors,

workrooms on the next two floors, and a kitchen, dining-room and assistants' sitting-rooms at the top. There was, however, no sleeping accommodation for staff, who lodged in nearby houses.

In the early 1900s Edward VII's mistress, Alice Keppel, would bring her two young daughters down from Edinburgh four times a year to shop at Woollands. Sonia Keppel recalled:

In those days, the 'Juvenile Department' at Woollands was situated on the third or fourth floor. Grimly, the lift man shut his concertina-gates on us, and very, very slowly we ascended to our appointment with 'No. 10'.
We never discovered whether 'No. 10' had had Christian baptism and a name of her own. To Violet and me, she remained a numerical cypher that sucked pins. Always she was bent double at our feet, measuring our skirts, slithering round on her poor, old knees.[116]

Up-to-date at the turn of the century, by the 1930s Woollands had come to seem old and cramped.[117] No further rebuilding took place, although in 1913 the firm had acquired the freehold, not only of the store, but of almost the entire block between William and Seville Streets, including the houses on the north side of Lowndes Square (these last, however, were disbarred by covenant from being put to business use).[118] In 1949 Woollands was acquired by the Debenham group, already in possession of its next-door rival, Harvey Nichols. For some years Debenhams maintained the distinctive character of each establishment, but by the mid-1960s the co-existence of the two large stores had ceased to be viable, and in 1967, the site having been sold for redevelopment, Woollands closed. The premises were demolished two years later for the building of what is now the Sheraton Park Tower hotel.[119]

Sheraton Park Tower Hotel

Plans for a hotel on the island site then occupied by Woollands store and residential buildings on the north side of Lowndes Square were drawn up by Seifert & Partners for Capital and Counties Property in 1966. The present rather stocky building (Plates 17c, 112), reminiscent of Seifert's earlier Space House in Kingsway, was conceived in 1968, successive designs for a much taller hotel having failed to obtain planning consent. Construction, by Y. J. Lovell & Company, began in 1970, and the hotel was opened in 1973 as the Skyline Park Tower Hotel, part of the Canadian-owned Skyline chain.[120]

The 300-bedroom hotel consists of a fifteen-storey rotunda of pre-cast concrete components, built around a reinforced-concrete core and carried on pilotis descending through the two-storey 'podium' and basement floors. Its most distinctive features are the projecting window units, faced in ceramic mosaic, a characteristic Seifert motif giving the building a cellulated appearance likened by Charles Jencks to corn-on-the-cob.[121]

Along with many of the large hotels of the early 1970s, most of them the beneficiaries if not the actual progeny of the Development of Tourism Act of 1969, which provided government subsidies for hotel-building, the Park Tower was generally not well received by the architectural press (though the architectural qualities of the rotunda were acknowledged here and there). Critics saw it as 'gasometric' and 'keep-like', with a top storey 'like the stopper on a scent bottle'.[122] The themed interior decoration, by the Canadian designer Allan Edwards, which included a Tudor-style 'half-timbered' restaurant, was dismissed by some as not much more than kitsch.[123]

Harvey Nichols

The founder of the famous store on the corner of Knightsbridge and Sloane Street, Benjamin Harvey, was one of two Ipswich-born brothers both of whom became prominent drapers in Victorian London.[124] Joseph, the elder by a few years, built up a large establishment in Westminster Bridge Road, Lambeth, which did not long survive his death in 1876 at the age of 84. Benjamin, in contrast, died relatively young, but his store continued to flourish, reaching its peak many years later. The precise origins of their involvement in the drapery trade are obscure, but they were probably apprenticed at a London draper's. They had a close association with the firm of White and Greenwell, linen-drapers and haberdashers of Commerce House, Great Surrey Street, Blackfriars.

Benjamin Harvey (*c.*1796–1850) set up shop in Knightsbridge in 1831, at No. 9 (later 16) Lowndes Terrace, on the corner of Sloane Street. From this site he expanded, taking over the adjoining shop by 1835, and within ten years the next one as well, the combined premises being known as Commerce House. At about the same time as this third building was acquired, Harvey took into partnership his shopman, James Nichols, then in his late twenties. In 1848 Nichols married Harvey's wife's niece, consolidating his position in the business, which became Benjamin Harvey & Company.

Harvey was seemingly enlightened as well as expansionist, taking an active role in the Metropolitan Drapers' Association (from 1845 the Metropolitan Early Closing Association), which sought to improve the lot of shopworkers. But it was not until 1851, after his death, that 'early closing' was introduced at Commerce House, and trading ceased at 7 p.m. (instead of eight or nine o'clock, according to the season, then customary in the drapery trade).[125]

After Harvey's death the firm was run by his widow Ann and James Nichols, and in about 1854 it was redesignated Harvey Nichols & Company.

The growing prosperity of the business was reflected in the social aspirations of the two families. In the late 1850s Nichols, now styling himself 'esquire', left his rooms over the shop and moved to No. 10 The Boltons, South Kensington; some years later Mrs Harvey became his near neighbour at No. 5. She died in 1872, and Nichols himself died early in 1873, whereupon the Harveys' son, Benjamin

Charles, turned the firm into a limited company.

The expansion of the shop premises continued over the years. Considerable building work was carried out in 1874 (when only one house in the terrace still eluded the company). The architect, for some of it at least, was Alfred Williams, District Surveyor for South Kensington.[126] From 1878 Harvey Nichols occupied the entire Knightsbridge frontage between Seville Street and Sloane Street, and in the 1880s further adjoining properties were acquired in Sloane Street. In 1889 it was decided to undertake complete rebuilding.

By this time the business had long since begun to diversify. Brussels carpets, striped rugs, eiderdown quilts, evening dresses and millinery were among the lines displayed in the shop windows in 1873.[127] Diversification, however, did not lead to Harvey Nichols becoming a 'universal provider' like Whiteleys or Harrods. Drapery remained the core of the business, and the firm continued to be described in directories simply as 'drapers' until 1914.

The new shop (Plates 1, 15a, 17c, 112), built in stages between 1889 and 1894, was designed by the local architect C. W. Stephens, later responsible for the new Harrods store and Claridge's hotel, who produced a conventionally imposing edifice with pavilion roofs in the French style (Plate 15a). At least two firms of contractors were employed, Higgs & Hill in 1892–3, and John Shillitoe & Son of Bury St Edmunds in 1893–4.[128]

The plan was essentially L-shaped, with a large central light-well above first-floor level in the main range, fronting Knightsbridge. Alongside Sloane Street redevelopment was hampered by the firm's failure to obtain an uninterrupted run of frontage. Two sites at the north end, Nos 211 and 212, were incorporated into the overall architectural scheme; but the façade at Nos 208 and 209, cut off by a recalcitrant bootmaker's shop at No. 210, was treated separately, in an Italianate style.

Sales and display space was concentrated on the ground and first floors, and part of the second floor (fig. 8). The basement was given over to stockrooms, and the remainder of the second floor, and the whole of the upper floors, were used as staff accommodation, including bedrooms, and workrooms. Fire regulations at the time made it virtually impossible to have open showrooms in the upper storeys.

The first major alterations were made following the firm's acquisition of the freehold, and additional property in Harriet Mews and Seville Street, in 1904.[129] In 1910–11 the light-well was largely filled in to give more showroom space on the first floor, and in 1913 more room, for sales and for a tea-room on the third floor, was freed by the acquisition of two houses in Queen's Gate for use as staff hostels.[130]

Harvey Nichols was one of several important department stores to lose its independence after the First World War. In 1920 it was taken over by Debenham & Freebody, to whose wholesale division it had become heavily indebted. A consequence of this was that Harvey Nichols, which held a royal warrant from Queen Mary, became a little

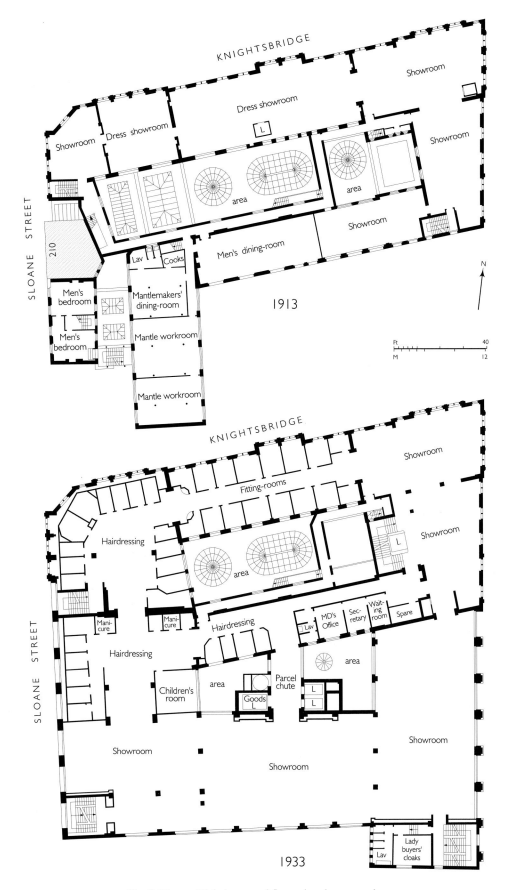

Fig. 8. Harvey Nichols, second floor, plans in 1913 and 1933

more populist in character, and for the first time advertisements began to appear, in journals such as the *Lady* (where the still independent Woollands advertised). The many departments, said a contemporary account, 'provide for practically every aspect of home and personal adornment':

The [carpet] salons have been an important feature from the inception of the business, and a wonderful variety and assortment of Oriental and British varieties, modern and antique, can always be seen. Their soft furnishing department is replete with decorated fabrics that display wonderful colours and skilful designs of all periods at extremely moderate prices, while the section of the house devoted to antique furniture is one of the first places visited when American and Continental connoisseurs come to London. Their fashion departments need no introduction . . . the choicest models of Paris, London, and New York in gowns, furs, footwear and hosiery are here gathered under one roof. The restful charm of the firm's Louis Seize Restaurant, well-known to the habitués of the store, and the *tout ensemble*, now form one of the finest and most popular shopping centres of the West End.[131]

Debenhams embarked on a scheme of capital investment, further expanding the site and undertaking an extensive programme of rebuilding in both Sloane Street (1922–8) and Seville Street (1928–34). Externally, the new work was carried out under the influence of the Beaux-Arts classicism of Selfridges, which had become the prototype for new British department stores (Plate 15c). The architects were Frederick Ernest Williams and Alfred Cox, successors to Alfred Williams' practice. Higgs & Hill were the builders.[132]

The rebuilding in Sloane Street, covering the sites of Nos 206–210, was possibly envisaged as the first stage in a southwards expansion of the store along a street which had become 'so fashionable that it is almost a rival to Bond Street'.[133] Harvey Nichols had acquired a reversionary lease of all the properties as far south as No. 190A, no doubt with an eye to rebuilding, and the new front seems to have been designed for easy duplication as the additional sites became available. In the event this expansion was never realized.

An odd feature of the rebuilding along Sloane Street was the addition of a second pavilion dome at the Knightsbridge corner, positioned on top of the short return front of the 1890s building and in the same, by then out-dated, style (Plates 15c, 112).

As work on the Sloane Street side came to an end in 1928, redevelopment began in Seville Street. Somewhat delayed by a dispute with the Lowndes Estate over the realignment of Harriet Mews (renamed Harriet Walk in 1932), it was completed in 1934. The clock in the middle of the Knightsbridge front was installed at this time, as one of the final touches.[134]

The revitalized Harvey Nichols was one of the most up-to-date department stores in London. There was one showroom in the basement, while the ground and first floors were entirely given over to display and sales areas.

On the second floor (fig. 8) were the fashion showrooms and fitting-rooms, each one 'decorated and furnished in the style of a different period, making delightful backgrounds for new frocks, and providing inspiration for decorative schemes at the same time'. Also on this floor was an extensive hairdressing and beauty department. The general colour scheme was green and pale yellow, with 'roomy and light' cubicles each done in a different pastel scheme.[135] A large restaurant was located on the third floor. Workrooms and facilities for employees occupied the fourth and fifth floors. These included common rooms, a restaurant for 'staff' and separate canteens for 'workers' and 'juniors'.[136]

Considerable internal reorganization followed the closure in 1967 of Woollands (by then also part of the Debenham group), and the transfer of some of its specialized departments and exclusive product lines, as well as most of its staff, to Harvey Nichols. Extensive and costly modernization was carried out in the 1970s, involving much internal demolition. In 1975 Maurice Broughton Associates were called in to redesign the ground floor and make other improvements. The object was to cater for a younger, more international clientele, and, following Harrods' lead, to provide 'shops-within-shops' for top specialist firms. On the fifth floor was created a restaurant and bar with a 'garden atmosphere', partially screened from the shop by a glass wall and curtain of running water. The window displays, designed by Andrew Wiles, became the most consistently striking in London, a tradition continued by Mary Portas.

In 1979, having reinforced Harvey Nichols' separate identity at enormous expense, Debenhams, by then suffering from the effects of out-of-town competition and unsuccessful diversification within their shops, put the store on the market. An offer from a property development consortium, who wished to redevelop the site, was ultimately rejected, and in 1985 Debenhams was taken over by the Burton Group. Under Burtons, Harvey Nichols continued to lose money and it required another change of ownership of the store (to Dickson Poon of Hong Kong, in 1991), and a yet more expensive make-over, to turn operating losses into profits. This remodelling, by the architects Wickham & Associates, involved the creation of a food hall, restaurant, café and bar, all on the fifth floor (Plate 15b). The food hall in particular, because of its upper-floor location, was seen as something of a gamble, though it has proved very successful.[137]

Harvey Nichols has long ceased to be a department store in the conventional sense and has become more of a 'fashion house', with a collection of designer-label counters occupying its otherwise anonymous-seeming sales floors. It has, with Harrods, done much to reinforce the reputation of Knightsbridge as an international shopping centre, and is probably better known now than at any time in its history.

CHAPTER II

Knightsbridge North Side:
Parkside to Albert Gate Court

Building on the north side of Knightsbridge as far west as Knightsbridge Barracks is confined to a narrow, tapering strip of ground bordering Hyde Park. The east end of this strip, truncated in the late 1950s for road-widening, formerly ran to a point, where the last building was a tiny sweet-shop built on to the park wall. At the west end, the barracks occupies part of the park itself. Bisecting this narrow tract of land is the Westbourne brook, now canalized under the roadway of Albert Gate. The Westbourne here is the boundary between the parishes of St George, Hanover Square, to the east (previously part of St Martin-in-the-Fields), and St Margaret, Westminster, to the west. The buildings on the eastern part were formerly called Park Side, those fronting the road on the broader western portion High Row. All of Park Side, and the eastern end of High Row (including the Hyde Park Hotel site), were formerly owned by the Dean and Chapter of Westminster Abbey as part of the manor of Knightsbridge and West-bourne Green, while the remainder of the ground to the west was, by the early eighteenth century, in private hands.

There was some building along the strip as far back as the Middle Ages, when a lazar-house or hospital was established on the east bank of the Westbourne (where the French Embassy now stands). The hospital continued in existence until the early eighteenth century; its chapel, long the chief place of worship in Knightsbridge, was rebuilt in the 1860s as Holy Trinity Church, which disappeared with the redevelopment of most of Park Side early in the twentieth century.

Although some earlier buildings stood westwards of the Westbourne, including two or more inns, High Row was largely a development of the 1720s and '30s, consisting in the main of good-sized terrace-houses. Among the other buildings erected here before the making of Albert Gate in the early 1840s were the small later-Georgian houses of Mills's Buildings and Park Row, and the Cannon Brewhouse of 1804, the latter falling victim to Thomas Cubitt's Albert Gate.

The creation of Albert Gate certainly helped put Knightsbridge on the map as part of fashionable London, but despite its improving effect on the vicinity did not encourage any further redevelopment in Park Side and High Row in the short or medium term. Its visual impact, however, as an architectural colossus bestriding what had previously been a filthy open drain, was considerable – an effect now entirely dissipated by the scale of later buildings on either side.

Much the most important of these is the Hyde Park Hotel of the late 1880s, whose great height in such close proximity to the park caused a furore when it was first projected. The hotel – originally residential 'chambers' and a club – was followed by several lesser apartment blocks near the barracks, but most of the eighteenth-century houses in High Row, together with Mills's Buildings and Park Row, survived until the Second World War, after which Bowater House was built on the site. Opposition to the erection of this gross office block recalled the arguments put forward against the building of the Hyde Park Hotel, and the issue of tall buildings on the north side of Knightsbridge was raised again a few years later with the designing of the new barracks.

Park Side

The area discussed here is the narrow triangle of ground extending from just south of the site of White Horse Gate in Hyde Park to Albert Gate (fig. 9). Historically, the greater part comprised the site and grounds of the Knightsbridge lazar-house. No. 1 Albert Gate, the French Embassy, which occupies the site of the lazar-house itself, latterly the White Hart tavern, is treated below with the Albert Gate development generally, as is its extension at No. 58 Knightsbridge.

The name Park Side was formally abolished in 1903, when the buildings were renumbered as part of Knightsbridge.

Old Park Side

Although development in Park Side dated back to the Middle Ages, with the establishment of the lazar-house, very little old building survived far into Victorian times. Trinity Chapel, which belonged to the lazar-house, had been reconstructed twice already since the early seventeenth century when it was rebuilt in 1860–1 as Holy Trinity Church. The old hospital buildings, and the Queen's Head tavern, which stood just east of the chapel and bore the date 1576, were all pulled down at or soon after the time of the Albert Gate development early in Queen Victoria's reign.[1]

East of the Queen's Head, the houses pulled down in 1904–5 for the Parkside flats development were probably of eighteenth- or nineteenth-century date. Further east,

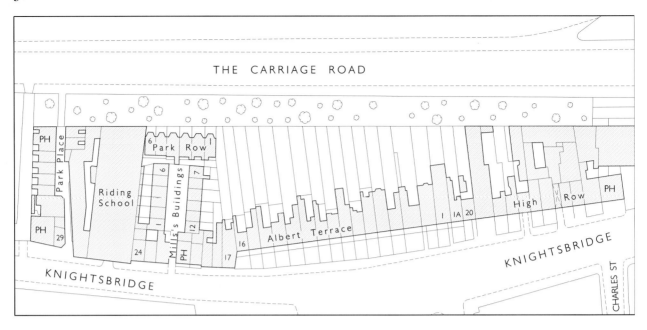

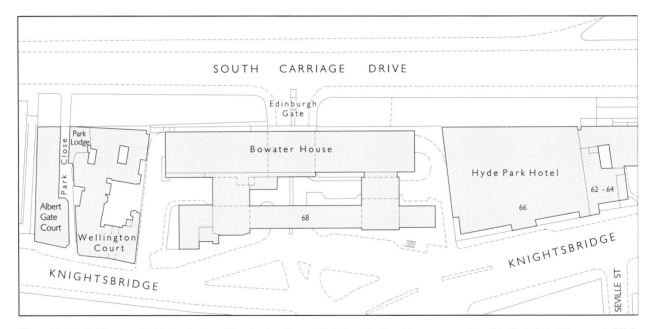

Fig. 9. Knightsbridge, north side, in the late 1860s (top) and 1991. Buildings in the 1860s were numbered in Park Side (Nos 1–22), High Row (Nos 1–20) and Albert Terrace (Nos 1A and 1–30)

beyond the lazar-house estate, the sites of Nos 2–26 Knightsbridge had, in the eighteenth century, been occupied by a smithy and a few cottages; near the east end, as late as 1805, stood the village stocks. By the 1830s the smithy and cottages had given place to a row of shops. Those at the east end were single-storey lock-ups only, the last, latterly a sweet-shop, not six feet square; they were used by W. Stocken as offices for his 'Knightsbridge Bank'.[2]

Most prominent of the buildings in this row was the tall stuccoed structure at Nos 10–14 Knightsbridge, the upper part of which had been the studio of the photographer H. Walter Barnett (Plate 22). The former Hyde Park Dairy at Nos 22–24 Knightsbridge was a pair of old houses refaced front and back in about 1880 (architect Robert Griggs). No. 26 had been rebuilt in 1897, to designs by M. C. Meaby, surveyor to the United Kingdom House Purchase and Investment Society Ltd.[3]

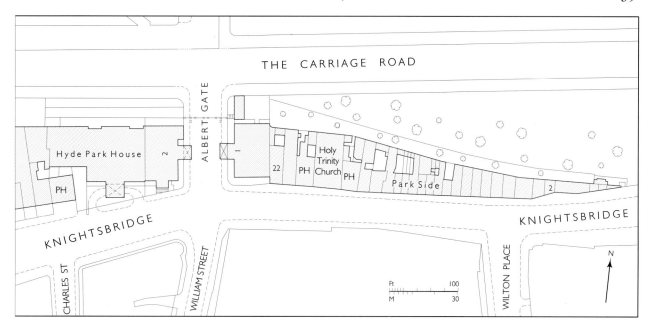

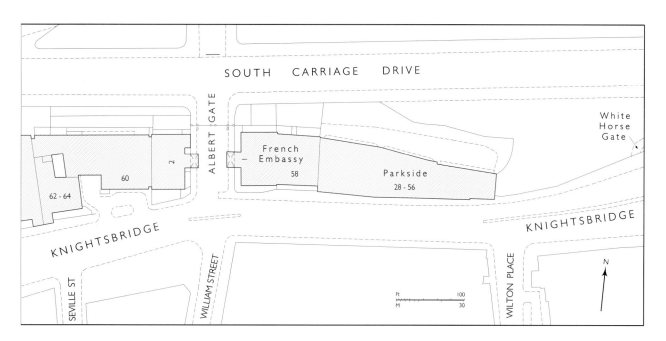

No-one seems to have seen anything remotely picturesque in old Park Side. As far back as the 1850s unfavourable comments were made about the meanness of the buildings, and in the early 1870s a proponent of a grand boulevard along Knightsbridge wrote of Park Side's 'paltry and antiquated shops'. The existing houses, it was said in 1904, 'interpose an unwelcome and purposeless interruption to the magnificent prospect which is London's chief asset of beauty, and their intrusion is almost as great a nuisance to the traffic as it is a blot upon the scenery'.[4]

Old Park Side may have lacked architectural distinction,

but it housed a great assortment of shops and businesses, ranging from jewellers' and art dealers' to a bird fancier's and a fishing-tackle shop (Plate 20d), and, more prosaically, makers and menders of boots and umbrellas. Knightsbridge's association with horses and riding was reflected in Colin Sleep's driving-glove shop, a branch of his big Oxford Street store.[5]

Park Side's most distinguished known resident was a Lancashire-born scientist and maker of mathematical instruments, John Read (1726–1814). He lived in Knightsbridge for nearly sixty years, and carried out research into atmospheric electricity at his house there, No. 10 Park Side, using an electrometer mounted on the roof. In Victorian times, Park Side was occupied almost entirely by shopkeepers and tradespeople and their lodgers.[6]

The building of the Parkside flats at Nos 28–56 Knightsbridge left the ultimate fate of the rest of Park Side – Nos 2–26 Knightsbridge – uncertain. The freehold had been broken up, and the shallow plots offered little scope for redevelopment. Plans for rebuilding No. 20 as a shop and apartments were drawn up by the architect Leonard Martin for the owner, the builder Mark Bromet, in 1917. However, fearing inflated building costs after the war, and reluctant to pay for a Crown licence for windows and balconies overlooking the park, Bromet abandoned the scheme.[7]

Nos 2–26 survived until 1959 when they were pulled down for road-widening in connection with the Hyde Park Corner to Marble Arch improvement scheme, which turned Park Lane into a dual carriageway: this widening permitted the making of an additional tunnel for the new Piccadilly underpass. Although themselves of no special architectural interest, these buildings were almost the last vestiges of the old pattern of development along the north side of Knightsbridge, and with them finally disappeared any lingering sense of Knightsbridge as a 'village' street.

The Lazar-house (demolished)

The date of foundation of the lazar-house is not known, and the earliest reference to come to light is quite a late one. This is a deed of 1473, granting an eighty-year lease of the 'lazercotes' property to Thomas Clowgh and Richard Thomson, yeomen of Knightsbridge. Although the hospital had presumably been set up specifically to accommodate lepers, by this time leprosy had largely disappeared from England and most existing lazar-houses were turned to other purposes: in the London area several, including that at Knightsbridge, became 'outhouses' for the chronic sick from the main hospitals. The Knightsbridge lazar-house was receiving patients from Bart's and St Thomas's certainly by the 1590s. A petition of the Commonwealth period refers to 'the curing of Lazars and poore cripled persons according to the use and Custome of the said Hospitall' at Knightsbridge.[8]

From Elizabethan times until about 1660, the lazar-house was particularly associated with a family named Glassington, and in 1654 a member of the family claimed that his ancestors had held the property time out of mind. This may have been an exaggeration, but several surgeons named Glassington were among the successive governors (or 'guiders') and lessees of the hospital.[9]

From just nineteen residents in 1570 (including the governor and his wife), the number of patients grew, so that by the mid-1590s there were about three dozen 'diseased, lame and impotent' poor at any time, who might stay for as long as three years. In two surviving annual reports, for 1595 and 1596, the governor, John Glassington, lists by name 55 and 78 people who, along with 'divers others', had been 'cured' in those years. As well as taking cases from the London hospitals, the lazar-house seems to have received patients from all over the country. Some were nominated by the governors of Westminster Abbey almshouse and school, while others were sent there by the parish of St Margaret, Westminster.[10]

Glassington outlines the inmates' regime: work in the mornings for those able to do any, according to their calling, with prayer in the chapel between eight and nine o'clock; dinner of warm meat and porridge served between ten and eleven, then back to work with a break between three and four for evening chapel, followed by supper, late chapel and bed. On Sundays and feast-days they were joined for morning and evening prayer by the local people.[11]

The hospital had no endowment, relying entirely on 'the charity of good people', which by the 1590s was 'much decayed from that it was wont to be'. There had, said Glassington, been some land, but this had been taken away and enclosed into Hyde Park. Leases of the hospital, however, included some ground to the east, originally orchard or garden, where the chapel and eventually houses were built, about a third of an acre on the south side of Knightsbridge (later the site of Knightsbridge Terrace), and a little plot on Knightsbridge Green. Two nearby fields, now occupied by Lowndes Square and Lowndes Street, were known as the Spittlefields and probably therefore once belonged to the hospital.[12]

When Glassington came to the lazar-house, it was 'reddy to fall downe', and its dilapidated state is confirmed by a survey carried out in 1570 by Robert Penythorne and Thomas Fowler. Fowler's report refers to an old house, 40ft high, with a roof in two unequal spans and a penthouse.[13]

In 1605 an order was made by James I for water to be piped to the hospital from a nearby spring in Hyde Park.[14]

The chapel was rebuilt twice during the seventeenth century, first in the early 1630s, and again in 1699. James Winter, a surgeon-governor, carried out building work at the hospital which was noted in a report made about 1653 by Adam Browne, the surveyor to Westminster Abbey:

I find that hee hath lately built there two Tenements with brick which he letts, And hee hath built up three of the rooms in his owne house now with brick, and eight Bed Rooms he hath made for the poore two of which are used already . . . And the house now standing is old decayed ready to fall & must be suddenly built.[15]

Winter was succeeded by another John Glassington about 1655, a former governor who was praised by the local people for his healing skill, but in 1668 the premises were let to a London goldsmith, Nicholas Birkhead, and seem never again to have been under the control of a medical man. According to a local tradition the hospital was used for the isolation of victims of the Great Plague, those who died being buried at Knightsbridge Green. The plot belonging to the hospital at the Green may have been the actual burial-place.[16]

Birkhead was probably a relation of the Glassingtons, for a later lessee of the lazar-house estate, the Rev. John Gamble, stated in 1809 that the property had been in his family's hands for more than two hundred years: Gamble himself was a descendant of Nicholas Birkhead's wife's niece, Ann Soley. From Birkhead's coming, the hospital continued in some form for half a century, but by 1718, when a new lease was granted to Mary Birkhead, the goldsmith's widowed daughter-in-law, it was defunct.[17]

Glassington's reports do not specifically refer to any children at the lazar-house, but 'poore Innocents' were kept at the hospital in the 1630s and '40s, according to the parish accounts of St Margaret's, Westminster. An orphanage or school at the lazar-house, for six boys and six girls, continued until at least 1720, when Mary Birkhead complained that reduced collections at the chapel had left her unable 'to Cloth ye twelve Children this year'.[18]

The old hospital buildings appear to have survived as a public house, the White Hart, and a ramshackle collection of low tenements, until the development of Albert Gate (Plate 5a–b).

Trinity Chapel and Holy Trinity Church (demolished)

In 1629 the inhabitants of Knightsbridge petitioned William Laud, Bishop of London, for permission to rebuild the ruinous chapel at the lazar-house, their usual place of worship, at their own expense. A licence was granted, with the proviso that they must attend their respective parish churches (St Margaret's, Westminster or St Martin's-in-the-Fields) at least once a quarter and also at Easter. By 1634 the chapel had been rebuilt. It was hoped that pew-rents would provide sufficient income for repairs and the cost of maintaining a curate.[19]

During the Commonwealth, and in the face of local opposition, Parliament appointed as minister Henry Walker, a former ironmonger turned anti-Royalist pamphleteer and newspaper editor or 'writer of weekly Newes'. In about 1658, after Walker's departure, the chapel began to acquire a reputation as a place for clandestine marriages and baptisms, and this continued until 1752, shortly before such marriages were outlawed.[20]

According to the Rev. Hibbert Binney, minister of the chapel from 1833, the lessees of the lazar-house estate sold leases on the chapel 'to the highest bidder', but the position was perhaps less scandalous than he claimed. Pew-rents over the years had been inadequate to pay the minister's stipend. Indeed, a decline in local affluence by the time of the Interregnum is suggested by a petition to Parliament from the people of Knightsbridge asking for money for the chapel from the proceeds of the sale of Dean and Chapter lands. Most of the sixty-eight or so Knightsbridge families were then 'very poore laboringe people' with many children, and 'Those that formerly were good Benefactors are many dead and the rest have left us . . . many of us anceyent lame and feeble'. At all events, effective control over the chapel had passed from the Bishop of London to the lessees, who sub-let the chapel, and the Dean and Chapter

of the Abbey, who routinely accepted the under-tenant as minister.[21]

In 1699 the chapel was rebuilt by the lessee, Nicholas Birkhead, goldsmith, and this building was enlarged and re-fronted in 1789, presumably for Dixon Gamble, of Bungay, Suffolk, who had succeeded Ann Soley as lessee in 1788 (Plate 19a–b).[22]

The extended chapel, containing 300 seats, was arranged conventionally, with galleries along three sides, reached by stairs near the street entrance. H. G. Davis, the Knightsbridge historian, records that the organ was built by Hancock in 1770. The bell too, which hung in the cupola at the front of the building, predated the enlargement, having been given by Mary Birkhead in 1733.[23]

A charity school, housed in a room at the rear, gave elementary education to boys and girls. It was set up in 1783, largely on the initiative of John Read, the scientist and mathematical-instrument maker, who lived near by.[24]

When Binney became minister he found the chapel so dilapidated and uncomfortable that it was difficult to keep a congregation during the winter, but his efforts to regularize its status, obtain an endowment and rebuild on a bigger scale came to nothing. It was not until 1859 that effective steps were taken to provide a new building, when a committee was set up headed by William Tite MP. By that time pressure of population on local churches was such that the chapel was 'constantly full'.[25]

The new church, a building in the Early Decorated style with seating for 600, was designed in competition by Raphael Brandon and Henry M. Eyton (Plate 19c–d). S. S. Teulon and Charles Gray were among the unsuccessful competitors.[26] The central entrance was flanked by two tiers of blind arcading; above was a large 'west' window, and, at the south-east corner, a bell-turret with a spirelet. Inside, the chief feature of interest was a hammer-beam roof with foliated spandrels. The old schoolroom was incorporated into the site, but hopes, briefly entertained, that land beyond in Hyde Park, little frequented at this point, might be obtained to make a larger overall site were not realized. As it was, the narrow, hemmed-in situation made galleries and a clerestory necessary. To avoid hanging rods inside the church, access for opening and shutting the clerestory windows was provided along outside passageways.[27]

Building work began in February 1860, and the church was completed a few days before its consecration by the Bishop of London on 30 March 1861, the entire cost, £3,600, being met by subscription. The contractors were Dove Brothers.[28]

Both the neighbouring houses were pubs: the Queen's Head to the east, and the White Hart, rebuilt eastwards of its old site following its demolition for Albert Gate. This situation gave rise to the soubriquet 'the heaven between two hells'. In fact the pubs seem to have been quite respectable, and one landlord of the White Hart was a highly regarded churchwarden.[29]

The building had a fairly short life. Proposals were put forward in 1899 which, despite local protest, led to a new

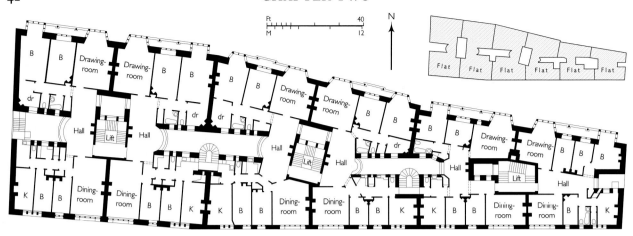

Fig. 10. Parkside, typical upper-floor plan, and diagram showing arrangement of flats. A. H. Hart and Leslie Waterhouse, architects, 1906–7

Holy Trinity Church being built on ground provided by the 1851 Commissioners in Prince Consort Road. The old church was pulled down in 1904 and its site, along with much of Park Side, was redeveloped with shops and flats (Parkside).[30]

Parkside

Large-scale redevelopment of the remnants of the Westminster Abbey estate in Knightsbridge began in 1902–3 when the houses in St George's Place between Wilton Place and William Street were rebuilt (see page 28). Once that block was completed, the Ecclesiastical Commissioners invited selected developers to tender for an 80-year building lease of a large site on the north side of the road comprising Nos 28–54 Knightsbridge and Holy Trinity Church. (A comparatively small site immediately west of the church had recently been redeveloped on a long lease from the Commissioners as the French Embassy extension.) Holy Trinity was pulled down in September 1904 and by May the following year the rest of the site had been cleared.[31]

The requirements were that the new building was to cost at least £50,000 and be the work of an architect 'of high standing': it was also to be no higher than the French Embassy at No. 1 Albert Gate (a condition which seems to have been either relaxed or not strictly adhered to). The lessee would be liable to the Commissioners of Works for an annual charge of ten shillings for each window overlooking Hyde Park. Occupying tenants of the old shops on the site were offered premises in the new development, but, as with St George's Place, there was no compensation for those higher up the leasehold chain, some of whose families had held the properties for generations.[32]

Henry Bailey, whose London Estates Company Ltd made the best bid, subsequently managed to negotiate himself a 90-year term, but did not undertake the development himself. After mortgaging his interest to the former Chelsea MP Sir Charles Dilke, Bailey entered into agreement with Sir Thomas Henry Brooke-Hitching, who

carried out the work on an 80-year underlease. (Brooke-Hitching had been a tenant of the Ecclesiastical Commissioners in St George's Place, but in the delay over its redevelopment he let slip his chance of a building lease by sub-letting his premises.) In 1907 the head lease of the new block, known as Parkside, was acquired by the Clerical Medical & General Life Assurance Society.[33]

Parkside was designed by A. H. Hart and Leslie Waterhouse and erected in 1906–7 by the Waring White Building Company Ltd. It is built of red bricks, supplied by T. Lawrence & Sons of Bracknell, with dressings of Hartham Park stone. The stonework was carved by H. H. Martyn & Company of Cheltenham (Plate 35b–e).[34]

The new building comprised twelve shops and forty-odd flats, the block being divided vertically into three parts, each with its own entrance and lifts, and divided into individual apartments running the full depth of the building (fig. 10). Dining-rooms and staff accommodation were placed on the Knightsbridge side to allow – trees permitting – park views from the principal bedrooms and reception rooms.[35]

Externally, the building is adequately summed up by Brooke-Hitching's own description: 'expensive and dignified' (Plates 35a, 115d). In the 1900s it seemed a considerable intrusion on the view across Hyde Park. King Edward VII complained that it was too high, and the park authorities refused to cut back some old poplars near by which made the flats so dark that they were at first difficult to let.[36]

Immediately west of Parkside is the French Embassy extension, a three-storey stucco-fronted building erected in 1899–1902 (see page 50).

High Row

High Row was the name generally used until the late nineteenth century for the buildings fronting the north side of Knightsbridge on the belt of land between the Westbourne (the site of Albert Gate) and Knightsbridge Barracks. The greater part of this ground was unbuilt on until the 1720s and '30s, when a terrace of houses was erected over most of its length. High Row was subsequently numbered as two sequences, High Row and High Row West, and in 1843 part of High Row West (Nos 1–16) was, 'in an absurd spirit of sycophancy', renamed Albert Terrace. The remainder of High Row West, Nos 17–30, retained its old name until c.1860, when it too was incorporated into Albert Terrace. The names High Row and Albert Terrace were abolished in 1877, when the properties there were renumbered as 4–44 Albert Gate. Under a further renumbering in 1903 they became 62–124 (even) Knightsbridge.

Included among the buildings discussed here are the principal redevelopments of parts of High Row carried out prior to the Albert Gate scheme. Later redevelopments, including all the present-day buildings westwards of Albert Gate to the barracks, are described further below, where a sketch of the history of the Park Close area at the west end of High Row is also given.

High Row: John Clarke's Estate

In 1719 John Clark(e) of St Martin-in-the-Fields, baker, acquired the two properties – one leasehold, the other freehold – lying between the Westbourne and a cluster of buildings in the vicinity of what is now Park Close. (He also acquired some leasehold land on the south side of Knightsbridge, near Hyde Park Corner).[37]

The eastern (leasehold) property, a one-acre close belonging to Westminster Abbey, had been bought by Henry VIII with other lands for enclosing into Hyde Park, but was in the event excluded as it would have 'brought the pale out of square'. Restored to the Abbey, it was let during the latter part of the sixteenth century successively to Robert Hatfield and William Muschamp of Kensington, and in 1607 was leased to Sir William Cecil (whose father and grandfather were in succession High Stewards of the Manors of Westminster Abbey).[38]

In 1612 a new lease was made out to Edmund Hooper, the composer and organist, in recognition of his long service at the Abbey. The lease – a lifehold secured on three of his children – required him to build a house within two years. However, no house seems to have been built, and the covenant was repeated when a new lease was granted to one of his daughters in 1670. It was repeated again in further grants, to Nicholas Birkhead, goldsmith, in 1673, and Edward Billings, tobacconist, in 1700. Billings, evidently, was the man responsible for building the Fox alehouse there, in about 1702.[39]

Clarke's freehold, three acres in extent, comprised the site now occupied by Bowater House. At one time the property of Sir Hugh Vaughan and then of Edmundishaw Muschamp, it too had come into the possession of the Billings family, Clarke acquiring it from James Billings, carpenter, of Boston in Lincolnshire. The ground then consisted of pasture, with the Swan inn at the west end.[40]

In 1722 Clarke began granting building leases on both his freehold and leasehold fields, and by the end of the decade there were more than forty new houses here, including cottages in a court called Park Prospect. At the Swan (which he let on a long lease to Edward Billings' widow) tenements had been built or portioned out of the old premises. Work continued until by the late 1730s the whole of this stretch of Knightsbridge had been built up (Plates 2b, 3, 4, 5a, 21).[41]

Among the lessees and other parties to the leases granted by Clarke was William Grant, a carpenter, who took several houses on the eastern one-acre piece. On Clarke's freehold, the lessees included the West End carpenter-builder Benjamin Timbrell, who took at least one house-plot – at 25ft, wider than most of those on the freehold ground, which averaged about 18ft. Plots on the leasehold ground were generally narrower, and at the east end the buildings seem to have been of a significantly lower order. H. G. Davis (not writing from first-hand knowledge) describes the houses there, demolished for the Cannon Brewhouse, as having been 'a row of mean dwellings, with open cellars at the front, and at the west end a filthy court [Park Prospect]'.[42]

In 1764, after the death of Clarke's widow, the leasehold property was split up.[43]

Later history of High Row

High Row, for most of its existence, was not obviously fashionable, but there was a sprinkling of rank and title among the ratepayers throughout the eighteenth and nineteenth centuries, and the secession in 1843 of Nos 1–16 High Row West – all private residences or lodging-houses – to form 'Albert Terrace' is doubtless indicative of social aspiration.[44]

It was at about the time of the naming of Albert Terrace that the architects Thomas Chawner and James Pennethorne inspected the area for the Commissioners of Woods and Forests, who were troubled by the growing number of encroachments on Hyde Park – such as unauthorized windows overlooking the park, and trellises on the park wall. They found the High Row houses 'very unsightly'. A number had notices of apartments to let on display, and it was evident that some of the residents were in the habit of throwing their rubbish into the park.[45]

In the second half of the nineteenth century and in Edwardian days the former Albert Terrace became increasingly smart. Many of the houses were extensively modernized and improved, if not largely rebuilt, with rear extensions, bay-windows, verandahs and covered ways (Plate 21). In the back gardens, summer-houses of varying degrees of sophistication were built or re-built, sometimes bringing owners into conflict with the park authorities.

As far back as the late eighteenth century, the park authorities had expressed concern over such encroachments as the cutting of windows and hen-holes in the park wall all along High Row and Park Side, and in the 1840s a system of licences was introduced. By the late nineteenth century encroachments typically involved the installation of guttering and flashing to deflect rainwater from garden buildings close to the park wall.[46]

Personal access to the park was in theory out of the question, but, extraordinarily, in 1865 Lord Henry Gordon Lennox managed to obtain it. With special permission from the Ranger, the Duke of Cambridge, Lennox had a doorway made in the wall behind his garden at No. 13 Albert Terrace; recognizing a *fait accompli* the Commissioners of Woods and Forests issued him a licence. More remarkably, after Lennox moved and the doorway was stopped up in 1870, a later occupant of the house, Florence Adamson, not only managed to get permission from the Ranger to open it up again so that she could take her dogs into the park, but contrived to get permission for a personal gate in the railings along the carriage road in the park, so as to avoid the indignity of climbing over them. Mrs Adamson enjoyed this unique privilege until her departure some years later.[47]

The novelist and playwright Charles Reade lived at No. 2 Albert Terrace (later No. 19 Albert Gate and eventually No. 70 Knightsbridge) from 1867 until the early 1880s (Plates 1, 21b–c). The house, apparently bought with the proceeds from *The Cloister and the Hearth*, he had extended to provide a 'palatial apartment' opening on to the garden, which served in turn throughout the day as breakfast-room, study, reception room, dining-room and drawing-room. The arrangement was described by Reade in *A Terrible Temptation*, published in 1871. From a long room at the front of the house, decorated in scarlet, white and gold with green velvet curtains and upholstery, glass folding-doors gave on to 'a small conservatory walled like a grotto, with ferns sprouting out of rocky fissures, and spars sparkling; water dripping'. Beyond, through another set of folding-doors, was a large room lined with mirrors from floor to ceiling and opening through French windows to the garden, with a view of trees in the park. This mirrored room was furnished with highly polished oak and marquetry and a 'gigantic' writing-table, and decorated with rubber trees and one or two 'masterpieces of painting'.[48]

Reade was greatly attached to the house, which he defended spiritedly against the property developer Lord Beaumont (see page 54).[49]

The east end of High Row was redeveloped in 1804 with the Cannon Brewhouse, itself pulled down in 1841 for the Albert Gate development. The remainder of John Clarke's former leasehold ground was cleared for Lord Beaumont's 'Empress Gate' scheme in the 1870s, staying vacant until the late 1880s, when the construction of Hyde Park Court began (Plate 30c). The remaining High Row houses were bought up for redevelopment in the 1930s and despite various schemes stood empty until their demolition in December 1942. Bowater House was built on the site in the 1950s.[50]

Some residents of High Row

Before Charles Reade came to live at Albert Terrace, his nephew, William Winwood Reade, author of *The Martyr-*

dom of Man, lived at No. 8. The Tory politician Sir Henry Drummond Wolff occupied No. 8 (by then No. 25 Albert Gate) in the late 1870s.

Among several theatrical residents of High Row was Paul Bedford, the comedian – famous for the catch-phrase 'I believe you, my boy' – who lived at No. 18 High Row in the 1850s and afterwards at No. 16 Albert Terrace.

In the late 1820s Lady Ann Hamilton, the friend and former lady-in-waiting of Queen Caroline, and the author of the *Secret History of the Court of England*, lived immediately west of the Cannon Brewhouse at No. 11 High Row, a house rebuilt around 1813. Later occupants included George White, naturalist and dealer in animals, who kept a menagerie there, and Mr Woodburn, an authority on 'ancient art' – probably Samuel Woodburn, the picture dealer who helped put together several important art collections, including that of John Sheepshanks of Rutland Gate.

A 'Matthew Brettingham Esq.', perhaps the Norwich architect Matthew Brettingham junior (1725–1803), was the ratepayer of a house in High Row (later No. 72 Knightsbridge) in 1778–83. Another architect, Harvey Lonsdale Elmes, who was involved in the design of Princes Gate, was living at No. 15 High Row West in 1841. The sculptor Hamilton MacCarthy, who with his brother Carlton specialized in modelling racehorses and was associated with Tattersalls, lived at No. 17 Albert Terrace with his family (including his son, Hamilton Plantagenet MacCarthy, who also became a sculptor).

Several artists were residents of High Row, the most distinguished of them being Sir Edward J. Poynter, who lived for many years at No. 28 Albert Gate (later No. 88 Knightsbridge). The painter Ozias Humphry lived at No. 13 High Row for some years until his death in 1810. Charles Hancock, artist, was living at No. 21 High Row in 1841; Captain Charles Mercier, artist and portrait painter, lived at No. 12 Albert Terrace in the 1870s; and Henry S. Watkins, landscape painter, was living at No. 34 Albert Gate in 1881.[51]

The Fox and Bull (demolished)

The Knightsbridge chronicler H. G. Davis described the Fox and Bull as 'a celebrated inn . . . traditionally said to have been founded in the time of Elizabeth, and used by her on her visits to Lord Burleigh at Brompton'. With its panelled and carved rooms, 'immense' fireplaces and ornamented ceilings, it was, Davis insisted, 'undoubtedly of Elizabethan build' – though if he himself had recollections of the place, they can only have been those of a small child, as he was about six years old when it was demolished. In this inn artists and others are said to have gathered in a sort of informal club, Sir Joshua Reynolds and George Morland among them; Reynolds once painted the inn-sign.[52]

However, it does not seem that the Fox and Bull possessed such a long a history as Davis supposed. The site had been subject to repeated building leases since 1612 (see above), but rate books indicate that the tavern was built on hitherto vacant ground about 1702; a deed of 1707 describes the building as 'new'. It is referred to by name in deeds from 1719, as the Fox Alehouse. There was, however, a tavern in Knightsbridge called the Fox some years before 1702, and mention was made in 1710 of an 'Old Fox' at Knightsbridge in Steele's *Tatler*.[53]

Salway's survey shows the Fox to have been a fair-sized, unromantic-looking house, standing some fifteen or twenty feet from the Westbourne (Plate 5a).

The body of Shelley's first wife, Harriet Westbrook, is said to have been taken to the Fox, through a doorway in the park wall, after it was recovered from the Serpentine in December 1816.[54]

In 1818 the Fox was acquired by the brewer Thomas Goding and renamed the Fox and Bull. It was rebuilt in 1836, presumably to the designs of Goding's architect Francis Edwards, its site shifted a little eastwards, as far as the plot would allow, to the bank of the Westbourne, apparently to make way for an extension to the Cannon Brewhouse. The new building, taller and narrower than its predecessor, had only a short existence, being pulled down in 1841 along with the brewery for Thomas Cubitt's Albert Gate. The 'Royal Harmonic Hall' at the Fox and Bull tavern, for which a playbill dated March 1841 survives, was possibly a temporary conversion of part of the brewery during its last days.

Cubitt replaced the building with another on the western part of the brewery site. This third Fox and Bull – a 'staring compoed public-house' as it was brusquely referred to in 1856 – was licensed for public entertainments from the late 1840s to the late 1850s, and survived into the 1880s when it was demolished for the London and County Bank (see below).[55]

Cannon Brewhouse (demolished)

The Cannon Brewhouse was built for Thomas and James Goding, wine merchants and brewers, in 1804. The site, with a road frontage of over 95ft and formerly on lease to Jonathan Clarke, was one of the portions into which John Clarke's leasehold estate had been split up in 1764. The architect was George Byfield, estate surveyor to the Dean and Chapter of Westminster Abbey, the freeholders.[56]

H. G. Davis remembered the brewhouse as an 'unsightly' edifice: on the other hand the impression given by Salway is of a not unhandsome building with a classical though windowless façade (Plate 5a). A tall range on the western side, of warehouse-like appearance, was built about 1812 on the site of Park Prospect. Goding further enlarged the premises, obtaining in 1818 a new lease of the expanded site, which included the Fox alehouse adjoining (thereafter the Fox and Bull).[57]

Additions were made about 1835 by Francis Edwards, a former assistant of Byfield's partner in his late years, H. H. Seward. These appear to have included an extension partly on the site of the Fox and Bull, which was itself rebuilt

around this time, presumably to Edwards' design.[58]

A few years later the brewery's 'eternal smoke' became the bugbear of Lady Sydney Morgan – recently arrived in the district – and Thomas Cubitt, the co-proponents of a scheme for a new entrance into the park close by, ultimately realized as Albert Gate. Together they plotted the brewery's removal, and in 1841 Cubitt bought and demolished both the Cannon Brewhouse and the Fox and Bull. Before being pulled down, the brewery housed bricklayers and their families, probably Cubitt's employees working on the Lowndes estate or the new Fox and Bull at the western end of the site. The wooden cannon which had stood on the parapet of the brewhouse was removed to adorn a pub in Warwick Street, Pimlico. The remainder of the site was left undeveloped until the building there in 1851 of a temporary structure for the Chinese exhibition (see page 52).[59] This was replaced a few years later by Hyde Park House, itself pulled down in the 1960s for the building of the present No. 60 Knightsbridge.

The Swan (demolished)

The Swan inn stood at the west end of the site now occupied by Bowater House. There was a Swan inn at Knightsbridge as far back as the 1630s, when it was mentioned in a rhyme by the 'water-poet' John Taylor. The Swan made further literary appearances in the seventeenth and eighteenth centuries, notably in the work of the satirists Thomas Brown and 'Peter Pindar', and in Thomas Otway's *Soldier's Fortune*, in which Sir Davy Dunce asserts 'tis a damned house, that *Swan*; that *Swan* at Knightsbridge is a confounded house!'. Traditionally, Knightsbridge inns did not have a good reputation, and as well as being apparently a rendezvous for illicit liaisons, the Swan was used by the ringleaders of a Jacobite plot to assassinate William III in 1694; in 1723 it was the scene of a murder.[60]

In 1756 the landlord built a new Swan inn on the south side of Knightsbridge, at the top of Brompton Road. The old Swan remained standing until about 1776, when it was acquired for redevelopment by Ralph Mills.[61]

Mills's Buildings and Park Row (demolished)

In 1776 Ralph Mills, a Knightsbridge carpenter-builder, took a long lease of the old Swan inn and adjoining tenements from John Clarke's heirs, and proceeded to redevelop the site. Over the next dozen years twenty-six houses were built there, comprising Park Row, Mill's or Mills's Buildings, and eight houses in High Row, subsequently Nos 17–24 Albert Terrace, and eventually Nos 100–114 Knightsbridge (see fig. 9). The new houses in High Row were all inhabited by 1777, and the dozen houses in Mills's Buildings were first rated in 1779. Three houses in Park Row followed in 1781, but it was several years before they were inhabited; three more appeared in 1787, and the entire row was occupied by 1789.[62]

Most of Mills's High Row houses were shops by the second decade of the nineteenth century (Plate 4c), and one was a pub, the Queen's Arms (later No. 108 Knightsbridge). Rebuilt in 1894 (Plate 20b), the Queen's Arms closed in the early 1930s, when it was converted into two shops, with offices and flats above.[63]

The houses in Mills's Buildings, though small, were superior to the cottages often found in such courts, with elegant doorcases (Plate 20a). It is possible that a surveyor, Godfrey Wilson the younger of Bryanston Square, may have had a hand in their design; he was among the first lessees of the houses.[64]

Whatever its original status may have been, Mills's Buildings was of lowly character by the late 1820s when several ratepayers there were described as 'poor' or 'very poor and aged'. The houses seem to have been in multi-occupation by working-class tenants throughout the Victorian period, before undergoing some gentrification after the First World War.[65]

Henry George Davis (1830–57), much of whose short life was devoted to the compilation of *The Memorials of the Hamlet of Knightsbridge*, published posthumously under his brother Charles's editorship, was born at No. 4 Mills's Buildings.[66]

In Park Row (renamed Hyde Park Row in 1939) the houses were larger than those in Mills's Buildings, with segmental bays facing the park.[67] They probably always had a higher social status, and the first occupants included a doctor of divinity, the Rev. John Trotter. Two notable occupants in the 1820s were the author, publisher and vegetarian Sir Richard Phillips, and Olive Wilmot, who styled herself 'Princess Olive' and claimed to be married to the Duke of Cumberland. According to the writer John Timbs, Phillips and Princess Olive were next-door neighbours, but in fact they both seem to have lived at No. 4, Phillips moving in after Olive's departure in 1829.[68]

The Chartist, poet and lecturer Thomas Cooper lived at No. 5 – 'the pleasantest house I had ever had in my life' – from 1848 until 1855:

The access to it was through 'Mill's Buildings,' a 'long square' tenanted chiefly by workpeople and washerwomen, and, therefore, not likely to attract fashionables. But the houses forming 'Park Row,' though somewhat old, were large and roomy, and must have been tenanted by 'considerable' sort of people, formerly. We had no access to Hyde Park, but we looked into it from our really beautiful parlour; and had daily views of the Guards, and Royalty, and great people, passing by, in the Park.[69]

Several years before Cooper's arrival, the residents of Park Row had included clerks, a secretary, and a young practising barrister, and there were on average only half-a-dozen people to each house (compared to fourteen in Mills's Buildings). Park Row retained a preponderance of middle-class residents (often lodgers) throughout the Victorian period; from the 1860s to the 1880s, No. 6 was occupied as lodgings, mostly by Swiss and French governesses and ladies' maids.

Jerome K. Jerome lived at No. 5 from the mid-1890s until the early 1900s. Other residents of Park Row at various times include: Frank Matthews, actor; George Henry Francis, editor of the *Morning Post* and other newspapers (No. 5, 1861); Charles Bruce Allen, architect (No. 6, 1861); George Kenyon, architect (No. 1, 1891); James H. D'Egville, watercolour artist (No. 3, 1861); George Mears, marine painter (No. 3, 1871); John Rogers, composer (No. 5, 1871); Sara Nelson, dramatic and illustrative artist (No. 4, 1881); (Sir) George Alexander, actor-manager (No. 6, 1891).[70]

Albert Gate

The creation of Albert Gate in the early 1840s by the greatest speculative builder of the day, Thomas Cubitt, gave early Victorian London a landmark whose original effect has long been lost and is now difficult to envisage. Cubitt's two mansions, famously dubbed 'Malta' and 'Gibraltar' because they were so large they 'would never be taken', attract little attention today on account of their size. When new, however, they towered prominently over the neighbouring buildings. Moreover, since the opening of Edinburgh Gate in the late 1950s, Albert Gate has been closed to traffic, and its redundancy serves to emphasize a certain obscurity of position – aligned not with a major road but the relatively minor William Street.

The core of Cubitt's development – the two great Italianate houses flanking the gateway – remains essentially as built, though No. 1 Albert Gate (the French Embassy) was extended in the early 1900s in similar style. An even larger third mansion, Hyde Park House, built by Cubitt a decade after the first two, was replaced in the 1960s with the present Modernist block, No. 60 Knightsbridge.

The origins of Albert Gate go back to January 1838, when Sir Charles Morgan and his wife Sydney, the Irish popular novelist, took up residence in a new house in William Street, on Cubitt's Lowndes estate development. Building on the estate was in its early stages – two or three houses only being erected in William Street, and Lowndes Square not yet begun – and the district still retained something of a rural air. Conscious that the pretty 'green swards' over the way from her new house would soon be lost to building, Lady Morgan focused her considerable energies on obtaining an entrance into Hyde Park opposite the top of William Street. From here the trees in the park were tantalizingly visible beyond the buildings on the road-side strip belonging to Westminster Abbey. In August 1838, supported by other local residents, Lady Morgan petitioned the First Commissioner of Woods and Forests, Lord Duncannon, to re-open what she claimed to be 'an ancient gate' on the site of the Fox and Bull inn. Her authority for this claim was 'a curious account' of the district given her by the poet Henry Milman, Prebend of Westminster Abbey, which linked the spot with the Knights of St John of Jerusalem and the monks of the Abbey. Cubitt, her landlord, 'a good, little, complying man' with whom Lady Morgan had developed a particular rapport, also supported the plan, to the extent of being 'willing to incur the expense of

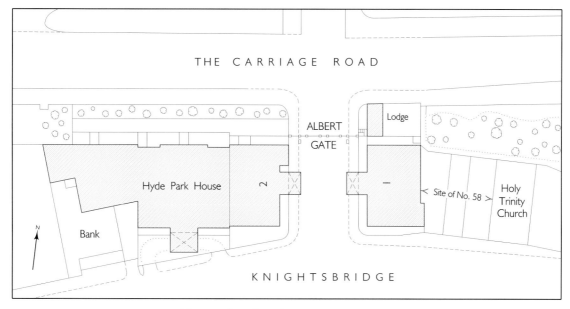

Fig. 11. Albert Gate, site plan in the mid-1890s

the alteration'. But it was turned down by Duncannon, who was worried that consent would encourage a rash of similar requests elsewhere around the park. Lady Morgan then appealed directly to the Queen, with a petition signed by the Duke of Wellington and 'all the respectable inhabitants of Cubittopolis'. She also won the support of the Duchess of Kent, the Queen's mother and Ranger of Hyde Park. Duncannon had eventually to concede defeat, but saw no reason to modify his own view of the scheme, which, he later wrote, 'had been urged on the Queen by other parties'.[71]

Quite apart from the simple opening of a gate into the park, Lady Morgan's campaign had a wider aim, the improvement of the Abbey land opposite William Street. Historical associations notwithstanding, this was now a far from beguiling spot. It was crossed by the Westbourne brook, a 'ditch of filth and infection' flowing through the narrow gap between the buildings in High Row and Park Side. There were two public houses here, the Fox and Bull and the White Hart, the former prosaic in its newness, the other old, but shabby and unprepossessing. Worst of all was the Cannon Brewhouse, casting a permanent pall of smoke over the whole neighbourhood. As early as May 1838, according to Lady Morgan's diaries, Cubitt had declared his intention of buying out the brewhouse, and without waiting for a decision on the gate he went ahead and bid for the brewery and other properties on the site. Presumably he planned to recoup the cost through a considerably more ambitious development than the gate and 'sort of little rustic bridge' that Lady Morgan had in mind.[72]

After this initial flurry of activity the project hung fire, for reasons not entirely clear. Duncannon's continuing hostility was doubtless one factor. Another may have been uncertainty over the future of an official proposal, also sug-

gested in 1838, for a new road into Hyde Park from Knightsbridge, opposite Sloane Street, which, had it gone ahead, would seem to have made another entrance into the park so near as William Street quite superfluous.[73]

Consideration was evidently given to a much grander Albert Gate project than that eventually adopted. Various undated drawings, of unknown provenance but possibly produced by Cubitt's office for submission to the park authorities, show the proposed gateway opposite William Street as part of a scheme incorporating Nash-like terraces of palatial houses, set back from Knightsbridge behind plantations. One variant would have involved the complete redevelopment of Park Side, another the rebuilding of the whole of High Row as well.[74] The work would certainly have needed the consent of the Dean and Chapter of Westminster, and it was perhaps with this grand scheme before him that in March 1841 Duncannon sought out their feeling as to granting long leases on their property, subject to statutory powers being obtained. In principle they had no objection.[75]

Cubitt was now in a position to break the impasse. With the Cannon Brewhouse and Fox and Bull already in the bag, and negotiations for the White Hart and other property east of the Westbourne continuing, he made an offer to Duncannon to construct the new opening to the park at his own expense, arching over the watercourse, erecting a lodge and gates, and undertaking to build houses on long lease over the adjoining ground, 'so as to form good looking sides to the new Entrance'. Duncannon, while remaining 'very averse' to the idea of a new gate, had to concede that it offered an opportunity to improve the district, which, in his words to Lord Melbourne, the Prime Minister, 'is not to be overlooked'.[76]

The sticking-point now was the question of the ownership of the ground. It was essential, in Duncannon's view,

that the Crown should have more control of the development than leaseholds from Westminster Abbey offered
(Cubitt was, presumably, offering to build on sub-leases
from the Crown). In practical terms this meant buying the
freehold not just of the gateway but of 'reasonable space of
ground on either side', without which any plan of this kind
would be 'highly inexpedient'.[77] A clause allowing the
Dean and Chapter to sell their freehold or grant long leases was accordingly added to a new Metropolis Improvements Bill, which was passed in May 1841.[78]

The ground covered by the Act comprised the Cannon
Brewhouse site and the strip extending eastwards as far as
No. 22 Park Side. But the Westminster Abbey authorities
proved reluctant to give up more land than was absolutely
necessary, and at first agreed only to sell part of the autho-
rized site, with the bed of the Westbourne well off-centre.
It was not until June 1842, nearly a year later, that the
Crown was able to buy the remainder of the ground delin-
eated by the Act.[79]

As the bed of the Westbourne, where a brick sewer had
to be constructed, dictated the line of the new roadway, it
was impossible for Cubitt to achieve a formal symmetry,
and his initial plan, based on the reduced site, was distinctly lop-sided. In this first version, the roadway, narrower
than eventually laid out, was divided at the north end by a
small island with a gatekeeper's lodge and closed off by
railings, with a single gate, not wide enough to admit carriages, between the lodge and the western house. The
scheme was shown to the Queen and approved in May
1841. Among the drawings submitted to her were eye-
catching 'before' and 'after' views, the latter for some reason omitting the lodge and railings altogether (Plate 114a).
This view suggests that a substantial brick terrace was in
mind for the site adjoining the eastern house, should it
become available.[80] After the rest of the site was secured in
1842 the proportions of the layout were changed: the eastern house plot was deepened and that of the western house
curtailed, the intervening roadway was widened and fitted
with gates broad enough to admit carriages, and the central
island dispensed with altogether.

The additional land to the west, where the Cannon
Brewhouse had stood, was sufficiently large to allow for the
building of one or more extra houses, and when it was
eventually built over in the 1850s, the effect was even more
unbalanced than the 1841 scheme had been. Having
obtained the freehold of the site of the new gate and the two
flanking houses, the Crown had little interest in retaining
that of the large western plot, which was later sold to
Cubitt for £10,534. However, the Crown wished to retain
the right to approve any building erected on the ground.
Cubitt resisted this, but agreed to submit the parkside elevation to the Commissioners of Woods and Forests for
approval, a condition he was not entirely scrupulous about
observing (see page 53).[81]

It is not clear when the name Albert Gate was first suggested. Lady Morgan in her published memoirs refers to
'My first shaking of the Albert Gate!' in a diary entry of

May 1838. But this was well before the Queen and Prince
Albert were formally engaged, and it seems likely that this
comment is a considerably later interpolation.[82] Following
the Queen's marriage, in February 1840, the name was a
fairly obvious one to choose, given the Queen's personal
involvement in approving the design of the entrance, and
the fact that her own name had already been appropriated
for a new park gate in Bayswater Road.

The gates and lodge

The entrance into the park originally comprised a short
stretch of new roadway between Knightsbridge and South
Carriage Drive, a set of gates, and a residence for the gate-
keeper. The gates were modest in scale and comparatively
simple in design, their chief decoration being a pair of
bronze stags on the outer piers. And these were not new:
attributed to the Dublin-born sculptor, Peter Turnerelli,
after prints by Bartolozzi,[83] they formerly graced the Piccadilly entrance to the Deputy Ranger's Lodge in Green
Park. This lodge having been earmarked for demolition,
Cubitt stepped in to acquire the stags for Albert Gate: 'it
occurs to me that the piers . . . with the 2 handsome stags
on the top might be worked into an appropriate design to
form part of the new entrance'. But demolition was
delayed, and while he obtained possession of the stags, the
stone gate-piers could not be dismantled in time for him to
make use of them at Knightsbridge.[84]

This was probably the reason behind a late change in the
intended disposition of gates and piers. A drawing published with Cubitt's authority in March 1844 shows he had
planned to site the stone piers between the pavement and
roadway, flanking the carriage-gates. In the changed
arrangement the stags were placed on new brick-and-stucco
plinths built into the adjoining garden walls. The gates
themselves, made of iron and 'of a very chaste design', were
fixed in August 1845.[85] Originally there were three pairs of
cast-iron piers, each decorated with a pattern of oak-leaves
and acorns and surmounted by a large gas-lamp. Two piers
were removed before the end of the century to widen the
carriage openings, when the original gates were presumably
enlarged or replaced. In the 1950s the gates, though not the
piers, were dismantled and apparently sold or destroyed:
their present-day replacements were erected in 1984–5.[86]

Once the island in the centre of the roadway intended in
1841 had been sacrificed for wider gates, there was no room
for a gatekeeper's lodge at street level, and Cubitt provided
one as unobtrusively as possible in the garden of the eastern house (fig. 11). Semi-submerged, so as not to interfere
with the view from the house, this two-room dwelling, with
an outside wash-house and w.c., gave trouble from the
start. By 1853 what the *Builder* dubbed the 'living sepul-
chre' at Albert Gate had claimed the lives of two keepers
'through diseases arising from its unwholesomeness and
dampness'. But a Board of Health inspection found the
rooms to be 'as good as those which are inhabited by the
great majority of the servants of the nobility of the West

KNIGHTSBRIDGE, NORTH SIDE

end of the Metropolis'. (Cubitt had said much the same himself, when submitting the plans in 1843.) Complaints about dampness continued and eventually the lodge was deemed unfit for occupation and the keeper moved to Prince of Wales Gate, where a second (east) lodge had been built at the time of the Great Exhibition as a temporary police station. The old dwelling was not removed until 1901. Latterly it was occupied by squatters: in 1898 the two rooms were home to a family of seven.[87]

Beneath the roadway at Albert Gate, the Westbourne was canalized into a brick sewer, but further north the stream bed remained open. In April 1844, citing the 'great objections' made, perhaps by prospective house-buyers, to the 'drain-like appearance' of the channel, Cubitt persuaded the Commissioners to allow him, at their joint expense, to do away with it by extending the Albert Gate sewer as far as Rotten Row. This work was completed in November 1844.[88]

The Albert Gate houses, 1843–5

Building work on the two mansions began in 1843. By the autumn the eastern house (No. 1) was in carcase, and in the following May both houses were said to be nearly completed, though in all probability work continued into 1845. Prince Albert viewed them in April of that year, when he was thinking about plans for the new Osborne. No. 1 was leased to Cubitt by the Crown in January 1846, and No. 2 in December 1847; both leases were for 99 years from 1845.[89]

Designed in Cubitt's office, the buildings are Italianate in style, with fully stuccoed façades, originally intended to be coloured and jointed in imitation of Bath stone.[90] The elevations were adapted from those approved by the Queen in 1841 (Plate 114a), to fit the altered dimensions of the plots – a consequence of the enlargement of the site. No. 2, in 1841 a bigger house with five-bay fronts to Knightsbridge and the park, was shorn of a bay on its north and south sides, while at No. 1 the original three-bay elevations were simply stretched to fill the extra space (Plate 23a).

Other modifications were made to the 1841 designs. At each house the porch was extended over the pavement, the main cornice was raised to the top of the building, balconies were added to the second-floor windows, and on the park side an intended full-height segmental bay, not unlike that at Cubitt's own house in Clapham Park, was dispensed with altogether.[91]

Rising to over 75 feet, with five full storeys, the two mansions were the largest speculative houses yet seen in London, and they were soon the best known, featuring in cartoons and the target of smart witticisms. The most famous quip, likening the houses to Malta and Gibraltar 'because they would never be taken', proved prophetic in the case of No. 2, which, unlettable in its original state, stood empty for many years. H. G. Davis damned them for their size and, as he saw it, lack of architectural quality: 'Though so gigantic, they are not imposing; of an unusual altitude, they are destitute of ornament'.[92] As a type, how-

ever, they proved very influential. John Elger's development at nearby Princes Gate was designed under their shadow, and their progeny can be seen all over South Kensington. The greatest tribute, however, came from the Queen and Prince Albert, who chose Cubitt to rebuild Osborne House for them, and in the 'Cubitt style' as redefined by the new houses at Albert Gate.

In building these exceptionally tall houses Cubitt made use of a hoist, a device then still sufficiently uncommon to merit a comment in the pages of the Builder.[93] At No. 2 (as recent works have revealed) and probably also at No. 1, he experimented with iron floor-joists in conjunction with traditional timber ones.

Within, the houses were planned along similar lines around three sides of a central top-lit hall and staircase compartment, with an entrance, under a stone-columned portico, in the centre of the Albert Gate front. At No. 1 the accommodation comprised: on the ground-floor, a 'great dining-room' facing the park, and two other rooms 'suitable for a library and a reception room'; on the first floor, a suite of drawing-rooms; on the second floor, six rooms of varying size 'intended for sleeping apartments for the family'; and on the upper two floors, 'smaller chambers for superior domestics'. However, the amount of floor space was soon being criticized as rather meagre, considering the height of the building, and to a disproportionate extent taken up by the staircase.[94] The planning at No. 2, no doubt originally intended to mirror that at No. 1, had to be adjusted to suit the peculiar circumstances of its original occupation (see below).

No. 1 Albert Gate: the French Embassy

In March 1844 the Illustrated London News published a view and a laudatory account of Albert Gate which claimed that various noblemen were 'desirous of inhabiting this splendid edifice [No. 1], as soon as completed'. However, it was not an aristocrat, but an archetypal Victorian self-made man, George Hudson, MP, the Yorkshire linen-draper turned railway promoter, who bought it. He paid the purchase price of £13,667 13s out of the large sum which 'admirers' had subscribed as a testimony of their respect (in hope, no doubt, of receiving an allotment of shares): Mrs Hudson reputedly spent another £14,000 on furnishings and decoration. The purchase was completed in January 1846, when Cubitt granted Hudson a 75-year lease at an annual rent of £150; at the same time Hudson took a separate lease of a coach-house and stable in William Mews, another Cubitt development, behind Lowndes Square.[95]

Already dubbed the 'Railway King' and 'Napoleon of the Railways', Hudson bought No. 1 at the height of his fame and in furtherance of his social ambitions; and while his star remained in the ascendant the great and the good readily overlooked his uncouth manners to pay him court there. The journalist G. A. Sala mocked their avaricious sycophancy:

came the nobles of the land, humbling themselves on their gartered knees, and pressing the earth with their coroneted brows, and calling him King of Men, that he might give them shares.[96]

But Hudson's fraudulent share dealings eventually caught up with him and he was obliged to give up the house, which he sub-let in 1853 to the French ambassador, Count Walewski, for £1,800 a year. A few months earlier Walewski had been interested in leasing the still unoccupied No. 2, and had wanted Cubitt to make a carriage-entrance there, closer to the house. To help Hudson secure the ambassador's tenancy for No. 1, Cubitt undertook £600-worth of work in the house, at 'great inconvenience' to himself. Hudson footed the bill, but had to be pressed hard for the money.[97]

Ambassadorial entertaining drew Queen Victoria and Prince Albert to No. 1 for a *Bal Costumé* in 1854, when the house was fitted up for the occasion by Cubitt. Generally the early ambassadors were not thought to be much of an improvement on the first occupant; nevertheless, as Sala observed when writing about Walewski's successor, De Persigny, 'the nobles and princes were as glad to come to his merry-makings as in the old time, when the now broken-down Railway Stag held high court there'.[98a]

No. 1 has been continuously occupied as the French Embassy since 1853, although in 1947 it ceased to be the ambassador's residence. In 1898 the French Government purchased the freehold from the Crown. The Embassy's lease (renegotiated in 1859–60) was not due to expire until 1920, but the ambassador, concerned about rising property prices in the latter part of the 1890s, had urged his government to move speedily: 'the market trend would be greatly accelerated in the event of a change of sovereign and the more continuous residence of the Court in the Capital'.[100]

A condition of the sale prohibited unauthorized alterations to the elevations of the building, and the exterior remains relatively little changed. A conservatory, now removed, was built over the porch in 1903 (Plate 23c),[101] and an extra attic storey was added in 1997–8.

The interior, on the other hand, has been much altered. Since official entertaining moved out with the ambassadors to Kensington Palace Gardens after the war, the Albert Gate building has been used chiefly for offices, and the fine interiors recorded in photographs, showcases of French art and taste, have largely disappeared. Much of the decoration of these rooms was carried out in 1900–2.[102] Particularly convincing were the first-floor drawing-rooms, where gilded and painted plasterwork and *boiseries* (some of it possibly authentic) re-created the interior of a Parisian hôtel of the Louis Seize period (Plate 24a). The sixteenth century was evoked in the library (on the ground floor overlooking the park) where the walls were adorned with carved wood panelling in the style of the sculptor Jean Goujon.

Cubitt's staircase compartment in the centre of the house remained more or less unaltered until the 1930s, when the lower part was remodelled by Fernand Billerey, the embassy's official architect, and the upper flights of the cantilevered staircase, between the first and second floors, were removed.[103] Surviving original features include the domed skylight, the decorative plasterwork, and the arcaded passage all around the compartment at fourth-floor level – an arrangement also found in some of Cubitt's houses in Eaton Square (Plate 24b–c). The servants' staircase in the south-east corner of the building is also original: lit by windows looking on to Knightsbridge, it is, somewhat surprisingly, visible from the street.[b]

No. 58 Knightsbridge: French Embassy extension

By the mid-1890s the French Embassy had outgrown its accommodation at No. 1 Albert Gate. New chancellery premises and a reception room were deemed to be 'absolutely necessary', and while the ambassador urged the case for more space with the Quai d'Orsay, he sounded out the Ecclesiastical Commissioners as to the possibility of building an extension on their land next door.[104]

Negotiations were protracted, partly because the minister at Holy Trinity was concerned about the effect such a building might have on the already inadequate natural lighting in his church. Eventually an accommodation was reached, and in 1899 the Ecclesiastical Commissioners granted the French Government a 999-year lease of all the ground between No. 1 and Holy Trinity (which included the site of the White Hart).[105]

The new building was designed by Olivier Carré, assistant architect at the Ministère des Affaires Étrangères. However, he was constrained by covenants restricting the height and external detailing of the building, and the result is a relatively plain block, three storeys high above a basement, with stuccoed elevations and some Italianate touches echoing Cubitt's adjoining house.

Building began in 1899, but soon ran into difficulties. The rising price of labour and materials, blamed on the Boer War, resulted in a considerable overspend and there was a marked slowing down in the rate of progress. It was not until the end of 1901 that the superstructure was complete, though not yet stuccoed. Concerned about the management of the project, the authorities in Paris sent over Louis Bernier fils, architecte des Bâtiments Civils, to investigate. He criticized Carré's professional conduct, and a subsequent enquiry found that because Carré was over-

---

[a] It has been claimed that the word stag in the sense of someone who acquires an allotment of shares for immediate resale at a profit was coined to characterize Hudson's share-dealings, by allusion to the stag outside his house in Albert Gate. In fact, Thackeray seems to have used it with this meaning in 1845, the year before Hudson bought his house.[99]

[b] Later developers who based the planning of their end-of-terrace houses on Albert Gate, like C. J. Freake at Nos 49 and 58 Princes Gate, usually contrived to place the servants' stair behind the principal staircase, well out of sight.

stretched by other commitments his tender documents had been insufficiently detailed and the specifications inadequate.[c] Meanwhile, work continued under the supervision of Edward Goldie, the local site-architect who was also responsible for the ordinary maintenance of the embassy building. Early in 1902 Carré was relieved of his responsibilities for the extension, which was completed later that year under Bernier's superintendence.

The shell was conventionally constructed (by Pattinson & Sons) with stuccoed brick walls. But for the floors, brackets and balconies Carré employed Hennebique's 'indestructible and absolutely fire-proof' system of reinforced- ('ferro-') concrete construction, not yet widely adopted in London, owing to the London County Council's reluctance to sanction its use. Exempted by reason of its diplomatic status from the requirements of the 1894 London Building Act, No. 58 is almost certainly the first significant non-industrial building in London to utilize structural reinforced concrete: earlier use had been largely confined to structures erected on land belonging to the dock and railway companies, where the LCC's writ did not run. The council took an interest in the work and early in 1900 its Architect inspected the floors; later that year an official LCC report concluded that Hennebique's concrete was acceptable, provided it was constructed with care. The floors at the embassy extension were formally tested early in 1902 by the Ingénieur en Chef des Ponts et Chaussées, in the presence of Goldie, the contractors for the concrete (A. Jackaman & Sons), the agent for Hennebique's patents in England (L. G. Mouchel), and two civil engineers.[106]

The self-effacing exterior was in marked contrast to the interior, where the first floor was given over to a lavishly decorated pair of state reception rooms – a banqueting-room on the Knightsbridge side and a ballroom overlooking the park (Plate 25). In the ballroom – 'probably without a rival in London', in the view of a contemporary magazine – the long north and south walls were lined with projecting pairs of sumptuously modelled Corinthian columns below a compartmented and ornately decorated plaster ceiling, the heavy plasterwork being fixed to the underpart of the concrete beams forming the floor above. Concrete was also used in the construction of the columns, though probably only for the core, the decoration of the capitals and the shafts being presumably modelled in plaster. Double doors in the south wall of the ballroom communicated with the adjoining banqueting-room, where, under another ornate plaster ceiling, the walls were hung with Louis Quatorze tapestries. In 1904 Mouchel singled out these apartments as good examples of how admirably reinforced concrete 'lends itself to ornamentation'.[107]

These rooms no longer survive, having been converted into a series of utilitarian offices opening off a newly formed central corridor.

No. 2 Albert Gate

Although reported in March 1846 to have been bought by a Sir Roger Palmer, No. 2 remained empty and on the market for ten years.[108] Cubitt's hopes of finding a buyer during that time were more than once disappointed: a proposal to establish a club there in 1851 soon petered out, and in 1853 a potential tenant in the person of the French ambassador was lost when he settled instead for No. 1.[109] When No. 2 was eventually occupied late in 1856, it was not as a single dwelling but divided in two, the southern part being let to the London and County Bank, which had its own separate entrance in Knightsbridge.[110] This part-commercial occupation lasted until the bank moved to a new building near by in 1885, but it does not seem to have blighted the residential eligibility of the northern half, where the first private inhabitant, from 1856 to 1868, was Colonel Fulke Greville, MP. He was fortuitously absent in September 1858 when a gas explosion rocked the house, severely injuring three female servants, one fatally.[111] Greville's successors here were the 1st Earl of Feversham, followed in 1875 by the banker Arthur David Sassoon, a younger brother of Sir Albert Sassoon, who added a conservatory over the portico (now removed).[112]

After the departure of the bank, Sassoon took over the old premises and reinstated the two halves of the building as a single house. At the same time the interior was lavishly redecorated by G. Jackson & Sons of Rathbone Place, specialists in papier mâché, carton pierre and composition ornament, with the builders Sprake & Foreman of Pont Street (Plates 26–7).[113] The most spectacular new feature was an opulent marble staircase, with a gilded balustrade incorporating lyres, torches and foliage (Plate 26a–b). The staircase walls were lined with variegated marbles, offset by large tapestry panels set in marble frames. Elsewhere, the decoration though sumptuous was more conventional (Plate 27). Several of the principal rooms, including the large ballroom on the first floor, were in the French taste (Plate 26c).

The new décor made a suitably luxurious backdrop for the Sassoons' renowned hospitality, which reached its apogee in 1889 when the Shah of Persia was their guest, both here in Albert Gate and at their house in Brighton.[114] Sassoon died in 1912, but his widow lived on in the house for another thirty years, until her own death in 1943. After the war No. 2 was occupied commercially, and a mansard floor added. In 1993–5 the building was expensively refurbished as the Kuwaiti Embassy by the Whinney Mackay-Lewis Partnership.

Of Sassoon's fine interiors the only substantial survival is the marble staircase, now, however, shorn of its tapestry panels (pieces of damask have been substituted), and with a modern glass lift-shaft inserted into the well. The panelled segmental-vaulted passage from the front door to the

[c] The Paris-based Carré's other responsibilities included the preparation of plans, estimates and contracts for work in Peking (reconstructing the French Legation destroyed in the Boxer rebellion), Washington (the French Embassy), Constantinople (the French hospital), Tangiers (a temporary hospital) and Vienna.

staircase compartment is probably another relic from the Sassoon years. The decoration of the other principal rooms is mostly post-war work: it includes, on the ground floor, a marbled former banking hall.

The Chinese Collection at Albert Gate in 1851

With No. 2 standing empty and no tenant in prospect, Cubitt was reluctant to press ahead with more speculative development on the large plot to the west (where the Cannon Brewhouse had stood): 'I would rather not venture upon a further outlay at present', he told the Commissioners of Woods and Forests in January 1847. What he really wanted was 'a Commission to erect a House or Houses in accordance with the views of a Customer'. In the meantime he laid the area to turf, restored the boundary wall on the park side and put up an iron railing along Knightsbridge. In 1851, no taker having yet come forward, he allowed the site (by then his freehold) to be used for a re-run of the Chinese Collection, an exhibition of Chinese artefacts first shown in London in the 1840s at St George's Place (see page 24).[115]

After closing in 1846, this exhibition had toured the English provinces, before returning to America in 1850, where P. T. Barnum displayed it at his American Museum in New York.[116] The prime mover in its restaging at Albert Gate was the curator, William B. Langdon, who seems to have acquired the collection after the death in 1844 of the original owner, Nathan Dunn. Francis George Herbert of Queen's Buildings, Brompton Road, a silversmith, with whom Langdon stayed in 1851, organized the construction of the exhibition hall.[117]

In mid-April 1851 *The Times* carried an advertisement for the show:

the celebrated Chinese Collection in the newly erected Celestial Palace, Albert-gate . . . is now in a forward state of completion, the whole collection having been re-arranged, enlarged, and beautified.[118]

This was somewhat disingenuous: the truth was that after its travels, far from being enlarged, the collection had dwindled to less than half its original size.[119]

The pretentiously named 'Celestial Palace' was a single-storey gallery 100ft long, with a raised central section and subdivided internally (Plate 126a). The only known illustration of the front – a small vignette – shows a symmetrical and classically proportioned structure, not unlike a Nonconformist chapel, the raised section having a small pediment and a cupola-like feature, possibly a ventilator. Panels and friezes of Chinese characters decorated the exterior. The entrance was in the centre of the Knightsbridge front, through a decorated porch faintly echoing the style of Brighton Pavilion. The 'Palace' was substantially constructed, with brick walls, finished with a stone cornice, and, apparently, a wood-and-canvas roof. The builder was Walter Longhurst, also of Queen's Buildings. It was later claimed that the promoters had been obliged to provide a

more strongly built structure than the 'merely temporary' one originally intended, and had lost money thereby.[120]

The Collection opened to the public on 21 April 1851. A highlight of the show was the series of daily concerts performed by a Chinese family, previously engaged by Barnum for the exhibition in New York. They made their first appearance at Albert Gate on 1 May 1851, the same day that the Great Exhibition itself opened. The 'family' consisted of a professor of music, his two young children, a lady vocalist (with feet 'of the most aristocratic proportions'), her maid, and an interpreter.[121] Hector Berlioz, an official judge at the Great Exhibition, went to hear them: 'I have never heard anything so strange in my life', he wrote of the professor's voice, 'hideous snorts, and groans, very much like the sounds dogs make when they wake up'. By comparison the lady vocalist had a heavenly voice, but Berlioz doubted if she was as 'small footed as she would have you believe'.[122]

Although the Collection was ideally placed to catch the Great Exhibition crowds, and at first did so, it had a poor and ultimately loss-making season. After closing, the Collection was sold at auction and dispersed, and early in 1852 the Celestial Palace itself was demolished.[123] Two years later, William Langdon, the former curator, sailed for Australia, where he died in 1868.[124]

Hyde Park House, No. 60 Knightsbridge (demolished)

By the time the Celestial Palace was being demolished, Cubitt had found a single 'customer' for the site, who commissioned a mansion there for his own occupation. He was Captain Thomas Leyland (born Naylor), of Westbourne Terrace, the eldest of three wealthy brothers whose family fortune was founded on banking interests in Liverpool. All three spent lavishly on building and collecting fine art, and Thomas's Knightsbridge house was as much a showcase for his collections as a private residence.[125] Begun in 1852, but still incomplete at the time of Cubitt's death three years later, the house was on a truly palatial scale, the interior vying in opulence with any in the metropolis (Plates 23b, 28–29).

Architecturally, the exterior was not remarkable. Like the two earlier houses in Albert Gate, Leyland's was designed in Cubitt's office, and the elevations, although 'arranged to meet the ideas of Captn. Leyland', were in exactly the same style. James Pennethorne, who vetted them for the Commissioners of Woods and Forests, was unimpressed and condescending: 'they are not superior to the ordinary character usually adopted for the Street Architecture in London'. He nevertheless let them pass, 'as the House from its size will be quite of the first class and suitable only for the residence of a very wealthy person'.[126]

As first intended the house was almost square in plan, with an eleven-bay façade on the park side and a nine-bay front to Knightsbridge. To this core was soon added a west wing of five bays, facing the park, but only after Cubitt had routed the Commissioners in a dispute over the design.

Not anticipating any problem, he had agreed to build the wing before obtaining approval for the elevation, and this was withheld because the Commissioners disliked the difference in height between the proposed three-storey wing and the five-storey house. Taken aback, Cubitt responded with a spirited letter (which he failed to sign) in which he justified his action by drawing a dubious distinction between the architectural design, 'which is the Commissioners' business', and the height of the building, 'which is not'. He also reminded them of all he had done for Hyde Park – removed an offensive brewery and 'a nest of houses occupied by the lowest class of persons', replacing them with mansions, and sustaining a heavy loss in the process. It was a brazen strategy but it worked and the Commissioners withdrew their objection.[127]

In November 1855, less than a month before his death, Cubitt sold the freehold to Leyland. Work continued for at least another two years, and the house was not occupied until 1858.[128] Known as Hyde Park House, it was numbered 3 Albert Gate in 1877, and renumbered 60 Knightsbridge in 1903.

Like Nos 1 and 2 Albert Gate, Leyland's house was planned around a central, top-lit staircase compartment, though on a very much larger scale (Plates 28a–b, 29a). From the outer hall a short flight of steps, flanked by two recumbent lions in white marble, led under a stone arch to an imposing imperial staircase with a highly decorated bronze balustrade, clearly derived from those at Northumberland House and Buckingham Palace. This led to a spacious first-floor landing or gallery extending round three sides of the compartment, with triple-arched openings supported on Corinthian columns of variegated marble.

On the ground floor the principal apartment was the dining-room on the park side, which had an elaborately modelled plaster ceiling and cornice, damask-hung walls, and a servery at one end divided from the dining-area by a pair of marble Corinthian columns.

On the first floor was a suite of drawing-rooms, the largest of which, in the centre of the north front, was also used as a ballroom (Plate 29b). Two screens of Corinthian columns, here fluted, divided this long room into one large compartment, with two smaller ones at either end. Photographs taken in the early years of the twentieth century suggest that the drawing-rooms had been redecorated in the French taste. By contrast, the décor of the dining-room and staircase was probably still the original.

Also on the first floor was Leyland's picture gallery, a top-lit apartment on the west side of the house, with a mirrored end-wall to give the impression of a room twice its length (Plate 28c). A description of the gallery in 1898 mentions paintings by Breughel, Gainsborough, Luini, Memling, Pisano, Rubens, Tintoretto and Van Dyck. In addition to the pictures the gallery was packed with furniture and *objets d'art*, including sculpture, porcelain, and metalwork. More sculpture was displayed around the hall, landing and staircase, and in the glazed conservatory above the porch – here an original feature, unlike those at Nos 1 and 2.[129]

In 1883–4 Leyland built some additional stables immediately to the west of the house, on the northern part of the site of No. 11 High Row. The freehold of No. 11, and of the adjoining Fox and Bull public house at No. 10, had been purchased by his son, Colonel Tom Naylor-Leyland, also of Hyde Park House, who let the rest of this ground to the London and County Bank for new premises.[130]

After Captain Leyland's death in 1891 the house descended to his grandson (Sir) Herbert Naylor-Leyland, his son having predeceased him. Herbert's American wife, Jennie, was a leading society hostess, and in the 1890s Hyde Park House provided the setting for parties and receptions attended by the cream of late-Victorian society, from the Prince of Wales downwards.

Though widowed while still young by her husband's death in 1899 aged only 35, Lady Naylor-Leyland continued to occupy the house and to host receptions there until 1923. In that year it was bought by the Royal Thames Yacht Club, which removed here from Piccadilly.[131] After nearly forty years in the building the yacht club found the cost of upkeep too onerous, and in 1961 Hyde Park House was demolished.

West of Albert Gate

The buildings discussed here are the various redevelopments between Albert Gate and the barracks carried out from the late 1850s, when Thomas Cubitt's final Albert Gate mansion, Hyde Park House, was being completed. They include the present-day successor to Hyde Park House. Some account is also given of the earlier history of the Park Close area, adjoining the barracks.

No. 60 Knightsbridge

The redevelopment of Hyde Park House, the Royal Thames Yacht Club's palatial home, was planned as much to exploit the high commercial value of the site as to provide a new clubhouse. Thus, in addition to new and more compact premises for the members, the scheme, by Guy Morgan & Partners, included extensive accommodation for letting.

Erected in 1961–4, the building is a typical 1960s design, comprising an L-shaped block faced in grey Spanish granite, raised on an irregularly shaped two-storey podium clad in dark Vallon marble (Plate 17b). The yacht club occupies the podium and the lowest storey of the superstructure. Above are five floors of offices and, on the long side only, a tier of two-storey maisonettes or penthouses. This horizontal division of the building between the various users is reflected in the elevational treatment.[132]

The club rooms, designed by Brian O'Rorke, incorporated features and fittings from the old house, including the two marble lions from the outer hall, which were installed on either side of the entrance to the new smoking-room. Teak panelling was used to engender a nautical atmosphere. Between 1994 and 1999 these 'comfortable but utilitarian' interiors – 'a curious cocktail of conservative Modernism' – were redecorated by Robin Moore Ede to add depth and colour while retaining their essential character. The re-vamp followed the abandonment of a proposed redevelopment of the entire building and its replacement by new club premises and a hotel. This scheme, by Sir Norman Foster, was refused planning permission in 1992.[133]

Nos 62–64 Knightsbridge

In 1883 the London and County Bank, which was then occupying part of No. 2 Albert Gate, secured a lease from Colonel Tom Naylor-Leyland of Hyde Park House of ground for a new branch building. This plot, abutting east on Hyde Park House (Plate 30c), comprised the site of the Fox and Bull and most of that formerly occupied by No. 11 High Row.[134]

The new building, a handsome stone-faced *palazzo* with correct classical detail (Plate 20c) was designed by Frederick W. Porter, something of a specialist in the design of banks, and built in 1884–5 by Trollope & Sons.[135]

The banking hall (No. 64), had been remodelled internally before the closure of the building as a bank in 1996. The upper floors (No. 62), previously the manager's residence, were occupied from the 1920s to the 1990s by the Danish Club, the oldest foreign club in London. The club dining-room contained a series of mural panels showing Danish scenes, painted in the 1930s by Mogens Lorentzen. In 1937 the club built a conservatory over the porch, now demolished.[136] The building is currently (2000) being refurbished as offices, with residential accommodation on the third floor.

Mandarin Oriental Hyde Park (formerly Hyde Park Hotel)

The Hyde Park Hotel, No. 66 Knightsbridge, was built in 1888–91 as apartments, one of the speculations associated with Jabez Spencer Balfour of the Liberator Building Society. Its height caused a controversy, and there were allegations of corruption over the way in which consent for the building came to be given by the Metropolitan Board of Works (MBW). In 1898, six years after Balfour's spectacular downfall, the building was bought from the Liberator's administrators and was subsequently turned into a hotel. It has particular associations with several famous patrons, including members of the royal family, Winston Churchill, Lord Beaverbrook, and Evelyn Waugh.

The Empress Gate and Rosebery House schemes

Plans for flats on the site were aired as early as 1877. In May that year Henry Stapleton, 9th Baron Beaumont, having acquired the leases of several properties in High Row,

agreed with the Ecclesiastical Commissioners, the freeholders, to redevelop the ground on lease over the next six years. His architect was Thomas Dudley, who was also involved with the development of Beaumont's estate in Fulham at that time. Beaumont's wider plans involved the creation of a road into Hyde Park at the top of Sloane Street – an idea first suggested forty years earlier (see page 47) – but the scheme foundered, at least in part because of the efforts of Charles Reade, whose home stood in the way. Denouncing Beaumont as a latter-day King Ahab, Reade had the sign 'Naboth's Vineyard' displayed on his gate-piers, and enlisted the support of Henry James (later Lord James of Hereford) to attack Beaumont's plans in the Commons, following which the Bill was withdrawn.[137]

The flats at Beaumont's proposed 'Empress Gate' were reportedly to have housed about 200 families. Towards the end of 1877 the site was cleared, but the project had already run into trouble over the line of frontage to be adopted.[138]

By the new year Beaumont's property had grown with his acquisition of the Fox and Bull, and several plots to the west, but a legal snag prevented his getting an assignment of the lease of No. 19 High Row and thus consolidating a very considerable development site (fig. 12). Nevertheless, a new building agreement was entered into. But when after nearly two years there had been no progress, Beaumont made a successful £30,000 offer for the freehold of the entire strip which, except for the Fox and Bull, he almost at once disposed of to the 5th Earl of Rosebery.[139]

Rosebery wanted this large site entirely for a new residence for himself. Having 'outgrown' his house at No. 107 Piccadilly, he chose the Parisian architect, Henri Parent (1819–95), to produce designs for a magnificent mansion here.[140d] One of London's great might-have-beens, it was entirely French in character, and planned for spectacular entertaining, with a ballroom and reception hall approached by a vast central *escalier d'honneur* ringed with galleries. Lord and Lady Rosebery's personal apartments were grouped in the eastern half of the house, approached by the main entrance across a *cour d'honneur* screened from the street by gates and railings. A second big courtyard, to the west, was an enclosed *cour des écuries* giving on to the extensive stables and a coach-house for eight vehicles. Architectural formality was concentrated on the north, with a symmetrical palace façade occupying the whole park front of the building, behind which were ranged some of the Roseberys' private rooms and a series of grand salons.

Parent drew up at least two versions of the design, dated January and March 1881 (Plate 30a–b). In the later version a long park-side terrace was added (though this would have involved building over a strip of the park itself, hardly a realistic proposition) and the stable court was covered over with an iron-and-glass dome. The extensive stabling and associated accommodation reflected the earl's passionate interest in horses. At the west end of the park-side range, for instance, was a tack-room nearly 30ft square. Another of the

---

[d]   Parent's works include the former Hôtel Edouard André, now the Musée Jacquemart-André, in the Boulevard Hausmann.

earl's great interests, book collecting, was reflected in the amount of library space. The main library, situated on the first floor above the tack-room and more than forty-six feet long, would have been one of the largest rooms in the house. Lord Rosebery would also have had a library for his own use, on only a slightly smaller scale and again overlooking the park, in his suite of personal apartments to the east.

Parent's plans appear to have been shown to a leading builder, William Cubitt & Company, probably for costing. One of the drawings is faintly annotated with the name of one of the partners, William R. Rogers, and the company's address in Gray's Inn Road.

While the scheme was in contemplation, Rosebery rented Lansdowne House in Berkeley Square, and a few years later, after the Knightsbridge project had been abandoned, he acquired No. 38 Berkeley Square, commissioning extensive improvements to this comparatively small house, which remained his London residence for the rest of his life.[141]

It is likely that the Rosebery House scheme had already been scrapped when, in July 1883, a strip at the east end of the ground, adjoining the site of the Fox and Bull, was sold to Colonel Tom Naylor-Leyland of Hyde Park House, who leased part of it, together with the pub site, to the London and County Bank for building a new branch (see above).[142]

In October 1886 Rosebery agreed to let the remainder of the land on a 90-year lease (with an option on the freehold) to T. J. Steele of Blackheath, a land agent associated with Jabez Balfour. Within a month, Steele's interest had been transferred to J. W. Hobbs & Company Ltd, the large building concern belonging to the Balfour empire.[143]

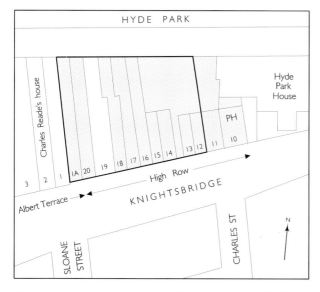

Fig. 12. Plan showing properties in High Row acquired by Baron Beaumont for his Empress Gate scheme. Stippled areas are those covered by Beaumont's building agreements with the Ecclesiastical Commissioners, 1877–8. Thicker line indicates site acquired by J. W. Hobbs & Co. Ltd in 1886 for Hyde Park Court (Hyde Park Hotel)

The building of Hyde Park Court

The extent of Jabez Balfour's role in the development of the 'Rosebery House' site is not known, but it seems from the start to have been very much the project of his close associate, the South London builder James William Hobbs. Neither Balfour nor Hobbs, however, were among the shareholders or directors of Hyde Park Court Ltd, the company incorporated in July 1887 to front the development, which was then described as 'a Residential Club or Buildings'. In the same month, Hobbs reached provisional agreement with the District Board of Works regarding the Knightsbridge line of frontage, and in August a scheme for '500 residential chambers', to be designed by Thomas Archer and Arthur Green, was announced.[144]

Progress was held up by the refusal of the MBW to approve the intended line of frontage (which was forward of the London and County Bank next door), and things were still unresolved in February 1888 when work began, 'it being', as Hobbs complained, 'a matter of ruin to the undertaking to delay operations longer'. The dispute was settled in April, and not on the developers' terms, for in addition to having to set the frontage back (and give up the ground in front to widen the pavement) they had to reduce the intended height of the building and make other alterations. Hobbs later claimed that he had given up two storeys to satisfy the Board, but this was not enough to placate at least one member, Alan de Tatton Egerton MP, nor to allay a spate of criticism in the press.[145]

Newspapers spoke of 'Outrage' and 'Horror' at Albert Gate, likening the building to a new Tower of Babel, and the question of whether the Commissioners of Works could restrict the building's height was raised in Parliament. There was laughter in the Commons at the First Commissioner's suggestion that a wall might be built between the park and the new building, but the erection of hoardings to block out light to the lower floors and so intimidate Hobbs into reducing the number of storeys was seriously considered by the department. A dissentient voice amidst the growing hysteria was that of the *Illustrated London News*, which felt that the building would add to the 'architectural dignity' of the West End.[146]

A bad precedent in tall buildings had been set in the 1870s by the erection of Queen Anne's Mansions at Queen Anne's Gate, fourteen storeys high and a monstrosity. Hyde Park Court was acknowledged to be of considerable architectural merit, but coming as it did at the same time as plans to extend Queen Anne's Mansions, it was to some extent tarred with the same critical brush.

Although the height of buildings in new London streets had been restricted by the 1844 Metropolitan Building Act and an amending Act of 1862, there was in the 1880s no limit for buildings in existing streets beyond an implicit requirement (in the 1855 London Building Act) that special consent was needed for residential and commercial buildings above 100 feet. Critics of Hyde Park Court, however, were less bothered about the building's height in relation to the street

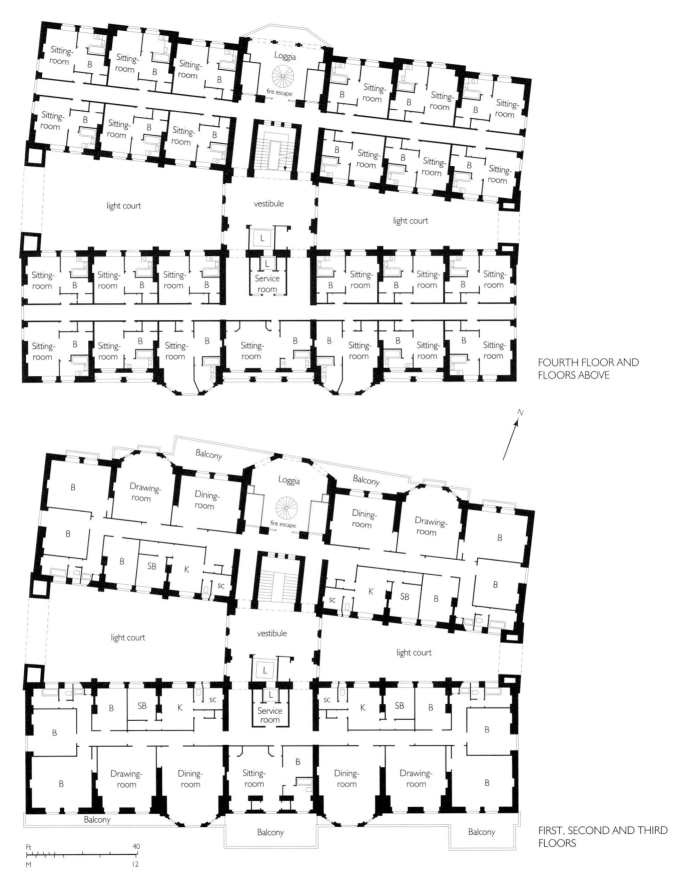

FOURTH FLOOR AND FLOORS ABOVE

FIRST, SECOND AND THIRD FLOORS

Fig. 13. Hyde Park Court, upper-floor plans. Thomas Archer and Arthur Green, architects, 1888–92

than with its effect on Hyde Park; they feared it would cast a shadow over the Serpentine. Among the complainants was the Metropolitan Public Gardens Association, which, concerned for light and air, singled out both Hyde Park Court and Queen Anne's Mansions for condemnation.

Tatton Egerton persisted in his opposition – Hobbs attributed this to pique at his failure to browbeat colleagues at the MBW over the line-of-frontage dispute – and the affair was muddied further by accusations from the London and County Bank that an abusive Arthur Green had boasted of 'influence enough at the Board to carry anything I please'. The charge, published in April 1888, was repeated some weeks later at the Commission of Inquiry into the allegedly corrupt running of the MBW.[147]

The upshot was that Egerton and others brought in an unsuccessful Bill to restrict the height of buildings in London (excluding churches) to sixty feet, or to the width of the street in streets wider than sixty feet.[e] A truce was reached with the bank, by which modifications and restrictions were agreed, including the carrying up of the bank's chimneys into those of the taller building (Plate 31a).[148]

Hyde Park Court was still unfinished, although partly tenanted, when the Liberator Building Society collapsed in 'Black September' 1892, bringing down Hobbs & Company and the entire Balfour edifice. Hobbs was among those subsequently jailed for their parts in the fraudulent running of the business, as, eventually, was Balfour himself. Under new management brought in by the Official Receiver, Hobbs's staff returned to work to complete both Hyde Park Court and 'Hobbs's Folly', the far-from-finished hotel in the Strand belonging to the Balfour group, which eventually opened as the Hotel Cecil.[149]

Design and decoration

When Thomas Archer and Arthur Green were appointed architects to Hyde Park Court they had been partners fifteen years and were experienced in comparable projects, including Whitehall Court, the Balfour apartment block on Victoria Embankment. They broke up somewhat acrimoniously in 1889, and Hyde Park Court was finished by Archer, with his new partner Francis Hooper.

The exterior, of red brick and Portland stone, is in the eclectic (predominantly Franco-Flemish) 'Free Renaissance' style already used by them at Whitehall Court. Considerable skill was deployed to articulate and modulate the great height and breadth, and in the creation of a dramatically picturesque skyline (Plates 31, 115c). The building was planned as two blocks with courts between, linked by a central vestibule giving access to the stairs and containing a hydraulic passenger-lift able to carry ten people (fig. 13). Communal loggias, connected by a circular iron staircase serving as a fire-escape, provided 'a pleasant summer's evening lounge and promenade' overlooking the park.[150]

The first, second and third floors were each laid out to provide four self-contained family suites, and a small bachelor's suite overlooking Knightsbridge, the latter comprising a sitting-room and a bedroom, with a combined bath- and dressing-room. The upper floors were divided into similar bachelor suites of varying size, twenty-five to a floor. Families who so wished could have their kitchen and scullery converted into extra bedrooms and take their meals *en pension*.[151]

The palatial interior decoration was no doubt designed in emulation of West End club-houses, its lavish use of marbles and gilding being years ahead of even the best London hotels of that date (Plate 116a–b). The hall, entered from Knightsbridge through swing doors of carved walnut, was lined with coloured marbles and had a panelled and frescoed ceiling, and a marble chimneypiece graced with a marble clock. Stairs of white marble flanked with marble balustrades led to the upper ground floor. This style of decoration continued in the principal communal rooms, including the breakfast- and dining-room, overlooking Hyde Park. Upstairs, the corridors had oak-block flooring; inside, individual suites were decorated and furnished to suit incoming tenants.[152]

The accommodation included three billiard-rooms on the lower ground floor, looking on to Knightsbridge, together with such conveniences as a hairdressing salon. The eastern entrance led to the rooms of the Hyde Park Club, a separate establishment occupying the basement and ground floors of the south-eastern quarter of the building.[153]

A sensational fire in 1899, which caused some damage to the top three floors of the Knightsbridge wing and destroyed part of the roof, including the central iron-and-glass turret, drew attention to the potential risks of such tall buildings. The fire-brigade's extension ladders reached only half-way up the walls, and although everyone made a successful escape, hardly anyone used the loggia staircase, which was cut off by smoke on the upper floors. In 1900–02 the present external fire-escape staircases were erected by the St Pancras Ironwork Company. Reinstatement after the fire, carried out by Colls & Sons, involved a somewhat redesigned turret.[154]

From residential mansion to hotel

The builder J. W. Hobbs had described Hyde Park Court as 'designed to meet the requirements of a large section of the upper classes, being men of first class social standing, but whose means may not permit them to go to a great expense in housekeeping'.[155] The annual cost of living at Hyde Park Court was at first projected at a modest level, £150 to £200. There was from the start an emphasis on serving the needs of bachelors, and it was the original intention that women would not be admitted as residents. An echo of this is heard early in Galsworthy's *Forsyte Saga*, where the old bachelor Swithin Forsyte (1811–91) is pictured in 1886 'in the lone-

---

[e] Subsequently, the London Council (General Powers) Act, 1890, essentially limited the heights of buildings to 90 feet plus two storeys in the roof; this figure was reduced by 10 feet in the London Building Act of 1894.

ly glory of orange and blue chambers in Hyde Park Mansions'.[f] In the 1930s, when the building had been a hotel for many years, the long-term residents were typically 'crotchety bachelor businessmen'.[156] But this impression of bachelor chambers is far from the whole picture, and following the Balfour débâcle the receiver's policy was evidently to let apartments to men or women. In 1898, of seventy-odd tenants more than twenty were women, many of them unmarried. Getting on for half of the tenants were occupying two or more suites, usually contiguous or nearly so; one woman was occupying six.[157]

In 1898 Hyde Park Court was bought from the receiver by Herbert Bennett, of the Sloane Street estate agency Marler and Bennett, a director of Harrods and the owner of Queen Anne's Mansions, where he lived. At first there was apparently little change in the regime. In 1899, when a full beer, wine and spirit licence was obtained (as was becoming *de rigueur* at similar establishments), it was described as 'really a hotel', with all the hundred and fifty residents catered for by the proprietors.[158]

The Hyde Park Club closed in December 1901,[159] and in 1902 the formal change from residential mansion to hotel was made, when Bennett set up The Hyde Park Hotel Ltd to put the business on a new footing. Similar transformations had already been made at St Ermin's Mansions in Westminster, and the Walsingham House Hotel in Piccadilly. Also involved in the venture were Edward Rawlings, another resident of Queen Anne's Mansions with hotel interests, and William Harris, chairman of both the Ritz and Carlton hotel companies. César Ritz himself acted as consultant, and he and the chef at the Carlton, Auguste Escoffier, each had stakes in the company, along with Samuel Waring (later Lord Waring), the founder of the furniture company Waring & Gillow. The architects for some, if not all, of the alterations and improvements to the building were Charles Mewès and A. J. Davis.[160]

Mewès, the planner of the Paris Ritz, and Davis, with whom he had designed the interiors at the Carlton Hotel, were the obvious choice for adapting the building to its new role. The involvement of the firm of Mewès & Davis with the hotel lasted from 1901 until at least the mid-1920s, long after Mewès's death. Theirs was not, however, the only architectural practice employed during that time, some alterations of *c.*1920 being designed by Bishop & Etherington-Smith.[161]

In May 1902 the *Caterer and Hotel-Keepers' Gazette* reported the hotel was 'fast approaching completion, and will leave little to desire in the way of sumptuous appointment. It has been decorated in elaborate style'. Among the most important changes was the filling-in of the loggias on the park front, to make an additional large room with *en suite* bathroom on each floor.[162]

The commercialization of the hotel soon led to friction with the authorities at Hyde Park, notably over the erection of the hotel name in large gilt letters facing the park, to which the King objected. An agreement, originally made with Hobbs, for the park ground immediately in front of the hotel to be planted with flowers was revoked, but it took the threat of the erection of trellis screens to persuade Bennett to take the lettering down.[163]

For many years before the First World War the hotel enjoyed great prosperity, at a time when there were fears that the London luxury hotel market was becoming saturated and some hotels were paying poor dividends. By 1910 the hotel comprised 268 rooms for letting, with smoking-room, restaurant (with orchestra gallery), drawing-rooms, grill room, American and buffet bars. The ballroom, on the ground floor overlooking Hyde Park in the eastern part of the building, was considerably enlarged in 1911–12 and redecorated in a Frenchified style; the architect was almost certainly Charles Mewès (Plate 33a).[164] Not until 1925 was a palm court – long regarded as indispensable in a top hotel – built (Plate 32a). Situated in the western light-well, it was designed, in a broadly Art Deco style, by the firm of Mewès & Davis, who remodelled several of the principal rooms at this time in a more conservative 'Louis Quinze' style. The Palm Court's chief features of interest concerned its lighting: a large flood-lit lay-light of elliptical shape, with an amber-glass surround, and enormous lamps in the form of vases on mock Sienna marble pedestals. A large arched window at the west end provided the setting for an orchestra gallery and ornamental fountain. Among other alterations overseen by Mewès & Davis at this time was the redecoration of the restaurant (Plates 33b, 116c), for which tiled panels (after paintings by Hubert Robert) were supplied by Georges Rémon et Cie of Paris. The Palm Court was remodelled in 1950 as a bar and lounge, when a suspended ceiling was installed and the 1920s fittings stripped out.[165]

There were originally no doors on the park side, but in 1926 emergency exits were put in, and these were first used for non-emergency purposes at the time of the coronation of George VI in 1937, when the Crown gave special permission for certain distinguished guests – including members of the Japanese imperial family and the South African Prime Minister, General Hertzog – to use the park entrance.[166]

Following the takeover of Trusthouse Forte, which owned the hotel for many years, it was sold for a record sum in 1996 to Mandarin Oriental International, becoming the Mandarin Oriental Hyde Park.

While the exterior remains essentially as designed by Archer & Green (the only significant changes being on the park side), the interior of the hotel today reflects successive rounds of alteration and redecoration. Among survivals of the original decorative scheme are, probably, some of the plasterwork ceilings, including those of the Rosebery Rooms, formerly the smoking-room (Plate 32b). The

---

[f] Hyde Park Court, which was loosely known as Hyde Park Mansions and was indeed 'not two minutes' from Soames Forsyte's house in Montpelier Square, was presumably intended, rather than distant Hyde Park Mansions in Marylebone; the chronology is of course a few years out.

entrance hall, staircase and upper lobby almost certainly retain most of their original décor of *c*.1890, chiefly remarkable for its use of variously coloured marbles (Plate 116a–b). The most recent round of internal improvements was completed in May 2000 for Mandarin Oriental. Stylistically, the most avant-garde element, displacing some of the Beaux-Arts formality of Mewès & Davis, is the work by the New York designer Adam Tihany. As well as remodelling the bar area (on the Palm Court site) Tihany has transformed the vast former restaurant facing Hyde Park into two distinct apartments: the Café on the Park, and the smaller, split-level Foliage restaurant approached from the bar through a showpiece glazed 'wine-cellar'. Screened from the wine racks by a partition of opaque glass and sheet metal, Foliage takes the trees in the park as its decorative theme, with large glass panels on the walls incorporating silk leaf-shapes. These are illuminated at night – in colours appropriate to the season – as the park itself fades from view.

Bowater House and Edinburgh Gate

Designed by Guy Morgan and Partners for The Land Securities Investment Trust Ltd, Bowater House was built in 1956–8 by Taylor Woodrow Construction; Bylander, Waddell and Partners were the consulting engineers. The whole building was pre-let to the Bowater Paper Corporation Ltd for their London headquarters, Bowater occupying two-thirds of the space and subletting the rest.

When excavation began in June 1956 the ground had long been vacant. Plans for its redevelopment dated back to 1935, in which year the greater part of the site was acquired by Ernest Payton of the Austin Motor Company for building shops and flats, and a design for a block of flats here was exhibited at the Royal Academy.[167] That design was by Messrs Gordon Jeeves, but subsequently several other architects were involved in schemes for the site, including Curtis Green, and, apparently, C. Howard Crane of Chicago (whose English representative for the construction of the Earl's Court Exhibition building had been Gordon Jeeves). Most of the houses were pulled down in 1942. After Payton's death in 1946, the site was sold to the property developer Sir John Mactaggart, and by the mid-1950s the entire block between Hyde Park Hotel and Wellington Court was in the possession of Land Securities.[168]

The London County Council was determined that the development should include much-needed road improvements, and accordingly the Land Securities scheme incorporated a new dual-carriageway entrance to South Carriage Drive in Hyde Park from Knightsbridge, and service roads for the building leading to underground car-parks. The new park entrance was named Edinburgh Gate in honour of the Queen's consort.

Bowater House consists of four main blocks: one running the full width of the site alongside the Park, a pair of unequal towers flanking the Knightsbridge entrance to Edinburgh Gate, and a low bridging block between the towers, carried on pilotis (Plate 18a). The taller tower was intended to be a skyscraper, but was whittled down in the planning stage, in the face of concern about its effect on the view from Hyde Park. Low-level wings on the Knightsbridge front complete the ensemble. On the north side, the road is carried under the building beneath a curved canopy to deflect noise and pollution.

The building's structure is of reinforced concrete cast *in situ* and expressed externally with differently coloured claddings for the various elements.[169] Most of the building is carried by pairs of widely spaced internal columns and peripheral mullions. The slab floors are carried on the columns and mullions using the 'balanced cantilever' principle, avoiding the need for beams. Exceptions to this general arrangement include the top storey of the park block, where the roof slab is cantilevered out, the mullions there being dispensed with to allow for glass curtain-walling.

The exterior is clad in polished granite with some brick and some Portland stone. Three sorts of granite were used: blue pearl, from Sweden; pink, from Peterhead, and grey, from Creetown in Galloway. The facing bricks are Uxbridge greys and dark blues from Tunbridge Wells. Portland stone was used on the low blocks and generally for copings.

The use of 'first class natural materials', upon which Guy Morgan placed great emphasis,[170] was continued inside. In the entrance hall – a spacious double-height area with a gallery – polished marble in a range of colours was used on the walls and floor, the floor incorporating a mosaic of the Bowater logo (now removed); in the offices, oak-block floors were laid. A stylish open-tread staircase was designed for the entrance hall to give access to the gallery. Cantilevered out from the floor on a reinforced-concrete spine, it stopped just short of the gallery to give a 'floating' sensation. The staircase was demolished in the late 1980s.[171]

To complement the building, Sir Harold Samuel, the chairman of Land Securities, commissioned a sculpture from Sir Jacob Epstein in November 1957. The 'Bowater group' was to be the very last piece on which Epstein worked: he made the finishing touches to the plaster model on the night he died in August 1959. The bronze, a gift from Land Securities to the nation, was cast at the Morris Singer Foundry and erected at Edinburgh Gate in April 1961.[172] Epstein's maquette for the work is displayed in the foyer of Bowater House.

Long and narrow, the sculpture was purposely designed by Epstein for its present position on the central reservation at Edinburgh Gate – though the Royal Fine Arts Commission doubted that it would be seen to advantage there. Variously known as *The Return of Spring*, *The Family*, or simply the *Pan Group*, it is made up of the nude figures of a man, a woman and a child, racing with their dog towards the park, Pan at their heels piping them on their way (Plate 18b). 'Epstein at his happiest', says his biographer;[173] Ian Nairn, who saw it as a 'sad end' to Epstein's career, was put in mind of 'an incestuous family fleeing into Hyde Park from the Vice Squad'.[174]

Park Close area

Today a narrow cleft between tall apartment blocks of late-Victorian date, Park Close – so named in 1938 – is the only survivor of the three passageways or courts laid out here in the 1720s and '30s (Plate 5c). These were Park Place, originally and for many years called Park Court; Bear Court or Nag's Head Court (the present Park Close, to which the name Park Place was transferred in the 1820s); and Jobbins Court. However, the occupation of the site goes back well before the creation of these courts, houses here being mentioned in a will of 1635.[175]

Old Park Place (Park Court), at the east end of the future barracks site and dating from the mid-1720s, was socially the most elevated of the three. Ratepayers in the eighteenth and early nineteenth centuries included Sir Philip Jennings, Lady Barrington, Burkat Shudi, son of the celebrated harpsichord maker, a foreign count, and one Charles Lewis, reported 'sick at Bath' (and then dead) in 1793. The houses, all on the east side of the passageway, were pulled down about 1824 and rebuilt fronting the west side of old Bear Court, which now assumed the name Park Place.[176]

Also dating from the mid-1720s, Bear Court took its name from a public house, the White (or Brown) Bear, on the east corner of old Park Place and Knightsbridge. The houses in Bear Court were ranged along the east side, originally looking across to the backs of the houses in old Park Place. At the east corner of Bear Court and Knightsbridge was another pub, the Nag's Head, later renamed the Life Guardsman (Plate 4c).[177]

Jobbins Court, between Bear Court and the Swan inn, was developed in the late 1730s by James Jobbins, a local bricklayer (Plate 4c). The first houses here were very lowly rated and their inhabitants 'poor'. They were pulled down and rebuilt by Jobbins in the early 1750s, only for most of the new houses to stand empty for a good many years.[178]

The houses built on the west side of Park Place (the former Bear Court) in the 1820s soon fell into a state of neglect, judging by the account of Mortimer Bayntun, gentleman (late of the 98th Regiment of Foot), who moved into the northernmost house in 1839. Bayntun spoke of the broken windows and 'time worn, crumbling and mud stained walls' of his home. His 'principle inducement' for moving there was to 'enjoy the invigorating influence of the salubrious Air from the Park – suffering at the Time from the effects of previous indisposition'. He paid out a substantial sum on repairs to make the house a credit to the neighbourhood, and, to take the air, had a balcony built overhanging the park wall. Worried that the authorities were going to demand its removal as an encroachment, Bayntun let it be known that a brewer was waiting ready to turn the house into 'a low Beershop'; and without a balcony, he said, the house would be 'utterly useless to any other respectable Resident'.[179]

In the event the balcony was allowed to remain, but his old home (united with the house next door) became a pub nevertheless, the Queen and Prince Albert. The concen-

tration of pubs, the nearness of the barracks and soldiers' lodgings, and the existence of a wicket-gate into the park at the end encouraged small shopkeepers and street-traders along Park Place, so that in Victorian times it seems to have been a fairly rowdy area.[180]

Williams Cottages, two dwellings which stood near the park wall at the back of Jobbins Court, attracted a higher class of tenant than most of the houses near by, presumably because of their parkside location. Their occupants in 1841 included a secretary, a clerk, and a music-teacher.[181]

John Lilwall, a leading campaigner in the early-closing and half-holiday movement, was living in lodgings at Nos 7–8 Park Place in 1851.[182]

The Duke of Wellington's Riding-School (demolished)

The redevelopment of the Park Place area began in the 1850s with the demolition of the Life Guardsman pub and a few houses to the east, and the complete obliteration of Jobbins Court. They were replaced by a building which became as well known as a venue for fashionable bazaars and banquets as for its chief purpose, that of a riding-school and stables. This institution was the personal project of the 2nd Duke of Wellington (son of the Iron Duke),

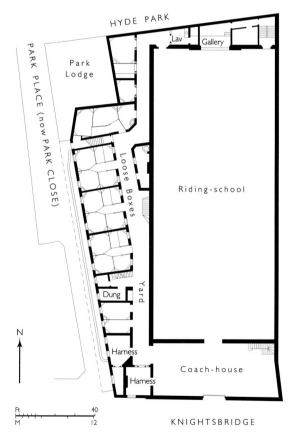

Fig. 14. Duke of Wellington's Riding-school, plan. Philip Hardwick, architect, 1856–7. *Demolished*

a great horseman and animal-lover.[g] He acquired the greater part of the site in 1853 (the year he became the Queen's Master of Horse), but it was only in 1856 that he was able to obtain the public house.[184]

The site (fig. 9) comprised almost the entire block from the west side of Mills's Buildings to the east side of Park Place, excluding only the north-west corner (where Park Lodge now is) which seems to have eluded the duke. The loss of the Life Guardsman pub, with its outside 'tippling-seats' and a row of costermongers' stalls along the passage, was seen as a great improvement, though congestion in the alley caused by refreshment stands and the crush of visitors to the park continued.[185]

The riding-school was built by Cubitts in 1856–7. The architect was Philip Hardwick RA, who had been employed by the duke to carry out alterations to Apsley House. His son, P. C. Hardwick, to whom the building has been attributed, would almost certainly have supervised its construction in view of his father's chronic illness.[186]

Classical in style, with a prominent pediment over the arched street entrance,[h] the riding-school attracted attention 'as possessing architectural merit seldom looked for in such buildings'.[188] It comprised a large arena or concourse with viewing galleries at one end, and an extensive range of stabling and coach-houses with living accommodation above for grooms and coachmen (fig. 14). The exterior was faced in tuck-pointed malms with Portland-cement dressings. A slated iron roof, 'light and elegant' in design with a skylight running its whole length, covered the concourse, additional light being provided by lunettes at either end and along the west side; artificial light was supplied by three gasoliers. Stained and varnished deal covered the internal walls to a height of six feet. The floor was made up of compressed puddled clay, spread with a hard cement of 'iron scales' and bullocks' blood, and covered in sea sand.[189]

One of the first big events recorded at the riding-school was a display by Mr Rarey, 'the celebrated American horse-tamer', given in a front of a large crowd of fashionable visitors. Before the show a number of aristocratic ladies were privately instructed in Rarey's methods of 'subjugating the horse'. In 1872 there was a near-riot when a meeting of Chelsea residents, held to denounce the republican sentiments of their MP, Sir Charles Dilke, was invaded by pro-Dilke 'roughs' who threw the seats about and tried to set fire to the platform. Among other notable functions was the party hosted by the duke himself – a lifelong Tory – in honour of Lord Beaconsfield and Lord Salisbury on their triumphant return from the Congress of Berlin in 1878.

The duke died in 1884: in 1891 'the famous bazaar ground of fashionable London' was put up for auction by his nephew, the 3rd Duke, and after brisk bidding was sold for £60,000. Within a few years a block of flats had risen on the site.[190]

Wellington Court

The buyer of the riding-school was (Sir) Charles Oppenheimer, a diplomat. In 1892 Wellington Court Ltd, in which Oppenheimer subsequently had a large stake, was set up to redevelop the site as mansion flats. Sir Charles's son Albert became a director, as did the builder of the flats, Henry Lovatt (who took an apartment there). Others involved in the company were a civil engineer, Henry Ward of Cannon Street, and two architects, also City-based, H. H. Collins and his son Marcus Evelyn Collins, and it was M. E. Collins who designed Wellington Court and oversaw its construction in 1893–5. The freehold was bought by the Crown from Oppenheimer in 1898 for £98,000.[191]

Wellington Court as built provided thirty suites of varying size on one or two floors, including three 'bachelor' apartments with a small sitting- and coffee-room for common use (fig. 15). Internal construction was of steel framing, to facilitate re-planning of individual suites. These contained accommodation for servants, but servants' rooms were also available on the top floor, and could be connected to apartments by speaking-tubes or electric bells. Interior finishings, said to 'show an advance on buildings of this class', included ornamental ceilings in the reception rooms by Jacksons of Rathbone Place, and, lining the lobby and staircase walls, embossed Japanese wallpaper in crimson and gold. The courtyard, with a rubber-paved approach, was laid out 'in the French manner' and adorned with shrubs and hanging plants.[192] By 1896 rentals ranged from £200 for four rooms to £800 for a thirteen-room suite, with the option of full service and meals prepared under the supervision of Colonel Kenney-Herbert, author of *Common Sense Cookery* – enabling residents 'to do away with the trouble of servants to a very great extent'.[193]

Externally, Wellington Court is of a familiar mansion block type, well built in brick and stone, and ponderously ornamented in an eclectic manner (Plates 36c, 37b). The brickwork is of Fareham reds and the dressings, now painted, of red Mansfield stone and Lascelles patent stone (courtyard and park front). The gates and other decorative ironwork were supplied by W. T. Allen & Company. Among the details is a sundial on the courtyard wall, possibly a reference to Sun Dial House, mentioned in 1719 as one of the buildings then on the site.[194]

Park Lodge

By the time the riding-school was sold in 1891 a small apartment block was already being erected at the north-east corner of Park Place, on the site which the Duke of Wellington failed to secure in the 1850s. This was Park Lodge, built in 1890–2 to designs by the architects G. D. Martin and E. K. Purchase, Martin himself having

---

[g] The duke was a man of enthusiasms, which included at various times Kashmir goats, donkeys, silkworm culture and beekeeping.[183]
[h] An intended entrance on the Hyde Park side was apparently vetoed by the Queen.[187]

GROUND FLOOR

SECOND FLOOR

Fig. 15. Wellington Court, ground- and second-floor plans, and diagrams showing arrangement of flats. M. E. Collins, architect, 1893–5

acquired an option to buy the site. The builder was Frank Kirk of Abingdon Street. As part of the development new gates into the park were installed, with an ornamental over-throw and gas-lantern, and the existing stepped approach made into a slope.[195]

Built of red brick and stone, Park Lodge is rather less ornamental than originally intended – the roofline was to have been enlivened with a Flemish gable and ball-finials, and the oriel at the north-west corner was curtailed at the

Fig. 16. Park Lodge, typical floor-plan. G. D. Martin and E. K. Purchase, architects, 1890–2

LCC's insistence so as not to encroach on the narrow foot-way of Park Place (Plate 36c–d). Inside, each floor was iden-tically planned as an individual suite (fig. 16); the basement comprised the steward's or housekeeper's rooms, service kitchen and cellarage. The apartments were well appointed with 'every contrivance known to modern club life', includ-ing telephones, speaking-tubes, electric bells, electric light (backed up by gas) and a hydraulic passenger lift.[196]

Albert Gate Court

In about 1886 the west side of Park Place, including the Brown Bear and the Queen and Prince Albert public hou-ses, was acquired by James Baker, a builder in Cadogan Terrace. 'I shall be making a great improvement', said Baker of his plans to erect a block of 'first class' residences and shops. His scheme would not only do away with the 'very great nuisance' of the Queen and Prince Albert pub but would mean that the street would no longer be used as a children's playground, and the intended new shops would make it both more attractive and better lighted.

Baker's building, known at first by its principal address,

No. 45 Albert Gate, was designed by Henry Charles New-march FSI of Lincoln's Inn Fields and built by Baker in 1887. It was acquired by the Law Land Company Ltd in 1904 and renamed Albert Gate Court.[197]

Minor problems arose from the nearness of the barracks. A forge and shoeing-shed there were so darkened by the new flats they could not be used, and legal proceedings were started against Baker, who agreed to build replacements. But there was so little space available that in the end a royal war-rant had to be obtained for building them on park ground adjoining the west end of the barracks site. Whether or not connected with this dispute, in 1889 screens were fixed to the ends of the balconies on the park front of the flats to shield from view a urinal in the barrack yard.[198]

The original accommodation (fig. 17) comprised shops in Knightsbridge and Park Place, a three-bedroom maisonette in Park Place, and two family flats, of five or six bedrooms, on each of the upper floors. Minimal ser-vice was provided.[199] Externally, Albert Gate Court is a fairly standard example of the mansion-flat genre, built of red brick with stone dressings and iron balconettes (Plate 36a).

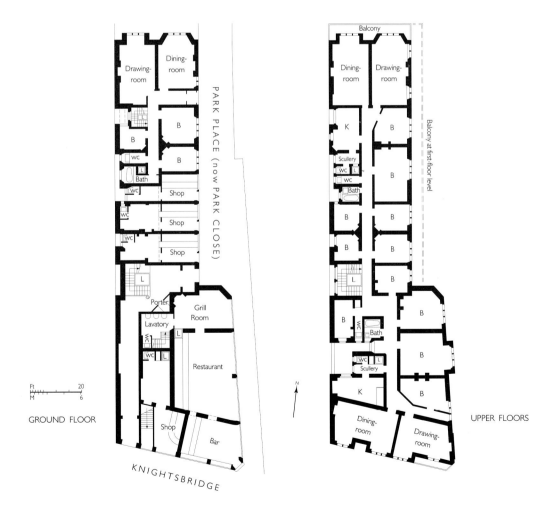

Fig. 17. Albert Gate Court, plans. H. C. Newmarch, architect, 1887

CHAPTER III

Knightsbridge Barracks

Conceived in the late 1950s, but not built until 1967–70, Sir Basil Spence's barracks for the Household Cavalry is architecturally the most remarkable post-war development in Knightsbridge. With its high tower, the principal landmark of the district and a conspicuous presence on the Hyde Park skyline, it is also the most controversial.

Spence's buildings are the third generation of cavalry barracks on the site. The construction of the first, started in 1792–3, coincided with the beginning of a systematic barrack-building programme throughout England. The original structures, obsolete as well as dilapidated, were replaced in the late 1870s by palatial buildings appropriate both to the prestige of the Household Cavalry and the importance of the site. By the 1950s not only had the imperial splendour they reflected become dim, but they in turn were felt to have reached the end of their useful existence.

The First Barracks, 1792–1877

The circumstances in which the first Knightsbridge cavalry barracks came to be built are not known.[a]

The timing is suggestive, though perhaps misleadingly so. Plans by the architect James Johnson were submitted to George III for approval on 28 March 1792.[1] This was only weeks before government panic at civil unrest led to the hasty construction of cavalry barracks in several English towns, the beginning of a countrywide barrack-building campaign which continued into the early nineteenth century.

Until this time, soldiers were mostly accommodated in temporary camps or in billets, often at public houses. The continuance of this system was a legacy of the civil strife and constitutional upheavals of the seventeenth century. Permanent barracks smacked of France and absolutism; they did exist in England, but were mostly confined to coastal garrison towns. Billeting, on the other hand, was felt to act as a check on the army. Troops were less likely to become estranged from the people if they were in daily close contact with them. This closeness, and the dispersal of the soldiers at various addresses, made it doubly difficult, it was reasoned, for a commander to indoctrinate troops for his own political purposes.

Following the French Revolution and the growth of popular radicalism, concern was felt that soldiers might side with an increasingly disaffected populace against the established order. In 1792 urban riots brought things to a head. On 21 May George III issued a proclamation against seditious writings and meetings, and the government sent Colonel Oliver De Lancey, deputy adjutant-general at the Horse Guards, to assess the reliability, in the event of civil insurrection, of troops quartered in manufacturing towns. In De Lancey's view, the building of barracks offered the best way of keeping troops isolated from revolutionary influences. During that summer, De Lancey organized the building of cavalry barracks in towns in the Midlands and North, at Norwich, and west of London at Hounslow. The plans for these barracks were all provided by Johnson.[2] War with France in 1793, and the danger of a French invasion, prompted further barrack-building, under De Lancey's control as head of a new Barracks Department, with Johnson as his principal architect and surveyor. By 1797 dozens of new barracks had been erected in England and Scotland.[3]

The volatile atmosphere of 1792 may have forced the government's hand, but the building of barracks was long overdue in the interest of efficiency, and it was probably for this reason, rather than counter-rebellion, that the cavalry barracks at Knightsbridge was built. There are two reasons for thinking so.

Firstly, the haste seen in De Lancey's initial building programme seems to have been lacking at Knightsbridge. The barracks, presumably begun soon after the plans had been passed, was still in progress in January 1793 and it was not occupied until December that year, when the 1st Regiment of Life Guards moved in.[4] Moreover, the buildings at this stage consisted only of a quadrangle of stables and troop rooms. The officers' quarters, and probably the main ancillary buildings, appear not to have been begun until 1795. Had it seemed that serious civil disorder in London was imminent, the barracks would presumably have been completed as quickly as possible.

Secondly, there was another fairly large barracks in Knightsbridge (see page 23), which had been extensively improved in 1789–90 and which was reportedly to have been used as a model in a general barrack-building programme.[5] Intended for the use of the Foot Guards – that is, the Coldstream and Grenadier Guards – this 'Knights-

---

[a] The barracks was usually known as Hyde Park Cavalry Barracks, the name Knightsbridge Barracks having been appropriated for the earlier foot-guards barracks on the south side of Knightsbridge. Since the later nineteenth century the names have been used interchangeably, but with the rebuilding in the 1960s Knightsbridge Barracks has become the preferred alternative.

bridge Barracks' was built on an essentially quadrangular plan, reminiscent of the later cavalry barracks (fig. 3). Such a layout was comparatively rare in English barracks at that time, but 'typical of the military quarters built in the unstable political climate of the 1790s'.[6] It was, however, a common one for stabling, and was the arrangement found in various West End mews used by Guards regiments in the eighteenth century. The Knightsbridge foot-guards barracks had itself originated, around 1760, as horse-guards stables.

The site of the new barracks was on a narrow, tapering strip belonging to Hyde Park, between Park Place and the Halfway House tavern (see Plates 2b, 5c). No formal grant appears to have been made of the land, which was apparently occupied simply with the King's permission, as were other military buildings in the park.[7] The Life Guards had earlier occupied a barracks or stables in the park on a much smaller but otherwise comparable site. This building, called Life Guard House, was in Kensington Gardens facing the Kensington road, at the south end of the Broad Walk (which did not then reach as far as the road).[8]

The arrangement of the barracks buildings – strung out in a line – was quite different from earlier cavalry barracks designs, such as William Gibson's model plans of 1784, produced for the Barrack Board in Ireland (fig. 18, Plate 2b).[9] This was more or less unavoidable for such a large complex given the shape of the site, but in any case the barracks was the product of three phases of construction, and not necessarily conceived as a whole in 1792.

The largest of the buildings was the **Barrack Block** at the eastern end of the site (Plates 2b, 39b). Over 400ft in length and rising to three storeys, it was built around a rectangular parade-ground and was arranged in the traditional cavalry barracks manner, with the animals on the ground floor and the men above. There was stabling for 385 horses, and living quarters for 368 non-commissioned officers and privates. The monotony of the building's long elevations to Knightsbridge and Hyde Park was broken by shallow pediments over the three central bays, beneath which double-height archways gave access to the courtyard. The only embellishments were pairs of decorative panels of military trophies on either side of the archways and, in the pediments above, oval plaques bearing the royal arms.[b]

The first-floor plan of the Barrack Block in figure 18 shows the later partitioning of the original large but low-ceilinged troop rooms to provide married quarters, consisting of a common living-room with a fireplace, and separate bedrooms, large but poorly lit and unheated. This was carried out some time after 1838, and replaced a far more unsatisfactory scheme in which a number of small rooms, one for each family, had been partitioned off along one side of the troop rooms. These cubicle-like spaces had been ill-lit and inadequately ventilated. The improved arrangement itself seems to have been fairly inconvenient, for cooking and washing facilities were situated far away in the eastern wing of the building. The second-floor troop rooms, too, were probably partitioned from large, open-plan dormitories.[11]

The wash-houses, on the first floor at the western corners of the barrack block, each contained an open fireplace, a row of coppers and a drying closet. There were two ablution rooms, fitted with slate benches. Baths were situated in a separate building, next to the guard room, to the south of the barrack block.

West of the barrack block, and separated from it by a narrow passage, were the **Hospital** and three blocks grouped around a courtyard facing the park: the **Officers' Quarters** (or Governor's House), the **Forage Barn** and the **Horse Infirmary** (Plates 4a, 7, 39a,c). The hospital was a two-storey building with rooms including a surgery and consulting-room on the ground floor, and three wards above for up to 36 patients.

The officers' quarters comprised a pedimented house of three storeys over a raised basement. Of eleven bays, it had a central doorway at the top of a short flight of steps. The two flanking buildings were both lower, the ensemble closely resembling a gentleman's seat laid out on Palladian lines with service wings. The upper floor of the horse infirmary was used (at least by the middle of the nineteenth century) as staff officers' quarters, providing accommodation for the riding-masters, adjutants and quartermasters, and a servants' kitchen.

Westwards of this group was the **Riding-school**, a single-storey building under a hipped roof enclosing a large rectangular arena for riding instruction and drill, lit by a clerestory of Diocletian windows (Plates 4a, 7). The riding-school was probably built at the same time as the officers' quarters, barn and infirmary, in 1795 or soon afterwards: all these buildings had been completed by July 1797 when views were published in the *Gentleman's Magazine*.

Beyond the riding-school, alongside the Knightsbridge boundary wall, were the **Officers' Stables**. This range was built *c*.1803 as part of alterations made to the barracks so that it could accommodate some of the 1st Life Guards then stationed at Uxbridge. The other changes made at this time included the conversion of the barn to stables, with a first-floor forage loft.[12]

Several small ancillary buildings were fitted in against the southern boundary wall or at the west end of the site, including punishment cells and various sheds and workshops.

In 1851 a small block of model dwellings was erected in

[b] When the barracks was rebuilt in 1878–80 one set of royal arms was saved for installation in the small pediment on the Knightsbridge front of the new Officers' Quarters. The supporters were replaced (apparently because the original lion and unicorn were on the wrong sides).[10] The coat of arms (but not the supporters) was again saved when the barracks was rebuilt in 1967–70 and now adorns the ante-room in the officers' mess, the only known fragment of the original building to survive.

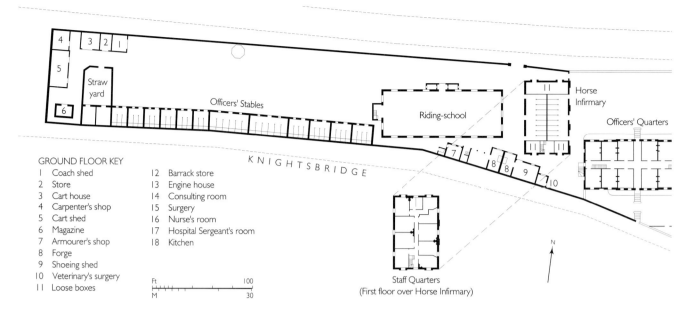

GROUND FLOOR KEY

1	Coach shed	12	Barrack store
2	Store	13	Engine house
3	Cart house	14	Consulting room
4	Carpenter's shop	15	Surgery
5	Cart shed	16	Nurse's room
6	Magazine	17	Hospital Sergeant's room
7	Armourer's shop	18	Kitchen
8	Forge		
9	Shoeing shed		
10	Veterinary's surgery		
11	Loose boxes		

Fig. 18. Knightsbridge Barracks of 1792–3, plans in 1861. James Johnson, architect. *Demolished*

the yard in front of the officers' stables by the Society for Improving the Condition of the Labouring Classes, as part of the Great Exhibition (see Plate 7). The building was paid for by the society's president, Prince Albert, who, mindful of public opposition to any raising of bricks and mortar in the park itself, had negotiated the site – just across the road from the Crystal Palace – from the Duke of Wellington, as Commander-in-Chief of the army. The designer was Henry Roberts, the Society's architect.[13]

Known as the Prince Consort's Model Lodge, this modest but influential building had been seen by 250,000 visitors by the time the Great Exhibition closed. Wellington declined the Prince's offer to leave the lodge at the barracks for the use of soldiers' families, on the grounds that its superior accommodation might provoke unfavourable comparisons with the rest of the quarters. After being dismantled, the block was re-erected in Kennington Park, Lambeth, where it remains.[14]

The duke's reasoning was doubtless well founded, for living conditions at Knightsbridge Barracks, in common with those at many British barracks, were becoming a scandal. In 1854 a War Office committee was appointed to look into the matter of soldiers' accommodation. This led in 1855 to the holding of an open architectural competition for designs – embodying the committee's recommendations – for both infantry and cavalry barracks.[15] First prize for the cavalry barracks design was won by the brothers Thomas Henry and Matthew Digby Wyatt. No building programme followed at this time, but public outrage over the conditions at military hospitals in the Crimea indirectly focused attention on the state of army establishments at home.

In 1857 the Barracks and Hospitals Commission was set up to investigate more fully the conditions of British barracks and barrack hospitals. The Commission's report of 1861, and lengthy appendix published in 1863, added up to a damning critique of the buildings occupied by soldiers throughout the country.[16] At Knightsbridge there was a catalogue of defects, with dampness, darkness and poor air-circulation among the most widespread problems. The stench of the stables pervaded the whole site.

One of the worst buildings was the hospital, which had long been a cause for concern, the mortality rate there being significantly higher than at the Regent's Park and Windsor cavalry barracks. In the barrack block, most rooms were overcrowded and poorly ventilated. Fumes from the stables, rising through a lath-and-plaster ceiling to the troop rooms, led to chronic chest complaints and conjunctivitis. The staff-officers' quarters, over the horse infirmary, were 'much complained of', presumably for similar reasons.

Latrines and ablution rooms were thoroughly insanitary.[17] The kitchens had no ovens or any means of cooking other than boiling. This must have made the diet even poorer than usual for the rank and file and their families, putting many 'Simple Recipes for Cooking in Barracks', such as toad-in-the-hole (made without eggs), and 'Nabob's Pie' – spiced meat with a suet-based stuffing, baked under a pastry crust – beyond their reach.[c]

Then there were the detention cells, damp and with only a small grating each for light and air. 'Even in punishing men, their health should be considered', commented the *Builder*, when some years earlier it published an illustration

---

[c] This collection of recipes was appended to the Report of the Barracks and Hospitals Commission, published in 1863.[18]

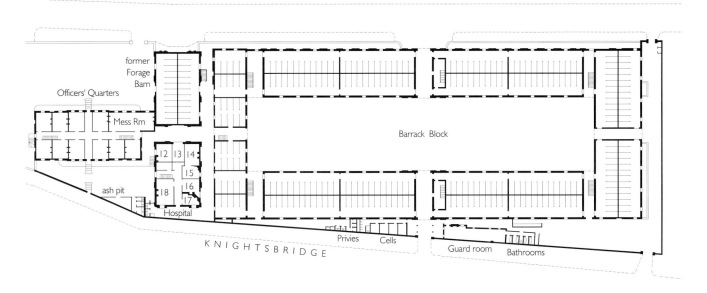

HYDE PARK

former Forage Barn

Officers' Quarters

Mess Rm

Barrack Block

ash pit

12 13 14

15

16

18

17

Hospital

Privies Cells

Guard room Bathrooms

KNIGHTSBRIDGE

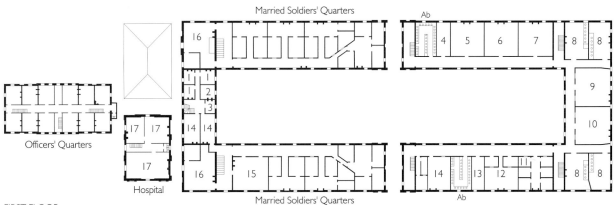

Married Soldiers' Quarters

Ab

16

4 5 6 7 8 8

9

10

Officers' Quarters

17 17

17

14 14

14 13 12 8 8

Hospital

16 15

Ab

Married Soldiers' Quarters

FIRST FLOOR

1	Barrack Sergeants' quarters	6	Quartermaster's store and office	11	Troop stores	15	Barrack store
2	Barrack Master's office	7	Band and lecture room	12	Saddler's shop	16	Wash-house
3	Barrack office	8	Kitchen	13	Boot-maker's shop	17	Ward
4	Cleaning-room	9	Infant school	14	Orderly room	Ab	Ablutions
5	Tailor's shop	10	NCOs' mess room				

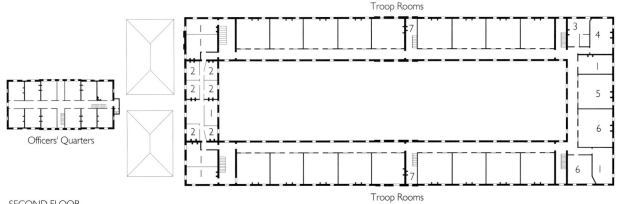

Troop Rooms

1

7

3

4

2 2

2 2

1

1

5

2 2

6

7

6 1

Officers' Quarters

Troop Rooms

SECOND FLOOR

1	Staff Sergeants' quarters	4	Schoolroom	6	Troop room
2	Troop Corporals' married quarters	5	Library and reading-room	7	Troop Corporal Major's room
3	Schoolmaster's quarters				

of one of these cells above the caption 'Black-hole for the Cavalry'.[19] The Commission evidently agreed.

Such were the official findings. Local householders too had cause to voice complaint, and during the 1860s and '70s pressure mounted from the residents of the smart west end of Knightsbridge to close the barracks down. Their concern, of course, was not with the living conditions of the troops, but with property values and the blight cast locally by their shabby neighbour across the road. Its influence was held responsible for the prevailing bad character of the area further east, where public houses and music-halls flourished, and drunkenness, brawling, and prostitution were rife.[20] Following publication of the official report, angry residents formed the Knightsbridge Barrack Memorial Committee to press for the removal of the barracks altogether. Their spokesman, John Elsworth of Trevor Terrace, described the sordid character of the area near the barracks in a pamphlet issued by the committee in 1867.[21] The Rt Hon. Robert Lowe MP, of Lowndes Square, a member of a deputation to Sir John Pakington, the War Secretary, condemned the barracks as 'an isthmus of barbarism': Sir John's bland response was that 'the residents had come to the barracks, and not the barracks to the residents'.[22] Serious consideration, however, was given to a proposal for moving the barracks to the site of Millbank Penitentiary. This scheme was still in contemplation when Lowe became Chancellor of the Exchequer in 1868, and he was in hopes that the sale of the Knightsbridge site would help pay for new buildings at Millbank. Nothing came of it, nor of Lowe's earlier suggestion that the cavalry at Knightsbridge should take over Chelsea Hospital (whose inmates would have been re-housed in the country).[23]

Meanwhile, the buildings continued to deteriorate as their future remained undecided. In May 1869 many of the officers were driven from their quarters by a disgusting smell. Almost incredibly, it was not until floors had been lifted, drains examined and ventilators installed that the cause was traced to the rotting paste, fungi and maggots between some fourteen layers of wallpaper.[24]

Local residents did not give up the fight and in the summer of 1875 the Knightsbridge Improvement Committee attempted to gain the support of Lord Henry Lennox, First Commissioner of Works.[25] The matter was vigorously debated in Parliament – in the Lords, the Earl of Lucan denounced the campaigners as 'no more than a cabal of builders, house-agents, and shopkeepers'. Elsworth produced a second pamphlet repeating the arguments for removing the barracks, but all to no avail. The War Office determined to rebuild on the same site.[26] By this time the barracks were in a perilous condition. In places the foundations had given way, and parts of the buildings threatened 'to fall and remove themselves if left untended much longer'.[27]

Demolition began towards the end of 1876. The old materials, owing particularly to a shortage of bricks,

fetched good prices, the proceeds from the barrack block alone amounting to some £4,300.[28] By the end of March 1877, all but the officers' quarters had been cleared and the troops dispersed to St John's Wood and other barracks.[29]

The Victorian Barracks, 1878–1965

With 'commendable justice',[30] the War Office gave the commission for designing the new barracks to T. H. Wyatt, the winner (with his brother M. D. Wyatt) of the cavalry barracks competition of 1855.[d] In doing so the War Office was following the precedent set at the infantry barracks at Chelsea, rebuilt in the early 1860s to the designs of the aged George Morgan, winner of the first premium in the infantry section of the 1855 competition. But any thought that the Wyatts' competition scheme, for an imaginary site of some twenty-two acres, could be adapted to fit the comparatively tiny space available at Knightsbridge was obviously vain. No sooner had proposals for demolishing the old buildings been announced than the site was further restricted by the paring away of a strip of ground for road-widening (a necessary public improvement which had been in prospect for some years).[31]

In the event, the planning of the new complex bore no resemblance to the competition scheme: on the contrary, the arrangement of the Victorian barracks was to follow quite closely that of its derided Georgian predecessor. The competition scheme had the men's quarters and stables along three sides of a large quadrangle, in the centre of which, approached by covered ways from each side, were a riding-school, kitchens, dining-rooms, a library and reading-room. In front of the quadrangle was the parade-ground, flanked by the officers' quarters on one side, and the sergeants' quarters, hospital, canteen and chapel on the other. At the back, another covered way led to the horse infirmary. The buildings at Knightsbridge could not have been arranged on such a spacious plan without considerable enlargement of the site. Stabling, living accommodation and ancillary rooms were to a large extent stacked one over another in large blocks rather than disposed horizontally about the site.

Wyatt's appointment may have been just, but it appears that his role from the start was essentially limited to that of providing attractive façades for a project which enjoyed little if any public favour. As one of the contractors employed on the rebuilding explained:

it is no secret that the War Department, in virtue of a long-standing arrangement with Mr Wyatt, selected his drawings for the elevations, and reserved to themselves the right of providing their own specifications and quantities and furnishing also their preparatory plans for all the internal arrangements.[32]

Preliminary designs for the barracks may have been in hand before Wyatt was officially appointed, probably in late

---

[d] M. D. Wyatt had become seriously ill and consequently was unable to share the commission.

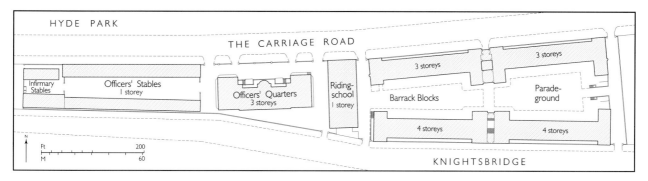

HYDE PARK

THE CARRIAGE ROAD

Infirmary Stables

Officers' Stables
I storey

Officers' Quarters
3 storeys

Riding-school
I storey

3 storeys

3 storeys

Barrack Blocks

Parade-ground

4 storeys

4 storeys

N

Ft 200
M 60

KNIGHTSBRIDGE

Fig. 19. Knightsbridge Barracks of 1878–80, site plan. T. H. Wyatt, architect. *Demolished*

1875.[33] The Royal Engineers' architect, Lieut. H. H. Cole, was certainly engaged in 1875 in 'making new plans for Knightsbridge Barracks'.[34] Three other Royal Engineers officers are known to have been involved in the project. Colonel E. C. Gordon, later commandant of the School of Engineering at Chatham, was named in 1880 as the officer superintending the rebuilding, and a Colonel Scott, probably Henry Y. D. Scott, architect of the Royal Albert Hall, as having supervision of the work. Gordon's name appeared on plans dated January 1877, which were in existence when the barracks was again rebuilt in the late 1960s.[35] The third man was Captain Elliott Wood, the executive officer appointed to the Royal Engineers' London district in 1876. 'Eighty great sheets of plans for Knightsbridge were given me', recalled Wood in his memoirs, 'and I found important structural alterations to be necessary'.[36] Just whose plans they were is not known.

Although the rebuilding was total, it was not at first intended that it should be, and it was for this reason, as much as because of the shape of the site, that the layout was so similar to the old. The original proposal was that the officers' quarters should be retained (with a new mess wing), together with the existing riding-school. When it was decided to rebuild these as well, the lack of space made it necessary to align the new and much larger riding-school north–south instead of east–west as before.[37]

The arrangement (fig. 19) may have recalled the old barracks, but the scale of building was considerably greater and the architectural treatment contrastingly lavish. This, at least, was some compensation for local residents. As Wyatt wrote to the prospective purchaser of South Lodge on the south side of Knightsbridge in 1877:

instead of the Barn-like looking Riding School which used to face the road nearby to the house in question we shall now have the most important front of the Barracks (being the Officers' Quarters) immediately facing the road. I cannot doubt but that the rebuilding of the Barracks on an improved and more ornamental scale, and the widening of the roadway immediately adjoining will have the effect of improving the value of all this neighbourhood.[38]

The new barracks provided accommodation for 23 officers, 352 NCOs and single men, 40 married men and their families, 386 troop horses and 76 officers' chargers. Construc-

tion began in 1878 and was completed in May 1880, when the Royal Horse Guards (The Blues) moved in to their new quarters from Albany Street Barracks.[39] The general contractor was George Shaw of Earl Street, Westminster, late of the firm Jackson and Shaw, whose estimate for the work was £150,000.[40]

The buildings, of 'palatial appearance and magnitude', were in a mixed classical style, chiefly Renaissance Italian but with a strong French influence evident, particularly in the roofs of the main barrack blocks – most appropriate to the boulevard-like location (Plates 40–3). They were faced in red brick with Portland-stone dressings and sculptured decoration. (Plain stock brick sufficed for the comparatively dour 'internal' elevations.) Two sorts of red brick were used, both pointed with black mortar: red Suffolks for the elevations to Knightsbridge, and 'deep crimson' Hampshires for the park fronts.[41] Sculptural ornament, though nowhere used in great profusion, was heaviest on the Hyde Park side. It was all carried out by Thomas Earp.

The two principal ranges, the **Barrack Blocks**, were designed as grand *palazzi* with prominent pavilions beneath tall mansarded roofs (Plate 40). The basements and ground-floor fronts were arcaded and heavily rusticated, and the façades were divided into bays by giant-order pilasters of similarly rusticated brickwork. Although in the same general style, the two blocks were not identical, partly on account of the site, and partly because of the different accommodation within.

The Knightsbridge block, with 'a façade of dignified simplicity', was the taller building by a full upper storey, and, taking advantage of the fall of the ground from north to south, also had a basement for storage. Stabling occupied the ground floor, above which were the married soldiers' quarters, together with orderly-rooms and recreation rooms. The stables in this block were lighted from the parade-ground side, and were screened from the street by a blind wall, pierced only with small ventilation gratings. The basement underneath was arcaded, but this aspect of the design was all but invisible from the street behind the barracks wall. The entrance to the parade-ground was in the centre of the block, a tall archway between close-set pavilions, framed by a pedimented surround with engaged columns ornamented with squared vermiculated bands (Plate 42b). At either end of the range were large gateways to the barrack-yard, the copings to the gate-piers bristling with sculpted trophies.

A particular feature of the Knightsbridge range was the large number of chimney stacks, rising above the rusticated pilasters (Plate 40c). These reflected the many individual apartments within, each with their own fireplaces. Married privates were allocated a self-contained flat with balcony access from the parade-ground side of the building. Each consisted of a sitting-room about 15ft square (and a lofty 14ft high), with a cooking-stove, a 'large' bedroom and a scullery. In the west pavilion at first-floor level was the sick bay, comprising a dispensary, two wards (one a detention ward), and the orderly's quarters. A communal laundry was provided at attic level, with hot-air closets and space outside on the roof for drying. There was also a children's playground on the roof. The flats were said to be based on those in model dwellings, and the internal elevations of both barrack blocks resembled such utilitarian apartment buildings (Plate 43a).[42]

The lower park-side range was similarly composed, with terminal and central pavilions, the latter topped by domes and tall finials, rather than mansards. An open terrace and loggias under the domes were designed to give the men somewhere to relax and smoke. There were few chimneys, the rooms being mostly on a large scale for communal use. The entrance here, with carvings of the royal arms in the tympanum of the archway and military accoutrements in the arch spandrels, was flanked by niches containing two life-sized sculptures of guardsmen, one in the uniform of 1879, the other in that of 1779 (Plate 42c). These statues are preserved in the NCOs' mess of the present barracks and the royal arms now decorate the wall of the staircase leading to the mess. This block contained stables on the ground floor, and accommodation for unmarried troopers above. On the third floor were ancillary rooms, including a kitchen and dining-room, cleaning-rooms, lavatories and baths, a tailor's shop, a fencing-room and a schoolroom.[43]

Of course, with stabling immediately beneath the soldiers' living quarters, the barrack blocks perpetuated the very arrangement that had been found so objectionable in the old barracks. However, the floors between the stables and the quarters above were now thickly constructed of iron and concrete on the fireproof, and hopefully fume-proof, Fox & Barrett system.

Next to the barrack blocks, occupying the full depth of the site and dividing them from the officers' quarters further west, was the **Riding-school** (Plates 42a, 43b). Considerably larger than its predecessor, it was stylistically rather similar, on the conventional riding-school pattern with Diocletian windows at high level. There were entrances on either side, for troopers and officers respectively; inside, the walls, lined with timber to a high dado rail, were battered so as to protect the riders' legs when their horses were close to the edge of the concourse. The roof was iron-trussed, with a louvred skylight along the ridge. A viewing gallery was provided at the south end, in a short projecting annexe with an ogee-domed staircase tower.

The riding-school's front to Hyde Park was one of the most appealing features of the whole barracks (Plate 43b). Because of the sloping site, the exposed wall at this end was greatly reduced, giving the impression of an unusually low building and greatly emphasising the weight of Earp's carved stone pediment filling the gable end. Here the function of the building was vividly expressed in stone by the heads and forequarters of rearing horses emerging from scrolling acanthus leaves. When the barracks was demolished the pediment was saved and incorporated into the new main gateway (Plate 115b).

On the west side of the riding-school was the third of the principal blocks, the **Officers' Quarters** (Plate 41). While its predecessor had resembled a gentleman's country house, the new building, on a considerably larger scale, with a prominent clock-turret, had more the architectural character of a town hall or hospital. But on the park front its militaristic nature was made obvious by its ornamentation. The building was of E-shaped plan, with the wings extending towards the park.

The front to Knightsbridge, from which it was partly screened by the high boundary wall topped by big ball finials (which carried on to the west end of the barracks), was much the plainest of the two chief elevations. Lacking the exaggerated pavilion towers of the barrack blocks, the great width of the façade was kept from monotony by shallow breaks in the frontage, a pediment over the middle three windows, and by variation in the fenestration pattern – close-set at the centre, widely spaced at the ends. Sculptured ornament was restricted to the royal arms in the central pediment (a relic of the old barracks) and a crown in an arched panel a couple of floors below.

The park façade was the most ornate of all the elevations of the three main blocks, with the greatest concentration of sculptured decoration. As on the Knightsbridge front, the centrepiece was tightly proportioned. A bow window on the ground floor, with a balcony over, was flanked by an attractive garden terrace (Plate 41b). Carved portrait heads of former army commanders – Wellington, Marlborough, Combermere, Anglesey and Oxford – gazed from laurel-wreathed niches over the bow window. Busts of four more military worthies – Somerset, Raglan, Londonderry and Hill – perched on brackets on the wall to either side. These last have been preserved in the officers' mess of the present barracks (Plate 45a, c).

Living quarters were on the upper floors, the senior officers having apartments overlooking the park. The mess, a narrowly proportioned room, ran the full depth of the building on the ground floor, terminating with the bow window looking out to Hyde Park. It was ornamented in a ponderous classical manner, its chief features being a screen of Corinthian columns at the Knightsbridge end and a deeply coved moulded plaster ceiling. There was a massive carved marble fireplace, above which latterly hung Sir Alfred Munnings' painting of a drum horse (Plate 41c).

Today this picture hangs in the new officers' mess.

Beyond the officers' quarters, at the narrow western end of the site, were two long rows comprising the **Officers' Stables**, and beyond these, at the far end of the site, the **Infirmary Stables**, which could accommodate fifteen horses. On the Knightsbridge side, only the roof of the stables was visible over the barracks wall. The park-side range, with squat mansarded end-pavilions and a pedimented centrepiece, was set back slightly behind a dwarf wall and railings.

The barracks façades were among T. H. Wyatt's most accomplished public-building designs, and the new barracks itself was acknowledged by the army to be 'the finest in the kingdom' in its standards of accommodation and sanitation.[44] The *Building News* was sufficiently impressed to feel that 'even the well-founded objections raised at first against the appropriation of such a site to barrack accommodation, now appear to lose somewhat of their force'.[45] But some reactions were so coloured by the long-standing campaign to have the barracks moved to a less important site as to be unjust. One critic, far from convinced of the wisdom of replacing the old buildings on the same spot, found the barracks, not yet finished, 'more presentable (though still sufficiently ugly)'. It was probably the same writer who, after their completion, did not feel that the buildings were 'quite equal to what might have been wished for in so very conspicuous a site'.[46] A more extreme view was expressed by the London correspondent of the *Leeds Mercury*, who, while glad to see the back of the 'wretched collection of dirty sheds' comprising the old barracks, dismissed the new as no more than 'a tasteless muddle of red brick and stone, which do not even suggest its use and purpose'.[47]

In 1922, as part of the post-war restructuring of the army, the 2nd Life Guards (then at Knightsbridge) and the 1st Life Guards (at Albany Street) were amalgamated. Knightsbridge Barracks had inadequate space and facilities either to drill the augmented regiment, or for training and riding instruction, and so Albany Street became the Life Guards' new home.[48] The future of Knightsbridge Barracks remained uncertain for some years, but the War Office had nothing to gain from its disposal as the site would have reverted to the Crown. In 1925 half a battalion of Foot Guards were moved there: this left the stabling still largely unused (except to a limited extent as storage), a situation which aroused some criticism.[49] Scenting opportunity, developers began making enquiries about the site. In 1931 the Frank Committee, appointed to consider the disposal of surplus government property, recommended that the barracks should be relinquished by the Army and the site let commercially on a building lease. The barracks were valued tentatively at £500,000, but after discussions between the Commissioners of Crown Lands, the Office of Works and the Treasury no mutually satisfactory scheme could be found.[50] The disruption to traffic caused by the Life Guards' journeys between Albany Street and White-

hall led the Metropolitan Police to press for the Household Cavalry to re-occupy Knightsbridge Barracks, which it did in autumn 1932.[51]

The barracks escaped serious damage during the Second World War, but behind the seemingly well-preserved façades living conditions were becoming intolerable. The cookhouse, for instance, was on the third floor of the park-side barrack block, and the stores on the third floor of the Knightsbridge block. Whenever the decrepit lift up to the cookhouse broke down a fatigue party had to carry the food up the stairs. Access to the married quarters was equally poor, and small children, prams and shopping had to be carried up two flights of stairs. The children used the barrack yard as a playground, and the balconies were a favourite vantage point from which to drop milk bottles on to the officers below. The familiar complaint of the stench of horse urine pervading the living quarters was voiced once again, in addition to which there was an infestation of rats. By the early 1960s the barracks was considered to be a military slum.[52] But by that time plans for rebuilding the entire complex were well in hand.

The New Barracks, 1967–70

In June 1956 the War Office made its proposal to demolish the Victorian buildings and erect a new barracks on the same site. Writing in the following February, William Hare, the Secretary of State for War, dismissed the old buildings as 'completely out of date'.[53] A year later Basil Spence was given a brief for the project. No other architects are known to have been approached. In November 1959 he officially accepted the commission to rebuild the barracks, 'to your own design', using the Ministry of Public Building and Works' general specifications for army barracks.[54]

Once again, the government had turned to an architect in private practice to come up with a prestigious design for what was almost certain to become a controversial project. A few years later, and the question of conservation of the old buildings might have been an important consideration. But as in the 1860s and '70s, it was the apparent inadequacy of the site for the necessary buildings, their likely impact upon Hyde Park, and the opportunity for improving the park offered by demolition, which were the principal points at issue. Victorian campaigners had believed that the site belonged to the public and should be cleared of buildings and restored to Hyde Park. As one writer had expressed it in 1865, 'to build a range of mansions or a lofty barrack here would be sacrilege'.[55]

Dilapidation, obsolescence, and, perhaps just as importantly, the unsympathetic light in which Victorian architecture was still generally viewed in the 1960s, had revived the old controversy. Despite all the objections to Spence's designs that were to be raised, none seems to have been made to the complete destruction of the Victorian buildings, although in 1958 F. J. Root, Under-Secretary at the Ministry of Works, had checked with the Chief Inspector

72

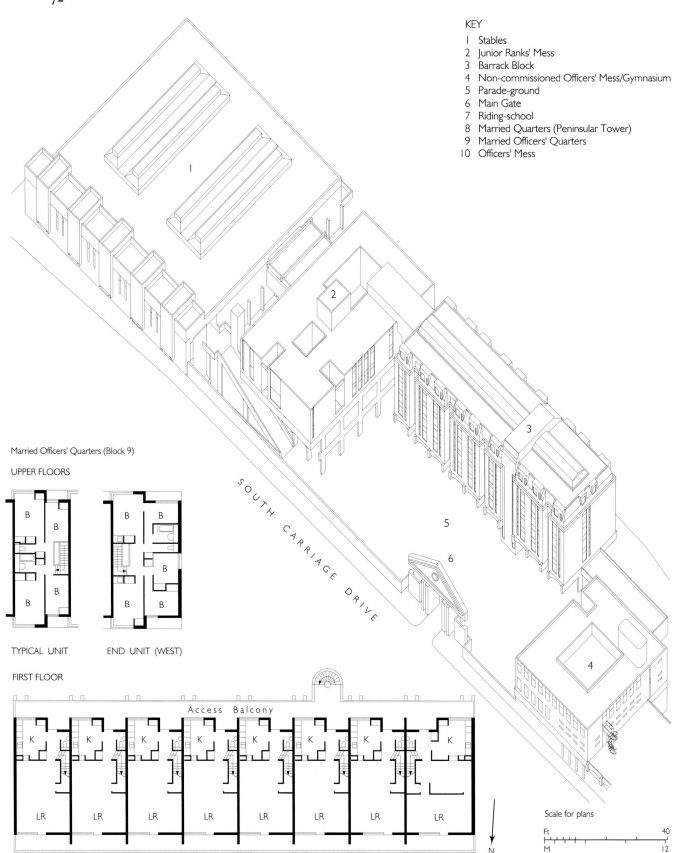

KEY

1 Stables
2 Junior Ranks' Mess
3 Barrack Block
4 Non-commissioned Officers' Mess/Gymnasium
5 Parade-ground
6 Main Gate
7 Riding-school
8 Married Quarters (Peninsular Tower)
9 Married Officers' Quarters
10 Officers' Mess

Married Officers' Quarters (Block 9)

UPPER FLOORS

TYPICAL UNIT   END UNIT (WEST)

FIRST FLOOR

Access Balcony

SOUTH CARRIAGE DRIVE

Scale for plans

Fig. 20. Knightsbridge Barracks of 1967–70, axonometric view looking south-east, and plans of the Officers' Mess, Married Officers' Quarters, and Married Quarters. Sir Basil Spence, architect

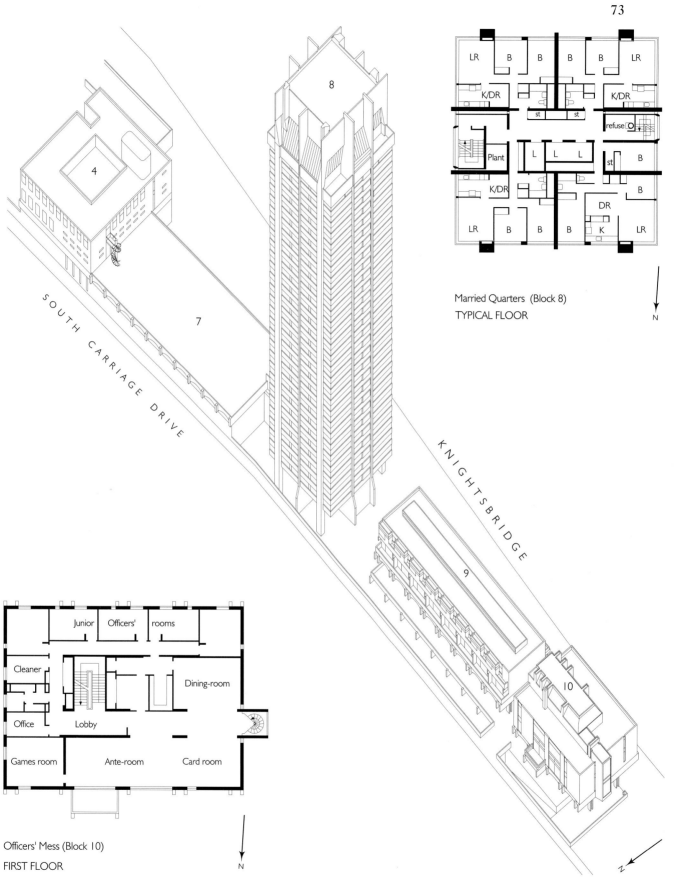

Married Quarters (Block 8)
TYPICAL FLOOR

LR B B B B LR
K/DR K/DR
st st refuse
Plant L L L st B
B
K/DR DR
LR B B B K LR

N

SOUTH CARRIAGE DRIVE

KNIGHTSBRIDGE

8

4

7

9

10

Officers' Mess (Block 10)
FIRST FLOOR

Junior Officers' rooms
Cleaner
Dining-room
Office Lobby
Games room Ante-room Card room

N

of Ancient Monuments, Paul Baillie Reynolds: 'I assume that we do not regard these buildings as worthy of preservation but it would be useful to have your confirmation'.[56] In early 1960 the initial plans, centred on a high tower, were submitted to the Royal Fine Arts Commission and (a matter of courtesy only, since Crown immunity exempted the barracks from normal planning controls) to the London County Council (LCC).

The Fine Arts Commission saw architectural merit in the design, but was generally against high buildings being built on the fringes of the royal parks, and felt that the tower would 'seriously damage local amenities'. Besides, 'it would be the more regrettable if the Government itself were to be the first body to put up a building of this height in such a position'.[57] John Profumo, who had taken over as Secretary of State for War, expressed his disappointment at the Commission's reservations: 'to avoid undue delay Spence is going ahead with another project designed to meet the objections of the commission, but, oh dear, it does seem a pity if we are to lose what promised to be an imaginative and attractive piece of architecture'.[58] Spence's alternative design placed the married quarters in a much lower 'slab' block instead of the tower. The Fine Arts Commission thought this preferable, but was concerned that it made the development at the west end of the site too dense.[59] Spence's own view was that a tower would cut out less light to the park than a slab block, and would not prevent people in buildings over the way from seeing across the barracks to the park. He cited the example of Bowater House near by, where the architects' original plans for a high tower had been rejected in favour of a lower but bulkier building. The Commission was, in due course, won round to the original concept. The adoption of a tower block made it possible to meet two crucial requirements of the barracks brief – a bigger riding-school, and a parade-ground large enough to mount both squadrons of cavalry, something impossible in the former barrack yard.[60]

The LCC had been involved with the Fine Arts Commission in drawing up a policy for high buildings in London aimed at limiting such buildings to just 100ft, and now objected to a tower block so near to the boundary of Hyde Park. In particular, it was unhappy about the relationship of the tower, as viewed from the park, with a group of high buildings then proposed to be built at Knightsbridge Green (see page 93). More fundamentally, the LCC felt that the barracks tower would be without visual or civic significance in relation to the district as a whole – a point block without point.[61] The only aesthetic justifications for erecting towers were held to be, either that a single tower should mark a 'nodal' position in the cityscape, or that a group of towers should form a carefully arranged cluster. In the case of the barracks, Spence had apparently believed that his tower would group itself with the higher Knightsbridge Green blocks (which were never built).[62]

Despite LCC and public opposition, Spence's original scheme was duly adopted, the only major alteration being the relocation of the officers' mess from the top of the tower to a separate block at the west end of the site.[e] The plans were officially approved at the end of July 1963. The *Builder*, readily accepting the tower as the only alternative to a slab block, which would have been 'intolerable by any standards', nevertheless drew a depressing conclusion from the whole controversy:

That an architect of no less eminence than Sir Basil, with the minister and the Royal Fine Art Commission behind him, can believe in the rightness of his tower, whilst a planning authority with the knowledge and experience of the LCC can believe it wrong, demonstrates a tragic failure of resolution about fundamental principles of planning.[64]

The old buildings were demolished in the latter half of 1965, the cavalry having been transferred to Wellington Barracks, where temporary accommodation had been provided to Spence's designs (at a cost of some £135,000).[65] There was delay when a survey of the cleared site led to the revision of certain measurements, and some re-planning became necessary. Construction, by Sir Robert McAlpine & Sons Ltd, began in February 1967, with November 1969 as the target completion date. Spence's job architect was his partner and son-in-law Anthony Blee. The structural engineers were Ove Arup & Partners.[66]

Continuing modifications to the plans made it impossible to keep to the intended timetable and budget. The crown of the tower, for instance, intended to dispel flue gases, had to be re-designed for technical reasons, while anti-corrosion and waterproofing measures in the stable block proved more involved than originally envisaged. Extra expenses were incurred to maintain a high standard of fittings and finishes. As a consequence, the buildings were not completed until October 1970 and at a cost of well over £4 million, against the original estimate of £3,175,000.[67] As late as 1974, the Public Services Agency (as the Ministry of Public Building and Works had become) initiated an investigation into the over-spend and delay. Though the Department of the Environment went so far as to issue a writ against Spence and McAlpines, eventually all accusations of negligence levelled at the architects and contractors proved unfounded.[68]

Accommodation was provided for 23 officers, 60 warrant officers and NCOs, 431 rank and file, and 273 horses. All the buildings are of reinforced-concrete construction (Plates 44–7). The Corbusier-inspired treatment largely adopted was one of several reprises by Spence of the idiom first used by him at Sussex University, begun in 1960. Based on the rhythmic use of shallow concrete arches and vaults offset by contrasting brickwork (red with raked joints), it was specifically chosen here in deference to the several large buildings of red brick and stone in the vicini-

---

[e] One of the reasons for this alteration was that it was not possible to provide a lift within the tower into which a horse could be ridden, it being a tradition, on occasion, to ride into the officers' mess.[63]

ty.[69] Where exposed, concrete was generally left in its board-marked finish. The tower was given a quite different treatment, with its trabeated concrete structure left entirely exposed, the edge-beams with a hammered finish, and the columns and exposed ends of the cross-walls lightly ground to reveal the aggregate. Exposed concrete on the north side of the stables, alongside South Carriage Drive, was also hammered.

There are eight individual blocks, including the tower, disposed along the site, with the main entrance gateway on the north side opening on to South Carriage Drive from the parade-ground (fig. 20).[70] The intention was to separate as far as possible horse traffic from pedestrians and motor-vehicles, with the former entering and leaving by the north gate, and the rest using entrances to other areas of the barracks on the Knightsbridge side. The ceremonial nature of the main gate is made plain by its large pediment incorporating the carved tympanum, by Thomas Earp, from the Victorian riding-school, the original oculus being filled by a clock (Plate 115b).

At the eastern end of the site are the **Stables** (Plates 46–47a). These are arranged on two floors over a basement and connected to the yard or parade-ground by ramps which can be heated to prevent icing-over in the winter. Each of the upper floors has five parallel lines of stalls. On the Knightsbridge side there is a balcony at first-floor level, cantilevered out over the boundary wall, with a fire-escape ramp at one end. In the basement is a dung collection chamber, served by chutes, and a forage barn, with lifts to the stables. Dung passes straight from the chutes into containers which are conveyed by railway to a collection point for daily removal by lorry.

Mechanical ventilation had to be particularly powerful to keep down the ammonia content in the atmosphere of the stables (corrosive of reinforced concrete as well as noxious to health). It was also necessary to provide space for gullies to cope with frequent floor-washing, this being accomplished by casting the secondary beams supporting the floors in a trough section.

Next to the stables are two ranges at right-angles to each other and enclosing the south and east sides of the parade-ground. The first is a four-storey building comprising the **Junior Ranks' Mess Block**. The ground floor on the west side is left open to provide a sheltered area for the guard to form up for inspection in bad weather. The mess itself is a large hall for dining and recreation purposes. Other facilities, including a club and games rooms, are on the upper floors. At ground-floor level is the Forge, comprising a shoeing-shed and a smithy with four furnaces and anvils (Plate 47b). In the basement is the saddlers' workshop.

The second range, on the south side of the parade-ground, is the **Barrack Block**, originally flat-roofed but since raised by the addition of a mansard storey (Plate 45b). This block was designed to provide four floors of barrack-rooms – single rooms for corporals and four-man rooms for troopers. The lower floors are given over to the Guard Room and offices.

West of the parade-ground is a four-storey block containing the **Non-Commissioned Officers' Mess Block**. In the basement are stores and workshops, and on the ground floor a gymnasium, which has a viewing gallery shared with the riding-school in the block adjoining. Under the gym is a rifle range and armoury. The mess is on the first floor, a large open-plan space combining a dining-area, bar, and dance-floor. There are mementoes of the Victorian barracks here: a stone coat-of-arms on the staircase wall, and, in the ante-room to the mess, two statues of guardsmen. The ante-room occupies the bottom of a light-well, around which the upper-floor rooms, mostly bedrooms for individual NCOs, are arranged.

Attached to the west end of the NCOs' mess is the **Riding-school**. The interior, with its battered timber walls and clerestory lighting, echoes its Victorian predecessor, although, at 150ft by 50ft, it is considerably larger. The entrance is on the south side, the doors being operated electrically from a high-level control panel. The ceiling is composed of shallow concrete arches, over which the flat roof was originally intended to serve as a children's playground.[71]

Beyond the riding-school are the **Married Quarters**, housed in the 'Peninsular Tower', 66ft square and rising to just over 310ft with a zinc-clad crown (Plates 44a, 115a). Its principal vertical structural elements make up a core: two east–west walls running the full width of the building, two central north–south walls dividing the flats, and two columns at the edges of the north and south fronts. Floor slabs are carried on the core walls at the centre of the building, and on edge beams cantilevered out from the core.

The tower has 28 floors each containing four two- and three-bedroom flats, above which are four more levels containing box- and plant-rooms, squash courts and a viewing gallery. Boiler plant and a laundry are housed in the basement and lower-ground floor.

Immediately behind the tower are the **Married Officers' Quarters**, a block of eight maisonettes with car-parking underneath at parade-ground level. Seven of the maisonettes have four bedrooms; the eighth, for the Commanding Officer, has five.[72]

Separated from the maisonettes by a narrow space is the **Officers' Mess**, also built over a car-park. The main entrance hall is at upper-ground level, and beyond its glass walls and doors are placed the stone busts of Somerset, Raglan, Londonderry and Hill from the park front of the former officers' quarters, mounted on tall plinths (Plate 45a, c). Never having been designed to be seen at such close quarters, they have a rather startlingly crude appearance, with little differentiation in their features beyond the varying length of their sideburns.

From the hall, stairs lead up to the mess rooms on the first floor. Of these, the ante-room is the most impressive, rising through two floors and lit by full-height windows overlooking the park (Plate 117c). The comfortable leather chesterfields and armchairs, and the various paintings and *objets* retained from the earlier barracks may seem rather at odds with Basil Spence's austere angular space, though it is a contrast which he seems to have felt quite successful.[f] There is a similar clash of styles in the adjacent dining-room where the long table, silverware, and deep-red walls hung with oil-paintings are overshadowed by an obtrusive concrete bridge reached by a spiral stair, features which might seem more at home in a multi-storey car park (Plate 117d). The dining-table proved a matter of some contention. Spence's original idea that the table should be finished in dull rosewood had to be abandoned when the Commanding Officer insisted that it should be of 'gleaming mahogany . . . in which the image of the Regimental silver would be reflected'.[74]

A report by the army made in 1971 suggests that the occupants were favourably impressed by their new buildings. Almost inevitably, there were a number of complaints on the grounds of inadequate space: the riding-school was felt to be too narrow, staircases in the officers' maisonettes too tight for easy furniture-moving, and storage for offi-cers' uniforms and the regimental silver inadequate.[75] Only in the officers' mess building was it felt that style had been allowed to take precedence over function, resulting in poor security, and difficulties with lighting and maintenance. The wider critical response to the new barracks was mixed, with the tower provoking the most negative responses, on account of its perceived inappropriateness to the pastoral view across Hyde Park. *Building*, acknowledging the flats as more or less unavoidable given the confines of the site, praised the new complex as 'elegant and immaculately detailed'.[76] Spence evidently did not feel that the brutalist style of the architecture clashed with the Ruritanian pageantry of the occupants. 'I did not want this to be a mimsy-pimsy building', he is reported as saying. 'It is for soldiers. On horses. In armour'.[77] The tower has remained a sore point with commentators: 'It is not clear', complains a contemporary guidebook, 'why living accommodation for soldiers should have been allowed to spoil 400 years of Crown and public investment in Hyde Park'.[78]

---

[f] The relics preserved here include an oval panel of the arms of the House of Hanover from the original barracks (see Plate 117c).[73]

CHAPTER IV

Knightsbridge Green Area

Redevelopment after the Second World War robbed the Knightsbridge Green area of much of its character, substituting soulless large commercial buildings for what had been a varied mixture of mostly Victorian development (figs 22, 27). Two features remain essentially intact: the narrow passageway of Knightsbridge Green, and the enormous bulk of Park Mansions at Scotch Corner – the junction of Knightsbridge and Brompton Road. But Knightsbridge west of Park Mansions has lost its 'high street' bustle, and the seedy lodging-house quarter of Raphael Street, obscurely placed behind the main-road shops, restaurants, hotels and mansion flats of pre-war days, has been entirely destroyed. Also vanished is Tattersalls' horse-mart, one of Knightsbridge's most celebrated institutions and, with its classical-style gateway, a distinctive architectural presence on the Green.

The oldest building hereabouts is the former All Saints' School of 1875, on the north side of the Green.

Landownership before development

Early development in this area was concentrated along the main Kensington road (known here as the High Road) and at Knightsbridge Green itself. However, a rather fragmented landownership (fig. 21) did not encourage a very orderly or ambitious pattern of building. In the early eighteenth century Philip Moreau acquired the greater part of the land around the Green (and more extensive ground further west), but portions remained in other hands, and in any case Moreau's estate was broken up in 1759. By that time much of the area was becoming fairly densely built over, with rows of small houses filling up gaps in the frontages to the roads and the Green. However, it was not until the construction of Raphael Street from 1844 that it began to take on a distinctly urban character. Successive redevelopments have entirely transformed the scale of building since then, and few of the old property boundaries are still apparent today.

The most important line to survive is along the west side of the present-day Knightsbridge Green, dividing the historical Green – the triangle of manorial land between the two main roads, belonging formerly to Westminster Abbey – from the variously owned land to the west.

These various landholdings included a piece of ground belonging from 1719 to the Trevor family, from whose larger estate further west it was separated by a narrow strip.[1] The development of this ground (latterly occupied by Albert Gate Mansions and Prince's Club, its boundaries now obliterated by redevelopment) was tied up with that of the High Road generally and its history is therefore given here rather than in the chapter describing the main Trevor estate.

Philip Moreau (1656–1733) belonged to a wealthy Huguenot merchant family from Picardy, and was at the centre of a small enclave of French *émigrés* settled in Knightsbridge in the early eighteenth century. Among them was the surgeon and anatomist Paul Buissière (or Bussière), who lived for more than twenty years until his death in 1739 in a house north of the Moreaus' own residence on the west side of Knightsbridge Green. A favourite of the royal family, Buissière attended Queen Caroline during her last illness. His house was later owned by another *émigré*, John Larpent the elder, chief clerk in the Foreign Office.[2]

The Moreau estate originated as the Knightsbridge portions of a hundred-acre landholding, mostly in Kensington and Chelsea, belonging to Sir William Blake but dispersed after his death in 1630.[3] Moreau first acquired, in 1705, a mansion house which had been part of Blake's property. This stood just to the west of the Green at its southern end. In 1718 he obtained the rest of the former Blake ground in Knightsbridge: a large area along the north side of the Brompton road, extending northwards to include the Rose and Crown inn fronting the High Road, and the future site of Montpelier Square, together with a detached piece of land now covered by parts of Princes Gate and Ennismore Gardens.[4]

Over the next few years Moreau completed his local acquisitions by obtaining the tenure of most of the manorial land belonging to Westminster Abbey at the junction of the Kensington and Brompton roads, including an inn, then called the Sun, forerunner of the present-day Paxton's Head. Middle Row (North), a terrace fronting the Kensington road, was built there shortly afterwards.[5]

In 1744 Philip Moreau's son and heir, Captain James Philip Moreau, negotiated an agreement with the neighbouring landowner Arthur Trevor, guaranteeing the maintenance of a driftway (eventually to become Lancelot Place) for the use of Moreau's tenants between the Brompton road and the Rose and Crown. From Captain Moreau, who rebuilt the family house at the Green, the estate eventually descended to Charles Frederick Moreau, his grandson, who put it up for auction in several lots in 1759.[6]

The site of the Moreaus' house and garden, latterly occupied by Tattersalls' horse and carriage mart, retained

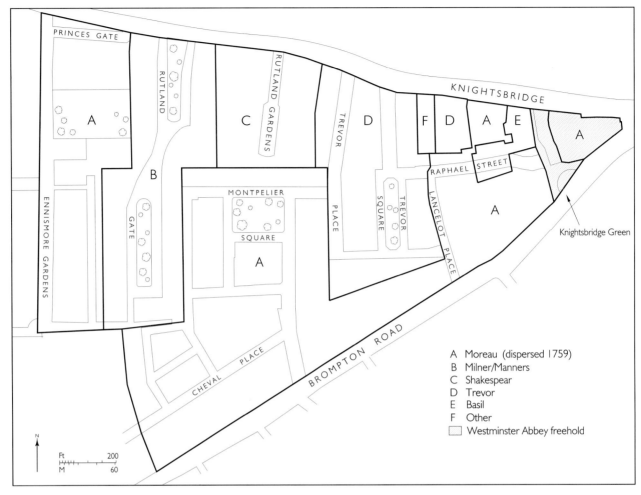

Fig. 21. Landownership in central Knightsbridge in the first half of the eighteenth century

its separate identity until redevelopment in the 1950s. Dr Buissière's old house, eventually to become the Pakenham Tavern, and the more extensive Rose and Crown property, each passed into separate ownership at the sale, but were eventually brought back together as part of the estate of the gunmaker Durs Egg. The ground south of the Moreaus' house (or Grosvenor House, as it became), fronting the Brompton road, was mostly built up in the late eighteenth and early nineteenth centuries (Plate 5c).

Middle Row and the Sun inn property also passed into separate ownerships at the sale, but were later reunited and ultimately redeveloped as Park Mansions.

The remaining portion of Moreau land near the Green was the World's End or Fulham Bridge inn, fronting the Brompton road on the plot between the Moreaus' garden and the driftway. The inn itself was subsequently rebuilt, and houses and shops erected along the Brompton road frontage.[7] The northern part of this deep plot was developed after the Moreau sale as a mews (Fulham Bridge Yard, later Tullett Place) with a ride for exercising and showing horses. In the 1830s houses were built on the east side, but

extensive stabling remained.[8] The mews and houses were largely redeveloped with garaging before the Second World War. This site also lost its separate identity as a result of post-war redevelopment.

Besides the land belonging to the Moreaus and Westminster Abbey, there was one more estate in immediate proximity to the Green in the eighteenth century. This consisted of an irregularly shaped plot fronting the Kensington road (E on fig. 21), extending from the west side of the Green to the boundaries of the Rose and Crown property and the gardens of Dr Buissière and the Moreaus. On it stood a house of 1688 and various small houses and outbuildings. By 1704 the ground belonged to Martin Cawfield Basil, a Lincoln's Inn barrister with estates in Ireland and Buckinghamshire, after whose death in 1735 it was partly redeveloped.[9] Basil's estate was later acquired by Durs Egg.

Durs Egg's estate, through which Raphael Street was ultimately to be carved, was assembled by him in 1799–1803 and amounted to about four acres. As well as Basil's old property, it consisted of the Rose and Crown and its grounds extending to the driftway, and Dr Buissière's house, where Egg lived until his death.[10]

A German-Swiss by birth, Durs Egg was one of the finest gunsmiths in England, patronized by the royal family. But his latter years were clouded by mental illness, litigation and family strife. He took against his children, and towards the end of his life carried loaded pistols, believing 'all those that approached him had designs upon his life'. When he died in 1831, at the age of 82, he left a will which would have largely disinherited his family. This was successfully contested on the grounds of his insanity, but the Knightsbridge Green estate, encumbered by a £5,000 mortgage, was not disposed of for several years. A purchase agreement with William Nokes of Denton Court, Kent, made in 1833, ultimately fell through, apparently because of remaining uncertainty over the title to the property. Egg's estate was eventually sold in 1838 to Lewis Raphael of Hendon, who initiated its partial redevelopment.[11]

Scotch Corner and the High Road

The High Road

Until 1903, the properties along the south side of Knightsbridge between Brompton Road and Trevor Street were mostly numbered as part of the High Road, sometimes known as the High Street. At the east end, on the Brompton Road corner, a terrace of houses, then recently replaced by Park Mansions, had been separately numbered under the name Middle Row, or Middle Row North, since its construction in the 1720s (fig. 22).[12] At the other end of the High Road, on the corner of Trevor Street, the last few houses formed the eastern half of Trevor Terrace, built in the early nineteenth century (see page 97). When the old names were abolished and the premises all renumbered as part of Knightsbridge, High Road was coming to the end of a period of piecemeal redevelopment, begun in the 1870s, which transformed the character of this part of Knightsbridge, socially and commercially as well as architecturally.

By the 1860s, the High Road had become one of the least salubrious parts of Knightsbridge, a centre for low pleasures in sharp contrast to the increasingly select character of the district in general. From Knightsbridge Green all along the High Road was 'a succession of music-halls, taverns, beer-stores, oyster saloons, & cheap tobacconists', that would have been 'a disgrace to any portion of London', the nightly meeting-place of disorderly men and women whose behaviour made the area 'quite as unseemly as the Haymarket'.[13] Not three hundred yards long, the south side of the High Road accommodated five public houses, two or three of them with purpose-built music-halls attached, while on the north side there was a concentration of shops, pubs and lodging-houses adjoining Knightsbridge Barracks in and around Park Place and Mills's Buildings.

The High Road's rambunctious nocturnal character stemmed naturally enough from the combined presence of several old inns and the cavalry barracks. The Marquis of Granby, the immediate precursor of the present-day Paxton's Head, was one of the oldest-established of these inns, dating back at least as far as 1632, when it was called the King's Arms – it was later known as the Golden Lion, the Red Lion and the Sun.[14] Perhaps the earliest was the Rose and Crown, formerly the Rose, a few doors along at No. 16 High Road, said in the 1850s to have been licensed more than 300 years. This establishment, reputedly used as quarters by Cromwell's troops, was called the Oliver Cromwell in the 1840s.[15] Further west, the King's Head or Old King's Head, No. 24 High Road, was certainly in existence by the 1790s.[16] Both the Rising Sun at No. 26, and the Trevor Arms in Trevor Terrace, had opened comparatively recently, the former about 1830, and the latter in 1844.[17]

A harbinger of things to come was Mr Neat's concert room at the Old King's Head, opened by about 1840 and conducted by Mr Paulyneo, manager or proprietor of several London concert rooms and 'himself a very good comic singer'.[18]

In 1849 residents of High Row, Lowndes Terrace, Trevor Terrace, Rutland Gate and elsewhere petitioned against the granting of music and dancing licences to various public houses in the district, including the Marquis of Granby, Rose and Crown, King's Head and Rising Sun, on the grounds that 'if such licences were granted immorality of all kinds in the neighbourhood already greatly abounding owing to its close proximity to the Barracks would be vastly increased'.[19] They referred to police action the previous year to put a stop to unlicensed music and dancing carried on in some of these pubs. But local opposition notwithstanding, the High Road enjoyed a musical heyday through the 1850s and '60s, echoes of which were still to be heard in the late 1880s.

The Rose and Crown was licensed for music and dancing from 1852 to 1876, and the King's Head from 1851 until 1858.[20] The Sun Music Hall began as a concert room built at the back of the Rising Sun in 1851, and was rebuilt on a grander scale in the 1860s. At the rear of the Trevor Arms, the Trevor Music Hall was first licensed in 1854.

The High Road's popularity as a place of entertainment in early to mid-Victorian days does not seem to have done much to improve its general appearance, nor to have resulted in any significant rebuilding along the road frontage. Middle Row in the 1850s was 'a medley of very inferior houses' and the buildings further along were 'generally of a mean description'.[21] The new concert halls were obscurely placed, at the back of narrow sites.

Probably the oldest structure at this time was the Rose and Crown, which bore the date 1679, and had timber-built galleries at the rear, overlooking a spacious stable-yard (Plate 48a).[22] The building then occupied as the Rising Sun was also, apparently, of seventeenth-century date. Another old house, between the Rising Sun and the King's Head, had been pulled down about 1801 and a row of three houses built on the site.[23]

Chatham House, No. 13A High Road, had been built in

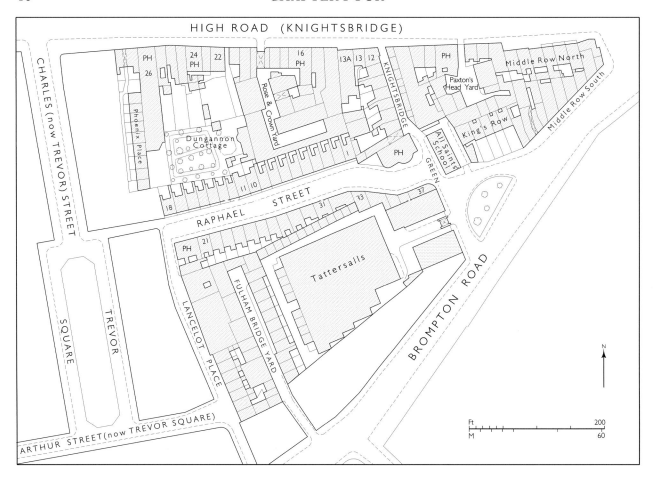

Fig. 22. Knightsbridge Green area in the mid-1860s

1688 on the site of a tavern called the Grave Maurice. Adjoining Chatham House at Nos 12 and 13 was a pair of houses built in 1736–7 along with a row of small houses behind on the west side of Knightsbridge Green.[24] A photograph of *c*.1904 shows Nos 12 and 13 as plain, rendered houses of three storeys, two windows wide, both in a state of some dilapidation.[25] They were then the last-surviving old buildings in the High Road.

Redevelopment of the High Road got under way in the mid-1870s, shortly before the rebuilding of the barracks and the widening of the roadway at that point. The Rose and Crown and the adjoining houses, west of Chatham House, were pulled down and rebuilt in 1874–5 on a much larger scale. The new buildings, six storeys high, were designed by Henry Pafoot Foster, architect, and erected by Thomas Elkington of Golden Lane. The Rose and Crown itself was re-created as the Rose and Crown Coffee Palace, later a 'temperance hotel'; it was 'practically rebuilt' in 1917 as the Royal Park Hotel.[26]

In 1876 Chatham House was rebuilt for Captain Charles Mercier, an artist who resided in High Row. The new Chatham House was designed by the architect Alexander Payne and constructed by Robert Lacy of Clapham. A curious building with a shaped gable of eccentric design on the street front, it apparently incorporated a top-lit studio for Captain Mercier on the second floor. Though considerably loftier than the old houses next door at Nos 12 and 13 High Road, it was nevertheless out of scale with redevelopment in the High Road generally. Foster's buildings dwarfed it, as in time did Park Mansions, on the other side of Knightsbridge Green.[27]

Gradually, the whole of the High Road was pulled down and largely replaced by mansion flats and shops, one of the last parts to go being the new Chatham House itself. Together with its decrepit neighbours, Chatham House was demolished a few years before the First World War for the building of the Knightsbridge Palace (later Normandie) Hotel.

Not all redevelopment, however, was of this sort, and the High Road continued to provide places of public amusement. In the 1880s Humphreys' Hall, which evolved from a former roller-skating rink on land behind the King's Head, became an important venue for high-class exhibitions and bazaars, including the famous Japanese Village, before being redeveloped as the exclusive sports centre Prince's Club.

In general, shops, restaurants, tea-rooms, hotels and residential apartments characterized the former High Road until the Second World War, and a little of this character remains at the east end today. Rutland Yard, formerly the stable-yard of the Rose and Crown, continued to be used for stabling into the twentieth century. It was latterly converted for warehousing and garaging before being obliterated in the 1950s, along with much of the rest of the High Road, for the building of Mercury House. Nos 171 and 173, part of H. P. Foster's 1870s rebuilding, survived, at least in part, into the 1990s.

The Marquis of Granby was rebuilt or remodelled in 1851 and renamed the Paxton's Head, in honour of the designer of the Crystal Palace:[28] it was again rebuilt in the early 1900s as part of the Park Mansions development. It is the only public house in Knightsbridge which originated as a village inn.

Statue of Lord Strathnairn (removed)

As long ago as 1836 the intersection of the Kensington and Brompton roads had been identified as an eligible spot for a public monument,[29] but it was not until 1895 that one was erected, and then the site was a substitute for the more prestigious one originally intended.

Hugh Rose, Field Marshal Lord Strathnairn, one of the chief suppressors of the Indian Mutiny, died in 1885 at the age of 84, and a few years later steps were taken to provide a public memorial. There was some suggestion that this should take the form of funding for some useful purpose connected with the Army, and, chairing a meeting to inaugurate the project in May 1890, the Duke of Cambridge remarked that statues were 'very expensive and not always good'. However, this idea was set aside. During that summer some £2,700 was raised in subscriptions, including 50 guineas from the Prince of Wales, and later in the year the sculptor E. Onslow Ford was commissioned to design an equestrian statue. It was hoped this would stand in Whitehall between the Horse Guards and the Admiralty. Official sanction was not forthcoming, and in due course the memorial committee settled for the Brompton Road corner site offered by Westminster Vestry.[30]

Ford's statue, showing Strathnairn in uniform with the helmet prescribed for Indian service, was unveiled by the Duke of Grafton on 19 June 1895 (Plates 1, 37a, 38a). It was cast by G. Broad & Son, using bronze from guns taken in 1858 by the Central India Field Force (under Strathnairn's command) and presented by the Indian Government. The Portland-stone pedestal bore panels with the names of the Field Marshal's principal battles. Much gilding was used on both horse and rider, which, in the words of the *Builder*, 'though it may be objected to as too realistic, certainly gives a better decorative effect, in London atmosphere, than a bronze statue in its ordinary state'.[31]

Taken down in 1931, during work on a new subway for Knightsbridge underground station, the monument languished in storage until 1964, when Westminster Council decided to give it away on condition of reasonable public access. The successful bidder was Vernon F. Northcott, on whose estate at Foley Manor in Liphook, Hampshire, it still stands.[32]

Park Mansions

The triangle east of Knightsbridge Green is largely occupied by Park Mansions, a block of flats and shops erected in 1897–1902. The site was assembled in 1887–90 by Frederick Yeats Edwards of Hampstead and Robert Clarke Edwards, an architect then in practice in Norfolk Street, Strand – presumably with an eye to complete redevelopment. Some of the old buildings on the corner of Brompton Road and Knightsbridge were pulled down at this time. Whatever plans the Edwardses had came to nothing, and the property – 'long disfigured by unsightly hoardings and sheds of corrugated iron' – was acquired in 1897–8 by Abram or Abraham Kellett, a contractor of Castle Bar, Ealing and Old Oak Wharf, Willesden.[33]

Kellett, his architect G. D. Martin, and their solicitor were originally to have undertaken the development through a specially formed company, backed by the light-opera impresario and property developer Richard D'Oyly Carte. However, this scheme seems to have fallen through, possibly because of Carte's illness early in 1897, and at least part of the project was financed by a loan to Kellett from the Bradford Commercial Joint Stock Bank, whose successor, the Knightsbridge and Bradford Estate Company Ltd, subsequently owned Park Mansions until its dissolution in the 1930s.[34]

The site was developed in two phases: the eastern corner in 1897–8, and the western part in 1900–2. The Paxton's Head public house was rebuilt as part of the western section. Between the two parts was built the Park Mansions Arcade, with a central octagon under a glazed cupola. The arcade was originally to have had an entrance on Knightsbridge Green, as well as on Knightsbridge and Brompton Road, but this was abandoned, along with a proposed third section on the site of All Saints' School – a plan to which the toothing of the brickwork on the south-west corner of the mansions still testifies. The old school building, however, was subsequently incorporated into the Park Mansions premises.[35]

The completed Park Mansions provided space for nearly forty shops, with a mezzanine for showrooms and basement stores. Well over a hundred flats of one and two bedrooms, most with an additional servant's room, were arranged on the six upper floors (fig. 23). The smaller suites, without kitchens, were intended for bachelors and clubmen, for whom a service room and a large kitchen 'fitted with every requisite' were situated on the top floor.[36] Among the first residents were numerous military men, a sprinkling of peers and gentlemen, and many 'Misses'. The eighteen apartments at Nos 159 and 161 Knightsbridge (on

FIRST FLOOR

The Paxton's Head

DR B DR LR B DR DR B DR K K B SB DR K
B B B B SB K LR B SB DR B LR
DR L L K B DR L B SB B K DR DR
DR SB SB SB SB B DR SB K B
B DR DR B K B DR
DR B SB K DR
SB K B B B DR B
B DR K DR B
DR SB K B SB B
LR

KNIGHTSBRIDGE

1-B Flat PH 2-B Flat 2-B Flat 1-B Flat
1-B Flat 1-B Flat 2-B Flat 2-B Flat
1-B Flat 2-B Flat 2-B Flat
1-B Flat 1-B Flat 1-B 2-B Flat
1-B Flat Flat 1-B Flat
1-B Flat 2-B Flat
1-B Flat 2-B Flat 2-B Flat
2-B Flat

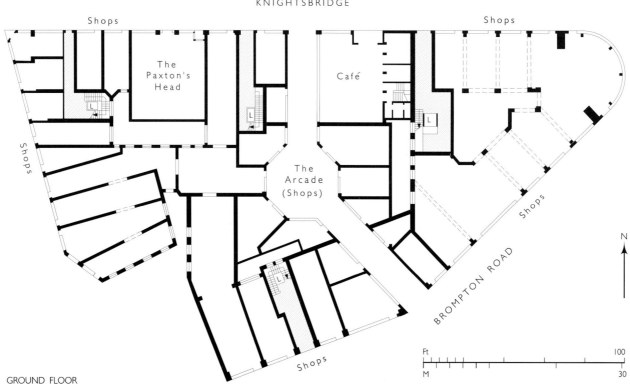

Shops   Shops

The
Paxton's
Head   Café

L   L   L

Shops

The
Arcade
(Shops)

L

BROMPTON ROAD Shops

N

Shops

Ft   100
M   30

GROUND FLOOR

the corner of Knightsbridge Green) were known as 'Hyde Park Chambers': in the 1960s these were converted into the Knightsbridge Green Hotel.

G. D. Martin dealt pragmatically with the architectural and commercial requirements of the development, producing a conventionally ornamental edifice, faced in red-brick and Bath stone, with red granite pilasters, but with an abundance of glass in the ground-floor shopfronts (Plates 36b, 37a). This necessary concession to the needs of the retail trade inevitably affronted the purists, among them a correspondent to the *Pall Mall Gazette*, Percy A. Johnson:

Where there should be stone, there is glass; where strength is expected, there is weakness, where lightness, an overpowering weight . . . The feeling of insecurity is paramount; it is as if a mammoth were seen to be reposing on cucumber-frames.[37]

The first commercial tenant was the clothing firm of Gardiner & Company Ltd, which took the prime corner site at Nos 2–8 Brompton Road for its Scotch House shop, which has given the informal name Scotch Corner to the junction of Knightsbridge and Brompton Road. Among the other early business occupants were East India merchants Cursetji & Cooverji, a hat manufacturer, an art dealer, and several automobile companies. The Scotch House was modernized in 1958 with a front in the Festival of Britain style, by Charles Baker & Company Ltd of Edmonton.[38]

Park Mansions Arcade (latterly Knight's Arcade) was closed in the early 1990s. The octagon and southern arm have now been incorporated into the Jaeger shop on Brompton Road; the northern portion has been subsumed into the Isola restaurant on Knightsbridge.

Former Normandie Hotel, Nos 163–169 Knightsbridge

The Normandie was built as the Knightsbridge Palace Hotel in 1910–11 for the Land and Leasehold Securities Company Ltd, and leased to the West End Hotel Syndicate Ltd, which ran several London hotels. The contractors were E. G. and F. C. Simpson of Chandos Street, trading as the General Building Company.[39]

The hotel was designed by the Viennese-born architect Paul Hoffmann, a specialist in large office and apartment blocks, and, appropriately for Knightsbridge with its equestrian traditions, a well-known owner of hackney and show horses.[40] According to an early report, the building was to have been faced in 'solid English granite', but in the event red brick with stone dressings was used. The style has some flavour of Edwardian Baroque (Plate 50d). Suites of rooms for guests were arranged around a central core containing a lift and stairs, with bay-windowed sitting-rooms overlooking Knightsbridge. The principal public

rooms (Plate 51) were fairly richly decorated: a large dining-room with a rather overbearing Jacobethan ceiling, a colonial-looking ground-floor lounge, and in the basement a 'charming' ballroom for up to 300 dancers, decorated in rose-pink and white. Private rooms, though 'furnished in excellent style', were unpretentious.[41]

In 1937 the Knightsbridge Hotel ('Palace' having been dropped by 1918) was renamed the Normandie. It closed *c*.1977 and the upper floors were then converted to apartments for 'holiday' lets. Since 1987 the building has been awaiting redevelopment.[42]

Humphreys' Hall and Albert Gate Mansions (demolished)

Humphreys' Hall and Albert Gate Mansions occupied the small detached eastern portion of the Trevor estate, the mansions later expanding into the freeholds on either side. The ground was previously occupied by old houses and shops along the High Road, including the King's Head public house at No. 24, and by Dungannon Cottage (named after one of the Trevor family titles), which stood in a large garden at the rear of the High Road buildings (fig. 22).

Humphreys' Hall became well known to the late-Victorian public as the venue for a series of exhibitions: the longest-running and most remarkable of these was the Japanese Native Village of 1885–7 (see below); others included a War Exhibition, the Food Exhibition of 1882, and the Medical and Pharmaceutical and Bread Reform Exhibitions of 1884.[43] The original building, previously used for roller-skating, and greatly enlarged before the opening of the Japanese exhibition, was destroyed in May 1885 when the village caught fire. Both hall and village were subsequently rebuilt. After the final closure of the Japanese Village, the new Humphreys' Hall was extensively reconstructed as Prince's Racquets and Tennis Club. Albert Gate Mansions were built along the High Road frontage when the original hall was enlarged in the early 1880s; they too were later extended.

The roller-skating rink which became the first Humphreys' Hall probably originated with premises at Dungannon Cottage used for manufacturing bicycles and sports equipment. Thomas Sparrow, bicycle maker and agent for the Coventry Machinists Company Ltd, and the firm of Sparrow & Spencer, manufacturers of gymnastic apparatus and government contractors for military gymnasia, occupied these premises, known as No. 21A High Road, for several years in the early and mid-1870s (at which time they also had a shop in Piccadilly). The skating rink, known as Dungannon Rink or Dungannon Cottage Skating Rink, was set up about 1876, during a brief mania for the sport.[44]

Like many others, this rink had fallen out of use by 1880, when it was refitted, by Edward Witts, architect, for the

Fig. 23 (opposite). Park Mansions, ground- and first-floor plans as originally designed by G. D. Martin, *c*.1897, and diagram showing arrangement of flats. The design was modified before construction, particularly by the addition of prominent corner bay windows on the first floor

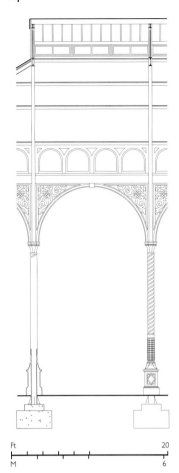

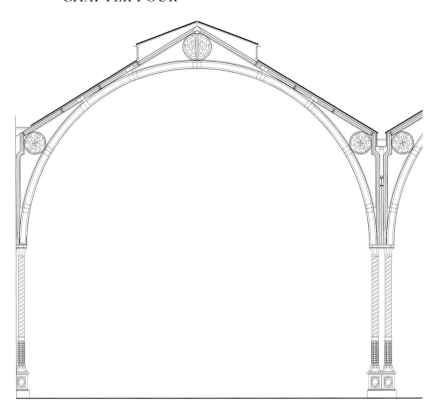

Fig. 24. Humphreys' Hall and adjoining premises belonging to
J. C. Humphreys. Plan in early 1886, and part sections through
Humphreys' Hall. *All demolished*

United Service Provision Market Ltd. This concern, soon
defunct, supplied cut-price food and general produce to its
shareholders and their friends.[45] In 1882 Dungannon Hall,
as the premises had become known, was taken over by
James Charlton Humphreys, the iron-buildings manufacturer, who adapted or rebuilt it for public use. Samples of
his buildings were displayed on the ground adjoining.[46]

Humphreys' building was said to be 'externally, a handsome one', and internally 'very open, light, and exceedingly well ventilated', with a single-span arched roof, a raised
skylight and a white marble floor. There was a gallery at
either end. One of the first functions held there, in October
1882, was a banquet given by prominent local residents for
the 1st Life Guards, recently returned from Egypt.[47]

The success of the hall encouraged Humphreys to build
a second hall, of similar construction, alongside the old in
1883–4. The two halls were available separately or might be
thrown together for large functions. As a further part of the
development (carried out on long leases from Lord Trevor,
the freeholder), the buildings on the High Road north of
the hall were replaced with flats. These were at first known

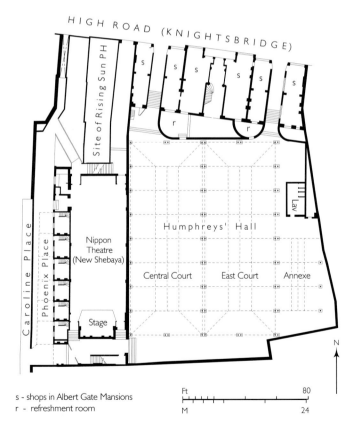

s - shops in Albert Gate Mansions
r - refreshment room

as Humphreys' Mansions or Humphreys' Hall Mansions, but soon took the more up-market name of Albert Gate Mansions.[48]

Designed by Romaine-Walker and Tanner in a northern Renaissance style, the flats were faced in rubbed and gauged red brick, with balconies, oriels and ornamentation of Portland stone (Plate 37c). Their construction generally was carried out by Humphreys' own workforce; the carving was by J. W. Seale of Walworth. Humphreys Ltd had offices in the building, which included a row of shops (fig. 24). On the first, second and third floors were high-class flats, offered at rentals of between £100 and £300 per annum, while the top floor (originally to have included a reception room for residents or societies) was divided into artists' studios, with large north-facing windows at the front and 'chambers' behind. Directories do not suggest that these studios found favour with artists. There was extensive provision for kitchens in the basement and an 'elaborately decorated' restaurant above, with a service lift to the other floors.[49]

Following the disastrous fire in May 1885, Humphreys employed the architect Spencer Chadwick to design a new hall conforming to the Metropolitan Board of Works' stringent safety regulations. The new building, with an iron roof in three arched spans, was constructed by Humphreys Ltd between June and December 1885 (fig. 24).[50]

Further development was carried out by Humphreys over the next few years on the ground adjoining to the west, then occupied by the Rising Sun public house and Nos 27–28 High Road, the Sun Music Hall and Phoenix Place.[a] He had acquired all or most of this property just before the fire. A block of apartments was built here in 1886 fronting the High Road, with a large restaurant on the ground floor occupying the site of the Rising Sun (fig. 25). These new premises were briefly run as the Princes Gate Hotel by the caterers Bertram & Company, but the apartments were later let as private flats, becoming part of Albert Gate Mansions. The restaurant and the Sun Music Hall at the rear were subsequently used as public rooms under the collective name Knightsbridge Hall (see below).[52]

In 1898 Nos 19–21 High Road were rebuilt as an eastern extension of Albert Gate Mansions. The architect of the new building, which was in the same style as the original block, was C. W. Stephens.[53]

The Japanese Native Village

The last and most ambitious show at Humphreys' Hall was the Japanese Native Village of 1885–7, a working replica of a Japanese village centre, inhabited by Japanese craftsmen and artistes and their families – more than a hundred people in all. The promoter was Tannaker Buhicrosan of Lewisham, a Japan merchant with premises in Milton Street, Finsbury, and for some years the proprietor and

director of a travelling 'Japanese Troupe'. In December 1883 Buhicrosan set up The Japanese Native Village Exhibition and Trading Company Limited with a number of associates, including Cornelius B. Pare, a Japan and China merchant in the City, Ambrose Austin, a concert agent, and John Miles, a Wardour Street printer. As managing director of the new venture, Buhicrosan was to receive a salary of at least £1,000. Although to all appearances set up as a commercial venture, the Japanese Village exhibition opened, a little under a year later, under a banner of altruism. Buhicrosan, it was reported, proposed to give the profits to his wife, a Japanese who had converted to Christianity and wanted to organize a mission to improve the social position of women in her native country.[54]

The exhibition was formally opened on 10 January 1885 by Sir Rutherford Alcock, former consul-general in Japan and the author of *Art and Art Industries in Japan*.[55] Housed in the older part of Humphreys' Hall, and built by Japanese workmen from authentic Japanese materials, the village comprised a broad street of houses and shops set against backdrops of painted scenery. These were constructed of bamboo, wood, and paper, with shingled or thatched roofs. There were further rows of smaller shops along one side, a Buddhist temple at the end, and a Japanese garden (Plate 53a). Individual shops displayed all manner of manufactures – including pottery, carvings in wood and ivory, toys, fans, cabinets, chased and inlaid metalwork and *cloisonné*, lacquer-work, textiles and embroidery. One shop was devoted to music and musical instruments.

Everything possible was done to bring the village to life: those attending could watch craftsmen at work in their shops (although the 'wares' were not actually for sale), and take refreshment Japanese-style in traditional tea-houses, where tea was served from lacquer trays by attendants in kimonos (Plate 53b). Priests officiated at the temple daily. A further attraction was in the newer part of the hall, where displays of kendo and other martial arts were staged.

The exhibition took place at the height of a vogue for Japanese arts and crafts; indeed, by this time Western demand for Japanese goods had already led to vulgarization and over-production in some manufacturing fields. An early visitor was the designer Christopher Dresser, who had been to Japan and had done much to promote appreciation of Japanese design and craftsmanship. He was generally impressed by the replica village, especially the 'manner in which the industries are carried on in the little open shops, where the goods would be sold'.[56]

The opportunity offered to study Japanese culture at first hand was not missed by W. S. Gilbert, whose idea for *The Mikado* coincided with the exhibition's arrival. When the new opera opened at the Savoy Theatre in March 1885 the cast had been coached in authentic deportment and use of the fan by inhabitants of the village, as the programme duly acknowledged.[57]

[a] The tiny cottages in Phoenix Place (fig. 24) had been built in the early nineteenth century, at about the same time as those in Caroline Place on the adjoining Trevor estate.[51]

The exhibition was an immediate success, attracting 250,000 visitors in its first few months (and in time spawning 'many wretched imitations' – as Buhicrosan's publicity called them – in provincial towns).[58]

The Metropolitan Board of Works had been pressing for some time for structural improvements to the hall to bring it up to the required safety standards when, on 2 May 1885, the village burned down, destroying Humphreys' Hall, damaging Albert Gate Mansions, and killing a Japanese woodcarver. Buhicrosan at once announced his intention of reconstructing the village. It had earlier been arranged that the Japanese would take their exhibition to the continent, and, pending the rebuilding, they travelled to Berlin, setting up new quarters at the Exhibition Park.[59]

By the end of the year Humphreys' Hall had been rebuilt and a new Japanese village erected, taking up the entire space. It re-opened on 2 December. In addition to several streets of shops (where goods were now offered for sale), there were two temples and various free-standing idols, and a pool spanned by a rustic bridge. The Sun Music Hall adjoining, which had been acquired by J. C. Humphreys just before the fire, was re-opened in conjunction with the new village as the Nippon Theatre or New Shebaya[b] concert hall, promising 'astounding entertainments' by Japanese artistes.[60]

Buhicrosan's company ran into financial difficulties, however, and in February 1887 went into liquidation. The exhibition was taken over by a new company with which he seems not to have been directly involved. The Nippon Theatre was turned over in part to conventional music-hall and concert entertainers, including the comic singer Charles Coborn (writer and performer of 'Two Lovely Black Eyes') and George Bohee, 'banjoist to their Royal Highnesses the Prince and Princess of Wales'. The band of the Victoria Rifles and the Italian Opera Company also performed there. It was reported in May that the Japanese Village was as popular as when it first opened, but it closed soon afterwards, on 25 June.[61]

Prince's Racquets and Tennis Club (demolished)

In 1888–9 Humphreys' Hall was converted into a clubhouse and sports centre for Prince's, one of the most august and exclusive of English sporting clubs, which had been forced to relinquish its old grounds on the Cadogan estate in Chelsea for redevelopment. A long lease of the hall was negotiated with J. C. Humphreys, and the new club premises, designed by the architect Edward Herbert Bourchier and constructed by Peto Brothers, was formally opened by its most celebrated member, the Prince of Wales, on 18 May 1889.[62]

Although patronized by the prince, the club in fact took its name from the brothers George and James Prince, who seem to have founded it at their wine and cigar shop in Regent Street about 1853. Whatever its original character,

Prince's was established within a few years as a sports club with spacious premises including a cricket pitch and tennis and racquets courts off Hans Place; the site is now largely covered by Lennox Gardens, Clabon Mews and part of Cadogan Square. The club was incorporated in 1864 as Prince's Racquets & Tennis Club Company Ltd by George, James and Theodore Prince and others, among them (Sir) William Hart-Dyke, a distinguished racquets player, later president of the club. In time, the range of the club's facilities was expanded to include squash racquets, lawn tennis and ice-skating. Prince's became famous not only for sports but for its snobbish exclusivity.[63]

By the mid-1880s Prince's Club was occupying new or greatly reduced premises in Pont Street. One of the founders, George Prince, was acting as secretary. The prime mover in the relocation to Knightsbridge, however, was Robert Hippisley Cox of the Coldstream Guards, surgeon, the vice-chairman of the club company, which was reconstituted in April 1888.[64]

Bourchier's adaptation of Humphreys' Hall involved cutting away many of the stanchions carrying the three arched roofs, and sub-dividing the space along new lines (Plate 53c). The principal sports facilities, designed in consultation with the tennis champion Charles Saunders, comprised two courts for racquets and one for real tennis (including the traditional 'dedans' for viewing), with a high-level gallery arranged so as to overlook play in all three.

In addition, there were grand club-rooms, comparable to those at the largest of the West End clubhouses. The entrance from Knightsbridge gave on to the Lounge, a high pillared hall with a barrel-vaulted roof. Adjoining this was the 45ft-square Oak Room, occupying the full width of one of the two main bays of the original structure of the building. This was a lofty saloon in the Elizabethan style, panelled and tapestry-hung, with a music-gallery at one end. Its coffered ceiling was designed by a member of the club, George Donaldson, who was responsible for overseeing the decoration and furnishing throughout the building, some of which was carried out by Campbell, Smith & Company.

Not the least impressive part of the clubhouse was the accommodation for bathing. As well as a range of hot and cold water baths, sitz and needle baths and a Russian vapour bath, there was a Turkish bath, 'without doubt the most elegant in London', decorated in the Pompeian style with painting and mosaic work executed by 'Signor Marolda and a staff of Italian artists', and a Roman-style plunge bath, 5ft 2ins deep throughout, lined in blue glass mosaic. Finally, there was a bath for the private use of the Prince of Wales, made entirely of marble. The contractor for the baths and other plumbing and sanitary fittings was John Smeaton of Great Queen Street (grandson of the civil engineer John Smeaton, of Eddystone Lighthouse fame).

In 1889–90 a second tennis court and a gymnasium were built, to Bourchier's designs, on the site of cottages in

---

[b] Seemingly a conflation of the Japanese *shibai jaya*, a theatre tea-house.

Phoenix Place, Caroline Place and Petwin Place, separated from the main club premises by the Sun Music Hall (figs 22, 28; Plate 57b). Later Prince's Club rented the basement of Knightsbridge Hall, as the Sun Music Hall became, for a bowling alley.[65]

Prince's Club remained in existence until just before the Second World War, during which the clubhouse was requisitioned by the War Department as headquarters for the Army Post Office. It continued in use by the army until about 1952, and was subsequently pulled down for the construction of Mercury House.[66]

The Rising Sun, Sun Music Hall and Knightsbridge Hall (all demolished)

The Rising Sun tavern at No. 26 High Road was opened about 1830 in an old red-brick house of 'neat appearance', containing 'much carved work' and 'a plain, old-fashioned staircase'. It was probably built in the seventeenth century – an indistinct inscription on the coping was variously interpreted as 16— or 1611: in recent years it had been occupied by Major Robert Eyre, a veteran of the American War of Independence and the founder, in 1803, of the Knightsbridge Volunteers.[67]

In 1851 the Rising Sun was licensed for music and dancing, and a concert room was erected at the rear of the premises. This 'Sun Music Hall' was rebuilt in 1864–6 to designs by the architects Finch Hill & Paraire. Ranking 'with the first class establishments of the metropolis', the new Sun Music Hall was 100ft long and 35ft wide with a cantilevered gallery along three sides, and ornamented with wall panels of allegorical reliefs and a decorative balcony front of *carton pierre*. It was at the Sun that George Leybourne first performed 'Champagne Charlie', in 1867, and G. H. Macdermott the great hit of 1878, 'By Jingo'.[68]

Extensive improvements to bring the hall up to fire-safety standards were ordered by the Metropolitan Board of Works in 1884, but before they were carried out the premises were sold, in April 1885, to J. C. Humphreys, owner of Humphreys' Hall adjoining, which was destroyed a few days later, when the Japanese Village exhibition there caught fire.[69]

Humphreys refitted the Sun Music Hall as a concert room for 'musical entertainments of a high class'. By January 1886 the old Rising Sun had been demolished, to be replaced later in the year by a restaurant or coffee-room with apartments above – effectively a western extension to Albert Gate Mansions with which it was later united. This work seems to have been carried out by Humphreys' architect for the rebuilding of Humphreys' Hall, Spencer Chadwick, in conjunction with the theatre and restaurant architect Thomas Verity. The new apartments, together with the restaurant, were run for a time as the Princes or Princes Gate Hotel.[70]

With the Japanese Village exhibition recreated in the new Humphreys' Hall, the refurbished Sun Music Hall became the Nippon Theatre, or New Shebaya concert hall, used for Japanese as well as conventional Western-style musical entertainments.

Following the closure of the village in 1887 the theatre enjoyed a brief renaissance under its old name the Sun Music Hall. On Boxing Night 1888 the Great Vance, clad in judicial robes and wig, sang his last song, 'Are You Guilty?', before collapsing in the wings with a fatal heart attack.[71] Figure 25 shows the Sun Music Hall in its latter days, when the premises were apparently associated with the restaurant and buffet on the ground floor of the Princes Gate Hotel.

The Sun, together with the former restaurant and buffet, was subsequently hired out for receptions and meetings as Knightsbridge Hall, Humphreys having given an undertaking to the London County Council that it would never again be used as a music-hall.[72] Knightsbridge Hall was later taken over by the John Griffiths Cycle Corporation Ltd as a cycle-riding school and showroom, which it

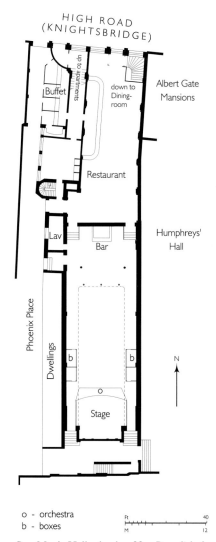

o - orchestra
b - boxes

Fig. 25. Sun Music Hall, plan in 1889. *Demolished*

remained for some years. In 1905 a plan to use the building as a restaurant was abandoned when Humphreys was refused a renewal of the licence, which he had held for ten years without making use of it.[73]

An extension to Knightsbridge Hall, on the sites of Nos 225–229 Knightsbridge (the former Nos 1–3 Trevor Terrace), was erected in 1918 by J. C. Humphreys' firm, Humphreys Ltd. About 1921 the enlarged premises, known as the Knightsbridge Halls, were taken by the decorators and furnishers Robersons Ltd and fitted out as galleries for displaying panelled interiors salvaged from historic houses.[74]

By the late 1930s the Knightsbridge Halls were used for motor-trading. They were demolished after the Second World War for the building of Mercury House.

Knightsbridge Green

The encroachment of building over the village green at Knightsbridge (part of the manorial ground belonging to Westminster Abbey) took place over a long period, reaching approximately its present-day extent by the 1850s. Some of the old rural character of the green survived into the early nineteenth century, when a cattle-market was still held and there was even a maypole. An inn, then called the Sun, and later the Marquis of Granby, had been built on part of the green by the seventeenth century. The open land was much diminished in the 1720s by the building of Middle Row. This was later renamed Middle Row North when houses fronting the Brompton road were built over the gardens, forming Middle Row South.[75]

King's Row was built in 1784–5 over a garden behind the Sun, reducing the open space to little more than a broad tree-lined strip running north to the Kensington road.[76] Plans put forward in 1836 for a railway terminus and covered market at Knightsbridge Green having come to nothing,[c] a piece of this strip was taken for the building of parochial schools in 1839.

By 1851 the northern part of Knightsbridge Green had been further reduced, by the erection of various wooden sheds along the east side, to the narrow footway that exists today (Plate 50c). In that year Chrisostome Mouflet, a victualler, replaced the sheds with a row of lean-to shops, at the same time building a short-lived 'Crystal Palace Hotel' adjoining, just north of All Saints' School. An attempt by the vestry to widen the passageway in 1899 failed, owing to the difficulty of obtaining the ground on either side.[77]

On the west side of the Green, towards the south end, formerly stood two substantial houses – the Moreaus' residence, later the site of Tattersalls, and Dr Buissière's house, converted into the Pakenham Tavern in the 1840s. Northwards of Dr Buissière's house, several houses were built in 1736-7 on the ground adjoining Martin Basil's old house (No. 13A High Road, otherwise Chatham House).[78]

The sites of these houses (a short row fronting the Green and Nos 12 and 13 High Road), together with that of Chatham House, are now occupied by the former Normandie Hotel.

The undeveloped southern remnant of the Green was let to successive occupiers of the old Moreau residence, and in 1857 was acquired with it – on lease – by Tattersalls. Apparently treeless, the small plot was then surrounded by a wall and iron railings. Plans by Westminster Vestry to plant the 'vacant' ground with trees in 1879 met with an angry response from local traders and cabmen, who saw the improvement as likely to interfere with their business and filled in the holes dug in preparation. However, by 1908 trees had been planted on the enclosure, which was then being looked after by Tattersalls. After the Second World War Tattersalls undertook a restoration of the enclosure, creating a 'Temple Garden' with a bronze figure. Intended as a contribution to the 1951 Festival of Britain, this project was carried out by Ralph Hancock & Son, landscape architects of Park Mansions Arcade, under the direction of Tattersalls' architects, Stone, Toms & Partners.[79]

Today the 'Green', as popularly understood – the triangular remnant of open space off Brompton Road – is a nondescript traffic island, occupied by a couple of plane trees and a forlorn drinking fountain. There is a long tradition that this piece of ground was used for a plague pit. What is known is that from 1640 a small strip immediately to the north-east (now occupied by the shops of Nos 16–22 Brompton Road) belonged to the Knightsbridge lazarhouse property – also part of the Westminster Abbey estate – on the north side of Knightsbridge. It is possible that this strip, which in about 1784 was taken to provide gardens for the new houses of King's Row, was used to bury plague victims dying at the lazar-house. Human bones found in 1808 on the site of William Street were reinterred at the Green, as this was felt to be the most appropriate place.[80]

Grosvenor House (demolished)

The old mansion owned by Sir William Blake (see page 77) was occupied after his death in 1630 by, among others, Katherine, Viscountess Ranelagh, the sister of the scientist Robert Boyle. About 1740 it was rebuilt by Philip Moreau's son and heir, Captain James Philip Moreau. Eventually to become known as Grosvenor House, Moreau's new house was a substantial brick building, sashed and slated, squarish in plan with four rooms and two closets to each floor, 'all wainscotted and floored in the best Manner, and compleatly fitted up with marble and other Chimney Pieces'. There was a stable wing and outbuildings to the side and a large garden behind, laid out with gravel walks, 'Grass Plats, Seats, Espalier Hedges, Wilderness and Shrubbery, all enclosed with a Brick Wall, and well planted with Fruit

---

[c] See *Survey of London*, volume XLI, page 5 and Plate 10c.

Trees in great perfection'.[81] Salway included a view of the property in his 1811 survey of the Brompton road.[d]

The Moreaus seem not to have lived at the house after the death of Captain Moreau's widow in 1753, but it was purchased by a member of the family at the sale in 1759. It soon passed, however, via Admiral Thomas Broderick, to the Rev. Martin Madan. A Methodist, Madan was chaplain of the Lock Hospital in Grosvenor Place, and the author of a controversial book advocating polygamy, published in 1780. Later owners included Nathaniel Gosling, of the prominent banking family.[82]

In 1857 Grosvenor House and its grounds, together with a lease of the remaining part of the old Green in front of it, were bought by Tattersalls to replace their Hyde Park Corner auction yard. It had been pulled down by 1863.

Tattersalls (demolished)

For more than seventy years Knightsbridge Green was home to Tattersalls, the renowned horse and bloodstock auctioneers and one of the great institutions of the equine world. The firm moved here in 1865, to newly built premises on the west side where a stone archway, flanked by ancillary buildings, gave access to the large covered auction yard (Plates 48b, 49, fig. 26). Between 1865 and 1939 Tattersalls' yard was the scene of regular weekly, and in the season twice weekly, horse sales, events as much social as commercial where the bluest-blooded of aristocrats rubbed shoulders with the shabbiest of sporting 'characters'.

Since it was founded in the early 1770s by Richard Tattersall, a former groom and trainer to the Duke of Kingston, the firm had occupied pleasant, almost rural, premises behind St George's Hospital, close to Hyde Park Corner (see Plate 5c). But this was a leasehold property, on which the leases ran out in 1865, and the Marquess of Westminster, who owned the land, would not extend the firm's tenure because the site was required to complete the building of Grosvenor Crescent.[83] That Tattersalls would eventually have to move must have been apparent as far back as 1832, when the line of Grosvenor Crescent was settled. In 1853 it was reported that they were planning to open new premises on the site of the old Fishmongers' Almshouses at the Elephant and Castle; nothing came of that scheme and in 1857 Tattersalls bought Grosvenor House on Knightsbridge Green. Adjoining Fulham Bridge Yard, where horse-dealing had been a well-established tradition, and only a short distance from Hyde Park Corner and the beau monde, this was a freehold property, and at two acres at least as large as the old, if not slightly larger.[84]

Construction work at Knightsbridge Green began in the summer of 1863 and the new buildings were completed in the spring of 1865, the first sale there taking place on 10 April.[85] Planned by the two partners, Richard and Edmund Tattersall, great-grandsons of the founder, and erected under their general supervision, the new establishment was designed by the architect Charles Freeman, who according to his obituary was 'probably best known as surveyor to the Sun Fire Assurance Company'.[86] He does not appear to have had any special expertise in designing buildings for equine purposes.[e] The contractors were Holland & Hannen.

Architectural display, of a fairly modest order, was concentrated on the street front. Here, a stone archway with iron gates, flanked by lower entrances for pedestrians, formed the centrepiece, framed by a matching pair of buildings in yellow-grey brick with stone dressings and balustrade which screened the back part of the premises from public view (Plates 48b, 49c). The *Sporting Review* was unimpressed: 'plain and unpretending enough' it might have been the front of 'a bazaar or some well-conducted manufactory'.[88]

The building to the south of the gateway was a subscription room for off-course betting, a long-standing custom at Tattersalls which the promoters of the 1853 Betting Act had been unwilling to disturb for fear of offending its aristocratic patrons.[89] Apart from providing a room, Tattersalls themselves had no direct involvement with the betting, which was under the control of the Jockey Club. The entrance, on the north side, was railed off 'so as to preserve to its frequenters the utmost privacy'. Inside, the subscription room was decorated with green and gold panelled walls, and an encaustic-tile floor worthy of 'a Genoese palace, so rich and harmonious are its colours' (Plate 49b). Two glass domes boosted the natural lighting, while a third dome contained a large gas 'sunburner'. At the west end folding doors, flanked by two stone lions from the old premises, opened on to a paved courtyard which was used for outside betting and had a telegraph-office adjoining.[90]

The corresponding building to the north comprised the manager's house, offices, a private room for the partners, and, on the upper floor, accommodation for the 'Rhadamanthuses of the Jockey Club'.[91]

Between the offices and the subscription room a granite roadway led to the auction yard, the heart of the whole complex. Enclosed within a large but plain two-storey building, this was a rectangular galleried court, 60ft by 108ft, covered by a soaring glass roof with deeply coved sides (Plate 49a, fig. 26). The roof was carried on iron girders and glazed with panes of Hartley's patent glass, which could be opened for ventilation. A fully covered yard was an innovation for Tattersalls, perhaps suggested by the iron-and-glass roofed yard at Aldridge's, a rival establishment in St Martin's Lane, rebuilt in the early 1840s.[92]

In the middle stood the drinking-fountain known as the Fox, which had been the centrepiece of the old yard.

---

[d] Reproduced in *Survey of London*, volume XLI, Plate 4.

[e] The designing of the new premises might have been kept wholly within the Tattersall family but for the premature death in 1849 of Richard's younger brother, George, a professional architect. In the 1840s George designed stables for the firm's stud-farm in Willesden and a new subscription room at Hyde Park Corner.[87]

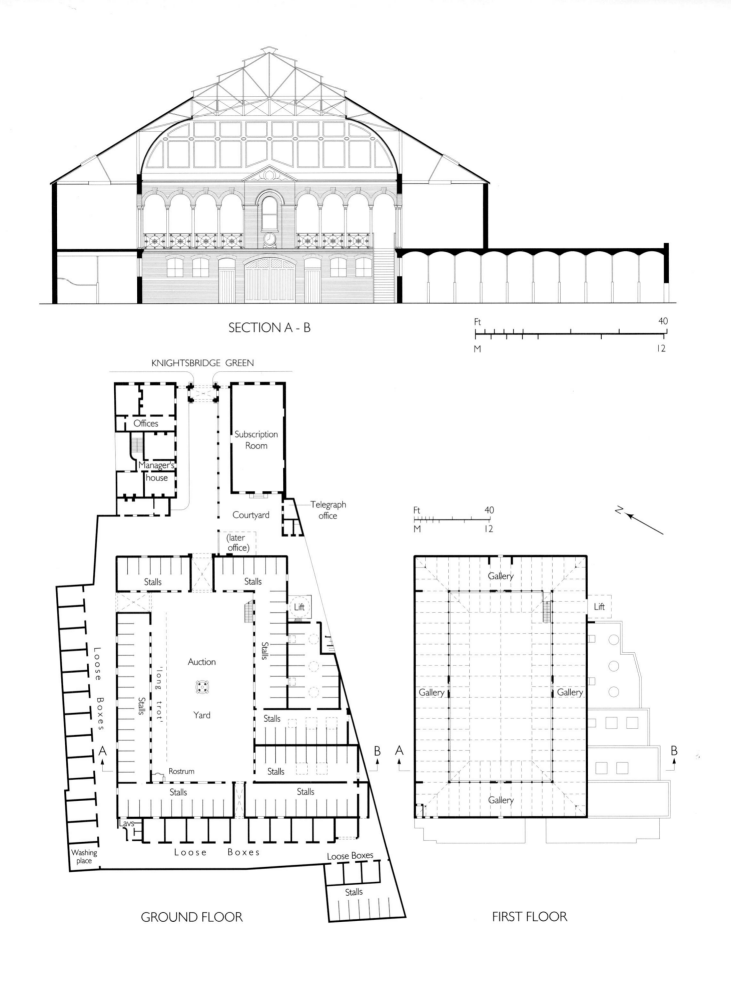

SECTION A - B

Ft   40
M   12

KNIGHTSBRIDGE GREEN

Offices

Manager's
house

Subscription
Room

Courtyard

Telegraph
office

(later
office)

Stalls   Stalls

Lift

Stalls

Loose Boxes

Stalls

Auction

'long trot'

Yard

Stalls

Rostrum

Stalls

Stalls   Stalls

Lavs

Washing
place

Loose   Boxes

Loose Boxes

Stalls

GROUND FLOOR

Ft   40
M   12

Gallery

Gallery   Gallery

Lift

Gallery

FIRST FLOOR

A

B   A   B

Housed within a classical stone cupola, the fountain was surmounted by the figure of a fox with raised paw, and the cupola by a bust of George IV. The latter was said to symbolize the firm's royal connections, the fox its links with hunting, which went back to the early days of the firm when hunters and hounds rather than racehorses were the mainstay of the business.

The auctioneer conducted the horse sales from a wooden rostrum in the north-west corner facing down the ride or 'long trot', where the horses showed their paces. Carriage and harness sales were held in the arcaded gallery, another feature probably suggested by Aldridge's, where carriage sales took place in a gallery along one side of the auction yard. At Tattersalls the carriages were raised to first-floor level on a hydraulic lift supplied by Easton Amos & Sons. Popular with spectators, the gallery also provided a useful vantage point for buyers 'who do not care to encounter the busy throng below'.[93]

Surrounding the auction yard at ground-floor level, but only partially covered by the main roof, was the stabling – originally comprising 95 single stalls, and 20 loose-boxes for stallions and mares with foals. Spacious and properly drained, with water and gas laid on, the stalls were constructed of wood, iron and polished grey marble, and had patent asphalt floors. The generously proportioned loose-boxes, top lit by ventilating louvres, occupied separate single-storey ranges on the west wall of the auction yard and the northern boundary of the site.

While there was some regret at the passing of the old 'Corner', with its lawns and gravel walks, the press found much to praise at the Green. The new yard 'is as superior to that at Hyde Park Corner as the Agricultural Hall is as a show-place to the Baker-street Bazaar' was the verdict of the *Sporting Review*, one of the more critical journals. The *Illustrated Times* was pleased to find the ambience little changed: 'still the same dealing for horses on one side and laying of wagers on the other: the same motley assemblage of characters who have made the place belonging to the firm their head-quarters for the last century'.[94]

Auction sales continued to be held at Knightsbridge Green up to the outbreak of war in September 1939, when they were transferred to Newmarket, never to return. The Fox too was taken to Newmarket for safe-keeping, fortunately, for in August 1944 a flying-bomb severely damaged the auction yard and stabling. After the war Tattersalls sold the buildings to Oetzmann & Company, home furnishers, who occupied the old subscription room and the patched-up auction yard as furniture galleries; Tattersalls themselves retained their offices in the north wing. When, in 1955, the old premises were demolished for redevelopment, the entrance arch was saved and, like the Fox, re-erected at Newmarket.[95] The entire site is now covered by part of Caltex House, but the name of Tattersalls lingers on in an eponymous, though modern, public house on Knightsbridge Green.

Former All Saints' School, Knightsbridge Green

In 1839 a piece of the Green was given by the Dean and Chapter of Westminster Abbey to the Rector and Church-wardens of St Margaret's, Westminster, as the site for parochial schools. Designed by the Knightsbridge architect W. F. Pocock, these were erected in 1839–40 on what was effectively an island site, as traffic had to be free to pass round on all sides (fig. 22). Construction costs were largely met by an anonymous benefactress.[96]

By 1851 St Margaret's Schools had been transferred to the Ecclesiastical District of All Saints, Knightsbridge, becoming All Saints' National School. In 1875 it was rebuilt to designs by Robert Hesketh, an architect with considerable experience of educational buildings, who produced a simple red-brick 'three-decker' in the Board School manner (Plate 50a–b). The contractors were T. H. Adamson & Sons.[97]

All Saints' School closed in 1900 and narrowly escaped demolition for a proposed extension of Park Mansions. Eventually, in 1908–9, the site was purchased by the owners of Park Mansions, who converted the old building into shops, workshops, showrooms, and accommodation for servants employed in the flats, to which it was connected by a glazed iron staircase; the architects were T. H. & M. A. Watson. The building is now numbered 24–26 Brompton Road and 15–17 Knightsbridge Green.[98]

Raphael Street

Raphael Street was laid out on part of the former estate of the gunmaker Durs Egg by Lewis Raphael of Hendon, who bought it from Egg's heirs in 1838. A member of an affluent Roman Catholic family of Armenian descent, Raphael was a dairy farmer with a mansion and a splendid estate at Bush Hill Park, Edmonton.

In November 1843 Raphael entered into a building agreement with Edward Nangle, builder (later 'surveyor'). Nangle laid out a new road, called Raphael Street, running from Lancelot Place eastward to Knightsbridge Green, where it curved southwards to avoid Egg's former house (fig. 22).[99]

Nangle's building operations began in 1844, with the conversion and enlargement of the old house as the Pakenham Tavern, and the erection of terrace-houses along the north side of the new road. The Pakenham, which took the address of Knightsbridge Green not Raphael Street, was perhaps named as a compliment to the Duke of Wellington, whose wife was a Pakenham. Nangle himself became its first landlord, in 1848, when at his direction the pub was leased to the brewers Elliot & Watney of Pimlico. (This was the only house on the estate to be leased to Nangle or his nominees.)

With the exception of two houses, Nos 10 and 11, the

Fig. 26 (opposite). Tattersalls, plans and section. Charles Freeman, architect, 1863–5. *Demolished*

north side of Raphael Street was completed by 1847 and mostly occupied over the next two or three years. The sites of Nos 10 and 11, somewhat larger than the rest, were probably left at the time with a view to a future roadway as part of development on the Rose and Crown or the neighbouring Dungannon Cottage properties.[100]

On the south side of the street and the corner of Lancelot Place, Nangle got into difficulties, probably as a consequence of the widespread depression at that time, and development was halted, leaving six houses still only partly built. Several years later, in March 1849, Nangle gave notice that he was resuming work on two, but does not appear to have completed them: at the time he was being pursued in court for debt.[101]

Further activity in Raphael Street took place in 1852–3 with the erection of a row of five shops (which became Nos 33–37) on the shallow plots opposite the Pakenham. They were the work of a Kensington builder, Francis J. Attfield. Another builder, George Day of New Kent Road, was responsible for the remainder of the south side of the street, built up in 1854–5, and Nos 10 and 11 on the north side, built in 1854. Both Attfield and Day were presumably working under contract not as speculators, for in August 1853 all their houses and Nangle's (apart from the Pakenham), together with the Rose and Crown property, were leased directly by Raphael's heirs to a West End solicitor, Frederick William Dolman, to whom Nangle had mortgaged his interest in the estate in 1847.[102]

Nangle's houses were of three storeys over half-basements, two windows wide, with stuccoed ground-floor fronts and iron balconettes at the first-floor windows (Plate 52a). Day's houses, on shorter plots, were built close to the pavement edge, with gratings to light the basements or cellars. They had stuccoed window surrounds and round-arched entrances. The Pakenham Tavern was large and showy; its curved and fully stuccoed façade was echoed across the road by Attfield's shops (Plate 52b–c).

On the corner of Lancelot Place, Nos 19 and 20 were later knocked together to form the Royal Oak public house.

From the beginning the houses of Raphael Street were in multi-occupancy, the tenants including many grooms and coachmen, as well as soldiers, clerks and domestic servants.[103] By the early 1860s the respectability of the street was threatened by the popularity of several singing and dancing venues near by, including the Pakenham Tavern, where 'Free and Easy' musical evenings were prone to lead to disturbances and fights. Householders complained that respectable early rising workpeople were giving up their lodgings because of the noise.[104]

Arnold Bennett lodged in Raphael Street around 1890, in his early days in London, as did the hero of his first novel, *A Man From the North* (1898).

In the twentieth century, if not earlier, many of the houses were overcrowded, dilapidated and insanitary, attracting the attention of Westminster City Council.[105] Boarding- or lodging-houses continued to dominate. 'Very handy for poor but respectable gentlemen like myself,' says a charac-

ter, not without irony, in a novel of 1926, 'Single ladies not taken without luggage and references. Very good address for out-of-work actors or lady typists . . . Almost as good as Rutland Gate, if you don't happen to have seen the cards in the windows'.[106] But many of the 'lodging-houses' were occupied by prostitutes and prosecutions for brothel-keeping in Raphael Street were frequent. The seediness of the area was usually blamed on its proximity to the barracks.

The Pakenham and the Raphael Street houses survived the Second World War largely intact, and were pulled down about 1956–7 for office development.

Post-War Redevelopment

Between 1955 and 1960 office-building greatly altered the appearance of the Knightsbridge Green area (fig. 27). The opportunity was taken to carry out some road-widening at this time, both in Knightsbridge and Brompton Road, but no important changes were made to the rather congested road pattern, and the overall effect of the redevelopment fell far short of complete transformation. In the late 1950s, however, plans for Knightsbridge Green were put forward which, had they been implemented, would have turned the road intersection at Scotch Corner into a roundabout comparable to those at Marble Arch and Hyde Park Corner, overlooked by some of the biggest tower-blocks in central London. The Knightsbridge Green development, it was confidently asserted in the early 1960s, reached back 'over the town planning chaos of recent years to recapture London's diverse and vital character'.[107] The utopian vision lingered until 1965, when it faded away in the light of changed economic conditions.

The scheme, which effectively originated with the London County Council (LCC), began to take shape during the planning of Land Securities' Bowater House a few years earlier (see page 59).[108] It was intimated then that the new entrance to Hyde Park under Bowater House at Edinburgh Gate (replacing that at Albert Gate) would be the first stage in a long-term plan to improve traffic circulation, the intended centrepiece being the roundabout at Scotch Corner. Subsequently the LCC Town Planning Committee liaised closely with the owner of almost all the ground likely to be affected by such a scheme, Capital and Counties Property Ltd, to produce a development plan satisfactory from road-traffic, commercial, and 'civic' angles.

Early plans drawn up by Capital and Counties' architects Guy Morgan & Partners featured blocks of 116ft and 126ft, but the Committee felt that there was a strong case for a much higher building on civic grounds. The LCC, under its Architect Hubert Bennett and Senior Planning Officer Leslie W. Lane, accordingly produced a modified scheme. This proposed a colossal slab-block on a podium (320ft high in all) between Sloane Street and Brompton Road, facing Bowater House across the roundabout, where a smaller slab-block was to be sited. By 1962 the great roundabout, which was to take in the entire Park Mansions

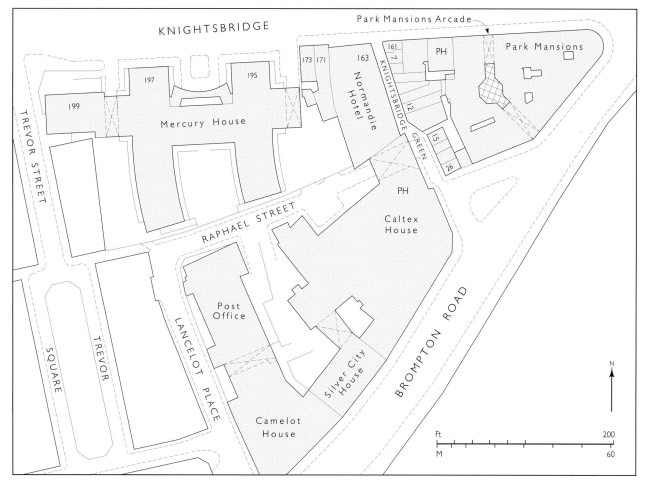

Fig. 27. Knightsbridge Green area in 1991

site, had been freed from buildings altogether, taking on the form of a sunken 'piazza'. Instead of the large slab-block there were to be three tower-blocks containing flats, offices, and a hotel, mounted over a shopping precinct connected by escalators to the Underground and more shops at basement level. The scale of the cluster of towers – the tallest more than 400ft high – was such as to have dwarfed Bowater House. At the new Knightsbridge Barracks, then in the planning stage, Sir Basil Spence's intended point-block was designed to form a visually appealing group with this civilian trio.

In July 1965, however, Capital and Counties announced that their project was unlikely to be carried out, citing a number of reasons including the increased cost of building, technical difficulties to do with the relocation of Basil Street fire-station as part of the development, and the problem posed by protected residential tenancies under the forthcoming 1965 Rent Act. Without the associated property development, it was out of the question for the LCC to finance the road improvements and the entire project fell by the wayside.

No special architectural or 'townscape' interest attaches to any of the post-war blocks already erected hereabouts when the Knightsbridge Green scheme was formulated. **Caltex House** (No. 1 Knightsbridge Green and Nos 44–58 Brompton Road), was designed by Stone, Toms & Partners for Edger Investments Limited (a subsidiary of the Alliance Assurance Company), and built in 1955–7 by Sir Robert McAlpine & Sons Limited.[109] Occupying the site of Tattersalls' auction yard and adjoining properties, the building incorporates Tattersall's Tavern, a new public house replacing the Pakenham Tavern, the demolition of which allowed the eastern end of Raphael Street to be straightened.[110] As a further nod to the history of the site, Caltex House is adorned with a sculpture representing horses, *Triga*, by Franta Belsky, made of reinforced concrete coated with plastic metal.[111]

Adjoining Caltex House to the west is **Silver City House** (Nos 58A–64 Brompton Road), designed by Frank Scarlett for Beaufort Estates and constructed *c.*1956–8 by Harry Neal Limited.[112] Like Caltex House, this presents a low range of shops to Brompton Road, with taller offices behind. Also facing Brompton Road, and largely outside the old parish boundary of St Margaret's, **Camelot House** (Nos 66–76 Brompton Road) was designed by Gunton & Gunton and built in 1960 for the City of London Real Property Company Limited; it was originally called Lionel House. The development includes a Post Office and depot in Lancelot Place.[113]

To the north of Raphael Street, **Mercury House** (Nos 195–199 Knightsbridge) was built in 1956–9 to designs by Guy Morgan & Partners. It comprises three linked office buildings with views north over Hyde Park (Plate 18d). The inspiration for the development is said to have come from Sir Aynsley Bridgland, chairman both of Haleybridge Investment Trust Limited, the owners, and of the old Knightsbridge firm Humphreys Ltd, who built it.[114] In front of the buildings stands *The Seer*, a bronze figure-group of 1957 by Gilbert Ledward (Plate 18c).

Prudential Assurance, the owner of Caltex House, bought Mercury House in 1986 and subsequently obtained the adjoining properties between Knightsbridge Green and Lancelot Place, with the exceptions of Silver City House, the Normandie Hotel and the sites of Nos 171–3 Knightsbridge.[115] A scheme for the complete redevelopment of this enormous site was proposed but ultimately did not go ahead, and Mercury House has since been sold off separately. At the time of writing (2000), refurbishment rather than wholesale replacement of all this property seems in prospect.

CHAPTER V

Trevor Square Area

Of the small area described in this chapter (fig. 28), the greater part comprises the well-preserved Regency development consisting largely of Trevor Square and Trevor Street. Subtly different in character are the early-Victorian houses of Trevor Place. To the south is the former Harrods depot, an early-twentieth-century interloper belonging with the commercial hurly-burly of Brompton Road.

Among a number of demolished buildings, much the most important was Smith & Baber's floorcloth factory of the 1820s, a substantial part of which remained until the 1970s. The story of the housing development now occupying the factory site, on the west side of Trevor Place, is bound up with that of South Lodge and is described in Chapter VII.

Powis House and the Trevor Estate

Trevor Square and Trevor Street were laid out on the site of Powis House, a late-seventeenth-century mansion belonging to the Trevor family of Brynkinalt in Denbighshire, but named after an eighteenth-century occupant, the 1st Earl of Powis. Standing a little way back from the Kensington road, Powis House was probably built in the late 1680s. The first ratepayer, in 1690, was the 2nd Earl of Peterborough, the Royalist and Catholic convert (who spent most of 1690 in the Tower). His successor there in 1691 was William of Orange's right-hand man, William Bentinck, 1st Earl of Portland. By 1700 the house was in the occupation of another prominent Whig, Lord Haversham. The residence there of Sir John Trevor (1637/8–1717), the politically corrupt Master of the Rolls, began about 1704.[1] Sir John also had a house in Clement's Lane in the City, where he died, as well as his Welsh seat.

The architect W. W. Pocock (whose father oversaw the development of the Trevor estate) described Powis House as 'widespread rather than lofty', built of plain brick, with a central doorway and wings on either side containing offices. His description, based on a drawing he had once seen, tallies more or less with the rear view of the house depicted on Rhodes's map of 1766 (Plate 2a). Though plain externally, it was evidently well fitted up inside, for Pocock recalled his father showing him some marble chimney-pieces which he had had made from the 'handrails' of the main staircase.[2]

Powis House occupied part of what had once been the estate of Sir William Blake, who at his death in 1630 owned extensive property in and around Kensington and Chelsea.

For some years, Sir John Trevor appears to have rented the place from a descendant of Blake, Anna Maria Browne, but he later obtained the freehold – probably about 1715, when he acquired some adjacent property (including the future site of Smith & Baber's floorcloth factory) from Anna Maria and her second husband John Thurloe Brace.[3]

Prudentia Trevor, Sir John's spinster daughter, kept the house after her father's death, living there and in Golden Square. She also obtained more property near by, including about an acre of partly built-up ground east of Powis House and separated from it by a narrow strip of ground not belonging to her.[4] At the time of her death in 1739, therefore, she owned two nearly conterminous freeholds in Knightsbridge; together they amounted to over six acres (see fig. 21 on page 78). The development of the smaller, eastern, portion of the estate (now covered by part of Mercury House) is described in Chapter IV.

Prudentia Trevor bequeathed the Knightsbridge property to her brother Arthur, who died in 1758 leaving it to his nephew Arthur Hill (later Viscount Dungannon), who took the additional name of Trevor.[5] He died in 1771, and it was his grandson Arthur Hill-Trevor, 2nd Viscount Dungannon (1763–1837), who initiated the development of the ground. Following the death of his son, the 3rd Viscount, in 1862, the estate was inherited by Lord Arthur Hill, who took the additional name of Trevor by royal licence and was made Baron Trevor of Brynkinalt in 1880.[6] His son, the 2nd Baron, was the last member of the Hill-Trevor family to hold the land, which was sold in 1909 to the Knightsbridge iron-buildings manufacturer and property developer, James Charlton Humphreys.

Following Arthur Trevor's death, Powis House was let to a succession of tenants, among them George II's mistress, the Countess of Yarmouth, who lived there for a while after the king's death before returning to her native Germany. The 1st Earl of Powis, a former Comptroller and Treasurer of the Household, after whom the house was named, resided there for several years from the late 1760s.

In the 1780s and '90s, Powis House was occupied by Thomas Harris, the proprietor and manager of Covent Garden Theatre, who, in collaboration with R. B. Sheridan and others, planned in the early 1780s to build a theatre or opera house near by, on the Lowndes estate, east of Sloane Street. Henry Holland was to have been the architect, but the scheme was ultimately abandoned.[7] Harris reportedly lost a collection of manuscript plays when in 1794 the fire which destroyed the floorcloth factory next door to Powis House spread to his outbuildings.[8]

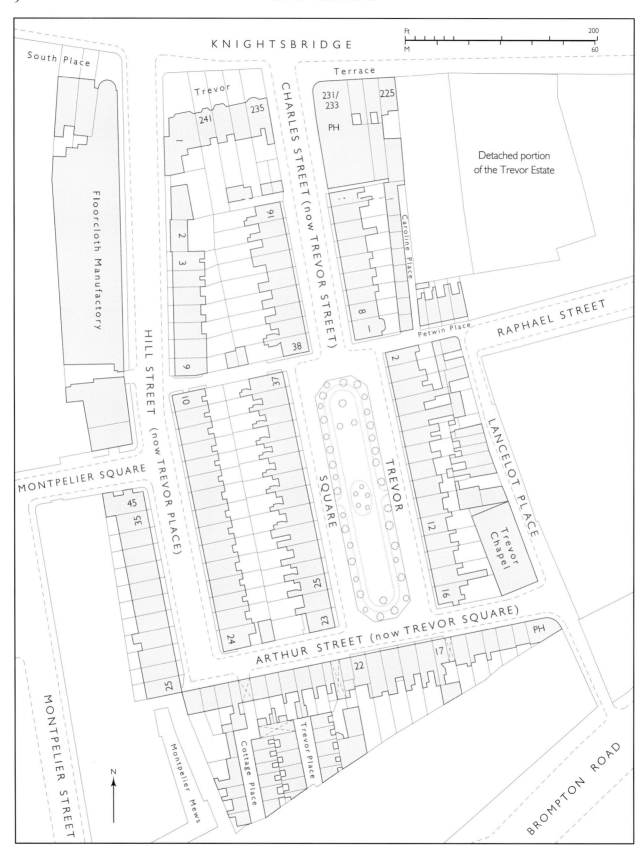

Fig. 28. Trevor Square area in the mid-1860s: Trevor Terrace is shown with post-1903 (Knightsbridge) numbers. The development of the detached portion of the Trevor Estate is described in Chapter IV

By this time, however, the building of the Life Guards barracks immediately opposite Powis House had spoiled both the view of Hyde Park and much of the sylvan charm of the locality. Within a few years, it was decided to pull down the old mansion. The last occupant, who lived there from 1801 until 1810, was a John Bruce, possibly the historian and keeper of the State Paper Office.[9a]

Adjoining Powis House on the east (being perhaps part of the original building, or built on the site of a service wing) was a house once occupied by a celebrated dentist, John March, who died there in 1802. Born in Sweden, March served as a French army officer before taking up his profession. As dentist to the nobility, he was said to have taken higher fees than had ever been charged before, but he also gave free treatment to artists and others of lesser means.[11]

Development of the Estate

By the late eighteenth century the larger (western) portion of the Trevor estate had been divided into two parts, comprising Powis House and its grounds and, to the west, a field with a workshop used for manufacturing floorcloth. The two parts were developed at different times, and much of the dividing-line between them is preserved in the present-day property divisions, along the boundaries between the houses on the west side of Trevor Street and Trevor Square and those on the east side of Trevor Place. It is presumably their separate development that accounts for the attenuated shape of Trevor Square (fig. 28). Both phases of development were handled by the same man, the architect William Fuller Pocock (1779–1849), the work being completed after his death by his son, William Willmer Pocock.

W. F. Pocock's professional involvement with the development of the Trevor estate seems to have begun about 1810, when he advised Lord Dungannon to pull down Powis House and lay out the ground for building, procuring reports from Philip Hardwick and others 'in confirming of his own views'.[12b] His plan was roughly symmetrical: an axial street leading off the Kensington road and opening out into a narrow 'square'. The south side of the square formed part of Arthur Street, a cross-street communicating with an old trackway (subsequently Lancelot Place) running northwards from the Brompton road. The remaining spaces, on the south and east sides of the estate, were set aside for other buildings, chiefly small cottages and a chapel. There was no mews as such, but there was some stabling at the back of the western part of Trevor Ter-race, the line of houses built fronting the Kensington road.

Work on laying out the Powis House grounds started in 1811, when the old house was demolished, but the development proceeded slowly. Building began at either end of the estate, with the first houses in Trevor Terrace and some smaller houses in Arthur Street. Few houses were completed before 1820, and it was not until about 1827 that the last were finished. By that time the redevelopment of the floorcloth factory site was also in progress, and there the work turned out to be even more protracted. It was still incomplete at the time of W. F. Pocock's death in 1849.

The Trevor estate development was to a very great extent Pocock's own creation and took up much of his time for some years, as his son later recalled. In addition to designing the layout he was responsible, at least in general terms, for the appearance of all the new buildings, and he carried out parts of the development as his own speculation, later expressing regret that he had not taken on the whole. On the Powis House grounds, his 'take' was limited to Trevor Terrace, Arthur Street, and a few other houses including No. 1 Trevor Square; for the second phase of development, on the western part of the estate, he did take every house-plot himself.[14]

Trevor Terrace

Trevor Terrace was the collective name given to the two markedly different rows of houses fronting the Kensington road on either side of the present Trevor Street (fig. 28). Of the ten houses eventually built here, the earliest, now Nos 237 and 239 Knightsbridge, were finished and occupied by 1813. No. 235, and five houses to the east of Trevor Street (all now demolished) followed in 1818–21.[15] The demolition of the old floorcloth factory, which adjoined the present No. 239 on the west, provided space for two more houses to be added to the row. Pocock took out agreements for building these two (and No. 2 Trevor Place) in 1823, but they were not completed until the late 1820s. They are now No. 241 Knightsbridge and No. 1 Trevor Place (Hill House).[16]

As well as being the developer of Trevor Terrace, Pocock had his own residence there. He first occupied the corner house in the east range, later No. 233 Knightsbridge, living there from 1817 until c.1828, when he moved to its counterpart in the west range, now No. 1 Trevor Place (then No. 1 Hill Street).[17] The builder of the terrace, or part of it at least, was the bricklayer Thomas Emmins of Chelsea, to whom, or to whose nominees, Pocock sublet two of the houses.[18]

---

[a] In his memoirs, W. W. Pocock stated that his father had lived in part of Powis House during the early stages of the redevelopment of the grounds, and that he himself had been born there (in 1813). This is not supported by the ratebooks, which record Powis House as having been empty for two or more years from the time of John Bruce's departure, and show that Pocock was occupying another house near by.[10]

[b] According to W. W. Pocock, the introduction between Lord Dungannon and W. F. Pocock was made through Dungannon's lawyer, Stratford Robinson. There may have been some prior connection between the two families, however, for Prudentia Trevor left £10 in her will to one William Pocock, and people named Pocock lived next door to Powis House in the 1760s and early 1770s.[13]

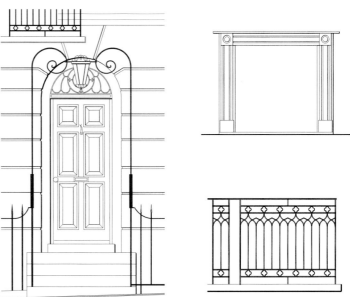

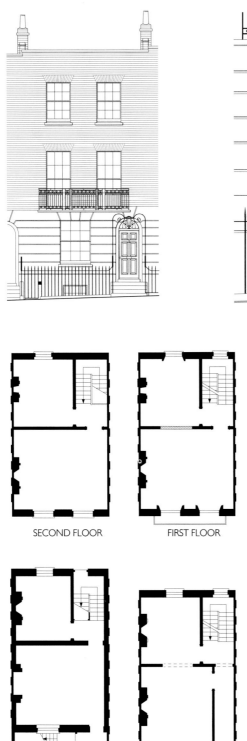

SECOND FLOOR   FIRST FLOOR

BASEMENT   GROUND FLOOR

Ft   20
M   6   ➝ z

Fig. 29. No. 31 Trevor Square, elevation, plans and details.
Thomas Allen, building lessee, *c*.1825–7

The houses in the surviving, western, half of Trevor
Terrace – the product of three phases of construction – are
tall and substantial, with front gardens of appreciable
depth (Plate 55a). The first three (Nos 235–239) were
designed as a more or less balanced group, the middle
house flat-fronted and the outer two with bows. The later
two houses have front bay windows, of a different pattern.
In contrast, the houses forming the eastern range had no
front gardens and were all flat-fronted (although the original intention does appear to have been for a corresponding
mixture of bowed and flat fronts).[19]

The physical difference between the halves of the terrace came to be matched by differences in use and social
status. Before many years had passed the eastern half had
lost its residential character, becoming drawn into the racy
and increasingly disreputable ambience of the High Road.
Nos 1 and 2 became shops, as did No. 3, after many years
in the occupation of surgeons, and in 1844 Nos 4 and 5
Trevor Terrace were converted into a public house, the
Trevor Tavern, later the Trevor Arms, at the back of which
a music-hall was built in the 1850s (see below).[20]

In 1911 Nos 225, 2, and 3 (by then Nos 225–229 Knightsbridge) were pulled down by J. C. Humphreys, the purchaser of the Trevor estate. It was announced in August
1914 that bachelor flats were to be built on the site, to
designs by Messrs Palgrave and Partners, but the scheme
was not carried out, presumably on account of the war.[21]
Four years later Humphreys used the vacant ground for a
western extension to Knightsbridge Hall (see page 88). Its
site, together with that of the Trevor Arms and the music-
hall, is now covered by part of Mercury House.

The western range of Trevor Terrace retained its residential character, becoming the most select part of the estate. After W. F. Pocock's death, his son W. W. Pocock continued to reside at No. 1 Trevor Place until the 1860s.[22] The back drawing-room in this house had 'a great deal of wood carving around the walls', possibly some of the oak work acquired by the elder Pocock from Wanstead House, Essex (pulled down in 1824), which he is said to have incorporated into the building.[23] No. 1 Trevor Place and the other surviving houses have been variously altered, the chief external change being the full stuccoing of the front at No. 239 Knightsbridge.

Past residents of Trevor Terrace include: Francis Augustus Bonney, surgeon and contributor of verse to the *European Magazine* and other journals (No. 3, later No. 229 Knightsbridge, c.1847–57); Jonathan Thomas Carr, founder of Bedford Park (No. 7, now No. 237 Knightsbridge, 1870s); and Tristram Ellis, artist and traveller (No. 8, now No. 239 Knightsbridge, 1890s).

Trevor Square and Trevor Street

Development in Trevor Square and Trevor Street (called Charles Street until 1936) was slow to take off. In 1816 John Souter, a bricklayer, leased a plot for houses on the east side of the square, at the south end, with a chapel at the back on the corner of Arthur Street and Lancelot Place. A plan with Souter's lease suggests that the square was then envisaged as laid out with the houses arranged in semi-detached pairs.[24] Trevor Chapel was duly completed later in the year, but no houses were built, and when work on the square began in earnest in about 1818 or 1819 the semi-detached arrangement had given way to standard terraces. Leases of new houses forming the east side of the square north of Souter's ground were granted between December 1819 and July 1821, one to a Chelsea bricklayer, James Binns, and the rest to nominees of the elder James Bonnin, the carpenter-builder responsible for much building in Brompton and Chelsea during the 1820s and '30s. Leases of five houses went to Lancelot Edward Wood, a stonemason, who, like Bonnin, was active elsewhere on the estate.[25]

The first houses to be completed in Trevor Square appear to have been Nos 9 and 10 on the east side, and No. 17, part of W. F. Pocock's own 'take' along Arthur Street, which were first rated and inhabited in 1819. The rest of the east side (including the five houses, Nos 12–16, on Souter's plot) had been completed and was largely occupied by 1821; the remainder of the south side followed by 1823.[26]

Leases of the three southernmost houses on the west side were granted during this period to Wood and another of Bonnin's nominees,[27] but only one house (No. 25) seems to have been completed at the time, the other two not being finished until about 1826. The remainder of the west side was completed c.1825–7.[28] So far as is known, neither Bonnin nor Wood was involved in these slightly later houses, the leases of which were mostly made direct to various

tradespeople. Two were leased by direction of Thomas Allen, a carpenter of High Street, Kensington, who himself took two houses on lease.[29]

The first and last houses numbered in the square are the end houses at the bottom of Trevor Street. No. 1 was first rated and occupied in 1823, No. 38 in the following year.[30]

Building in Trevor Street began about 1819. No. 5 appears to have been the first house to be occupied, in 1821, and the rest of the street was finished and fully occupied a couple of years later.[31] Thomas Emmins was involved in the building of some of these houses, and one was leased to another bricklayer, William Bennett of Soho.[32] Pocock took a lease on the last three houses on the east side (Nos 7 and 8 and No. 1 Trevor Square), together with an L-shaped plot adjoining on which were subsequently built cottages in Caroline Place and a range of four houses which became known as Petwin Place (fig. 28).[33]

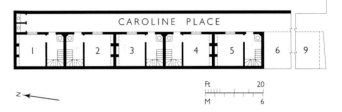

Fig. 30. Nos 1–9 Caroline Place, 1820–2, ground-floor plans. *Demolished*

Caroline Place was a row of dwellings of the most basic description (fig. 30). Originally known as Emmins Place, it was built by Thomas Emmins and another Chelsea bricklayer, Charles Hawkins, in 1820–2.[34] In 1889–90 both Caroline Place and Petwin Place were pulled down and incorporated into the site of a new tennis court for the nearby Prince's Club (see Plate 57b).

The architecture of Trevor Street and Trevor Square is characteristic of the late Georgian to Regency period, and, though engaging – as long ago as 1909 *The Times* spoke of the square's 'old world charm'[35] – calls for little comment. The houses are of standard side-passage plan, and built of yellow brick with gauged window-heads and channelled stucco to the ground-floor fronts. Their only external decorative features are patterned fanlights and balconies (fig. 29, Plates 55b–c, 56a–b). While some mansards have been added and rear wings reconstructed, the houses remain essentially unaltered in their outward appearance. The notable exception is No. 38 Trevor Square, much enlarged and embellished with stuccowork some time before the First World War (Plate 55d).[36] Indoors, some houses retain their original door-frames and matching wooden chimneypieces of a pattern similar to one shown in W. F. Pocock's *Modern furnishings for rooms* of 1811 (fig. 29).

Trevor Lodge, on the west side of Trevor Street, is entirely new, a neo-Regency essay of 1990 by John Green, a restorer of period houses.[37]

The most famous past resident of Trevor Square is the

courtesan Harriette Wilson, who lived at No. 16 from 1828 to about 1830, a few years after the publication of her celebrated *Memoirs*. Her novel *Clara Gazul* (1831) was probably written at the house.

Inhabitants of the square before the First World War included several artists, among them George Fripp (No. 10, 1841); Claude Langlois (No. 24, 1840s), John Swindles (No. 20, 1861) and Westley Horton (No. 30, 1880s–90s); a sculptor, Thomas McCarthy (No. 22, 1881); a comedian, Richard Leggett, and his vocalist wife Emma (No. 1, 1871), and a 'dramatic writer', William Brownlow (No. 32, 1840s–60s). Later occupants include the novelist Radclyffe Hall and her companion Lady Troubridge (No. 7), Leon Quartermaine, actor (No. 4), and the playwright Ben Travers (No. 10).

Past residents of Trevor Street include John Chapman Mathews, artist (No. 16), and the architect Herbert Osborn Cresswell (No. 12).

Arthur Street

Development in Arthur Street began a little earlier than in Trevor Square. On 1 July 1812 Daniel Pontifex of Holborn, mercer, took out an agreement with Lord Dungannon to build four houses there, but within a few days he had transferred the agreement to W. F. Pocock. About a year later Pocock obtained leases on three plots comprising the entire south side of the street (including the south side of the square and the sites of two back courts, Cottage Place and Trevor Place). It was not until about 1815, however, that the first four houses appeared, and not until the early 1820s that the majority of these plots was built up. The easternmost house became a pub in the 1840s, the Earl Grey.[38] Censuses show this part of the estate to have been mainly working-class throughout the Victorian period (though the larger houses at Nos 17–22 Trevor Square seem to have retained a generally higher-class character until the mid-century).

On the north side of the street, at the corner with Lancelot Place, stood the Trevor Chapel, built in 1816 for an Independent congregation led by Dr John Morison, who had resigned as minister of Union Chapel in Sloane Street, following differences of opinion there. Pending the opening of the new chapel, in December 1816, Smith & Baber's floorcloth factory provided a temporary meeting-place. The builder was a member of the congregation, John Souter, to whom the site, together with ground for houses in Trevor Square, had been leased some months earlier.[39]

The chapel was greatly enlarged during the 1830s, and in 1840 schoolrooms were added at the top of the building, when funds were also raised for the intended purchase of the property (though this was evidently not accomplished). Among the donations received was £300 from the developer Seth Smith.[40] A gallery was later installed, perhaps during alterations in 1865.[41]

Trevor Chapel (latterly Trevor Congregational Church) closed about 1902, in which year the building was taken over by Harrods and converted for use as a showroom and garage for motor-carriages and accessories. It was later used as a warehouse until its demolition in the early 1950s.[42]

All the old houses on the south side of Arthur Street were swept away about 1913 for the building of a large warehouse and factory for Harrods. The name was abolished in 1918, since when the whole street has been regarded as forming the south side of Trevor Square.

Lancelot Place (west side)

Lancelot Place takes its name from Lancelot Edward Wood, the stonemason involved in the development of houses in Trevor Square. The roadway itself originated as a driftway from the Brompton road to the back of the Rose and Crown on the Kensington road, and dates back to the eighteenth century or earlier.

The southern end was taken up by the Trevor Chapel, the site of which was redeveloped in 1953 with a row of neo-Georgian houses designed by Jack E. Dalling, LRIBA (Plate 58b).[43]

North of the chapel, Lancelot Place was built up with small cottages and shops *c*.1819–20, much of it being included in leases of houses on the east side of the square.[44] None of these survive, and this part of the street is now occupied by post-war houses and lock-up garages, the most recent building being Lancelot House at the north end (1995, by the Halpern Partnership).[45]

Soldiers' Dwellings, Trevor Street (demolished)

At the back of the Trevor Arms in Trevor Terrace a small block of flats was built about 1890, on the site previously occupied by the Trevor Music Hall, and subsequently adapted as married quarters for soldiers from Knightsbridge Barracks.

The music hall, first licensed in 1854, was the westernmost of several such places of popular entertainment which flourished in early to mid-Victorian Knightsbridge. With

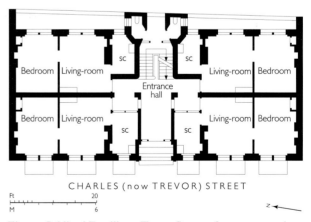

Fig. 31. Soldiers' Dwellings, Trevor Street, 1890–92, ground-floor plan. *Demolished*

Fig. 32. Nos 11–23 Trevor Place, typical elevation. W. F. Pocock, architect, 1840–3

Fig. 33. Nos 3–8 Trevor Place, typical elevation. W. F. Pocock, architect, 1844–5

galleries on three sides, the hall could seat 800.[46]

A reconstruction on a grander scale, to designs by J. W. Brooker, was planned in 1889 but did not go forward, apparently because Lord Trevor was not willing to grant a new lease for such a purpose. The following year the landlord of the Trevor Arms, George Young, did obtain a new lease of the site, which he redeveloped as flats (soon let to the War Office), with a basement billiard-room communicating with the pub though under separate management.[47] The six-storey block was built of red brick with stone dressings: bay windows were added to the upper floors in 1892 by the War Office. Except on the top (mansard) floor, where a communal laundry and wash-house were situated, each level was divided into four apartments, of three or four rooms (fig. 31).[48]

The building was demolished after the Second World War for the Mercury House development.

Trevor Place

The planning of Hill Street (renamed Trevor Place in 1936) dates back to about 1822, when W. F. Pocock began work on the replacement of Smith & Baber's floorcloth factory, which then stood towards the north end of a large enclosure on the west side of the estate (immediately west of the present No. 239 Knightsbridge). But it was only in 1827, when additional land was acquired from the neighbouring landowner, T. W. Marriott, that the present layout became possible. The extra ground allowed houses to be built on the west side of the street south of the new factory. As part of the deal, Marriott was able to join his roadway at the top of Montpelier Square to the new street, thus connecting his estate, which he was then in the process of developing, with the Kensington road.[49]

Although by 1828 building agreements had been made

for houses all along the east side of Hill Street, only two houses were built there at this time, both on leases to W. F. Pocock under an agreement of 1823: these were No. 1 Trevor Place (see under Trevor Terrace above) and No. 2 (otherwise known as Hill Street House). A wide-fronted, shallow house, No. 2 was built adjoining some stables, now enlarged or rebuilt as dwellings, at the rear of the large plot occupied by No. 1. Nothing further was built until about 1840, presumably as a consequence of the general slump in the building trades in the late 1820s and '30s.

All the remaining plots were let to Pocock in a series of leases made between 1840 and 1843, but several houses had yet to be erected by the time of his death in 1849; they were completed by his son William Willmer Pocock. Building began with the south-eastern range (Nos 10–24). Four houses were standing, two of them occupied, by 1840, and the rest were completed by 1843. The northern range (Nos 3–9) was built in 1844–5, but was not fully occupied until the early 1850s. Of the south-western range, Nos 29–35 and the corner house were first rated in 1847; the last four houses, Nos 25–28, were completed but as yet uninhabited in 1852.[50] The corner house, formerly No. 36 Hill Street, is now numbered 45 Montpelier Square.

Although the earlier houses on the Trevor estate were apparently built of bricks made on site, some at least of those in Hill Street were constructed with bricks made by the Pococks at their brickfield in Battersea. This had been bought by W. F. Pocock in 1844, with the aim of cashing in on the brick shortage caused by the rush to complete buildings in the London suburbs before the new Building Act (with its revised definition of the metropolitan area) came into force.[51]

Stylistically, the 1840s and '50s houses in Trevor Place show how architectural fashion had moved on since Trevor Square was built (Plates 56c, 57a; figs 32–3). Semi-circular fanlights have given way to plain rectangles, unadorned window openings with gauged heads to stuccoed surrounds, and there are thick stucco cornices along the parapets. The three ranges are not identically treated: the taller end houses in the southern half of the street, for instance, have the additional emphasis of cursorily defined giant pilaster orders. On the northern terrace the houses have full-width balconies, while those to the south have only minimal iron enclosures to each window.

Former residents of Trevor Place include: Henry Whittaker, artist (No. 14, late 1840s); Charles Digby Harrod, son of the founder of Harrods, largely responsible for the firm's expansion from the 1860s (No. 2, 1860s–70s); the composer Constant Lambert (No. 10, late 1930s), the architect and designer Felix Harbord (No. 1, 1940s–50s), and the novelist Henry Green (No. 16, 1940s–50s).

Social Character

The Trevor Square development was clearly designed to attract residents of moderately prosperous middle-class character, a working-class contingent being provided for by cottages on the fringes of the estate.

Early Victorian census returns show that the square was by no means solidly middle-class, some houses being occupied by artisans and other workpeople. There was a tendency for later middle-class residents to be lodgers rather than householders, and by 1861 most houses were lodging-houses or otherwise in multiple occupation. The most striking social phenomenon, redolent of lower-middle-class gentility, was the colonization of Trevor Square by the drapery trade. In 1861 the census recorded seven houses in the occupation of drapers, all of them young or youngish Scotsmen. Taking into account lodgers and assistants living with them, there were about two dozen Scottish drapers in the square in that year. Scottish drapers remained a substantial proportion of the population of the square and near by into the 1890s.

Trevor Square did not really begin to lose the ambiguous social position typical of a lodging-house district until the twentieth century, long after neighbouring Montpelier Square had begun to attract a number of fashionable or well-to-do residents. There was, however, at least one aristocrat living in the square as early as the 1890s. This was Earl Cowley, who occupied No. 1 for several years from about 1896 (shortly before his first divorce).

Ostensibly a dull street mostly of lodging-houses, Trevor Place (then Hill Street) had a moment of particular notoriety in 1886 when No. 9 was revealed as a house of ill-repute in the celebrated Crawford divorce proceedings, which blighted the political career of Sir Charles Dilke. Dilke himself does not seem to have made use of the house, but it was visited by both Mrs Crawford, who claimed to have had an adulterous relationship with him, and her sister Helen (sister-in-law of the writer Frederic Harrison), to pursue their affairs with one Captain Forster.[52]

The Estate since 1909

In 1909 the freehold of the Trevor estate was sold by Lord Trevor to James Charlton Humphreys, the iron-buildings manufacturer, for close on £200,000. The iron-buildings business, which at one time had occupied the former floor-cloth factory in Hill Street (Trevor Place), was now largely carried on in Pimlico, the company's offices and showrooms remaining at Albert Gate Mansions, on the detached portion of the estate. Humphreys himself – 'small in stature . . . big in business' – was a well-known local figure, not only as an industrialist and property-owner but also as a member of the Westminster Vestry and a Volunteer officer.[53]

Humphreys soon determined on a complete rebuilding of the main part of the estate, where many of the original leases were shortly to fall in, and in 1911 an architectural competition was held to find the best redevelopment scheme. It was won by Horace Field & Simmons and Cyril Farey: the runners-up were H. S. Goodhart-Rendel (second), Ernest Schaufelberg (third) and W. G. Wilson (fourth). All of the four premiated designs were similar in that they retained most of the existing pattern of streets (while re-aligning or otherwise altering the square itself), and by their reliance on terraces of tall houses rather than horizontally planned blocks of flats (though some of these were planned). The winning scheme was a rather grandiose affair with a vista along a lengthened Charles (Trevor) Street to a crescent at the south end of the estate (Plate 58a). It was not alone in proposing to cut off the estate entirely from any communication with down-market Raphael Street (see page 10).[54]

The top four entries showed a taste for classical styles, and each made use of tall mansard roofs containing one or two floors. Both the winning design and that by Schaufelberg adhered to a fashionable Beaux-Arts classicism, Wilson, in some contrast, adopting an ornateness reminiscent of the houses of an earlier generation in and around Princes Gate. Goodhart-Rendel's own comparatively stripped-down style (making use of windows grouped in threes on his flats for the sites north of the square, another echo of Princes Gate) was criticized by the *Builder* as depending 'too much on its detail, workmanship, and choice of material' for its success.

Despite the competition, no redevelopment scheme was put in hand, and by 1912 the estate was again on the mar-ket. Harrods considered buying it, but the directors backed away from the idea on the grounds that property speculation was not part of their business, even though it offered an ideal site for much-needed expansion. However, the managing director, (Sir) Richard Burbidge, was determined that the opportunity should not be lost altogether, and as Humphreys was only prepared to consider a sale of the whole property, more space than Harrods could reasonably require, he formed the Trevor Syndicate Ltd with a Mr Mendel and another member of the Harrods board, and Humphreys himself, to acquire the entire freehold. The site for the Harrods building on the south side of Arthur Street was then leased from the syndicate in 1913, together with Nos 2–37 Trevor Square and the west side of Lancelot Place north of Arthur Street.[55]

After the First World War, the freehold of most of the property was sold off, leaving only a fraction in the ownership of the Trevor Estate, successor to the syndicate, today.[56]

Former Harrods Depot

In 1913 the entire south side of Arthur Street was leased by the newly formed Trevor Syndicate Ltd to Harrods for the construction of a warehouse and depot. All the old houses (together with the stables and cottages on the east side of

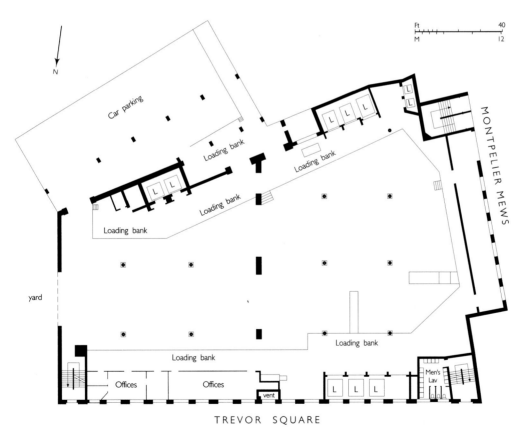

Fig. 34. Former Harrods depot, Trevor Square, ground-floor plan. Munt and Stephens, architects, 1913–*c*.1920

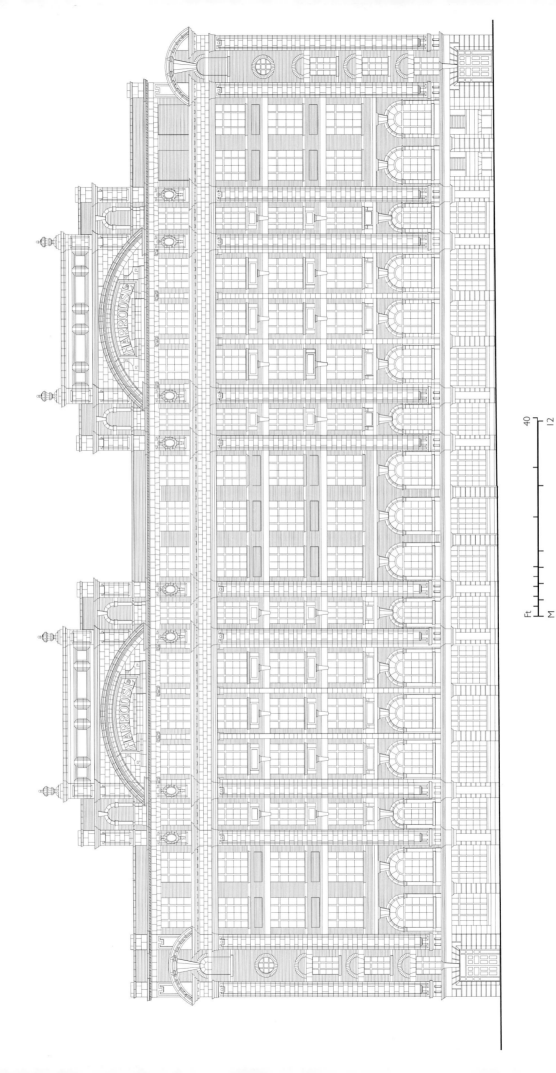

Fig. 35. Former Harrods depot, Trevor Square, north elevation. Munt and Stephens, architects, 1913–c.1920

Montpelier Mews) were pulled down for the new building, which was designed by C. W. Stephens, architect of the Harrods store in Brompton Road, and his new partner, formerly his assistant, E. J. Munt. Preliminary work, involving demolition, excavation, and making a subway to the shop under Brompton Road (designed by Harley H. Dalrymple-Hay) was carried out by John Mowlem & Company. Construction, by James Carmichael of Wandsworth, began in 1913, but the outbreak of war and the building workers' strike brought it to a stop by late 1914, leaving only the basements and ground floor usable. Work resumed in 1919 and was completed by the early 1920s.[57]

Faced with red brick and terracotta, the former Harrods depot is a building of palatial proportions, designed for a range of activities including warehousing, packing, despatch, manufacturing, processing and repair work (figs 34–5; Plate 57c). The production of own-brand goods, including baking, chocolate-making and tea-blending, continued there until the 1970s, since when it has been used largely for storage and garaging. Long-standing plans to convert the building into the 'Harrods House Hotel', together with the redevelopment of No. 100 Brompton Road, are still in abeyance at the time of writing.

Smith & Baber's Floorcloth Factory

Before the construction of the Harrods depot the dominating building on the Trevor estate was Smith & Baber's floorcloth factory, on the west side of Trevor Place. Built in the early 1820s, this was one of several noteworthy structures, most of them now destroyed, erected in London for the manufacture of ornamental painted floorcloth, an industry particularly associated with the capital. With its tall belvedere tower, Smith & Baber's factory was for some seventy years a distinctive local landmark. The tower was demolished in the 1890s, but the shell of the building survived into the 1970s.

It was the firm's third factory. The first was erected in the mid-eighteenth century for Nathan Smith, whose son-in-law, James Baber, later claimed that Smith had founded the works in 1754. In fact a date some ten years later is more likely to be correct. Baber's further assertion that it had been the first floorcloth manufactory was more or less specious. (Both claims were embodied in a prominent inscription on the 1820s building.)[58] There certainly were earlier factories – one of them in Knightsbridge, just east of what is now Sloane Street (see page 31) – though they were not necessarily on such a large scale as Smith's, nor perhaps were their products comparable with his in quality and durability.

It was in March 1763 that Nathan Smith, a painter-stainer of Fenchurch Street, patented a composition and machinery for making floorcloth. Oil-cloth used as a relatively inexpensive floor-covering had then been around for many years, since the very early eighteenth century if not before.[59] It was also utilized for awnings, tents and garden buildings. The manufacturing process involved covering the canvas base with several thick coats of paint, and then applying a printed pattern with wooden blocks. By the late eighteenth century techniques had reached a high degree of sophistication, allowing production of very large and elaborately patterned cloths.

A problem with the earlier floorcloths was that the water-soluble size or glue used to prime the canvas backing would go soft if the cloth was washed down, causing the paint to peel. Smith's patent composition, which had to be pressed into the cloth by a rolling apparatus, was intended to supersede sizing.[60] He is also credited with introducing two further innovations in floorcloth manufacture: block-printing instead of stencilling for making patterns; and 'seamless' floorcloth, achieved at first by sewing canvases together without a raised seam, and later by using specially woven canvas of exceptional width.[61]

Whatever his earlier involvement, if any, in floorcloth making, it seems certain that Smith's factory originated as a workshop built on ground adjoining Powis House in 1764.[62] The exact circumstances of the building of the factory, however, and the nature of Smith's tenancy, are unclear. Possibly the building was erected for manufacturing floorcloth using his newly patented process, though the first ratepayer was Jonathan Durden esquire, who lived at a neighbouring house in South Place for a few years, and Smith's name does not appear in the ratebooks in connection with this building until 1766. In 1785 a lease of the factory site (about an acre in extent) was granted by the Trevors to the builder Henry Holland, during the lives of two of his sons, Henry (the architect) and Richard, and the Prince of Wales. Holland assigned this lease to another son, John, who appears to have continued to hold it for many years. Smith presumably, therefore, became an undertenant of John Holland, and it may be that the Hollands had some interest in the business.[63]

In February 1794 a fire destroyed the original factory. The cost of the damage, including the loss of £15,000-worth of materials for the cavalry and other government contracts, amounted to £20,000, and as nothing was insured a collection was set up to help the proprietors, which managed to raise about £500. Within a couple of years a new factory had been built on the same site, together with a dwelling-house; a second house was built later (see Plate 5c).[64] A design for the new factory was shown at the Royal Academy in 1794 by W. S. Newman (who had earlier exhibited at the Academy giving his address as Mr Smith's, Knightsbridge).[65]

Although a building with some pretensions to style, the 'Phoenix' floorcloth factory was, according to W. W. Pocock, only made of wood (Plate 54d).[66] It stood well back from the road behind a grass area with a goldfish pond and a statue of Time standing near by, holding his scythe and hour-glass.[67]

Nathan Smith seems to have retired in 1798,[68] evidently to Brighton (if he was the Brighthelmestone gentleman named Nathan Smith who, late that year, patented a vapour-bath contraption for treating gout).[69] The factory was taken over by his son-in-law James Baber, a man of humble origin who had trained as a mason and stonecutter, and with whom Soane is said to have worked at one time.[70]

Between 1822 and 1824 Baber's factory was rebuilt on a much grander scale than previously. The new site, which was a portion of the field in which the original factory had been built, had a narrow frontage to Knightsbridge and extended southwards along the west side of what is now Trevor Place. It was extended further south in 1828, as far as the roadway at the north end of Montpelier Square, on ground recently acquired by Lord Dungannon from T. W. Marriott.[71] Two houses (Nos 1 and 2 South Place), also included in the site, were occupied for many years by the Baber family or their employees.[72]

The new factory was designed by W. F. Pocock, Lord Dungannon's estate surveyor. It was an architectural composition of some distinction, shown to good effect in a contemporary perspective view, probably drawn by Pocock himself (Plate 54a).[73] Visitors entered through a domed rotunda at the north end, which gave on to a single-storey showroom, south of which lay the manufactory itself. This comprised a large block of more than double-storey height containing the framing- and drying-rooms, where the floorcloths spent the greater part of the time-consuming manufacturing process, mounted in wooden frames for priming and painting or simply hanging up to dry (Plate 54b). The interim stage of block-printing was carried out above in the lower stage of the central tower. Particularly long floorcloths were hung up to dry from the tower, reaching down into the drying-room. Other activities, including paint-making, block-making, and carpentry repairs, were carried out in smaller rooms at the south end of the premises. The tower, which may not have been completed for several years after the opening of the factory, was built to a different design from that shown in Pocock's perspective (Plate 6b). The engraving used on the firm's stationery, as much as two years before the new factory can have been in use, shows the tower completed only up to its first stage;[74] an increase in rateable value in 1828 may mark its completion.[75]

Smith & Baber's products had a considerable reputation, and the manufacturing techniques used at the factory (where nineteen men were employed in 1851)[76] were well-publicized during its heyday.[77]

After the closure of the floorcloth factory about 1888, the premises were acquired by J. C. Humphreys (the future purchaser of the Trevor estate) and used by him for several years for manufacturing iron buildings. Humphreys had entered into an agreement to redevelop the site with houses or flats,[78] but this scheme was ultimately abandoned and in 1894 he let the factory to an ice-skating company. There was strong opposition from some nearby residents (including Lord Llangattock at South Lodge), and a music and dancing licence for the proposed 'Pôle Nord' was refused by the London County Council.[c] When the project did go ahead, as Prince's Skating Club – an offshoot of the nearby Prince's Club – there were various restrictions to ensure that it did not become a nuisance, including a ban on alcohol, singing and late-night opening. Moreover, ice-skating was restricted to a six-month season, with 'high class entertainments' only to be held during the rest of the year.[80]

Opened in September 1896, the Prince's Skating Club retained little of the old factory beyond a large part of the shell. The tower went, a new iron-and-glass roof was erected, and the principal block, comprising the former framing- and drying-rooms, was extended southwards as far as Montpelier Square (Plate 54c).[81] The south extension followed the plain round-arched style of the factory; at the north end, the main entrance was at the corner of a single-storey wing, somewhat showier with stone dressings and ball finials on the parapet. Replacing or converted from the old floorcloth showroom, this building, latterly No. 243 Knightsbridge, contained a lounge, refreshment room and offices. Two more storeys were later added.[82]

Although a 'brilliant success', the skating-club was put up for sale in 1897, probably because of the difficulties over licensing. But no buyer was found until 1903, when it was purchased by the Duchess of Bedford – the future 'Flying Duchess' was a keen skater and determined to keep the place open. The building had already housed, in 1902, an exhibition of Austrian art and furnishings, and a succession of exhibitions and bazaars followed over the years leading up to the First World War.[83] The Olympic winter sports were held there in 1908, and in the following year it was used for an exhibition by the Women's Political Union, when the hall was decorated with purple, white and green murals to Sylvia Pankhurst's designs. The rather cloying blend of Pre-Raphaelite, Biblical and pagan symbolism, with a female sower and angels as the centrepiece, was heavily influenced by Walter Crane's socialist imagery.[84]

After the First World War the building became a car-hire depot, and this it remained until its demolition in the mid-1970s for the South Lodge redevelopment (see page 134).[85]

---

[c] The name was apparently taken from the Pôle Nord in Paris, with which the patentees of the ice-making apparatus for the proposed rink, two engineers both living in Paris, Edouard de Stoppani and Ernest Herrmann, may have been concerned.[79]

Montpelier Square Area

The square and adjacent streets known collectively as 'the Montpeliers' (fig. 36) were laid out in the mid-1820s, but they were not fully developed until the 1850s and the corresponding range of stylistic treatments of the buildings is a particular feature of the area. Phases of social change, as fashionable newcomers took over run-down or unmodernized properties, are reflected in later alterations – late Victorian and Edwardian in Montpelier Square, 1920s and '30s in the small houses and cottages of the side streets. The most notable building erected here since the nineteenth century is the German Christuskirche of 1904, a distinguished example of late Gothic Revival architecture.

The Montpelier Estate

Formerly part of the Moreau family property broken up in 1759 (see page 77 and fig. 21), the Montpelier estate came into separate being in September 1824 with the sale by Elisha Biscoe junior of some 7½ acres of undeveloped land behind Brompton Row, his father's development along the north side of Brompton Road.[a] John Robins, of the well-known family of auctioneers, paid £6,000 for the ground, nearly all of it in the parish of St Margaret, Westminster, the exception being a portion belonging to Kensington parish at the south end. The property included the last house in Brompton Row (later No. 188 Brompton Road) and with it a passageway to the Brompton road. Robins sold on the estate shortly afterwards, for £4,735 down and £5,000 payable at interest by way of a mortgage, to John Betts esquire of Brompton Row, and Thomas Weatherley Marriott, an ironmonger of High Row, Knightsbridge.[1]

Marriott was the son of Solomon Marriott of Knightsbridge, himself an ironmonger, and his wife, Mary Weatherley of Uxbridge. Not recently illustrious, the family was descended from a figure of some standing, Richard Marryott J.P. (c.1626–1703) of Finchingfield, Essex, and Worlingworth, Suffolk, whose career as accountant and estate agent included senior appointments with the Duke of Norfolk, the Council of Queen Catherine of Braganza, the Bedford Level Corporation and the Duchy of Lancaster.[2]

Over the next couple of years, Betts and Marriott laid out streets and a square, set up brickworks and began letting plots on building leases. The name of the new estate

had been adopted by November 1824, when a building plan was presented to the Westminster Commissioners of Sewers on their behalf by a Chelsea builder, Samuel Symons.[3] Whether spelt with a single or double 'l', 'Montpelier' was already becoming something of a cliché as a name for new developments, intended to evoke images of fashionable salubrity.[b]

Robins was soon paid off, and a series of mortgages was taken out in the new year. Betts 'agreed to retire' from the concern in August 1826, selling out to his partner for £3,000.[4]

A significant drawback to the estate in the early stages of its development was the absence of any road access to the north. This was overcome in 1827, when Marriott sold a strip of land north of Montpelier Mews to Lord Dungannon, owner of the neighbouring Trevor estate: part of the strip was set aside for a roadway connecting Montpelier Square with a new street, the present Trevor Place, and thence with the Kensington road.[5]

In 1830 Marriott took a £10,000 mortgage loan from Robert Lawton esquire, of Devon, and he continued to borrow on the estate. Parts were sold off freehold. In 1839 he tried unsuccessfully to obtain finance from the Corporation of London Assurance to carry on the development,[6] and in 1842 he re-mortgaged much of the estate to Charles Chatfield, Edward Layton and Henry Snook.[7] In the 1850s, the freeholds of several properties were sold to or bought for John Snook the younger, a merchant.

On T. W. Marriott's death in 1857, the Montpelier estate, somewhat reduced, passed to his numerous children, subject to a trust administered by his son Thomas Weatherley Montague Marriott for paying off the mortgages. In time, following the death of another son, who died intestate, a law suit became necessary to determine the distribution of his estate, and by order of the Court the Marriott property in Montpelier Square and adjacent streets was disposed of at auctions in the early 1890s.[8]

In 1896, after Snook's death, most of his property was bought from his trustees, his relations Henry Snook and Sir Charles Dilke, by the governors of Queen Anne's Bounty. The Ecclesiastical Commissioners, as successors to the Bounty, sold their freeholds during the 1930s and '40s, as leases began to fall in, since when there has been no large landlord in the area with the exception of Harrods,

---

[a] See *Survey of London*, volume XLI.
[b] For example, in contemporary or near-contemporary developments in Brighton, Cheltenham and Harrogate. In the London area, one of the earliest instances of its use was at Montpelier Row, Twickenham, in the early 1720s.

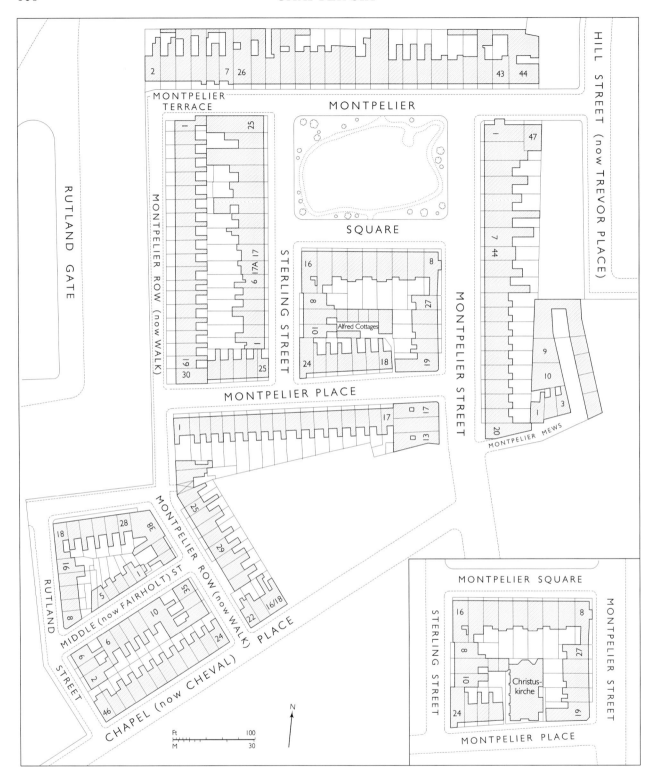

Fig. 36. Montpelier Square area in the mid-1860s. Insert shows part of the north side of Montpelier Place in 1906, after the building of the Christuskirche

which had acquired a number of properties by the First World War (now disposed of).

Building on the estate made fastest progress in the south and west, where Montpelier Walk, Montpelier Place, Cheval Place, Rutland Street and Fairholt Street were mostly built up between 1825 and 1830. To the east, much of Montpelier Street, and most of Montpelier Mews, remained unbuilt-on until the late 1830s. The south side of Montpelier Square went up as planned in the mid-to-late 1820s, but remained untenanted for several years; the other sides saw little further progress until the east and west sides were completed in the early to middle 1840s, and half the north side remained vacant until the early 1850s, when Montpelier Terrace was also built. A few cottages off Montpelier Place more or less completed the development in 1852–3. T. W. M. Marriott was refused permission in 1857 to build on a spare piece of ground, probably behind Nos 24 and 25 Montpelier Square.[9]

Socially and physically, the area underwent a noticeable change between the wars. The hitherto working-class streets to the south and west were transformed from the mid-1920s, as leases expired and freeholds were snapped up by those in search of conveniently placed, easily managed residences. 'All these little back streets are in a transition state and require bathroom and lavatory accommodation', wrote the architect Baillie Scott in 1925.[10] The newcomers, most of them from the upper-middle and upper classes, often single women, wanted more than plumbing of course, and many houses were extended, remodelled or entirely rebuilt. Some were provided with integral garages. By the mid-1930s, however, demand was falling off and unmodernized little houses (especially those with basements) were proving difficult either to let or sell.[11]

In this inter-war period, residents of the square and near neighbours fought off incursions into what had become a fairly select enclave. Harrods was thwarted in its attempt to build a large bakery with warehousing and despatch facilities on Montpelier Street. There was opposition to the establishment of lodging-houses or businesses, such as a domestic service agency, and concern that the Eresby House development in Rutland Gate would generate traffic to and from its rear entrance in Montpelier Terrace. The area escaped severe damage during the Second World War, since when little has been rebuilt and relatively few of the larger houses have been made into flats.

Montpelier Square

'Something about the atmosphere of the place gripped me', wrote Arthur Koestler's wife Cynthia of her first, chance, sight of Montpelier Square on a winter morning in the early 1950s. 'It struck me as the most beautiful square I had ever seen.'[12]

Montpelier Square owes much of its appeal to its seclusion and smallish scale, gently sloping situation, and well-planted garden (Plate 59a). The architecture of the houses is mixed, reflecting not only a process of development stretching over nearly three decades from 1824, but also the tastes of successive house-improvers (fig. 37). There were originally to have been three similar terraces of nine houses each, forming three sides of the square, with a longer range to the north. But construction work, begun at the peak of a development boom, came to a premature halt when the boom collapsed. The leading builder was bankrupted, and only the south side – a fully stuccoed range – was completed as originally intended. Part of the northern terrace, and the two northernmost houses on the west side, were built between the mid-1820s and the late 1830s, the plain, late-Georgian aspect of the earlier houses contrasting somewhat with the more ornamental manner of a few years later. The entire east side was built up in the early 1840s, the remainder of the west side about 1845. The north side of the square was finally completed in the early 1850s, together with Montpelier Terrace. The variations in design of these later houses are the more interesting in that most were the work of the same builder.

In 1867 the communal garden was vested by the Metropolitan Board of Works in a residents' committee, under the Gardens in Towns Protection Act of 1863.[13] The surviving paths in the half-acre plot still follow in part the original layout of curvilinear walks, and there are venerable trees – planes, chestnut and sycamore – amidst lawn and shrubbery. In the 1980s new railings replaced those razed during the Second World War.

Street-numbering

Montpelier Square's protracted genesis led to some oddities of numbering. The present Nos 8–16 on the south side were originally numbered 10–18, in anticipation of the nine houses planned to have been built on the east side. Only seven were ultimately built there: in the meantime the present-day Nos 25 and 24 had been built on the west side and had taken the numbers 1 and 2, throwing the intended sequence into disorder. On completion the west side was renumbered 19–27 in continuation of the flawed sequence already established on the south side. The earlier houses on the north side were originally numbered separately under the name Montpelier Terrace. Although this name was soon dropped, and they were recognized as part of the square, they retained their old numbers for some years. When the north side was completed, the present Nos 26 and 27 were at first numbered 8 and 9 in the new Montpelier Terrace (to the west), and subsequently 26A and 27A Montpelier Square. Some anomalies were put right as the square developed, but for many years there were no houses numbered 8 and 9. The numbering was regularized in 1865, since when the only changes have concerned houses not strictly speaking on the square: No. 17A (formerly No. 7 Sterling Street); No. 25A (otherwise No. 7 Montpelier Terrace); and Nos 44A–B and Nos 45–7 (at the corners of Trevor Place and the north-east entry to the square).

South side: Nos 8–16

The builder most closely associated with the early development of Montpelier Square was William Darby (*c.*1800–48), otherwise known as William Absolom Darby, of Darby & Son, carpenters and builders. Darby, with others including members of his family, seems to have been chiefly responsible for building the south side of the square, together with two houses at the back, in Sterling and Montpelier Streets. He intended to construct at least some houses on the west side of the square, using the same design as for the southern range, and there is evidence that he was planning to build on the east side too.

The firm of Darby & Son was based at Wilton Street, Grosvenor Place, from the 1820s to the 1830s. William Darby's father Isaac, who died in 1837, seems to have been in business there on his own from about 1833.[14] William, who undertook to build on the Bishop of London's Paddington estate at about the same time as he became involved with Montpelier Square, went bankrupt in 1828, resurfacing in the 1840s as a surveyor in Marylebone and Westbourne Park. He may have been the William Darby who in the interim ran a shop at Queen's Buildings, Brompton Road.[15] His son William Henry Darby became a builder himself in Upper George Street, Marylebone, where he employed five men in 1851 and shared premises with his brother Frederick, an estate agent and surveyor.[16] The Darbys may possibly have been related to a family of that name from Sunbury (where T. W. Marriott himself lived in retirement), and thus to the St Quintins, owners of the Notting Barns estate in North Kensington.[17] It does not appear that they were involved in building on the estate other than in this most ambitious part. The other builders were mainly from around Chelsea and Brompton.

Ninety-nine-year leases of the five eastern houses on the south side were granted by Marriott and Betts at the end of May 1826, on the direction of William Darby, with whom building agreements had been made. Besides Darby, the lessees were Isaac Darby, described as a plumber, of York Terrace, Marylebone; Edward Darby, painter, and Marshall Hill Smith, mason, both of Belgravia; and Jonathan Turner, a Soho timber merchant. Rents were set at fourteen guineas from the third year.[18] Marriott and Betts soon disposed of the freehold of these houses and that of the unbuilt west side of the square to Alexander Anderson, a surgeon of Brompton Row. In August 1826, just before Betts withdrew from the development, the freehold of the rest of the south side was sold to William Bromley, a Gray's Inn solicitor much involved in property transactions. Bromley's purchase included the present No. 8 Sterling Street and its counterpart 'about to be built' in Montpelier Street (No. 27). Leases of Bromley's houses were granted

to William Darby, and Richard Darby esquire of Pollen Street, Hanover Square, towards the end of the year.[19]

Not until 1830 were the first few houses on the south side rated, and it was only in the mid-1830s that the whole terrace was occupied.[20] The stucco-fronted buildings (fig. 37, Plate 59b) form a unified architectural composition, characteristically Regency, slightly marred by later alterations. William Darby, as a future surveyor, may himself have been the architect, but it is conceivable that the Richard Darby who leased No. 14 was the R. Darby practising as a surveyor a year or so earlier in Jermyn Street,[21] and if so that he was involved in the design.[c] The outer two houses at each end are treated as pavilions, with a slight break forwards and a giant pilaster order applied, giving a touch of grandeur to buildings of no great scale, the frontages being only about eighteen feet.

Externally, the stucco detailing is minimal, and the area railings and balconies are of standard patterns; there is some variety in the balcony-brackets used, not all of which appear to be original. Plans are of conventional side-passage type (the corner houses have their entrances on the return walls). Particulars of No. 13 in 1889 appear typical of the houses at that time. In the basement were two kitchens and the scullery, with a wine-cellar and two coal-cellars under the pavement. The large dining-room on the ground floor could be divided into two rooms by folding doors; there was no such partition in the corresponding double drawing-room upstairs (where the chimneypieces were of marble). The upper floors each comprised two bedrooms, with various cupboards; there was a w.c. on the ground floor, another on the top floor, but no bathroom.[22]

T. W. Marriott took a lease of the partly built No. 8 from Alexander Anderson in 1828.[23] This corner house, which was for some years the residence of his son T. W. M. Marriott, has been much altered at various times. By 1861 it accommodated two households and for most of the rest of the century was a lodging-house. Residents in 1891 included the author Robert S. Hichens, who became well known with his novel *The Green Carnation*, published in 1894.[24] Its strongest literary association, however, is with the Hungarian-born writer Arthur Koestler, who bought the house on a characteristically sudden fancy while flat-hunting in 1952; it remained his London base for work and entertaining for the rest of his life. His study, which he had lined with old pine panelling, was at the top, and the whole house – from its exterior grey wash and the blind windows of the entrance front – became known to his circle as 'Bachelor's Fortress'. Koestler was in fact married three times, but had many girlfriends (the cause of angry scenes at the house, such as when caviar was hurled through the kitchen window and a hapless guest thrown into the street).[25] In 1983, when he was terminally ill, Koestler and his third wife

---

[c] Another possibility is that the designer was Marriott's brother Edward Evans Marriott, the lessee of several houses on the estate, who was variously described as a surveyor or brickmaker. Ernest Oswald Coe, an architect who witnessed a number of deeds relating to property on the estate, appears merely to have been a relation of one of T. W. Marriott's many mortgagees and of a solicitor who probably arranged the loans.

Cynthia committed suicide at the house. It has been remodelled internally since (Plate 63c).

No. 9 was occupied from about 1848 by Mary Rimbault, her wood-engraver sons Charles, Edward and John, their sister Emma, and their lodger Frederick W. Fairholt, the wood-engraver and illustrator, and the author of *Costume in England*. In about 1864 the household moved to No. 22, and it was there that Fairholt died.[26]

The windows at No. 14 have been enriched with Italianate stucco pediments, perhaps by the architect Harvey Lonsdale Elmes, whose father-in-law, Charles Terry, was a long-term occupant of the house (then numbered 16).

No. 15 was for many years occupied by the politician Anthony (Lord) Barber, who designed the penthouse floor, added in the 1960s.

Other former residents include: the painters Thomas Brigstocke (No. 11, in 1841), William Bromet (No. 14, in 1835–7)[27] and John Hanson Walker (No. 14, in the early 1870s); Vice-Admiral Sir Michael Culme-Seymour, Second Sea Lord and Chief of Naval Personnel (No. 16, from c.1900); Dr John Muir, former Inspector-General of Hospitals (lodging at No. 16 in 1881); Sir George Augustus Stevenson, Private Secretary to the Treasury Secretary, later Commissioner of Public Works in Ireland (No. 15).

North side: Nos 26–44

The north side of the square was originally called Montpelier Terrace. Built at several dates and variously altered, the house fronts here are more of a mixture than those elsewhere in the square, the earliest, at the east end, being the plainest (fig. 37). The frontages vary from 17 to 20 feet.

A particular feature of the north side is the number of houses with shallow bay-windows inserted on the ground-floor fronts, in place of the original sashes and often in widened openings, most of which seem to have been done in the late Victorian and Edwardian periods. Deeper bay-windows, projecting beyond the building line, required special permission under the Building Acts, which was unlikely to be granted.[28] No. 28 received such a window in 1906–7, apparently in emulation of the house next door.[29]

The earliest houses on the north side were the King George IV public house at No. 44, and No. 37, first rated in 1827 and 1829 respectively. Nos 36 and 38, 40 and 41 were completed and occupied by c.1830. The builder, of Nos 36–38 at least, appears to have been John Souter of Chelsea, a bricklayer who had earlier built Trevor Chapel behind Trevor Square and who was also involved in building in Montpelier Walk.[30]

For many years from 1852, No. 38 was the home of a well-known comedian, Walter Lacy (whose real name was Walter Williams) and his former-actress wife Harriette

(née Taylor), 'the best Ophelia of her day'.[31d] Later occupants include Louis Waldstein of New York, pathologist and author of *The Subconscious Self* (1897).

Though a lease of the site of No. 39 was granted in 1826, the house remained unbuilt or incomplete until about 1835.[32] It forms a group with the earlier Nos 40 and 41, the three houses having channelled stucco on the ground floor, and stucco surrounds to the upper windows.

In 1851 the architect Matthew Digby Wyatt was living at No. 40, then a lodging-house and presumably a convenient base while he was involved with the Great Exhibition.[33]

The architect Horace Farquharson lived at No. 41 in the early twentieth century.

No. 44, the King George IV public house (Plate 60d), built c.1827, was leased to Marriott's brother Edward Evans Marriott (who did not run it himself).[34] It was a haunt of the novelist Henry Green, who lived in Trevor Place in the 1940s and '50s. A third storey was added in 1992, but the pub closed in 1995 and was pulled down two years later. To the east, Nos 44A and 44B, built as part of the South Lodge redevelopment and occupied for some years as the Omani embassy, were demolished at the same time as the King George IV. Four traditional-style houses were built on the site of Nos 44, 44A and 44B in 1998–9.

By 1832 the sites of Nos 42 and 43 had been leased, for a 63-year term, to one Archibald Ritchie,[35] but he had left the scene by 1838 when the plots (whether or not built up), formed part of a demise to Charles Bowler, a Fetter Lane baker.[36] Still unfinished, No. 43 was leased to a grocer in March 1839.[37] A grocer-and-cheesemonger's shop throughout the 1840s, it was taken over about 1850 by a young Scottish draper, and a draper's it remained. This shop and the pub, with the dairy and the stationer's over the road (see Nos 45–47, below) and later a general practitioner at No. 42, gave to this corner a business character of which no trace remains.

After the draper's closed, No. 43 was considerably altered c.1927, when the old-fashioned double shop-front was replaced by a fanlighted doorway and a garage entrance (where the gates call to mind modern faux-Georgian 'fanlight' doors). The alterations, for Major Sir John Prestige, were designed by the architect Walter Godfrey (one of the editors of the *Survey of London*).[38]

No. 42 was completed by late 1840, when it was let to Sarah Rosetta Lane, widow.[39] It was altered and enlarged c.1891 by the architects Habershon & Fawckner for Robert de Burgh d'Arcy, the London County Council (LCC) allowing a front bay to be built.[40]

No. 35 was built about 1849 by W. J. Adams of Montpelier Street for James William Wimsett, also of Montpelier Street, who bought the site freehold in 1848 (and a strip to widen it the following year).[41]

---

[d] Many of the north-side houses have had connections with the performing arts world. Apart from actors and others who took lodgings there in Victorian times, No. 28 was once the home of the composer Lionel Monckton and his mother, the actress Lady Monckton; No. 29 was the birthplace of Joyce Grenfell; Madame Belle Cole, an American-born singer, formerly of No. 24 Montpelier Square, lived at No. 36 in the 1890s; and Leslie Caron and her theatre-director husband (Sir) Peter Hall lived at No. 31 in the 1960s.

26   27   28   29   30   31   32   33   34   35

1851-3   1849

North

17   18   19   20   21   22   23   24   25

c.1845   1835

West

8   9   10   11   12   13   14   15   16

1826 - c.1830

South

Ft   40
M   12

Fig. 37. Montpelier Square, elevations as in 1996–7

Nos 27–34 were all started in 1851 by the builder John Gooch the younger.[42] (Gooch and his father, also a builder, were formerly near neighbours of T. W. Marriott's in High Row, Marriott at No. 15, the Gooches at No. 16 High Row West, later Albert Terrace.) Leases of these houses, none of them yet finished and one or two hardly begun, were granted by May 1851 and all were occupied by 1853.[43] Their construction was evidently taken over from Gooch (who died in 1851) by Henry William Atkinson of Cheyne Walk, who took the leases of Nos 30–33.[c] The other lessees were Edwyn Allum (Nos 27, 28, 34), a local shopkeeper with

leasehold interests in houses on the west side of the square, and the Misses Savill, of Michael's Place, Brompton (No. 29).[44]

The Gooch-Atkinson houses follow the general pattern of the houses which Gooch had already built on the east side of the square, but are more ornamental with balustraded parapets. The frontages, however, are less generous. Nos 27–34, and No. 35, all carry on the established cornice line, dentilated at Nos 28 and 35 where the houses break forward very slightly and have the additional emphasis of rusticated quoins, window pediments, and round-arched doorways

[c] Atkinson and Gooch had both been prominent, though not in partnership, in the development of the Thurloe Square area in the 1840s (see *Survey of London*, volume XLI).

with fanlights. Also continued is the balcony line, where the ironwork is similar to that on the east side of the square.

No. 28 underwent one of the first thorough modernizations in the row. This was done in 1906–7 for Sir Henry Chartres Biron, a well-known magistrate, by the decorative specialists George Jackson & Sons of Rathbone Place. Among the improvements, which included the fitting of new chimneypieces and mahogany doors, were two fairly standard modifications to houses of traditional side-passage plan: the turning round of the foot of the stairs to face the partly opened-up back room, and the building of a top-lit ground-floor extension for dining and entertaining. This room was finished in Parian cement, with an ornamental 'waggon' ceiling.[45]

No. 34 has a minimal iron-columned portico of 1861.[46]

No. 35 owes much of its imposing appearance to relatively recent features – such as the big first-floor window dating from a 1935 remodelling for General Blackett-Swiny (Plate 60c). It had already been extended. In 1914 the accommodation included a smoking-room and a sitting-room on the ground floor, with a dining-room built over the garden and served by a lift from the basement; on the first floor, the drawing-room ran the full depth of the main house to a small conservatory. A bathroom – the first in the house – was built out at the back on the second floor in 1931; a second, for an intended 'large indoor staff', was refused by the LCC in 1935.[47]

No. 26 was built in 1851–2, together with Montpelier Terrace, by Joseph Liddiatt.[48] It was altered and much enlarged some time before the First World War. Tall, with its own cornice-line, No. 26 has five full storeys, the top two floors being expressed as a double attic. In 1913 a portico similar to that at No. 34 was added.[49] T. W. M. Marriott was the first occupant of the house, from 1852 – when it was numbered 8 Montpelier Terrace – until about 1880. It was next occupied by the philosophical and scientific writer Edmund Gurney, a founder of the Society for Psychical Research. Gurney was the principal author of the pioneering work on hallucination and experimental telepathy, *Phantasms of the Living* (1886); visiting him, Sir Oliver Lodge found the sitting-room 'completely covered with little piles of printed slips' containing the case-histories used in its compilation.[50] After Gurney's mysterious death in Brighton, his widow continued to live at the house for some time with her second husband, Thomas N. A. Grove, the founder and editor of *New Review*.[51]

West side: Nos 17–25

By June 1826 William Darby had taken out an agreement with T. W. Marriott and John Betts to build three houses at the south end of the west side of Montpelier Square. These and the other six plots were intended to be built up to the same elevational design as the houses on the south side, but nothing came of these initial plans, doubtless because of Darby's bankruptcy.[52]

When building did begin, some years later, it was to a plainer pattern, though in size and plan the new houses were similar to those on the south side (figs 37–8). The first houses, Nos 24 and 25, were first rated in 1835. No. 25 was from 1848 the home of Dr John Morison, the founder-minister of Trevor Chapel and long-serving editor of the *Evangelical Magazine*. From the late 1890s until *c*.1914 it was occupied by Leopold Maxse, owner-editor of the imperialist *National Review*. The house was much altered in 1914 when it was extended and 'incorporated' with No. 1 Montpelier Row.[53]

Occupants of No. 24 have included the Rev. Edward Charles Mackenzie Walcott, writer on ecclesiological, antiquarian and topographical subjects, who had lodgings there about 1857, and the artist Charles William Campbell, *c*.1884.[54]

Fig. 38. No. 24 Montpelier Square, *c*.1835, plans

Nothing was done with the ground south of No. 24 until 1845, when Nos 17–23 were built there by John Gooch the younger.[55] The ground-floor fronts have round-arched openings and recessed doorways, several with ornamental fanlights.

No. 23 was modernized in 1991–2 (by Christian Stocker Associates, architects), when a galleried steel-and-timber conservatory was added (Plate 63b).

Nos 19 and 20 were used together for most of the later nineteenth century as a boarding-house, to which No. 21 had been annexed by 1891; the establishment then comprised the landlord's family, about twenty guests and a staff of seven.[56]

William Morris's *Oxford and Cambridge Magazine* was edited at No. 18 (then a lodging-house and numbered 20) in 1856. The editors, William Fulford and Wilfred Heeley, moved to the house and for a while it became a meeting-place for the contributors. Losses and Morris's growing preoccupation with painting led to the magazine's early closure.[57]

East side: Nos 1–7

Little is known of William Darby's intentions for the east side. He cut a drain there, presumably as a preliminary to building, but without having first received official permission, and in March 1827 the Sewer Commissioners ordered the drain to be destroyed and fined him £18.[58] Darby was no longer involved when in 1838 the vacant ground was demised by T. W. Marriott to Charles Bowler, baker, of Fetter Lane.[59] A building agreement for the construction of Nos 3–7 was made in April 1841 between Marriott and John Gooch the younger, but more than a year later the houses had not been built. By that time Nos 1 and 2, probably built at Marriott's expense, were standing but unfinished. Leases of Nos 3–7 were granted to Gooch in February 1843, and tenants began moving in during that year; Nos 1 and 2 stayed empty for several years.[60]

There was no attempt to make the east side of the square conformable to the southern range. Seven houses, not the originally intended nine, were built, giving frontages of about 20 feet, and the resulting houses (fig. 37) are that much grander than those on the south side. A mixture of stucco and yellowish brick was used instead of full stucco, the doorcases are larger and more ornate, and ironwork of a more elaborate pattern, with a bellied profile, was used for the balconies. The end pair, Nos 1 and 2, have particular prominence, not only from their slight break forwards and their full fourth floor, but from their position at the upper end of the sloping site. As on the southern range, the entrance to the corner house, No. 1, is on the return front. The original porch at No. 1 was extended in 1904, and it has been ornamented by a stone eagle since the early 1970s.[61] Nos 3–7 follow the end houses in their general proportions, the chief modification in design being the different treatment of the ground-floor windows (flat-arched as opposed to round-headed) and the lack of an attic floor. The greater width allows the windows to be paired, thus giving more individual identity to the houses; a slight emphasis is given to the middle house by means of segmental arches over the first-floor windows.

An early resident was R. Kirkman Lane, an attorney, at No. 1 (perhaps related to Mrs Lane at No. 42 opposite), and there were at least three early households with East Indies connections. No. 7 was the last home of T. W. M. Marriott; he died there in 1889. Nos 1 and 2 had both become lodging-houses by the 1870s, and they were later run as a single establishment.[62]

At No. 3, a dining-room at the rear was added in 1931 for the new owner, Major Philip Le Grand Gribble. Designed by Douglas Wells, architect, and built by Maurice H. Turner Ltd of Beauchamp Place, it was painted by 'an unknown Italian artist' with *trompe-l'oeil* landscapes, sky and trellised vines.[63]

Nos 45–47

No. 45 Montpelier Square (Plate 56c), formerly No. 36 Hill Street, is part of the Trevor estate development (see page 102). The single-bay addition to the side, formerly No. 46 but now incorporated with it, was built in 1858 as a house and shop, despite objections from T. W. M. Marriott and others that it would restrict air to the neighbouring houses.[64] The shop was for many years a stationer's and newsagent's. Next door the 'Princes Gate Dairy', which opened about 1850, was converted from or replaced a stable originally belonging to No. 1 Montpelier Square.[65] At first known as No. 1A Montpelier Square (or No. 2 Montpelier Terrace), it became No. 45 in 1865 and No. 47 in 1891. The present No. 47, replacing the recently closed dairy, was designed and built in 1938 by T. M. England & Company Ltd of Kinnerton Street.[66] Among its occupiers have been the Dowager Viscountess Craigavon, widow of the first Prime Minister of Northern Ireland.

Social character

Censuses and directories suggest that the Victorian square was predominantly middle-class, while far from solidly well-to-do. Residents appear often to have taken in one or more paying guests, and there were several lodging- or boarding-houses (a few comprising two or even three neighbouring properties). Many households had a cook and a maid, sometimes a nursemaid as well; a few managed larger staffs with perhaps a butler and coachman. Mrs Smith, for instance, an Irish actress, employed a lady's maid, cook, housemaid and groom at No. 32 in 1871; a few doors away, the Reverend Whichcote and his wife also had four servants.

Many of the inhabitants up to the mid-century claimed private means: others included barristers, army officers, doctors and a dentist, wine merchants, a brewer's agent, an upholsterer, teachers, artists, an architect, a clerk of works, and a distinguished Nonconformist minister, Dr Morison.[67] No. 6, a school run by the young Misses Ramsay, one of whom had been born in Calcutta, accommodated more than a dozen girls mostly born in India.[68] By 1861 the obviously commercial householders included a blind-maker (employer of sixteen men and boys), a coal agent, a confectioner and a decorator. Later a funeral furnisher, a Jewish commercial traveller and a musician in the Life Guards took houses there.

If the inhabitants were mixed, there was also continuity. Some early and later residents stayed for decades. T. W. M. Marriott, a non-practising barrister (whose local interests included membership of Westminster District Board of Works), lived successively at three houses in the square until his death.

Yet Montpelier Square acquired an enduring bad reputation. It was this that prompted T. W. M. Marriott's application, rejected by the Metropolitan Board of Works early in 1863, to have the square and Montpelier Street renamed. In 1867 it was said that both Montpelier and Trevor Squares 'if they are still dull and shabby, have lost the ill-name that generally attached to them'.[69] Nevertheless more than eight years later residents petitioned for the square to be renamed Beaufort Square, on the grounds that although it was now occupied by 'a different class of persons' its old reputation still depressed property values.[70] The matter was raised more determinedly in the late 1880s and early '90s by residents claiming that houses were difficult to let and had depreciated. A Mrs Silvertop, newly arrived at No. 30, suggested the names Princes, Rutland Gate, Ennismore, Knightsbridge or Beaufort Gardens Square.[71] But by that time perhaps the aim was really to acquire a name with instant cachet.

The censuses suggest very few possibly dubious houses. Lodging-houses may have attracted some undesirables, but only proliferated in later years and may have been as much the product as the cause of the bad reputation. Of five houses uninhabited in 1871, four were later used as lodging-houses. In 1861 the lodging-houses (excluding addresses with only one or two lodgers) appear to have been at Nos 22–24, run by the same man; but by the 1870s and '80s Nos 1–2 and 36, and many of the houses on the south and west sides could be so described.[72] Moreover, with residents such as the Reverend Walcott, the ecclesiologist, M. D. Wyatt, the architect, and members of William Morris's circle (all these in the 1850s), the lodging-houses were doubtless largely respectable.

John Galsworthy's choice of a house in the square ('No. 62') as the fictional address of Soames Forsyte in 1886 was no doubt an informed one, and it is interesting that he makes something of the square's appeal to the Forsytes for investment, as well as having a 'capital position' for their own residential purposes. Soames's father James had been after another house in the square for the past two years, but baulked at the price – James's brother Jolyon (with an eye also on Soho) has just bought this house himself when the family saga opens.[73]

As a solicitor, Soames would not have been out of place at that time. In the 1880s and '90s householders on the north side included at least one solicitor, a civil engineer, a Parliamentary agent, a retired major-general, and several men and women of independent means.[74]

By the 1890s the residents of the square were confident of its rising status, and in petitioning against the opening of a skating-rink in the old floorcloth factory on the west side of Trevor Place dissociated their own 'very much improved' neighbourhood from Trevor Square and Trevor Street.[75] The architect Henry Currey, reporting on properties there in 1896, emphasized the 'rather special' character of the houses, small but desirable because so near the parks (precisely the Forsyte assessment).[76]

In the 1920s the novelist Sir Philip Gibbs chose the square as the home of an unconventional ménage (socially of much higher antecedents than the Forsytes), headed by a professional gambler turned Bond Street milliner. The house, paid for by her soldier husband (deserted by her long ago but now under a cloud himself following a massacre in the Punjab), is seen as a 'find' for people who before the First World War would have aspired to some-

thing grander; as with 'No. 62' in *The Man of Property*, its smallness and cosy charm are stressed.[77]

In the mid-1930s Montpelier Square could be described as 'the best residential square in the district',[78] though it still contained boarding-houses and continued to do so until after the Second World War. By the 1960s the square was firmly established as a fashionable address. No. 31, the home of the actress and hostess Leslie Caron, was mentioned in the *Time* article which made famous the phrase 'Swinging London': it was the only private house shown on an accompanying map of the London 'scene'.[79]

Other Streets

Montpelier Terrace

The name Montpelier Terrace was originally used for the north side of the square and for shop premises on the south side of the street – on the sites of the present No. 47 Montpelier Square and No. 8 Montpelier Terrace. The latter is the site of the original No. 1 Montpelier Terrace, a property long gone, which seems to have been built on to the rear of No. 1 Montpelier Row in about 1833.[80] Nos 2–7 Montpelier Terrace, on the north side, were originally a row of six similar houses built in the early 1850s: of these, only Nos 5, 6 and 7 survive. Nos 26 and 27 Montpelier Square were once known as Nos 8 and 9 Montpelier Terrace. The present Nos 8–10, on the other side of the street, are recent buildings.

The development of the north side of Montpelier Terrace was originally undertaken by Joseph Liddiatt, builder, of Nottingham Terrace, Regent's Park, who in 1851–2 erected Nos 2–7 and was the lessee of four of these houses. Gloucestershire-born Liddiatt, then in his early thirties, is probably identifiable with a plasterer of that name living in Montpelier Row in 1841.[81] The other lessees were William Parker of Eaton Mews South, coachman, and George Park, gentleman, of Islington – neither bought for their own occupation.[82]

With their small scale, stucco ornamentation and rococo balcony-ironwork, the six houses must have formed a particularly pretty row (Plate 60a). Although of a convenient size for small households with perhaps one servant, the houses soon seem to have acquired an inferior social status to those in the square, and for some years there was a high turnover of tenants. Early occupants did, however, include a couple of 'esquires' and a Captain; No. 3, briefly, housed a preparatory school. By the later 1850s no residents (except for T. W. M. Marriott at the then No. 8) appeared in the *Post Office Directory*, and from 1861 to 1887 Montpelier Terrace was not listed. Heads of households recorded in the 1861 census included a baker, a telegraph clerk, a private soldier, a plasterer, and a dressmaker. The occupants of No. 5 may have been more genteel – an independent widow and her offspring, respectively a clerk and a governess, with one maidservant and a lodger – but the composition of other households hardly suggests conventional respectability. At No. 6, for instance, the single household comprised a 23-year-old unmarried woman of no occupation, and her six-year-old daughter. There is a local tradition that the houses were once occupied by mistresses of officers from Knightsbridge Barracks (though this is often said of houses generally in the vicinity).

By the 1880s most houses in the terrace were lodging-houses. No. 7 was for several years the headquarters of the Middlesex Yeomanry (Duke of Cambridge's Hussars).[83] Doubtless a sign of social aspiration, No. 7 was unofficially redesignated No. 25A Montpelier Square in 1899.[84]

Nos 2 and 3 were held for some years until 1913 by Lord Howard of Glossop, the occupier of No. 19 Rutland Gate, perhaps for staff accommodation, and in 1916 the whole row was acquired by the new owner of that house, the Earl of Ancaster.[85] Nos 2–4 appear to have been rebuilt in 1919, probably as a garage.[86] At the remaining houses, residents between the wars included the actor and man-about-town Ernest Thesiger at No. 6. Thesiger, an accomplished artist and embroiderer, is said to have done much of his interior decorating, working his own carpets and painting a sky on his wife's bedroom ceiling.[87]

Garages with living accommodation above were built on the site of Nos 2–4 about 1933, in connection with the new Eresby House flats (see page 153); the slightly prissy façade, by T. P. Bennett and Son (Plate 62d), superseded a bolder design rejected by the LCC.[88] Numbered 3 and 4, they are now private residences.

At the rear of Nos 6–7 is a high screen wall built in 1914, a relic of the alterations made at No. 19 Rutland Gate for the ill-fated Dr Pearson (see page 149).[89]

The south side of Montpelier Terrace comprises three houses (Nos 8, 9 and 10), between No. 25 Montpelier Square and No. 1 Montpelier Walk. Both No. 8 and No. 1 Montpelier Walk are by the architect Charles Bernard Brown, who, about 1964, acquired No. 25 Montpelier Square, to which No. 1 Montpelier Walk had long formed an annexe. No. 1 was rebuilt in 1965 as a bijou house of quite distinguished design. The doll's house-like north façade is scaled down and given false windows to create the illusion of an additional storey (Plate 62a–b). In the same spirit, the basement dining-room was given a fanciful view in the form of a *trompe-l'oeil* garden painted on the area wall. Plate 63a shows the drawing-room in the newly completed house. For his own occupation, Brown built No. 8 Montpelier Terrace (incorporating part of the rear extension to No. 25 Montpelier Square). In the late 1970s he clad the exterior with pvc weatherboarding, a material he had used a few years earlier to face Nos 62 and 64 Cheval Place.[90]

A single house and garage, No. 9 Montpelier Terrace, was converted from the back extension to No. 25 Montpelier Square in about 1974. The architects were Michael Twigg, Brown & Partners (a firm unconnected with Charles Bernard Brown). It has since been made into two dwellings, Nos 9 and 10.[91]

Montpelier Street

Montpelier Street today consists of the former Rawstorne Street[f] and its northern continuation to Montpelier Square. That part on the former Montpelier estate comprises Nos 13–27 on the west side, and Nos 20–44 on the east. Rawstorne Street was merged with Montpelier Street in 1862 and the old name abolished.[92]

The southern part of the street has always been a mixture of shops and commercial premises; northwards the houses become larger and blend into the residential milieu of the square. The houses are of the most ordinary description, with plain brick fronts stuccoed on the ground floor (a few now fully rendered or painted over). Several have alterations characteristic of pre-Second World War gentrification, such as wooden canopies over the front doors and widened ground-floor windows. The ironwork of the first-floor window-guards is mostly of the same design as that on the balconies of the south and west sides, and part of the north side, of Montpelier Square: a simple pattern of fleurs-de-lis and rosettes. A somewhat more florid design is used on the balconies at Nos 40–44.

The earliest house, No. 27, was erected by William Darby in 1826, on lease from the new freeholder, William Bromley. Nos 23 and 25 were built the following year by Henry Cullingham, carpenter.[93]

The trio at Nos 13–17 was built by 1831. No. 21 and the Talbot Tavern or Hotel (now the Tea Clipper) at No. 19, had followed by about 1839.[94] They are similar in style, with rounded corners and prominent cement cornices (Plate 61c).

Nos 28 and 30 date from 1827–8, No. 30 being leased in early 1828 to William Sparks, carpenter, of Sloane Street; No. 28 was leased back by T. W. Marriott from a mortgagee at the end of the year.[95] The rest of the houses on the east side, Nos 20–26 and 32–44, date from the late 1830s and were probably all or largely the work of John Gooch the elder and his son, also John. The younger Gooch, who went on to build up most of the remaining vacant plots in Montpelier Square, later took leases of some of them and a workshop behind in Montpelier Mews; the Gooches lived at No. 38 Montpelier Street. The other lessees included William Parker, who also took Nos 1, 2 and 3 in the mews. The original appearance of Nos 20–38 was presumably similar to the houses on the other side of the street; the northernmost three, Nos 40–44, are somewhat grander, befitting their place on the fringe of the square.[96]

Former residents of the street include the artist Joseph Austin Benwell, a specialist in pictures of India, who was

---

[f] Described in *Survey of London* volume XLI. Since the publication of that volume in 1983 Nos 1–11 (odd) Montpelier Street, erected in 1865–6, have been rebuilt in replica.

living at No. 44 in 1871, and the painter William Henry Haines, who died at No. 44 in 1884. Another artist, Frederick S. Thomas, was living at No. 32 in 1841. The Arts and Crafts architect James MacLaren lived at No. 40 with his brother Thomas, later also an architect, in the early 1880s. Dyneley Hussey, the music-critic, lived at No. 22 in the 1920s.

Montpelier Mews

Montpelier Mews was developed over several years from c.1837, although James Sams, dairyman, had taken a lease of a presumably new yard and stabling there – the site of the present Nos 9 and 10 – from T. W. Marriott in 1830. Nos 1, 2 and 3 (Plate 78c) were erected in 1839–40. The eastern side, built up with stabling, workshops and a cottage, is now occupied by the former Harrods depot in Trevor Square; the south side, not part of the Montpelier estate, was formerly occupied by stabling and flats called Montpelier Buildings, and has been rebuilt in recent years.[97]

Sterling Street

At first called Harriet Street, and then Alfred Street, Sterling Street was renamed in 1890 after Edward Sterling of *The Times*, who lived in South Place.

The earliest house is No. 8, begun in 1825–6 by William Darby. He took a 99-year lease from William Bromley (who had recently bought the freehold) in January 1827. Darby then raised a loan from John Collins, a Fetter Lane butcher, committing himself to finishing the building and paying an annuity out of the anticipated rack-rent, but before the work was completed Darby was bankrupt. The house was assigned to Edward Aldred of Fulham, a timber merchant, and sold to its first occupier, Hannah Rayner Woodward, a widow previously of Rutland Terrace, in 1829.[98] Like Darby's houses in the square it is stucco-fronted, and it has similar balcony ironwork.

Nos 9 and 10, built for T. W. M. Marriott in 1852–3,[99] are similar in style to the larger contemporary houses on the north side of Montpelier Square.

On the west side of the street, No. 6 and the former No. 7 (now 17A Montpelier Square) were leased, still incomplete, in late 1831 to George Symons, carpenter. Things must have gone wrong, however, for the houses do not seem to have been rated and occupied until 1837–9, and Marriott was able to grant a 60-year lease of No. 7 in 1848.[100]

The other houses on the west side, Nos 1–5, were built in 1845–6 (though No. 5 was still incomplete in 1849). The first lessees were William Balch, tailor, James Beazley, gentleman, and George Bird, paper-hanger.[101]

Quaintly dissimilar now (Plate 60b), all these houses may originally have been fairly uniform. The fronts of Nos 2–4, with their plain stucco cornices and sunk panels (a feature of the earlier No. 6), can probably be taken as showing the original design. No. 7 is distinguished by a tented iron veranda of indeterminate Victorian date incorporating the original balcony railing (Plates 60b, 61a). Most of the houses have narrow overdoor lights; No. 6 has a decorative 'fan' incorporating a lantern. No. 3 has a larger opening, with a cobweb-pattern fanlight.[102]

The houses were generally in working-class occupation throughout the nineteenth century, as lodging-houses or tenements. James Campbell, a Cornish-born portrait and landscape painter, lived at No. 3 from the 1860s to the 1880s. In 1891 residents were typically dressmakers, clerks, and shop assistants, and No. 9 subsequently became a hostel for shopworkers at Woollands the drapers.[103]

An early hint of gentrification is given by the LCC's order in 1899 against the 'improper description' of No. 7 by its socially aspiring occupant as No. 17A Montpelier Square. Though earlier a working-class lodging-house, by 1891 No. 7 had risen socially, and was occupied by three young sisters and their two servants, who called it (perhaps in reference to the balcony) 'The Wigwam'. By 1909 No. 7 was occupied by the Hon. Mrs Hamilton Tollemache, and it was in the next few years that the street generally began to attract people of obviously high social position, and the shop assistants and self-employed workpeople – such as the dressmaker and the lace-cleaner listed in the directories – departed. As in other streets near by, the small houses particularly appealed to women and army officers.[104]

No. 5, for instance, was bought in 1929 by a widow, Mrs May Shephard, then living in Hill Street, and remodelled (by G. Smith, architect and surveyor) as a residence suitable for a lady. The house was partly re-planned and extended with a dining-room built over the garden. On the front, the balcony was removed and the first-floor windows were made into bays (fig. 39; Plate 60b). The house was occupied for many years from the mid-1930s by the Misses Arup, who practised there as high-class masseuses.[105]

In some contrast to the alterations at No. 5 was the remodelling of No. 3, carried out in 1938 by Serge Chermayeff for John Mathias, a documentary film-maker, and his wife. Here there was a characteristically Modernist emphasis on bathrooms, which were placed, together with storage space for clothes and linen, in a new closet-wing (fig. 39). This addition was built of solid white-brick walls, with metal-casement windows, and a flat roof of asphalted timber construction. The long, narrow proportions of the wing were presumably designed to make the most of the garden and the west-facing living-room and study in the main part of the house. Other features included a generous provision of built-in wardrobes and other fitted furniture, a sliding door between the bedrooms, wall-mounted lights, and central heating.[106] The house has been altered and extended since, and none of the fixtures and fittings designed by Chermayeff remain.

In the early 1920s, No. 10 Sterling Street was the home of the writer Radclyffe Hall and Lady Una Troubridge (who had herself been brought up at No. 23 Montpelier Square). They had earlier lived in Trevor Square. The house was extensively renovated for them, but in the end it proved too small.[107]

Fig. 39. Nos 3 and 5 Sterling Street, built 1845–6, as remodelled by Serge Chermayeff, architect, 1938 (No. 3) and G. Smith, architect, 1929–30 (No. 5)

A Blue Plaque at No. 1 commemorates the First World War cartoonist Captain Bruce Bairnsfather, of 'better 'ole' fame, who lived and worked there in 1919–21.

Montpelier Walk

Montpelier Row, as it was called until 1939, was built up in the late 1820s. The earliest house was probably No. 1, erected *c*.1826 but since rebuilt (see above under Montpelier Terrace). Nos 1–4 appear to have been the work of John Souter, who also put up some of the first houses in Montpelier Square. Neither Souter nor any nominee of his seems to have taken up leases of any of his houses, but he was party to subsequent conveyances of the properties. The new owners included Alexander Anderson, who had bought a large part of the square, and a syndicate of building-materials suppliers who may have had some part in the development: Thomas Hill of Swan Wharf, Chelsea, timber merchant; George Bird of Hammersmith, brickmaker; William Freeman of Millbank, stone merchant, and George Bazley White of Nine Elms, cement manufacturer.[108]

Most of the other houses were let to various building tradesmen, including T. W. Marriott's brickmaker brother Edward Evans Marriott.[109g] Between Montpelier Terrace and Montpelier Place the building line was set back, allowing tiny front gardens but little space for back yards.

Early Victorian occupants of the Row included artisans, labourers, servants, sailors, soldiers, musicians, dressmakers, and laundresses; a similar pattern held throughout the rest of the reign. Several houses were let as apartments by

---

[g] Others (all of Chelsea or Brompton) were James Smith, bricklayer, Richard Beauchamp, William Blore, William Henry Edmonds, John Greenacre, Daniel Spalding, and John Thomas, carpenters.

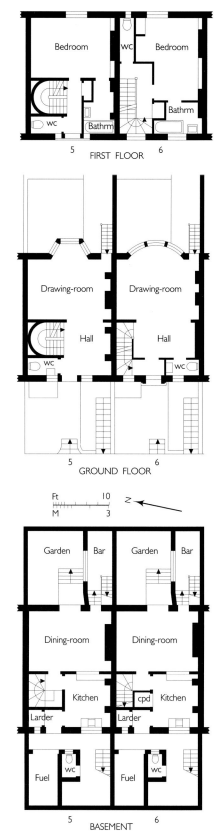

Fig. 40. Nos 5 and 6 Montpelier Walk, built late 1820s, as
remodelled by Hugh Vaux, architect, 1937

the 1860s if not earlier. Inhabitants were overwhelmingly
English, the few foreigners being mostly lodgers. They
included (in 1871) a French actress, a Stockholm-born
family of milliners and a couple of Italians – a tailor and a
print-seller; and (in 1881) two German bakers and a
French chef.[110]

No. 9 was used as one of the first Metropolitan Police
stations, in 1829–31.[111]

The houses were transformed in the late 1920s and '30s
from nondescript working-class dwellings to desirable residences. Two attractive modernizations were those carried
out at Nos 5 and 6 in 1937 by Hugh Vaux, architect, for
Mrs Sefton-Cohen, wife of an Assistant Director of Public
Prosecutions (fig. 40). Both houses were recast internally,
partly rebuilt, and given an additional floor in a mansard,
comprising bedrooms and an extra bathroom. The fronts
were made distinctive by ornamental windows – Venetian

at No. 5, oval with cobweb glazing-bars at No. 6. The Sefton-Cohens' own residence, No. 4, was modernized in 1938–9, the house being extended backwards and upwards but with the old side-passage plan retained.[112] No. 6 was the home in the late 1940s of the choreographer John Cranko.[113]

A typical modernization was that of No. 17, done for Lady Cecil Douglas in 1928–30 by the surveyors Fleetwood, Eversden & King. Here again a mansard was added, this time with the parapet dropped, but the basic pattern of openings at the front was retained. At No. 19, in 1927, the façade was carried up in the original style to accommodate an additional storey; the architect was William Doddington.[114]

No. 22 was modernized and enlarged in 1927 by Baillie Scott & Beresford for Lieut.-Commander S. Alun Maurice-Jones; the new accommodation included a top-lit studio.[115]

Nos 23–24 were rebuilt in 1929 for The Freehold Syndicate Ltd of Pall Mall as flats with garaging, in a staid neo-Georgian style. No. 23, which had a cartway entrance to sheds at the rear, was originally the premises of William Emmins, builder, and prior to rebuilding was occupied by the builders Hammond & Barr. That firm carried out a modernization of No. 26, which they owned, in 1925. Instead of knocking into one the front and back ground-floor rooms, they threw together the front room and passage, adding an outside porch; this arrangement has since been altered.[116]

The remaining houses to the south on this side of Montpelier Walk were also remodelled in the late 1920s and '30s. Similar remodellings are seen on the other side of the road south of Rutland Street; No. 35, for instance, was extensively rebuilt in 1927 to designs by C. H. Roberts, with a bay-windowed front and lozenge-shaped windows looking on to Fairholt Street.[117]

No. 38, built as a public house, the Montpelier, in 1826–7, was turned into a private residence, Montpelier House, in 1927. The conversion was designed by Eric Taylor, of Church Stretton, Shropshire, for his wife. The old pub, which had been enlarged to include the first house in Rutland Terrace (now part of Rutland Street) and much remodelled, was given an imposing entrance (with a wooden classical-style surround) on the street corner. The building has been extensively altered since.[118]

Montpelier Place and Alfred Cottages

Montpelier Place was begun in 1828–9 and largely completed during the next few years. The builders and most of the first lessees were carpenters and bricklayers, there being no obvious leading developer.[119h]

Although many of the houses have been altered and prettified, the original plain character of the south side of the street is still apparent: two-bay terrace-houses of three storeys with basements, the fronts stuccoed up to the first-floor sills (fig. 41, Plate 61b).

Fig. 41. No. 10 Montpelier Place, c.1830

Throughout the nineteenth century, Montpelier Place was occupied by a mixture of skilled and unskilled workmen, married soldiers, domestic servants, laundresses and dressmakers. Annie Chapman, who eventually became a victim of Jack the Ripper, was living at No. 29 at the time of her marriage in 1869; her mother was still living there many years later.[120] There were several small businessmen, including by 1910 a printer, a bootmaker, a decorator and a bath-chair proprietor.[121]

No. 14 was used as one of the first Metropolitan Police stations, though only for two or three years. The engineer John Lum Stothert, of the crane-makers Stothert & Pitt, was lodging at the house in 1851.[122]

---

h Among the building tradesmen to whom, or on whose nomination, many of the original leases were granted were Henry Debruno Austin of Marylebone, Philip Bennett of Islington, and William Emmins of Chelsea (bricklayers); Joseph Bennett, Henry Cullingham, John Greenacre, George Symons, John Walton – all living locally – and Edward Thomas of Marylebone (carpenters).

Fig. 42. No. 3 Fairholt Street, elevation and plans. Stanley Hicks & Son, surveyors, 1927–8

No. 1 was much altered and extended in 1927, the corner site allowing the original side-passage plan to be dispensed with (A. V. J. Kirkham, architect); a mansard floor has since been added. Nos 2 and 3 may have been remodelled at about the same time, although a scheme for their complete rebuilding seems to have been abandoned.[123]

Nos 4 and 5 were altered in 1931 to designs by Stanley C. Ramsey, making for a single handsome villa with a mansard roof (since removed) and stucco dressings.[124]

On the north side of the street, No. 22 ('The Yellow House') was formerly Nos 21 and 22. They were knocked into one in 1922–3 for Miss Ethel Snagge (later responsible for some redevelopment in Fairholt Street) and further altered in 1930 by George Val Myer, the architect and portrait painter, who lived there in the 1930s.[125]

The Nelson beerhouse at No. 24 was rebuilt c.1938–9 for Mann Crossman & Paulin, to designs by Stewart & Hendry;[126] it is now a private residence.

No. 25, now much reconstructed and extended, was a cowkeeper's house until the mid-1860s and later a boot-maker's.[127] Nos 26 and 28 were modernized and given an additional floor in 1927, to designs by C. H. Roberts, mak-

ing four-bedroom family houses of them.[128] No. 30, formerly a general shop, was rebuilt in 1927–8 to designs by William Doddington, with modish green pantiles (Plate 62c). A rebuilding scheme by Baillie Scott & Beresford had come to naught a few years earlier, apparently over the LCC's refusal to let the building line on Montpelier Walk be brought forward.[129]

Alfred Cottages (originally Alfred Mews), in a court on the north side of Montpelier Place, were built for T. W. M. Marriott in 1852.[130] The two surviving cottages, subsequently Nos 19 and 20 Montpelier Place (and since 1980 a single house) were described c.1910 as one-up one-downs, with a w.c. upstairs and a sink downstairs. There was a communal wash-house in the yard.[131] As one-family buildings they were no doubt preferable to many houses in multi-occupancy: censuses show that families tended to stay there for very many years. Victorian householders included coachmen, labourers, a police constable and a Swiss basket-maker.[132]

Three of the cottages, and three houses in Montpelier Place, were demolished about 1903 for the building of the German Christuskirche, described below.

Rutland Street

The northern arm of Rutland Street, originally Rutland Terrace ('Michael Street' on Ruff's map of 1835), was incorporated with the southern arm in 1874, when the whole street was renumbered.[133] No. 30 (formerly No. 1 Rutland Terrace) now forms part of No. 38 Montpelier Walk. The cottages on the west side were built by William Farlar, the developer of Brompton Square, who acquired the ground in 1830.[i]

On the eastern side of the street, built up from 1826 to c.1830, the chief builder seems to have been Henry Adams, a bricklayer formerly of Pimlico and later of Rutland Terrace, who in 1851 was employing eight men.[134]

Variously enlarged with extra floors and back additions, many of the houses have the bay windows, jalousies and front-door canopies typical of inter-war modernizations. No. 24, for instance, was much rebuilt in 1929 (by Christopher Wright, architect). No. 18 was altered and enlarged in 1932 (following a similar but abortive scheme of a few years earlier by Baillie Scott & Beresford), the improved accommodation including a garage: Percy E. Bacon of Tooting Common was the architect.[135]

Of post-war work the most obvious is at No. 8, where the early 1950s plain brick façades are linked by a (presumably original) rounded-off corner. The architect of the new building (and alterations to No. 10 to provide maisonettes, a flat and shop premises) was Michael Brashier. Before the Second World War No. 8 was a dairy, and earlier had been a general shop.[136]

Fairholt Street

Fairholt Street, originally Middle Street, was renamed in 1937 after the artist and writer F. W. Fairholt, who lived in Montpelier Square. The earliest houses, on the north side, were built in 1827–8 by William Henry Edmonds, carpenter, of Symonds Street, Chelsea. They were small basement cottages, with (originally) one room on each of three floors. The south side was built up ten years or so later with houses of basement, ground and two upper floors, the builders there being William Emmins of Montpelier Row and the younger John Gooch.[137]

Before the First World War, Middle Street was unhealthily crowded, with a high rate of deaths from tuberculosis, pneumonia, and alcoholism. High rents forced tenants to take lodgers or sub-let. The cottages on the north side were particularly squalid, their low-ceilinged basement rooms lit only by part-glazed doors giving on to miniscule areas.[138]

By about 1925 all the private houses in the street had been acquired by Ethel Fanny Snagge of Sloane Street, a judge's daughter. On the north side, the two westernmost cottages – No. 5 and a former fried-fish shop at No. 5A (also known as No. 6A) – were rebuilt as one house in 1925–6 to the designs of Baillie Scott & Beresford. Of four windows' width, the front is faced in re-used stocks, with gauged window-heads and a mansard hung with pantiles.[139]

The overall style was continued (in a taller, more condensed form and with plain tiles instead of pantiles) at Nos 3 and 4, which followed in 1927–8. The plans for No. 3 at least, however, were prepared not by Baillie Scott & Beresford but by a firm of surveyors, Stanley Hicks & Son of High Holborn. Different builders were involved too. Perhaps intended as Miss Snagge's own residence (she died before the works were completed), No. 3 has her initials on a date-stone over the rainwater head, and a stone pediment over the doorway, with a stylized tulip carved in low relief (fig. 42). Both houses were planned with central staircases; No. 4 has a small three-sided bay at the rear instead of the larger projection at No. 3.[140]

Miss Snagge's death in 1928 seems to have halted the intended rebuilding of Nos 1 and 2 under Stanley Hicks's direction. In 1933 they were replaced by a single house, No. 1, built, and probably designed, by W. J. Mitchell & Son Ltd of Dulwich Village. The new house, quite different in style, was intended as a family residence incorporating a maid's room and nurseries.[141]

On the south side the houses were improved in 1931, by T. M. England & Company, when jalousies were fixed at the windows. No. 11, the Prince of Wales beershop, had been amalgamated with No. 10 by the 1860s; the enlarged premises were rebuilt for Watney Combe Reid in 1908. The interior was remodelled and the front altered in the late 1940s by Watneys' architect Charles John Bailey; the pub is now called The Swag and Tails.[142]

Cheval Place (Nos 16–46)

The name Cheval Place applied originally just to the narrow western arm of the street, entered through the archway at what became No. 188 Brompton Road. The main part, successively called Chapel Row and Chapel Place, was incorporated with Cheval Place in 1910.

On the north side, the terrace west of Montpelier Walk (Nos 24–46) was part of the original Montpelier estate development, the earliest leases of houses there running from Christmas 1824. Building was more or less completed by 1830.[143i] Commercial as much as residential, Cheval Place was gentrified later than the streets to the north. A few houses were extended and improved in the mid-1930s, but many of the mansard floors in the street were only constructed in the 1960s or later.[144] The very plain houses, mostly without basements, open straight on to the pavement and are today gaily painted in a variety of colours.

---

[i] See *Survey of London*, volume XLI, page 44.

[i] Building tradesmen who took leases or nominated lessees here included George Aberdeen, mason; Peter Blackborow, mason; William Blore, carpenter; James Handy, plumber; and Daniel Spalding, carpenter.

Cheval House at Nos 16–22 was erected in 1907–8 as a warehouse for Harrods, replacing several old cottages. It was converted to a shop and flats in 1967 by Little, McClure & Knight, architects, providing three floors of one- and two-bedroom apartments and a grander penthouse flat. The basement was fitted up as the Shezan Restaurant in 1969 (Sten Eric Dahlstrom, architect).[145]

Deutsche Evangelische Christuskirche, Montpelier Place

This attractive Edwardian building on the north side of Montpelier Place (fig. 36) came into being in unusual and somewhat controversial circumstances.

The church traces its origins to the late 1660s, when a Lutheran congregation was formed from within the German and Scandinavian merchant community in the City of London. The first building, in Trinity Lane (erected on the site of Holy Trinity-the-Less, which had been destroyed in the Great Fire), survived until the 1860s, when it was replaced by the Hamburg Lutheran Church, adjoining the German Hospital in Dalston.[146]

The German offshoot of this congregation from which the church in Montpelier Place derives enjoyed a long royal association, meeting for several years at the Savoy Chapel, and later at St James's Palace. From 1781 the church met in what is now the Queen's Chapel, adjoining Marlborough House, which became known as the German Chapel (or German Chapel Royal).[147] In 1901 Edward VII, who before his accession had been a regular attender at the Anglican Sunday-morning service there, brought this custom to an abrupt end.[148]

Natural enough in Hanoverian days, by the early twentieth century the existence of a German Chapel Royal might, in view of the growing imperial rivalry between

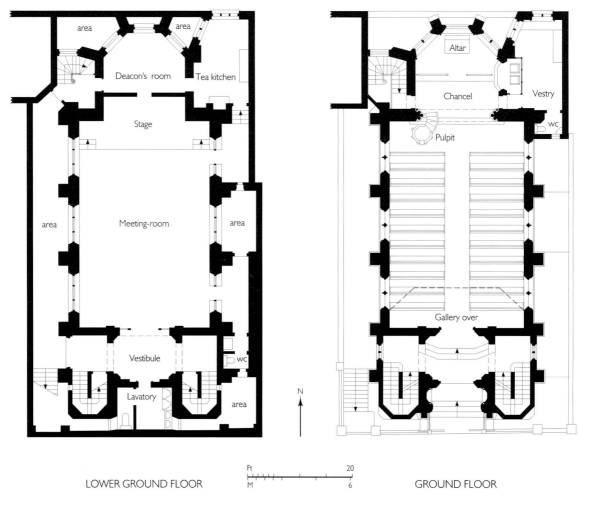

LOWER GROUND FLOOR   GROUND FLOOR

Fig. 43. Deutsche Evangelische Christuskirche, Montpelier Place, plans. Charles G. F. Rees and Edward Boehmer, architects, 1904

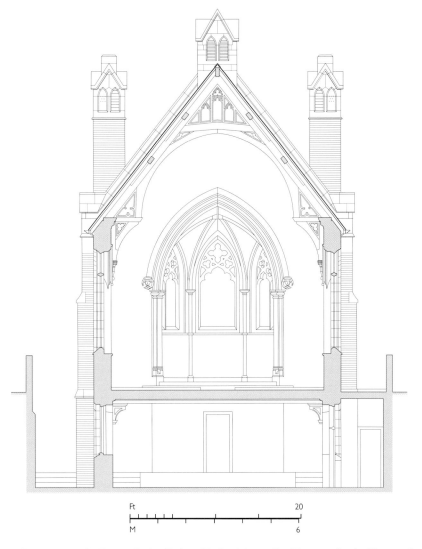

Fig. 44. Deutsche Evangelische Christuskirche, Montpelier Place, section looking north

Great Britain and Germany, have come to seem anomalous, and tradition has it that the King put a stop to the German services on the grounds that their continuance was incompatible with his position as head of the Church of England. There is, however, little doubt that the closure of the German Chapel Royal was brought about essentially to reduce expenditure in the Lord Chamberlain's department. Such other considerations as there were seem to have been personal rather than nationalistic.

In April 1901 Dr Edgar Sheppard, Sub-Dean of the Chapels Royal, proposed two money-saving measures: a reduction in the number of sinecures associated with the Chapels Royal, and the 'eventual abolition' of the chaplaincy attached to the German Chapel. Such was Sheppard's official line, but in a private note to the Comptroller of the Lord Chamberlain's department, he urged that the chaplaincy should be abolished 'in the immediate present'.[149]

The weekly German service attracted only a small congregation, drawn mainly from the suburbs, yet the associated costs, met by the department, were substantial. They included the pay of the chaplain and chapel staff, and the maintenance of furnished rooms in St James's Palace for the chapel-keeper and organist, Dr Weber. These rooms, in earlier times the Sub-Dean's official lodgings, had been given up by a predecessor of Sheppard's, much to the annoyance of successive Bishops of London, as well as of Sheppard himself, who had to live at a distance. In 1895 he had attempted to oust Dr Weber, but there was a 'rumpus' and the scheme fell through. By 1901 the circumstances were more favourable to change: the chaplain, the Rev. Dr Frisius (who was also the minister at Dalston), was a fairly recent appointee with no local connections – his predecessor having been, like Weber, elderly and long-serving.

As a result of Sheppard's recommendations, a royal

decree dated 1 July 1901 required the German services to cease in three weeks; and on the same day the Lord Chamberlain gave notice that the chapel-keeper's rooms would again become the Sub-Dean's lodgings. The staff were at once pensioned off or otherwise discharged. Diplomatic pressure was brought to bear on the King to postpone the closure until after Easter, but the deadline was merely shifted from 22 July to 4 August. Dr Frisius (who was to become the first pastor of the Christuskirche) subsequently complained, with some justice, of the 'insulting manner' in which a long tradition had been ended.[150] That the Danish services were allowed to continue there made it all the more galling, but then Queen Alexandra was Danish. Thenceforth the building was known as Marlborough House Chapel.[151]

For some time the congregation met in Eccleston Hall in Victoria.[152] The present church was erected at the expense of the Anglo-German merchant banker Baron Sir John Henry William Schröder (1825–1910), who had been involved in the negotiations over the closure of the German Chapel Royal. It was intended both to provide a permanent home for the congregation and to serve as a memorial to his late wife, Evelina.

The building was designed jointly by Edward Boehmer and a comparatively obscure architect, Charles G. F. Rees. Boehmer (who Anglicized his name to Bomer during the First World War) was born in Philadelphia of Pennsylvanian-German parents, and was educated and trained in Germany. He completed his training in London, in the office of Archer and Green. Rees, an architect, surveyor and estate agent with an office near Stanmore railway station from the 1890s, designed at least one other church for the Schröders, the Markuskirche in Kelvedon Road, Fulham (1911). He was also surveyor to the German Hospital in Dalston (of which the Schröders were benefactors), designing two substantial additions to that institution in 1911–12.[153]

The Knightsbridge church is the only work Rees and Boehmer are known to have done in collaboration, and their respective roles in this presumably *ad hoc* partnership (based apparently in Boehmer's Spring Gardens office), are not known, although there are indications that Rees's was the senior position. His name appears before Boehmer's on the contract drawings[154] and on a perspective view of the building (Plate 64a), as well as in their initial application to the London County Council regarding the church. Rees alone was named as architect in published reports of the consecration ceremony. And he, moreover, received a decoration from the Kaiser on the completion of the church.[155] There is, however, nothing in the comparatively coarse design of Rees's other known buildings to suggest affinity with the Christuskirche, and Boehmer's may be presumed to have been the guiding hand in the finer points of the design. It is a building of quality, and may perhaps be seen as something of an architectural riposte to the King's action. There was no prestige in the location, however, for Montpelier Place in the early 1900s was at best an indifferent address.

The site, then occupied by Nos 18–20 Montpelier Place and Nos 1–3 Alfred Cottages, was acquired about 1903, the plans of the new building being approved by the LCC in November that year.[156] Construction was carried out by Dove Brothers at a cost of more than £8,600.[157] The foundation-stone was laid at a ceremony in June 1904 and the building consecrated in the following November, the service being attended by Kaiser Wilhelm II's representative Count Bernstorff, Prince Christian, Princess Louise Augusta of Schleswig-Holstein, Prince and Princess Louis of Battenburg, and Baron von Schröder.[158]

The Christuskirche is a diminutive church, Decorated in style and built of orange brick with plentiful stone dressings (Plate 64a–b). Short staircase turrets with stone spirelets flank the entrance and the geometrical 'west' window. Along the frontage are iron railings with sliding gates (fig. 45). Despite the confines of the site, it is very much a church 'in the round', the sides being as well finished as the front. There is no tower, but a ventilation-shaft rises, belfry-like, over the chancel arch.

The aisleless interior (figs 43–4; Plates 64c, 65a) is simply treated, with a plain hammer-beam roof with arched braces, white-painted walls and a tessellated floor bearing a fleur-de-lis motif. A late addition to the design was the inclusion of the German ambassador's or 'royal' pew, set to the side of the chancel behind an archway and a balustrade of curvilinear tracery (Plate 65c).[159]

Beneath the church is a large meeting-room with well-preserved original features, tiled to dado level in coloured Burmantofts faience, together with various ancillary rooms (fig. 43, Plate 65d).

Fittings and furnishings

Many of the interior fixtures and fittings, and all the stained and painted windows, were made in Germany.

Two Munich glass-workshops, F. X. Zettler, glass-painters to the Bavarian court (Königliche Bayerische Hofglasmalerei), and Ostermann & Hartwein, made the figurative glass for the three chancel windows and the two central windows of the nave. A Cologne firm of glass-makers, Schneiders & Schmolz (Kunstglasmalerei), produced the leaf-patterned glass in greenish monochrome which fills the remaining windows in the nave, and the large west window (Plate 125e). All the glass is signed by the makers. The figurative glass illustrates New Testament subjects:

Chancel. The Nativity and the Crucifixion (Zettler, Plate 125d,f); the Resurrection (Ostermann & Hartwein; Plate 125b)

Nave. 'Suffer Little Children' (Zettler; Plate 125a): the Good Samaritan (Ostermann & Hartwein; Plate 125c)

The communion vessels, with a crucifix and other pieces of plate, were given by the Kaiser, from whose own designs they were made by Professor Otto Rohloff.[160] The brass memorial plaque to Baroness von Schröder in the entrance lobby was cast in 1904 by P. Stotz of Stuttgart.

The conventional octagonal wooden pulpit was carved in Berlin.

The font, a stone basin with a bulbous wooden cover, the whole mounted on a wooden stand with barley-sugar twist uprights, is said to be of late-seventeenth-century date and a relic of the German church in Trinity Lane (Plate 65b).

In 1980 the original organ, made in Germany, was replaced by a new and highly regarded baroque-style instrument by the Danish organ-builders Peter Bruhn & Son (Plate 65a).

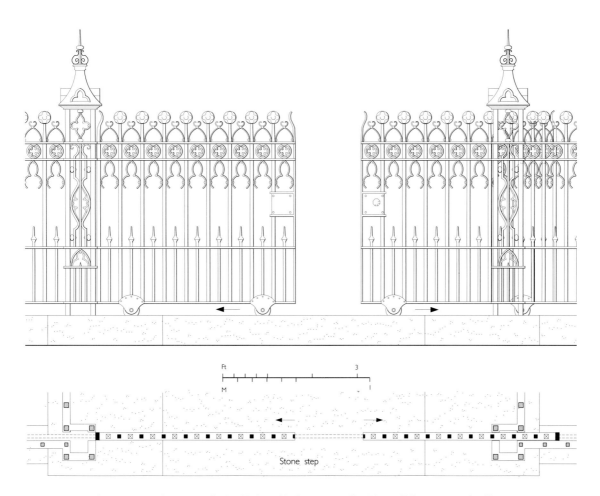

Fig. 45. Deutsche Evangelische Christuskirche, Montpelier Place, sliding gates and railings

CHAPTER VII

Rutland Gardens and South Place

Rutland Gardens was laid out in 1870–1 by Mitchell Henry, an Anglo-Irish businessman and politician who had acquired the freehold of the ground a few years earlier. The small estate was then occupied by two old mansions: Kent House and Stratheden House. The new development involved the demolition of Kent House but left Stratheden House, which was Henry's own London residence. This house was pulled down about 1900 and replaced by the blocks of flats comprising Rutland Court.

Development on Henry's estate petered out after the building in the early 1870s of a new Kent House, a few smaller houses, and a mews (Kent Yard). In the 1880s and '90s the remaining vacant sites were bought and partly built up in connection with South Lodge, a large house on the strip of ground between Henry's property and the old floorcloth factory at the corner of Trevor Place and Knightsbridge. The sites of South Lodge and the factory are now occupied by offices and housing built in the late 1970s. (The history of the factory is given in Chapter V.)

The development of the area from c.1770

Until 1862, the ground now occupied by Rutland Gardens, and the South Lodge site, formed a single freehold property, which in the eighteenth century belonged to a family named Shakespear. The eastern part, where South Lodge eventually came to be built, was by the 1760s occupied by a largish house and some cottages, but the rest of the ground was undeveloped.[1] In the early 1770s a large plot on the west side was leased for the building of the mansion later called Stratheden House, and the existing house was rebuilt or improved by the master carpenter and builder George Shakespear, on a long lease from his relations William and John Shakespear.[2] This house was later known as No. 3 South Place. A third house, the kernel of the future Kent House, followed in the early 1790s, by which time George Shakespear had become the freeholder of the whole estate. On his death, the property passed to his niece Mary Phillips, the daughter of his brother-in-law and partner John Phillips; she married Shakespear's Pimlico neighbour and trustee, William North,[3] whose family retained the land until 1862. No. 3 South Place was then sold to the sitting tenant, Sir Anthony Sterling, who built South Lodge over part of the garden at the back of the house.[4] The rest of the ground, with Kent House and Stratheden House, was sold to George Duddell of Albemarle Street, who disposed of it in November 1863 to Mitchell Henry.[5] In April 1864 Henry acquired the short residue of the orig-

inal leases of Stratheden House and its stabling; the leasehold interest in Kent House he did not acquire until 1866.[6]

Henry carried out lavish improvements at Stratheden House before turning his attention to the development of the Kent House estate. In the summer of 1870 Kent House was pulled down, and the German-born architect and decorator Frederick Sang, Henry's interior designer at Stratheden House, sought approval from the Metropolitan Board of Works on Henry's behalf for a plan to build a road (Rutland Gardens) and houses on the site.[7]

The main-road frontage of the Kent House estate was divided into three large plots for mansions, but in the event only the westernmost plot was sold, where work on the present Kent House began in 1872. Sang entered into an agreement with Henry to buy the rest of the Kent House estate,[8] but a portion of it, at the rear of the new Kent House, was sold in 1872 to Colonel R. C. S. Clifford for a 'family mansion', together with a plot for stables in what became Kent Yard.[9] Sang's purchase was never completed, though he did build one house in Rutland Gardens – Rutland Lodge, at the corner of Kent Yard.

Instead of a single mansion, Clifford built a row of four houses on his ground (Rutland House and Nos 1, 2 and 3 Rutland Gardens), at which point the development stalled. Apart from the replacement of Stratheden House with flats, the subsequent nineteenth-century building up of Rutland Gardens, and of the vacant ground adjoining Kent House, consisted essentially of improvements to the South Lodge estate. Rutland Gardens Mews was created as part of this process.

South Place and South Lodge

This section describes the development of the ground between Rutland Gardens and the floorcloth factory in Trevor Place, concluding with the joint redevelopment of most of this site and that of the factory in the 1970s.

South Place

In the nineteenth century the name South Place was the address of two, and eventually four, houses. It was abolished in 1903, when the houses were renumbered as part of Knightsbridge. No. 1 South Place was a house attached to the floorcloth factory built on the Trevor estate in the 1820s. George Shakespear's old house became No. 2 South Place, and from c.1845 (when another house was built at

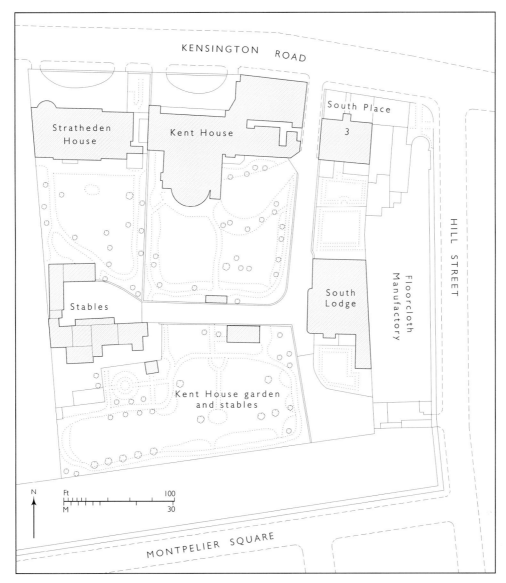

Fig. 46. Rutland Gardens and South Place area in the mid-1860s, before development

the factory) No. 3. It was the residence from 1801 until his death in 1811 of the Rev. John Gamble, minister of Trinity Chapel in Knightsbridge. An authority on telegraphy, Gamble held several appointments including chaplaincies to the armed forces, and to the Duke of York, Commander-in-Chief of the army.[10] From the mid-1820s the house was occupied by Edward Sterling, known from his leader-writing as the 'Thunderer of *The Times*'. A frequent visitor here was his elder son John, a writer who died young of consumption and is chiefly remembered as the subject of a biography by his friend Carlyle. The house is shown on two aerial views of 1851 (Plates 6b, 7).

After his father's retirement in 1843 the younger son, Anthony Coningham Sterling, took over the house, where

he lived with his wife and his late brother's children.[11] By profession a soldier, Anthony Sterling was military secretary to Sir Colin Campbell (later Baron Clyde) during the suppression of the Indian Mutiny; he was knighted in 1860.

In 1851 or slightly earlier he constructed a 'studio' in the garden behind the house, and, having acquired the freehold in 1862, set about turning this building, which seems to have been known for a while as the 'White Cottage', into a substantial house called South Lodge. The building in its presumed original form is clearly discernible in one of the aerial views published in 1851 (Plate 6b).[12] No. 3, meanwhile, was taken over by his nephew and heir, John Barton Sterling, who had now come of age. In 1873 J. B. Sterling

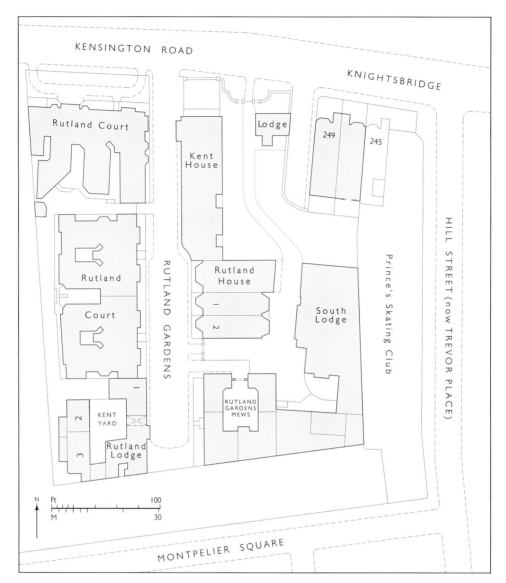

Fig. 47. Rutland Gardens and South Place area in 1906

replaced No. 3 with a pair of houses, Nos 3–4 South Place, one of which became his own residence (see Nos 247–249 Knightsbridge below).

South Lodge (demolished)

Sir Anthony's architect in the transformation of the 1851 'studio' into South Lodge was Henry Clutton, a member of the well-known family of surveyors and third cousin to the distinguished architect of the same name who later designed the new Kent House.[13a]

Little is known of the old studio other than that it was of oblong plan, corresponding to the entrance hall and library of South Lodge (fig. 48). The work seems to have involved making a new upper floor, building a large south extension, and removing the entrance from the north front to the west. The result, judging from its much later appearance, was dignified with stucco and classical detail if slightly odd in its proportions (Plate 69b).

South Lodge was sold by J. B. Sterling in 1871 to Baron Henry De Worms (later Baron Pirbright), who became a Conservative minister and a prominent figure in Anglo-Jewish affairs. De Worms extended the house and had some elaborate decoration carried out, much of it by Con-

---

[a] Sterling was a near neighbour of the Cluttons in Surrey, his country residence there, Headley Grove, being not far from the Cluttons' at Hartswood Manor.

A Sir Anthony Sterling's Studio, 1851

B House enlarged by Henry Clutton
   for Sir Anthony Sterling, 1862

C House enlarged by Henry Petit
   for Baron De Worms, 1871-7

D Wing added for Lord Llangattock,
   1907

GROUND FLOOR   FIRST FLOOR

Fig. 48. South Lodge, plans in 1967, and diagram showing building phases, 1851–1907. *Demolished*

tinental artists. Henry Petit of Welbeck Street, a young London architect with strong Continental connections himself, superintended the various works.[14b]

In 1877 South Lodge was bought by John Allan Rolls (from 1892 Baron Llangattock), who, like his contemporary De Worms, became a Conservative MP in 1880.

T. H. Wyatt, Rolls's architect for alterations at his Monmouthshire seat, The Hendre, who looked over South Lodge for him, had found it unusual and refined, furnished and decorated 'very much beyond the average of London houses'. But there were obvious drawbacks to the site, which was hemmed in and already overlooked by houses on the as yet only partly built-up Kent House estate.[16] Over the years Rolls was able, by dint of considerable expenditure, to alleviate these problems. In 1881 he bought the vacant ground south of Clifford's four houses in Rutland Gardens; then in 1882 he purchased No. 3, the southern-

most of these 'horrid houses', as he called them, and demolished it. He used the space to make a side entrance to South Lodge. This was built over in the 1970s as part of the South Lodge redevelopment, but the gates, with his initials prominent in the ironwork, remain (fig. 49). On the vacant ground, he built a range of stables called Rutland Gardens Mews. Rolls subsequently further enhanced the outlook from South Lodge by acquiring and improving the stable and coach-house (now called Balcony House) at the back of Rutland House.[17]

In 1893 Rolls bought the long-vacant ground east of Kent House, which enabled him to make a new and spacious approach to South Lodge from Knightsbridge, with imposing gates and a two-storey lodge (fig. 55, Plate 69a). The finely detailed ensemble, suggestive of extensive grounds beyond, was designed by the architectural practice of Boulnois & Warner.[18] The lodge was demolished

[b] Born *c*.1847 in London to French parents (his father was a dancing master), Petit had trained in France.[15]

Fig. 49. South Lodge, Rutland Gardens entrance, gates erected c.1882

in the 1970s for the South Lodge redevelopment, but the gates still stand, somewhat overshadowed by the tall modern block behind them.

The interior of South Lodge was rambling and probably most inconvenient. Figure 48 shows the ground and first floors as they were in 1967 and had been, in all essentials, in Rolls's day. The third floor comprised bedrooms and a bathroom, with servants' bedrooms in the south wing. Menservants had their bedrooms in the basement, where the servants' hall and housekeeper's room were also located.[19]

Of the decorative work carried out for De Worms, the painted and gilded ceiling in the first-floor ballroom, or salon as it was called during Rolls's occupancy, was by John G. Crace & Son (Plate 70a). The ceiling in the first-floor ante-room, depicting night, morning and the seasons, was painted by Kriepenkerl, a pupil of Rahl and Piloti of Munich. In the drawing-room (Plate 71), the richly ornate ceiling was painted with representations of the continents and attributes of the arts and sciences by Eduard Charlemont of Vienna, a pupil of the fashionable artist Hans Makart. The rest of the room was decorated by Kieser, also of Vienna, with Renaissance-style woodwork in oak and walnut, and large panels of old-gold silk.[20]

Rolls commissioned some striking decoration himself, of which the most ambitious was for the Eastern Room, described below, and he seems to have continued to improve the house more or less for the rest of his life. The entrance hall, in 1902 furnished with old oak, but later redecorated in classical style and lined with columns, led to

an inner hall with the main staircase. This had ornately carved walnut balustrading incorporating the initial double letter of his title.[21]

The room behind the entrance hall, furnished as a morning room in 1902, was subsequently made into a library (with ornate brass-pillared bookcases), perhaps as part of alterations in 1907, when a bow-fronted smoking-room was added on the north side.[c] In the library was a carved wooden chimneypiece of 1640, and the walls were covered with Italian leather, also said to be of seventeenth-century date.[23] The other large room on the ground floor was the dining-room, hung with red and gold embossed leather and a Flemish tapestry.[24]

Upstairs, the windows of the salon were fitted with mirrored sliding shutters. Strong colours characterized two of the smaller rooms: crimson velvet for the walls of the ante-room, and a predominantly turquoise-blue scheme in the Louis Seize-style boudoir or small drawing-room.[25]

Against these decorative backdrops and some good furniture and paintings, Rolls displayed a collection of conversation pieces, ranging from a Sedan chair to the fly-swat with which the Dey of Algiers, by striking the French ambassador, precipitated the Franco-Algerian War of 1830.[26]

From the boudoir a few steps led down to the Eastern Room, which also communicated with the downstairs dining-room. This Arabian fantasy (Plate 70b) was created for Rolls in 1883 by the decorators H. & J. Cooper of Soho at a cost of about £736. A certain amount of old work was incorporated in the scheme, notably pieces of

---

[c] The architect for this may have been Sir Aston Webb, who carried out minor alterations to the house in 1912, and who had partly remodelled The Hendre in 1897.[22]

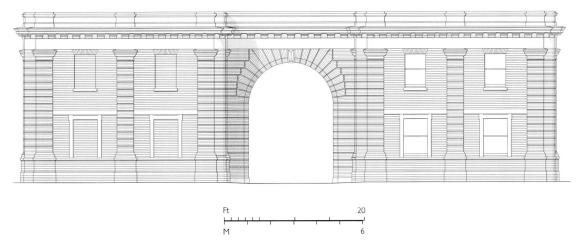

Fig. 50. Rutland Gardens Mews, north elevation. Holland & Hannen, builders, 1882

Musharabeŷeh lattice, Persian tiles, and 'two real old Damascus alcoves'. Lattice screening and a fretwork cornice comprised the main background, the ceiling was tented in striped Madagascar drapes, and more latticing covered the 'porthole' rooflights. Other hangings were of patterned muslins, yellow and blue Indian matting, and Persian-style unglazed chintzes. Red and blue distemper, black marble, bronze stencilling, green-stained or ebonized furniture, drapes and upholstery in various sorts of embroidery, damask, velvet and plush, all added to the variety of colour and texture. As well as a collection of china, numerous antiques and curios were on display, including weapons, a Koran stand, mosque lamps, punkahs and a hookah. A cabinet (to display china and conceal hot-air pipes) was copied from a piece at the South Kensington Museum.[27]

The Llangattocks lived at South Lodge with their three bachelor sons and their daughter. The second son, Charles Stewart Rolls, was the pioneer motorist and aviator who co-founded the firm of Rolls-Royce. By 1899 he had an engineering workshop in the stables at the rear of the house; the business was moved to Fulham in 1902.[28]

The last member of the family to live here was Lady Shelley-Rolls, C. S. Rolls's widowed sister, who died in 1961. Uncertainty then overshadowed South Lodge and its grounds for some years. Plans by Westminster City Council to build a fire station there as part of a comprehensive redevelopment of the whole site between Rutland Gardens and Trevor Place were vetoed by the London County Council as constituting overdevelopment.[29] Having escaped compulsory purchase, the South Lodge property was sold by the Shelley-Rolls family in 1967. Shortly afterwards it was acquired by the Royal Academy of Dancing, which, under its president Dame Margot Fonteyn, had ambitious plans for the site. South Lodge and its best interiors were to have been refurbished as the Academy's head-

quarters and study centre, and the outbuildings replaced by a studio and student accommodation. However, it proved impossible to raise the money needed and within weeks of the Academy's taking up residence in 1969 the scheme had to be abandoned and the property put on the market.[30] The Academy remained there until August 1972, when the site was cleared for redevelopment.[31]

Rutland Gardens Mews

This group of stables and coach-houses, with living accommodation over (fig. 50; Plate 78a), was built in 1882 for J. A. Rolls of South Lodge, the four units being let by him on leases or short tenancies. The builders were Holland & Hannen; the architect's name is not known.[32] A glazed shelter formerly ran along the inside edge of the quadrangle.[33] The South Lodge stables adjoining on the east side, now demolished, were of broadly similar style and probably built at or about the same time.

In the 1920s and '30s the buildings were converted into private dwellings.[34] A plaque on the wall at No. 2 commemorates two former residents: Dame Margot Fonteyn, who lived there during the Royal Academy's spell at South Lodge, and the cellist Jacqueline du Pré.

Nos 247–249 Knightsbridge (demolished)

Known until 1903 as Nos 3 and 4 South Place, these tall Italianate-style houses were built in 1873 for J. B. Sterling, on the site of the old No. 3 South Place. They were designed by J. W. Sanders[d] and erected by T. H. Adamson & Sons of Putney (who were building houses at about the same time for Colonel Clifford in Rutland Gardens).[35]

After the Second World War the two buildings, which had been knocked together and occupied by a bridge club, were made into flats (Plate 69c). The cosmetician Helena

---

[d] Probably John Williams Sanders of Lincoln's Inn Fields, surveyor.

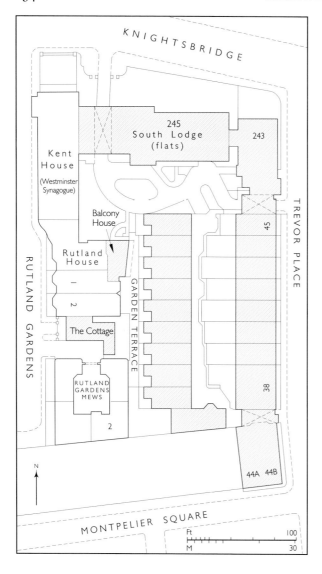

Fig. 51. South Lodge area in 1991. Development by Chapman
Taylor Partners, architects, 1974–81

Rubinstein had a flat with a roof terrace here in the early
1960s. They were demolished in the early 1970s for the
South Lodge area redevelopment.[36]

Redevelopment of South Lodge and Nos 243–249 Knightsbridge

The large site occupied by South Lodge, the former floorcloth factory (latterly car-hire depot) in Trevor Place, its
entrance premises at No. 243 Knightsbridge, and the
houses at Nos 245–249, was redeveloped in the 1970s by
Trafalgar House Developments (fig. 51). Of the existing
structures on the site only the two pairs of gates to South
Lodge, in Knightsbridge and Rutland Gardens, and the

Balcony House at the rear of Rutland House, were
retained. The architects of the scheme were Chapman
Taylor Partners.

The first buildings to be erected, in 1974–7, were an
office block on the corner of Trevor Place (No. 243
Knightsbridge), and a block of flats (No. 245) called South
Lodge. The others followed in the late 1970s and were
completed by about 1981. They consist largely of two rows
of houses, in Trevor Place and Garden Terrace. Two houses
forming the southernmost part of the development, Nos
44A and 44B Montpelier Square, occupied for some years as
the embassy of Oman, were demolished in 1997 and have
been replaced by a pair of traditional-style family houses.
In Rutland Gardens a period-looking 'cottage' was built on
the site of the side entrance to South Lodge.[37]

The development was one of the most expensive of its
day in central London, aimed particularly at Middle- and
Far-Eastern buyers. A feature of the show-house in Trevor
Place, fitted out at great expense by Faith Panton of Property Plan, was a 12-metre 'chandelier' of polycarbonate
tubes, containing 600 light bulbs, running through the
house from basement to third floor in the well of the D-
shaped staircase.[38] Externally, the buildings are modern in
style, mostly faced in brick, with some stucco (Plate
58c–d).

Kent House and the Kent House Estate Development

This section deals with the area formerly occupied by Kent
House and its grounds, which was redeveloped by Mitchell
Henry in the early 1870s as the east and south-west sides of
Rutland Gardens (see fig. 47). Rutland Gardens Mews,
which formed part of the Kent House estate, was built by
the owner of South Lodge and is described above.

Old Kent House (demolished)

Kent House took its name from Queen Victoria's father
Prince Edward, Duke of Kent and Strathearn. The prince
was not yet 31 when, following a riding accident, he was
invalided to England late in 1798 after a military career
overseas. Taking a house in St James's while apartments at
Kensington Palace were being fitted up for his occupation,
he installed his mistress of some years' standing, Madame
de St Laurent, in what was then a modest-sized newish
house in Knightsbridge. The duke, as he became in 1799,
spent part of 1799–1800 commanding the British forces in
America, and a period in 1802–3 in Gibraltar as governor,
after which he stayed in England until 1815.[39]

The Knightsbridge house, first rated in 1793, was held
by Thomas Jones esquire on a long lease from George
Shakespear and had briefly been occupied first by Lady
Reeve and then a Mr Palmer.[40] It was occupied in
1799–1800 (while the duke and, presumably, Mme de St
Laurent were in America) by Thomas Pownall, the aged

former governor of Massachusetts and South Carolina. The building was greatly enlarged in 1801 at the duke's behest, expanding across 20ft-wide strips on either side of the original plot. For these and further ground at the rear Jones obtained an additional, concurrent, lease, himself granting a 28-year sub-lease of the house to the duke.[41]

Mme de St Laurent's relationship with the duke did not end until 1817 (when she withdrew to a convent in order to clear the way for him to marry in the interests of the succession), and it was no doubt for financial reasons that 'Knightsbridge House' and its contents were put up for auction in July 1808 (earlier attempts to find a private buyer having failed). No expense had been spared by the duke, whose tastes were exacting and extravagant beyond his means. It was a magnificent residence, superbly equipped, and decorated and furnished lavishly throughout (though not perhaps comparing with the duke's country residence at Castle Hill Park in Ealing). The principal reception room was a lofty drawing-room forty feet by twenty-six; there were two dining-rooms, a library, morning and music-rooms, boudoirs and apartments *en suite*. Decoration in white and gold, with mirrors, statues and marble chimneypieces, was offset by coloured hangings (predominantly blue), carpets and upholstery. Furniture included a set of thirty white parcel-gilt chairs upholstered with 'curtain seats' of blue silk damask; dining-room chairs, and some other pieces, were in the Grecian style. Blue and white Persian silk curtains hung at many of the windows.

Balconies at front and back gave views over Hyde Park and distant Surrey, while the grounds themselves were laid out with pleasure gardens, complemented by a large semicircular greenhouse, a hothouse, a kitchen garden and fruit trees.[42]

After the departure of the duke and Mme de St Laurent, the house was occupied by Lord Boringdon, later 1st Earl of Morley. He divided it, living in part and letting the rest to his sister and her husband, the Hon. George Villiers. A large garden with stables (now covered by Kent Yard and Rutland Gardens Mews) and a wide strip of ground on the east side of the house, with outbuildings, were formally added to the property under a third concurrent lease in 1829, the earl taking an assignment of all three leases from Thomas Jones of Droitwich in 1831.[43]

A bird's-eye view of the house and its well-screened garden in 1851 is given on Plate 7.

Kent House remained in the occupation of the two families for many years. The 2nd Earl lived there until *c*.1860. The Villiers's daughter Theresa, and her second husband, the statesman Sir George Cornewall Lewis, lived in 'Kent House B' (the western half) until their deaths in the 1860s. 'Kent House A' was last occupied by Sir John Ogilvy, Bart, for some years MP for Dundee.[44] The whole building was pulled down in 1870 by the freeholder, Mitchell Henry of Stratheden House.[45] Not long afterwards its name was to be transferred to a new house built partly on the site of the old.

Kent House: The Westminster Synagogue

This dignified mansion of red brick and stone at the northeast corner of Rutland Gardens was built in 1872–4 for Louisa, Lady Ashburton, widow of William Baring Bingham, 2nd Baron Ashburton. It was the first house to be erected on the newly laid out Kent House estate, and the only one to be built on ground facing the park, where the development plan had called for a row of three large houses. As the first person to take a building plot on the estate, Lady Ashburton was allowed to appropriate the name, resonant with royal association, of the former mansion on the site. The new house was designed by Henry Clutton, architect of the Ashburtons' Jacobethan country seat, Melchet Court in Hampshire (1863–8).[46]

Widowed, with a young daughter, Lady Ashburton was rich, independent-minded and intensely interested in art, especially painting and sculpture. She was at the centre of a wide circle of artistic and literary figures, and numbered among her friends Thomas Carlyle, the painters G. F. Watts and Edward Lear, Sir Coutts Lindsay, the art connoisseur, and John Forster, the biographer of Dickens. With the American-born but Rome-based sculptress, Harriet Hosmer, of whom she was an important patron, her friendship developed into an intensely romantic relationship. Some of these figures became caught up in the saga of Kent House, as did her close friend Lady Marian Alford, another art-loving widow of substantial means and herself a friend and patron of Harriet Hosmer.

In deciding to build a town house rather than rent an existing property, Lady Ashburton could well have been influenced by Lady Alford, whose own new residence in Ennismore Gardens was then nearing completion (see page 175). Whether or not in conscious emulation of her friend, Lady Ashburton's choice of site closely mirrored that of Lady Alford's house – a corner plot, facing the Kensington road with a long return frontage.

Clutton's plans for the new house were put out to tender in the autumn of 1871, and half-a-dozen leading builders competed for the contract, the winner being William Brass of Old Street. At £14,945 his tender was the lowest.[47] (This did not include the quite separate and expensive stable block which Brass built for Lady Ashburton in Kent Yard, see below.) Once building was under way, in the spring of 1872, Lady Ashburton completed the purchase of the site, paying £18,000 to Mitchell Henry for the freehold.[48]

It is unlikely that Clutton counted Kent House among his more enjoyable commissions. Lady Ashburton could be difficult to deal with, as even her close friends admitted. 'Lady Ashburton is too absurd, a perfect dingle dousie', wrote Carlyle, while Harriet Hosmer called her 'erratic and immeasurable'. As her long-standing architectural adviser Clutton was no doubt used to her ways. But when, late in 1872, she went abroad for an extended stay he found himself beleaguered by the orders, criticisms and comments of her amateur lieutenants, who could be as exasperating as Lady Ashburton herself. Chief among them was Forster, who was left virtually in charge of her building projects, which by then included the reconstruction of Melchet after a disastrous fire. Living near by, in Palace Gate, Forster was effectively her agent on the spot, itself not an easy role, and although he wanted Clutton to look on him as 'your friend in this matter' relations between them were sometimes strained. More than once Forster wrote to Lady Ashburton that he would 'have been glad to get rid of Mr Clutton altogether'.[49]

Both Sir Coutts Lindsay and Lady Marian Alford were consulted over the interior decorations, and Lady Alford seems to have been behind the late decision to move the dining-room from the first to the ground floor – a major change of plan which not only caused delay but added another £1,300 to the costs. From Rome, Harriet Hosmer contributed her own salvos of criticism and suggestions.

To make matters worse Lady Ashburton's friends had little time or respect for Clutton himself. Hosmer called him 'the old Jesuit', and Carlyle 'that arch-quack and son of Beelzebub, Architect Clutton!'.[50] Hosmer had been urging Lady Ashburton to allow her to make a copy of an antique vase in the Vatican for the hall at Kent House, and she was not best pleased when Clutton objected that the vase (and its pedestal) were on too large a scale for the intended situation. Mockingly she wrote to Lady Ashburton:

Clutton's note amuses me & is all froth and bellow like himself – all nonsense – what a string of words to say that the bigger a thing is the more important it looks, which is what I suppose he means by the following – 'the supremacy of scale over every other element is the art of design'.[51]

Clutton was generally blamed for the slow progress of the work, though Lady Ashburton's absence and indecision contributed to this, as did the late change of plan. In April 1873 Forster had advised her that the house would be finished by September, but this forecast proved over optimistic. Delayed perhaps by Clutton's illness, work on the interior decoration was still in progress in November, and Lady Ashburton does not appear to have taken up residence until 1874.

The exterior of Kent House (Plate 66a), which Carlyle called 'very stately and fashionable',[52] is an early essay in the worthy if slightly dull French Renaissance manner which Clutton seems to have felt appropriate for secular buildings in London. He used it again at No. 39 Upper Grosvenor Street, and also around the Piazza in Covent Garden. On both the front elevation and the long return to Rutland Gardens the dark red brickwork is relieved by extensive use of Portland-stone dressings. These originally included a substantial balustraded parapet, now removed. A mason fell to his death during its construction, when scaffolding gave way under the weight of one of the component blocks.[53] The plain eastern elevation, intended to abut the proposed house on the adjacent plot, was originally windowless.

Figure 52 shows the former planning of the ground floor, not exactly as built but essentially so. Originally the house was some 15ft longer and had two more rooms on the ground floor at the southern end – an additional servant's bedroom and a larder. This part of the building, with its curved frontage to Rutland Gardens (Plate 68a), was sold in 1902 and incorporated into Rutland House adjoining.[54] In Clutton's original scheme (before the dining-room was moved downstairs) the ground floor was predominantly the servants' domain, the only family room there, apart from the hall and staircase, being the morning room. This idiosyncratic allocation was doubtless due to Lady Ashburton, who stipulated that 'the offices should be really first class – plenty of good air and sufficient light'. She could afford to be generous with prime space, given that this large house was built for the convenience of just two people – herself and her daughter.

The re-siting of the dining-room made it necessary to consign some of the domestic offices, including the servants' hall and the housekeeper's room, to the basement. But Clutton assured Forster that only the housekeeper's room would be 'inferior', because the window was too high up to give a view, although still 'very good compared with other London houses'.[55] Both the kitchen and scullery remained on the ground floor and they, like the other rooms on the west side, had windows looking on to Rutland Gardens.

The northern end of the ground floor was wholly given over to the saloon hall, a high-ceilinged room with a marble-and-stone floor and windows overlooking the main road and the park. At the west end, adjoining the front door, was a small entrance lobby created by a 6ft-high walnut screen with carved oriental wood and rolled-glass panels. The chimneypiece in the hall, of rouge marble, was embellished with a large carved stone frieze of a hunting scene, possibly of some antiquity.

South of the hall, but not directly communicating, was the morning room, from where folding doors gave access to the dining-room. The walls in both these rooms were hung with embossed and gilded leather. In the dining-room (where Clutton had been told to work closely with Lady Alford), the dominant feature was the black-and-gold wooden chimneypiece (Plates 66c, 118d). Inscribed with the motto EAT TO LIVE & LIVE TO SERVE, it had flanking barley-sugar columns on plinths embellished with the owner's monogram. In the overmantel was Edward Lear's painting *The Crag that fronts the Even*. Lear himself was delighted with its 'vast black frame': 'Never saw anything so fine of my own doing before and walked ever afterwards with a nelevated and superb deportment and a sweet smile on everybody I met'. Other paintings by Lear were also hung in the dining-room, which Forster had described as having a 'gallery character'.[56]

Clutton placed the principal staircase and inner hall in a top-lit compartment on the windowless east side, behind the saloon hall. Rising only to the first floor, the staircase is both broad and shallow, with cantilevered stone treads and gilded-iron scroll-balusters of an early-eighteenth-century character (Plates 66b, 67a). Lady Ashburton planned to

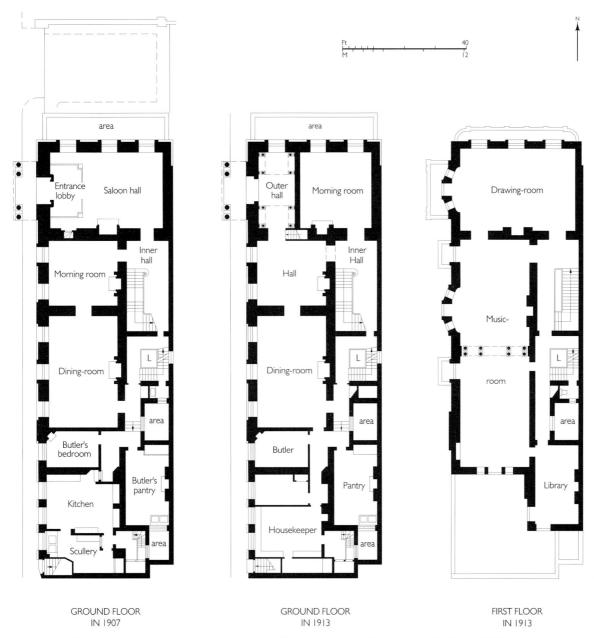

| Ft | | | | 40 |
| M | | | | 12 |

GROUND FLOOR
IN 1907

GROUND FLOOR
IN 1913

FIRST FLOOR
IN 1913

Fig. 52. Kent House, plans in 1907 and 1913. Henry Clutton, architect, 1872–3; altered by Reginald Blomfield, c.1910

display paintings and other works of art here, and in August 1873 Sir Coutts Lindsay superintended the installation of a large sculptural relief, *Virgilia*, by Thomas Woolner. It was not a success and soon removed.

The staircase compartment was probably in Lady Ashburton's mind when in 1874 she discussed with G. F. Watts ideas for a great wall picture at Kent House. Nothing came of this, and in 1875 Augustus Hare noticed 'semi-ruined cartoons of Paolo Veronese upon the staircase'.[57] They were set off by stencilling on the walls – a pretty honeycomb pattern, incorporating flowers, the initial A, and the motto SALVE (Plate 66b). The designer was L. W. Collmann, who also worked at Melchet, assisted there by Alfred Stevens.[58]

The first floor was given over to a suite of three intercommunicating drawing-rooms and a small library. Much the best preserved of the apartments created for Lady Ashburton, the library has fitted bookcases and a marble chimneypiece with Egyptianizing colonettes and inset panels of red marble carved with hunting scenes and putti treading grapes (Plate 118c). This chimneypiece is probably one of several which Lady Ashburton had in her possession and wanted re-used in the new house.[59] (The blue and brown Delft tiles on the hearth-cheeks post-date Lady Ashburton's occupancy.)

On the second floor were four bedrooms, three with communicating dressing-rooms, a bathroom and water-closets, and on the top floor were seven bedrooms, a linen room, housemaid's room and w.c.

Kent House remained Lady Ashburton's London home until her death in 1903. She was frequently joined there by Harriet Hosmer, who, disenchanted with post-unification Rome, spent more and more of her time in England. Lady Ashburton provided her with a studio in Albert Gate Studios in William Street.[60]

After Lady Ashburton's death the house stood empty for several years. An auction in 1907 failed to attract a buyer, and in 1909 it was purchased by the industrialist (Sir) Saxton Noble, a director of Armstrong Whitworth, the armaments manufacturers. Noble and his wife (a grand-daughter of I. K. Brunel) occupied Kent House until 1940. Princess Marie-Louise, great grand-daughter of the Duke of Kent, who gave his name to the original Kent House, was their guest here for a couple of years.[61]

Before taking up residence the Nobles called in Reginald Blomfield to spruce up parts of the by-then old-fashioned and somewhat dingy interior.[62] On the ground floor Blomfield reorganized the entrance arrangements, dividing Clutton's large saloon hall to create an outer hall or vestibule with a new morning room behind, and turning the old morning room into a new hall entered from the vestibule by a door in the south wall (fig. 52). Though small, the outer hall is a striking example of Blomfield's skill as a designer of neo-classical interiors (Plate 66d). Predominately white in tone, it is divided into three compartments, the central space being flanked by alcoves with coffered vaults and entablatures carried on paired Doric columns.[c] In the new hall Blomfield removed the embossed-leather wall-hangings, and installed a black-and-white stone floor (Plate 67b).

In the inner hall Blomfield retained Clutton's staircase, but the upper parts of the walls he covered with classically detailed panelling, and on the second-floor landing he introduced a series of arched openings overlooking the stairwell, a change which necessitated raising the ceiling and the oval domed skylight. The result is an impressive if over-tall compartment which proved difficult to heat (Plate 67a).

On the first floor Blomfield combined the second and third drawing-rooms to make a large music-room, over seventy feet in length. Musical parties were a regular feature of the entertainments provided at Kent House by Noble and his wife (a former pupil of Clara Schumann), and many leading instrumentalists performed here, including Casals, Suggia, Myra Hess and the d'Aranyi sisters. Blomfield replaced the dividing-wall between the two drawing-rooms with a screen of paired Ionic columns under a deep entab-

lature, decorated with a frieze of festoons and bucrania (Plate 67c). The original design for this screen had included a central archway, with coffered soffit matching the alcoves in the new entrance vestibule. However, this was ruled out when the removal of the dividing-wall brought to light a steel girder, and a continuous deep entablature was adopted instead. The frieze decoration, at first applied only to the entablature over the screen, was subsequently extended around the other walls of the music-room.[63f]

Within only a couple of years, however, this coolly neo-classical space was transformed into a decorative extravaganza with the installation of mural paintings by José Maria Sert y Badia, the fashionable Catalan artist and decorator.[g] Painted in Sert's Paris studios, the murals were installed at Kent House in June 1914, under the artist's personal supervision: the Nobles, who had accepted the work 'sight unseen', were delighted.[65] In the northern half of the music-room Sert's murals covered the whole of the north and west walls (Blomfield's frieze here being entirely removed). They were capriccio-like, faintly Dali-esque compositions in brown and gold, featuring classical temples perched on precipitous heights, bridges, waterfalls, fireworks, a canal, a procession of elephants and numerous nudes. In the southern part of the room the murals were smaller and fixed to the walls in frames, the surrounding areas being marbled in lapis lazuli blue. The columns in the screen were similarly treated and gilding was applied to both the capitals and the frieze. This work was carried out by W. H. Haynes, upholsterer, of Spring Street, Paddington.[66]

During the Second World War Kent House was let to the Red Cross as a repository for stores. After the war it was occupied as offices by a telephone company. In 1959 Sir Saxton's son sold the freehold and in the following year the house was bought by the Westminster Synagogue (previously the New London Jewish Congregation).[67] It has since undergone a further round of changes, particularly affecting the first and second floors. Blomfield's work on the ground floor and in the staircase compartment remains mostly intact, but the former music-room, now the synagogue, has been stripped of its columned screen, frieze and mural decorations, painted white and given a lowered ceiling. In the former dining-room (now the Rutland Room), Lady Ashburton's embossed-leather hangings survive, painted over white, but Clutton's chimneypiece has been removed to the synagogue above, where it has been adapted to make an Ark of the Covenant (Plate 118d). The marble chimneypiece in the morning room (now the Reinhart Library) has lost its sculptured frieze.

Since 1964 the third (top) floor of Kent House has been

---

[c] Blomfield remodelled the hall at No. 40 Upper Grosvenor Street (now demolished) in a similar manner, though on a larger scale.

[f] The Nobles evidently liked Blomfield's work, for they commissioned him to design their neo-Wrennish country house in Norfolk, Wretham Hall (1911–12), but there relations between the architect and his clients were somewhat strained.[64]

[g] Sert's clientele, the international rich, stretched from Barcelona to Palm Beach. He also designed ballet sets for Diaghilev. In England Sir Philip Sassoon employed him at both No. 25 Park Lane and Port Lymne, and he painted another set of panels for the Nobles at Wretham.

occupied as the Czech Memorial Scrolls Centre, where some 1,500 Torah scrolls purchased from the Jewish Museum in Prague have been stored and repaired before being allocated to Jewish congregations around the world.

Rutland House and Nos 1 and 2 Rutland Gardens

These tall and severely plain houses were built in 1872–3 by T. H. Adamson & Sons of Putney for Colonel (later Sir) Robert Cavendish Spencer Clifford, the largest, Rutland House, as his own residence. The architects were Walker & Elsam.[68] There was originally a fourth house, No. 3, which was bought in 1882 by J. A. Rolls of South Lodge and demolished, principally to improve the view from his own residence. Later Rolls also purchased the coach-house and stabling at the rear of Rutland House, which he made more attractive externally and turned into a laundry for South Lodge. The owner of Rutland House retained use of the roof, which was laid out as an ornamental garden. This building, made into living accommodation in the 1960s, is now known as Balcony House (see fig. 51).[69]

Rutland House was bought in 1899 by Colonel Charles St Clair Anstruther-Thomson, who initially employed (Sir) Edwin Lutyens to design some decorative alterations. These involved the incorporation of a set of four large spiral columns into one or other of the principal reception rooms.[70] A group of 'five Spanish paintings' mentioned by Lutyens in correspondence in 1900, and intended by him for the ground-floor dining-room, may have been the 'five valuable oil-paintings' still in the house when it was put up for sale in 1967. They were then mounted in carved oak wall-panels in the back sitting-room on the first floor.[71]

In 1902 Anstruther-Thomson extended the building with the acquisition of the south end of Kent House (Plate 68a). The attendant alterations, carried out by Harrods, included the filling in of the gap between the addition and the front bay-window of Rutland House to create annexes to the front rooms. On the first floor the annexe, used as a studio, was decorated in Moorish taste, with tiling and mosaic flooring.[72]

Plate 68c shows the entrance hall of Rutland House as decorated in 1906 by 'Cavaliere Formelli' – doubtless the architect and decorative artist Commendatore Cesare T. G. Formilli, who was later responsible for the redecoration of the Brompton Oratory. The roundels, depicting Roman emperors, were modelled by Panicelli of Hammersmith Broadway, and the variegated marble was from the demolished St James's Hall in Piccadilly. Some remnants of this scheme were still in existence in 1993, including the imperial portraits.[73]

Rutland Lodge and Kent Yard

Kent Yard seems originally to have been envisaged as a quadrangle of stables and carriage-houses with a screen wall in front, but the first building to be erected there was a dwelling-house. This was Rutland Lodge, built by Thorn

& Company for Frederick Sang, the architect and decorator who laid out Rutland Gardens on the Kent House estate for Mitchell Henry. The building of the house, presumably to Sang's designs, began in the summer of 1872, at about the same time as Colonel Clifford's houses were being erected opposite.[74] A large stable for Kent House was built in the following year adjoining Rutland Lodge (see No. 1 Kent Yard below), and subsequently two smaller stables were built at the back of the site (Nos 2 and 3 Kent Yard), one of them for Clifford.[75]

Rutland Lodge has a stucco-dressed front of Italianate character, with a sculpted head decorating the wall below the two-storey oriel window, and other, slightly effete, decoration in relief (Plate 68b). The house was first occupied about 1874 by an American theatrical impresario, 'Colonel'

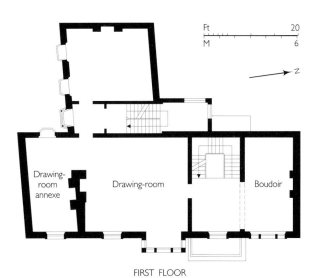

FIRST FLOOR

GROUND FLOOR

Fig. 53. Rutland Lodge, plans in 1929. Frederick Sang, architect, 1872–3

H. L. Bateman.[76h] He had settled in England with his wife Sidney, the daughter of an English comedian, Joe Cowell, who had emigrated to America. Two of their daughters, Kate and Ellen, were famous as child actors, touring under the management of P. T. Barnum, and it was to promote another daughter, Isabel, that Bateman took over the Lyceum Theatre in 1871. She was not the hoped-for success, but that same year Bateman's then little-known leading man at the Lyceum, Henry Irving, made a spectacular hit with *The Bells*. Bateman – known for his fiery temper – died at Rutland Lodge in 1875 following a fracas at a restaurant dinner hosted by Irving, apparently started when the police requested the party to break up as required by the licensing laws.[78] Afterwards, Mrs Bateman ran the Lyceum for a few years before relinquishing it in somewhat acrimonious circumstances to Irving and herself taking over Sadler's Wells. She appears to have left Rutland Lodge soon after the colonel's death.

Rutland Lodge has been much altered over the years, and little remains of the original interior features. Figure 53 shows the layout in 1929, by which time the house had been much enlarged. The stable and coach-house added in 1879 were probably the origin of the west 'wing'; the annexe at the south end also seems to be an addition. Rutland Lodge was further enlarged and made into five apartments in the 1960s. It has been occupied as the Turkish Consulate General since the mid-1970s.[79]

No. 1 Kent Yard, adjoining Rutland Lodge, was built in 1873 by William Brass for Lady Ashburton of Kent House.[80] Four-storeyed and of L-shaped plan, it was designed by Henry Clutton, Lady Ashburton's coachman being consulted over the details. On the ground floor were a coach-house for several vehicles and two loose-boxes. A ramp in the southern arm of the building led up to stalls for six horses on the first floor, above which were a balcony and a harness room, and, at the top of the building, living quarters for the coachman and grooms. The accommodation was much greater than had been in mind when the site was taken in 1871, and it was to avoid buying more ground (for which Mitchell Henry was asking what Clutton felt to be an exorbitant price) that the four-storey layout was devised. It was nevertheless a very expensive building, costing well over £3,000, and fully in line with Lady Ashburton's requirement that service accommodation for Kent House should be of the highest standard. Her close friend Harriet Hosmer found it 'palatial'.[81]

About 1910 No. 1 was converted to a garage and chauffeur's house for Saxton Noble, Lady Ashburton's successor at Kent House. It has undergone successive remodellings since, most recently in 1986–7, and now comprises six floors, including basement, arranged as two dwellings.[82]

Nos 2–5 Kent Yard are four houses built in 1961–2 on the site of the former Nos 2 and 3, two stables built in the 1870s. They were designed by Collins and Babister, architects, of Leverstock Green, Hertfordshire (Plate 79b).[83]

Stratheden House and Rutland Court

This section deals with the west side of Rutland Gardens north of Kent Yard. Now covered by Edwardian flats, it was formerly occupied by a single dwelling, latterly known as Stratheden House.

Stratheden House (demolished)

The mansion which became known in the nineteenth century as Stratheden House was designed by Sir William Chambers for the politician and army contractor John Calcraft the elder (1726–72), who took a long lease from the freeholders, William and John Shakespear.[84] It was built in 1770–2 on a joint contract by Chambers and the decorative plasterer Thomas Collins. The house is described by Chambers's biographer as square in plan with a handsome staircase, but containing only 'a small number of rooms suitable to the needs of a bachelor' – a somewhat ambiguous description, in view of the fact that Calcraft fathered at least two illegitimate families.[85] He owned several estates, including much of the town of Wareham in Dorset; early death, however, denied him the chance of settling in at Knightsbridge. Little is known of the appearance of the house. Distant views indicate a tall, plain building with a hipped roof (Plates 6b, 7).

Calcraft's house was for many years the residence of William Marsh, senior partner in a banking house which failed in 1824 following embezzlement by another of the partners, Henry Fauntleroy, who was hanged in consequence, despite widespread protest.[86] Subsequently the house was occupied by Lord de Dunstanville, formerly MP for Penryn, and became known as Dunstanville House. The best known occupant, however, was Lord Campbell, Lord Chief Justice in 1850 and later the Lord Chancellor, and it was from his wife, Baroness Stratheden of Cupar, that the house took its final name. Campbell bought it from de Dunstanville's daughter, Baroness Basset, in 1842. Savouring the view over Hyde Park and air as pure, he felt, as any in England, he set about his great work, *The Lives of the Chancellors*.[87] Later his view was marred by the erection of the Crystal Palace. On the closure of the Great Exhibition, Campbell took an active part in the debate on whether to preserve or demolish the building. 'I have been the leader of the *pulling-down* faction', he recorded, 'and our triumph has covered me with glory, although I have been scurrilously abused in the newspapers, and at all the public meetings which have been held'.[88]

The last occupant was Mitchell Henry MP (1826–1910), who purchased the freehold of the Stratheden House and

---

[h] His first names were Hezekiah Linthicum, but he disliked Hezekiah, the choice of his Welsh Methodist mother, and was generally known as H. L. or Henry L. Bateman.[77]

Kent House estate in 1863. Born in Manchester of Irish stock, he was the son of Alexander Henry, a textile merchant and Liberal MP for South Lancashire. Mitchell trained and practised as a surgeon, but after his father's death joined the family firm, A. & S. Henry, and went into politics, becoming a significant figure in Irish affairs as MP for County Galway. He also acquired a large estate in Galway, where he built a vast Gothic pile called Kylemore Castle (now well known as Kylemore Abbey, a Benedictine convent). The Campbell family, too, had links with Galway, but whether this had any bearing on Henry's acquisition of Stratheden House is not known.

Mitchell Henry transformed Stratheden House in keeping with his status as both public figure and connoisseur of the arts. The work was carried out by the architect T. H. Wyatt and, as decorator, the architect Frederick Sang. Most of the ornamentation was Italianate in style, befitting a collection of furniture and *objets d'art* which ranged from an antique bust of Agrippa to a carved settee from a Florentine mansion. The furniture also included modern Italian replicas of originals in the Vatican and the Pitti Palace. One of the most elaborate rooms was the library, fitted up with ebonized woodwork and gold mouldings, green silk-hung walls, and an ornate ceiling and frieze in Venetian cinquecento style, embellished with portraits of philosophers and poets. The showpiece of the house was *The Pompeian Mother*, Giosuè Meli's statue of a woman and child fleeing from the eruption of Vesuvius. This was displayed in its own Pompeian-style temple within the house. Among other items in the Henry collection were a *Puck* by J. G. Lough (another example of which is in the V & A) and statuary by Woolf of Rome.[89]

Possibly as a result of extravagance in building and collecting, Henry's financial position deteriorated; and his life seems to have been marred by family tragedies. Having retired as chairman of A. & S. Henry in 1893, he disposed of all his holding in the firm over the next few years.[90] Stratheden House was sold up and pulled down about 1900; the site is now occupied by Rutland Court. Kylemore was sold at a heavy loss in 1902,[91] and Henry died a few years later, leaving barely £400.[92]

Rutland Court

In 1899 plans were proposed for a block of flats on the site of Stratheden House. The building, designed by the architect William Isaac Chambers, was to have comprised a number of balconied apartments, each of fourteen large rooms.[93] Nothing came of this scheme, however. In June 1900 the cleared ground was put up for auction but was withdrawn when bidding failed to go higher than £89,000. It had been sold, reportedly for £85,000, by September 1901, when work began on the blocks of apartments which make up Rutland Court. The architect of the new building was Delissa Joseph, and the builder Henry Lovatt of Wolverhampton.[94] The 'developer' was probably the North British Mercantile Insurance Company, Mitchell Henry's

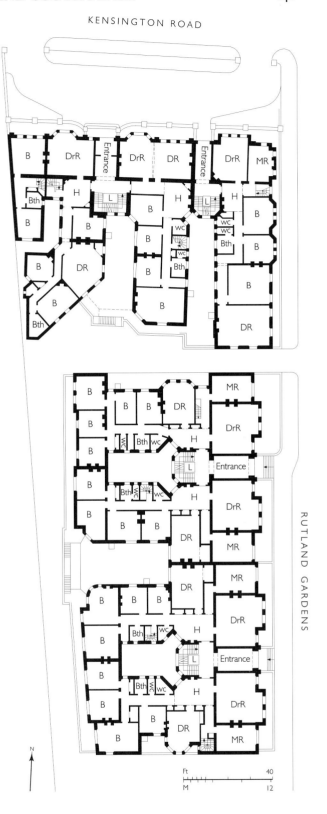

KENSINGTON ROAD

RUTLAND GARDENS

Fig. 54. Rutland Court, ground-floor plan. Delissa Joseph, architect, 1901–3

mortgagee, which was named as the freeholder some years later.[95] Finished in 1903, Rutland Court cost £120,000 to build.[96]

The complex was planned as a mixture of flats and maisonettes (fig. 54). Faced in red brick and Portland stone, it has the French-inspired appearance of much of Delissa Joseph's work and some well-executed ornamental details (Plate 34). The tall main block fronting Kensington Road, of nine storeys, is surmounted by a Baroque dome and cupola; the portico is an attenuated substitute for that intended, which the London County Council would not allow.[97] The blocks to the rear, fronting Rutland Gardens, are lower in height and much plainer.

The photographer Cecil Beaton occupied a flat in Rutland Court (Plate 111c) for a few years until the outbreak of the Second World War.

Ft   10
M   3

Fig. 55. South Lodge, Knightsbridge entrance, gates erected c.1895

CHAPTER VIII

Rutland Gate

Rutland Gate was developed over a period of more than twenty years following the demolition in 1836 of Rutland House, an aristocratic mansion which had stood here since the middle of the eighteenth century. The original houses are largely the work of two builders: John Tombs, who built up the northern half of the street in the late 1830s and '40s, and John Elger, who completed Rutland Gate after a hiatus in its development during the early 1850s. Tombs was a relatively minor figure in the building world, with limited speculative involvement. Elger, by contrast, was an established property baron, combining in himself the roles of freeholder, developer and builder. His work in Rutland Gate followed on from his development on the Kingston House estate to the west, and, barring a few later houses in Rutland Gardens, it marks the eastern extent of a large area of Knightsbridge built up speculatively with very high-class houses during the mid- to late nineteenth century.

Many of the original houses, or at least their façades, have survived, and their broadly Italianate style remains the predominating architectural flavour of the street (Plates 73–5).

The numbering is divided between an odd and an even sequence in the upper or northern part of Rutland Gate and a consecutive sequence in the lower. The consecutive numbers begin with No. 27. There is no No. 21.

The Rutland House Estate

The site of Rutland Gate was formerly two adjoining three-acre fields known as Wellfields. The lower or southern field lay directly behind the upper field, but slightly offset, and this 'displacement' is preserved in the shape of the development. In the seventeenth century Wellfields belonged to the extensive estate of William Muschamp of Kensington. By 1752, when John Manners, 3rd Duke of Rutland, built Rutland House there, they were owned by John Milner, whose uncle had bought them in 1699, and they formed an independent freehold estate. The duke's lease covered the whole property, the upper field being the site of the house and gardens, while the lower was used as a paddock.[1]

A Chancery suit following Milner's death led to a public auction in 1771, when the freehold was bought by Jacob Whitbread, who ten years later sold it to Edward Manners of Goadby Marwood in Leicestershire, believed to have been the 3rd Duke of Rutland's illegitimate son.[2] Manners died in 1811, leaving the property for life to Ann Stafford, and on her death to the ten children he had fathered by her. A complex legal dispute after she died was not resolved until 1836–7, when the entire freehold effectively passed to Elizabeth Manners, the widow of the eldest son, Fursan. By drastically reducing the number of parties required to be involved in any legal transaction concerning the estate, this greatly facilitated its development on building leases.[3]

The Manners family retained the freehold of the entire estate until 1853, when the southern half was sold to the developer John Elger. The northern half was in the possession of Cubitt Estates before the First World War.

Rutland House (demolished)

Rutland House was built in 1752–3 by John Manners, 3rd Duke of Rutland, as a residence for himself, his companion Mrs Elizabeth Drake, and their son Edward Manners, then aged about seven.[a] The middling-sized mansion was among the earliest of the string of detached houses erected in the mid-eighteenth century along the south side of the Kensington road, between the older Powis House to the east and Kensington House to the west. It was also one of the first to disappear, being pulled down in the 1830s.

Doubtless the irregular nature of Mrs Drake's relationship with the duke, a widower in his mid-50s, was a factor in the choice of an out-of-town location. Nevertheless, there was nothing particularly clandestine about the arrangement. The duke's eldest son and heir, the famous Marquess of Granby, Commander-in-Chief of land forces in Great Britain, was a regular visitor. One of his daughters was born in the house in 1772, and the marquess himself, who predeceased his father, died there in 1773.

The site was taken by the duke on an 80-year lease from John Milner in March 1752. Building work began immediately and the house was substantially complete by the summer of 1753. It cost just under £4,432, of which £1,771 was paid to the bricklayer, Richard Stanton, and £1,317 to the carpenter, John Wright.[b] Extras included payments to a

---

[a] That Edward Manners was indeed the duke's natural son seems almost certain. He benefited very substantially under the duke's will, and, in addition to the family name, adopted the Manners arms (which appear on his biographically uninformative tomb in Goadby Marwood church).

[b] The other building tradesmen involved were Thomas Okill, mason (£319), John Whitehead, plasterer (£196), Richard Troubridge,

watchman for 440 nights at 1s a night (and £1 5s for meat for his cat), and £7 8s 3d for a 'raising dinner' given to the men.[4]

Nowhere in the building accounts is there a mention of the architect, who is thought to have been John Vardy. The evidence for his involvement is a sheet of drawings, unsigned and undated but endorsed 'John Vardy 1763' (Plate 72b).[5] The date is puzzling, and raises the question whether the endorsement is contemporary. Vardy's absence from the accounts might be explained if he did no more than provide a draught of the house. A 'Mr Morris', perhaps the surveyor and architectural writer Robert Morris, was responsible for measuring the builders' work.

Rutland House was built of red brick, with some Portland-stone dressings. It was a squarish building, five bays wide with a pedimented centre, flanked by lower service wings and linking arcades – the classic Palladian disposition. At the time of its demolition the house had three full storeys plus an attic (Plate 72a), but both the 'Vardy' drawing and Rhodes's map of 1766 (Plate 2a) show a two-storey building. The elevations were plain, embellished only with simple bandcourses and a central stone frontispiece embracing the pedimented and columned doorcase and the window surround on the floor above. The mason was paid extra for altering the frontispiece 'from what was first intended'.

The interior was conventionally planned (Plate 72b). On the ground floor was a large entrance hall, dining-room, drawing-room, and another room called the library in a later survey. The staircase, a wooden one, was relegated to a compartment behind the hall. On the first or principal floor were four bedrooms and several closets. According to the Vardy plan only the western of the two single-storey 'arcade' rooms communicated directly with the house itself. The stables were in the east service wing, the kitchens in the west wing.

The building accounts do not convey the impression of an elaborately decorated interior. In the principal rooms the walls appear to have been mostly hung with fabric, above wainscotted dados, and there were enriched plaster cornices. Stone and marble chimneypieces, carved by James Whittle & Son, were installed in the dining- and drawing-rooms and in the first-floor rooms, the most expensive decorated with carved tablets – 'Diana's head & her Trophies' (dining-room), and 'Apollo's Head in Glory' (drawing-room).

After the death of the duke in 1779, the property and most of its contents passed to Elizabeth Drake,[6] who seems to have gone on living there until she died, about 1800. For much of that time the rates were paid by her son, Edward Manners, by then the freehold owner of the estate. He succeeded his mother as the occupant, and on his own death in 1811, the house passed to his common-law wife Ann Stafford, who shared it with her eldest son, Fursan Manners.[7]

Following Ann Stafford's death in 1827, Rutland House stood empty for several years while the estate languished in the limbo of litigation. Then in 1833 it was put on the market, and George Robins, the auctioneer, issued particulars balancing some eye-catching views of the house (Plate 72a) against a frank assessment of the problems and potential of the property:[8]

A few years since . . . it had the misfortune to be visited with a fearful attack from the Court of Chancery, which on the outset paralyzed almost every limb . . . It is now happily convalescent, but it would be uncandid to deny that there are 'outward and visible signs' that a termination of this protracted suit was most devoutly to be wished.

In its present condition the 'house would be inadequate to the high pretensions of a Nobleman without encountering a large outlay'. On the other hand, a 'Minister of State would find it difficult to resist this expenditure, or adopting the alternative to erect a more splendid habitation, when it is remembered that all the *agrémens* of a Town and Country abode are contained at a distance of ten minutes drive from the Great Offices of State'.

Alternatively, the site offered an opportunity for development on an 'extended Scale', being 'suitable for an Immense Square of First-Rate Houses or a group of detached Villas'.

For all the auctioneer's blandishments, Rutland House failed to attract a buyer. Empty and unwanted, the neglected mansion survived until January 1836 when it was pulled down for redevelopment, Robins being called in again to sell the materials.[9]

Early Development of Rutland Gate, 1836–c.1847

In January 1836, as Rutland House was being demolished, the first of several agreements was made with Elizabeth Manners, as *de facto* freeholder, for developing the estate, and by the end of the following year much of the northern half of the ground had been let as building plots.[10]

Development had been in mind for some years, and in 1832 a plan of the Brompton road area had shown the southern part of the ground marked out for building along lines similar to those subsequently adopted.[11] The scheme eventually drawn up by Mrs Manners' surveyor, the architect Edward Cresy the elder, is shown on a rather perfunctory plan which he submitted with an application to build sewers in October 1836.[12] Cresy's scheme was for a wide road through the middle of the ground, divided into two carriageways by a central communal garden running its full length, and lined on either side by continuous terraces of houses. Short terraces were to occupy the frontages to the Kensington road. At the south end, side roads were planned so that the estate could be linked up

plumber (£217), Richard Hughes, slater (£172), Thomas Phillips, paviour (£100), John Speed, smith (£80), Philip Hinde, ironmonger (£88), William Pickering, painter (£72), James Phillips, glazier (£64), and James Whittle & Son, carvers (£32).

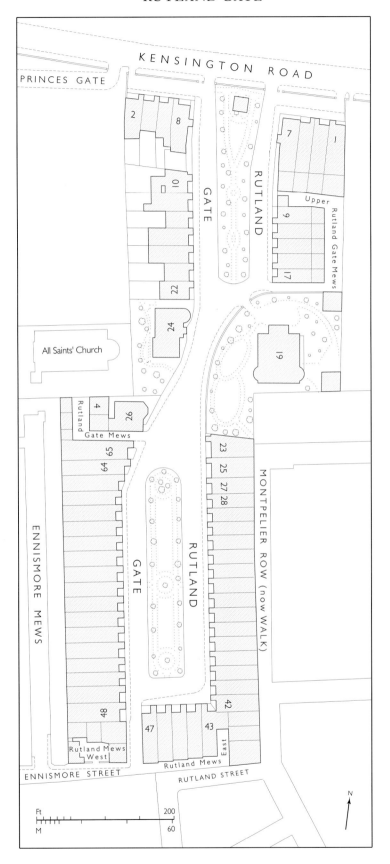

Fig. 56. Rutland Gate
in the mid-1860s

with developments present or future on adjoining proper- ties. The central roadway, following the alignment of the ground, took an offset bend which, together with the near- ness of Hyde Park, presumably suggested the original name of the development: Serpentine Terrace.

The first prospective builder on the scene was George Crowne of Foley Place, Marylebone, who undertook to construct a dozen houses on the north-eastern sector of the ground. But at the end of 1836, having built nothing, he sold his interest to the architect (Sir) Matthew Wyatt.[13] Nine houses were ultimately erected under Crowne's agreement, some on widened plots, together with coach- houses and stabling in Upper Rutland Gate Mews (now Gate Mews). Three of these houses, Nos 3–7, were leased jointly to Wyatt and his partner John Howell in December 1837. Leases of six more houses, Nos 1 and 9–17, were granted to Howell almost exactly two years later.[14c] A party to these latter leases was John Tombs, who was by then under agreement to build houses on ground south of No. 17, and on the west side of Serpentine Terrace. He was, very likely, the executant builder of all nine houses, which had been completed and occupied by 1840.[16]

Tombs's address was then in Church Street, Millbank, but he had been in business for some years previously in Southwark, initially in partnership with Thomas Tombs: they had described themselves variously as bricklayers, builders and timber merchants. Another member of the family, George Tombs, a plasterer, was living at No. 18 in 1841 and was presumably involved in the building work.[17] In 1840–1 John Tombs was the ratepayer at No. 12 Rutland Gate, which was probably being occupied as a site office.[18]

On the north-western sector of the ground, building was largely carried out under two agreements, dated May 1836 and October 1837. The first was made with Thomas Ross esquire, of Blackheath (who developed much of Blackheath Park in the 1820s and '30s).[19] Ross undertook to build four houses (Nos 2–8) fronting the Kensington road. Two of these houses were subsequently leased to him, and the others by his direction to George Ross, possibly Thomas's brother, a surveyor based near Tombs's old home in South- wark.[20] As with the corresponding eastern range, the site had originally been earmarked for five houses. The second agreement, taken out by Tombs, covered the sites of Nos 12–20 on the west side of the new road, and a large plot, for eight houses, on the east side, just on the bend.[21] Leases of Nos 12–18 were taken up by Tombs in May 1838 and immediately mortgaged to Cresy, who, at the same time, himself took the lease on No. 10, which may be presumed to have been built for him by Tombs.[22] In September, Tombs took the lease of another new house, No. 20.[23] Like Howell, Tombs financed his venture through the London

Assurance Corporation, to which he was able to report, in July 1840, that four of his houses were finished, and two of them let.[24] Apart from No. 10, which remained empty until 1845, the houses were soon occupied.[25]

Although Tombs's involvement with Rutland Gate con- tinued for some years, he did not build the intended hous- es on the east side of the road. By August 1839 he had made only a small incursion into his site there, in the form of a coach-house and stables at the north-east corner, for Thomas Ross.[26] The remainder of the plot was made over to William Jones, a rich Monmouthshire landowner and art collector, as the site for a big detached mansion known as Clytha House which was leased to him in 1840. Early in the following year Jones took two building plots on the other side of the road (the sites of Nos 22 and 26, and Rutland Gate Mews). They were separated by a larger plot already under agreement to another art collector, John Sheepshanks, also for a detached house.[27] The building of these two free-standing houses (separate accounts of which are given below) was the first important departure from Cresy's original development plan.

Jones's Clytha House and Sheepshanks's future house – strongholds of dissimilar artistic tastes – might have faced each other across the neutral zone of the communal garden, but within a few weeks of acquiring the plots of Nos 22 and 26 Jones obtained a sweep of additional land to the west and south of Clytha House, taking a large bite out of the eastern roadway and the garden.[28] The upshot was a further modi- fication of the layout, constricting the middle portion to a single roadway with no garden 'reservation', and giving the development its distinctive hour-glass shape (fig. 56). It was now in effect two garden squares, with the large hous- es standing in their own gardens forming a 'buffer zone' between them. The northernmost square was already more or less complete; its intended counterpart was slightly re- cast to have a semi-circular south end, with terrace-houses or detached villas occupying the two quadrant sites on either side of the entrance into a mews.[29]

It was at about this time that the name Serpentine Terrace – having thus become less apt – was changed to Rutland Gate. With its aristocratic connotation this had a grander sound. The entrance to the development was now railed and gated (the original plan had been for an open junction with the main road), and provided with a gate- keeper's or gardener's lodge, but a hoped-for entrance across the road into Hyde Park did not materialize.[30d]

The lodge, a stuccoed building, with an attached order of palm-headed columns similar to those on the porticoes of Tombs's houses in Rutland Gate, stood in the upper garden slightly forward of the general building line (Plate 73a). It was demolished in 1969, having

---

c Wyatt and Howell were responsible at about this time for developing Victoria Square, near Buckingham Palace, and the building at Knightsbridge was almost certainly financed by loans taken out by Howell from the London Assurance Corporation on the security of the Victoria Square houses.[15]

d In 1859, following the development of southern Rutland Gate, residents paid for a wicket-gate to be made into the park just west of the barracks, Prince of Wales Gate, opened in 1848, being regarded by them as too out of the way.[31]

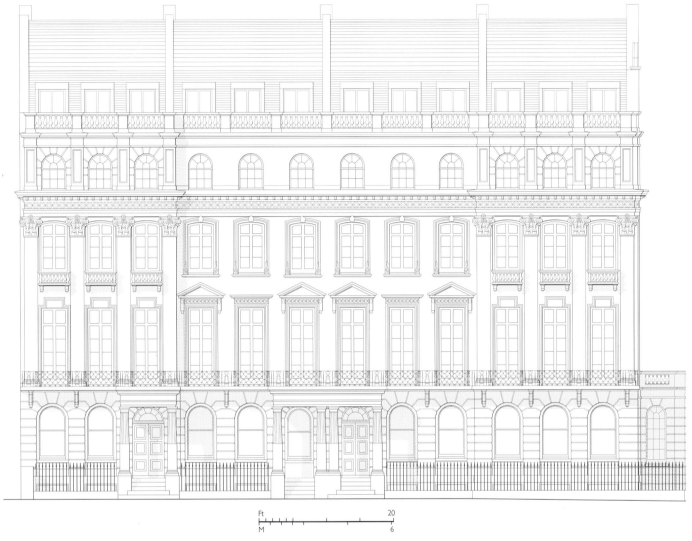

Fig. 57. Nos 1 and 3, formerly Nos 1–7 (odd) Rutland Gate, 1837–9; elevation in 1997. *Attic storey reconstructed in the 1970s*

been allowed to become semi-ruinous.[32e]

In 1841 the northernmost of William Jones's two plots on the west side of Rutland Gate was leased to the Hon. Edmund Villiers, a brother of the 4th Earl of Clarendon, who occupied the new end-of-terrace house there (No. 22) until his death in 1843.[34] Jones's other plot was partially laid out by Tombs as Rutland Gate Mews, but apart from a stable for Villiers it was not built up until about 1845.[35] Tombs, by then resident in Chelsea, followed this in 1846–7 with a substantial, and to all intents and purposes detached, house (No. 26), partly overlooking the planned new church on the Kingston House estate. It seems to have been Tombs's last work at Rutland Gate. The house was evidently built speculatively, for, writing to the Ecclesiastical Commissioners in January 1847, Tombs stated that it

would be of the full size for a second-rate house, 'and will therefore be occupied by a family of the first respectability'. Although large, it had no garden, unlike Clytha House and No. 24. The lease was taken in due course by a City solicitor, Frederick Pratt Barlow, previously the first occupant of No. 17.[36] In the 1920s and '30s No. 26 was the London residence of Lord Redesdale, the father of the celebrated Mitford sisters. During Lord Redesdale's day the house was little-used, the rooms dust-sheeted for months on end. It was requisitioned for housing evacuees from the East End during the Second World War, and fell into disrepair before being restored by Patrick De Laszlo, son of the society portrait-painter Philip De Laszlo, who made the ballroom available for Conservative party meetings. In the late 1960s the ballroom was transformed into a private

[e] A plan to build a house on the site of the lodge, following the sale of the freehold of the upper garden in 1972, was successfully resisted by local residents.[33]

cinema, as part of a Hollywood-style remodelling of the interior carried out for Richard Gangel, the American friend and business associate of the financier Bernie Corn-feld. When their company Investors Overseas Services collapsed and Gangel went bankrupt, the house was put on the market for a then record sum, attracting some attention for the extravagance of its decorations and fittings.[37]

South of Clytha House, the development had continued in 1842 with a pair of plain semi-detached villas set back from the originally intended building line (see Plate 7). Who built them is not known. These modest houses, then numbered 21 and 23, were first occupied in 1843, by the artist and (later) royal drawing-master Edward Henry Corbould, and an architect, John Forbes Hardy. Corbould's house, No. 21, like its bigger neighbours Clytha House and No. 24, incorporated a 'gallery' – in his case, probably more a working studio.[38] The pair was rebuilt by John Elger in 1857–8 as Nos 23 and 25 (see below).

In 1847–8 more houses were proposed, perhaps started,[39] but by then, with the building trade in recession, the first phase of Rutland Gate's development was effectively over.[f]

The architecture of upper Rutland Gate

As built, upper Rutland Gate presented two contrasting faces to the passer-by. At the north end, overlooking the park, were two showy ranges with fully stuccoed *palazzo*-style façades, ultimately deriving from Nash's Regent's Park terraces (fig. 57, Plates 34a, 73a, 74a, 77a). By contrast the houses behind were much plainer, with predominantly brick façades (Plate 74b). There were, in addition, comparatively minor differences in treatment between the two northernmost ranges and between the two ranges to the south. The estate surveyor, Edward Cresy, must have approved of the contrasting styles, but who was responsible for the actual designs is not known.

Matthew Wyatt, as a prominent architect who is known to have designed the houses on his own development at Victoria Square, is an obvious candidate. George Ross, the surveyor who took the leases of Nos 2 and 4, may himself have made some architectural contribution. The north-eastern range, Nos 1–7, which Wyatt developed jointly with John Howell, had the more sophisticated façade of the two terraces fronting the Kensington road, but its design may have been his improved version of that at Nos 2–8 rather than an original concept of his own. Certainly, the decision to make the north-western range of four not five houses (the wider frontages making it possible to erect houses on a somewhat grander scale) had been taken by the time of Thomas Ross's building agreement in May 1836. Wyatt is not known to have had any involvement in the development of the estate until December 1836, when he bought out George Crowne's interest on the as yet virtually untouched north-eastern corner. He too proceeded to

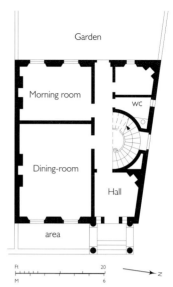

Fig. 58. No. 10 Rutland Gate, 1838, ground-floor plan

build a row of four houses facing the Kensington road, rather than the five stipulated in Crowne's agreement. Wyatt's houses at Nos 1–7 were distinguished from Nos 2–8 by the varied shapes of window used, the greater degree of stucco enrichment, and the breaking forward of the end houses to give the effect of pavilions.

The plainest of all the houses were those comprising the eastern range, Nos 9–17, of which only Nos 9 and 11 survive. These houses all had the comparatively narrow frontages indicated on Cresy's original development plan. Although here too fewer houses were built than first intended, the plots were not enlarged, the spare ground being taken for coach-houses in what is now Gate Mews. On the opposite side of the road, Nos 10–22 are built on wider plots and have a more ornamental treatment, with string-courses and stuccoed window surrounds (Plate 74b). The bow window at No. 14 is a 1920s addition, and it is probable that No. 22 in its original form was not very different from the rest. A feature common to the houses on both sides of the road is a pillared portico with distinctive palm capitals.

Whether Cresy's role of estate surveyor included architectural design in any detail is not known. Possibly he designed the porticoes of the east and west ranges, and it seems likely that he was responsible for the planning of No. 10, of which he was the lessee (though not the occupant). While conforming in elevation to its neighbours, this house is distinguished by a semi-circular staircase (fig. 58). The design of contemporary staircases was a subject on which Cresy developed strong views – dismissing those in most English houses as too much like stepladders, but also criticizing the French taste for radial plans on the grounds of safety and convenience.[40]

---

[f] The census records two houses 'building' in 1851: these were probably the 'Nos 25 and 27' for which notice was given in 1848, but which seem ultimately to have been abandoned.

The plans of the other houses, on both sides of the road, seem to have been entirely unremarkable, with convention-al dog-leg staircases.[41]

The detached houses at the southern end of the devel-opment show a greater diversity. Of the three, No. 24, while lower in height and alone in having a bow at the front, was originally closest in appearance to its northern neighbours, with a brick front and the standard portico. Clytha House was wholly stuccoed with a symmetrical plan, semi-circu-lar bays and a grand Ionic portico. No. 26, Tombs's last house, also originally stuccoed, was angular and asymmet-ric with a Doric portico. It has, apart perhaps from the treatment of the windows, no particular stylistic resem-blance to his other houses. The balconies at Nos 24 and 26 have similar cast-iron balustrading, with plain supports at No. 24 and ornate brackets at No. 26.

Clytha House, No. 19 Rutland Gate (demolished)

Built around 1840 for William Jones (later Herbert), a Roman Catholic landowner and art collector, this neo-clas-sical mansion was the largest house in Rutland Gate. Named after Jones's Monmouthshire estate, it stood well back from the road, in the centre of a large plot on the east side of the street originally allocated for a row of eight houses (fig. 56). Latterly the building was screened from view by trees. The site is now occupied by an inter-war block of flats called Eresby House.

Little is known about the construction of Jones's man-sion, first occupied by him in 1841, and the only illustra-tions appear to be some distant glimpses in general views (Plates 6b, 7). From these, and written sources, it emerges as a stucco-faced house of two storeys plus an attic, square on plan, with a full-height tetrastyle Ionic portico on the north front and a picture gallery with bowed ends at the back.[42] In certain respects the house seems to have been modelled on Jones's neo-classical country seat, Clytha, which had been rebuilt for him in the 1820s by Edward Haycock, the Shropshire-based architect. There is, how-ever, no documentary evidence to connect Haycock, or any other architect, with the Rutland Gate house.

The principal rooms were all on the ground floor. Arranged *en suite* for the reception of company, they com-prised 'a handsome entrance paved with variegated marble opening to a vestibule', two drawing-rooms 'uniformly and superbly embellished by a celebrated foreign artist', 'a noble saloon or picture gallery with embayed ends and costly parquetrie floor' and a 'grand eating room'.[43] The unidentified foreign artist could have been Jones's friend Ludwig Grüner, the Dresden-born painter and engraver. Grüner seems to have been living at Clytha House when in

October 1842 he witnessed Jones's signature, signing him-self 'Lewis Gruner of Rutland Gate, engraver'.[44g]

The accommodation on the upper floors comprised a lady's morning room and seventeen bedrooms and dress-ing-rooms. The 'ample and convenient' domestic offices and servants' apartments included a separate stable and coach-house at the south-east corner of the site.[46]

Jones's occupation of this expensive house was relatively brief. In 1852 he withdrew to Monmouthshire, put Clytha House on the market, and disposed of the paintings and other contents at auction.[47] The lease was bought in June 1853 by Lord Edward Howard, another Catholic landowner, who in 1869 was created Baron Howard of Glossop.[48] Lord Howard occupied No. 19 (the name Clytha House fell into disuse) until his death there in 1883, and the house remained in the hands of his descendants until *c.*1912.[49]

The succeeding owners were an American couple, Dr Fred Stark Pearson and his wife, Mabel, on whose behalf it was purchased in 1914 by a trust company. Dr Pearson was an electrical engineer and entrepreneur, who had made his fortune through a series of public works enterprises includ-ing the electrification of the tramcar systems in New York and Boston, and the construction of hydroelectric-power stations around the world. He also had interests in mining, railways, forestry and irrigation.

With Thomas Henry Smith as their architect, the Pear-sons embarked on an expensive modernization and enlargement of the by-then rather shabby and old-fash-ioned house. Smith raised the height of the building, which he extended on three sides, leaving only the north front unchanged. In the process Jones's bow-ended gallery was subsumed into a large oblong music-room-cum-drawing-room, at the east end of which there was to have been a grand organ with its pipe-chamber in the basement below.[50]

The Pearsons never lived here, however. In May 1915, while work was still in progress, they were lost when the liner *Lusitania*, on which they were returning to England from New York, was torpedoed off Ireland. After some delay their representatives decided to complete the 'rebuilding' with a view to selling the house, which was bought in 1916 by the 2nd Earl of Ancaster.[51] The earl lived here until 1931, during which time No. 19 was known as Eresby House, after one of his titles. By April 1931 plans were already afoot to build a block of flats on the site (see Eresby House below) and the old house succumbed to the demolition contractors in 1932.[52]

No. 24 Rutland Gate: Park House

Distinguished by a conspicuous bow rising through four storeys, this is the house, now much extended, built in 1841

[g] Grüner had dedicated his first book, published in Rome in 1839, to Jones, whom he describes as a true friend, with whose unfaltering support ('conforti di lui non cessanti') he had gone to Rome to educate himself in the masterpieces of art.[45] In England Grüner's princi-pal patrons were Prince Albert and Queen Victoria, for whom he worked at Buckingham Palace, Osborne and Frogmore. Like Prince Albert, Jones was one of the few collectors at that time of pre-1500 Italian paintings, and may have made some of his acquisitions through Grüner, as did the prince.

for John Sheepshanks, the art collector and former Leeds cloth manufacturer, who occupied it until his death in 1863 (fig. 59, Plate 74c).[53] After retiring early from business, Sheepshanks had settled in London, in Bond Street and later at Blackheath. In the 1830s, having built up and disposed of an unrivalled collection of Dutch and Flemish prints, he began acquiring contemporary British paintings, which his new house in Rutland Gate, with its integral picture gallery, was designed in part to display. In 1857 he presented this collection, which included several Constables and Turners, to the nation.

When new, No. 24 was fully detached and had fewer storeys, as is shown in a bird's-eye view of the area in 1851 (Plate 7). The present top storey and, almost certainly, the second storey are later additions. Justifying his reluctance to admit visitors to the collection, Sheepshanks, a bachelor, explained that the house was 'of limited dimensions' with

'only a very small establishment of servants'.[54] One visitor whom Sheepshanks did not discourage was Henry Cole, the future first Director of the South Kensington Museum, to which the collection was entrusted in 1857. On one of his regular trips there, in February 1845, Cole was accompanied by Turner.

The house was originally faced in brick, yellow malms being specified in the building agreement for the front elevation (now mostly stuccoed) and grey stocks for the remainder.[55] Even with a brick façade, No. 24 must always have stood apart from its northern neighbours on account of its bow and, originally, its much lower height. That it has the standard pillared porch may be due to the estate surveyor, Edward Cresy, to whom the plans had to be submitted for approval, rather than to Sheepshanks's (unknown) architect. A possible candidate for this role is the surveyor George Ross. As has been seen, Ross and his relation

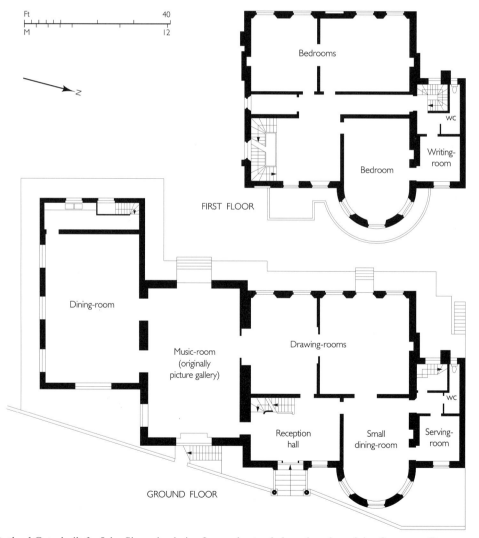

Fig. 59. No. 24 Rutland Gate, built for John Sheepshanks in 1841, and extended north and south in 1899–1900. Room-names are those in use c.1911, during the residence of Baron d'Erlanger

Thomas Ross, a developer in Sheepshanks's former home district, Blackheath, were both involved in the early development of Rutland Gate.

All the principal rooms are on the ground floor. In Sheepshanks's day these comprised, besides the entrance hall, a drawing-room, dining-room and breakfast-room, and, in a single-storey wing to the south, the 'well-lighted' picture gallery. Sheepshanks's paintings were not confined just to the gallery, but hung in all the principal rooms.[56]

After Sheepshanks's death, the house was occupied by Eric Carrington Smith, a prominent banker and notable patron of the Vernacular Revival architect George Devey. It was presumably Smith, a family man with seven children and a large domestic staff,[h] who had the extra storeys built: a substantial increase in the rateable value of the house in 1864 doubtless reflects this addition.[58] The main staircase, still in the house today, was extended in matching style: early Victorian in character, with restrained iron balusters, it rises seamlessly from the hall to the top floor. Soon after taking up residence Smith laid a path across his garden to All Saints' Church in Ennismore Gardens, with gates which he opened for a short time before and after services for the convenience of local churchgoers.[59] Smith's successor here in 1885 was William Sheepshanks MP, a great-nephew of the original owner.

The next occupant, from 1899, was Baron Frédéric d'Erlanger of the well-known international banking family, some other members of which, including his father, were already living in Rutland Gate. Baron Frédéric successfully combined the careers of banker and composer. No less a virtuoso than Fritz Kreisler premiered his violin concerto, and his operas, though now sunk without trace, were heard at Covent Garden and in opera houses across Europe and in America.

The present appearance of No. 24 owes much to the alterations and additions carried out for d'Erlanger in 1899–1900 by Green & Abbott of Oxford Street, a decorating firm.[60] At the southern end d'Erlanger built a large single-storey dining-room next to Sheepshanks's gallery, which became his music-room, and at the northern end he added a four-storey extension, closing the gap between No. 24 and No. 22. The stuccoing of the front elevation up to third-floor level probably also dates from this time. Jalousies and some faintly Art-Nouveau-style windows in the old gallery and new dining-room testify to the Parisian-born d'Erlanger's essentially French taste. Internally this is exemplified in the plasterwork and panelling of the principal rooms, latterly painted white but originally gilded.[61]

D'Erlanger lived at No. 24, which he named Park House, until his death in 1943. Post-war occupants have included Frank T. Sabin, the fine-art dealers (1948–63), and the

Accademia Italiana delle Arti e delle Arti Applicate (1989–94). During the Accademia's time the ground floor was regularly used for exhibitions.

John Elger's Development, 1853–59

By the end of the 1840s building in Rutland Gate had petered out, but early in 1851 an agreement was drafted between Elizabeth Manners and John Elger, who had been developing the adjoining Kingston House estate since the mid-1840s, for completing the southern part of the street. However, it was not until 1853 that work got under way. Several houses were started in the autumn, and soon afterwards Elger bought the freehold of all the remaining vacant ground from the Manners family.[62]

During the next six years the whole of southern Rutland Gate was built up by Elger (Plate 73b), together with Rutland Mews East and West and a roadway linking Rutland Gate with his development on the Kingston House estate. It was presumably at this time that the high brick wall along the south side of Ennismore Street was built, shutting off Brompton Road and its northern hinterland from the exclusive culs-de-sac opposite Hyde Park.[i]

Elger also acquired the two little villas, Nos 21 and 23, to the south of Clytha House, rebuilding them in the late 1850s. The new houses (wider, but otherwise similar to the rest of Elger's houses in Rutland Gate) were numbered 23 and 25. This rather suggests that there was some idea of building a new No. 21 to the north, on part of the Clytha House garden. Whether or not this formed part of his plans, Elger appears to have been sufficiently determined to replace the existing villas that he had resort to strong-arm tactics. E. H. Corbould, 'extremely comfortable' in his home and studio at No. 21, refused to sell, whereupon Elger seems to have pulled down the adjoining house and dug out new foundations. In Corbould's version of the story, his 'unpleasant neighbour started to dig a tremendously deep hole under the house, which shattered and cracked the walls', forcing him to leave. Corbould complained that Elger was in breach of the law in building forward of the established building line, and he was apparently successful in gaining substantial compensation.[63]

That Elger was, strictly speaking, the 'builder' of all the houses in lower Rutland Gate is not perhaps quite accurate, for by 1858 the building work seems to have been at least partly in the hands of the firm of Welchman & Gale, whose partners were former clerks of Elger and who shared premises or next-door premises with him in Rutland Gate for a while. However, they do not appear to have had any significant speculative interest in the development.[64]

---

[h] In 1871 the Smith household contained 20 persons, of whom 11 were servants; Sheepshanks, by contrast, had lived alone with a staff of four or five maidservants.[57]

[i] Since the Second World War a footway has been opened between Rutland Mews East and Rutland Street, which goes some way to alleviating the isolation of Rutland Gate from Brompton Road and the area of Montpelier Square. For Elger's opposition to a proposed roadway linking Brompton Square with the Kensington road see page 164.

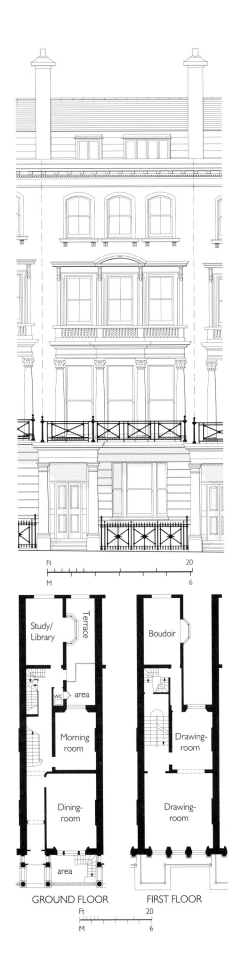

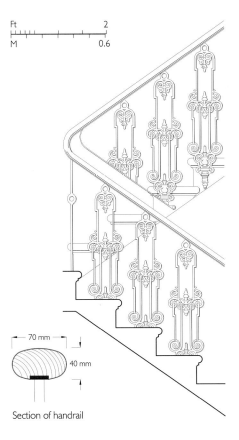

Section of handrail

Fig. 60. Nos 27–47 Rutland Gate, typical elevation, plans and staircase detail. John Elger, builder, 1853–9

It is not known who designed the houses, but their standard elevation clearly derives from designs made for Elger by H. L. Elmes in the 1840s (see page 165), and which provided the basis for the fronts of the houses built by Elger and others on the Kingston House estate. They are much more 'Victorian' in style than Tombs's houses of the late 1830s and '40s, including the putative Matthew Wyatt houses at Nos 1–7, both in their breaking away from strict Georgian proportions and in their ornamentation and robust ironwork (fig. 60, Plate 75a–b).

Inside, in their original state, the houses were of conventional side-passage plan with main and service staircases of stone. As with houses on the Kingston House estate, they are of considerable depth, which allowed for a third main room at the rear on the ground and first floors, ideally suited to uses requiring privacy and quiet (fig. 60).[65]

Twentieth-Century Redevelopments

Rutland Gate changed little before the First World War. A few of the original houses were altered prior to that, but mostly with little or no jarring impact. The enlargement and remodelling of the corner house, No. 8, for instance, carried out in the late 1880s to designs by Fairfax Wade, conformed externally to the existing style in general terms.[66]

A minor work of some interest is the roof-garden and penthouse at the rear of No. 64 (extending over the roofs of the stabling in Ennismore Mews), created prior to 1913 for the Rt Hon. Frederick Huth-Jackson (Plate 76).[67]

Internally, one or two noteworthy decorative schemes are known. In 1921, for example, some of Deane & Braddell's fairly recent work for Viscount Erleigh at No. 65 appeared in *Academy Architecture*. Two rooms were shown: the neo-Adam drawing-room and an early-Georgian-style boudoir.[68] The previous year the first issue of *House and Gardens* had published photographs of Huth-Jackson's remodelled entrance hall at No. 64, and a view of the interior of the garden penthouse.[69]

In the 1930s the architectural harmony of Rutland Gate was disturbed by the redevelopment of the former Clytha House and of Nos 4–8 Rutland Gate with flats and houses in the Modern style. (Both developments are described below.) The loss of Nos 4–8 is not quite so obvious today, as the site has again been redeveloped with a building superficially at least 'in keeping' with the 1830s range at Nos 1–7.

Since the Second World War, the majority of the houses have been made into flats – many by means of 'lateral' conversions, so that the individual identity of the houses, behind the mostly unaltered façades, has been lost. In the mid-1950s all the Elger houses on the west side of Rutland Gate (Nos 48–65), which had been requisitioned during the war, were made into flats. The developers were Tillings, the haulage contractors, and great emphasis was placed on the provision of garages for the tenants. These are at basement level at the rear of the flats.[70]

There are two post-war blocks of flats, neither of which show any great regard for the neighbouring houses. **Rutland Gate House (Nos 43–44)**, designed by Walter and Eva Segal and built in 1955–8, probably gains from the stylistic contrast with the old houses, being on the same overall scale. The front is attractively simple, faced in light-coloured brick with strip windows, the overall horizontality offset by a vertical pattern of casement windows and the uprights of the area railings and window guard-rails. The two flats to each floor are clearly expressed (Plate 77b).[71]

The block of flats at **No. 15**, shown in its original form in Plate 77c, was built in 1968–70 for Hillbrow Estates on the site of Nos 13–17. The old houses were being underpinned as part of a scheme to convert them to flats, with the addition of a penthouse floor and basement car-park, when they collapsed in November 1967. The architects of both the ill-fated conversion scheme and the eventual rebuilding were Leslie Sacks and Partners. Three cottages at the rear of the houses, in **Gate Mews**, were rebuilt as part of the same development (Plate 79c).[72] In 1996 an insensitive two-storey extension was built on top of the flats.[73]

Both of the original ranges of houses in Rutland Gate facing the park have been redeveloped. **Nos 1–7**, saved from total demolition at the eleventh hour in 1971,[74] were largely rebuilt in the late 1970s by AB International, preserving the original façades to the main road, but with a wholly reconstructed attic storey (fig. 57). The architects of the scheme, which included houses to the flank and rear, in Rutland Gate and Gate Mews, were Richard Matthew and Colin Woodiwiss.[75]

Nos 2–8, built in 1985–7, were designed by the architects YRM, who won the commission in a limited competition in 1982. They replace the original No. 2 Rutland Gate and a group of Modern Movement houses built in the 1930s (see Nos 4–8A below). One of YRM's least Modern designs,[i] the building comprises a rather bland white *palazzo*. A very expensive development, it consists of only four residential units, each with its own swimming-pool.[77]

Of those houses in Rutland Gate that remain single dwellings, the most remarkable is **No. 14**, which was internally transformed in the early 1990s by Eva Jiricna Architects. The house had already undergone several re-vampings, including one in 1927 by the architects Wimperis, Simpson & Guthrie, when it was extended and given bow windows at front and back.[78] As remodelled by Eva Jiricna the interior is minimalistic, monochromatic, and spot-lit, characterized by hard surfaces and precisely engineered materials such as stainless steel, glass and stone. This combination is relieved by softer materials here and there, such as sisal insets in the stone floors, and sliding window shutters of hand-made paper in wooden frames. The overall simplicity of the design – the doors, for instance, are full-height and frameless – acts as a foil to the complexity of the central feature, a spiral staircase of steel with sand-blasted glass treads (Plate 117a–b).[79]

At the south end of the street, **No. 47** was remodelled internally as a speculation in the early 1990s by the fashionable designers David Champion and Anthony Collett. In accordance with their stylistic principles, reportedly influenced by ethnic African design, the house is characterized by joinery in a variety of hardwoods.[80]

Eresby House

This smart inter-war apartment block, conspicuously situated aslant the bend in the road, occupies the site of the nineteenth-century mansion of the same name, originally called Clytha House (Plates 73b, 108). The present building was erected in 1933–4 to designs by T. P. Bennett & Son (a slightly earlier scheme by Wimperis, Simpson & Guthrie having been abandoned). The main contractor was J. Gerrard & Sons Ltd of Swinton, Manchester.[81]

Comprising a central block flanked by projecting wings, Eresby House has a symmetrical plan (fig. 61) designed to provide seven floors of two- and three-bedroom flats with

[i] Perhaps one of the few 'wobblies' the architect John Winter had in mind when assessing YRM's contribution to the Modernist tradition during the 'architectural chaos and disillusion' of the 1980s.[76]

reception rooms looking out to Rutland Gate, most with a view of the upper communal garden. The central section contains two flats per floor while the wings have three, grouped around their own staircase and common areas. Here the entrance lobbies and staircase halls have stylish elliptical and semi-circular plans. An extra floor over the central section, designed as bedrooms and bathrooms for servants, has since been converted to private flats. Much of the basement was originally fitted out as box-rooms for the tenants.[82]

The exterior of the building is faced in brick, rusticated on the ground floor, with minimal Portland-stone dressings. Curved corners on the projecting front wings give a slightly streamlined effect. The brickwork of the balcony fronts is laid in a basket-weave pattern, but otherwise ornamentation is mostly reserved for the main entrance (Plate 108a–b). The stone relief of a horse and rider above the central doorway is by Eric Aumonier (Plate 108c), as is the turquoise faience relief of two female musicians in classical dress over the fireplace in the main entrance hall.[83] In the common areas wood veneers and marquetry are used to produce a look of suave modernity (Plate 108d). Similar in feeling are the Travertine marble stairs with their steel banisters and chromed handrails.

At the back of the flats are lock-up garages, including a pair with maisonettes over in Montpelier Terrace (see page 117).

Nos 4–8A Rutland Gate (demolished)

In 1936 three of the four houses facing Hyde Park on the west side of Rutland Gate were pulled down for a new development (fig. 62) whose clean lines could hardly have been in greater contrast to the stuccoed classicism of the old buildings (Plate 77a). The new houses, Nos 4–8A, were designed for Cubitt Estates by Francis Lorne of Sir John Burnet, Tait & Lorne, and built in 1936–7 by Holland & Hannen and Cubitts.[84]

Externally, they had a thoroughly Modern look, with flat roofs, oblong metal-casement windows, and porthole lights to the stairways. Particular attention was paid to the

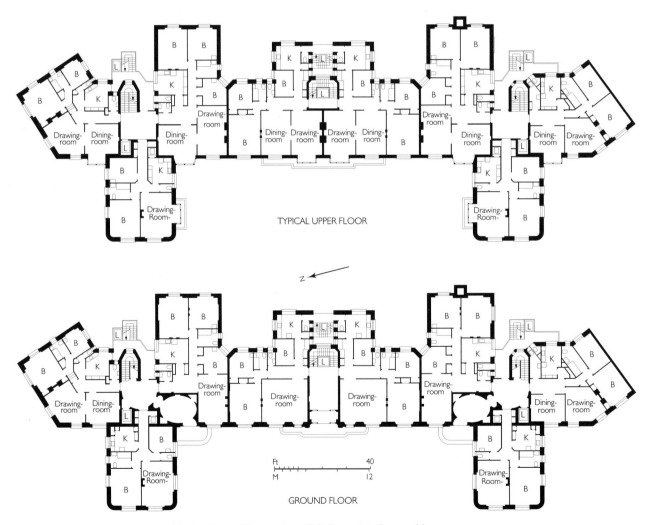

Fig. 61. Eresby House, plans. T. P. Bennett & Son, architects, 1933–4

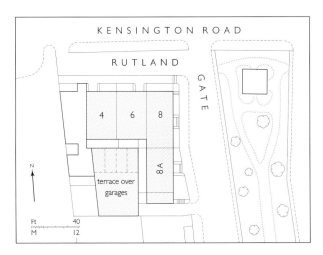

Fig. 62. Nos 4–8A Rutland Gate, redeveloped 1936–7: site plan.
Demolished

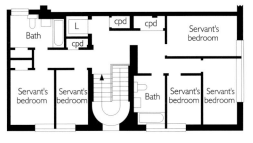

THIRD FLOOR

SECOND FLOOR

FIRST FLOOR

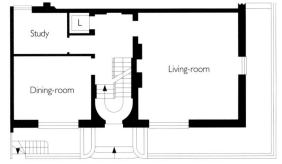

GROUND FLOOR

brickwork in order to create a 'monolithic' effect. All the exposed walls were faced in narrow (two-inch) stocks of light 'silver grey' colour, laid with thick colour-matched joints in a bond of one header to two stretchers along each course. In contrast, to achieve the effect of compression and horizontality, the brickwork of the plinth and the door surrounds was carried out in dark grey pressed bricks laid in thick white horizontal and dark vertical joints. The area walls and integral flower-boxes were similarly treated, and had the extra refinement of 'streamline' corners.

Structurally, the houses were conventional, with wooden joisted floors and wooden staircases, American oak being used for the stairs and the flooring at ground level and on the landings. The asphalted flat roofs too were of timber construction. Pre-cast terrazzo was used for the entrance canopies.

The accommodation was an up-dated version of the traditional upper-middle-class home, with rooms for numerous servants. Ample bathrooms, lifts, central heating, fitted pantry-kitchens and plenty of cupboards were provided. There were, however, no grand reception rooms. Each house had its own garage in a row at the back, the roof of which provided a terrace for common use. Figure 63 shows the layout of the corner house, No. 8.

The site was redeveloped in the mid-1980s (see above).

Rutland Gate Mews

This mews was laid out *c.*1841 by John Tombs and built up by him over the next few years.[85] No. 4 was leased to the first occupant of No. 26 Rutland Gate and remained in the same ownership as that house. The stabling was converted to take cars in 1914.[86] Jessica Mitford, whose family's London home was at No. 26, described 'camping out' as a child with her sisters and nanny in the rooms over the garage, which

Fig. 63. No. 8 Rutland Gate, plans. Francis Lorne, architect, 1936–7. *Demolished*

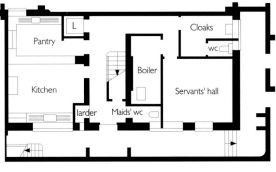

BASEMENT

were entered from the main house. In the 1930s, Diana and Unity Mitford are said to have engraved the windows with a hammer and sickle, a swastika and 'Heil Hitler', symbolic of their respective allegiances.[87]

Nos 1–3, on the west side, were rebuilt in the early 1990s – in planner-approved neo-Victorian style – as three-bedroomed houses with integral garages. The architect was Paul Brookes.[88]

Rutland Mews East and West, and Montpelier Walk

Both mews are part of John Elger's development of southern Rutland Gate and date from the mid-1850s.[89] The most striking of the buildings here is Clock House, formerly No. 3 Rutland Mews West (Plate 75c). Its name and the basic pattern of the openings on the Rutland Gate front belong to its pre-Second World War conversion to bijou residence. Much of the ornamental treatment, including the statues on the parapet, dates from the early 1960s, when the house was remodelled for Sir Henry Aylwen, a former Lord Mayor of London. His architect was Austin Blomfield.[90]

A scheme to build a five-storey block of flats at Nos 3 and 4 Rutland Mews East, on the corner of Rutland Street and Montpelier Walk, was put forward in 1934 by the architect E. Kingdon Rowe; Erno Goldfinger later seriously considered buying the property himself to redevelop with flats, but ultimately nothing came of the idea.[91] The old buildings, converted to flats and much altered, are now Nos 39–41 Montpelier Walk.

Neither these nor any other of the buildings on the west side of Montpelier Walk north of Rutland Street call for architectural comment. They are essentially rear extensions of the houses in Rutland Gate, altered and extended at various dates (Plate 73b). Several have been converted into separate dwellings.

Social Character and Notable Residents

The social character of Rutland Gate changed little if at all throughout the Victorian period and beyond. Householders were typically merchants, bankers, lawyers, politicians, civil servants, senior army and naval officers, rentiers and others of independent means; a small proportion were members of the aristocracy. The houses made ideal lets for families coming to town for the season.

The following is a selective list of noteworthy past occupants of houses in Rutland Gate, excluding those already mentioned.

No. 3   Richard Meinerzhagen, naturalist and Intelligence officer; Frederic (Lord) Maugham, Lord Chancellor, brother of W. Somerset Maugham; Edward Turner Boyd Twisleton, politician, contributor to the debate over the authorship of the 'Junius' letters

No. 5   Archibald Hastie MP, owner of Robert Burns's punch bowl and promoter of 'Burns Night'; George Ward Hunt, chancellor of the exchequer in Disraeli's first administration

No. 6 (dem.)   Miss A. E. Barker, artist

No. 8 (dem.)   Sir James Colvile, chief justice of the supreme court of Bengal; George Wightwick Rendel, civil engineer

No. 9   George Lyall, Governor of the Bank of England

No. 10   Sir John Bell, general; Hugh de Grey, Marquess of Hertford (as Earl of Yarmouth), courtier

No. 12   Lord Noel-Buxton, Liberal and Labour politician, philanthropist

No. 13 (dem.)   Sir George Russell Clerk, permanent under-secretary of state for India, governor of Bombay

No. 15 (dem.)   Robert Sullivan, poet and playwright; Sir Henry Charles Drummond Wolff, Conservative politician and diplomatist

No. 16   Frederick Marrable, Superintending Architect of the Metropolitan Board of Works

No. 17 (dem.)   Lord Northcote, governor-general of the Australian Commonwealth; Sir John St George, general

No. 18   Sir Eyre Massey Shaw, head of the London Metropolitan Fire Brigade

No 22   Sir Thomas Bladen Capel, admiral; Sir Stuart Alexander Donaldson, Australian businessman and statesman

No. 25   Sir Henry Thurstan Holland (Lord Knutsford), Conservative politician

No. 27   The Hon. Arthur R. D. Elliot, Liberal Unionist politician, editor of the *Edinburgh Review*; Sir Edward Fanshawe, admiral

No. 32   Sir Herbert Lawrence, soldier and banker; Sir Montague Edward Browning, admiral

No. 34   Sir Hew Dalrymple-Ross, field-marshal

No. 38   Frank McClean, civil engineer and astronomer; Frederick A. Maxse, admiral and political writer; Sir Edward McArthur, military commander in Australia, sometime acting governor of Victoria

No. 39   T. D. H. Browne, artist; Lord Carson, advocate and Ulster Unionist leader

No. 41   Sir Robert Donald, editor of the *Daily Chronicle*; Sir Thomas Gardner Horridge, judge

No. 42   Sir Francis Galton, founder of eugenics and pioneer of fingerprinting

No. 43 (dem.)   Sir Archibald Alison, general

No. 45   Sir John Edmund Commerell, VC, Admiral of the Fleet; the 3rd Earl of Morley, Liberal politician

No. 48   7th Earl of Albemarle, Liberal and Conservative politician

No. 51   Sir Frederick John Dealtry Lugard, later Baron Lugard of Abinger, colonial administrator

No. 52   Sir Robert Craigie, diplomatist

No. 58   Sir James Bailey, founder of Bailey's Hotel; Sir Austen Chamberlain, Conservative statesman

No. 59   Sir Claude Henry Mason Buckle, admiral; Sir Philip Rose, founder of Brompton Hospital

No. 61   William Forsyth, writer and Conservative MP, editor of the *Annual Register*

No. 62   Henry Reeve, editor of the *Edinburgh Review*; Sir Cecil Harcourt-Smith, director of the Victoria and Albert Museum

No. 63   Lord Calthorpe, agriculturist, benefactor of Birmingham University

CHAPTER IX

Princes Gate and Ennismore Gardens: The Kingston House Estate

Extending over twenty-one acres, the Kingston House estate was one of the largest property holdings in Knightsbridge. At its centre was Kingston House itself, built in the mid-eighteenth century for the celebrated Elizabeth Chudleigh, soi-disant Duchess of Kingston. Bounded on three sides by fields, this mansion originally commanded uninterrupted views towards Surrey. Increasingly encroached upon by building, it survived until the 1930s, the last of the big houses of old Knightsbridge.

The development of the estate (figs 64, 82) took place in stages between the 1840s and the 1960s. Of the four principal phases, only three are represented today by buildings on the ground. The earliest, begun by one of the great Victorian speculative builders, John Elger, lasted almost a decade, and saw the construction of two ranges of large houses in Princes Gate, east and west of Kingston House, and the lesser houses on the eastern side of Ennismore Gardens. The other three sides of Ennismore Gardens belong to the second wave of development, undertaken in the late 1860s and early '70s by the contractors Peter and Alexander Thorn.

A rather disjointed third phase, overlapping with the second and continuing into the 1880s, produced a cluster of large detached houses in the northern part of Ennismore Gardens, on the eastern and southern fringes of Kingston House garden. In the 1930s a protracted fourth phase began. While preserving the leafy and spacious character of the area, this swept away old Kingston House, the later Victorian mansions to the south and east, and the early Victorian eastern range of Princes Gate, replacing them with a mix of apartment blocks and town-houses, the last of which were not completed until the late 1960s.

Almost all of the mews houses associated with the two earlier phases of development survive. Endlessly prettified, they provide a picturesque counterpoint to the prevailing *gravitas*, and occasional banality, of their neighbours. In these surroundings, the Lombardic architecture of the former All Saints' Church (now a Russian Orthodox cathedral) strikes an unexpectedly exotic note.

Kingston House and the Kingston House Estate

When its development began in the 1840s, the Kingston House estate had existed as an entity for barely half a cen-

tury. There were four main constituent parts, which are to a large extent discernible in the present-day pattern of streets and buildings. Just under a third of the ground was freehold. The remainder, formerly part of the extensive property of the Brompton nurseryman John Swinhoe, was copyhold of the manor of Knightsbridge and Westbourne Green, belonging to the Dean and Chapter of Westminster Abbey.[1]

At the core of the estate were the three acres of copyhold ground acquired in 1757 by Elizabeth Chudleigh for the building of Kingston House, occupied today by Kingston House North and its garden. The land adjoining to the west, a four-acre copyhold field, now occupied by Nos 14–25 Princes Gate and their communal garden, was purchased by the 2nd Duke of Kingston in 1759. Two freehold fields to the east of Kingston House, but separated from it by a narrow strip of ground, were bought in the same year by Elizabeth Chudleigh. Known as West Mead or Wett Meads, and together containing 6½ acres, these fields had hitherto formed the westernmost portion of the Moreau family's property in the Knightsbridge area (see fig. 21 on page 78).[2] Today this ground comprises the main north–south roadway of Ennismore Gardens, together with the whole east side of that street, Nos 1–7 Princes Gate and their communal garden, the site of the Russian Orthodox cathedral, and Ennismore Mews.

When the Duke of Kingston died in 1773 all this property descended to his wife (as he believed), Elizabeth Chudleigh, for her lifetime, and upon her death in 1788 to his nephew Charles Meadows, who under the terms of his uncle's will took the surname Pierrepont.[3]

The narrow strip of ground between Kingston House and the two freehold fields to the east purchased in 1759 was connected at its southern end to another copyhold field lying behind the house. In 1793 Charles Pierrepont took this whole piece of land, about 7½ acres in extent, on long lease, thus consolidating as well as greatly enlarging the estate. These 7½ acres continued to be held on lease until the 1860s, when the 3rd Earl of Listowel, the then owner of the Kingston House estate, was admitted as copyholder and secured the ground's enfranchisement from manorial control.[4] On the ground today are Nos 1–35 Ennismore Gardens, Ennismore Gardens Mews, Moncorvo Close and the two blocks of Kingston House South; the slip itself is occupied by Kingston House East and the houses comprising Bolney Gate.

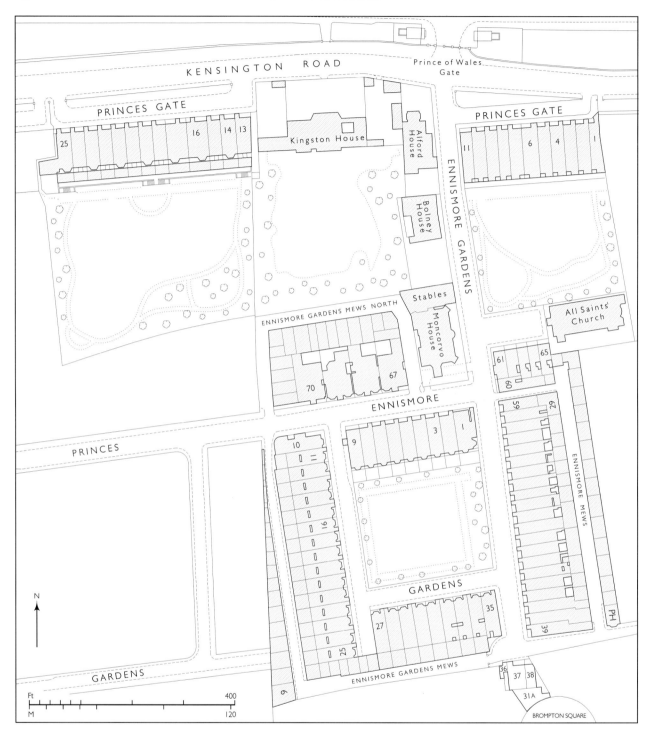

Fig. 64. Princes Gate and Ennismore Gardens in the mid-1890s: the Kingston House Estate

In 1807–8 Pierrepont, by then 1st Earl Manvers, gave the property to his second son, Henry Manvers Pierrepont, who in 1813 sold it for £20,000 to William Hare, Baron Ennismore, later 1st Earl of Listowel (1751–1837).[5]

In 1855 the substantial portion of the estate built up with houses and stables in the 1840s and early '50s was sold by the 2nd Earl, but the greater part, including Kingston House itself, remained in the possession of the Hare family until shortly before the Second World War.[6]

With the death of the 4th Earl in 1931, the estate passed

not to his eldest son, the socialist 5th Earl, but on trust to a younger son, John Hare, later Viscount Blakenham.[7] In 1935 an agreement was made with property developers for the sale of Kingston House, together with the neighbouring houses to the east and south built in the 1870s and '80s. Later the rump of the estate – the mid-Victorian houses at Nos 1–35 Ennismore Gardens and Ennismore Gardens Mews – passed into the possession of the Egerton family, Earls of Ellesmere (now Dukes of Sutherland). In 1996 the freehold of these large houses, now known as the Ennismore Gardens Estate, was acquired by the Wellcome Trust. Most of the properties in the mews have been enfranchised under the 1967 Leasehold Reform Act.[8]

Kingston House (demolished)

Of the string of aristocratic mansions built along the south side of the Kensington road in the late seventeenth and eighteenth centuries, Kingston House was the only one not to succumb to redevelopment in the nineteenth. A remarkable survival, it was well photographed before being pulled down in 1937 (Plates 80–1); but the records of its building history appear largely to have been lost.[9]

Elizabeth Chudleigh (1720–88), for whom the house was built in 1757–8 – probably at the expense of the Duke of Kingston – was the daughter of a lieutenant-governor of Chelsea Hospital. A maid of honour to the Princess of Wales, she formed a series of relationships with high-ranking noblemen, and became somewhat notorious for flouting the conventions of polite society. Many years before her involvement with the Duke of Kingston, she had secretly, and ill-advisedly, married the Hon. Augustus Hervey, later Earl of Bristol. It was eventually determined in court that the marriage had never taken place; but evidence of its validity was blatantly suppressed, with the eventual result that, after the duke's death, the judgement was overturned and Elizabeth Chudleigh was indicted and found guilty of bigamy.[10]

Miss Chudleigh is listed as the ratepayer of Kingston House from 1758 until 1769, the year she and the duke married, and they lived there together thereafter, until his death in 1773. Following her trial in 1776, Elizabeth Chudleigh (correctly the Countess of Bristol) fled abroad to escape legal proceedings brought by the duke's family to recover his property. However, the duke's will, leaving his real estate to her for life, was upheld by the courts and she continued to enjoy the profits until she died in France more than ten years later.[11]

From Elizabeth Chudleigh, Kingston House descended to the duke's nephew, and it remained in his family's possession until the estate was sold in 1813. For some of this time the house was occupied by tenants. Sir George Warren lived there from 1789 to 1803, and in December 1790 was reported to be making 'considerable', though unspecified, alterations. (He also contrived to have a private carriage-entrance into Hyde Park built immediately opposite, which apparently remained in use until the opening of Prince of Wales Gate in 1848; a pedestrian gate now occupies the site.)[12] The 6th Earl of Stair is said to have lived at Kingston House after Warren, though he is not listed in the ratebooks, and between 1805 and 1808 the rates were paid by Edward Lovedon Lovedon. Lord Ennismore took up residence in the house after purchasing the estate in 1813, and made 'many alterations and additions'.[13]

In its original form, Kingston House was a conventional Palladian villa, comprising a squarish three-storey block flanked by lower wings containing stables and kitchens (Plate 80a).[a] Architectural display was concentrated on the north front, where the central bay was embellished with two Venetian windows under a shallow pediment. Between the house and the service wings were two small courtyards, enclosed on the south side by single-storey linking corridors, and on the north by walls with pedimented gateways. Though the architect is not known, a possible candidate is Henry Flitcroft, who undertook commissions for both the 1st and 2nd Dukes of Kingston.[15]

Behind the house were originally formal gardens and a grotto.[16]

An impression of Kingston House (or Chudleigh House as it was then called) was recorded by a visitor in 1762:

[Miss Chudleigh's] house can justly be called a gem; it contains a quantity of handsome and costly furniture and other curiosities and objects of value, chosen and arranged with the greatest taste, so that you cannot fail to admire it greatly. There is hardly a place in the whole house left bare or without decoration, like a doll's house. Everything is in perfect harmony. The view, over Hyde Park, and at the back over Chelsea, is considered with truth one of the finest that could be pictured.[17]

Parts of the mid-Georgian interior décor, including the staircase, survived until the house was pulled down (Plate 81a). The photographs taken in 1937 show a lobby on the second floor decorated in the Chinese taste.

Some Regency-style additions in the form of a colonnaded *porte-cochère*, bow windows at the front and a full-width Trafalgar balcony at the back (Plate 80a, c) were most likely part of Lord Ennismore's improvements. He is known to have made two major additions at the back before 1820: a grand first-floor saloon, built over the west service wing and linking corridor, and beyond it, at the same level, a 75ft-long Gothick-style conservatory of cast iron and glass (Plates 80b, 81b, d).[18] The saloon was opulently decorated in the style of Nash, with green scagliola columns, red damask wall-hangings and coffered coving. Together with the two existing drawing-rooms on the first floor, the saloon and conservatory made up an interconnecting sequence of apartments along the garden front. According to H. G. Davis, the Knightsbridge historian, the conservatory originally contained a painted window by John Martin

[a] An early illustration, in 1766, shows the house as a two-storey building, but its reliability is called into question by the survival, until demolition, of mid-eighteenth-century features on the second floor.[14]

of a garden scene.[19] This had disappeared by the 1930s, but another painted window by Martin, 'Woman cloathed with the Sun', inspired by a passage in the Book of Revelations, survived in the ante-room or corridor on the north side of the saloon.

The appearance of the interior was enhanced by fine furniture and the Hare family's very considerable collection of Old Master paintings, which included works by Rembrandt, Van Dyck, Holbein, Poussin, Murillo and Velázquez.[20]

That Kingston House survived well into the twentieth century is all the more remarkable in that neither the 2nd Earl of Listowel nor, initially, the 3rd Earl seem to have had any particular attachment to the place. After the death of the 1st Earl in 1837, the house was let to the Duke of Wellington's brother, Richard, Marquess Wellesley, who died there in 1842. In 1864 the house attracted a purchase offer – through the agency of C. J. Freake, the developer of the adjoining ground to the west – from Baron Lionel de Rothschild, who had been living there since about 1859. Nothing came of this, but the 3rd Earl was actively pursuing the enfranchisement of the property at this time, presumably as a preliminary to a proposed redevelopment of the ground, and there is evidence that the demolition of Kingston House was in mind during the 1870s.[21]

Possibly the difficulties encountered by the developer of the north side of Ennismore Gardens in the 1880s discouraged further development and so helped to stave off the destruction of the old house. The 3rd Earl died at Kingston House in 1924, and the last occupant was his widow, who in turn died there in December 1936. In March 1937 the contents were sold and that autumn the house itself was demolished for the building of flats (see Kingston House North below).[22]

Development by Elger, Kelk and Mayhew from 1845

William Hare, 1st Earl of Listowel, died at Kingston House on 13 July 1837, aged 85, and was succeeded by his grandson.

By 1836, when the 1st Earl's will was drawn up, the estate's twenty-one acres were becoming ripe for development. Rutland House, the neighbouring mansion to the east, had already been demolished and work was under way on laying out its grounds for building. Recognizing his property's potential, the earl made provisions permitting his heir and trustees to grant long leases for building and improvement on the freehold part of the estate.[23]

However, the impetus for development came not from the 2nd Earl, but from John Elger (1802–88), a Bedford carpenter's son who had made his name in the 1820s and '30s as a speculative builder in the South Street area of Mayfair.[24] He approached Lord Listowel (who resided for only short spells at Kingston House) with proposals for building on parts of the estate, and by February 1840 was already discussing terms with the earl's surveyor, George Gutch.[25]

By the end of September 1840 an agreement had been drafted, but progress came to a halt when the Birmingham, Bristol and Thames Junction Railway Company announced plans for a branch line across the estate to a terminus at Knightsbridge Green. Elger promptly withdrew from further discussions, for, as Lord Listowel's lawyer recorded, 'it would be impossible in the event of a Railway to build the class of Houses he had contemplated with any chance of success'.[26]

The railway threat duly receded, and negotiations were resumed in January 1842. But Elger procrastinated, possibly waiting for the enfranchisement of the prime site to the west of Kingston House, and it was not until May 1843 that a new draft agreement was prepared. By then he had submitted a layout plan for the eastern, freehold portion to the Westminster Commissioners of Sewers. This showed a terrace of eleven houses fronting the Kensington road east of Kingston House, with an ornamental communal garden at the back, and a new north–south street running towards Brompton Square, with a terrace of twenty-four houses on the east side and a mews street behind.[27] The *Builder*, evidently aware that this was likely to be only the first phase of a large-scale development, reported that Kingston House itself was to be pulled down – for 'a beautiful square of the first class houses' – and that a church was also 'in contemplation'.[28]

Between May 1843 and January 1845, when the building agreement was finalized, the plan was modified to include the western, copyhold ground (soon to be enfranchised), and a site was allocated for a church in a cul-de-sac off the north–south road.[29]

The agreement stipulated that Elger was to construct no more than fifty-one houses, with as much stabling as he considered necessary. Twenty-four or twenty-five houses were to face the park in two ranges, one either side of Kingston House. These houses were to be larger and of greater value – about £3,000 each – than those fronting the new street, which were to be worth £1,800 each. All houses were to be of brick, the principal façades rendered in blue lias or other cement, and those facing the Kensington road were to be set back from the highway behind carriage drives.

Leases were to be for 99 years from Michaelmas 1844, at rents rising to more than £1,500 in total after nine years.[30] According to Lord Listowel, the terms took into account the nuisance factor of the Halfway House tavern in the Kensington road, an eyesore removed by Elger in 1846.[31]

The architect and artist Thomas Allom produced a panoramic view of the intended development, showing the two ranges of Princes Gate in matching style, a Gothic church with a spire on the site of All Saints', Ennismore Gardens, and a single long range of houses south of the church (Plate 82a).

Instead of taking their names from Kingston House or Lord Ennismore, as was at first intended, the terraces along the Kensington road were called Princes Gate, relating them to Prince of Wales Gate, the new entrance into Hyde Park directly opposite. This important improvement, which followed the removal of the Halfway House, was accomplished in 1847–8, largely at Elger's instigation and expense (see below). At the same time the north–south road, originally Ennismore Terrace, was renamed Princes Terrace: in 1874 it was renumbered as part of Ennismore Gardens, along with the houses fronting the cul-de-sac leading to All Saints' Church, hitherto called Ennismore Place.[32]

Elger had at first intended to undertake the entire development himself, using designs by the architect Harvey Lonsdale Elmes. In the event, he relinquished parts of the ground to two other speculators, both of whom brought in their own architects. The contractor (Sir) John Kelk, who was briefly in partnership with Elger in the mid-1840s, took the large plot to the east of Kingston House, where he built Nos 1–11 Princes Gate and laid out the communal garden at the back. He also contributed £1,500 towards the removal of the Halfway House and the making of Prince of Wales Gate.[33] Before taking on responsibility for Nos 1–11, however, Kelk seems to have been involved in the development as the executant builder of John Pearce's house at No. 14 Princes Gate and his stable in Ennismore Mews.[34] A comparatively small plot behind Kelk's was taken by the builder G. W. Mayhew, who built six houses there, now Nos 60–65 Ennismore Gardens. Elger himself was responsible for the western range of Princes Gate, originally Nos 13–25 (Kingston House itself being No. 12), and the houses south of Mayhew's, now Nos 39–59 Ennismore Gardens.

All three developers erected coach-houses and stables in Ennismore Mews, where building on the estate began in 1845, with the construction by Elger of a public house, the Ennismore Arms. Kelk and Mayhew had completed their respective developments, and Elger his houses in Princes Gate, by about 1850. Elger's Ennismore Gardens houses were built between 1849 and 1854. The houses generally had filled up with tenants by 1855.[35]

Elger and the creation of Prince of Wales Gate

A potential obstacle to the success of the Kingston House estate development was the continued presence of the old Halfway House tavern opposite the top end of Elger's new north–south street. Formerly the King's Arms, and dating back at least to 1733, the tavern occupied a narrow site between the highway and the footpath alongside Hyde Park (Plate 2a). A night-house, it was a favourite stop for waggoners, whose vehicles often blocked the road.[36]

The question of its removal was raised in 1841 by the Metropolis Roads Commissioners, who had long wished to incorporate the site into the roadway. With this end in view, they bought the freehold (from the Dean and Chapter of Westminster Abbey), selling it on to the Crown under an agreement that the tavern would be demolished on rever-

sion in the 1860s and the road widened. (The commissioners' finances, weakened since the opening of the Great Western Railway, prevented them from keeping the freehold themselves.)

For Elger the clearance of the Halfway House was a matter of some urgency. In November 1845, having agreed to buy the leasehold and business, he offered terms to the Commissioners of Woods and Forests and the roads commissioners for removing the building: £1,000 each to be contributed by the respective commissions, the remaining £1,000-plus to be paid by himself. When this proposition was declined, he threatened 'to make the best I can of my Purchase' by selling out to a brewing company, 'with a condition to remove such portions of the premises, as are calculated to be injurious to my Interest' – a course which 'would do little for the Public'. Support for Elger came from the Countess of Blessington, of nearby Gore House, who urged on the Commissioners of Woods and Forests the destruction of

one of the greatest nuisances that ever disgraced any entrance to a great Capital . . . If you could best know the stoppages occasioned by the Carts and Horses continually in front of the public house and in the open stables adjoining, the dreadful odour, and the filth they accumulate you would pity those who are obliged to pass this terrible spot twice and thrice a day.[37]

Eventually the two commissions agreed to contribute £800 each, and in September 1846 Elger demolished the Halfway House. By that time, however, he had a further improvement in mind: the creation of a gate into the park where the tavern had stood. Lord Auckland, Lady Blessington's neighbour at Eden Lodge, acted as intermediary, forwarding plans and a memorial to the Commissioners of Woods and Forests.

In October 1847 Elger was behind a further memorial in support of a new entrance, to be called Prince of Wales Gate, signed by, among others, the countess, Auckland, Lord Listowel, Lord Campbell (of Stratheden House) and the Earl of Morley (of Kent House). The authorities agreed, provided that Elger built the gateway and a lodge at his own expense, to plans drawn up by their architect, Decimus Burton. Elger was also to pay the gatekeeper's salary for ten years, as it was thought the gate would chiefly benefit local people rather than the general public. Opened in October 1848, Prince of Wales Gate was, however, soon admitting thousands to the Great Exhibition, when a second (east) lodge was built as a temporary police station (fig. 64; Plates 7–8).

Elger and Kelk at Princes Gate

The two rows of houses comprising Princes Gate were envisaged as matching ranges, as shown in Thomas Allom's view (Plate 82a). The frontages of the proposed houses were of similar size, and the two sites, although of unequal length, were of comparable prominence viewed from the road or park. Both terraces, moreover, looked

Fig. 65. Nos 13–25 Princes Gate, typical elevation. H. L. Elmes,
architect, John Elger, builder, 1846–50

Fig. 66. Nos 1–11 Princes Gate, typical elevation. John Johnson,
architect, John Kelk, builder, c.1848–50. *Demolished*

across spacious communal gardens to the south. Elger,
however, regarded the western plot as the finer, and
reserved its development to himself. He began building
there in October 1846, and the last three houses were started in March 1849. Six were sufficiently advanced for the
leases to be granted in 1848; the remaining houses were
leased between December 1849 and November 1850.[38]

The original plan had been for a symmetrical west range
of fourteen houses, ten with 26ft frontages and the pairs at
each end a couple of feet wider and set forward slightly,
with the further emphasis of rusticated quoins. At some
point this plan was altered to give only thirteen houses, Nos
16 and 17 together occupying three plots – their façades
follow the rhythm of the rest of the terrace, the central bay,
where the party wall is, having blank windows.

The end house, No. 25, was also of exceptional size,
achieved in this instance by utilizing a kink in the bound-

ary between Lord Listowel's land and the neighbouring
property to add a substantial wing.

Kelk, who brought in John Johnson as his architect, had
four houses under way by November 1848. The remaining
seven were begun in the following February, and all eleven
were finished in carcase before the end of 1849, when leases were issued by Lord Listowel.[39]

Elger's houses initially 'went' well, five tenants taking up
residence in 1849. But with the building of the Crystal
Palace opposite Princes Gate, blocking the view and bringing noise and disruption to the area, prospective tenants
began to be put off (Plate 7). Elger's 'lordly mansions', it was
reported, were 'much depreciated in value'.[40] Four of his
houses were still empty in 1851, when he complained that it
was 'impossible to calculate the injury to individuals who
have expended money on the faith that the parks will always
continue open'.[41] It was not until 1853–4, by which time the

Fig. 67. Nos 60–65 Ennismore Gardens, typical elevation. Charles Mayhew, architect, G. W. Mayhew, builder, *c.*1847–50

Fig. 68. Nos 39–59 Ennismore Gardens, typical elevation. John Elger, builder, 1849–54

Crystal Palace was being re-erected at Sydenham, that the last three houses – Nos 20, 22 and 25 – were occupied.

Kelk's development, having started later, was worse affected. He told the inquiry into the future of the Crystal Palace that sales of three houses had been lost solely because of the spoiled view. Before the Great Exhibition his speculation had gone 'as fast as ever it could' and 'would have been the best thing I ever touched': it would be ruined if the exhibition building remained where it was. Several people had been 'about the houses' lately, but all wanted to know the fate of the Crystal Palace.[42] Six of his houses remained unlet until 1852–3, the large corner house, No. 11, being the last to be occupied.[43]

Elger and Mayhew at Ennismore Gardens

The building up of the east side of Ennismore Gardens

('Princes Terrace' and 'Ennismore Place') was carried out between 1846 and 1854 (fig. 64). The houses here are inferior to those in Princes Gate, being smaller and having neither park views nor access to communal gardens, but they are closely related to them stylistically, and, when new, they looked west over the walled grounds of Kingston House.

Elger's original plan had been for a continuous terrace running the full length of the street south of the garden behind Nos 1–11 Princes Gate, with a mews behind, but this was modified about 1845 to provide a site for a church at the end of a short turning, Ennismore Place, which offered excellent frontages for five houses looking towards the Princes Gate garden. The plan was further modified to take advantage of this, and to demarcate these houses from the main terrace by making a northern entrance to the mews.[44]

The small block so formed was sub-let by Elger to the

builder George William Mayhew, together with ground for coach-houses at the top of Ennismore Mews, under agreements made in June and July 1846.[45] Curtailing the backs of the plots and dispensing with porticoes, Mayhew fitted in a sixth, west-facing, house with a coach-house at the back. These houses, originally Nos 1–4 Ennismore Place and Nos 1 and 2 Princes Terrace, were renumbered 60–65 Ennismore Gardens in 1874.

Like Kelk, Mayhew, although himself a trained architect, brought in his own man to design the houses, in this case his brother Charles, whose practice he later took over. It was to some extent a joint development, for Charles Mayhew (and another relative, Frederick Mayhew) provided finance, and subsequently acquired the freehold of four of the houses.[46]

Nos 61 and 62 were built first, by late 1847; Nos 63–65 were completed about a year later, and No. 60 and its stabling were finished by late 1849. All six houses were occupied by the end of 1851.[47]

In January 1849, with building on Mayhew's portion nearing completion, Elger began work on the remainder of the east side of the street. Nos 47–59 were completed in 1852 and occupied by the following year. The remaining eight houses (Nos 39–46) were built between 1852 and 1854 and occupied by 1855.[48] The architect of Elger's houses here is not known, but their appearance suggests that he drew upon the designs by Elmes he had used at Princes Gate.

If the houses of Princes Terrace were of a lesser rank than those of Princes Gate, they were still superior to the residences of Brompton Square to their immediate south. The developers of the north end of the square had reasonably enough expected that in time it would be possible to make a road northwards from the square to the Kensington road, and a gap had been left in the houses there for this purpose. But it was too great a threat to the exclusivity of Elger's development, and as early as January 1844 he had strongly opposed the road plan.[49] The issue generated much bad feeling and led to the promotion of an unsuccessful Bill, opposed by Lord Listowel on the grounds that the road would destroy the 'extreme privacy' of his estate and connect it to property of 'a greatly inferior description'.[50] Some residents of Princes Terrace, however, were themselves in favour of the road. Elger settled the matter in 1854–5 by buying up the interest in the Brompton Square gap, and, much to the vexation of the residents of Brompton, inelegantly plugging this hole with buildings (now rebuilt as Nos 36–38 Ennismore Gardens and No. 31A Brompton Square; see fig. 64).[51]

Design and planning

Of the three architects known to have been involved in the first phase of building in Princes Gate and Ennismore Gardens, much the most important was Harvey Lonsdale Elmes (1814–47).

Elmes, who came to prominence in 1839 when he secured the prestigious commission for designing St

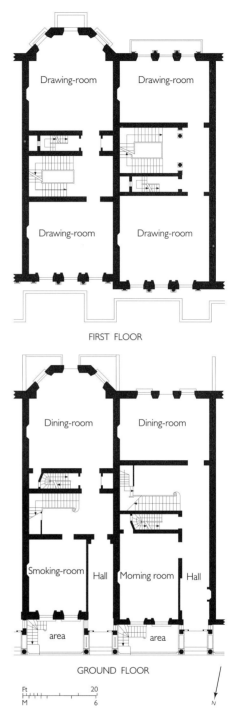

FIRST FLOOR

GROUND FLOOR

Fig. 69. Nos 23 and 24 Princes Gate, plans of the ground and first floors (partially reconstructed). H. L. Elmes, architect, John Elger, builder, 1846–50. Room-names are those in use in 1914

George's Hall in Liverpool, was closely associated with John Elger for much of his short career. He also had family ties with the Knightsbridge area. His father-in-law, Charles Terry, lived for many years in Montpelier Square,

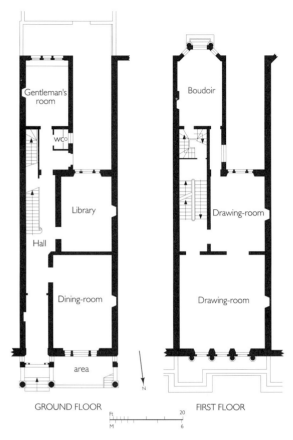

GROUND FLOOR   FIRST FLOOR

Fig. 70. Nos 1–11 Princes Gate, typical plans. John Johnson, architect, John Kelk, builder, c.1848–50. *Demolished*

and after his marriage Elmes and his wife lived near by in High Row.[52]

Elmes made a great many drawings for the Kingston House estate. Those that survive date from the period 1844–7, when he was preoccupied with work on St George's Hall and in poor health. Among them are elevations, plans, sections, sketches and site plans. Not all are inscribed, but most appear to be for the two ranges of Princes Gate facing Hyde Park.[53]

Designed no doubt under the influence of Thomas Cubitt's two recent mansions in Albert Gate, these large houses were Italianate in style, after the manner of Charles Barry (Plate 23a). The earlier drawings show Elmes experimenting with *palazzo*-style terraces of four- or five-storey houses, with windows evenly spaced all along the façade, except in the pavilion houses at either end. From these designs he developed a more original scheme in which the terraces were broken down into individual units by grouping together the windows of each house-front. At the same time a sense of unity was maintained by the continuous cornice and entablature, punctured by regularly spaced attic windows.

The level of architectural display exhibited in some of the drawings is exceptionally high for speculative houses,

even on this scale, and doubtless could not be justified on cost grounds. One sketch shows an ornate Adam-esque staircase under a coffered dome, with columns and statuary. A suggested treatment for the garden front has the rear wings linked by arcaded loggias adorned with urns and statues (Plate 83a).

By the time house-building began in 1846, Elmes's health had given way. He was obliged to spend more and more time trying to recuperate, both at home and abroad, and in November 1847 he died.[54] None of his surviving drawings precisely matches what was built. Only in the earlier, western terrace of Princes Gate (Nos 13–25) do the elevations correspond at all closely to Elmes's drawings, in particular one dated 1844 and inscribed 'for John Pearce Esqr', the first lessee of No. 14 (fig. 65; Plate 82b–c). However, the influence of Elmes's designs is clearly seen in the other houses erected during this phase of development, even though they are from the hands of other architects.

The generic façade was Italianate, three windows wide and of four or five storeys over a basement. All the houses were stuccoed, with ground-floor rustication, and most had porticoed entrances, but their most important family characteristic was the grouping of the windows (figs 65–8; Plates 82b–c, 84a–b). This simple device, in marked contrast to the regularity seen in the terraces of Belgravia and Regent's Park, was taken up by C. J. Freake and others near by in western Princes Gate and Queen's Gate in the 1850s and '60s. The effect is to exaggerate the height as well as to stress the individuality of each house. It was no doubt this impression, particularly marked in the slightly taller and narrower houses designed by John Johnson for John Kelk, which prompted Leigh Hunt to compare Princes Gate to 'a set of tall thin gentlemen, squeezing together to look at something over the way'.[55]

Elger's Princes Gate houses follow Elmes's surviving designs with Ionic porticoes, balustraded balconies, and first-floor window surrounds of engaged columns, pilasters and triangular pediments. The principal deviation from them is in the treatment of the attic windows, which are rectangular and grouped in threes, rather than circular and evenly spaced. The garden elevations of these houses, too, were built much as suggested by Elmes, with alternating bayed and flat fronts (Plates 83c, 114b).

The terrace designed by Johnson for Kelk at Nos 1–11 Princes Gate, though still derived from Elmes's designs, was somewhat more French in feeling (fig. 66). The repetition of upper windows in groups of three followed Elmes's precedent, but Johnson united the first- and second-floor windows in a composition of superimposed orders, under a segmental pediment. The awkwardness of the arrangement, with the porches well offset from the grouped windows, which were not centrally placed, was noted at the time.[56]

At either end of the range, the houses had oblong attic windows set within the mansard roof, behind a balustraded parapet. The central house, No. 6, was wider than the rest, and the three middle houses were together distin-

Fig. 71. No. 24 Princes Gate, staircase detail

guished by a deep entablature with round attic windows and festoons in high relief, making them closer to Elger's own Princes Gate houses. This taller group was also defined by rusticated quoins.[57]

Elmes's influence was evident here too in the fairly elaborate architectural design of the backs of the houses.

The elevational treatment of the Mayhews' houses at Nos 60–65 Ennismore Gardens (fig. 67; Plate 84a), still deriving from the Elmes designs, is again characterized by triplet windows, with rather heavy ornamentation (thrown into greater prominence by the absence of porticoes, a consequence of the restricted site). The first-floor windows have alternate triangular and segmental pediments.

This last feature reappears on Elger's houses at Nos 39–59 Ennismore Gardens, which are essentially a watered-down version of his Princes Gate terrace. These houses originally had deeply projecting enriched cornices, few of which have survived (fig. 68; Plate 84b).

In planning, as in elevational treatment, the three developers appear broadly to have followed Elmes's designs, which offered two layouts.[58] The wider buildings at Nos 16 and 17 apart, Elger's Princes Gate houses had single rooms front and back on the ground and first floors, separated by a top-lit, central main staircase to the second floor (figs 69, 74).

In contrast, Kelk adopted the more conventional plan of side-passage entrance and L-shaped double drawing-rooms on the first floor (as did Elger at Nos 16 and 17), but added large private rooms in a two-storey rear wing (fig.

70). In his evidence to the inquiry into the future of the Crystal Palace, Kelk claimed, somewhat opaquely, that these houses were 'almost different to any houses in London', having been specially planned to make the most of the view over Hyde Park (which the Crystal Palace had, of course, obscured). 'I have given [them] a narrow frontage and an increased depth', he explained, 'I never did that anywhere else, and I have been building houses on speculation all my life'.[59] Quite how this arrangement satisfied Kelk's intentions remains open to question, but at all events variants on this plan became popular with London house-builders in the later 1850s and '60s.

As well as being of exceptional depth, Kelk's houses were built to unusually high specifications, with stone stairs and brick floors from attic to basement. In such a situation, Kelk said, 'I thought they deserved to be done as well as they could be'.[60]

The smaller houses in Ennismore Gardens, too, conformed generally to the traditional side-passage plan, with the two principal ground-floor rooms opening off the hall, and a third, more private room behind the staircase. On the first floor this allowed for a boudoir at the back, as well as the usual L-shaped double drawing-room.[61]

Internally, surviving details suggest that Elger's houses were finished elegantly but plainly, with simple cornicing (usually with dentils or egg-and-dart mouldings), ceiling roses and doorcase surrounds. However, comparatively little of the original décor survives, most of the houses having been subject to extensive redecoration, particularly in the late nineteenth and early twentieth centuries. French panelling and Adam Revival embellishments from this period are much in evidence. New staircases or balustrades, such as the Rococo-style banisters at No. 24 Princes Gate (fig. 71) were fitted on occasion; other contemporary improvements included the installation of electric passenger-lifts.[62] An exotic example of late-Victorian taste was Sir William and Lady Marriott's oriental drawing-room of c.1890 at No. 56 Ennismore Gardens, with genuine Eastern embroidered couches and draperies, Moorish arches, mirrored panels and 'yielding Turkish carpets'. The room was inspired by Sir William's experiences in the Middle East in the late 1880s, where he acted as counsel for the ex-Khedive Ismail Pasha in an action against the Egyptian government.[63]

Ennismore Mews

Some thirty-two stables and coach-houses were built in the mews street between 1845 and 1852, most by Elger, eleven by Kelk (one each for his houses), and at least two by G. W. Mayhew (Plate 78d). Most of the houses on the east side of what became Ennismore Gardens were let without stabling.[64]

The mews buildings, two storeys high, of plain brick with slate roofs, varied greatly in size, with frontages ranging from about 12ft to over 50ft. The largest, No. 29, with space for four carriages, four stalls and three loose-boxes

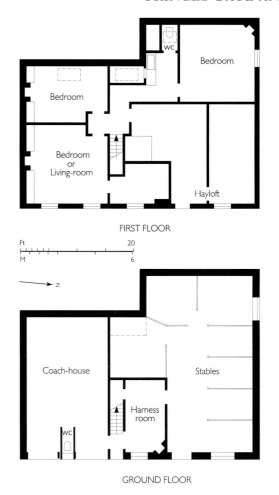

FIRST FLOOR

Ft ————————— 20
M ————————— 6

→ z

Coach-house   Stables

Harness
room

wc

GROUND FLOOR

Fig. 72. No. 29 (now Nos 29 and 29A) Ennismore Mews, plans in
1926. John Elger, builder, c.1850

(fig. 72), was let to Henry William Eaton, a silk broker, who occupied one of the largest houses, No. 16 Princes Gate.[65]

The Ennismore Arms, at the south end of the street, the only public house in the locality and the first building in the development to go up, was built by Elger in 1845–7. Designed by H. L. Elmes, it was a stuccoed building of three storeys over a basement, with a full-height canted bay at its southern end. The present brick-faced building of the same name is a 1950s reconstruction carried out for Watneys following wartime bomb damage.[66]

At the opposite corner, No. 1 was rebuilt as a townhouse in 1920–1 to the designs of Alfred Matthew Cawthorne, architect, apparently as his own speculation. Cawthorne's first proposal, in 1919, was wildly outlandish – a picturesque 'Wealden' hall house, half-timbered and with a jettied first floor. This was hardly likely to satisfy the strict London building regulations, and by the time that London County Council sanction for the scheme was obtained, the house had been transmuted into a neat Tudor-style dwelling with a tall hipped roof and rendered

façades (Plate 79a). The new building, entered on the south side, took the address No. 1 Ennismore Street (this part of the mews being renamed Ennismore Street in 1922). Over the next year or two Cawthorne rebuilt Nos 2–8 on the opposite side of the road in a similar manner.[67] By and large, however, the mews buildings have simply been converted, initially to garaging and subsequently (mostly since the Second World War) to private houses.

No. 14 Princes Gate

Formerly two houses, Nos 13 and 14, this building received its present stately Beaux-Arts front in 1925–6, when it was remodelled as the official London residence of the American ambassador by Thomas Hastings, of the eminent New York architectural firm Carrère & Hastings.[68]

Both the original houses, part of John Elger's development, were completed in 1848, No. 14 apparently being constructed by Elger's associate John Kelk. No. 13 was first occupied in 1849, by the Lambeth-based contractor, and builder of All Saints', Ennismore Gardens, George Baker. At No. 14 the lessee (and later the freeholder) was John Pearce, whose name appears on an elevational drawing for the house by H. L. Elmes dated 1844 (Plate 82b). Pearce did not live there, however, and it was first occupied in 1852 by Edward Wyndham Harrington Schenley, a former soldier and commissioner for the suppression of the slave trade. Schenley later bought the freehold from Pearce.[69]

For a few years in the mid-1850s Schenley appears to have shared No. 14 with the American merchant banker Junius Spencer Morgan, both names being listed in directories. In 1858 Morgan took a lease of No. 13, buying the freehold in 1870,[70] and he stayed there regularly until his death in 1890, when the house passed to his son John Pierpont Morgan, the great banker and art collector. For tax reasons Pierpont Morgan kept his collection (though not his library) in England, much of it at this house. By 1902 he had redecorated some at least of the principal rooms, this work probably being undertaken by Cowtan & Sons, the Belgravia decorators whom the Morgan family employed both in London and the USA. The front drawing-room, where Morgan displayed his Sèvres porcelain, was decorated in Louis-Quinze style, with ornate panelling. In the rear drawing-room (known as the Red Drawing Room) the walls were hung with red damask as a background for Old Master paintings, including Gainsborough's *Duchess of Devonshire* and works by Rembrandt, Frans Hals, Velázquez, Van Dyck and Turner.

In 1904, needing more space, Morgan bought No. 14 from Schenley's widow and threw the two properties into one. Externally they retained the character of separate houses (Plate 90a), but inside there was some remodelling and more redecoration. On this occasion Morgan turned to Henry and (Sir) Joseph Joel Duveen, the international art dealers, who engaged a specialist Parisian firm of decorators and furniture-makers, Carlhian & Beaumetz, with whom they had a long-standing arrangement.[71]

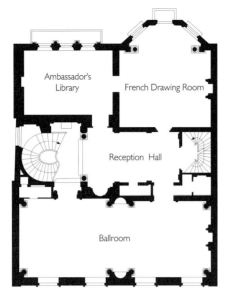

FIRST FLOOR

GROUND FLOOR

Fig. 73. No. 14 Princes Gate after remodelling in 1925–6 as the American Ambassador's residence; Thomas Hastings, architect. Plans *c*.1954: room-names are those used in 1926

The principal structural change was the replacement of the main staircase at No. 14 with an octagonal hall, faced in grey Caen stone (Plate 91c), and, on the floor above, a lobby with marble columns. Behind the new hall, the rear

ground-floor room was transformed into an elaborate parlour for guests, with Louis-Quatorze-style panelled walls: the furniture here had been given by Louis XV to the king of Denmark. Carlhian & Beaumetz were also responsible for decorating the two rooms on the first floor: a Louis-Seize drawing-room at the back (Plates 91a, 118a), and the Fragonard Room, formerly the front drawing-room, where the walls were specially adapted to accommodate ten panel paintings by Fragonard from his ensemble *The Progress of Love*.

After Pierpont Morgan's death in 1913 his son, John Pierpont Morgan junior, chose not to live at Princes Gate, and during the First World War lent the building to the Professional Classes War Relief Council for offices and a maternity home. In 1919 he offered the house as a gift to the United States government 'for Embassy purposes'. Although unsuitable for the entire consulate, it had potential as a residence for the American ambassador, who at this time was not provided with an official home in London. The reaction of some sections of the American press was distinctly hostile: the state might have been remiss in failing to provide suitable residences for its diplomatic representatives, but had no need of patronage from a money-lender like J. P. Morgan.[72] After some hesitation Morgan's offer was formally accepted in March 1921.

Cowtans (with the support of embassy staff) submitted proposals for the necessary refurbishing, but the State Department insisted on employing an American architect. Carrère & Hastings emerged as the principal contender during the summer of 1922 and had been given the commission by February 1924. On their recommendation, Holland & Hannen and Cubitts were awarded the building contract.[b] Although Cowtans had been promised the final phase of interior decoration, they were underbid for most of this by the main contractor. Work was carried out between June 1925 and June 1926.[74]

The major alterations were the recasting of the front elevation, the installation of a new grand staircase, and the opening-up and remodelling of rooms on the ground and first floors as apartments suitable for large-scale entertaining (fig. 73). Hastings described his design for the new façade as

somewhat based upon the [Palazzo] Farnese and the [Villa] Madama, and other Italian Renaissance buildings. Again, it is somewhat in character with McKim's design of the University Club in New York.

It was not wholly new, however, in that it incorporated the upper parts of the existing front, including the cornice and frieze. The Renaissance character of Hastings' design was diluted in the finished building, where, for economy, stucco was substituted for stone and the heavy ground-floor rustication simplified. Furthermore, the carvings of classi-

---

[b] Hastings was already involved with Holland & Hannen and Cubitts at Devonshire House, Piccadilly (1924–6), his only other known work in England.[73]

cal masks on the keystones of the ground-floor windows, intended by Hastings to match those in the frieze above, were superseded by striking if rather incongruous heads of native American Indians (Plate 90b).[75]

Inside, two of Pierpont Morgan's rooms were allowed to remain more or less unaltered: the octagonal hall (known as the Circular Hall), and the Louis-Seize drawing-room (called the French Drawing Room). Hastings removed the original stairs from the old No. 13, replacing them with a neo-Adam staircase leading off the Circular Hall (Plate 91b). At the rear of the ground floor he fashioned a full-width State Dining Room out of the two existing rooms. The new ambassador, Alanson B. Houghton, had hoped to retain Morgan's French panelling here as the basis of the new room, but was too late to prevent Hastings and the contractors from removing and selling it.[c] Instead Hastings installed neo-Georgian panelling and a heavily moulded plaster ceiling.

On the first floor, Hastings created a central Reception Hall and an Ambassador's Ballroom or State Drawing Room, both decorated in the neo-Adam taste (Plates 90c, 119b). The ballroom, overlooking Hyde Park, was another full-width apartment, formed out of Morgan's Fragonard Room and the Louis-Quinze drawing-room. It was to have been of double height, but considerations of space for staff bedrooms above prevailed. Hastings was also responsible for the pale buff Caen stone walls in the Ambassador's Study on the ground floor (formerly part of Morgan's dining-room). The Ambassador's Library (formerly the Red Drawing Room) was redecorated with a sepia paper depicting landscape views of London; this was replaced in the late 1930s by the present wooden panelling.

Houghton, who had been in London since April 1925, took up residence here in the summer of 1926. The first official receptions at Princes Gate were reported in May 1927, by which time the number '13' had been dropped from the address.[77] Other ambassadors who have lived and entertained here include Andrew Mellon, the art collector, and Joseph Kennedy, whose family of nine children, among them the future President John F. Kennedy, spilled over into the staff accommodation.[78] No. 14 continued as the ambassador's official residence until 1955, when Winthrop Aldrich, unhappy with the mid-1930s block of flats next door (Kingston House North), moved to an even larger house in Regent's Park.

No. 14 then became the headquarters of the Independent Television Authority. The building was refitted by Cowtans, who divided the ballroom and enlarged the attic windows. In 1962 it was purchased for £175,000 by its present occupant, the Royal College of General Practitioners, which has since annexed No. 15. The College has divided the former State Dining Room on the ground floor, but removed the division in the Ambassador's Ballroom, now the Long Room, which is used for meetings and as a dining-room.

No. 16 Princes Gate

This house was acquired by the Iranian government in the late 1960s for use as an embassy to ease overcrowding at the ambassador's residence at No. 26. It gained international notoriety in April and May 1980, when the building and more than two dozen hostages were seized by Arab terrorists opposed to the regime of Ayatollah Khomeini in Iran. A six-day siege ended dramatically on 5 May with the storming of the building by soldiers of the SAS. In the process the embassy was severely damaged by fire and for more than ten years remained an empty shell.

In 1991–3 it was rebuilt by the Iranian government, the front and back elevations replicating the originals and the interior reflecting traditional Islamic design. The architects were Ali-Shaukat & Associates, with Norman & Dawbarn as consulting engineers; the contractors were Balfour Beatty.[79]

No. 25 Princes Gate

No. 25 is remarkable for its exceptional size and plan (fig. 74), and for the lavish decoration of its principal rooms. The L-shaped plan, unexpected in a terrace house, takes advantage of the kink in the boundary between the Kingston House estate and the Park House property to the west, which had left Elger with a small piece of ground at the western end of the terrace without a direct frontage to the Kensington road (fig. 64). In 1849 he turned this to account by adding a wing to the main house (on which work had begun in 1848), with a small private garden on the south side.[80] At first the wing had only two storeys and a basement, as can be seen in a view of Princes Gate in 1851 (Plate 7). Two more storeys were added subsequently, raising it to the full height of the house: most likely these were the unspecified 'additions' made by Elger in 1853.[81] The building of No. 26 Princes Gate on the former Park House property in 1856–7 blocked off the north and west faces of the wing, obscuring its elevational treatment.

Slow to sell, No. 25 was eventually taken by Edward Ladd Betts, senior partner in Peto & Betts, the railway contractors, who lived here for three years from 1854, acquiring the freehold in 1855. He was succeeded in 1857 by Samuel Gurney, MP, of the bill discounters Overend, Gurney & Company, whose failure precipitated the famous financial crash of May 1866 – Peto & Betts being one of the casualties. Only two months before this débâcle, Gurney sold No. 25 to Robert Cooper Lee Bevan, a prominent banker and future Chairman of the London Clearing Bankers. From Bevan it passed in 1884 to another financier, James Stern, of the merchant bankers Stern Brothers, whose widow stayed on here until her death in 1941.[82]

Between 1949 and 1987 the house was the headquarters of the Royal School of Needlework. Some rooms were adapted for institutional use, and in 1963 the upper three

[c] The panelling was re-used in the Grill Room (now Bracewell's restaurant) of the new Park Lane Hotel, where it remains.[76]

FIRST FLOOR

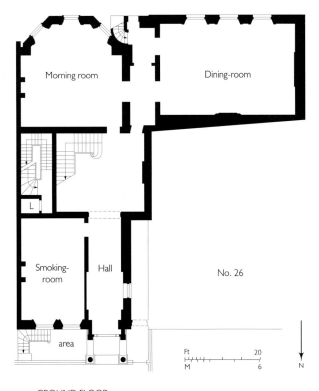

GROUND FLOOR

Fig. 74. No. 25 Princes Gate, plans. John Elger, builder, 1848–53.
Room-names are those in use in 1914

floors were converted to apartments. In the mid-1990s it was expensively refurbished and restored as a single residence, with a swimming-pool in the basement of the extension.[83]

The tastes of a succession of wealthy inhabitants have left their marks on the interior of the house, where very little of the original fabric has survived. The iron-and-stone back stair is Elger's, and a couple of chimneypieces may also be his. In the principal rooms the lavish décor is essentially late Victorian in character, though not necessarily all of the same date. Most striking is the large double drawing-room on the first floor, overlooking the communal garden, where the decoration is in the revived Louis-Quinze style particularly associated with the Rothschilds, who were relatives of the Sterns (Plate 119a). The dining-room, which occupies the entire ground floor of the wing, is decorated in the Renaissance manner with carved wooden panelling and a coffered ceiling (Plate 118b). It is similar in style to the dining-room, made by Gillows, which Sir Albert Sassoon installed at No. 25 Kensington Gore in the late 1870s.[84]

Between No. 25 and No. 26 is a gap of some eight feet where there was formerly a passageway, entered from Princes Gate, to allow the gardeners access to the communal gardens at the rear. It originally led directly under the new wing at No. 25 in a tunnel at basement level, but within a few years the tunnel was closed off and the passage re-routed around the western periphery of the site.[85]

Occupants

The houses built in the first phase of development on the estate were of a size and standard successfully calculated to appeal to wealthy members of the upper and upper-middle classes. Nevertheless, there was a significant distinction between the mansions of Princes Gate, where from the start residents were drawn from the ranks of the very rich, including landed aristocrats, merchants, bankers and industrialists, and the smaller houses of Princes Terrace, where professional men such as barristers, and officers of the armed services, were more likely to be found. The area maintained its exclusiveness into the 1920s and '30s, by which time the grand family town-house was in inexorable decline.

The following list includes all the first occupants of the houses built by Elger, Kelk and Mayhew on the Kingston House estate, with their dates of residence, and some later occupants of note.

Nos 1–25 Princes Gate (Nos 1–11 demolished)

No. 1 George J. D. Poulett Scrope, MP, geologist and political economist (1853–61)
No. 2 William Gore Langton, MP (1853–82); Sir Thomas Fowell Buxton, 3rd Bart, governor of Australia
No. 3 John Harris, art collector (1851–71)
No. 4 Elizabeth, Dowager Duchess of St Albans (1853–73)
No. 5 Richard William Jennings, proctor in Doctors' Commons

(1851–5); Edward Berkeley Portman, 1st Viscount Portman, Liberal politician and agriculturist

No. 6   Capt. George Cookes, soldier (1853–97)

No. 7   Frederick John Howard, civil servant (1853–64); Sir Robert Balfour, 1st Bart, merchant and politician

No. 8   Capt. William Edward Fitzmaurice, soldier, author and illustrator (1851–4); William Legge, Viscount Lewisham (later 7th Earl of Dartmouth), MP, Lord Great Chamberlain; Sir John Meir Astbury, MP, judge

No. 9   William Hallows Belli, retired East India Company servant (1851–7); Henry Louis Florence, architect

No. 10   John Horrocks (1851–8)

No. 11   Lady Marian Alford (1853–72)

No. 13   George Baker, timber merchant and contractor (1849–57)

No. 14   Edward Wyndham Harrington Schenley, slave trade commissioner (1852–78)

No. 15   Edmund Barker Ray (1849–74); Sir Sayaji Rao, Maharaja Gaekwar of Baroda, colonial administrator

No. 16   Henry William Eaton (1st Baron Cheylesmore), MP, silk broker (1851–91); house occupied late 1930s–60s by Royal Photographic Society

No. 17   Maj.-Gen. James Caulfield, CB, East India Company director (1849–52)

No. 18   William Tetlow Hibbert, West India merchant (1850–81)

No. 19   Miss Margaret E. Trafford Southwell (1851–82)

No. 20   John Aldridge, barrister (1853–92); Thomas Span, 2nd Baron Plunket, Bishop of Tuam, Killala and Achonry; Arthur Charles Churchman, 1st Baron Woodbridge, MP, soldier and politician

No. 21   Rt Hon. Justice Sir Cresswell Cresswell, judge (1850–63)

No. 22   Sir Robert Peel, 3rd Bart, MP, politician (1853–7)

No. 23   Hon. Misses Baring (1849–71/88); Gen. Hon. Sir Percy Feilding, Crimean veteran; Stuart Rendel, 1st Baron Rendel, Liberal politician

No. 24   John Gellibrand Hubbard (1st Baron Addington), MP, Russia merchant, Bank of England director (1849–89)

No. 25   Edward Ladd Betts, railway contractor (1854–7)

Nos 39–65 Ennismore Gardens

No. 39   Count Gustavus Batthyány, racehorse owner (1854–9)

No. 40   George Witt, FRS (1855–69)

No. 41   Henry White (1854–6)

No. 42   William Henry Merle (1854–78)

No. 43   (Sir) William Baliol Brett (Lord Esher), judge (1854–69); Rt Hon. Sir Maurice de Bunsen, 1st Bart, diplomat

No. 44   John Leopold F. Casimir De la Feld, Count of the German Empire (1854–67); Rt Hon. Sir Henry Primrose, civil servant

No. 45   John William Burmester, banker (1854–62)

No. 46   Rev. Thomas Mozley, Tractarian and journalist (1852–6); Sir Augustus Keppel Stephenson, Director of Public Prosecutions; Adm. Sir William Boyle, 12th Earl of Cork and Orrery, Commander-in-Chief of Home Fleet

No. 47   (Sir) John Blossett Maule, QC, barrister (1853–89)

No. 48   John Hambrough (1852–60)

No. 49   Rev. Robert Lovett (1852–7)

No. 50   William George Campbell, barrister, commissioner in lunacy (1852–81)

No. 51   Bonamy Price, political economist (1852–69)

No. 52   Charles James East, merchant (1852–5)

No. 53   (Sir) Arthur John Otway, MP, soldier and politician (1852–4); Sir Charles George Young, Garter King-of-Arms

No. 54   Sir Arthur James Rugge–Price, 5th Bart, merchant (1852–91); Charles Lyle, sugar refiner

No. 55   John Cotton Powell, wine merchant (1852–62); Sir William Dunbar, 7th Bart, MP, auditor-general of public accounts

No. 56   Lieut. Henry Raper, RN, writer on navigation (1852–8); Rt Hon. Sir William Thackeray Marriott, MP, Judge Advocate-General; Adm. Sir Dudley de Chair

No. 57   William Walter Cargill, soldier and barrister (1852–8)

No. 58   Hon. Miss Adelaide Sidney (1852–61)

No. 59   Capt. Orbell Oakes, RN (1852–5)

No. 60   Thomas Edward Dicey, railway director and newspaper proprietor (1850–8)

No. 61   John Macgregor, MP, politician, statistician, and historian (1849–55)

No. 62   Henry Reynolds-Moreton, Lord Moreton (later 3rd Earl of Ducie), MP (1850–3)

No. 63   William Thomas Carr, barrister (1849–54); Adm. Rt Hon. Lord Clarence Paget, KCB, PC; Lieut.-Col. Harry Norton Schofield, VC

No. 64   Rt Hon. Thomas Fitzmaurice, 5th Earl of Orkney (1850–69)

No. 65   Thomas Hayter Longden, soldier, JP (1851–74)

Development by Peter and Alexander Thorn, 1868–74

In 1855, when the 2nd Earl of Listowel sold all the houses and stables recently built on his estate, their reversionary value was estimated at £17,000 per annum, and it was said that Princes Gate had become 'equally valuable' with Park Lane. But, the acknowledged 'Westward movement of Noble and Wealthy Families' notwithstanding, no further effort was made towards development on the Kingston House estate for some years.[86]

In the 1860s the 3rd Earl, who had succeeded his father in 1856, began taking steps towards enfranchising the two remaining copyhold portions of the estate – an essential prerequisite for development. These comprised the site of Kingston House itself and its garden, and, much greater in extent, the area south of the garden, with the slip connecting it to the Kensington road. Though all this ground was copyhold, the larger piece was only held by the earl as a sub-tenant.

In February 1867 the earl secured freehold ownership of both areas and arrangements were made for development on the southern part of the former leasehold ground. Between 1868 and 1874 thirty-four large houses were built there, forming three sides of a new square (Nos 1–35 Ennismore Gardens), and stabling and coach-houses in Ennismore Gardens Mews (fig. 64, Plate 84c).

The builders and developers here were the Thorn brothers, Peter and Alexander, who had set up in business about 1860 as contractors, stone merchants and asphalt

manufacturers, with premises at Cremorne Wharf in what
is now Lots Road, Chelsea. Their most important commission was the new Blackfriars Bridge, built in 1864–9, under
the supervision of the civil engineer Joseph Cubitt, to
replace Robert Mylne's bridge of 1760–9. Peter Thorn
died in 1871, while Ennismore Gardens was still in
progress, and the development was completed by his
brother.[87] Under Alexander Thorn's direction, the firm
survived a period of insolvency in 1875, brought on by losses and difficulties in connection with the Blackfriars
Bridge contract, but following a second failure in 1886,
caused by the firm's inability to sell its houses, the business
seems to have come to an end.[88]

Chronology of development

By August 1867 a development plan had been drawn up for
the site opposite Princes Terrace (the present-day Nos
39–59 Ennismore Gardens). This site comprised the
greater, southern, part of the field added to the estate in
1793 by Charles Pierrepont. By October, the Thorns were
in negotiation for its development on lease.[89]

In the background, however, was John Elger, the developer of Princes Gate and Princes Terrace, now no longer a
speculative builder but a man of social standing and, since
the mid-1850s, the freeholder of much of Princes Terrace.
There had apparently been some sort of understanding
between Elger and the 2nd Earl that any future development on the estate would be carried out without detriment
to the houses in Princes Terrace. (For the time being, these
looked out across the roadway to a wall bounding the large
'shrubbery' south of the main garden of Kingston House.)
During the late summer and autumn of 1867, therefore,
whilst touring abroad, Elger was in regular correspondence with Lord Listowel's surveyor, W. F. Meakin,
demanding that nothing be done by the Thorns until he
had seen the latest plans.[90]

Several were drawn up. One, with houses arranged in
pairs and small groups in a U-shaped formation – open to
the east – around a central garden, and a mews along the
south side of the site, was apparently acceptable to both
Elger and the Thorns but did not go ahead. Another, with
a double row of mews buildings along the east side of the
site, was objected to by Elger as deleterious to his own
property.[91] He was also highly critical of a proposal to build
a mews on the strip of ground east of Kingston House,
which, he warned, would inflict 'the greatest possible
injury' to the northern part of the estate.[92]

In March 1868 Elger at last declared himself happy with
the Thorns' latest scheme, in which he himself seems to
have had a hand.[93] The arrangement consisted of three
rows of large houses, comprising Ennismore Gardens,
grouped around a central garden, with Princes Terrace
occupying the east side of the resultant square (fig. 64).

Stabling and coach-houses were confined to the western
and southern edges of the ground, in Ennismore Gardens
Mews.[94] This layout was submitted to the Metropolitan
Board of Works in April 1868, attracting complaints from
some of the inhabitants of Princes Gardens, immediately to
the west, who were unhappy that a mews was planned so
near to their houses.[95]

Work began shortly afterwards with the imposing northern range, Nos 1–9 Ennismore Gardens. With the exception of No. 7, used by the Thorns as their site office, these
houses had been completed and sold by May 1871, and the
first occupants had moved in by 1872. Most were let with
stabling and a coach-house on the west side of the mews,
backing on to Princes Gardens.[96]

Work on the southern range, Nos 27–35, was well
advanced in the spring of 1871, and the houses had been
completed by March 1872. They were fully occupied by
1873.[97] The construction of the western terrace, Nos
10–25, was more protracted, the houses here being built in
batches between the autumn of 1871 and 1874.[98] In a modification of the plan, the site of the intended southernmost
house in the western range, and that of the roadway in
front, opening into the mews, were appropriated for additional stables; the number 26 was consequently never used.
Residents moved in gradually from 1873 and all the houses were occupied by 1879, except for Nos 21 and 24, which
apparently stayed empty until 1889–90. The remainder of
the mews was built up at about the same time as the south
and west ranges.[99] The Thorns also laid out the central
garden, enclosing it with Portland-stone piers and cast-
iron railings.

Design and planning

It is not known who designed the Thorns' houses, which
were erected under the general supervision of W. F.
Meakin, as surveyor to Lord Listowel.[100d] The principal
elevations are of Italianate *palazzo* design, with channelled
masonry to the ground floor, pedimented first-floor windows and projecting Corinthian porches (Plate 85b). In
each terrace the three central houses are emphasised. Dispensing with the contemporary fashion for grouping
together the upper-floor windows of each house, introduced by H. L. Elmes at Princes Gate, the Thorns reverted to the traditional formula of evenly spaced windows.

Unusually for a Victorian speculation in London, the
houses are faced predominantly in stone, the result of circumstance as much as of architectural taste. The Thorns
had in hand a large quantity of Portland-stone ashlar
salvaged from Robert Mylne's Blackfriars Bridge of the
1760s, which they had acquired as the demolition contractors a few years earlier, and the building of these large
houses provided a fine opportunity to make use of it.
Reworking of the old stone was carried out at the Patent

[d] An obituary of Charles Mayhew in 1877 listed Ennismore Gardens (and Princes Gate) among his works, but as he had retired in 1858
this almost certainly refers to his earlier houses in Ennismore Place and Princes Terrace (by then Nos 60–65 Ennismore Gardens).[101]

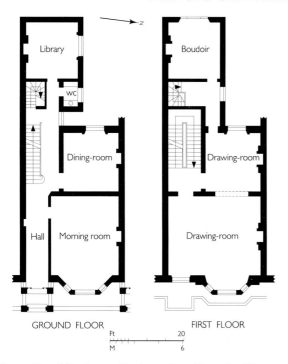

Fig. 75. No. 16 Ennismore Gardens, plans. Alexander Thorn, builder, 1872–3

ers' and other enrichments specified for the principal rooms – were provided by George Jackson & Sons. The houses typically had Portland-stone staircases, skirtings throughout moulded in Keene's Cement, and hall and vestibule floors paved with Minton tiles laid in concrete. Walls were generally painted, papered, or simply distempered, and woodwork, where not of hardwood, was likely to be finished in walnut varnish-stain or painted graining.[106]

No. 1 was finished for its first resident, Sir Thomas Edwards-Moss, 1st Bart, under the superintendence of Alfred Waterhouse, with stone carving by Farmer & Brindley: a black-and-green marble chimneypiece in the former drawing-room on the first-floor could be a remnant of this scheme. But the external embellishments proposed by Waterhouse – an open portico projecting over the footpath with a conservatory above, and then an overhanging bay-window on the front – all fell foul of the Metropolitan Board of Works' habitual dislike of interruptions to the building line.[107]

The high quality of the development was continued in the design of the stabling and coach-houses in Ennismore Gardens Mews. This is approached at its eastern entry through a stone screen of Ionic columns, carrying a deep entablature (Plate 79e). The buildings themselves, now variously altered and colour-washed, were in their original workaday form somewhat superior to the usual London mews. Their characteristic features are segmental-arched openings with prominent stone keys and sill courses (fig. 77, Plate 79d).

Stone-working Machinery Company's premises adjoining York Road station, Battersea, using Fothergill-Cooke & Hunter's patent machinery.[102]

Only the free-standing northern range, the grandest, and the first to be built and occupied, is entirely stone-faced (Plate 85a). The south and west ranges have just their principal fronts in stone, some return walls being of yellow malm bricks with stone dressings; the rear walls, adjoining the mews, are of ordinary stocks. The freestone facings, so distinctive in an area dominated by cream and white stucco, confer, in the words of Henry-Russell Hitchcock, 'a solid dignity almost unique in London'.[103]

The area and balcony railings were supplied by Messrs Benham, of Cadogan Works, Chelsea.[104]

The internal planning of the houses in the west and south ranges conformed to the side-passage type, with two main reception rooms off the entrance hall, and a smaller, private room at the back, behind the stairs (fig. 75). An L-shaped double drawing-room took up most of the first floor, with a short corridor leading to a rear boudoir. The north-side houses had central staircases, and were planned to present their best rooms to the south, with canted bays overlooking the garden (fig. 76).

The interiors were finished to a high standard of decoration. Among the craftsmen known to have worked on them was the carver and gilder Charles Moxon of Brook Street, who had worked for the architect S. W. Daukes at Dudley House, in Park Lane.[105] The plasterwork was by William John Taylor of Church Street, Chelsea, and the papier mâché decorations – presumably the ceiling 'centre flow-

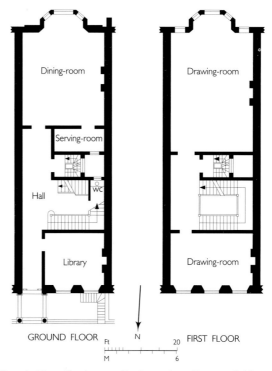

Fig. 76. No. 3 Ennismore Gardens, plans. Peter and Alexander Thorn, builders, 1868–71

Fig. 77. Ennismore Gardens Mews (north-east range), typical elevation (reconstructed). Alexander Thorn, builder, 1871–4

Occupants

As with the houses built under Elger's aegis some twenty years earlier, the Thorns' development was aimed at people of substantial wealth and connection. Again, there was a hierarchy: as Lord Listowel's estate agent later put it, the large houses of the northern range were intended for families 'of considerable affluence', while those of the western and southern ranges were suited to 'gentlemen of good position in the City', retired naval and army officers or other 'persons of standing'.[108]

The following list includes all the first occupants of the houses built by the Thorn brothers in Ennismore Gardens, with their dates of residence, and some later occupants of note.

No. 1 Sir Thomas Edwards-Moss, 1st Bart, banker (1872–90)

No. 2 John Gerald Potter, JP, papermaker (1872–91); Sir Patrick Playfair, merchant, sheriff of Calcutta

No. 3 Alexander Grant Dallas (1872–5)

No. 4 Etheldred, Dowager Countess of Hopetoun (1873–84)

No. 5 Albert George Sandeman, port-wine importer, Bank of England director (1872–9); Moubray St Andrew Thornton, 18th Baron St John of Bletsoe, soldier and politician

No. 6 Sir William Baliol Brett (Lord Esher), judge (1870–99)

No. 7 Allan Harvey Drummond, banker (1875–1913; house previously occupied by Thorn & Company)

No. 8 Mrs Reid (1872–5)

No. 9 Frederick Cox, army agent (1872–5); Sir John Tomlinson Brunner, 1st Bart, MP, industrialist

No. 10 Samuel Whitbread, MP, former Lord of the Admiralty (1873–99)

No. 11 Charles Morgan Norwood, merchant and ship-owner (1890–1; house previously occupied by Thorn & Company); Rt Hon. Walter Hume Long, 1st Viscount Long of Wraxall, statesman

No. 12 Maj. Gilbert Stirling (1875–89)

No. 13 James Guthrie, East India merchant (1874–88); (John) Arthur Godley, 1st Baron Kilbracken, civil servant; Very Rev. Thomas William Jex-Blake, headmaster of Rugby

No. 14 Vere Fane Bennett-Stanford, MP (1876–90)

No. 15 Lieut.-Col. Edward Henry Clive, Grenadier Guards, Crimean veteran (1875–87)

No. 16 Maj. Vaughan Hanning Vaughan-Lee, MP, Crimean veteran (1875–81)

No. 17 John Stirling, JP (1875–1908)

No. 18 Capt. Ellis Brooke Cunliffe, retired army officer (1875–93); Rt Hon. Victor Bruce, 9th Earl of Elgin, statesman; Hon. Sir Granville De Laune Ryrie, High Commissioner for Australia

No. 19 Michael Biddulph (later 1st Baron Biddulph), MP, banker, (1877–1915)

No. 20 Frederick Du Cane-Godman, zoologist (1875–82); Sir Edward Rae Davson, 1st Bart, chairman of British Empire Producers' Organization; Brig.-Gen. Charles Woodroffe, military secretary to the Prince of Wales (later Edward VIII)

No. 21 John Bazley White, jun., MP, Portland cement manufacturer (1889–90)

No. 22 Frederick Campbell, 2nd Viscount Emlyn (later 3rd Earl of Cawdor), MP, judge and Ecclesiastical Commissioner (1878–91); Herbert Plumer, 1st Viscount Plumer, field-marshal

No. 23 Fanny, Dowager Countess of Winchilsea and Nottingham (1877–90)

No. 24 Mrs Benthall (1890–1902)

No. 25 John Ulrich Truninger, merchant (1875–92)

No. 27 Emile G. Levita, merchant (1873–1908)

No. 28 Ralph Creyke, MP, JP, Unionist politician (1873–84)

No. 29 Jeffery Grimwood Grimwood, JP (1873–97); Arthur Hood, 1st Baron Hood of Avalon, admiral; Sir Peter Bark, banker, former Imperial Russian finance minister

No. 30 Sir Robert Hay, 8th Bart, golfer (1873–84); Alfred Emmott, 1st Baron Emmott, politician and cotton-spinner

No. 31 Henry Hansard (1873–80)

No. 32 Henry Yates Thompson, proprietor of the *Pall Mall Gazette*, collector of illuminated manuscripts (1873–7)

No. 33 James Mitchell, barrister (1873–94)

No. 34 Charles Allanson-Winn, 3rd Baron Headley, Baron Allanson and Winn of Aghadoe (1873–7); Sir Francis Oppenheimer, diplomat

No. 35 Walter Armstrong (1873–6); Sir Edward Durand, 1st Bart, colonial administrator

Development in Northern Ennismore Gardens, 1869–85

Elger and his associates, and then the Thorn brothers, developed much of the Kingston House estate in the time-honoured manner of the grander speculative builder, covering their large 'takes' with regular terraces of houses and spacious communal gardens. By contrast the remaining portion, comprising Kingston House, its large private garden and the L-shaped strip to the east and south, was developed somewhat differently. The most important factor here was Kingston House. While Lord Listowel and his family remained in occupation any development was effectively restricted to the ground beyond the garden wall. In the late 1860s Lord Listowel allowed a piece of this ground, immediately east of Kingston House, to be used for the building of a large detached residence, Alford

House. At this stage, however, there was no master-plan for dealing with the remaining vacant ground, let alone Kingston House itself.

Pressure on Lord Listowel to release more land for development grew in the early 1870s, when the builder Alexander Thorn, who was then on the verge of finishing his houses in southern Ennismore Gardens and keen to take on more speculative work in the area, made more than one offer for the vacant ground.[109] Perhaps as a consequence, an outline plan for building over the whole of the northern portion of the estate was drawn up in 1874, presumably by Listowel's surveyor, W. F. Meakin.[110] This showed a terrace of houses on the site of Kingston House itself, another along the eastern ground, south of Alford House, a mews on the west, and some large detached houses along the north side of Ennismore Gardens, opposite the Thorns' houses at Nos 1–9.

In July 1874 Thorn renewed his offer of a 'fair price' for the vacant land, promising that any building would be carried out 'with as much spirit and energy as the houses we have just completed'.[111] But he was to be disappointed and his only contribution to the development of this northern area was as a contract builder. The 1874 scheme was largely set aside and Kingston House and its garden survived for another half century. Further building was confined to the extra-mural strip, which was covered in stages with large detached houses and a mews during the late 1870s and early 1880s (fig. 64). Some of these houses were the work of a speculative builder. The others were designed by leading architects for wealthy individuals and were of outstanding architectural quality. Not one of them is still standing, the whole of this phase of development having been swept away for a comparatively undistinguished collection of flats and town-houses (see fig. 82).

Alford House (demolished)

Building on the strip of ground next to Kingston House garden began with the construction of a large detached residence at the corner of the Kensington road (fig. 64). This was Alford House, built in 1869–71 by Lady Marian(ne) Alford, the artistically inclined elder daughter of the 2nd Marquess of Northampton and, from 1851, widow of Viscount Alford, eldest son of the 1st Earl Brownlow.[e] Since 1853 Lady Alford's London home had been No. 11 Princes Gate, on the opposite corner to the future Alford House (Plates 7, 83b).

Negotiations for the site, immediately to the east of Kingston House, may have opened as early as 1866. But Lord Listowel seems to have prevaricated, and it was not until October 1868, after Lady Alford had personally asked him for a 'decisive reply' before she went abroad for the winter, that he finally agreed to let her have the ground. By

early January 1869 both the site and the basic shape of the new house had been settled. In June the Metropolitan Board of Works approved the line of the frontage, and in August the building agreement was signed. Lord Listowel undertook to let her have the ground for 80 years, from 1869, at an annual rent of £400 (raised to £535 in 1873, when an extra piece of land to the south was added). He would not allow any on-site stabling and in 1870 she bought the lease of the newly built stable and coach-house at No. 9 Ennismore Gardens Mews.[112]

The architect of Alford House was Sir Matthew Digby Wyatt, hardly a surprising choice, since he had been regularly employed by both Lady Alford's own family and her husband's for important commissions at their country seats – Ashridge, Compton Wynyates, and Castle Ashby. Wyatt's first designs were for a very large house in a style seemingly influenced by the younger Thomas Cundy's Grosvenor Gardens, with a square tower at the north-east corner, capped by a soaring pyramidal roof in the New Louvre manner (Plate 86a). Probably too big for Lady Alford, this design would almost certainly have been rejected by Lord Listowel, who made it a condition that the building should be no taller than Kingston House. The revised design was towerless and considerably reduced in size. Still Second Empire in feeling, with a steep-pitched French roof, it was given a veneer of 'Queen Anne' by the use of deep-red brick for the elevations, and tawny-coloured terracotta for the copious ornamentation (Plate 86b). When Wyatt exhibited a perspective in 1872 (Plate 86c) the *Builder* questioned what was to be gained from having 'such an array of great carved festoons under the cornice', but praised the ornamental ironwork.[113]

The latter, as it happened, had been designed by Lady Alford herself, aided by Wyatt's loan of 'the two French iron works books you need'.[114] An accomplished draughtswoman and amateur painter, she was regularly consulted by Wyatt, and personally devised some of the interior decoration. But the claim advanced by the *Dictionary of National Biography* that the house itself was built mainly from her own designs appears to be an exaggeration.[115]

There was also some slight contribution from her friend Harriet Hosmer, the American sculptress, whose proposal for a moulding may have been for the fountain room, where the centrepiece was one of Hosmer's own works (see below).[116]

Although designing for a largish site, with two road frontages, Wyatt was constrained by Lord Listowel's concern for his privacy and the fact that the northern part of the site abutted the Kingston House stable-yard. Prevented by Lord Listowel's conditions from having any important windows in the west elevation, Wyatt located most of the principal rooms on the east side and at the north end

---

[e] Like her friend and near neighbour Lady Ashburton of Kent House, who was also widowed at a young age, Lady Alford pursued her interest in the arts with boundless energy. Clever, witty and extravagant, she was a generous hostess and patroness. She also wrote a pioneering history of art needlework and used her connections to help establish the Royal School of Needlework.

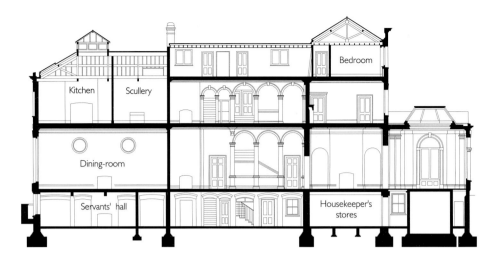

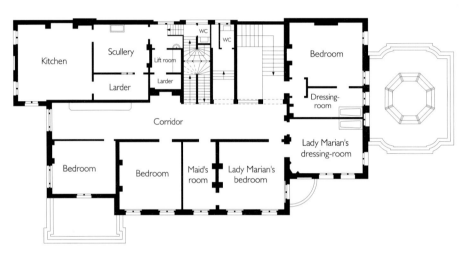

FIRST FLOOR

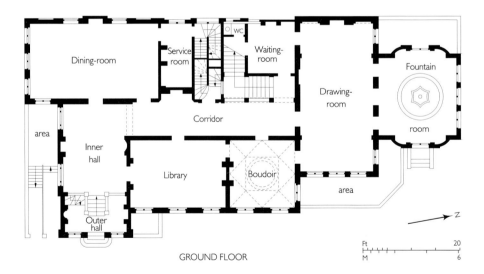

GROUND FLOOR

Ft 20
M 6

Fig. 78. Alford House, plans and section. Matthew Digby Wyatt, architect, 1869–72, for Lady Marian Alford.
Demolished

(fig. 78). Only the dining-room was on the west side, and his inclusion there of two high-level bull's-eye windows was initially objected to as likely 'to be an annoyance to Lord L by admitting the sound of what passes in the room to be overheard in his garden'.[117]

The most unusual feature of the plan was the siting of the kitchen and scullery on the first floor, directly over the dining-room. They were completely walled off from the rest of the first floor and could only be reached from the floors above and below by enclosed staircases. Both were top lit, and although the kitchen had two windows in the south wall, these had fixed sashes with ground-glass panes, to frustrate any servant tempted to steal a glimpse of Lord Listowel's garden.

A public drinking-fountain proposed for the Kensington road corner of the site (see Plate 86c) did not materialize, perhaps because of the problems foreseen by Wyatt: the possible annoyance of having 'children etc "larking" and "squalling" as they generally do in the neighbourhood of a drinking fountain', and the difficulty of obtaining the consent of the 'Parochial Authorities – "Bumble" and others'.[118]

Building began in 1869, and the house was substantially finished, except for some interior decoration, in 1871. The builders were Peter and Alexander Thorn, the developers of Ennismore Gardens and Ennismore Gardens Mews, who were paid between £15,000 and £17,000 for their work. J. M. Blashfield of Stamford provided all the terracotta, which included chimneypieces as well as external mouldings and decorations.

The interior decoration was evidently lavish and ornate, as is indicated by numerous queries on the subject in Wyatt's letters to Lady Alford, but the only record of the interior as executed appears to be a few meagre photographs of about 1931.

In both the drawing-room and the boudoir the walls were hung with silk under highly embellished plaster ceilings with 'hand painted' panels, perhaps executed by Lady Alford herself. The drawing-room ceiling contained a central octagonal panel 'depicting Seraphs and Cherubim in an ethereal setting'. In the boudoir, where the ceiling was vaulted, the spandrels were painted with angels and idealized views. The dining-room ceiling was based on one at Castle Ashby. In the library the walls were hung with silk, and the doorway to the inner hall was framed by an elaborately carved wooden doorcase, with female terms and baskets of fruit and flowers.

Most of these rooms contained carved chimneypieces; that in the inner hall was oddly Mannerist in design and reminiscent of Wyatt's work in the India Office (Plate 87b). Sculptural plaques and reliefs decorated the walls of the main staircase and first-floor landing. The stairs themselves were of stone, with stone balusters and a marble handrail.

That this was a new house did not preclude the use of architectural salvage, and the first floor was 'for the most part' panelled in 'old woodwork with a good deal of carving'. This may have been the pine panelling with a carved cornice which Wyatt had brought to Lady Alford's attention in May 1870, when it was being offered for sale cheaply with two Spanish mahogany chimneypieces. Wyatt recommended white paint for the panelling; for the doors he advised varnish, enlivened by 'a few lines of bright colour on the panels'. In Lady Alford's own bedroom and dressing-room the white paint was offset by gilding.[119]

At the northern end of the ground floor was the fountain room, a single-storey apartment with an octagonal glass dome containing the ornate fountain commissioned by Lady Alford from Harriet Hosmer while wintering in Rome in 1860–1 (Plate 87a). Hosmer wrote of this commission to a friend:

It is the Song of the Siren & while she sings the Amorini on their Dolphins stop to listen to her – the water falls from the three shells which form the vase so that they will be seen as it were under the water.[120]

Intended for the conservatory at No. 11 Princes Gate, but probably never installed there, the fountain was over seven feet tall and executed in three different shades of marble. Although it was said to be nearly finished in the spring of 1862, Lady Alford was still awaiting delivery when Queen Victoria visited No. 11 in March 1867, and had asked 'but where is Miss Hosmer's fountain – I want to see that Fountain'.[f] After the Queen's visit, Lady Alford told the sculptress, 'When I get it I am going to exhibit it and invite the Queen'.[122]

The walls and floor of the room were lined with marble, the floor being paved with an inlaid pattern, executed from Lady Alford's own designs by Henry Poole & Sons.[123]

Lady Alford took up residence in 1872, and occupied the house as her London home until 1887. In December of that year, less than two months before her death, she sold it to James Williamson (from 1895 Baron Ashton), the Lancastrian linoleum magnate and Liberal MP, who still owned the house at the time of his death in 1930. Ashton is known to have made some alterations, but the illustrated catalogue issued when the house was auctioned in 1931 suggests that both externally and internally it had not been significantly changed. It failed to sell and was bought in for only £5,250.[124]

In 1955–6 Alford House was demolished, seemingly unrecorded, for the building of Kingston House East.

Moncorvo House (demolished)

In 1874 the builder Alexander Thorn was negotiating on behalf of a client for the easternmost of the plots earmarked for large detached houses on the north side of Ennismore

---

[f] The Queen had come to see her cousin, Princess Mary of Teck, who was staying there with her husband and was 'unwell'.[121] At the time the Princess was seven months pregnant with the future Queen Mary.

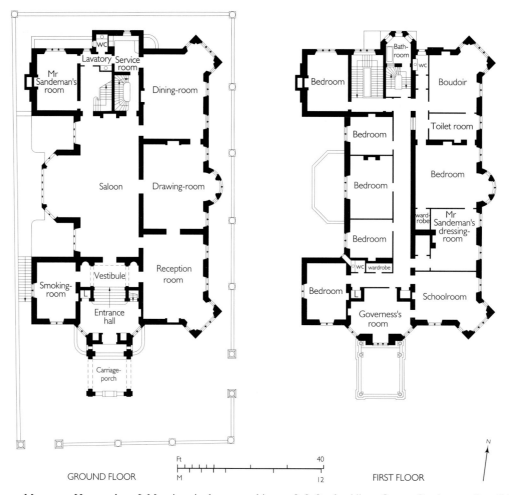

GROUND FLOOR   Ft   40   FIRST FLOOR
                                M   12

Fig. 79. Moncorvo House, plans. J. Macvicar Anderson, architect, 1878–80, for Albert George Sandeman. *Demolished*

Gardens.[125] Nothing came of this, but only a few years later Albert George Sandeman, who had secured the site under a leasing agreement in August 1877, employed Thorn to build a substantial mansion there. Sandeman, a wealthy member of the family of port and sherry shippers and a future Governor of the Bank of England, was then living across the road at No. 5 Ennismore Gardens. Building began early in 1878, the plot having been extended northwards to allow for stables, and the new house was substantially finished the following year.[126] First occupied about 1880, it was named in honour of Mrs Sandeman's family, her father, sometime Portuguese ambassador in London, being the Visconde Da Torre de Moncorvo.

Moncorvo House was one of the earliest works in London of the Scottish architect John Macvicar Anderson.[127] Resembling a modest French Renaissance château (Plate 88a–b), it was built of red brick, with plentiful stone dressings, and had a steeply pitched pavilion roof, which was interrupted by dormer windows trimmed with elaborate stone pediments, both triangular and segmental. The long east front was punctuated by a central bow, and on this side

the corners were opened out to form projecting splays. The principal entrance was at the south end of the sloping site, sheltered by a bulky stone carriage-porch (fig. 79).

The surviving contract drawings include only one for interior work – a single sheet of details for the hall – and some of the décor shown in later photographs may represent the taste of more recent owners. Several of the main rooms were decorated in neo-Georgian style, with Adamesque ceilings and eighteenth-century chimneypieces (Plate 89b–c). What is evidently Anderson's original décor can be glimpsed in the dining-room, and in the great saloon (later a ballroom), which had a coffered ceiling (Plate 89a). In the dining-room the dado was embellished with a floral frieze of decorative tiles above which the walls were hung with panels of stamped or embossed leather.

The Sandemans left Moncorvo House in 1886, and that September it was purchased, reputedly for £45,000, by the Duc D'Aumale, fourth son of King Louis Philippe, who had recently been exiled from France for protesting against being struck off the French army list. The duc brought with him from his château at Chantilly the greater part of his famous library, and favourite pictures and items of furniture 'avec lesquels il aime à vivre'. One visitor to Moncorvo House reported seeing Gerard's *Bonaparte*, a self-portrait by Ingres, Mignard's *Molière* and Raphael's *Three Graces*.[128]

Some months after taking up residence D'Aumale installed electric lighting, powered from a private generator supplied by Edison & Swan.[129]

The duc was famed for his hospitality and on one occasion in 1887 the guest-list for dinner included the kings of Greece and Denmark, two future kings of England, and assorted members of various European royal houses.[130]

D'Aumale returned to France in 1889 and the following year he sold the house to John Gretton of the Burton-on-Trent brewers Bass, Ratcliff & Gretton.[131] Some at least of the duc's furnishings seem to have been included in the sale, for an Aubusson carpet which had been made for him found its way to the drawing-room of the Grettons' Leicestershire house, Stapleford Park.[132] After Gretton's death in 1899, his son, the 1st Baron Gretton, inherited the property and lived there until 1921, except during the war, when it was used as a rest home by Canadian nurses.[133]

The last private occupant, from 1922 to 1941, was the American engineer and industrialist Arthur Graham Glasgow, co-founder in 1892 of the gas-engineering firm Humphreys & Glasgow.[134] After the Second World War Moncorvo House was variously occupied as ATS billets (1947), the London Headquarters of the Canadian Joint Staff Establishment (1951–63) and the Moroccan Embassy (1963). It was demolished in 1964. The eastern block of Kingston House South now stands on the site, but the name is perpetuated in the adjacent 1960s terraces called Moncorvo Close.

Bolney House (demolished)

The ground immediately to the south of Alford House, designated for terrace-houses in 1874, remained vacant until the building of Bolney House in 1883–5 for the bibliophile and connoisseur Alfred Henry Huth. The delay is perhaps explained by an unconfirmed story told many years later by the historian of All Saints' Church, Ethel Richardson. She recalled how an uncle of hers had himself intended building a house here but died before work began, leaving his family to pay the architect £1,000 for plans.[135] Huth's house, built by Perry & Company, and held on a 90-year lease, was named after the Sussex village where his father had a country seat. The architect was Richard Norman Shaw, whose work at Bedford Park had brought him into contact with Huth, a director of the development company. Huth may have employed Shaw to design some stables at his house in Kensington Square in 1881.[136] Bol-

THIRD FLOOR (ATTIC)

SECOND FLOOR

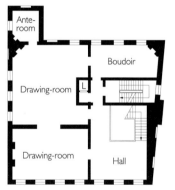

FIRST FLOOR

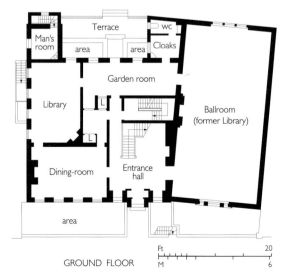

GROUND FLOOR

Fig. 80. Bolney House, plans in 1926. Richard Norman Shaw, architect, 1883–5, for Alfred Huth. *Demolished*

ney House was intended in part to provide accommodation
for the famous collection of incunabula and other rare
books which Huth had inherited from his father in 1878,
and the plans included two separate libraries, the larger
occupying an entire wing (fig. 80).[137]

Bolney House was Shaw's first uncompromisingly
'Georgian' town-house and the reserved red-brick front,
with some stone dressings, closely imitated the genuine
article (Plate 87c–d). The absolute regularity of the design
was broken only by the off-centre front door, and by the
library wing on the north side, a single-storey extension
with a Venetian window. The front doorcase was one of
several details altered after the contract drawings had been
signed, and its final form was not settled until February
1884, both versions of the design being in the hand of
Shaw's assistant, William Lethaby.[138] In another change the
library wing was lengthened and turned through several
degrees so that its front to Ennismore Gardens was slightly oblique to the rest of the house.

The Georgian character of Bolney House reflected
Alfred Huth's preference for English domestic architecture of the late seventeenth and early eighteenth centuries,
a taste which can be inferred from his occupation since
1874 of No. 17 Kensington Square, a well-preserved house
of the 1680s. Shaw may even have been influenced by No.
17 in designing Bolney House, where the ground and first-
floor plans (less the library wing) mirror those of the older
house. The drawings suggest the interior was quite simply
decorated, with straightforward wooden panelling. An
inspection of the property in 1914 mentions mahogany
panelling in the dining-room and a tessellated floor in the
hall.[139]

After Huth's departure in 1899, Bolney House was
occupied by another Shaw client, Henry Tate junior, a son
of the sugar magnate and arts benefactor, for whom Shaw
had designed Allerton Beeches, Liverpool (1883–4). Both
Tate, and, after his death in 1902, his widow, made alterations, including the addition of an iron-and-glass canopy
leading up to the front door.[140] While this did nothing to
enhance the appearance of the doorcase, it was a practical
appendage retained by subsequent occupants. A more substantial addition came in 1926, when Sydney Martineau,
the then occupant, had a two-storey rear extension built on
part of the flat roof of the former library. Designed by E. P.
Warren, it contained bathrooms, and bedrooms with bay
windows overlooking Kingston House garden.[141]

Martineau's widow was the last occupant of Bolney
House, which in later years became covered in a blanket of
Virginia creeper. It was demolished in the mid-1960s,
unrecorded, for the building of the row of houses called
Bolney Gate.

Nos 67–69 Ennismore Gardens and Ennismore Gardens Mews North (demolished)

The development of the remainder of the strip of ground
on the north side of Ennismore Gardens west of Moncor-

vo House, formerly the site of an ornamental lake, was to
prove a troublesome enterprise.[142] Work on the construction of Moncorvo House had not long begun when, in
March 1878, the first of several unsuccessful proposals for
a mews street here was made to the Metropolitan Board of
Works (MBW), by Lord Listowel's surveyor W. F. Meakin.
There was concerted opposition from nearby householders.[143] Eventually, approval was given to a revised plan, submitted in November 1879 by the builder William Radford,
who had entered into an agreement with Lord Listowel to
develop the whole strip.[144]

William Radford (c.1850–1939), then of Courtfield
Gardens, was the son of Francis Radford, one of the two
Devon-born brothers who built the grand Italianate villas
of Pembridge Square and Holland Park in the 1850s and
'60s.[145] Like his father and uncle, he was his own designer,
styling himself architect as well as builder.

At Ennismore Gardens Radford undertook to build a
closely spaced row of five large double-fronted houses
along the street, with stables and coach-houses hidden in a
through-road at the back. Although modified to satisfy the
MBW, this layout was in its essentials a less spacious version of the arrangement proposed in 1874 in the outline
development plan for the northern part of the estate.[146]

The mews buildings and the first three houses were
scheduled for completion in 1883. However, by then the
development was not going well and Radford had to ask
Lord Listowel for more time. He had finished only one
house (No. 67), together with the stables. Another house
(No. 68) was in carcase, and in due course he finished it, but
he only built one more house – No. 69, completed in 1884.
The adjoining plot he sold to a private buyer, who erected
his own house there (No. 70), and he used the westernmost
plot to build more stabling and coach-houses with an ornamental façade along the return to Ennismore Gardens.
This was not much to Lord Listowel's liking; for Radford,
however, the change of plan must have been necessary
damage-limitation.[147] Perhaps because of their exceptional
size, his three houses, erected at a time when demand for
new houses throughout London was falling, proved virtually unlettable.

While not forming a uniform row, all three houses kept
to the same basic double-fronted format and were faced
chiefly in red brick. None seems to have been of any particular architectural pretension or originality. In general
terms, they resembled the Radford brothers' double-fronted villas in northern Kensington, updated in style and
materials in an attempt to meet changing tastes.

No. 67, the earliest, was of three storeys plus basement
and attic. It was ornamented with quoining and banding
and other dressings in Portland stone, and had a conventional classical portico with paired pillars. The return front
to the mews street was given an ornamental treatment, as
required by covenants in the Moncorvo House lease, which
also restricted the height of the building (Plate 88b). No. 68
was more up-to-date, closer to the 'Queen Anne' style, and
had an extra storey to the back addition. Both houses had

mansard roofs with dormers, round-arched at No. 67, double-pitched at No. 68, on either side of a pyramid-roofed 'turret'. At No. 69, unlike the others, the main storeys were all of equal height, and there was also a full fourth floor (Plate 85b).

The architect Robert Griggs, a pupil of H. Saxon Snell, applied on Radford's behalf to the MBW in connection with the building of No. 68, but it is not known if he had any role in the designing of this or the other houses.[148] The only architect named on the original sales particulars for Nos 67 and 68 is Radford himself.

In the early 1890s, with Nos 67–69 still on his hands, Radford proposed converting them into a private hotel in an attempt to recover some of his losses. This Lord Listowel would not have, but he did agree to allow No. 69 to be turned into flats, which was done in 1893. By 1913 No. 67 had still not been taken; occupied only by a caretaker, it was said to require at least £2,000-worth of work to make it fit for letting.[149]

In 1904 No. 68 was at last let, to the Marquess of Breadalbane, who had the house (the only one to be occupied by a single tenant) fitted out under the superintendence of the architect Alfred Williams.[150] The marquess lived there until about 1922. In the mid-1920s Radford converted this house and No. 67 to flats.[151]

A resident at No. 68 from the 1940s to the 1960s was the literary hostess, and mistress of H. G. Wells, Moura Ignatevna, Baroness Budberg. Gide, Graham Greene, Hemingway, the Huxleys and Somerset Maugham were among the visitors to her second-floor salon here.[152] Edith (Baroness) Summerskill, the politician and writer, was a post-war occupant of a flat in No. 69.

The greater part of Ennismore Gardens Mews North was pulled down in the 1930s, along with No. 70 Ennismore Gardens, for the building of Kingston House South (Nos 1–32). Radford's houses at Nos 67–69, and the eastern remnant of the mews (renamed Ennismore Place in 1939) survived until the 1960s, when the site was cleared for the construction of Moncorvo Close.

No. 70 Ennismore Gardens (demolished)

In 1884, with the extent of the failure of his development becoming apparent, Radford was fortunate in being able to dispose of his one remaining house-plot to a private buyer. This was Gustav Natorp of Palace Gardens Terrace, a Hamburg-born dilettante, connoisseur and gastronome, who wanted to build an unusual house there for his own occupation.[153]

Natorp's architect was Basil Champneys, a follower of T. G. Jackson, and his eclectic neo-Jacobean façade, in red Fareham brick and Portland stone, contrasted sharply with Radford's stodgier work next door (Plates 85b, 88c).

FIRST FLOOR

GROUND FLOOR

Fig. 81. No. 70 Ennismore Gardens, plans. Basil Champneys, architect, 1884–5, for Gustav Natorp. *Demolished*

Champneys' design, published in 1886, differed from his other houses of this date, which were more 'Queen Anne' in style, and perhaps reflected the tastes of the owner.[154] The front elevation was enlivened by shaped gables, oriel windows and, appropriately for a client who had trained as a sculptor under Rodin, a mass of exuberant stone carving (although not all that shown in the published engraving was executed).

The intended builder was Albert Estcourt of Gloucester, then working close by on No. 2 Kensington Court, another house of individual character designed (by T. G. Jackson) for a client of refined tastes and a long purse. But within two months of starting work in February 1884 Estcourt was replaced by Mark Manley of St George's Road, Regent's Park.[155] The house was completed by November 1885, when it was photographed for Champneys by Bedford Lemere.[156]

Planned for a wealthy bachelor with overweening artistic and social pretensions, No. 70 was dominated by an enormous galleried studio occupying half the first floor and presumably needed for entertainment as much as for work. There was a smaller 'open-air' studio, or glasshouse, at the back (to the north), and a dining-room and a drawing-room at the front (fig. 81). Oak was extensively used, for floors, ceilings, panelling and other fittings, and there were various painted decorations, doubtless by Natorp himself. A painted panel which he exhibited at the Royal Academy in 1892 was probably created for the house. Intended as a frieze to go above oak panelling, it formed part of a decorative scheme on the theme of 'The Three Ages', and depicted 'Youth, the Toilers and the Idlers'.[157] Carved oak panelling and a painted frieze were features of the dining-room at No. 70 noted in 1914.[158]

Natorp took up residence in 1885 and remained there until c.1909. His successor, Ernest George Hawkings, converted the ground-floor front rooms to a full-sized billiard-room and a morning room. By 1931, when the house was offered for sale at auction, Natorp's studio had become a ballroom – 'probably one of the most beautiful Ball Rooms in London' – with an organ in the gallery.[159] No. 70 was demolished c.1936, along with the western section of Ennismore Gardens Mews North, for the building of Kingston House South (Nos 1–32).

The area since the 1920s

William Radford's failure to sell his large houses in northern Ennismore Gardens in the 1880s and after may have been a sign of over-supply in the market. The conversion of one of these houses into flats in 1893 was the precursor of a trend in Ennismore Gardens generally, which gathered pace in the years following the First World War, as demand for town mansions fell. 'Lateral' conversions of pairs of houses were favoured, so as to provide floor-space sufficient for high-class tenants, a number of properties in the south and west ranges of Ennismore Gardens being so

altered in the 1920s.[160] Most of Ennismore Gardens had become flats by the 1960s. A long-time resident at one of these flats, at No. 34, was the film-star Ava Gardner. The actor, Jack Hawkins, also had a flat at No. 34, and another actor, Charles Gray, occupied a flat in No. 30. Gentrification of the mews buildings in this area was largely delayed until after the Second World War.[161]

Kingston House, Princes Gate and the big houses in northern Ennismore Gardens attracted property developers during the flat-building boom of the 1930s. Two schemes were proposed, one involving the rebuilding of the eastern range of Princes Gate and the other the immediate redevelopment of Kingston House itself, and, as leases fell in, the adjoining properties south and east. In neither case, though for different reasons, did the buildings do justice to their sites.

Nos 1–7 Princes Gate

Redevelopment of the entire eastern range of Princes Gate was planned in the mid-1930s by the builder Harry Neal, with Septimus Warwick as his architect. But Warwick's architecturally coherent scheme was compromised by Neal's failure to secure the entire site, and an intended monumental block of flats became two blocks, separated first by the incongruous presence of Kelk's surviving central house (No. 6), and subsequently by its modish 1970s replacement (Plates 109a, 114c).

Warwick's original design in 1936 was for a ten-storey block with stepped-back upper floors and a mansard roof. Already modified to satisfy the requirements of the London County Council, the design underwent further alterations when it became clear that the building would have to be erected in sections as the individual properties were acquired, starting with the ends and working towards the centre. Consequently the intended block plan was superseded by a more open arrangement of two H-shaped blocks – one on each side of the one remaining house (fig. 82).[162]

Building began in 1937–8 with the western block (**No. 7**). The eastern half of the eastern block (**No. 1**) followed in 1939–40 (leaving the old house at No. 4 still standing, though not the old No. 5). The western half of this block (**No. 5**), on the site of the old Nos 4–5, was not built until 1949. This last was carried out under the supervision of Ernest W. Banfield & Son, successors to Warwick's practice.[163]

The Princes Gate flats are a more monumental version of Warwick's contemporary Albion Gate flats in Bayswater Road, also designed for Harry Neal.[164] They would have been more monumental still had not the LCC vetoed the two top storeys of the ten originally planned, so that, as Warwick himself put it, 'the main architectural feature of the scheme had to be abandoned': this despite the fact that the site was 'much less congested' than those north of the park in Bayswater where taller blocks had been permitted. Warwick used his experiences in the building of the Princes

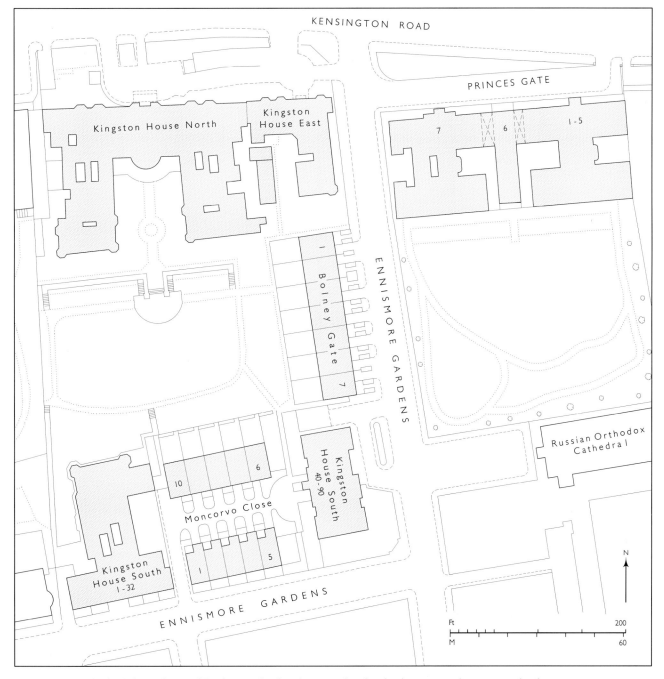

Fig. 82. Princes Gate and Ennismore Gardens in 1991: plan showing inter-war and post-war redevelopments

Gate flats to illustrate a sharp critique of the convoluted and sometimes perverse bureaucratic processes of the LCC.[165]

The buildings are of steel-framed construction, clad in silver-grey bricks and Portland stone, the principal elevational features being Lutyens-esque entrance porches framed by pairs of six-storey stone 'oriels', and columned aedicules capped with stone vases at the fifth- and sixth-floor levels.

No. 7 (the only part of the development to be occupied as flats from the start) contains three flats on a typical floor, the largest having, as originally planned, a drawing-room, dining-room and library overlooking the garden at the rear (fig. 83). The entrance halls and other common areas are sumptuously decorated, with fireplaces, floors, skirtings and architraves all of marble, mirror-lined walls and coffered ceilings (Plate 109b–c). The tunnel-vaulted garden hall and glass doorway was designed in 1939 by Braddell,

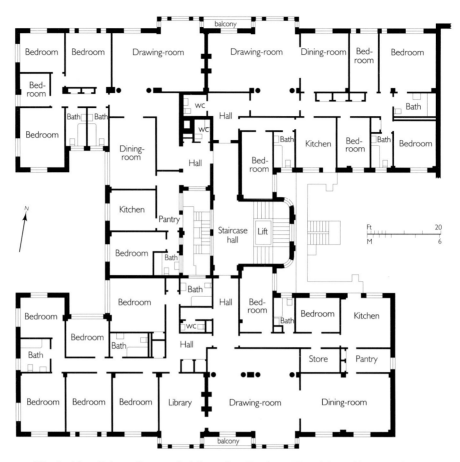

Fig. 83. No. 7 Princes Gate, typical floor-plan. Septimus Warwick, architect, 1938

Deane & Bird.[166] Two penthouse flats were added in 1987, by Chapman Taylor Partners.[167]

On completion, the shell of **No. 1** was taken over by the Combined Operations Branch and partitioned into offices; it was made into flats in 1965–6 and a penthouse flat was added in 1985–6. **No. 5** was used initially as offices by the Ministry of Works, and remains in office use.[168]

Kelk's old house at No. 6 survived into the early 1970s, when it was replaced by the present building, erected in 1972–4 by J. M. Hill & Sons. Designed by Turner Lansdown Holt & Partners, the new **No. 6** has been mistaken for the rebuilding of a portion of a complete original block, and perhaps, therefore, for a bolder piece of architecture than it actually is.[169] The building has bronzed aluminium curtain-walling with reflective double glazing. The lower floors are used as offices, and the three upper floors comprise a penthouse with a swimming-pool and a roof terrace.[170]

Kingston House redevelopment

The redevelopment of Kingston House and northern Ennismore Gardens began in 1937 and continued in stages over the next thirty years as leases fell in. All the buildings are the work of the Viennese-born architect Michael Rosen-

auer. They are, considering the opportunity offered by such a large-scale development, disappointingly bland. Of the six matching blocks of flats for the site originally designed by Rosenauer, only three were built, two before the war and one in the mid-1950s. The later buildings are another apartment block and three rows of town-houses (fig. 82).[171]

Tentative plans for flats on the Kingston House and Alford House sites, by O. Howard Leicester, were put forward by the contractors Sir Lindsay Parkinson & Company Ltd in January 1935, but at that stage no firm agreement for the sale of the property had been made. This first scheme was objected to by the London County Council as too dense and, at ten storeys over a basement, too high.

In September 1935 the Hare family and their trustees agreed to sell Kingston House and the adjoining properties on the north and west sides of Ennismore Gardens to Guardian Properties Ltd (a subsidiary of an investment company) for redevelopment. The price was £375,000. At the time Kingston House itself was still occupied by the elderly Dowager Countess of Listowel, as tenant for life under the will of her husband, the 3rd Earl. As she could not be disturbed, completion of the sale was held back until after her death in December 1936. Construction began in

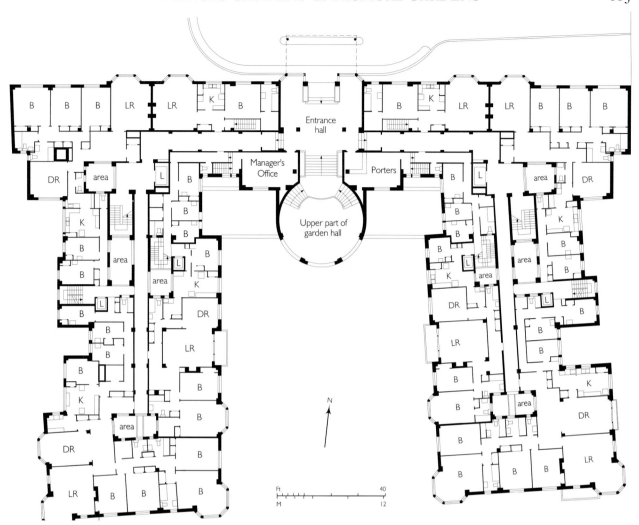

Fig. 84. Kingston House North, lower-ground-floor plan. Michael Rosenauer, architect, 1937

1937, under the aegis of a new company, Kingston House Ltd; the final stage was not completed until 1967.[172]

It was reported in January 1936 that the property was to be rebuilt, to designs by Messrs Gordon Jeeves, with family flats arranged around a central garden court, planned so as to contain 'a number of smaller rooms rather than a few large ones'. This was the essence of the scheme submitted to the local authorities in August 1936, but by that stage Jeeves had been supplanted by Michael Rosenauer.[173]

The first phase of building, carried out in 1937–8 by Holloway Brothers, comprised two blocks of flats, **Kingston House North** and **Kingston House South** (**Nos 1–32**).[174] Both buildings are of eight full storeys above the basements, steel-framed with brick cladding and Portland-stone dressings. Owing to the north–south fall of the site, Kingston House North has an additional, semi-basement, floor. The chief features of the exterior are full-height canted bays, doubled at the corners to give a turret effect, and cantilevered balconies with horizontal railings

(Plate 110b). At the main entrances are flat canopies carried on bronzed-steel piers.

Kingston House North, the centrepiece of the development, is built around a south-facing court. A circular hall, with a terrace above and communal lounges at either side on the lower-ground floor, looks out over the court and gardens, but the enclosure is too deep for its width to make the arrangement really effective. The building was planned with eight flats to a floor, varying in size from one-bedroom apartments to family suites containing four bedrooms, two reception rooms and accommodation for two or three maids (fig. 84).

Kingston House South (Nos 1–32) was intended as the western half of a symmetrical U-shaped block. A small wing at the north-east corner of the ground floor was added to the design at an early stage, presumably at the request of a prospective tenant; it was planned to comprise a music-room with an organ, and a dining-room.[175]

It was intended that both buildings should have ground-floor restaurants, but neither was fitted out and the spaces for them were converted into flats after the war.

Kingston House East, on the site of Alford House, was erected in 1955, by Gee, Walker & Slater Ltd. It matches Kingston House North in both internal organization and exterior style, and, indeed, the two buildings viewed from Kensington Road appear to be one.

With the completion of Kingston House East, no further attempt was made to complete the development on the pre-war lines, and Rosenauer drew up new plans for the remaining sites, which were built up in 1965–7.[176]

An eleven-storey tower block (**Nos 40–90 Kingston House South**) was built on the site of Moncorvo House. There are eight flats on each floor, mostly of two or three bedrooms. Externally, there is little, apart from some unobtrusive balconies and full-height stair-tower glazing, to relieve the plain brick cladding.

The remainder of the development took the form of short terraces of town-houses: **Nos 1–10 Moncorvo Close** on the site of Nos 67–69 Ennismore Gardens and the eastern part of Ennismore Gardens Mews North (Ennismore Place), and **Nos 1–7 Bolney Gate** on the site of Bolney House. They are all very plain brick buildings, loosely neo-Georgian in style, with integral ground-floor garages. Those forming Bolney Gate are the largest, with spacious accommodation arranged over five storeys, large bowed first-floor rear windows, and pedimented doorcases at the front.

Kingston House North accommodated the wartime Norwegian government-in-exile and, over the same period, Stephen Lanigan O'Keeffe, the Rhodesian High Commissioner. Post-war residents have included the actor Kenneth More and the writer Margaret Pedler. Lord Trenchard lived at No. 9 Kingston House South in the 1940s.

Russian Orthodox Cathedral, Ennismore Gardens (formerly All Saints' Church)

Standing at the east end of a little cul-de-sac off Ennismore Gardens, the former Anglican church of All Saints was erected in 1848–9, during the first phase of development on the Kingston House estate. Unusually, it is in the Lombardic style, which enjoyed a revival in the 1840s. Two striking features of the exterior were not, however, present when the church opened in 1849: the campanile, though contemporary in design, dates from about 1860, its construction having been deferred to save money; and the west front, an almost archaeological recreation of a twelfth-century Lombardic façade, is a rebuilding of 1891–2. Conspicuously un-English in its appearance, the building has been happily adopted by the Russian Orthodox Church since it ceased to be used for Anglican worship in the 1950s, and is now the Russian Orthodox Cathedral of the Dormition of the Mother of God and All Saints.

Although All Saints' was not erected until the late 1840s, the building of a new church to serve the developing district had been in contemplation since at least 1835, in which year the Church Building Commissioners made a grant of £2,000 for the purpose.[177] The delay was blamed on the difficulty of obtaining a suitable site in the district. In 1836 the Rev. Hibbert Binney, minister at the old Trinity Chapel on the north side of Knightsbridge, called for a 'spacious and well ordered' new church to be erected in a 'secluded' part of Hyde Park immediately behind his chapel, which, he suggested, should be demolished for a formal approach to the new building.[178] Nothing came of this – though it is possible that a design for a church in the park was prepared – and the subsequent building of St Paul's in Wilton Place, in 1840–3, reduced the need for another church at the eastern end of Knightsbridge.

The possibility of a site on the Kingston House property was first explored in 1840, when the Bishop of London asked John Elger to reserve a plot for a church on his proposed development there.[179] In April 1843 the building of a church on the estate was reportedly under consideration, but no agreement had yet been reached as to a site.[180] In fact it was only with 'great difficulty' that one was eventually secured on acceptable terms. The credit for this was due in large measure to the energy of the future first incumbent, the Rev. William Harness, then minister at the Brompton Chapel in Montpelier Street. Encouraged by the Rector of St Margaret's, Westminster, the mother church of the parish, Harness had set himself the task of securing a site and getting a church built. The former was accomplished in 1845, when Lord Listowel at last consented to sell some of his land. Although only a stone's throw from an existing large church, Holy Trinity, Brompton, this proximity was more apparent than real, since there was no direct access south to either the church or the Brompton road. The site, costing £1,250, was formally conveyed to the Ecclesiastical Commissioners in 1849.[181]

By June 1846, the versatile Lewis Vulliamy had been appointed architect and had produced plans for a church costing £8,514.[182] But instead of a conventional Gothic edifice like that shown in Thomas Allom's panoramic view of the Kingston House development (Plate 82a), Vulliamy proposed a building in the Lombardic style. According to the *Ecclesiologist*, his plans were not new, having been made in the mid-1830s for a site in Hyde Park – perhaps the site behind Trinity Chapel proposed by Binney in 1836.[183]

The dating of the design is significant. If, as claimed, it was made in the 1830s, it is a harbinger, albeit a tentative one, of the short-lived vogue for the Lombardic style, generally held to have arrived fully armed in England in 1840 with Wyatt & Brandon's St Mary and St Nicholas at Wilton. On the other hand, if All Saints' was designed in the mid-to-late 1840s it is a fairly tame specimen of the genre.

Construction could not begin immediately for financial reasons. A minimum of £7,000 was required before the Church Building Commissioners would allow work to start, and by 1848 the building fund was still short of this figure, in spite of Harness's efforts to drum up subscriptions.[g] The delay was undermining the morale of the building committee and Harness feared that unless a start was made soon the members might 'withdraw themselves in despair'. To cut costs they asked Vulliamy to make a reduced design, costing no more than £5,000. This he achieved largely by dispensing with the clerestory. But in the end the reduced version was not required and the committee was allowed to proceed on the basis of the original design, minus the campanile, the construction of which was postponed to save £1,400.[185] (Some bird's-eye views of the Crystal Palace in 1851 show the church in its original, towerless state, see Plates 6b and 7.)

Given the financial constraints, there was no money available for building a rectory, and Harness continued to reside at his house in Hyde Park Terrace, Kensington Gore. Subsequent incumbents occupied a succession of local houses, in Montpelier Square, Rutland Gate and elsewhere.

Building began in September 1848, with George Baker & Son of Lambeth as the contractor, and was completed in the summer of 1849, consecration taking place in July. Vulliamy was paid his fees, totalling £373, in November.[186] The church was assigned a district or parish which extended from Kensington Palace Gardens to Albert Gate and included the barracks and the streets and estates on the south side of the Kensington road. Socially this was a very mixed area, though most of its five thousand inhabitants lived in the poor and densely crowded neighbourhood near the barracks. Less than a third of the population could be accommodated in the new church, which had sittings for 1,308 (including 100 children): only 100 sittings were free.[187]

All Saints' has a typical basilican plan, with a nave flanked by lower, lean-to aisles, and an apse at the east end (fig. 85): the original west front (like its late-Victorian successor) was a clear expression of this plan. At ground level the central entrance was recessed behind an arcade (*Frontispiece*, Plate 92a). In the centre of the front was a wheel window – higher up and much smaller than its 1890s counterpart.

The exterior was to have been faced in stone.[188] In the event, and no doubt to save money, stone was used only for the west front and north side, which overlooks the communal gardens of Princes Gate. The east and south elevations are of brick (Plate 92c–d).

Inside, round-arched arcades with classical columns divide the nave from the aisles. Raised on brick plinths, the columns are of cast iron, originally 'polished to imitate marble'. Cast iron was also used for the bressummers or girders supporting the gallery fronts on the north, south and west sides. The original appearance of the interior was rather plain and severe, the prevailing tone being French grey. The *Ecclesiologist* was critical of the mean-looking ceiling in the nave – white, flat and dotted with large ventilators – a description which holds good today (Plate 93a, c). The only splash of colour was in the apse, where Owen Jones (a former pupil of Vulliamy) painted the semi-dome with a pattern of gold stars on a blue ground, and the windows were filled with coloured glass (long since removed).[189]

On the north side of the apse opening was a reading-desk, 'hoisted on a staircase', and on the south side a pulpit, reached from the vestry by a concealed staircase. The font was sited in the centre of the nave, among the block of free seats, and the organ in the children's gallery at the west end. None of these original fittings has survived.

During the incumbency of William Harness, which lasted until his death in 1869, the interior seems to have undergone little change. His curate, a Mr Tupper, repainted the Owen Jones decoration in the semi-dome, apparently turning the gold stars silver, and livened up the nave columns with red paint. Harness himself gave the three stained-glass windows in the apse (see below).[190] A new organ, by Holditch, was installed in 1851,[191] and it may have been then that the organ was moved from the west gallery to the easternmost bay of the north gallery.

Externally, the biggest change was the construction in about 1860 of the postponed bell-tower. Rising to some 120ft, it was built virtually as shown in Vulliamy's early sketch, though with a less pointed roof (Plate 92). This 'square topped' version dates from 1848, when he was cutting down his original design for the church to save money.[192] It is not known if Vulliamy himself oversaw the construction, or why the architect R. L. Roumieu should have prepared two spikily Gothic designs for the campanile (*Frontispiece*).[193h]

Originally the tower had only one clock face, on the west side. In 1872 a new eight-day movement by Gillett & Bland was installed and gilded copper dials put up on the other three sides. At the same time the old slate dial on the west side was gilded.[195]

Following the appointment in 1884 of a new and energetic incumbent, the Rev. Ravenscroft Stewart, plans were drawn up for enlarging and modernizing the church. These were the work of Charles Harrison Townsend, then a partner in the practice of Banks & Townsend, under whose imprint the drawings were prepared. There were three main components to this scheme: the re-ordering of the east end to create a raised chancel with choir seats in the easternmost bay of the nave; the complete rebuilding of the

---

[g] John Elger, who believed that a church would benefit his development, gave £300. This was the second largest private donation, exceeded only by the £500 from Henry Thomas Hope, the MP and patron of architectural art.[184]

[h] Vulliamy's design, a close adaptation of the early medieval campaniles at Murano and Torcello near Venice, seems uncannily to anticipate the work of Charles Harrison Townsend, who made important later alterations at All Saints'; indeed, the campanile has understandably been attributed to him.[194]

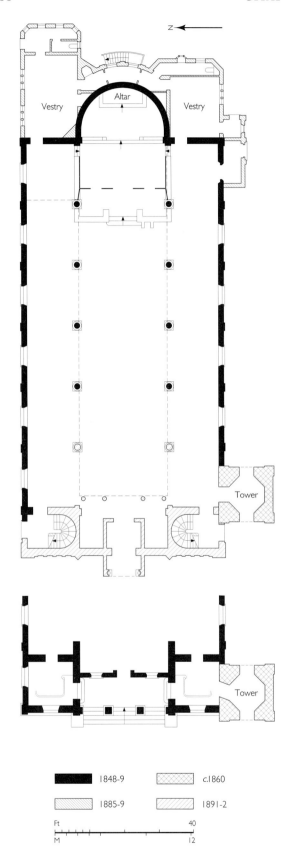

Vestry   Altar   Vestry

Tower

Tower

| 1848-9 | c.1860 |
| 1885-9 | 1891-2 |

Ft   40

M   12

west end some ten feet further forward, partly to make up for the seating space lost to the new chancel; and the building of new vestries at the north-east and north-west corners of the church, linked to each other by an ambulatory. With John T. Chappell of Pimlico as contractor, building work began in July 1885, but, as less than half the estimated cost of around £9,000 was actually in hand, the remodelling of the west end was postponed.[196] (While the work was in progress the congregation met in a temporary wood-and-iron building erected by J. C. Humphreys on part of the site of Humphreys' Hall, which itself was being rebuilt after a fire.[197])

To create the new chancel, Townsend provided a raised platform in the easternmost bay of the nave, and built up the floor level in the apse to make a sanctuary. The new chancel was paved with black-and-white marble squares, and the sanctuary in 'bastard white with a Sienna border'. At the same time the remainder of the nave was re-laid with wood blocks and reseated in oak, and the backs of the galleries were raised to improve the sight-lines.[198]

Townsend also designed several new fittings, including a high altar, a litany-desk, and a pulpit (Plate 93b). All three were made of carved oak, the altar and the pulpit by Messrs Daymond. The front of the altar, the only piece still in the church, was decorated with angels set within niches, and the pulpit with figures of Moses, Isaiah and Our Lord, representing the Law, the Prophets and the Gospel respectively. A design for a new square-shaped font of white statuary marble, decorated with low-relief carving and black marble inlay, was not executed.[199] Some years later, however, Townsend designed another font, which was installed in 1896 in the south-west bay of the nave on a specially laid paving of green cipollino marble. This font consisted of a large bowl of Mexican onyx with a lining of burnished copper, and an Art Nouveau cover of hand-beaten copper, made from Townsend's design by Llewellyn Rathbone at Menai Bridge.[200]

The rebuilding of the west end of the church eventually went ahead in 1891–2, but not in the form proposed in 1885. That scheme had included a semi-circular baptistery in the centre of the west front, flanked by columned porches leading to new vestibules at the western end of the nave.[201] Townsend's new design was closely modelled on the twelfth-century façade of S. Zeno Maggiore in Verona, which he had visited in 1886. His own characteristic style occasionally breaks through, however, for example in the treatment of the low-level windows on either side of the porch (Plate 92b, d). The new front was erected in 1892, by T. H. Adamson & Sons of Putney.[202]

Inside, the nave, having lost a bay for the new chancel in 1885, gained one at the west end in matching style, and the two westernmost columns are of this date, as is the present

Fig. 85. Russian Orthodox Cathedral (formerly All Saints' Church), Ennismore Gardens, plan c.1990. Lewis Vulliamy, architect, 1848–9; enlarged by C. H. Townsend, 1885–92. The original form of the west end is shown below

west gallery, with its supporting columns of carved wood.

Even before the western extension was begun plans were afoot to do something about the appearance of the interior, the decoration of the nave in particular being deemed 'chilly in the extreme'.[203] The authorities' first concern, however, was to embellish the re-ordered east end, and in 1891 the semi-dome was handed over to Thomas R. Spence for decoration. Recently moved to London from the north-east, Spence was a designer, decorator and architect, who had made a name for himself with St George's Church, Jesmond (1888–9). At All Saints' he painted the semi-dome 'after the manner of work characteristic of Northern Italy', with a view of an Eastern city surmounted by Christ in Majesty. On either side were standing figures of saints and above them a tier of angels. The predominant tones were yellow, russet and brown, on a rich blue background. Within only a few years, however, Spence's painting was obliterated, and no record of it appears to have survived, although a sketch model was shown at one of the Arts and Crafts Exhibitions.[204][i]

Spence's work was sacrificed for a much more ambitious programme of decoration, carried out between 1896 and 1903 by the Arts and Crafts designer Heywood Sumner. As part of this scheme the walls of the apse were faced with alabaster and the semi-dome coffered and gilded (Plates 94a, 122). The gilded frieze of vines in the apse is doubtless also Sumner's. In a somewhat different style are the three mosaic panels between the windows (Plate 124c). The designer of these is unknown. Sir William Richmond, the artist responsible for much mosaic work in St Paul's Cathedral, who was paid £31 for work at All Saints', may have been consulted about them, but the panels are not characteristic of his manner.[205]

The principal feature of Sumner's work at All Saints' is the arresting sequence of sgraffito decoration on the nave walls, his largest surviving scheme (Plates 122–3). This covers the clerestory and upper parts of the nave arcade, the chancel arch, and the arch over the west gallery. Sgraffito, a technique involving the scraping-back of layers of coloured plaster to produce decorative effects, was a particular speciality of Sumner, who first essayed it in 1885. Unlike earlier exponents, however, he used the medium in a pictorial way to create figurative and naturalistic images – well demonstrated in his first major commission, a series of panels illustrating the Benedicite, at Llanfair Kilgeddin church in Monmouthshire (1888–90).

The sgraffito decoration at All Saints', though conceived as a unity and executed as such, divides into two sequences: one, a cycle of scriptural scenes – from Creation to Calvary – the other, in the clerestory, a sequence of saints plus the Venerable Bede and the Holy Innocents. (A list of the subjects is given below.) The figures in the clerestory

are framed by oblong panels, on either side of the windows, while the scriptural scenes occupy roundels filling the spandrels of the nave arcade. The intervening wall spaces are covered with a design of trailing foliage and other patterns. As part of this scheme Sumner designed new stained glass for the clerestory and also for the new west front.

Work began at the east end, after a faculty for the decoration was issued in September 1896.[206] But progress was intermittent, being dependent on funds becoming available. In spite of this, the original programme was little changed: on the north wall St Anselm ousted St Cecilia, and on the western arch the proposed 'Promise to the World' from Genesis (presumably to be represented by a rainbow) gave way to a series of six roundels illustrating the six days of Creation. Only the Jesse tree intended to embrace the wheel window in the west wall failed to materialize, and this wall remains undecorated.

Between 1903 and 1955, when All Saints' was made redundant, changes to the interior were mostly of a minor character. A new organ had been installed in 1901, and in 1920 it was re-cased to a design by George Jack, carved by Joubert.[207] In 1927 a new oak lectern, designed by W. A. Forsyth, was installed, evidently replacing Townsend's reading-desk.[208] In 1939 F. C. Eden, an expert in church fittings and furniture who had trained with Bodley & Garner, designed a Renaissance-style altar for a small chapel to be formed out of the easternmost bay of the south aisle.[209]

It was not until 1924 that the church acquired a room for parochial activities. This was in a building erected before the First World War as a side addition to No. 65 Ennismore Gardens, above two former stables in Ennismore Mews. The principal room, formerly a dining-room, was oak-panelled, with a Jacobean-style plaster ceiling and a bow window overlooking the mews (see Plate 78d). The floor above was adapted as a flat for the vestry clerk, while the stables were let as garaging. The entrance to Church House, as it became known, was on the north side, through a round-headed stone doorcase decorated with a carved cross above the door. Since converted into a private residence and given another storey, it is now No. 66 Ennismore Gardens. The main room has lost its oak panelling, but retains its ornamental ceiling.[210]

Following closure in 1955, when the district was merged with that of Holy Trinity, Prince Consort Road, All Saints' was leased to the Russian Orthodox Church, which has since bought the freehold.[211] Before being handed over to the Orthodox congregation many of the fittings were removed, and their present whereabouts are mostly unknown.[j] The pews have been taken out of the nave and an iconostasis or icon screen installed at the eastern end (Plate

[i] Spence also designed a scheme (unexecuted) for decorating the roof and upper parts of the nave at another local church, Christ Church, Victoria Road, South Kensington.

[j] These include the font, the reading-desk, and the pulpit. The organ, made redundant because Orthodox services are sung unaccompanied, was re-installed at St John's, Mare Street, in Hackney.

122b). The Royal Gates in the centre of this screen were rescued from the old Czarist embassy chapel in Welbeck Street after the 1917 revolution. The icons on the screen were painted by pupils of the Russian iconographer, Leonid Ouspensky.[212]

In the early 1990s a parish hall and other ancillary buildings were erected along the south side of the church, and some of the existing structures, including the south-east vestry, demolished. Designed by M. P. Mandrigin, the new buildings are faced with fawn-coloured bricks, matched to the fabric of the church.[213]

Sgraffito decoration

Designed and executed by Heywood Sumner, 1896–1903 (Plates 93a, 94a, 122a, 123)

Chancel arch. Crucifixion (in a mandorla), flanked by symbols of the four Evangelists and a trellis of vines. The sgraffito work is embellished with gilded mosaic and mother-of-pearl.

North clerestory (west to east). St Agnes; St Swithin; St Giles; St George; St Christopher; St Paul; St Peter; St Francis; St Maurice; St Anselm; The Venerable Bede; St Columba.

North nave arcade (west to east). Angel (Heywood Sumner's initials, and the date 1903); Hortus Paradisi (Man before the Fall); Labor Terrae (Man after the Fall); Abraham Patriarcha; Moses Legislator; Esaias Propheta; Angel with scroll.

South clerestory (west to east). St Anne; St Catherine; St Margaret; Holy Innocents (two panels); St Aidan; St Hilda; St John; St Stephen; St Edmund; St Oswald; St Augustine.

South nave arcade (west to east). Angel; Ancilla Domini (the Annunciation); Filius Dei (Nativity scene); Verba Christi (Sermon on the Mount); Dolor Animae (Agony in the Garden); Via Crucis (Christ bearing the Cross); Angel with scroll.

Arch above west gallery. Six roundels illustrating the six days of Creation.

West porch. The Good Shepherd, in the tympanum over the west door, embellished with gold mosaic. This is the only external sgraffito.

Stained glass

Apse. The three round-headed windows (Plate 124c) are each filled with a figure under an architectural canopy in a representation of the Transfiguration – Christ flanked by Moses (left) and Elias. Little is known about these windows, which are of good quality and have been attributed to Clayton & Bell.[214] They were the gift of the first minister, William Harness, made partly in memory of his brother, who died in 1856, and must have been in place before William's own death in 1869.[215] The faintly Romanesque treatment of the canopies is appropriate in this architectural setting, if unexpected; Gothic would have been more usual.

Clerestory. The glass here was designed by Heywood Sumner to complement his sgraffito work (Plates 123e, 124b). Sumner himself thought the windows were too small and high up to be suitable for figure work, and he filled them with plant and tree forms of an almost domestic character. Religious imagery is confined to small emblematic roundels, although these are not present in every case. Re-glazing began at the east end and kept pace with the progress of the rest of the decoration.

West wall. All the glass is by Heywood Sumner, who exhibited the cartoon for the wheel window at the Arts and Crafts Exhibition of February 1903. Executed in Prior's glass, the wheel window contains an image of the Lamb of God in the central roundel, surrounded by twelve angels with inscriptions from the Te Deum (Plate 124a).[216] The small windows of the west front contain slightly sentimental figures of children with the text 'Suffer Little Children to Come unto Me', and angels' heads peeping out from folded wings with the words of the Trisagion (Plate 124b).

Sculpture

Memorial to William Wilson (d.1908), by Frank Derwent Wood, in the form of a reredos of three panels let into the alabaster dado of the apse. The central panel, inlaid on a marble ground with an oval in lapis lazuli and a vine in Mexican onyx, is flanked by carved white marble reliefs, in the early Renaissance style, of the Annunciation (Plate 94b) and a Pietà.[217] Wood exhibited the Pietà at the Royal Academy in 1910.

CHAPTER X

Princes Gate and Princes Gardens:
The Freake Estate

The streets and buildings discussed in this chapter were originally developed between the mid-1850s and the mid-1870s by (Sir) Charles James Freake, one of the most successful speculative builders in Victorian London of the generation after Cubitt.[1] Building on land which was partly his own freehold and partly leasehold, Freake erected ninety-five houses here, comprising the western end of Princes Gate (Nos 26–31) and its long return to Exhibition Road (Nos 32–72), together with the square called Princes Gardens. In addition to the houses he also built the substantial complex of stables and coach-houses making up Princes Gate Mews.

Even by Freake's standards, these were large houses, intended for the top end of the market, and as usual Freake seems to have been a shrewd judge of what that market would bear. The cautious pace of development, spread over almost twenty years, and Freake's deserved reputation as a sound builder, ensured that the houses let readily.

Within a couple of generations, however, such big houses were in little demand for private occupation. Redevelopment pressures, first manifest in the late 1930s when five houses in Princes Gate were replaced by a block of flats, re-surfaced after the Second World War. A scheme for rebuilding Princes Gardens as a campus for Imperial College, begun in the late 1950s, has yet to be completed. Almost two-thirds of Freake's original houses have now been demolished, and those that remain are all either sub-divided or in institutional use.

As is often the case, the mews properties have fared rather better than the houses they were built to serve, being transformed into attractive and sought-after dwellings.

The area before development

The ground on which Freake's houses were built (figs 86–7) had been part of the celebrated Brompton Park Nursery, founded in 1681.[2] By the mid-nineteenth century the greater part of this ground had come into the possession of Mary Plummer, through inheritance from a descendant of one of the nursery's proprietors. At that time it was occupied in two parts. The larger portion, covering 11½ acres and still used as a nursery until 1851, was connected to the Kensington road by a long, narrow strip on its west side. The other piece, on the east side of this strip and with a much wider frontage to the road, had been occupied since 1753 by a substantial mansion, latterly called Park House,

and its two-acre garden. Both pieces were copyhold of the Dean and Chapter of Westminster Abbey, and enfranchised on the eve of development.

Park House was built in 1753 by John Swinhoe, who had taken over the nursery in the early 1740s.[3] Set back from the road, it was a two-storey building with an attic and side wings. At the rear, the garden was formally laid out with parterres and an ornamental lake (Plate 2a). Swinhoe does not seem to have lived at the house. The ratepayer for about ten years was a Mrs Harrison, presumably the proprietress of the Brompton Park Boarding School, under which name the house appears on Rhodes's map of 1766. Between 1785 and 1822 it was the residence of James Vere, banker. The last occupant, from 1839 until 1855, was William Evans MP, of Allestree Hall near Derby.[4] Its final use, however, was as a site office for Freake's clerk of works.[5]

Development by C. J. Freake

Freake bought the 11½-acre rump of Brompton Park Nursery in 1851–2, but it was not until 1856 that he was ready to build there. During the intervening years, he had seen the value of his land increase greatly from the £24,000 that he had paid for it: he claimed to have turned down an offer of £75,000.[6]

The boost given to this whole area by the success of the Great Exhibition had set developers vying with each other for possession of the remaining open ground, chief among them the 1851 Exhibition Commissioners themselves, with their grand scheme for a permanent centre of cultural and scientific institutions here. Anxious to secure as much ground as possible, so that they could augment their long-term income through speculative property development, the Commissioners had initially hoped that Freake would be prepared to sell them the nursery ground at a modest profit to himself, but in the event it proved impossible to strike a deal on this basis. In any case, the Commissioners were perhaps more immediately concerned with trying (without success) to get possession of the much smaller Eden Lodge property, with its comparatively wide frontage to the Kensington road. This lay between Freake's ground and the old Gore House estate, the original nucleus of their holding, acquired in May–August 1852 (see fig. 86).[7]

Crucial to the development plans of both Freake and the

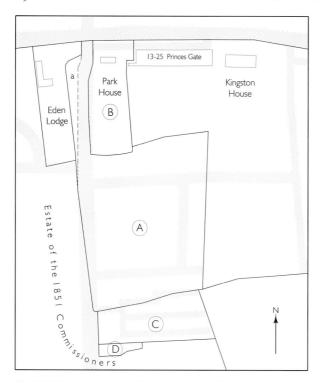

Fig. 86. The components of C. J. Freake's landholdings in Princes
Gate and Princes Gardens: modern roads stippled

Key:
A   Bought from the heirs of Mary Plummer, 1851–2
B   Developed under a building agreement with the heirs of
    Mary Plummer, 1855
C   Acquired in exchange for area marked 'a' from the 1851
    Commissioners, 1856–7
D   Bought from the Science and Art Department, 1865

Commissioners was the creation of Exhibition Road, the
second of two north–south streets over the Commissioners' estate between the Brompton and Kensington roads,
the other being Queen's Gate. Freake's possession of the
neck of land connecting the old nursery with the Kensington road, which offered the most promising northern exit
for the intended eastern street, gave him a trump card in
negotiations with the Commissioners. They had long since
abandoned the idea of buying his nursery ground when, in
1856, they reached agreement with him for the construction, at the joint expense of both parties, of the new street.
With their eyes still fixed on Eden Lodge, they entered into
an exchange of land with Freake which, in retrospect, must
have seemed a poor bargain. In return for the little slip of
ground left between the new road and the garden of Eden
Lodge they ceded to Freake a very substantial portion of
land immediately south of his property. This was sufficient
for him to build six houses on the road frontage (Nos 64–69

Princes Gate) and, at the back, a spacious mews for his
whole development. (The Commissioners' hopes that possession of the slip of ground would improve their negotiating position in the proposed purchase of Eden Lodge
proved unfounded, and in 1874 they sold it to William
Lowther, the new owner of the Eden Lodge property.)[8]

Freake, meanwhile, had consolidated his own position in
December 1855 by obtaining terms for building on the
recently enfranchised Park House property.[9a] With his
existing freehold land, this gave him a long uninterrupted
line of frontage to develop along the proposed Exhibition
Road, and a sizeable piece of the choice ground fronting
the Kensington road, opposite the park.

It was the intention of both Freake and the Commissioners that Exhibition Road should be secondary in
importance to Queen's Gate, a private road rather than a
public thoroughfare, and for this reason it was narrower
and the junction with the Kensington road was left somewhat constricted. Freake did not, however, take advantage
of the option of putting a gate at this end.[11]

Freake began building in 1856 on the Park House property. The first houses to be erected were Nos 26–31 Princes
Gate (completing the line of development at Nos 13–25
begun by John Elger on the Kingston House estate, but
demarcated from it by a railing and a passageway into the
communal garden there). These houses were leased to
Freake in March 1857, and were in the process of being finished internally at the beginning of September. Work was
also well advanced by then on building up the Exhibition
Road frontage, where Nos 32–35 Princes Gate were nearing completion and other carcases had been roofed in.[12]

Of the six houses facing Kensington Road, three were let
by Freake in 1858, and two more in 1860. The particularly
large house at No. 26, however, was not taken until the end
of 1862. Nos 32–44, fronting Exhibition Road, were variously let between 1859 and about 1861.[13] This row was
completed by four houses on Freake's freehold ground,
Nos 45–48 Princes Gate, which were first occupied
between 1860 and 1864.[14]

As this work proceeded Freake was already preparing
plans for much of the southern part of the estate. Proposals
for Princes Gardens were approved by the Metropolitan
Board of Works in October 1858.[15] The first houses there,
on the north side of the new square, were in carcase in 1859,
and one was let in that August.[16] Progress, however, was
hindered at this time by a strike which lasted for over two
months.[17b] By October 1860 the northern range was almost
completed, and several more properties there had been let.
Meanwhile the east side had also been built up, and the
square garden had been 'tastefully' laid out.[19] The first
houses on the south side were in carcase in 1861, and the
entire row was up in the following year. All the houses on

---

[a] The freehold of the Park House ground remained in the hands of Mary Plummer's heirs until 1881, when it was sold to W. H. 'Pinafore'
Smith, the politician and bookseller.[10]
[b] In April 1857 there had been a threat of strike action among Freake's workforce and several men were subjected to intimidation, for
which the ringleaders were prosecuted and jailed. Freake later became an advocate of arbitration in settling labour disputes.[18]

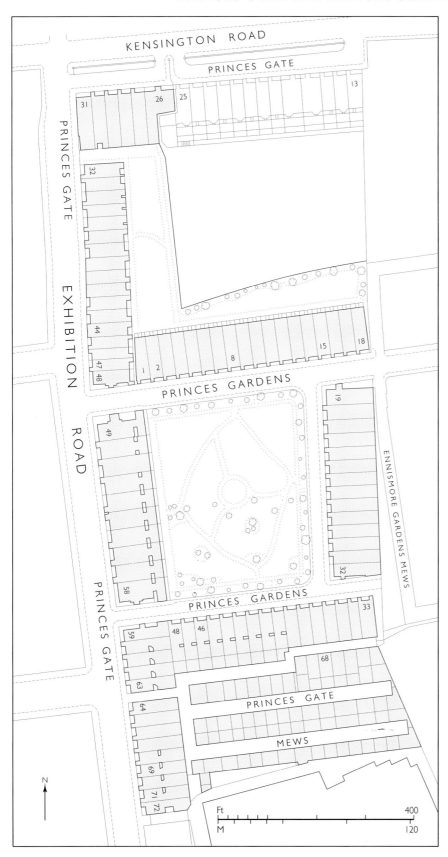

Fig. 87. The Freake Estate in Princes
Gate and Princes Gardens in the
mid-1890s

the east and south sides were occupied by about 1866.[20]

For the time being the Exhibition Road frontage on the west side of the square remained undeveloped. In 1862 Freake took advantage of the vacant site to set up an indoor market or 'International Bazaar' here, while the International Exhibition was being held across the road. Measuring 400ft by 100ft by 59ft high, this was a galleried wooden building alongside the street, adorned with flags and painted decorations by a Parisian firm, Delessert & Company, to give the requisite cosmopolitan flavour. The building was dismantled when the exhibition closed, but it was not until the late 1860s (having completed more houses further south in Princes Gate) that Freake ventured to erect houses on the plot.[21]

The houses on the bazaar site, numbered 49–58 Princes Gate (but carrying rights of access to the garden in the square), began to be occupied from 1869; the last to be taken, in 1875, was No. 57.[22] With the exception of No. 26 Princes Gate they were the largest houses on Freake's Knightsbridge estate.

To the south, the slightly earlier ranges at Nos 59–63 and 64–72 Princes Gate were first occupied between 1867 and 1873. The three southernmost houses, Nos 70–72, were built on an additional piece of ground, sold to Freake in 1865 by the Science and Art Department, which was then building the South Kensington Museum (now V & A) on the land adjoining. Their construction did not begin until after April 1867.[23]

Princes Gate Mews

This enclave, where Freake concentrated the stabling and coach-houses for his development, was built in 1859–61, well before many of the houses were even begun. Originally called Princes Mews, it was renamed in 1896.

Extensive though it is, the mews was not quite big enough. At least one house was leased with two adjacent properties in Princes Gate Mews, and some of the last of the Princes Gate houses to be built had to be let with stabling on his other developments, in Cromwell Mews and Reece Mews.[24]

The three parallel streets making up the mews are spaciously laid out, though with only one way to or from Exhibition Road. Resolutely plain in their original form, the buildings (the majority of them back-to-backs) have been variously altered and enlarged as private residences (Plate 78b).

Social character

Freake's houses in Princes Gate and Princes Gardens quickly became established as very good addresses. He was fortunate in securing three earls among his first tenants at Princes Gate: Earl Grosvenor at No. 28, the Earl of Ducie at No. 30, and Earl Somers at No. 33. Ten years later Somers removed to another, larger, new house on the estate, No. 49 Princes Gate.

Among the other first occupants of the earlier houses in Princes Gate were Charles Seeley, MP for Lincoln (No. 26); Sir Henry Bold Hoghton, a Lancashire baronet (No. 27); Robert Cooper Lee Bevan, banker (No. 31); Maj.-Gen. John Dawson Rawdon (No. 34), and the Dowager Marchioness of Bath (No. 39). John Augustus Beaumont, managing director of the County Fire Office (from which Freake obtained finance for the development) was the original occupant of No. 32.

The first houses to be completed on the north side of Princes Gardens attracted a few titled people, among them Viscount Hawarden and Lord Augustus Fitzroy (later 7th Duke of Grafton), four MPs and several judges.

On the east side of Princes Gardens there was a preponderance of commercial and professional men among the first or very early occupants. Three had close ties with New South Wales, two having been respectively the first Premier and Speaker of the Legislative Assembly there; the other was the son of the 'father of New South Wales', John Macarthur.

There was a comparable range of inhabitants on the south side of Princes Gardens and the southern part of Princes Gate. A good few were titled. Many were active in politics, the law, banking, the armed services, industry and commerce; most had country estates or at least a country residence.

Such large houses called for a fairly numerous indoor staff. The average complement was eight, typically consisting of butler, cook-housekeeper, lady's maid, a couple of housemaids, a kitchen maid and two footmen: governesses and nursemaids, and in grander households a page, might also be needed. There might be a dozen or so servants in all: in 1891 an MP and his wife and four children at No. 54 Princes Gate required fourteen.[25]

Lengths of occupancy varied greatly, the houses often being taken by a succession of short-term tenants. In at least ten of Freake's forty-seven Princes Gate houses, however, the first tenants or their families remained in occupation for twenty-five years or longer. In Princes Gardens, seven of the forty-eight houses remained in the hands of the first occupant or his family for at least thirty years (and in two cases sixty years).

Design and planning

Freake's success as a developer rested in large part on the single-mindedness with which he kept to just one section of the property market, and that largely within one locality. Having found a winning formula for catering to the requirements of the wealthy householder, moreover, he was not inclined to innovate. His houses, in consequence, epitomize the conservative taste of their day, providing conventionally grand exteriors acceptable alike to the artistically progressive (who might redecorate inside as they pleased) as to the more staid. In planning, too, allowing for the extra scope offered by their large scale, they were conventional. Equally important, they were soundly constructed on traditional lines. The *Building News* (which followed the progress of Freake's development with flattering assiduity) puffed the quality of the double-framed floors in Princes Gardens, which were finished in pitch pine 'without flaw, blemish or shrinkage, forming as a whole one of the best specimens of the sort we have seen'.[26]

In Princes Gate and Princes Gardens Freake's houses conform to the pattern repeated with variations across a large part of the South Kensington area during the 1850s and '60s. Three windows wide, fully stuccoed, with columned porticoes, they rise five full storeys over a basement. Within each range, the identity of each house is clearly expressed, but within a unified architectural treatment. By the time that Freake completed his last houses on the estate the fashion had become stale, and architectural taste was turning against these Italianate 'stucco classic' terraces altogether.

The houses here are closely related to those Freake was building at about the same time in Cromwell Road and Cromwell Place. The basic features of the type, however, were not introduced by him to this district. They were developed by John Elger and others building on the Kingston House and Rutland House estates from the 1840s, most grandiosely at Nos 13–25 Princes Gate, where a design by H. L. Elmes was used. Freake's own houses at Nos 26–31, similar in their elevational treatment to this earlier range, have the grandest façades on his estate, and were clearly intended to set the standard for the rest of the development (Plate 95a–b).

Unlike Elger, however, Freake preferred to place the main cornice between the two top floors, and his ornamentation was generally richer. Except for the area railings (where considerations of natural light to the basement, or perhaps security, dictated otherwise), exterior ironwork was shunned in favour of stone or stuccoed balustrading, giving the buildings a more committedly Italianate look.

Freake followed the design of his initial range fairly closely along Exhibition Road at Nos 32–48 Princes Gate (Plates 95c, 96c), but omitted the *alto relievo* swags over the attic windows. The attic window-heads here had keystones, and swags were used to decorate the spaces between the first- and second-floor windows. Among other minor changes, the quoining – long and short at Nos 26–31 and vermiculated on the ground floor – was made uniform. A feature of this whole range was that it was broken up irregularly as it stepped down the slope of Exhibition Road. Divisions were indicated by quoining and by the main cornice, but also by the arrangement of the porticoes. At the middle three houses (Nos 39–41), the porticoes took up the full width of each house, so as to form a colonnade (an effect reminiscent of C. J. Richardson's slightly later 'Albert Houses' in Queen's Gate). No. 44 also has a full-width colonnaded portico.

The considerably larger, later Princes Gate houses, Nos 49–58 (Plate 96a–b), are slightly plainer, without swags. None of the windows are round-arched. Instead of the

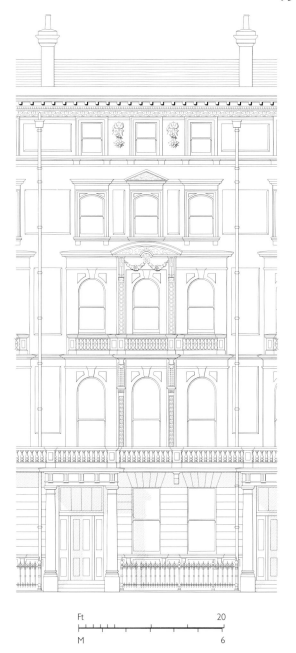

Fig. 88. Princes Gardens, north side, typical elevation. C. J. Freake, builder, 1858–9

Vitruvian scroll frieze beneath the main cornice there is a floral pattern.

The Princes Gardens houses are chiefly distinguished from those in Princes Gate by having the main cornice over the attic floor, beneath which there is a secondary cornice (Plate 97a–b). This arrangement was a favourite part of the architectural stock-in-trade of the various developers and builders active locally at this period, being found on many of the contemporary houses in and around Queen's Gate.

Of the three Princes Gardens ranges the most interesting was the northern, with a Mannerist elevational treatment ornamented with sprays and festoons (fig. 88). The eastern range (now entirely demolished) and the southern range (today represented by Nos 46–48 only) were given almost identical, more conventionally classical façades.

Nos 64–72 Princes Gate, and perhaps Nos 59–63 also, followed the Princes Gardens houses in having the attic storey beneath the main cornice (an additional modern attic storey has been added to the surviving houses at Nos 69–72).

Where the backs of the houses overlooked the communal gardens, they were stuccoed and given a modicum of ornamentation. The accretion of pipework and minor alterations has somewhat marred the original effect (Plate 97b). Small terraces or bridges over back areas give access to the gardens (fig. 89, Plate 96b).

Who designed the individual ranges is not known for certain. Freake himself aspired to the title of architect, but he had no professional training and there is no reason to suppose that he had the time to involve himself very deeply in architectural design and planning. Without doubt these matters devolved upon his various professional assistants. Chief among these was his right-hand man James Waller, who also came to style himself 'architect'. Another was William Tasker, who went on to establish his own successful architectural practice. According to an obituarist, Tasker 'planned many' of Freake's houses in Princes Gate and Cromwell Road.[27] George Edwards, who worked as Freake's 'pupil and assistant' from 1865 until 1874 and later practised independently, may also have been involved in design on the estate.[28] The architect W. H. Nash described himself as Freake's 'surveyor' in a letter of 1867 about the drainage in Princes Gate: he was then only about 17 years old.[29]

Freake's houses were planned as 'very complete family mansions' with all the 'necessary conveniences for a town residence required by a nobleman or gentleman'. Some had close on thirty rooms, including more than a dozen bedrooms. Except at some of the end-of-terrace houses the conventional side-passage plan was adopted, with a main dog-leg staircase.[30]

There was a large ground-floor dining-room, usually at the front (see fig. 94); that at No. 55 Princes Gate is perhaps typical in having a pair of columns at one end to define a servery. The other main ground-floor room might be arranged as a breakfast room, morning room, library or billiard-room. The smaller third room made a study or smoking-room. The main staircase was top lit, and had stone treads, a polished wooden handrail and cast-iron balustrading (fig. 90). Back stairs, also of stone, with simple iron balustrades, were provided for the use of servants.

On the north side of Princes Gardens the houses were built with an extra ground-floor room at the back, occupy-ing the full width of the house and opening on to the communal garden. They were typically used as dining-rooms (fig. 89, Plate 97b).

On the first floor, the usual arrangement was an L-shaped double drawing-room and a boudoir at the rear. The wider and deeper houses at Nos 50–57 Princes Gate had an oblong double drawing-room running the whole depth of the house, and front and back boudoirs (fig. 94). The other upper floors were given over to bedrooms, and the basement to the usual domestic offices.

End-of-terrace houses with side entrances had large central halls, open-well staircases, and reception rooms extending the full width of the building (see fig. 92).

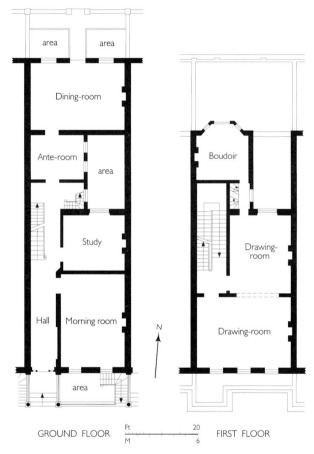

GROUND FLOOR   FIRST FLOOR

Fig. 89. Princes Gardens, north side, typical plans. C. J. Freake, builder, 1858–9

Uniquely, because of its irregular plot, No. 26 Princes Gate is on an L-shaped plan and double-fronted to the road. The central entrance hall, flanked by two reception rooms, turns into a top-lit staircase hall across the back of the eastern side of the house. On the deeper western side a third room (later furnished as a library) overlooks the communal garden. On the first floor a grand apartment occupies the entire front of the house, with another reception room behind, on the west side.[31]

Interiors

Freake's houses were finished to a high decorative standard, with much enriched plasterwork and other ornamentation (Plate 105a). Entrance halls were paved with encaustic tiles, variously by Minton or Maw & Company (Plate 121d). The main reception rooms, decorated 'in a most elaborate style', had ceiling 'centre-flowers' and coved cornices, gilded and coloured in 'a good display of polychromatic art'. Plate 103a shows the drawing-room at Lord Dinevor's residence, No. 19 Princes Gardens, in the 1860s, with its original cornicing. More unconventionally, at Nos 26–31 Princes Gate, and some at least of the other houses, the doorways of the drawing-rooms were designed with elliptical heads and architraves, formed in Keene's cement. The floors of the drawing-rooms and boudoirs had borders of inlaid parquetry made up of mahogany, walnut, sycamore and oak. The particularly fine parquetry floor in the drawing-room at No. 53 Princes Gate (fig. 91) was probably installed for an early occupant.[32]

Such large dwellings, suited to extensive households and entertaining on a princely scale,[c] were natural arenas for ambitious re-decorators. The most spectacular interiors, both in the Aesthetic taste, were at Nos 49 and 52 Princes Gate (described below). At **No. 27 Princes Gate**, the Hon. William Francis Cowper Temple (afterwards Baron Mount Temple) and his wife Mary, fired with enthusiasm by Rossetti himself, espoused the same fashion. A visitor in 1872 was ushered into 'a room like an emerald with dark bright green satin walls', hung with paintings including Rossetti's *Beatrice*. Smaller pictures were hung on a low gold-painted dado. The dining-room was 'panelled in green wood, with squares of gold let into the panels . . . each square being painted with a large sunflower, a blue iris, a branch of spindle tree with coral beads hanging by a thread, or some lovely tree or flower'. In a recess were painted windows by Morris, and window seats adorned with Italian pottery jars.[34]

Of the same period, but in a very different style, was the interior décor at an unidentified house in the Exhibition Road part of Princes Gate. The first-floor drawing-rooms had been thrown into one and sumptuously decorated in Louis-Quatorze style, with ornate over-mantel mirrors and a panelled ceiling ornamented in white on a pale turquoise ground. The walls were decorated with painted panels and pilasters, the panels with a fleur-de-lis pattern, and the pilasters (painted on zinc) with small symbolic representations of Architecture, Painting, Music, Sculpture, Literature, Science, Agriculture, and the Chase. All the woodwork was painted white, relieved by sparing use of gilding and silvering, and heightened with 'tints of tempered cerise and turquoise'. This work was designed and executed by the Baker Street house decorators W. Phillips & Son.[35]

The banker Herbert de Stern (afterwards Lord Michelham), an intimate of the Prince of Wales, commissioned some especially lavish redecoration at **No. 26 Princes Gate** in the early 1890s. This was carried out by H. Hanks, probably the decorator Herbert Hanks of Berners Street. A marble staircase was installed, the walls of the entrance hall and staircase were veneered in grey veined marble, and the floor was laid with marble mosaic (Plate 102a–b). An oak dado and scagliola columns were added to the dining-room, and the library was fitted with richly carved bookcases, a massive Renaissance chimneypiece and a Jacobethan-style moulded-plaster ceiling (Plate 102c).[36] The marble work in the hall and the staircase still survive.

Fig. 90. No. 53 Princes Gate, staircase balustrade

No. 58 Princes Gate has many decorative features dating from an expensive Edwardian make-over. Almost certainly carried out prior to 1909,[37] it was probably commissioned by George Alexander Lockett, of the Liverpool merchants William & John Lockett, whose London residence this was from about 1903 until his death in 1923.

The best-preserved interiors are the entrance hall and staircase compartment, and the full-sized billiard-room overlooking Exhibition Road on the first floor. The first two, in the French Beaux-Arts manner, are lined in pale

---

[c] Princes Gate, quipped an American dinner-guest at No. 52, was 'obviously a gate to high society': as his cab arrived, a footman on the steps 'unrolled long lengths of rich stair-carpeting to our feet, and at the door two other flunkeys relieved us of our wraps'.[33]

grey stone, with moulded panels and elaborately sculpted over-doors (Plate 105c). The hall, which has an ornate eighteenth-century-style plaster ceiling, is divided from the stairwell by a screen of fluted green marble columns, with gilded capitals and bases, carrying a deep entablature (Plate 119c). The staircase is of stone and perhaps original to the house, but the metal balustrading, with gilded enrichments incorporating the initial L, evidently forms part of the remodelling (Plate 105b).

Fig. 91. No. 53 Princes Gate, detail of parquetry floor in the first-floor drawing-room

The former billiard-room is done up in the Jacobethan style, with dark wooden panelling and a strapwork ceiling with pendants: the painted frieze is modern. On the ground floor, the former smoking-room is decorated in similar taste. The decoration of the former dining-room and morning room, in neo-Adam and mid-eighteenth-century English styles respectively, is also probably Edwardian work. The first-floor drawing-rooms have been showily redecorated more recently, with *boiseries* and painted panels in the early-eighteenth-century French fashion.

A final example of redecoration is the Georgian-style drawing-room at No. 6 Princes Gardens (now demolished), probably carried out in the 1920s (Plate 103b).

By the First World War a number of houses had undergone some internal structural alterations. At No. 53

Princes Gate there was now a double dining-room, running the full depth of the house and subdivided by a 'sinking wall'. Several houses on the south side of Princes Gardens had annexed parts of the buildings adjoining in Princes Gate Mews. In this way No. 48 had been provided with a new ground-floor billiard-room. In other instances, however, the former stabling and coach-houses in the mews were employed as motor-garages. Passenger-lifts were installed in some houses: at No. 54 Princes Gate a quaint glass-and-metal lift of 1920s appearance survived into the 1990s. Other houses were slow to receive more basic improvements. In the early twentieth century No. 11 Princes Gardens still had not a single bathroom or fitted bath.[38]

No. 49 Princes Gate

Outwardly unremarkable, this house claims a place in the history of art as the original home of a legendary piece of interior design – James McNeill Whistler's Peacock Room. Probably no other dining-room in London has been quite so celebrated, or received such extravagant encomiums – the 'World's Greatest Masterpiece of Decorative Art' in the not unbiased view of one Chicago newspaper – and the story of its creation, spiced with controversy, continues to fascinate.[39]

Much of the original publicity for the room was generated by the artist himself, somewhat to the embarrassment of its owner, F. R. Leyland, the Liverpool shipping magnate and art collector, and Whistler's principal patron. A private man, Leyland had preferred the relative anonymity of a speculative builder's house, albeit a large and superior example of the genre, to some outwardly individual mansion (Plate 96a–b): his previous London house, in Queen's Gate, was similarly an up-market speculative builder's job of the mid-1850s. Inside, however, he was prepared to lavish substantial sums on decoration. Contemporaries were struck by the contrast: 'Without is London, within is Italy'.[40]

The house was not new when Leyland acquired it. The first occupant, who bought it from the builder, C. J. Freake, on an eighty-year lease and lived there from 1869 to 1874, was Charles Somers, 3rd Earl Somers.[41] He too was a connoisseur and collector, particularly of armour, and, at his country seat Eastnor Castle, an enthusiastic and lavish interior decorator. If, however, he made any alterations to No. 49 these have not been identified.

Somers sold the house to Leyland (together with his coach-house at No. 68 Princes Gate Mews) in July 1874.[42] The remodelling of the interior must have begun almost immediately, and was to continue intermittently over the next decade. Designed to create opulent settings for Leyland's collection of pictures and antiques, this work was essentially decorative and largely carried out within the framework of Freake's original plan. During the early stages the house was presumably uninhabitable, and Leyland does not appear to have taken up residence until 1876.

Three designers are particularly associated with Leyland's refashioning of the interior: Whistler; the architect and designer Thomas Jeckyll; and the architect Richard Norman Shaw.

The first on the scene was Jeckyll, employed on the advice of Murray Marks, the Oxford Street china dealer, through whom Leyland had acquired his own collection of blue-and-white Kangxi porcelain.[43] The extent of Jeckyll's brief is not known, but seems to have included the remodelling of the hall and stairwell, the decoration of the dining-room, and the creation of a study or sanctum for Leyland himself.

The study was probably the first to be finished. Situated in the basement on the west side of the house, it was a long, low room reached by a staircase from a lobby in the south-west corner of the hall. Above a dado of American walnut, the walls were hung with old-gold Spanish leather, embossed with 'a soft floral design interspersed between bold red-brown arabesques'.[44] Henry Cole, a visitor in 1876, described the room as generally 'coloured green bronze on ceiling and walls and hung with Botticellis and the like'. He found it 'very harmonious – a rose modern piano only being incongruous'.[45] Dominating the room were some elaborate gas-lamps (doubtless incorporating a self-ventilating system to keep the fumes from harming the pictures and decorations), with bulbous shades resembling Japanese lanterns.

The remodelling of the hall and the dining-room proceeded in parallel. In the former (Plate 98a), Jeckyll presumably had the responsibility of adapting Freake's staircase to take the balustrade from the great stairs at Northumberland House, which Leyland acquired when the historic mansion was pulled down to make Northumberland Avenue. At the sale of the materials in September 1874, the balustrade, with its Spanish mahogany handrail, was knocked down for just £360.[46]

The balustrade is an exceptional piece of design – an enriched Vitruvian scroll highly decorated with foliage and flowers (Plate 105d). Dating from 1822–3, it was designed by the Duke of Northumberland's architect, Thomas Cundy the elder, and made of Grecian metal, a 'refined species of brass'. It was one of a number of metal and glass fittings at Northumberland House, including four 'superb' Grecian metal chandeliers costing £2,700, supplied and fitted by William Collins of the Strand, 'Glass Enameller and Glass Manufacturer to the King and the Royal Family'. His charge for the balustrade, including two nine-feet-high candelabra at the foot of the staircase, was £2,000.[47d]

Fitting a balustrade intended for a large imperial staircase to the shorter, steeper flights and sharper turns of a staircase in a terraced house, however large, must have required both ingenuity and skill, and perhaps used up more of the original than expected. For whatever reason, the balustrade as originally installed at No. 49 extended from the entrance hall only to the second-floor landing.

Presumably it was Jeckyll who designed the architectural features of the hall and staircase, and the prettily patterned mosaic floor, but the colour scheme was apparently entrusted to Whistler, his earliest involvement with the decoration at No. 49.[48] For the walls Whistler chose contrasting shades of green, to harmonize with the gilt balustrade; his most personal contribution, however, was a series of panels along the dado. Embellished with pink and white flowers on a background of dutch metal (imitation gold-leaf) under a lightly distressed green glaze, these were in progress in March 1876. Doubts as to the stability of the glaze caused the work to be suspended, and by the time they were resolved Whistler was preoccupied with the dining-room, and the intended series of panels in the hall was left incomplete.[49]

The history of Leyland's dining-room at No. 49 is of a room designed by Jeckyll, and, short of painting the woodwork, completed to his design, which was then raised to a higher aesthetic plane by Whistler's transforming brush (Plates 101a, 126b). Not that Jeckyll's scheme was deficient in artistic merit.[e] His task here was to devise a setting suitable for displaying Leyland's collection of blue-and-white china and Whistler's painting *La Princesse du pays de la porcelaine*, which had come into Leyland's possession probably in the early 1870s. To display the china, Jeckyll designed a range of open shelves or étagères, divided at intervals in the Japanese fashion. As a background, the walls were hung with gilt leather, painted with red flowers and green foliage, above the wooden dado. Whistler's *Princesse* was hung in a prominent position over the fireplace, which contained two of Jeckyll's distinctive sunflower andirons. Jeckyll's ceiling, made from wood and canvas, was divided by wooden ribs into a Tudoresque pattern of eight eight-pointed stars with a pendant in the centre of each (fig. 93). At the end of every pendant was a gas-lamp with a bulbous lantern-light, like those in the study. Although electric lighting was installed in parts of the house during Leyland's lifetime (very likely by the Edison & Swan Electric Light Company, of which he was a director), it did not entirely supersede the gas system.[50]

Jeckyll's dining-room, constructed by a local builder, Joseph W. Duffield of Jay Mews, Kensington, was fitted into the existing room on a framework independent of the walls and ceiling. It was thus capable of being dismantled and removed – a fortuitous circumstance, but for which the

[d] It has been questioned whether the elder Cundy, then aged 57, was capable of so sophisticated a design, anticipating Nash's grand staircase at Buckingham Palace. By this date he was working in partnership with his son, also Thomas, and their respective contributions are impossible to distinguish. For their almost contemporary recasting of Viscount Belgrave's house in Grosvenor Square, they designed a palatial new front with a deep, scrolly frieze not unlike the Northumberland House balustrade.

[e] A reconstruction of the dining-room as it may have appeared before Whistler started work there is given in Linda Merrill's recent study of the Peacock Room (fig. 5.1).

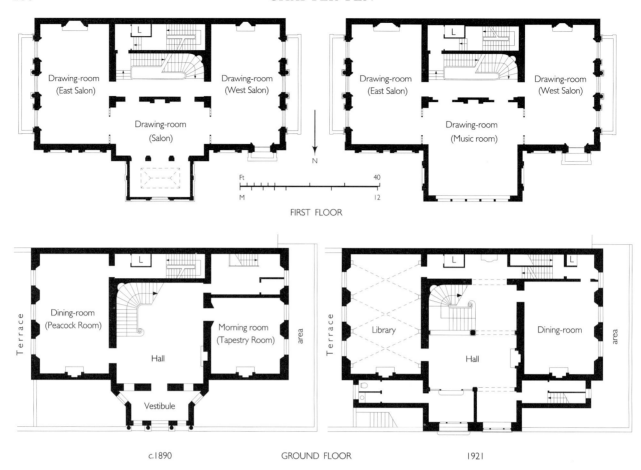

Fig. 92. No. 49 Princes Gate, plans in *c*.1890 and 1921, showing the ground and first floors as modified for F. R. Leyland (left) and after remodelling in 1895–7 for Mrs Watney. *Some details of Leyland's vestibule are conjectural*

room and Whistler's embellishments would certainly not have survived.[51]

Since one of his own paintings was to be the focal point of the decoration, Whistler doubtless kept an eye on what Jeckyll was doing in the dining-room, but he did not become involved there himself until quite a late stage. Jeckyll was close to finishing when in April 1876 Leyland consulted Whistler about the colouring of the woodwork, Jeckyll himself being still undecided – 'he speaks of two yellows and white'. Leyland wondered if it would be better treated like the hall dado, using dutch metal – 'I wish you would give him [Jeckyll] your ideas'.[52] Thus at Leyland's invitation Whistler was drawn into working on the decoration, and so began a series of 'adjustments' to Jeckyll's scheme out of which the Peacock Room emerged.

He began by applying dutch metal and a transparent greenish glaze to parts of the unpainted woodwork. In this work he was assisted by Walter and Henry Greaves. Pre-

sumably Jeckyll approved, but his health was already beginning to give way and by the summer he had left the scene altogether. Whistler next turned his attention to touching-up the gilt-leather wall-hangings with traces of yellow: he felt the red flowers clashed with the colours of the *Princesse*. In August, he wrote to Leyland in Liverpool that the room was all but finished, apart from a blue 'wave pattern' which he intended to apply to the 'green gold' of the cornice and dado – three days' work at the most. Leyland sanctioned this, but alone in London, unrestrained by his patron's wishes, Whistler allowed his imagination free rein, and his simple wave pattern evolved into a peacock-feather design which he carried over on to Jeckyll's ceiling. He also gilded the china shelving and painted large golden peacocks on the window shutters.

When, in October 1876, Leyland saw what Whistler had done to his dining-room he was apparently noncommittal. But he soon made his feelings clear when he declined to pay

Fig. 93 (opposite). No. 49 Princes Gate, ceiling plans. *The drawing-room ceilings (by Richard Norman Shaw) partially survive; the Peacock Room ceiling (by Thomas Jeckyll), removed with the rest of the room, is now in the Freer Gallery, Washington, DC; the morning room ceiling (by W. R. Lethaby) was destroyed in 1895–7*

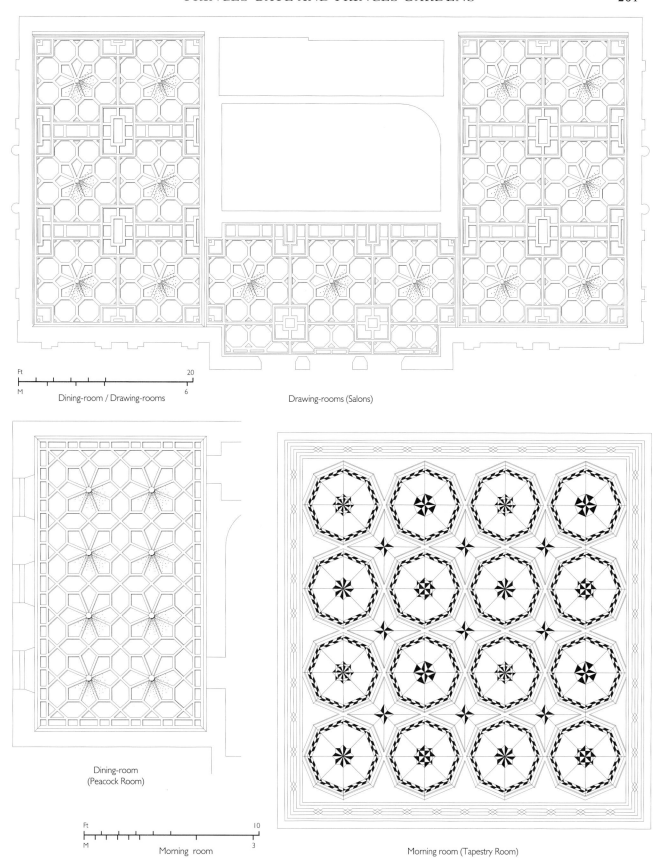

Ft 20
M 6
Dining-room / Drawing-rooms

Drawing-rooms (Salons)

Dining-room
(Peacock Room)

Ft 10
M 3
Morning room

Morning room (Tapestry Room)

the artist's fee, two thousand guineas, and a *froideur* descended on their relationship. Eventually, they agreed that Whistler could finish the work – it was so far advanced Leyland felt he had no choice in the matter – and that they both would share the cost. Leyland paid Whistler £1,000, itself a calculated snub, as artists, unlike tradesmen, were normally paid in guineas. The breach between them was never healed.

By the end of the month Whistler was back at work, painting peacock plumage on the wainscot. He completely obliterated the flowers on the gilt-leather hangings, and on the south wall, opposite the fireplace, he painted the famous mural intended to encapsulate his quarrel with Leyland. Artist and patron are depicted as peacocks themselves, identifiable by their respective attitudes and attributes. The bird on the right, angry and threatening, its neck features mimicking Leyland's habitual ruffled shirt-fronts, stands over a scatter of silver discs fallen from its plumage – the shillings deducted from Whistler's fee. The other bird, calm and dignified, has a silver crest in allusion to Whistler's own distinctive white forelock.

Without regard for the owner's privacy or feelings, Whistler entertained his friends and fellow artists in the room, and when nearly finished provoked a spate of publicity by inviting in the press. In March 1877 he added the final touches to the shutters and by the time Leyland returned to London for the season the work was finished and Whistler left the house, never again to see his self-styled 'Harmony in Blue and Gold'.

Two years later, Leyland turned his attention to redecorating the drawing-rooms on the first floor. By this time Jeckyll's health had totally collapsed, and instead he called in Richard Norman Shaw, again on the recommendation of Murray Marks, whose shop in Oxford Street had been designed by Shaw.[53] Working within the existing plan, Shaw created a suite of three drawing-rooms or salons, divided by two screens which could be removed to make one large U-shaped space (fig. 92, Plates 99, 100a). The design of the panelled walnut screens with their burnished-brass balusters (Plate 99) was apparently suggested by the rood-loft of the early-seventeenth-century marble-and-alabaster screen from the cathedral at s'Hertogenbosch (Bois-le-Duc), which Murray Marks had acquired and sold to the South Kensington Museum (now V & A).

For the drawing-room ceilings (fig. 93) Shaw devised a more elaborate version of Jeckyll's ribbed ceiling in the Peacock Room, with the same pendant lamps and shades:

I always thought them exceedingly well designed & indeed all his [Jeckyll's] work there was most admirable. I only wish I could have done anything half as good.[54][f]

The areas between the ribs were filled with gilded arabesque designs. American walnut was used for the ribs and also for the panelled dado and doors. Above the dado the walls were lined with silk damask, the colour of old gold. Leyland reserved the walls of the east salon for his Old Master paintings while his Pre-Raphaelite pictures were mostly displayed in the west. For the chimneypiece in the east salon, a 'handsome remnant of an Italian Renaissance house' presumably installed by Leyland, Shaw designed a carved wooden overmantel, with niches for oriental pots (Plate 100a).

Shaw also provided some additional wall space for pictures by building 'a gallery sort of place' above the entrance portico.[56] Opening off the middle drawing-room, from which it was separated by square piers, this little picture alcove was lit by a glass roof (fig. 92). Leyland used its windowless silk-covered walls to display a group of Pre-Raphaelite paintings, including six by Burne-Jones representing Day, Night and the Seasons. Externally the structure conformed to the general Italianate style of the house, with false window openings so as not to disturb the rhythm of the north front.[57]

The redecoration of the drawing-rooms was completed in 1880. Five years later Leyland turned to Shaw again to refashion the morning room on the ground floor. This room, used by the family for billiards, had served as a temporary dining-room while the decoration of the Peacock Room was in progress.[58] The new décor was designed to display a set of old Brussels tapestries, woven with scenes of rural life after Teniers. Though nominally by Shaw, the drawings for this work are in the hand of his assistant, W. R. Lethaby,[59] and the geometric style of the woodwork is rather more characteristic of Lethaby than of Shaw himself (Plate 100b). The *pièce de résistance* was a panelled oak ceiling inlaid with black and white woods (fig. 93).

Completed in 1886, the redecoration of the morning room was Leyland's last major undertaking here. In January 1892 he died of a seizure on the Underground: four months later his art collection was sold, and in June No. 49 was offered for sale. The auctioneers produced a sumptuous catalogue, but their efforts went unrewarded and the house was bought in for £20,100.[60] It was eventually sold, in September 1894, to Mrs Blanche Watney of Thorney Lodge, Palace Gate, widow of James Watney, the brewer and Liberal MP.[61] The previous month Thorney Lodge had been offered for sale by Mrs Watney's landlord, 'with possession on completion', but in the event she stayed on there until 1896, while No. 49 was being altered to suit her requirements.[62]

These alterations, designed by the architectural partnership of Ernest George and Alfred Yeates[g] and carried out by Trollope & Sons, were substantial and far reaching, but mainly concerned with the interior.[64] Externally only the

---

[f] Shaw's verdict, characteristically generous, was not universally shared. E. W. Godwin, for one, was an early critic: in his view the room should have been lit by candles.[55]

[g] The building application was made in the name of George & Peto, still the official name of the firm, though the original partnership had been dissolved.[63]

north front and the garden terrace were significantly changed.

On the north front the porch was enlarged, being both widened and raised a storey, and on the first floor a five-light window was inserted. At the same time two quite plain single-storey extensions were built on either side of the extended porch, containing lavatories and a staircase to the basement (fig. 92). The eastern extension has been demolished. For the garden terrace George & Yeates created a Renaissance-style enclosure with stone and marble walls, a carved wall-fountain, stone seats and a geometrically patterned brick-and-stone pavement.[65]

After the house had failed to find a buyer in 1892, Leyland's son-in-law, Val Prinsep, expressed the hope that its next owner would be 'wise enough to leave it in its present state'.[66] Mrs Watney, however, was not the right person for this. It was not that she had no interest in artistic matters – Millais, her neighbour in Palace Gate, was a friend, and she owned paintings by Leighton – but that Leyland's interiors were evidently not to her taste. Her alterations were correspondingly ruthless. Seeing the work in progress, the American architect Stanford White felt that the house had fallen into the hands of the Philistines.[67] Of particular concern to Whistler and his friends and admirers was the future of the Peacock Room, which the new owner initially dismissed as 'hideous' and planned to have 'entirely redecorated'.[68] That it was saved from this fate seems due to the artist W. Graham Robertson, who explained to Mrs Watney how the room could be dismantled and would command a high price if sold. Whistler himself encouraged the idea that it might be purchased for reconstruction in America, and at his behest Stanford White, accompanied by John Singer Sargent, visited No. 49 in 1895 to examine the room. But in Mrs Watney's absence they were unable to determine if it was actually for sale, and, as it turned out, she had changed her mind – for the time being it was neither to be sold nor redecorated.

While the Peacock Room received a stay of execution, other areas were, in White's words, 'gutted and torn down preparatory to furbishing up in the latest modern style'.[69] On the ground floor George & Yeates remodelled the hall in the Florentine Renaissance manner which the firm had earlier employed in an even more full-blooded make-over of the hall at No. 6 Carlton House Terrace in 1890 (Plate 98b). The Northumberland House balustrade survived this change with its lowest section turned through ninety degrees behind a stone screen dividing the hall in two, but the dado with its Whistler panels disappeared. Another casualty was Leyland's mosaic floor, replaced by a pavement of black and white marble squares. For the front hall the architects provided a large canopied stone chimneypiece, and in the back hall they constructed a stone alcove

under the staircase, decorated with gold mosaic, within which was set a sculptured marble fountain and basin.

To the west of the hall Leyland's morning room was lengthened, and the decoration entirely sacrificed, to make a new dining-room. Here, George & Yeates drew inspiration from 'Merrie England' to create a Jacobethan-style room with much oak woodwork, embossed Spanish leather wall hangings, and a strapwork ceiling. In the architects' drawing the windows along Exhibition Road are shown as casements filled with small leaded lights. Below the new dining-room Leyland's old basement study was turned into a servants' hall.

Shaw's work on the first floor fared better, though his overmantel in the east drawing-room was at some point removed. The chief casualty here was the little picture alcove, which was swallowed up to make an enlarged middle drawing-room or music-room extending over the widened porch. A carved marble-and-wood chimneypiece of late-Tudorish character, on the wall directly opposite the new five-light window, was probably inserted at the same time.

In 1904, the year after Whistler's death, Mrs Watney decided to dispose of the Peacock Room, but had several changes of mind before finally parting with it to Messrs Obach & Company, picture dealers in New Bond Street. Her asking price was 10,000 guineas. After removal from Princes Gate the Peacock Room was re-assembled for exhibition at the Obach gallery in June.[70h] Mrs Watney, meanwhile, called in (Sir) John Belcher, who was currently engaged on an extensive programme of works for her eldest son at Cornbury Park, the family's country house, to remodel the empty shell as a library. Belcher gave the room an elaborately decorated groined ceiling (modelled in fibrous plaster by the Veronese Company of Fulham), a new wooden chimneypiece, and ranges of open and closed bookcases. All the woodwork was executed in Italian walnut by Trollope & Colls. Belcher also designed the suite of six oxidized silver electric-light fittings, made by Geere Howard of Berners Street.[72] Photographs of the library (Plate 101b) show a spare, masculine-looking room of little charm. The ranges of book-shelves lining the walls were faintly reminiscent of Jeckyll's staging for Leyland's china collection. A more palpable link with Leyland's dining-room was the pair of Jeckyll's sunflower andirons in the grate, probably left behind when the rest of the room was sold.[73]

For all that it was 'most expensively fitted out', in 1910 the house still had only one bathroom.[74]

Mrs Watney occupied No. 49 until her death in 1915: it then stood empty for several years. In 1919 the house was put on the market but failed to attract a buyer and in 1921 it was converted into flats.[75] Although this was very

[h] Before the exhibition opened the room was purchased by Charles Lang Freer, an American industrialist and Whistler collector who had already acquired the *Princesse*, and it was subsequently shipped to America for re-erection at Freer's house in Detroit. Freer bequeathed the room to the American nation and after his death in 1919 it was removed to Washington, where as an exhibit in the Freer Gallery of Art it was first shown to the public in 1923 (Plate 126b).[71]

destructive, more of the interior decoration remains than has perhaps been recognized hitherto.

The most important feature is the Northumberland House staircase balustrade, which survives intact between the first- and second-floor landings (Plate 105d). The metalwork, which when new was said to have had a purity and richness of colour which 'approaches in no inconsiderable degree, gold', is now rather dulled.[76] Above the second floor the balustrade is original to the house, and of a pattern found elsewhere in Princes Gate (fig. 90). At the top of the stairwell, below the skylight, is a deep plaster frieze richly decorated with ribbons, wreaths and fruit in the manner of the late seventeenth century, which most likely dates from Mrs Watney's time.[i]

Throughout the common areas pilasters, friezes, ceiling beams and door architraves decorated with arabesques are all remnants of George & Yeates's work of the 1890s. Theirs too is the black-and-white marble paving in the hall and the wood-and-glass screen dividing the hall from the vestibule. Most remarkably, the Renaissance-style marble fountain and basin set within an arched alcove has been preserved. Formerly part of the decoration of Mrs Watney's hall, it has now been incorporated into the ground-floor flat. The pretty painted panels in the lift are probably another legacy of the Watney years. Outside, the garden terrace retains George & Yeates's fountain and some of their stone walls.

On the first floor, Norman Shaw's ceilings remain largely intact (though partly concealed, and with the wooden ribs painted white), and some of his walnut doorcases and sets of double doors have survived. In the former east salon Leyland's Italian stone chimneypiece with flanking herms is another survivor.

Of No. 49's most celebrated interior not a shred remains *in situ*, and all traces of its successor have been obliterated. Stripped of decoration, and with a lowered ceiling, this once-famous room has been rendered completely anonymous (Plate 101c).

No. 52 Princes Gate

The first occupants were Thomas Eustace Smith, Tyneside shipbuilder, 'advanced Liberal' MP and art collector, and his aesthetic wife Mary ('Eustacia' to her friends). They moved here in 1873 from No. 28 Princes Gardens.[77] Two or three years later, having bought the house on a long lease from Freake,[78] they commissioned the architect George Aitchison to decorate it in a manner commensurate with their social and artistic aspirations. The results were a brilliant success. To Whistler, working on Frederick Leyland's dining-room at No. 49, Aitchison's decorations were, if not a direct challenge to his creativity, at least a yardstick against which to measure his own achievement. Writing to Leyland in September 1876 of the emerging

'Peacock Room', he could boast there was nothing in London to match it and 'Mrs Eustace Smith is wiped out utterly!'[79] Subsequent depredations and many years of institutional occupation have taken their toll, but a surprising amount of Aitchison's décor remains. It confirms the impression of refinement and delicacy conveyed by his surviving drawings (Plate 120a–c).

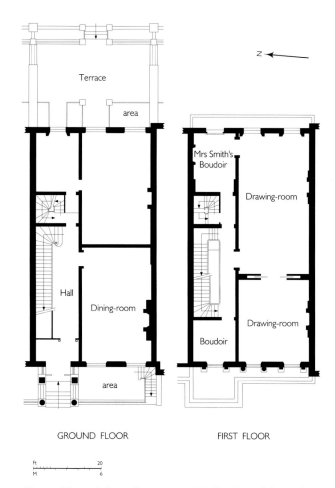

Fig. 94. No. 52 Princes Gate, plans. C. J. Freake, builder, *c.*1869. Room-names are those used by the first occupants, Mr and Mrs Eustace Smith

On the ground floor Aitchison's chief work was the decoration of the dining-room overlooking Exhibition Road, the scene of a memorable dinner recalled long afterwards by the American novelist Julian Hawthorne (son of Nathaniel). Among those also present on that occasion were Hawthorne's compatriot Henry James, the Liberal politician Sir Charles Dilke, and the painter Frederic Leighton. The principal features of the room were a large sideboard, against the east wall, and on the south wall a massive chimneypiece flanked by low bookcases (which

[i] An identical frieze at No. 8 Carlton House Terrace (now removed) appears to date from the 1890s, when the staircase there was remodelled for Earl Brownlow.

presumably carried on round the rest of the room or gave way to a dado of the same height). The upper parts of the walls were coloured pale green, with a delicate pattern of trailing foliage, and finished with a gilded floral frieze below a gilded cornice. Two large paintings by Aitchison's friend and colleague Thomas Armstrong were displayed in this room, both 'let into' the wall. One was *Woman with Calla Lilies*, now in the Laing Art Gallery.[80]

Of all this the only remnant still *in situ* is the walnut chimneypiece (Plate 104a), a classical pedimented structure that Hawthorne mistook for a second sideboard. In its centre, now replaced by a mirror, was a majolica relief of the Madonna and Child in the style of della Robbia, 'ravished' by the Smiths from a church in Italy (so Hawthorne was informed by Leighton). Either side of the mirror are inlaid figures of Pomona and Picus, with quotations from Horace: IMPVNE LICEBIT ÆSTIVAM SERMONE BENIGNO TENDERE NOCTEM and DONA PRÆSENTIS CAPE LÆTVS HORÆ ET LINQVE SEVERA.[j] The sideboard – 'looks like an organ', remarked Leighton – was also in classical style, though with a more Grecian flavour, and probably also of walnut.[81]

In a memoir of Thomas Armstrong the dining-room frieze – hardly the most striking feature of the decorations – is credited to Leighton. It is possible, however, that the writer was confusing his recollections of this room with Mrs Smith's boudoir on the first floor, where there was indeed an eye-catching frieze, though not by Leighton (see below). The Smiths knew Leighton well and may have consulted him over their plans. They owned a number of his pictures, including *Venus Disrobing for the Bath*, for which Mrs Smith claimed to have posed (though only, she insisted, for the feet).[82]

More of Aitchison's work survives on the first floor, where he made much use of inlaid wood in decorating the drawing-rooms and boudoirs. The jewel here was Eustacia's own inner sanctum looking into Princes Gardens (Plate 120b–e) – a scheme composed of reddish-orange walls with flowers picked out in gold, a black wooden dado inlaid with a floral pattern in ivory and mother-of-pearl, and a decorative plaster ceiling with a large central panel of foliage in low relief. The frieze, by Walter Crane, depicted 'white cockatoos with lemon and orange crests on a gold ground, connected by fanciful scroll-work in bronze green and red'. (Sir) Edward J. Poynter, who moved to a house in Knightsbridge at about this time, lent Crane his studio in Shepherd's Bush to 'work out' the frieze. This was the first time Crane had worked with Aitchison and it led to further collaborations elsewhere, including the Arab Hall in Leighton's house (1877–9). None of the painted decoration survives, but the dado remains intact, as do the inlaid doors and the pierced window shutters. Other survivals are the ceiling and the finely detailed Renaissance-style

chimneypiece carved in black marble (Plate 104c). The 'rose-and-scroll' and 'griffin' De Morgan tiles in the fireplace cheeks are doubtless original (Plate 121c).[83]

In the small front boudoir the only traces of Aitchison's scheme are the inlaid black window-shutters and a characteristic black-and-white frieze with ivory inlay.

The drawing-rooms at No. 52 originally communicated by means of sliding doors. These still exist, but the rooms are now cut off from each other by a passage formed across the rear room to give access from the landing to a new doorway into No. 53. For the larger room, at the back, Aitchison designed another inlaid floral dado, the sliding doors being embellished on this side with flower patterns inlaid in wood and mother-of-pearl (Plate 121a–b). The upper parts of the wall, long since redecorated, were coloured dull gold, with a frieze of arabesques and griffins, and had several large canvases inset (including the *Venus Disrobing*). The other surviving features of Aitchison's are the decorative plaster ceiling, with sunflowers in the border panels, and a plain black marble chimneypiece.[84]

In the front drawing-room the dado (with burr walnut panels) is much plainer, and the sliding doors on this side are unadorned. Some liveliness is provided by a plaster frieze of dolphins, which may originally have been coloured (Plate 104b). Twenty years later Aitchison produced a similar dolphin frieze for Leighton House, which was intended to be coloured, but on Leighton's instructions was painted white.[85]

The Smiths' tenure of No. 52 was ended abruptly when they were caught up in the trammels of the Crawford divorce case of 1886, in which Sir Charles Dilke was cited as co-respondent – Mrs Crawford being one of the Smiths' daughters. Bizarrely, the verdict appeared to exonerate Dilke of having committed adultery, while accepting Mrs Crawford's own admission of guilt. Especially embarrassing was the mention of Dilke's earlier indiscretions with Eustacia herself. His political ambitions were effectively ended by the scandal, and the Smiths fled into exile in Algiers. In 1887 they sold No. 52 and much of its contents to Alexander Henderson, a City financier with wide business interests, who was created Baron Faringdon in 1916.[86]

Henderson gave up No. 52 about 1904, having removed the della Robbia altar-piece from the dining-room to his country house, Buscot Park, where it remains.[k]

Redevelopment and Social Change

Increasingly unsuited to the needs of post-war society, several of the houses on the Freake estate were converted to high-class apartments or taken over by foreign legations in the 1920s and '30s. In the late 1930s a group of five was

[j] 'We will not be censured if we spend the summer night in pleasant conversation' (*Epistles*, book 1, epistle 5), and 'Gladly seize the gift of the present hour and lay aside serious matters' (*Odes*, book 3, ode 8).

[k] Also in the Faringdon Collection at Buscot are two of Eustace Smith's most important Pre-Raphaelite paintings: D. G. Rossetti's *Pandora* and G. F. Watts's *The Wife of Pygmalion*.

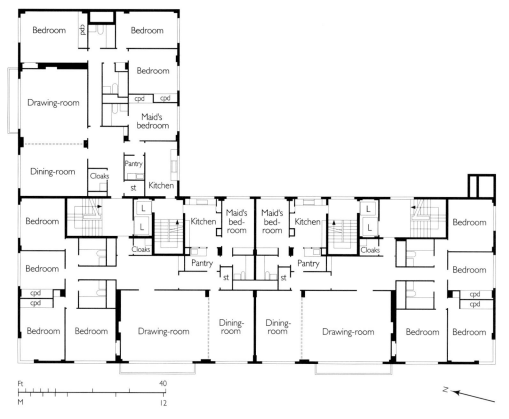

Fig. 95. Nos 59–63 Princes Gate, typical floor-plan. Adie, Button & Partners, architects, 1937–8

replaced by a purpose-built block of flats (Nos 59–63 Princes Gate). This trend continued after the Second World War, with the building of another large apartment block, Montrose Court, and most of the remaining houses sub-divided or turned over to institutional use. In the early 1960s a Mormon church was built on the site of Nos 64–68 Princes Gate.[1]

By the early 1950s only two or three houses in Princes Gate remained single dwellings. No. 56, the residence and private gallery of the art collector Count Antoine Seilern, who died in 1978, was probably the last: it is now in the occupation of an American university. Foreign cultural and academic bodies today occupy many of the surviving houses in Princes Gate. In Princes Gardens institutionalization has had a drastic impact on the building fabric, many of the original houses having been pulled down for redevelopment by Imperial College.

Nos 59–63 Princes Gate

This strikingly clean-cut apartment block (Plate 110a) was erected in 1937–8 to the designs of Adie, Button & Partners.[87] Built of reinforced concrete faced monolithically in reconstituted Portland stone and with 'wrap-around'

corner windows, it much resembles their contemporary Athenaeum Court in Piccadilly. Adie and Button were initially involved in the project, which dated back to 1933, as interior consultants. In April 1935 they took over as the architects from Gordon Jeeves, their Modernist design superseding his more traditional scheme in brick and stone or stucco. The main contractor was E. H. Burgess Ltd, the Trussed Concrete Steel Company Ltd acting as reinforced-concrete engineers.

It was the developers' intention to cover the site more densely, but the London County Council objected to the proposed wing alongside Princes Gate Mews. The resultant L-shaped block is ten full storeys high, over two basement levels, and contains three flats to a floor, with balconies facing Exhibition Road. To the rear is a paved terrace garden with a summer-house. The upper basement was designed as a car-park (entered from the mews) and store-rooms. The lower level was fitted up as a bomb- and gas-proof air-raid shelter, with air-locks, a decontamination chamber and provision for chemical toilets and emergency water and power supplies: proof of 'how the atavistic ideals of twentieth-century nationalism are driving us back to the dungeons and fastnesses of our mediaeval ancestors'.[88] This facility was conceived in order to utilize the

---

[1] Described in *Survey of London*, volume XXXVIII, page 356.

deep excavation necessitated by the site.

The original windows, by Crittall, were metal casements and (opening on to the balconies) sliding-folding doors.

The individual flats were planned with three or four bedrooms, two bathrooms, maid's quarters, and a large reception area divided by sliding doors into living- and dining-rooms (fig. 95, Plate 111a). Built-in wardrobes were provided in the bedrooms, and the kitchens were 'beautifully fitted with a most impressive array of drawers and cupboards, cellulosed white and having chromium handles'.[89] There was, however, no attempt at doctrinaire Modernism, and the main entrance halls to the block were conservatively decorated in Georgian style, with fibrous plaster mouldings and gilded capitals (Plate 111b).

Past residents of the flats include the thermodynamics expert Sir A. C. Glyn Egerton, professor of chemical technology at Imperial College. The Czechoslovak Prime Minister Eduard Beneš had offices in the building during the Second World War.

Montrose Court

In 1956 most of the original houses at Nos 32–43 Princes Gate were demolished for the building of Montrose Court.[90] This new development, a row of five eight-storey blocks of flats fronting Exhibition Road, and two ranges of four four-bedroom houses at the rear, was designed by Bowden, Son & Partners for Finborough Properties Ltd.[91]

The flats, of reinforced concrete clad in brick and cement render, were built by John Laing & Son, the first four blocks in 1957–8. Construction of the central block, delayed while No. 37 Princes Gate remained standing, was carried out in 1959–61 under the supervision of Clifford Culpin & Partners, architects.

The houses were built by Trollope & Sons in 1958–9. Separated from the flats by a service road, they occupy the former communal garden to the old buildings. Something of a surprise in central London, they are low and chalet-like, with pitched roofs and brick walls with Tyrolean render on the upper storey.

Various alterations and additions to Montrose Court, including penthouses over the flats, were made in 1997–8 (William Gower & Partners, architects).

Imperial College and the redevelopment of Princes Gardens

Almost all the houses in Princes Gardens were vacated during the Second World War, and although only a few suffered bomb-damage (Nos 33–35 alone being 'total losses'), requisitioning and neglect left them generally dilapidated. Wartime use as hostels and offices had altered the character of the area, and the big old houses now seemed obsolescent.

London County Council planners had visions of a National Science Centre in the Exhibition Road area, taking in the site of Princes Gardens, where buildings 'of great national importance' would be erected.[92] Nothing was to come of this, but the idea was to prove prescient. In the meantime, some sort of redevelopment seemed desirable, and in 1954–5 at least two schemes were in contemplation.

One was a straightforward conversion of the houses to flats, for which Lord Rendlesham obtained an agreement for a lease from the Freake Estate.[93] The other, by Wells Coates, would have entailed the demolition of all the existing buildings, apart from a few houses on the south side. Coates proposed two slab-blocks (135ft and 168ft long), aligned north–south, the internal layout of which was based on his pre-war flats in Palace Gate. They would have been built across the central garden, with the longer block

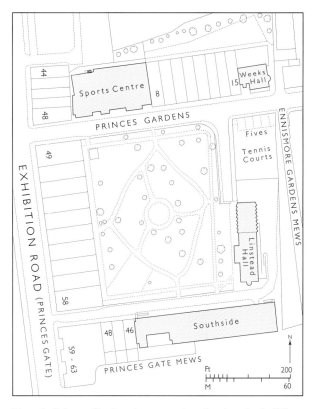

Fig. 96. Princes Gardens in 1991: plan showing the buildings erected for Imperial College

straddling the roadway on the north side. Most of the south side of the square would have been replaced by four-storey terraced houses.[94]

The availability of Princes Gardens for redevelopment coincided with the enlargement of the Imperial College of Science and Technology under a government initiative to improve training for industry, part of the general post-war expansion of higher education. Between 1953 and 1962 the college received some £17,000,000, mainly to fund building works, and saw its student roll almost double to 3,000.[95]

Attention was focused initially on the rebuilding of the congested 'island site' between Prince Consort Road and Imperial College Road, where the available development space was reduced by the decision to preserve T. E. Coll-cutt's Imperial Institute tower. A substantial new site had to be found if the necessary halls of residence and common rooms were to be provided. Just across the road from Imperial College, the six acres of Princes Gardens must have seemed like a campus-in-waiting. The Freake Estate was unwilling to allow partial redevelopment, which might have depressed the value of the remaining houses, and in March 1956 the College agreed to take all three sides on a 199-year building lease.[96m]

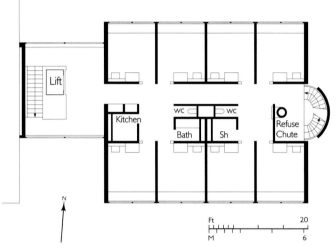

Fig. 97. Imperial College, Princes Gardens. Weeks Hall, typical floor-plan with eight study bedrooms. Richard Sheppard, Robson & Partners, architects, 1958–9

Norman & Dawbarn, the College's architects, were too heavily involved with work on the island site, and with building the BBC Television Centre at White City, to take on the new development. Accordingly, another firm was sought and in August 1956 Richard Sheppard, Robson & Partners were given the commission. By December the outlines had been agreed with the college planning committee, headed by the new Rector, Sir Patrick Linstead.[97]

The scheme provided for three eleven-storey ranges, comprising fourteen halls of residence, set round the square garden in the traditional collegiate manner (Plate 106c).

Refectories and common rooms were to be concentrated within the south block, scheduled to be developed first, while the northern range, the intended final stage, was to include an underground sports centre.

The new buildings, of reinforced-concrete cross-wall and slab-floor construction clad in precast concrete sections, were based on a module or 'set' of rooms, one set comprising eight study bedrooms, with bathroom, shower-room, and water-closets, served by an internal staircase.

Each hall of residence was to be built up from three-storey stacks of these sets, each stack having its own open-plan 'gallery' floor for communal recreational and service facilities. Within the individual halls, the planning was contrived to foster social contacts and a 'meaningful communal life'.[98]

Contemporary reaction to the scheme was generally favourable. The *Architects' Journal* welcomed 'the first attempt we have seen to interpret the collegiate idea of student accommodation in an acceptable, twentieth-century, architecture'. The *Spectator*, noting parallels between its 'boldly plastic architecture' and Le Corbusier's Pavillon Suisse of 1932 for the Paris University City, saw it as an 'exercise of symphonic complexity'. The *Builder*, however, was concerned at the 'shut-in feeling' conveyed by the architects' perspective exhibited at the Royal Academy summer show.[99] In the event, financial constraints obliged the College to develop the site piecemeal and not one side has been finished according to the original vision (fig. 96).

As it happened, the first building to be erected, **Weeks Hall** (Plate 97c), was an addition to the planned ensemble. Early in 1957 the engineering firm Vickers offered the College £150,000 to pay for a hall of residence. As no independent site was available, it was decided to accommodate the extra building at the eastern end of the proposed northern range (which was never built), where it was to act as a visual 'stop'. Named after Lord Weeks, the former chairman of Vickers, the hall was erected in 1958–9 by Tersons Ltd, for £126,000, and formally opened in September 1959.[100]

Vickers had asked that the building should have an individual character of its own, while relating to the character of the rest of the development. The result (fig. 97, Plate 97c) is a vertically arranged version of the blocks already planned, using a broadly similar modular set of eight rooms (though without an internal staircase). There are eight floors of study bedrooms and a warden's penthouse flat. Under the terms of Vickers' gift, the premises were to be made available to the company for conferences during student vacations, and a 50-seat assembly room was accordingly provided on the ground floor (Plate 107c).

In construction and finish, the building was closely modelled on the intended long ranges. Indeed, Weeks Hall became a 'testing-ground' for the detailed design of the later buildings. It is clad in precast concrete sections mostly faced with Cornish granite aggregate. Lighter-coloured Norwegian quartz aggregate is used for facing the sill units and the external secondary staircase on the eastern flank of the building. Where exposed to view, the concrete structure is toned with Cornish Lee Moor sand in the mix. The window frames of the study bedrooms are of teak, untreated externally; other windows have painted metal frames. On the west side is a fully glazed tower containing the main stairs and lift, intended as the buffer between the building

[m] Nos 49–58 Princes Gate, the backs of which comprise the fourth side of the square, were not included in the proposed redevelopment, although Imperial College did express an interest in the houses and has since taken over Nos 52 and 53.

and the proposed range to the west. The precast, semi-elliptical escape staircase on the east side was later adopted as the pattern for the access staircases in the south and east blocks.

Inside, the main structural walls were left in their board-marked state (the subject of some carping by a few early users of the building). In the study bedrooms the walls were plastered and white-painted, with some fitted furniture and a full-length window-seat finished in terrazzo.[101]

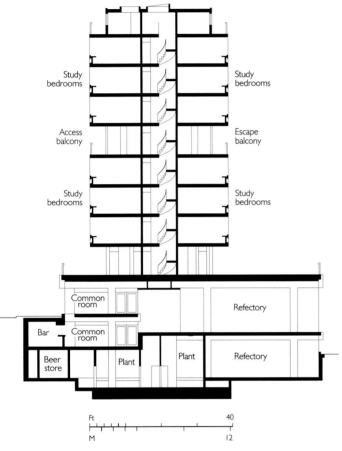

Fig. 98. Imperial College, Princes Gardens. Southside halls, section looking east. Richard Sheppard, Robson & Partners, architects, 1960–3

Weeks Hall was followed in 1960–3 by **Southside**, an eleven-storey range containing four halls of residence (Falmouth, Tizzard, Keogh and Selkirk), refectories, kitchens, bars and common rooms (fig. 98, Plate 106a–b). Built by Wilson Lovatt & Sons, and formally opened in October 1963, it takes up most of the south side. (The remaining houses, Nos 46–48, occupy the site of a now-abandoned extension.) As at Weeks Hall, the exterior is faced with panels of Cornish and Norwegian quartz aggregate, and the predominating interior finish is *béton brut*, 'well offset by warm, heavy timber ceilings, rich joinery, ample soft furniture and carpets' (Plate 107b).[102]

Two more buildings were erected in the later 1960s, both by Higgs & Hill to Sheppard, Robson's designs. **Linstead Hall**, built in 1966–8 as the first phase of the east-side development, carries on the architectural idiom established by Weeks Hall and Southside (Plate 106a). On the north side, the **Sports Centre** (1967–8), constructed within the basement space of the former Nos 1–7, was designed as the footing for further halls of residence, which have yet to be built.[103]

In 1973 Norman & Dawbarn, who had taken over from Sheppard, Robson as architects for the site, produced an ambitious three-phase plan for the completion of the north and east sides, beginning with a new hall over the sports centre.[104] The granting of Listed Building status to Nos 8–15 Princes Gardens, and local opposition to the height of the proposed buildings, necessitated considerable modifications. When construction work eventually began, in August 1978, it was confined to a relatively modest extension to Linstead Hall (Plate 107a), paid for by an anonymous benefaction. Built by Walter Lawrence & Sons Ltd, and completed in 1980, this comprises four storeys of living accommodation over a glazed semi-basement. The reinforced-concrete structure is clad in precast concrete panels faced with white calcium-silicate brick. All the study bedrooms along the 'serrated' main façade are angled to face south-west.[105] The rest of the east side remains undeveloped and is currently occupied by tennis and fives courts.

Now that the original Corbusian concept has been abandoned, the redevelopment of Princes Gardens seems set to continue incrementally as finances permit, and architecturally as the fashion of the day dictates. The issue of conservation, hardly in evidence in the 1950s, now looms large as a factor in the planning process. In 1992 a development scheme for the entire South Kensington campus was drawn up by Foster and Partners, and a number of new buildings have now been projected.

At the time of writing (2000) plans include the construction of additional living accommodation on the north and east sides. On the north side the proposed range, to be built over the existing sports centre, will 'echo' Freake's houses adjoining. It is also intended to build five mews-houses adjacent to Southside in Princes Gate Mews. They will be in a style 'sympathetic' to the 1960s block.[106]

Some Former Residents

This list excludes occupants mentioned above.

Princes Gate (Nos 32–43 and 59–68 demolished)

No. 30 Henry Huth, merchant banker and bibliophile
No. 31 Sir (William) Charles Wright, industrialist, chairman of Baldwins Ltd
No. 32 David Mocatta, architect; Robert Baden-Powell, founder of the Boy Scouts
No. 33 Henry William Ferdinand Bölckow, ironmaster, MP and art collector

No. 39 Lieut.-Col. Alexander Leith Wyllie, industrialist, chairman of the RSPCA; Sir Stuart Campbell, senior executive at *The Times* and *Daily Mail*; Charles Theodore te Water, South African diplomatist

No. 44 Sir Robert Elliott-Cooper, civil engineer

No. 46 Ernest Noel, chairman of the Artisans' Dwellings Company

No. 47 Walter Victor Hutchinson, publisher

No. 51 Alexander Brogden, industrialist and MP; (Sir) James Timmins Chance, glassmaker

No. 53 Earl Carrington, subsequently 1st Marquess of Lincolnshire, politician

No. 55 Sir Frank Hillyard Newnes, 2nd Bart, publisher and MP

No. 56 Sir Bernhard Samuelson, 1st Bart, industrialist and politician (previously at No. 69 Princes Gate)

No. 57 Sir (James John) Trevor Lawrence, 2nd Bart, MP, President of the Royal Horticultural Society

No. 59 Frank (Francis Augustus) Bevan, banker (previously at No. 72)

No. 60 Sir James Mills, Chairman of the Union Steamship Company of New Zealand

No. 62 Henry John Selwin-Ibbetson, 1st Baron Rookwood, politician

No. 65 Viscount Bury (later 7th Earl of Albemarle), politician

No. 69 see No. 56

No. 70 (Sir) Everard Alexander Hambro, merchant banker

No. 71 Hugh Colin Smith, Governor of the Bank of England; Sir Clement Anderson Montague Barlow, politician, chairman of Sothebys

No. 72 (see also No. 59) Lord Acton, historian; Joseph Chamberlain was briefly Acton's tenant here

Princes Gardens *(all except Nos 8–15 and 46–48 demolished)*

No. 2 Arthur Pease, industrialist and MP

No. 3 Sir John Barnard Byles, lawyer, author of *Byles on Bills*

No. 4 Sir George Markham Giffard, Lord Justice of Appeal; Rt Hon. Sir Charles Ernest Swann, 1st Bart, politician; Sir James Currie, educationist

No. 5 Clementina, Lady Hawarden, wife of 4th Viscount Hawarden, one of the earliest woman photographers and the first to achieve critical recognition (her studio and darkroom were on the first floor); Maj. Edward Howard Thornbrough Parsons, Chief Constable, Metropolitan Police

No. 7 Viscount Emlyn, later 3rd Earl of Cawdor, First Lord of the Admiralty, chairman of the Great Western Railway

No. 10 Peter Blackburn, Lord of the Treasury, chairman of the Edinburgh and Glasgow Railway

No. 11 Sir Henry Singer Keating, judge

No. 12 Sir William Erle, judge

No. 13 Sir George William Allen, founder of *Allahabad Pioneer* and *Civil and Military Gazette*; John Brownlee Lonsdale, later 1st Baron Armaghdale, Irish Unionist politician

No. 16 Baron Monk Bretton, Chairman of the London County Council

No. 17 Hugh Culling Eardley Childers, politician

No. 18 (Sir) Joseph Whitwell Pease, industrialist and MP, first Quaker to accept an honour from the Crown; William Rathbone, nursing reformer and politician; Sir Charles John Darling (later Lord Darling), judge

No. 19 Earl Jellicoe, Admiral of the Fleet

No. 20 Sir Daniel Cooper, 1st Bart, first Speaker of the New South Wales legislative assembly

No. 22 Sir Bartle Frere, colonial administrator and statesman; General Sir Richard Harrison, veteran of the Siege of Lucknow; Ossian Donner, Finnish diplomat and industrialist

No. 25 Walter Sydney Sichel, writer

No. 26 Sir Samuel Cunard, 1st Bart, shipowner

No. 27 Lieut.-Gen. Sir Edward Macarthur, Peninsular War veteran, acting Governor of Victoria

No. 32 Sir Stuart Alexander Donaldson, Australian businessman and statesman; Field Marshal the Earl of Cavan, Chief of the Imperial General Staff

No. 35 Sir Robert Williams, 1st Bart, engineer and colleague of Cecil Rhodes

No. 36 Gen. James Robertson Craufurd, Brigade of Guards commander in the Crimea

No. 39 Henry Austin Bruce, 1st Baron Aberdare of Duffryn, statesman

No. 40 Joseph Chamberlain and his son Austen, statesmen

No. 42 Marcus Gervais Beresford, Archbishop of Armagh

No. 44 Sir George Houstoun Reid, Australian Prime Minister

References

ABBREVIATIONS

AJ	*Architects' Journal*
AR	*Architectural Review*
B	*The Builder*, from 1966 *Building*
BAL	British Architectural Library, Royal Institute of British Architects
BL	British Library
BN	*Building News*
CERC	Church of England Record Centre
Chancellor	E. Beresford Chancellor, *Knightsbridge and Belgravia: Their History, Topography, and Famous Inhabitants*, 1909
Colvin	Howard Colvin, *A Biographical Dictionary of British Architects 1600–1840*, 3rd edn, 1995
Davis	Henry George Davis, *The Memorials of the Hamlet of Knightsbridge*, ed. Charles Davis, 1859
DNB	*Dictionary of National Biography*
DSR	District Surveyors' Returns in London Metropolitan Archives
GEC	*The Complete Peerage*, ed. G.E.C., 1910–59
GL	Guildhall Library
ICST	Imperial College of Science and Technology
ILN	*Illustrated London News*
KLS	Royal Borough of Kensington & Chelsea, Education and Libraries, Kensington Local Studies
LCC	London County Council
LMA	London Metropolitan Archives
MBW	Metropolitan Board of Works
MDR	Middlesex Deeds Registry, London Metropolitan Archives
NAL	National Art Library, Victoria & Albert Museum
NMR	National Monuments Record
OS	Ordnance Survey maps of London, 1:1056
POD	*Post Office Directories*
PP	*Parliamentary Papers*
PRO	Public Record Office
RB	Ratebooks
RO	Record Office
V&A	Victoria and Albert Museum
WA	Westminster Abbey Muniment Room
WBC	Westminster City Council, Building Control and Planning records
WCA	Westminster City Archives

Introduction

pp.1–17

1. *B*, 31 Oct 1857, p.629.
2. Davis, pp.51,244.
3. Reginald Colby, 'Knightsbridge: A London Hamlet', in *Country Life*, 18 Nov 1965, p.1340.
4. Correspondence printed in *The Blackmailing of the Chancellor*, ed. Kenneth Bourne, 1975.
5. *BN*, 26 Sept 1890, p.450.
6. Thomas Allen, *A New History of London and Westminster*, 1836, p.397.
7. *An Account of the Occasion and Manner of Erecting the Hospital at Lanesborough House ...*, 1733.
8. KLS, newspaper cutting 267e (1764).
9. Lord Hervey's Memoirs, quoted by Davis, p.25.
10. Newspaper cutting, quoted in James Ayres, *Building the Georgian City*, 1998, p.95.
11. Davis, p.30.
12. 7 Geo 4, c.cxlii, public and general.
13. Allen, *op.cit.*, p.396.
14. *Morning Chronicle*, 23 May 1799, cited in Edward Walford, *Old and New London*, Vol.V, 1897, p.17: Davis, p.27.
15. *London*, ed. Charles Knight, Vol. I, 1841, p.247.
16. CERC, Church Commissioners' file 15834/2.
17. Trevor May, *Gondolas and Growlers: The History of the London Horse Cab*, 1995, p.110: *B*, 20 Jan 1872, p.52.
18. PRO, IR58/91018/54.
19. Harold P. Clunn, *The Face of London*, 1932, pp.325–6,330,334.
20. *The World*, 28 Oct 1793.
21. *Ibid.*, 16 Aug 1791.
22. *B*, 11 June 1853, p.374.
23. *Ibid.*, 14 Jan 1871, p.25.
24. *Ibid.*, 6 Jan 1872, p.14; 14 Jan 1871, p.25.
25. Clunn, *op.cit.*, p.326.
26. *B*, 11 March 1876, p.238.
27. Davis, p.163.
28. Ethel M. Richardson, *The Story of All Saints Ennismore Gardens (Knightsbridge)*, n.d. [*c.*1935], p.51.
29. MBW *Mins*, 9 Nov 1877, p.533.
30. *BN*, 27 May 1898, p.744.
31. *B*, 25 July 1857, p.422.
32. *Letters of The Right Hon. Sir George Cornewall Lewis, Bart, to various Friends*, ed. Rev. Sir Gilbert Frankland Lewis, Bart, 1870, p.234: *Life of John, Lord Campbell, Lord High Chancellor of Great Britain*, ed. Hon. Mrs Hardcastle, 1881, p.289: information from the diaries of Sir George Cornwall Lewis, kindly communicated by Rev. Dr R.W.D. Fenn.
33. *B*, 18 Feb 1854, p.90.
34. Denis Kilcommons, *Matilda's Game*, 1992, p.257.
35. *B*, 2 June 1911, p.684.
36. WCA, Acc.1004/1.
37. *DNB*.
38. *Perfect Occurrences of Every Daie iournall in Parliament*, 7 May 1647, p.144 (BL, Thomason Tracts, E/386/8): Leslie Hotson, *The Commonwealth and Restoration Stage*, Cambridge, Mass., 1928, pp.23,28.
39. Davis, p.30.

CHAPTER I (pp.19–36)

Knightsbridge: South Side

1. WA, Register Books; WAM 17285: Buckinghamshire RO, D/LO/4/2; D/LO/6/9/27.
2. WA, Register Book xxv, ff.76–7; xxvi, ff.199–200; xxix, ff.277–8.
3. Davis, pp.214–15.
4. WA, WAM 17285; WAM 52247; Register Book xx, ff.441–3; xxiv, f.11.

5. WA, WAM 66064; Register Book LIV, ff.248–50; LVI, 2nd sequence, ff.3–5, 10–12.

6. RB: WA, WAM 52636: Davis, pp.146–7: R. Horwood, *Plan of the Cities of London and Westminster . . .*, 1792–9 edn.

7. MDR 1833/3/675.

8. NMR, photo AA63/06632: *POD*.

9. RB: LMA, WCS/71, p.97; WCS/73, pp.69–70.

10. *POD*: NMR, hospitals' file 10029: Anthony Blee, 'Report on St George's Hospital Site for The Sir Basil Spence Partnership', 1987, p.8.

11. WA, Register Book LII, ff.188–91; LVI, 2nd sequence, ff.10–12; WAM 66060: Davis, p.185: RB.

12. WA, WAM 66064; Register Book LIV, ff.248–50; LVI, 2nd sequence, ff.10–12; LVIII, f.181; LX, f.232: Davis, p.187.

13. Flintshire RO, Glynne–Gladstone MS 722.

14. MDR 1833/5/102–4: BL, Add.MS 44137 (Gladstone Papers), vol.LII, ff.16, 17.

15. Flintshire RO, Glynne–Gladstone MS 1527, extracts from affidavits by W.B.Smythe, 13 Nov 1863 and 24 May 1864.

16. WA, Register Book LXII, ff.97–9.

17. Flintshire RO, Glynne–Gladstone MS 1527, J.Litton to W.E.G., 15 Feb 1867; *The Architect's, Engineer's, and Building-Trades' Directory*, 1868: *POD*.

18. DSR 1847/426: *B*, 20 Nov 1847, p.560: MDR 1848/10/564–7; 1849/3/837; 1849/7/423; 1851/3/963: *Companion to the Almanac . . . for 1849*, p.249.

19. MDR 1850/11/49; 1857/10/323; 1858/3/502–6.

20. *B*, 1 Dec 1849, p.574: *BN*, 2 Jan 1857, p.21; 4 Sept 1857, p.931.

21. *BN*, 2 Jan 1857, p.21; 4 Sept 1857, p.931; 11 Dec 1857, p.1299.

22. MBW *Mins*, 27 Jan 1860, p.74: MDR 1861/8/640.

23. *POD*.

24. Colvin, p.335: *POD*: LMA, GLC/AR/BR/06/55907.

25. LMA, GLC/AR/BR/22/TP/14786: *Architect & Building News*, 22 Oct 1937, p.103.

26. See Christopher Wilk, 'Who was Betty Joel?', in *Apollo*, July 1995, pp.7–11.

27. *BN*, 2 Jan 1857, p.21; 11 Dec 1857, p.1299: MDR 1856/10/554; 1857/10/323: *POD*.

28. PRO, BT31/33968/462: MDR 1863/15/986–8.

29. *The Caterer and Hotel-Keeper's Gazette*, 16 Sept 1907, p.388.

30. *The Times*, 2 Aug 1864, p.7e: *B*, 2 Sept 1864, p.660: MBW *Mins*, 2 Dec 1864, p.1194; 24 March 1865, p.398; 22 Sept 1865, p.1032: *London: A Complete Guide to the Leading Hotels, Places of Amusement* (published by Henry Herbert, London), 1872, p.3.

31. *London: A Complete Guide to the Leading Hotels . . .*, 1872, p.3.

32. Derek Taylor and David Bush, *The Golden Age of British Hotels*, 1974, p.70.

33. *The Times*, 2 Nov 1897, p.12e–f; 25 March 1898, p.14c; 8 Aug 1900, p.11f.

34. *The Caterer and Hotel-Keeper's Gazette*, 16 Sept 1907, p.388: James Bone, *London Echoing*, 1948, p.102.

35. James Douet, *British Barracks 1600–1914*, 1998, p.62.

36. Davis, p.196: KLS, Deeds 3781 (bundle 6): PRO, WO55/2613.

37. *The Times*, 19 Oct 1789, p.3c; 28 Oct 1789, p.3c.

38. PRO, WORK16/434; WO40/5.

39. PRO, WO55/741: Davis, pp.196–7.

40. WCA, Grosvenor Estate Trustees Minute Books, 1049/5/13, pp.427, 444–5, 524; 1049/5/14, p.77: *B*, 5 March 1859, p.179.

41. *The Times*, 24 March 1952, p.2d.

42. *ILN*, 6 Aug 1842, p.204.

43. *Morning Post*, 21 June 1842, p.6.

44. W.B.Langdon, *A Descriptive Catalogue of the Chinese Collection*, 1844 edn, p.15.

45. The literature on the Chinese Collection and its successors is considerable. The following were extensively drawn on for this account – Richard D.Altick, *The Shows of London*, 1978: Elizabeth Phillips, 'A Pagoda in Knightsbridge', in *The Journal of Pre-Raphaelite Studies*, vol.iv, no.2, 1984, (New Hampshire), pp.37–42: and Helen Saxbee, 'An Orient Exhibited. The Exhibition of the Chinese Collection in England in the 1840s', RCA PhD thesis, 1990 (copy in NAL). Infor-

mation about W.B.Langdon was provided by his great-grand-daughters, Jeanette Parsons and Nancy McKay. See also Alan Cox, 'Pagoda and Celestial Palace', in *Westminster History Review 3*, 1999, pp.19–24.

46. *Morning Post*, 21 June 1842, p.6: LMA, MBW/OW/VP/3.

47. *ILN*, 6 Aug 1842, pp.204–5: *The Spectator*, 25 June 1842, p.616: George Mogridge, *Old Humphrey's Walks in London and Its Neighbourhood*, 1842, p.328.

48. *ILN*, 6 Aug 1842, p.205.

49. Langdon, *op.cit.*, 1844 edn, p.17.

50. *ILN*, 6 Aug 1842, p.205: Jean Gordon Lee, *Philadelphians and the China Trade 1784–1844*, Philadelphia Museum of Art, 1984, p.15: John Timbs, *Curiosities of London*, 1855 edn, p.432.

51. *The Times*, 9 Aug 1854, p.12d.

52. Lee, *op.cit.*, p.17: Phillips, *op.cit.*, p.38.

53. *The Spectator*, 25 June 1842, p.616: Phillips, *op.cit.*, p.38.

54. *The Spectator*, 2 July 1842, p.635: *The Times*, 13 Nov 1843, p.5d; 11 Dec 1844, p.7e; 26 Oct 1846, p.7c: Lee, *op.cit.*, pp.17–18.

55. *The Times*, 26 Oct 1846, p.7c; 12 Nov 1849, p.7e.

56. LMA, MBW/OW/VP/3: *The Times*, 8 Oct 1956, p.5c.

57. Phillips, *op.cit.*, p.40: copies of catalogues in NAL.

58. Altick, *op.cit.*, pp.290–1.

59. *The Art-Journal*, vol.12, 1850, pp.129, 201: *ILN*, 3 May 1851, p.356: advertisement of Jan 1853 in collection of GL.

60. Charles Dickens, 'The Noble Savage', in *Household Words*, vol.7, 1853, p.168.

61. *ILN*, 4 Feb 1854, p.99: *The Times*, 9 Aug 1854, p.12d: Jenny Elkan, 'Knightsbridge Could Not Go To Mahomet', in *Museums Journal*, vol.89, no.9, Dec 1989, pp.28–31.

62. RB.

63. *Texas Monthly*, June 1992, p.103: *AJ*, 14 Sept 1988, p.76: *B*, 14 Sept 1990, p.11: *The Times*, 7 Nov 1990, p.37: WBC.

64. PRO, CRES35/2653.

65. London Transport Museum, photo U58980.

66. LCC *Mins*, 10 Nov 1908, p.959: WBC.

67. PRO, BT31/4118/129301: Mary Cathcart Borer, *The British Hotel Through the Ages*, 1972, p.230: *POD*.

68. David Leboff, *London Underground Stations*, 1994, p.77.

69. LMA, Acc.3527/227; Acc.3527/285–6.

70. Except where otherwise indicated, this section is based upon PRO, CRES35/2653; CRES38/1556; CRES38/1722.

71. MDR 1847/5/588.

72. *B*, 12 Nov 1870, p.915.

73. *B*, 5 Nov 1870, p.894.

74. *POD*: information provided by the Royal Society for the Prevention of Accidents.

75. Information provided by Francis Baden-Powell.

76. John P.Morraby, 'Collector's Piece', in *AR*, Nov 1964, pp.380–2.

77. LMA, GLC/AR/BR/06/55494: *POD*.

78. WBC: *AR*, Nov 1964, pp.325–7.

79. LMA, GLC/AR/BR/17/29755: WBC.

80. *Daily Telegraph*, 22 Jan 1991, p.23; 29 Jan 1996, p.27: *B*, 2 Feb 1996, p.18: information provided by Hunter & Partners.

81. Account based on – LMA, GLC/AR/BR/13/104552; GLC/AR/BR/13/126636: WBC: *AR*, Sept 1972, p.139: *B*, 31 March 1972, p.41: *Interior Design*, Aug 1972, pp.528–9: *Stone Industries*, July/Aug 1973, p.20: Wendy Arnold, *The Historic Hotels of London*, 1981, p.15.

82. *Brick Builder*, Dec 1937, pp.13–16: *AR*, June 1938, p.300: WBC.

83. Percy J.Edwards, *History of London Street Improvements, 1855–1897*, 1898, p.205.

84. CERC, Church Commissioners' file 45481.

85. *Ibid.*, files 67785, 71092, 80655–65, 80769: *POD*.

86. *BN*, 30 Oct 1903, p.603.

87. *POD*.

88. CERC, Church Commissioners' files 80656, 80663.

89. *Ibid.*, file 67785: *The Caterer and Hotel-Keeper's Gazette*, 15 March 1915, p.133; 15 June 1916, p.225.

90. *POD*.

91. *Ibid.*

92. Buckinghamshire RO, D/LO/4/2 (abstract of title): Davis, p.149.
93. Davis, pp.150–2.
94. RB: 53 Geo III, c.205, loc. and pers: Davis, pp.155–9: Edward Walford, *Old and New London*, 1897 edn, vol.v, p.21.
95. Davis, p.155.
96. MDR 1748/1/69.
97. Illustrated in E.A.Entwisle, *A Literary History of Wallpaper*, 1960, Pl.35.
98. *POD*.
99. GL, MS 11936/298, policy no.454526: RB.
100. MDR 1791/4/189: RB: The Chelsea Society, *Annual Report*, 1956, pp.8–10: Tradecard in British Museum, Banks Collection (ref 30.18).
101. NAL, II.RC.H.10, Robert Barnes, 'Papers in connection with the Early FLOOR CLOTH MANUFACTURE', MS scrapbook, 1857, pp.42, 47: MDR 1799/4/450–1: *The Times*, 5 April 1873, p.5c: *POD*.
102. GL, MS 11936/298, policy no.454526: NAL, II.RC.H.10, Robert Barnes, 'Papers . . .', p.42: 53 Geo III, c.205, loc. and pers: Davis, pp.158–9.
103. Buckinghamshire RO, D/LO/4/2 (abstract of title); D/LO/6/9/27: Journals of the House of Commons, vol.20, reprinted 1803, pp.93, 127, 177.
104. 53 Geo III, c.205, loc. and pers: Buckinghamshire RO, D/LO/6/15/1a and 3: LMA, WCS/66, f.94, 23 April 1819; WCS/PR/60: Grosvenor Estate papers (Chester), Lowndes to Earl Grosvenor, 25 Jan 1810.
105. Hermione Hobhouse, *Thomas Cubitt*, 1971, p.152 *et seq.*
106. Buckinghamshire RO, D/LO/6/15/8, 9.
107. *Ibid.*, D/LO/6/15/9, 20: MDR 1826/1/529: 1832/3/558: Colvin, p.809.
108. MDR 1824/10/650–1; 1829/8/124.
109. Buckinghamshire RO, D/LO/6/15/8: BAL Archives, PoFam/1/2, p.63.
110. Buckinghamshire RO, D/LO/6/15/13(a–b).
111. Alison Adburgham, *Shops and Shopping 1800–1914*, 2nd edn, 1981, p.195.
112. *The Warehousemen and Drapers' Trade Journal*, vol.II, 18 Jan 1873, p.24.
113. RB: *POD*: Census (1891).
114. *The Gentlewoman*, 29 July 1893, p.138.
115. LMA, LCC/AR/BA/4/67, No.162; LCC/AR/BA/4/75, No.116: LCC *Mins*, 20 Jan 1897, p.31; 13 April 1897, p.421: *BN*, 23 Feb 1900, p.263.
116. Sonia Keppel, *Edwardian Daughter*, 1958, p.41.
117. Thelma H.Benjamin, *London Shops and Shopping*, 1934, pp.170–1.
118. LMA, B98/097, Box 3.
119. Maurice Corina, *Fine Silks & Oak Counters: Debenhams 1778–1978*, 1978, p.140: *Daily Telegraph*, 27 Sept 1966, p.1: *The Times*, 27 Sept 1966, p.1: *Harpers & Queen*, Feb 1980, p.74.
120. *The Times*, 27 Sept 1966, p.1; 14 Jan 1967, p.7: *Daily Telegraph*, 21 Feb 1968, p.15; 25 Jan 1969, p.16: *Construction Journal*, 11 March 1971: LMA, GLC/AR/DS/4/45; GLC/AR/DS/4/45–7: Kensington and Chelsea Borough Council, Building Control and Planning records.
121. Quoted in *The Times*, 21 Nov 1984, p.15.
122. *AR*, Sept 1972, p.136: *The Architect*, July 1973, p.38: *AJ*, 4 July 1973, p.7.
123. *Building Design*, 13 July 1973, p.4: *AJ*, 4 July 1973, p.8.
124. This account uses material compiled by Mary Cosh (history of Harvey Nichols) and Lucy Roe (genealogy of the Harvey and Nichols families).
125. Information from the Metropolitan Early Closing Association's Annual Reports, provided by Mary Cosh.
126. DSR 1872/214: *B*, 24 Oct 1874, p.898.
127. *The Warehousemen and Drapers' Trade Journal*, 18 Jan 1873, p.24.
128. LCC *Mins*, 30 June 1891, p.687; 27 Sept 1892, p.795: DSR 1892/125; 1893/167.
129. LMA, B98/097, Box 3.
130. *Ibid.*, GLC/AR/BR/17/035059: KLS, MS 2434.
131. *Who's Who in Royal Warrant Holders*, 1921, pp.239–40.
132. LMA, GLC/AR/BR/17/035059, plans dated 1922–3: *BN*, 26 Jan 1923, p.107: *B*, 16 Feb 1923, p.294: DSR.
133. Harold P. Clunn, *London Rebuilt 1897–1927*, 1927, p.249.
134. LMA, GLC/AR/BR/17/035059: DSR.
135. *The Lady*, 21 June 1934, p.1058; 11 Oct 1934, p.595.
136. LMA, GLC/AR/BR/17/035059.
137. *The Independent*, 3 Oct 1992, weekend section, p.33: *AR*, July 1993, pp.82–5.

CHAPTER II (pp.37–63)

Knightsbridge: North Side

1. Davis, p.163: WA, RCO 33.
2. WA, WAM 12847: Davis, pp.30, 160: Census (1851): RB: *POD*.
3. *BN*, 10 Feb 1882, p.185: PRO, WORK16/692.
4. *B*, 22 Nov 1853, p.737; 6 Jan 1872, p.14: *Pall Mall Gazette*, 12 Dec 1904, p.2.
5. *POD*.
6. Davis, pp.161–2: Censuses (1841–91): *POD*.
7. PRO, WORK16/917.
8. WA, WAM 16298; WAM 16312: *The Evolution of Hospitals in Britain*, ed. F.N.L.Poynter, 1964, pp.29, 34.
9. WA, WAM 16315.
10. WA, WAM 16311; WAM 43659; WAM 52243: Davis, pp.55–6: *The Evolution of Hospitals in Britain*, p.34.
11. WA, WAM 16311; WAM 52243.
12. WA, WAM 52243; Register Books, e.g. xx, f.241.
13. WA, WAM 1630; WAM 52243.
14. BL, Add.MS 5755, quoted in Davis, pp.52–4.
15. WA, WAM 16324.
16. WA, WAM 16316; Register Book XVIII, ff.130–2: Davis, p.57.
17. WA, RCO 33; Register Book XXIX, f.248: CERC, Church Commissioners' file 45481/2.
18. Davis, pp.56–7, 92: WA, WAM 52253A.
19. WA, RCO 33: Davis, pp.58–60.
20. WA, WAM 9409; RCO 33, letter of Rev. H.Binney, 8 July 1833; Davis pp.60–1.
21. WA, WAM 9407; WAM 43659.
22. Davis, pp.61–2: WA, Register Book LIII, f.75.
23. Davis, pp.61–2: plan in account book in WA, RCO 33.
24. Davis, pp.91–2: Thomas Allen, *A New History of London and Westminster*, 1836, p.396.
25. CERC, Church Commissioners' file 33082/1: PRO, WORK16/1183.
26. *B*, April 13 1861, p.244: Matthew Saunders, 'Samuel Sanders Teulon' in *The Architectural Outsiders*, ed. Roderick Brown, 1985, p.135.
27. *B*, 21 April 1860, pp.248–9; 13 April 1861, pp.248–9.
28. *Ibid*: PRO, WORK16/1183: CERC, Church Commissioners' files 24314, 33082/1.
29. CERC, Church Commissioners' file 45481.
30. *Ibid.*, file 33082/1–4.
31. *Ibid.*, files 81734, 33082/4.
32. *Ibid.*, file 81734.
33. *Ibid.*, files 45481, 81734.
34. *B*, 14 March 1908, p.309: *Academy Architecture*, vol.35, 1909', p.32.
35. *B*, 30 Nov 1907, p.586; 14 March 1908, p.309: CERC, Church Commissioners' file 81734.
36. PRO, WORK16/1183.
37. WA, Register Book XXX f.12: MDR 1720/5/214–5.
38. WA, WAM 16274; Register Books VII, f.24; X, f.120: L.E.Tanner, *Westminster Abbey Occasional Papers No. 9*, 1962, pp.3–4.
39. WA, Register Books XI, f.50; XIX, ff.59, 215; XXV, f.165: RB.
40. WA, Register Book XXVII, f.66: MDR 1720/5/214–15.
41. MDR: RB.
42. Davis, pp.113–14.
43. WA, Register Book XLII, ff.137–42.
44. RB.
45. PRO, WORK16/341.
46. *Ibid*; WORK16/912.

47. PRO, WORK16/363.
48. LCC, *Indication of Houses of Historical Interest in London*, vol.II, pp.69–71.
49. *DNB*: LCC, *op.cit.*, p.68.
50. Harold P.Clunn, *London Marches On*, 1947, pp.11, 132.
51. Davis, pp.114–15: RB: Censuses (1841–91).
52. Davis, pp.111–12.
53. RB: WA, Register Books XXVII, ff.66–8; XXX, f.12: Bryant Lillywhite, *London Signs*, 1972, p.196: *The Tatler*, no.259.
54. Davis, pp.112–13.
55. WA, Register Book LV, f.397: RB: Davis, p.113: *Land & Building News*, 9 Aug 1856, p.486: Diana Howard, *London Theatres and Music Halls 1850–1950*, 1970, p.87.
56. Davis, pp.113–14: Colvin, pp.202–3: WA, Register Book LV, f.397.
57. Davis, p.113: RB: WA, Register Books XLII, ff.137–42; LIX, ff.27–9.
58. Colvin, pp.334–5.
59. RB: Census (1841): Howard, *op.cit.*, 1970, p.87: Davis, pp.113–14.
60. Davis, pp.36–7, 176; Jacob Larwood and John Camden Hotten, *The History of Signboards, From the Earliest Times to the Present Day*, 1866 edn, p.214: Chancellor, pp.259, 264.
61. KLS, 58/5604, pp.217, 219–20: MDR 1776/4/513: RB: Davis, p.176.
62. MDR 1776/4/513: RB.
63. Inscription on building, see WCA, E138/43; WDP2/491: *POD*.
64. MDR 1778/1/95.
65. RB: Censuses (1841–91): *POD*.
66. Davis, p.iv.
67. WCA, Box 60, no.44B.
68. John Timbs, *Curiosities of London*, 1867 edn, p.492: RB.
69. Thomas Cooper, *Life of Thomas Cooper*, 1886, p.302.
70. Davis, p.117: Censuses (1861–91).
71. *Lady Morgan's Memoirs: Autobiography, Diaries and Correspondence*, vol.II, 1862, pp.432–3, 438–43, 470: PRO, WORK16/439.
72. *Lady Morgan's Memoirs . . .*, pp.432–3, 440, 442–3.
73. *Plan Shewing the Proposed Improvements to the Roads from London and Westminster through Chelsea, also the proposed Road into Hyde Park from Knightsbridge, 1838*.
74. PRO, MPE1367(1–3); WORK32/199.
75. PRO, WORK16/439.
76. *Ibid*.
77. *Ibid*.
78. 4 & 5 Vic, c.12.
79. WA, FA 12432B, 12434: PRO, CRES38/1539.
80. PRO, WORK16/439; WORK32/29.
81. PRO, WORK16/683; CRES2/650.
82. *Lady Morgan's Memoirs . . .*, p.442.
83. *ILN*, 31 Jan 1863, p.130.
84. PRO, WORK16/439.
85. Davis, p.101: *B*, 23 Aug 1845, p.400.
86. *The Observer*, 13 Nov 1983, p.40: information provided by the Royal Parks Agency.
87. PRO, CRES2/650; WORK16/439: *B*, 5 March 1853, p.152.
88. PRO, WORK16/334; MFQ595.
89. PRO, CRES2/650; WORK16/440; WORK16/683: *ILN*, 4 May 1844, p.287: Hermione Hobhouse, *Thomas Cubitt*, 1971, p.377.
90. PRO, WORK16/683.
91. PRO, WORK32/29.
92. Davis, p.102.
93. *B*, 16 July 1843, p.347.
94. *ILN*, 30 March 1844, p.202; 20 May 1854, p.474.
95. *Ibid*: MDR 1846/2/688–9; 1854/17/584: information provided by Hermione Hobhouse: Felix Barker and Denise Silvester-Carr, *The Black Plaque Guide to London*, 1987, p.187.
96. G.A.Sala, *Twice round the Clock*, 1858, pp.188–9.
97. Hobhouse, *op.cit.*, p.164: *ILN*, 22 Oct 1853, p.343: MDR 1854/17/584.
98. *ILN*, 20 May 1854, pp.472–4: Sala, *op.cit.*, p.189.
99. *Oxford English Dictionary*.
100. Centre des Archives Diplomatiques, Nantes, Fonds Comtabilité, Carton 321.
101. LMA, GLC/AR/BR/22/23234.
102. *The Gentlewoman*, 21 June 1902, p.870.
103. Oliver Curtis, 'Architecture of Today and Yesterday', in *Town and Country News*, 23 Feb 1934, p.7.
104. This account is based largely on information extracted by Mr Martin Meade from official French sources in the Centre des Archives Diplomatiques, Nantes, Fonds Comtabilité, Cartons 319–32.
105. CERC, Church Commissioners' file 45481/2.
106. *Journal of the Royal Institute of British Architects*, vol.XII, 3rd Series, 1905, p.59: P.G.Mouchel & Partners, file 66: LMA, GLC/AR/BA/3/1.
107. *The King*, 2 Aug 1902, pp.897–900: Mouchel-Hennebique Ferro-Concrete, *List of works executed in UK*, p.65: *Journal of the Royal Institute of British Architects*, vol.XII, 3rd Series, 1905, p.59.
108. *ILN*, 14 March 1846, p.174.
109. PRO, CRES2/650: information provided by Hermione Hobhouse.
110. *POD*: MDR 1858/11/382.
111. *The Times*, 16 Sept 1858, p.8f; 19 Oct 1858, p.6f.
112. PRO, WORK16/683.
113. NMR, Bedford Lemere day-books (interiors), 8821–32: DSR 1886/81.
114. Cecil Roth, *The Sassoon Dynasty*, 1941, p.132.
115. PRO, CRES2/650, 21 Jan 1847, 15 Jan 1851.
116. *The Times*, 26 Oct 1846, p.7c; 12 Nov 1849, p.7e: *The Life of P.T. Barnum Written by Himself*, 1855, p.347.
117. LMA, MBO 26, pp.257–68: PRO, HO107/1469, f.132v.
118. *The Times*, 15 April 1851, p.1e.
119. *The Art-Journal*, New Series, vol.iv, 1 Jan 1852, p.33.
120. LMA, MBO 26, pp.257–68; MBO 76, pp.329–44: PRO, MPE783: *The Times*, 20 Jan 1851, p.5e; 2 May 1851, p.3f: *The Art-Journal, op. et loc.cit*: Tallis's *Illustrated Plan of London and its Environs in Commemoration of the Great Exhibition*, 1851 (Tallis's vignette of the Celestial Palace is reproduced in *Westminster History Review 3*, 1999, p.22): John Timbs, *Curiosities of London*, 1855 edn, p.432.
121. *The Times*, 2 May 1851, p.3f: *ILN*, 10 May 1851, p.380.
122. A.W.Ganz, *Berlioz in London*, 1950, pp.94–6.
123. *The Art-Journal, op. et loc.cit*: Christies Archives, *Catalogue of the Celebrated Assemblage . . . collected by the late Nathan Dunn*, 10 Dec 1851: *B*, 20 Jan 1852, p.24.
124. Information provided by Langdon's great-grand-daughters, Jeanette Parsons and Nancy McKay.
125. Dianne Sachko Macleod, *Art and the Victorian middle class: Money and the making of cultural identity*, 1996, pp.456-7.
126. PRO, WORK16/676, 7, 17 Feb 1852.
127. PRO, WORK16/676.
128. MDR 1858/2/865: *Land & Building News*, 9 Aug 1856, p.486: Davis, p.114: *POD*.
129. *Ladies Field*, 16 July 1898, pp.226–33.
130. MDR 1882/21/528; 1883/30/719; 1884/15/141: PRO, WORK16/676.
131. *Antique Collector*, Aug–Sept 1973, p.191.
132. *AR*, Aug 1964, pp.130, 132: WBC.
133. *AR*, Aug 1964, pp.130, 132: *Antique Collector*, Aug–Sept 1973, pp.189–95: Jeremy Musson, 'Changing Rooms at the Club', in *Country Life*, 22 April 1999, pp.96–7: *Building Design*, 21 Feb 1992, p.24; 21 Aug 1992, p.3.
134. MDR 1883/30/179.
135. MBW *Mins*, 3 Aug 1883, p.289: LMA, GLC/AR/BR/22/088038; MBW/1725, no.204: English Heritage, Historians' file WM556.
136. Information provided by Mrs Savage of the Danish Club: English Heritage, Historians' file WM556.
137. CERC, Church Commissioners' file 55519: *B*, 19 May 1877, p.518; 26 May 1877, p.544: Coleman's *Life of Charles Reade*, quoted in Chancellor, p.48.
138. MBW *Mins*, 2 Nov 1877, p.514; 16 Nov 1877, p.575: LMA, MBW/751, 13 Nov 1877, p.57: *B*, 24 Nov 1877, p.1185.
139. CERC, Church Commissioners' file 55519: MDR 1880/28/31; 1880/30/349.
140. Parent's designs are in possession of the Earl of Rosebery at Dalmeny House.

141. Robert Rhodes James, *Rosebery: A Biography of Archibald Philip, Fifth Earl of Rosebery*, 1963, p.123: *DNB*.
142. MDR 1883/30/719; 1884/15/141.
143. MDR 1888/24/74–5.
144. PRO, BT31/3916/24762: *B*, 20 Aug 1887, p.286.
145. PRO, WORK16/381: MBW *Mins*, 13 April 1888, p.598.
146. PRO, WORK16/381: *ILN*, 26 May 1888, p.563.
147. *The Standard*, 24 April 1888: *B*, 16 June 1888, p.434.
148. Buildings (Metropolis) Bill, copy in LMA, LCC/AR/BA/1/2: MDR 1888/15/9.
149. Account of Balfour's career by Esmond J. Cleary in *Dictionary of Business Biography*, ed. David J. Jeremy, vol.4, 1984: contemporary reports in *Building Societies Gazette*, etc.
150. *BN*, 25 Nov 1892, p.735.
151. *Ibid.*
152. *Ibid.*
153. *Ibid*: *B*, 3 May 1890, p.323.
154. *The Times*, 18 April 1899, p.8; 20 April 1899, p.9: *B*, 15 March 1902, p.273: DSR.
155. PRO, WORK16/381.
156. Anthony Masters, *Inside Marbled Halls*, 1979, p.139.
157. PRO, BT31/7895/56574.
158. *Hotel World*, June 1899, p.xviii.
159. PRO, BT31/6540/46041.
160. Companies House, file 73251: Marie Louise Ritz, *César Ritz – Host to the World*, 1938, p.275: LMA, GLC/AR/BR/19/173.
161. LMA, GLC/AR/BR/19/173.
162. WAC, WDP2/489.
163. PRO, WORK16/381.
164. PRO, IR58/91028/522: *Caterer & Hotel Proprietor's Gazette*, 15 Jan 1912, p.2: *B*, 14 Aug 1914, p.184.
165. LMA, GLC/AR/BR/07/0173.
166. PRO, WORK16/1250.
167. *B*, 21 June 1997, p.1167: Clunn, *op.cit.* (note 50), p.132: *The Estate Exchange Year Book for 1935*, p.155: *B*, 13 Sept 1935, p.447.
168. PRO, WORK16/1187: Clunn, *op.cit.*, p.132: CERC, Church Commissioners' file 55519.
169. Description based on contemporary accounts including – *Concrete Quarterly*, Jan–March 1959, pp.37–40: *Contract Journal*, 12 Dec 1957, p.1347: *Architect & Building News*, 1 April 1959, p.407 *et seq.*: *AR*, March 1959, pp.167–73.
170. PRO, WORK16/1835.
171. Information provided by Ian Hedges.
172. PRO, WORK16/1835: Stephen Gardiner, *Epstein: Artist Against the Establishment*, 1992, pp.466–8, 475–6.
173. Gardiner, *op.cit.*, p.468.
174. Ian Nairn, *Modern Architecture in London*, 1964, p.46.
175. PRO, CRES38/1591: RB: John Lockie, *Topography of London . . .*, 1813.
176. MDR 1761/4/171: RB.
177. RB: PRO, CRES38/1591.
178. *Ibid.*
179. PRO, WORK16/903: RB.
180. *B*, 25 July 1857, p.422.
181. Census (1841).
182. Census (1851).
183. *The Reminiscences of Lady Dorothy Nevill*, ed. Ralph Nevill, 1906, chapter XIII.
184. MDR 1853/8/809–10: PRO, CRES35/2839.
185. *B*, 25 July 1857, p.422.
186. *BN*, 2 Jan 1857, p.21: Hermione Hobhouse, 'Philip and Philip Charles Hardwick: an architectural dynasty', in *Seven Victorian Architects*, 1977, ed. Jane Fawcett, pp.139, 152.
187. Information provided by Giles Worsley.
188. *Companion to the Almanac . . . for 1858*, p.249.
189. *BN*, 2 Jan 1857, p.21; 17 April 1857, p.383.
190. *The Times*, 1 April 1858, p.10b; 17 Jan 1872, p.5d; 29 July 1878, p.10a–f: *The Lady*, 3 March 1891, p.287: *B*, 21 March 1891, p.237.
191. PRO, BT31/15252/37055; CRES35/2839: MDR 1891/20/558; 1893/24/452; 1895/1/264–5.
192. *B*, 18 May 1895, p.381.
193. *Flats*, Sept 1896, supplement.
194. PRO, CRES38/1591.
195. PRO, WORK16/1184: MDR 1891/8/175.
196. *Ibid*: LCC *Mins*, 25 Nov 1890, p.1050: *BN* 30 Oct 1891, pp.618, 631.
197. PRO, WORK16/903: DSR 1887/173: LCC *Mins*, 6 May 1887, p.754; 1 July 1887, p.27.
198. PRO, WORK16/449.
199. PRO, WORK16/903; IR58/91028/505.

CHAPTER III (pp.64–76)

Knightsbridge Barracks

1. *B*, 2 Feb 1878, p.110 (the fate of these plans is not known).
2. *PP* 1806 (317), VI.115, *Second Report of the Commissioners of Military Enquiry: Establishment of the Barrack Office*, 18 July 1806, Appendix 19.
3. *PP*, *Reports from Committees of the House of Commons*, vol.XII, 1803, *20th Report from the Select Committee on Finance*, 19 July 1797, p.409.
4. *The Times*, 21 Dec 1793, p.3d.
5. *Ibid.*, 28 Oct 1789, p.3c.
6. James Douet, *British Barracks 1600–1914*, 1998, p.60.
7. PRO, WORK16/434.
8. John Rocque, *A Plan of the Palace Gardens and Town of Kensington*, 1754.
9. Colvin, *sub* Gandon: and see Maurice Craig, *The Architecture of Ireland from the earliest times to 1880*, 1982, pp.285–8: PRO, WORK38/1–4.
10. Maj.-Gen.Sir Elliott Wood, *Life and Adventure in Peace and War*, 1924, pp.82–3.
11. PRO, WO44/566.
12. *Ibid.*, WO40/19.
13. Royal Archives, F24/66; F24/74–5: *B*, 15 March 1851, p.174: James Stevens Curl, *The Life and Work of Henry Roberts*, 1983, pp.97–8.
14. Curl, *op.cit.*, pp.98–106: *Survey of London*, vol.XXVI, 1956, pp.34–6.
15. *PP* 1854–5 (405), XXXII.37, *Report . . . on Barrack Accommodation for the Army*, 17 July 1855: *B*, 1 March 1856, p.121.
16. *PP* 1861 (2839), XVI.1, *General Report of the Commission appointed for Improving the Sanitary Condition of Barracks and Hospitals*, 1861: *PP* 1863 (3084), XIII.117, *Appendix to the Report of the Commission for Improving the Sanitary Condition of Barracks and Hospitals (Interim Reports)*, 1863.
17. *PP* 1863 (3084), XIII.117, *Appendix to the Report of the Commission for Improving the Sanitary Condition of Barracks and Hospitals (Interim Reports)*, 1863, p.14: *B*, 1 May 1858, p.290.
18. *PP* 1863 (3084), XIII.117, *Appendix to the Report of the Commission for Improving the Sanitary Condition of Barracks and Hospitals (Interim Reports)*, 1863, pp.348–51.
19. *B*, 13 March 1858, p.170.
20. *B*, 11 June 1870, p.463.
21. John Elsworth, *The Knightsbridge Barracks & the Necessity for their removal*, 1867.
22. *B*, 6 July 1867, p.498.
23. Hansard, Commons 1876, vol.227, cols 1114–15, 9 March 1876.
24. *B*, 22 May 1869, p.414.
25. *B*, 26 June 1875, p.580.
26. Hansard, Commons 1876, vol.227, col.555, 21 Feb 1876; col.1118, 29 Feb 1876.
27. *B*, 22 Jan 1876, p.72: Hansard, Commons 1876, vol.227, col.1232, 2 March 1876.
28. *B*, 4 Nov 1876, p.1079.
29. *B*, 24 March 1877, p.299.
30. *B*, 11 March 1876, p.230.
31. 42 & 43 Vic, c.219: P.J.Edwards, *History of London Street Improvements, 1855–1897*, 1898, Plan XLIX, p.119: *B*, 1 July 1871, p.513.
32. *BN*, 28 Nov 1879, p.663.

33. *B*, 2 Feb 1878, p.110.
34. *Survey of London*, vol.XLVIII, 1975, p.217n.
35. Edmund Happold, *Reconstruction of the Household Cavalry Barracks*, 1970 (Paper no.31, given at Public Works and Municipal Services Congress and Exhibition, 1970): *ILN*, 15 May 1880, p.486: *BN*, 26 March 1880, p.383.
36. Wood, *op.cit.*, p.82.
37. *B*, 2 Feb 1878, p.110.
38. WCA, Acc.262.
39. *ILN*, 15 May 1880, p.486.
40. *The Architect*, 31 May 1879, p.325.
41. Description based largely on – *BN*, 26 Nov 1880, p.383: *The Architect*, 21 Nov 1879, p.602.
42. *ILN*, 15 May 1880, p.486.
43. Household Cavalry Museum, volume of plans dated 3 May 1911.
44. *Journal of the Household Brigade*, 1879, p.227.
45. *BN*, 26 March 1880, p.383.
46. *Companion to the Almanac . . . for 1879*, pp.159–60; *. . . for 1881*, p.153.
47. *BN*, 21 Nov 1879, p.602.
48. Hansard, Commons 1929–30, vol.231, cols 655–6, 4 Nov 1929.
49. Hansard, Commons 1924–5, vol.181, col.947, 9 March 1925.
50. PRO, CRES35/3118; WORK16/1834.
51. Happold, *op.cit.*, pp.788–9: *The Times*, 21 Sept 1932, p.5d.
52. *Guards Magazine*, Winter 1970–1, pp.203–4.
53. PRO, WORK16/1834, A.G.Offer to Ministry of Works, 26 June 1956; WORK16/1834, William Hare to Hugh Molson MP, 14 Feb 1957.
54. PRO, WORK16/1834, Maj.-Gen.J.H.Amers to Mr King, Ministry of Works, 11 Feb 1958: Anthony Blee archives, 25/F/1/L, memo from War Office to Basil Spence & Partners, 2 Nov 1959.
55. *B*, 25 Feb 1865, p.141.
56. PRO, WORK16/1834.
57. LMA, LCC/AR/TP/1/92, Godfrey Samuel to Director-General of Works, War Office, 4 Aug 1960.
58. PRO, WORK16/1834, Profumo to Lord John Hope, 15 Aug 1960.
59. LMA, LCC/AR/TP/1/92, Godfrey Samuel to Basil Spence & Partners, 13 Sept 1960.
60. *AR*, Oct 1963, p.227.
61. *B*, 2 Aug 1963, p.220.
62. Anthony Blee archives, 25/F/1/G, Anthony Blee to W.H.Mundy, 3 June 1970.
63. Information provided by Anthony Blee.
64. *B*, 2 Aug 1963, p.220.
65. *ARUP Journal*, vol.1, no.2, March 1967, pp.2–9.
66. *B*, 30 Oct 1970, p.61: Anthony Blee archives, 25/F/1/G.
67. *B*, 2 Aug 1963, p.219; 30 Oct 1970, pp.61–4.
68. Anthony Blee archives, 25/F/3/M.
69. *Concrete Quarterly*, April–Sept 1971, p.35.
70. The following account is based largely on – Ministry of Public Building and Works, *Hyde Park Barracks*, 1970: *AJ*, 28 Oct 1970, p.995: *B*, 30 Oct 1970, pp.62–4: Happold, *op.cit.*, pp.797–8.
71. *B*, 30 Oct 1970, p.63.
72. Ministry of Public Building and Works, *op.cit.*, p.37.
73. *Guards Magazine*, Winter 1970–1, p.200.
74. Anthony Blee archives, 25/F/2/J.
75. *Ibid.*, 25/F/2/K.
76. *B*, 30 Oct 1970, p.61.
77. *Concrete Quarterly*, April–Sept 1971, p.34.
78. Edward Jones and Christopher Woodward, *A Guide to the Architecture of London*, 1992, p.192.

CHAPTER IV (pp.77–94)

Knightsbridge Green Area

1. WA, WAM 52252: MDR 1719/1/181; 1719/5/202–4.
2. RB: WCA, Acc.1188, bundle II: KLS, MS 3471: *DNB*.
3. The histories of the Blake and Moreau estates generally are given in *Survey of London*, vol.XXXVIII, 1975, Chapter 1, and vol.XLI, 1983, Chapter III.
4. KLS, MS 3799: List of possessions of Sir William Blake at his death, in extra-illustrated copy of Thomas Faulkner, *History and Antiquities of Kensington*, 1820, in BL (press mark L.R. 271.c.3), b/w pp.440–1: LMA, C/96/47.
5. WA, Church Commissioners' Records, Box 441, Deed 292078, 11 March 1719/20; Register Book XXXI, ff.128v–129: MDR 1724/4/260; 1726/6/175.
6. KLS, MS 3799: WCA, Acc.1188, bundle II.
7. *Survey of London*, vol.XLI, 1983, p.34.
8. MDR 1760/2/153–5; 1762/3/259–61; 1778/2/328; 1793/3/226; 1793/3/229–31; 1795/3/300: RB.
9. KLS, MSS 3788, 3729–35: information provided by Victor Belcher.
10. KLS, MSS 3736–7, 3748–50, 3775–7.
11. MDR 1842/1/123–4: Claude Blair, 'The Egg Family Part 1', in *The Journal of the Arms and Armour Society*, vol.VII, nos 9–10, March–June 1973, pp.326–7.
12. MDR 1724/4/260; 1726/6/175.
13. *Daily Telegraph*, 24 May 1867, p.4: John Elsworth, *The Knightsbridge Barracks & the Necessity for their removal*, 1867, p.9.
14. WA, Church Commissioners' Records, Dean & Chapter Estates, Box 441, Deed 292079, Fine Book 1632–1877.
15. Davis, p.104.
16. RB: LMA, WR/LV/1798/1: MDR 1797/7/285.
17. Davis, pp.144–5.
18. KLS, cuttings (ref.266a).
19. LMA, MR/LMD/1849/4/81(b).
20. Diana Howard, *London Theatres and Music Halls 1850–1950*, 1970, pp.133, 199.
21. Davis, pp.103, 144.
22. PRO, C5/62/12: Chancellor, pp.265–6: Davis, p.104.
23. MDR 1802/3/723.
24. MDR 1737/3/214–26; 1738/2/260–2.
25. Postcard in Brian Girling collection (W005).
26. MBW *Mins*, 4 Dec 1874, p.637; 29 Jan 1875, p.126: DSR 1874/315–6: *POD*: *The Caterer and Hotel-Keeper's Gazette*, 15 Aug 1917, p.254.
27. *B*, 8 April 1876, p.350: DSR 1876/174: MBW *Mins*, 26 May 1876, p.772: postcard in Brian Girling collection (W005).
28. Davis, pp.144–5: DSR 1851/58.
29. *Architectural Magazine*, vol.III, 1836, p.327.
30. *The Times*, 23, 24 May 1890, pp.5e, 10b; 3 June 1890, p.7e; 7 Nov 1890, p.4f: PRO, CRES35/2601.
31. *The Times*, 25 Feb 1895, p.11e; 20 June 1895, p.7a: *Daily Graphic*, 20 June 1895, p.9: *B*, 22 June 1895, p.464.
32. Westminster City Council *Mins*, 15 Oct 1931, p.542; 22 Feb 1934, pp.97–8; 22 Oct 1964, pp.208, 231: *The Times*, 22 Oct 1964, p.24a; 23 Oct 1964, p.17e; 30 Nov 1964, p.12d.
33. *Pall Mall Gazette*, 1 Dec 1899, p.10: MDR 1885/16/999; 1887/32/678–9; 1890/7/893; 1890/32/308–9; 1898/13/391.
34. WCA, Deed 85/99: MDR 1899/40/811: PRO, BT31/2672/14273; BT31/31956/91284.
35. LMA, GLC/AR/BR/17/012546; GLC/AR/BR/23/027279: *BN*, 27 May 1898, p.744: DSR 1897/123; 1900/27; 1900/148; 1902/75: LCC *Mins*, 7 Oct 1902, p.1344.
36. *BN*, 27 May 1898, p.744.
37. *Pall Mall Gazette*, 1 Dec 1899, p.10.
38. LMA, GLC/AR/BR/17/012546.
39. *The Caterer and Hotel-Keeper's Gazette*, 14 May 1910, p.211; 15 May 1911, p.213: MDR 1910/10/406: PRO, BT31/3510/21370; BT31/18494/98881; IR58/91030/679.
40. LCC *Mins*, 28 March 1911, pp.785–6: *London at the Opening of the Twentieth Century*, ed. W.T.Pike, 1905, p.490.
41. *The Caterer and Hotel-Keeper's Gazette*, 14 May 1910, p.211; 15 May 1911, p.213: NMR, photos BL 21890/1–8.
42. Information provided by Daniel Smith.
43. *BN*, 12 Sept 1884, p.424.
44. DSR 1876/135: MBW *Mins*, 22 Dec 1876, p.818: *POD*: RB.

45. MDR 1879/4/263: RB: DSR 1880/310: *B*, 18 Dec 1880, p.740.
46. *The Times*, 4 Feb 1882, p.4c: PRO, BT31/2637/13995: DSR 1882/216; 1882/371: *B*, 1 Sept 1883, p.284.
47. *ILN*, 4 Nov 1882, p.472: *B*, 1 Sept 1883, pp.279, 284.
48. MDR 1884/2/523; 1884/6/1: *B*, 1 Sept 1883, p.284.
49. *B*, 1 Sept 1883, p.284: *BN*, 12 Sept 1884, p.424.
50. LMA, GLC/AR/BR/19/028; MBW 799, pp.511–13, 593, 630–2, 659–61.
51. RB.
52. *POD*: DSR: LMA, GLC/AR/BR/19/028; MBW 802, p.223: *Westminster and Pimlico News*, 28 April 1888, p.5.
53. LMA, GLC/AR/BR/22/TP/025753; GLC/AR/BR/22/036230: WCA, Plan E<538>.XLII.
54. PRO, BT31/3271/19257: *The Times*, 12 Jan 1885, p.10e: *POD*.
55. Except where otherwise indicated, the following account is based on – *The Times*, 20 Dec 1884, p.10e; 10 Jan 1885, p.6d; 12 Jan 1885, p.10e: *BN*, 16 Jan 1885, pp.77–8: Joan Bennett, 'Japan in London, 1885 – an unusual Victorian exhibition', in *The Lady*, 25 April 1985, pp.862–3, 874.
56. *BN*, 30 Jan 1885, p.189.
57. *The Lady*, 19 March 1885, p.147: Leslie Baily, *Gilbert & Sullivan and their world*, 1973, p.86.
58. *Daily Telegraph*, 11 April 1885 (advert): KLS, cutting No.121, 712.5 KEN/H, K60/307.
59. *The Times*, 4 May 1885, p.10f; 6 May 1885, p.9f; 4 June 1885, p.5e: LMA, MBW 799, pp.276–7, 290, 337–9, 405–6.
60. LMA, GLC/AR/BR/19/028: *The Standard*, 9 April 1886, advertisement.
61. PRO, BT31/3271/19257; BT31/3804/23840: *The Times*, 13 April 1887, p.10d; 31 May 1887: Bennett, *op.cit.*, p.874.
62. Except where otherwise indicated, this account is based on – *The Times*, 20 May 1889, p.10a: *B*, 15 June 1889, pp.448–9: *BN*, 11 Oct 1889, p.484: Ben Weinreb and Christopher Hibbert (eds), *The London Encyclopaedia*, 1983, p.621.
63. *POD*: Walford, *Old and New London*, 1897 edn, vol.V, pp.99–100: PRO, BT31/953/1285C.
64. PRO, BT31/4117/26476.
65. MDR 1889/35/380: WCA, rolled plan E<1779>: Denbighshire RO, DD/BK/94: LMA, GLC/AR/BR/07/2408.
66. LMA, GLC/AR/BR/06/046118.
67. Davis, p.106: WCA, D.Foster, *Inns, Taverns, Alehouses, Coffee Houses, Etc. In & Around London*, c.1900, vol.53, p.317.
68. DSR 1851/144: Howard, *op.cit.*, p.232: *BN*, 7 Sept 1866, p.602: LMA, GLC/AR/BR/19/028: Christopher Pulling, *They were Singing . . .*, 1952, p.178.
69. LMA, MBW 798, pp.719–23; MBW 799, pp.442, 484.
70. LMA, GLC/AR/BR/19/028; MBW 799, p.514; DSR; MBW 800, p.193: *POD*: *Westminster and Pimlico News*, 28 April 1888, p.5.
71. Archibald Haddon, *The Story of the Music Hall*, 1935, p.36: Pulling, *op.cit.*, p.178: *DNB*.
72. LMA, GLC/AR/BR/19/028.
73. OS: *POD*: PRO, BT31/5767/40406: *The Caterer and Hotel-Keeper's Gazette*, 15 March 1905, p.114.
74. DSR 1918/41, 1921/95: Charles L.Roberson, *Historical Rooms from the Manor Houses of England*, vol.I (n.d.), p.3, plan facing p.4.
75. Davis, pp.144–6: Chancellor, pp.19, 78–9: MDR 1724/4/260; 1726/6/175.
76. MDR 1784/1/558; 1784/2/404–5; 1784/3/464; 1784/4/102; 1785/5/289: R. Horwood, *Plan of the Cities of London and Westminster . . .*, 1792–9 edn.
77. LMA, MBO/Plans/446: DSR: MDR 1853/9/474; 1856/4/478–9: *Annual Report of the United Vestry of the Parishes of St Margaret and St John . . . 1899*, pp.15–16.
78. MDR 1737/3/214–26; 1738/2/260–2.
79. *The Times*, 20 March 1879, p.11b: CERC, Church Commissioners' file 46300: Vincent Orchard, *Tattersalls, Two Hundred Years of Sporting History*, 1953, p.304.
80. Davis, p.145.
81. RB: WCA, Acc.1188, bundle II.
82. KLS, MSS 3785, 3798: *DNB*: Davis, p.146.
83. Orchard, *op.cit.*, pp.92–6 *passim*: RB: WCA, 1049/4/50, p.72; 1049/5/14, p.410.
84. Hermione Hobhouse, *Thomas Cubitt*, 1971, p.137: *ILN*, 19 Feb 1857, p.147: MDR 1857/5/527–8.
85. *BN*, 3 July 1863, p.509: *B*, 9 Jan 1864, p.31: *ILN*, 22 April 1865, p.382.
86. *Illustrated Times*, 22 April 1865, p.245: *B*, 24 July 1869, p.590.
87. Colvin, p.958: *Sporting Review*, April 1865, p.275.
88. *Sporting Review*, April 1865, p.275.
89. *Penny Illustrated Paper*, 2 July 1869, pp.6–7.
90. *B*, 9 Jan 1864, p.31: *Illustrated Times*, 22 April 1865, p.245.
91. *Sporting Review*, Feb 1865, p.84.
92. *Survey of London*, vol.XXXIV, 1966, p.342, Pl.45b.
93. *B*, 9 Jan 1864, p.31: *Sporting Review*, April 1865, p.277.
94. *Sporting Review*, April 1865, p.276: *Illustrated Times*, 15 April 1865, p.245.
95. Orchard, *op.cit.*, pp.302–4: Peter Willett, *The Story of Tattersalls*, 1987, pp.91–2, 95: *The Sphere*, 12 June 1948, p.340.
96. WA, Register Book LXIII, ff.134v–5: BAL Archives, PoFam/1/4, p.32: *The Times*, 20 Feb 1841, p.5e.
97. CERC, Church Commissioners' file 46300: *The Architect*, 30 Oct 1875, p.242: DSR 1875/443.
98. CERC, National Society file no.5755: LMA, GLC/AR/BR/23/027279; GLC/AR/BR/22/032227.
99. MDR 1844/10/497: *POD*: LMA, WCS/P44/1457.
100. RB: DSR: MDR 1847/4/424; 1848/9/897: *POD*.
101. DSR: RB: MDR 1849/4/785.
102. DSR: WCA, E3998: RB: MDR 1847/4/424; 1854/1/338–75.
103. Censuses (1851–61).
104. LMA, MR/LMD/1862/3/57.
105. Westminster City Council *Mins*.
106. (Sir) Philip Gibbs, *Young Anarchy*, 1926, p.136.
107. *The Knightsbridge Item*, Christmas 1962, p.36.
108. Account based on – *Official Architecture and Planning*, Feb 1959, pp.82–3: *AR*, Dec 1959, pp.332–6: *B*, 23 March 1962, p.623; 29 Oct 1965, p.947: *Architect & Building News*, 21 March 1962, p.407; 17 April 1963, p.573: *The Knightsbridge Item*, Christmas 1962, pp.35–7: *The Times*, 17 Jan 1959, p.3e, 14 (ill.): LCC *Mins*, 1956–65: GLC *Mins*, 2 Nov 1965, pp.708–9.
109. *Architect & Building News*, 5 April 1956, p.331: *B*, 4 May 1956, p.454; 14 Nov 1958, p.817; 3 Aug 1962, p.218.
110. LMA, LCC/MIN/11787, 17 Jan 1957: PRO, MT78/131.
111. *B*, 14 Nov 1958, p.817.
112. *AR*, Jan 1957, p.28: *B*, 16 May 1958, pp.903–5.
113. *Survey of London*, vol.XLI, 1983, pp.35–6.
114. LMA, GLC/AR/BR/06/046118; GLC/AR/BR/22/TP/025753: *The Times*, 17 Feb 1969, p.13.
115. *Daily Telegraph*, 8 July 1986, p.21; 19 May 1997, p.26.

CHAPTER V (pp.95–106)

Trevor Square Area

1. RB.
2. BAL Archives, PoFam/1/3, p.1.
3. Denbighshire RO, DD/BK/101, marriage settlement of Anna Maria Brace, 1713: MDR 1715/2/163.
4. MDR 1719/5/202–4.
5. PRO, PROB11/699, f.247: *Gentleman's Magazine*, Jan 1759, p.46.
6. GEC.
7. *Survey of London*, vol.XXXV, 1970, p.5: Ian Donaldson, *Theatre Notebook*, XVI, 1962, pp.117–25: Dorothy Stroud, *Henry Holland, His Life and Architecture*, 1966, pp.123–4: Folger Shakespeare Library, manuscript W.B. 104.
8. *The World*, 25 April 1794.
9. RB.
10. BAL Archives, PoFam/1/3, pp.2, 5: RB.
11. RB: *Gentleman's Magazine*, Jan 1802, p.92.

12. BAL Archives, PoFam/1/2, pp.47–8; PoFam/1/3, p.2.
13. *Ibid*., PoFam/1/3, p.1: Denbighshire RO, DD/BK/92: RB.
14. BAL Archives, PoFam/1/2, p.2.
15. RB: MDR 1813/3/131; 1814/7/176; 1815/3/371–7; 1819/2/177; 1819/5/344.
16. Denbighshire RO, DD/BK/109: RB.
17. BAL Archives, PoFam/1/2, p.48: RB.
18. MDR 1819/2/177; 1819/5/344.
19. LMA, WCS/P/15/496; WCS/P/28/890.
20. RB: *POD*.
21. PRO, IR58/91032/764–6: *B*, 28 Aug 1914, p.218.
22. *POD*.
23. BAL Archives, PoFam/1/3, p.18; PoFam/1/5, p.17.
24. MDR 1816/6/557.
25. MDR 1820/2/326; 1820/3/54; 1820/4/449; 1821/1/136; 1821/2/216; 1821/3/741; 1823/1/121.
26. RB.
27. MDR 1820/8/234: Denbighshire RO, DD/BK/109.
28. RB.
29. MDR 1825/11/282; 1825/9/545; 1825/13/542; 1826/4/716; 1826/9/86; 1826/10/541: Denbighshire RO, DD/BK/109.
30. RB.
31. *Ibid*.
32. MDR 1821/3/30; 1821/3/742; 1821/6/737; 1821/7/181; 1821/8/49; 1821/8/134–5; 1822/1/648: Denbighshire RO, DD/BK/109.
33. MDR 1821/6/380; 1822/1/645–6.
34. MDR 1821/4/655; 1822/1/647: RB.
35. *The Times*, 8 July 1909, p.13c.
36. PRO, IR58/91048/1513.
37. *The Independent*, 9 March 1991, p.37: date on rainwater head.
38. LMA, O/105/9: RB: MDR 1814/1/592–3, 685.
39. MDR 1816/6/557: PRO, C54/9822(18): Rev. John Kennedy, *Service and Suffering: memoirs of the life of the Rev. John Morison DD LLD*, 1860, pp.60, 63.
40. *Evangelical Magazine*, Dec 1840, p.608: Kennedy, *op.cit.*, pp.69–70.
41. Harrods Archive photograph: *B*, 22 July 1865, p.531.
42. Harrods Archive, *Harrods Illustrated*, 1902 General Price List; letters in possession of Harrods: Nikolaus Pevsner, *The Buildings of England: London except the Cities of London and Westminster*, 1952, p.250.
43. Date-stone on building.
44. Denbighshire RO, DD/BK/109.
45. WBC.
46. Diana Howard, *London Theatres and Music Halls 1850–1950*, 1970, p.244.
47. LMA, AR/BR/19/08; LCC/MIN/10879, Session of Licensing Committee, 11 Oct 1894 (transcript of shorthand notes, pp.39–40): MDR 1890/11/754; 1892/23/867, 1892/36/225, 1892/37/119.
48. PRO, IR58/91032/767: LCC *Mins*, 26 Jan 1892, p.54: Household Cavalry Museum, volume of plans dated 3 May 1911.
49. Denbighshire RO, DD/BK/109: MDR 1827/10/98.
50. Denbighshire RO, DD/BK/109: RB.
51. BAL Archives, PoFam/1/2, p.48: PoFam/1/5, p.8.
52. Roy Jenkins, *Sir Charles Dilke: A Victorian Tragedy*, 1958, pp.316, 333–6, 340–1: David Nicholls, *The Lost Prime Minister: A Life of Sir Charles Dilke*, 1995, pp.189, 192.
53. *Westminster Times*, 10 Oct 1890, p.2: *The Times*, 8 July 1909, p.13c.
54. *B*, 15 Oct 1910, pp.xvi, 444; 2 June 1911, pp.684–7.
55. Harrods Archive, Minute Book No.5, pp.27, 29–30, 32–33; typescript paper stamped 11 Jan 1917.
56. Information provided by David C.Humphreys, and Michael Duncan of W.A.Ellis.
57. LMA, AR/BR/17/040352: Harrods Archive, Contractors' bills; Minute Book No.5, p.117; Minute Book No.6, p.311.
58. NAL, II.RC.H.10, Robert Barnes, 'Papers in connection with the Early FLOOR CLOTH MANUFACTURE', MS scrapbook, 1857, p.27.
59. Ian Bristow, '"They will look very well": Painted Floorcloths in the 18th Century', in SPAB News, vol.11, No.2, 1990, pp.11–13.
60. Patent No.787, 15 March 1763.
61. NAL, II.RC.H.10, Robert Barnes, 'Papers . . .', p.18.
62. RB.
63. MDR 1785/2/458; 1825/7/543.
64. *The Times*, 13 Feb 1794, p.3: *The World*, 14 Feb 1794: *Gentleman's Magazine*, Feb 1794, p.176: RB.
65. Colvin, p.701.
66. BAL Archives, PoFam/1/3, p.2.
67. GL, extra-illustrated copy of D.Lysons, *The Environs of London*, 1792, vol.2, Part 1, f.338: BAL Archives, PoFam/1/3, pp.2–3.
68. RB.
69. Patent 2271, 20 Nov 1798.
70. NAL, II.RC.H.10, Robert Barnes, 'Papers . . .', p.42.
71. MDR 1824/8/761.
72. RB: Censuses (1851–81).
73. BAL, Scrapbook compiled by W.W.Pocock, f.5r.
74. NAL, II.RC.H.10, Robert Barnes, 'Papers . . .', p.43 (Smith & Baber bill-head of 1822).
75. RB.
76. Census (1851).
77. e.g. George Dodd, *Days at the Factories*, 1843, pp.281–302.
78. Denbighshire RO, DD/BK/94, building agreement of 16 Dec 1889.
79. LMA, LCC/MIN/10879: PRO, BT31/5767/40406.
80. LMA, AR/BR/19/265.
81. LMA, LCC/MIN/10879; AR/BR/19/265: PRO, BT31/5767/40406.
82. LMA, AR/BR/19/265; LCC/MIN/10880: PRO, IR58/91032/772: Barbara Denny, *Kensington in old photographs*, 1974, Pl.108: LMA, photo 73/8203.
83. LMA, AR/BR/19/265; LCC/MIN/10880.
84. Illustrated in Lisa Tickner, *The Spectacle of Women*, 1987, pp.32–3.
85. *POD*.

CHAPTER VI (pp.107–127)

Montpelier Square Area

1. CERC, Ground Rents Purchases 26, abstract of title of T.W.Marriott.
2. Patricia S.Wolfston, 'Richard Marryott & Finchingfield', in *Essex Journal*, Spring 1980, pp.22–9.
3. LMA, WCS/P/19/619; WCS/179, p.117.
4. MDR 1826/9/507.
5. MDR 1827/10/98.
6. GL, MS 8733/9, pp.128–9.
7. CERC, Ground Rents Purchases 26, abstract of title of T.W.Marriott.
8. Information in the case of Marriott *v.* Cobbett (PRO, J15/1853; J54/532; J57/4293) provided by Dr A.E.L.Davis.
9. WCA, Westminster District Board of Works Letter Books E2757, pp.346, 348; E2758, p.20.
10. LMA, GLC/AR/BR/22/036413.
11. CERC, Ground Rents Sales 1268.
12. Arthur and Cynthia Koestler, *Stranger on the Square*, ed. Harold Harris, 1984, p.151.
13. MBW *Mins*, 28 June 1867, p.822.
14. *POD*.
15. *Ibid*: MDR 1828/7/84.
16. *POD*: Census (1851).
17. See *Survey of London*, vol.XXXVII, 1973, Chapter XII.
18. MDR 1826/8/587–90; 1832/4/790.
19. MDR 1826/10/514–15; 1827/1/4–5; 1827/2/417.
20. RB.
21. *Kent's London Directory*, 1825.
22. Sale particulars in WCA, Acc.964.
23. MDR 1828/10/995.
24. Census (1891).
25. Koestler and Koestler, *op.cit.*, pp.151–2, 184, 206.
26. RB: *POD*: Censuses (1851–61): *DNB*.
27. Paul Mellon Foundation for British Art, *List of A & B artists who resided in Westminster* (in WCA).
28. e.g. MBW *Mins*, 8 March 1878, p.401: LCC *Mins*, 27 Sept 1892, p.795.

29. CERC, Church Commissioners' file 1619.
30. MDR 1827/5/54: RB.
31. Frederic Boase, *Modern English Biography*, 1965 edn, vol.II, p.274.
32. RB.
33. Census (1851).
34. RB: MDR 1828/5/143.
35. MDR 1832/4/257.
36. MDR 1838/7/313.
37. MDR 1838/7/314.
38. WCA, WDP2/570.
39. MDR 1840/8/727.
40. LCC *Mins*, 24 Feb 1891, p.223.
41. RB: DSR: MDR 1848/4/840; 1849/2/722.
42. DSR.
43. RB.
44. CERC, Ground Rents Purchases 26, abstracts of deeds: MDR 1846/11/109; 1846/10/358.
45. CERC, Ground Rents Sales 1619.
46. MBW *Mins*, 17 May 1861, p.364.
47. WCA, WDP2/570: LMA, GLC/AR/BR/17/068566: PRO, IR58/91036/947.
48. DSR: RB.
49. LCC *Mins*, 3 June 1913, p.1251.
50. Alan Gauld, *The Founders of Psychical Research*, 1968, p.162.
51. *POD*: Census (1891).
52. MDR 1826/10/603–4.
53. PRO, IR58/91036/937: DSR: CERC, Ground Rents Sales 223.
54. *POD*: Chancellor, p.88.
55. MDR 1845/8/11; 1845/9/510–16: RB: DSR.
56. Census (1891).
57. Philip Henderson, *William Morris: his life, work and friends*, 1986 edn, pp.32–8.
58. LMA, WCS/69, 16 March 1827, p.446.
59. MDR 1838/7/313–14.
60. MDR 1842/7/405; 1843/2/188–92: RB.
61. LCC *Mins*, 3 May 1904, p.719: information provided by Mrs J.Virgin.
62. Censuses (1851–91): *POD*.
63. WCA, WDP2/569: 'At Home with the Pringles', in *Harper's Bazaar*, April 1968.
64. MBW *Mins*, 7 May 1858, p.324; 28 May 1858, pp.373–4; 4 June 1858, pp.385–6.
65. Census (1851): RB: DSR.
66. WCA, WDP2/570.
67. Censuses (1841, 1851): *POD*: RB.
68. Census (1851).
69. *Daily Telegraph*, 24 May 1867, p.4.
70. MBW *Mins*, 10 Dec 1875, p.664: LMA, MBW 776, report by the Superintending Architect, 5 Feb 1876.
71. LMA, LCC/MIN/1563, case no. 168.
72. RB: Censuses (1861–81).
73. John Galsworthy, *The Man of Property*, 1906.
74. Censuses (1881, 1891).
75. LMA, LCC/MIN/10879.
76. CERC, Ground Rents Purchases 26.
77. (Sir) Philip Gibbs, *The Reckless Lady*, 1924.
78. LMA, GLC/AR/BR/17/068566.
79. *Time*, 15 April 1966, p.32: map reproduced in Robert Hewison, *Too Much: Art and Society in the Sixties*, 1986.
80. RB.
81. Censuses (1841–51).
82. CERC, abstracts of deeds in Ground Rents Purchases 26: RB.
83. *POD*: Census (1891).
84. LCC *Mins*, 17 Oct 1899, p.1390.
85. CERC, Ground Rents Sales 223.
86. DSR: *POD*.
87. Michael Elliman and Frederick Roll, *The Pink Plaque Guide to London*, 1986, pp.202–3.
88. LMA, GLC/AR/BR/17/068338.
89. CERC, Ground Rents Sales 223.
90. WBC.
91. *Ibid*: WCA, WDP2/571.
92. MBW *Mins*, 6 June 1862, p.421.
93. MDR 1827/2/417; 1828/7/618–19.
94. MDR 1832/4/257; 1838/7/313: RB.
95. MDR 1828/3/640; 1836/1/291–2.
96. CERC, Ground Rents Purchases 26: RB: MDR 1839/9/209; 1840/8/981; 1842/7/405; 1842/8/736.
97. RB: MDR 1830/3/177; 1839/9/209.
98. WCA, Acc.964.
99. DSR: RB.
100. MDR 1848/7/345.
101. CERC, Ground Rents Purchases 26: MDR 1846/1/382; 1848/7/87; 1849/5/356–9.
102. Illustrated in John Sambrook, *Fanlights*, 1989, p.79.
103. Censuses (1861–91): PRO, IR58/91046/1454–63.
104. Census (1891): LCC *Mins*, 17 Oct 1899, p.1390: *POD*.
105. CERC, Ground Rents Sales 867: WCA, WDP2/818.
106. WCA, WDP2/818: BAL, Drawings Collection, RAN 8/M/8(2): information provided by Mrs Ludmilla Mathias.
107. Michael Baker, *Our Three Selves: a life of Radclyffe Hall*, 1985, pp.142–3, 166.
108. MDR 1828/8/276–7, 355.
109. MDR 1828–42.
110. RB: Censuses (1841–91).
111. PRO, MEPO 5/3.
112. WCA, WDP2/569.
113. Elliman and Roll, *op.cit.*, pp.54–5.
114. WCA, WDP2/569: LMA, GLC/AR/BR/06/060151.
115. LMA, GLC/AR/BR/06/59846.
116. WCA, WDP2/569.
117. WCA, WDP2/571.
118. MDR 1830/5/221: WCA, WDP2/569.
119. RB: MDR 1828–31.
120. Philip Sugden, *The Complete History of Jack the Ripper*, 1994, p.77.
121. Censuses (1841–91): *POD*.
122. RB: PRO, MEPO 5/3: Census (1851).
123. LMA, GLC/AR/BR/06/059536: WCA, WDP2/546.
124. WCA, WDP2/546.
125. WCA, WDP2/569.
126. WCA, WDP2/546.
127. *POD*.
128. WCA, WDP2/546: LMA, GLC/AR/BR/22/036413.
129. LMA, GLC/AR/BR/22/036413.
130. DSR: RB.
131. WCA, WDP2/546: PRO, IR58/91017/2.
132. Censuses (1861–91).
133. MBW *Mins*, 9 Oct 1874, p.364.
134. MDR 1828/2/114; 1829/2/767: Census (1851).
135. WCA, WDP2/756: LMA, GLC/AR/BR/06/060125.
136. WCA, WDP2/756: *POD*.
137. MDR 1827/10/703; 1837/7/379; 1840/9/42–3.
138. Report by Medical Officer of Health, 10 Nov 1911, copy in WCA, WDP2/1135.
139. WCA, WDP2/1135: LMA, GLC/AR/BR/6/55271.
140. *Ibid*: Principal Probate Registry, will of Ethel Snagge.
141. WCA, WDP2/1135.
142. *Ibid*: PRO, IR58/91033/828.
143. MDR 1826/2/464; 1827/3/315–6; 1828/4/461; 1830/7/470.
144. WBC: WCA, WDP2/343.
145. WCA, WDP2/343.
146. Based on account in booklet *Deutsche Evangelische Christuskirche*, n.d., published by the church.
147. *History of the King's Works*, vol.v, pp.253–4.
148. PRO, LC1/735.
149. *Ibid*.
150. *Daily News*, 21 Oct 1901, p.5.
151. PRO, LC1/735.
152. *Deutsche Evangelische Christuskirche*.
153. LCC *Mins*, 12–13 Oct 1909, p.561; 24 Jan 1911, p.58: City and

Hackney Health Authority Archives, Ha62/11, German Hospital Board of Management Minutes, 1908–13.

154. BAL, Drawings Collection, W5/2.
155. LCC *Mins*, 13 Oct 1903, p.1529: *The Times*, 28 Nov 1904, p.9f: *B*, 10 Dec 1904, p.611.
156. LCC *Mins*, 17 Nov 1903, p.1827; 22 Dec 1903, p.2119.
157. David Braithwaite, *Building in the Blood: the story of Dove Brothers of Islington 1781–1981*, 1981, p.129.
158. Date-stone: *B*, 10 Dec 1904, p.611: *The Times*, 28 Nov 1904, p.9f.
159. PRO, IR58/91017/2.
160. *Deutsche Evangelische Christuskirche*: *BN*, 1 Sept 1905, p.290.

CHAPTER VII (pp.128–142)

Rutland Gardens and South Lodge

1. Joshua Rhodes, *A Topographical Survey of the Parish of Kensington*, 1766.
2. MDR 1773/2/350: RB.
3. MDR 1797/4/266.
4. WCA, Acc.879: MDR 1862/11/520.
5. MDR 1862/11/450: Title deeds of Rutland House.
6. MDR 1862/11/450; 1864/11/627; 1866/19/693.
7. MBW *Mins*, 5 Aug 1870, p.227; 10 March 1871, pp.41–2; 28 April 1871, p.613: *B*, 18 May 1872, p.393.
8. MDR 1874/19/333.
9. *B*, 11 May 1872, p.373; 7 March 1874, p.206.
10. Davis, p.107: *DNB*.
11. Census (1851).
12. WCA, Acc.262; Acc.879: MDR 1862/11/520: Census (1861): *POD*.
13. *B*, 24 May 1862, p.378: Cluttons, *Cluttons 1765–1965*, 1965.
14. MDR 1871/18/992: WCA, Acc.262.
15. Census (1871): RIBA, *Directory of British Architects 1834–1900*, 1993.
16. WCA, Acc.262.
17. *Ibid*: Title deeds of Rutland House.
18. NMR, Bedford Lemere day-book, Nos 13835–6: LMA, LCC/MIN/10879.
19. PRO, IR58/91026/468.
20. V&A, Prints & Drawings, Acc.no.E810–1981, design by J.G.Crace: *The King*, 12 July 1902, p.778: WCA, Acc.262.
21. *The King*, 12 July 1902, p.774.
22. WCA, WDP2/489.
23. WCA, WDP2/479: Royal Academy of Dancing, *The New Home of the Royal Academy of Dancing*, brochure, c.1968.
24. *The King*, 12 July 1902, p.774.
25. *Ibid*., p.778.
26. *Ibid*.
27. Gwent RO, D.361.F1.1.1.
28. Lord Montagu of Beaulieu, *Rolls of Rolls-Royce*, 1966, p.30.
29. Westminster City Council *Mins*, 16 July 1963, pp.514–15.
30. *Royal Academy of Dancing Gazette*, Feb 1968, p.1.
31. *Dance Gazette*, 1972, No.2, p.8.
32. DSR 1882/59–62, 214: WCA, Acc.262: PRO, IR58/91043/1320–3.
33. OS 1894–6, 1906.
34. WCA, WDP2/754.
35. *B*, 11 Nov 1871, p.896: DSR 1872/71–2: MBW *Mins*, 13 Oct 1871, p.352; 9 April 1873, p.481; 2 May 1873, p.541.
36. PRO, IR58/91032/774–5: *POD*: LMA, GLC/AR/BR/06/052347.
37. WBC.
38. *Interior Design*, Nov 1980, pp.39–41.
39. *DNB*: Mollie Gillen, *The Prince and His Lady*, 1970, p.120: RB.
40. MDR 1796/3/573: RB: *The Observer*, 2 Dec 1798.
41. MDR 1811/7/761; 1831/3/103.
42. *The Times*, 10 March 1808, p.4c: *The Star*, 11 July 1808, p.4.
43. MDR 1831/5/403.
44. *POD*.
45. *The Times*, 26 June 1870, p.7e.
46. This account of Lady Ashburton and the building of Kent House draws on the following sources – Letters addressed to Lady Ashburton, principally from John Forster and Harriet Hosmer, in the Baring Collection now in the National Library of Scotland: Virginia Surtees, *The Ludovisi Goddess: The Life of Louisa Lady Ashburton*, 1984: Dolly Sherwood, *Harriet Hosmer: American Sculptor, 1830–1908*, 1991: and Debenham, Tewson, Richardson & Co., *Kent House, Knightsbridge*, sale particulars of Nov 1907 (copy in NMR).
47. *B*, 18 Nov 1871, p.915.
48. DSR 1872/134: Title deeds of Rutland House: *B*, 18 May 1872, p.393.
49. Surtees, *op.cit.*, p.165: Baring Collection, John Forster to Lady Ashburton, 29 Sept 1873.
50. Surtees, *op.cit.*, pp.164–5.
51. Baring Collection, Harriet Hosmer to Lady Ashburton, n.d.
52. Surtees, *op.cit.*, p.164.
53. *The Times*, 31 Oct 1872, p.8c.
54. Title deeds of Rutland House, conveyance of 29 Sept 1902.
55. Baring Collection, John Forster to Lady Ashburton, 4, 29 April 1873.
56. *Ibid*., John Forster to Lady Ashburton, 4 April 1873: Surtees, *op.cit.*, pp.171, 177.
57. Surtees. *op.cit.*, p.157: Baring Collection, G.F.Watts to Lady Ashburton, 3 June 1874: Augustus Hare, *The Story of My Life*, 1900, vol.IV, p.329.
58. V&A, Prints & Drawings, Collmann drawings, pm Q.11.a.
59. Baring Collection, John Forster to Lady Ashburton, 4 April 1873.
60. *Ibid*., John Forster to Lady Ashburton, 17 Feb 1878.
61. *The Diaries of Cynthia Gladwyn*, ed. Miles Jebb, 1995, p.121n.
62. *Country Life*, 1 Nov 1913, *Architectural Supplement*.
63. Humphrey Noble, *Life in Noble Houses*, 1967, p.97, Pl.IX: *Country Life*, 1 Nov 1913, *Architectural Supplement*.
64. Information provided by Lord Gladwyn.
65. *Ibid*.
66. *Ibid*: Noble, *op.cit.*, p.98, Pl.X.
67. *The Czech Memorial Scrolls Centre: A Historical Account*, ed. Phillipa Bernard, 1988, p.38: *The Times*, 15 Dec 1959, p.7c.
68. *B*, 10 Aug 1872, p.635.
69. Title deeds of Rutland House: WBC.
70. BAL, Drawings Collection, Lut 159: Correspondence in Charleton House Papers (copies held by Royal Commission on the Ancient and Historical Monuments of Scotland).
71. Hampton & Sons' sale particulars, in possession of Rutland Trust plc.
72. DSR 1902/125: PRO, IR58/91043/1317.
73. Title deeds of Rutland House: copies of annotated photographs in Charleton House Papers (RCAHMS D10318).
74. MDR 1878/18/342: Title deeds of Rutland House: *B*, 13 July 1872, p.554: DSR 1872/317.
75. MDR 1879/8/290; 1880/5/502.
76. *POD*.
77. Robert Samuel Badal, 'Kate and Ellen Bateman: A Study in Precocity', thesis submitted to Northwestern University, USA, 1971, p.4 (copy in Theatre Museum).
78. *Ibid*., p.38: *The Times*, 24 March 1875, p.8c.
79. DSR 1879/284: WCA, WDP2/754.
80. DSR 1873/225.
81. Baring Collection, John Forster to Lady Ashburton, 14 May 1873; Harriet Hosmer to Lady Ashburton, n.d.
82. PRO, IR58/91043/1320: WCA, WDP2/754: WBC.
83. WBC.
84. MDR 1771/6/262.
85. John Harris, *Sir William Chambers*, 1970, p.223: *DNB*.
86. Chancellor, p.182: *DNB*.
87. *Life of John, Lord Campbell, Lord High Chancellor of Great Britain*, ed. Hon. Mrs Hardcastle, 1881, pp.170–2.
88. *Ibid*., pp.306–7.
89. *B*, 24 Oct 1868, p.776.
90. *DNB*: Companies House file 30306.
91. *Kylemore Abbey, An Historic Essay* (booklet provided by the Abbey, n.d.).
92. Principal Probate Registry, will of Mitchell Henry.
93. *B*, 18 March 1899, p.282; 7 Sept 1901, p.210.

94. *B*, 23 June 1900, p.622; 7 Sept 1901, p.210; 14 Sept 1901, p.237.
95. MDR 1902/25/721: PRO, IR58/91043/1324.
96. *BN*, 21 Aug 1903, p.239; 28 Aug 1903, p.293.
97. LCC *Mins*, 28 Oct 1902, p.1563; 18 Nov 1902, p.1692.

CHAPTER VIII (pp.143–156)

Rutland Gate

1. KLS, MSS 2778, 2799–2800: WCA, Acc.1188.
2. WCA, Acc.1188, abstract of title.
3. *Ibid*.
4. Belvoir Castle Muniments, Acc.no.633.
5. V&A, Prints & Drawings, 6821/4.
6. PRO, PROB11/1054.
7. RB: PRO, C13/2627/1; PROB11/1524: T.Faulkner, *History and Antiquities of Kensington*, 1820, p.445.
8. GL, sale catalogues 105.
9. WCA, Acc.1188, valuation, April 1837.
10. WCA, Acc.1188(II).
11. LMA, WCS/P28/890.
12. LMA, WCS/P35/1082.
13. WCA, Acc.1188(II).
14. MDR 1837/8/755–7; 1840/1/404–9.
15. GL, MSS 8733/9, pp.84–5, 92, 98–9, 105; 8733/10, pp.24–5, 64.
16. WCA, Acc.1188(I): RB.
17. *POD*: Census (1841).
18. RB.
19. Neil Rhind, *Blackheath Village and Environs 1790–1970*, vol.2, 1983.
20. WCA, Acc.1188(II): MDR 1837/8/686–9.
21. WCA, Acc.1188(I).
22. MDR 1838/5/165–70.
23. MDR 1838/7/742.
24. GL, MSS 8733/10, p.439; 8733/11, pp.8, 153–4, 158.
25. RB.
26. MDR 1842/3/840.
27. RB: MDR 1840/7/9: WCA, Acc.1188(II), articles of agreement 4 Jan 1841.
28. MDR 1841/4/644.
29. LMA, WCS/P41/1329: WCA, Acc.1188(III).
30. WCA, Acc.1188(I).
31. PRO, WORK16/353.
32. WBC.
33. *Evening Standard*, 1 Aug 1990, p.23: WBC.
34. MDR 1841/7/280: RB.
35. MDR 1845/9/291–2.
36. DSR 1846/183: CERC, Church Commissioners' file 15834/2: MDR 1848/4/82: RB.
37. Leslie Field, '26 Rutland Gate' (typescript), 1971.
38. MDR 1842/7/205–6: LMA, WCS/P41/1329: RB.
39. DSR 1847/140, 157; 1848/183–4.
40. Annotation by Cresy in copy of his wife's translation of Milizia's *Lives of Celebrated Architects*, 1826, vol.I, facing p.liv, in BAL (reference provided by Diana Burfield).
41. e.g. MDR 1838/5/156; 1838/7/742; 1840/1/404; 1841/7/280.
42. RB: MDR 1840/7/9: *The Times*, 6 May 1852, p.16f: PRO, IR58/91045/1371.
43. *The Times*, 6 May 1852, p.16f.
44. MDR 1843/2/495.
45. L.Grüner, *I Mosaici della Cupola nella Cappella Chigiana di S. Maria del Popolo in Roma*, 1839.
46. *The Times*, 6 May 1852, p.16f.
47. *Ibid*.
48. Davis, p.178: *The Athenaeum*, 1 May 1852, p.475: MDR 1853/9/139.
49. *POD*: GEC: PRO, IR58/91045/1371.
50. CERC, Ground Rents Sale, bundle No.223: WCA, WDP2/754: DSR 1914/48: PRO, IR58/91045/1371.

51. WCA, WDP2/754; WDP2R/309: CERC, Ground Rents Sales, bundle No. 223: DSR 1916/111.
52. *POD*: LMA, GLC/AR/BR/17/68338.
53. WCA, Acc.1188, articles of agreement, 25 March 1841: RB: MDR 1847/12/43.
54. Martin Royalton-Kisch, 'John Sheepshanks (1787–1863) and his Dutch and Flemish Etchings', *Landmarks in Print Collecting: Connoisseurs and Donors at the British Museum since 1753*, ed. Antony Griffiths, 1996, p.73.
55. WCA, Acc.1188, articles of agreement, 25 March 1841.
56. Gustav Waagen, *Treasures of Art in Great Britain*, 1854, vol.II, pp.299–307.
57. Censuses (1851–71).
58. RB.
59. Ethel M.Richardson, *The Story of All Saints Ennismore Gardens (Knightsbridge)*, n.d. [c.1935], pp.35–6.
60. DSR 1899/37.
61. PRO, IR58/81046/1424.
62. WCA, Acc.1188, draft articles of agreement, 20 March 1851: DSR: MDR 1853/18/186.
63. RB: MBW *Mins*, 25 Sept 1857, p.702; 12 Feb 1858, p.154: A.M.W.Stirling, *Victorian Sidelights*, 1954, p.209.
64. RB: POD: *Survey of London*, vol.XLII, 1986, p.142.
65. *Land & Building News*, 20 Dec 1856, p.945.
66. WCA, Acc.1188.
67. PRO, IR58/91046/1411: NMR, Bedford Lemere day-books.
68. DSR 1919/85: *Academy Architecture*, vol.52, 1921, pp.18–19.
69. *House and Garden*, Nov 1920, pp.9, 25, 28.
70. WBC.
71. *Ibid*.
72. *Ibid*.
73. *35th Annual Report of The Knightsbridge Association*, Dec 1996, p.27.
74. WCA, Westminster City Council News Bulletin dated 11 May 1971: *The Times*, 12 May 1971, p.3d: *Daily Telegraph*, 24 Feb 1972, p.13.
75. Sale brochure, c.1978: *The Living History of Westminster*, ed. Gillian Darley and Ian Lacey, 1985, pp.50–1.
76. John Winter, 'YRM, where are they now?', in Alan Powers, *In the Line of Development: FRS Yorke, E Rosenberg and CS Mardall to YRM, 1930–1992*, 1992.
77. *Building*, 25 Oct 1985, p.11: WBC.
78. LMA, GLC/BR/AR/06/060326.
79. *Domus*, April 1992, pp.60–5: WBC.
80. *The Independent*, 19 Feb 1994, p.30: WBC.
81. LMA, GLC/AR/BR/17/68338: WCA, WDP2/754.
82. WBC.
83. *Architect & Building News*, 23 March 1934, p.370.
84. This account is based on – *Brick Builder*, March 1937, pp.37–8: *Architect & Building News*, 12 Feb 1937, pp.196, 203–7: *AJ*, 22 April 1937, pp.702–5, 709.
85. MDR 1845/9/291–2.
86. DSR 1914/47.
87. Jessica Mitford, *Hons and Rebels*, 1960, pp.42–3: Leslie Field, '26 Rutland Gate' (typescript), 1971.
88. WBC: advert in *House and Garden*, Feb 1994.
89. Principal Probate Registry, will of John Elger, 1888.
90. *POD*: WBC.
91. WBC: *B*, 1 May 1936, p.890: BAL Archives, GolER/249/8: WCA, WDP2/571.

CHAPTER IX (pp.157–190)

The Kingston House Estate

1. WA, WAM 16459: CERC, Church Commissioners' file 292078: WCA, Acc.943/2.
2. WA, WAM 16461: CERC, Church Commissioners' file 292078: WCA, Acc.943/2: MDR 1760/2/154.
3. WCA, Acc.943/2, 3.

4. WCA, Acc.943/2.
5. MDR 1813/4/46–7, 291–2: WCA, Acc.943/2: CERC, Church Commissioners' file 15834/1.
6. WCA, Acc.943/2, bundle 1.
7. Principal Probate Registry, will of 4th Earl of Listowel.
8. Information provided by W.T.S.Digby-Seymour, and Alan Flint of Cluttons Daniel Smith.
9. Unless otherwise indicated, the following paragraphs are based largely on *Country Life*, 20 March 1937, pp.300–5: *Architect & Building News* (Supplement), 1 Oct 1937; 8 Oct 1937: RB.
10. *DNB*.
11. *Ibid*.
12. *The World*, 10 Dec 1790: PRO, WORK16/661: Chancellor, p.194.
13. WCA, Acc.943/2: MDR 1813/4/291–2: Thomas Faulkner, *History and Antiquities of Kensington*, 1820, p.445.
14. Joshua Rhodes, *A Topographical Survey of the Parish of Kensington*, 1766.
15. Colvin, pp.367, 369.
16. Rhodes, *op.cit*: National Library of Wales, Peniarth MS 418D, ff.79–116.
17. Diary of Count Kilmansegge, quoted in Chancellor, pp.184–5.
18. Faulkner, *op.cit.*, p.445.
19. Davis, p.164.
20. Faulkner, *op.cit.*, pp.445–9: Gustav Waagen, *Treasures of Art in Great Britain*, 1854, vol.II, pp.311–12.
21. *B*, 8 April 1843, p.112: GEC: WCA, Acc.943/2/1; Acc.1004, Box 7.
22. *Country Life*, 20 March 1937, p.300: *Architect & Building News* (Supplement), 1 Oct 1937; 8 Oct 1937.
23. PRO, PROB11/1883, ff.87r–88r: MDR 1855/9/187; 1855/10/548.
24. *Survey of London*, vol.XXXIX, 1977, p.131; vol.XL, 1980, pp.186, 247, 285, 336.
25. WCA, Acc.943/4: *The Times*, 18 July 1851, p.8e.
26. PRO, RAIL733/1–3, 16 Aug 1836, 11 Nov 1840: WCA, Acc.943/4.
27. WCA, Acc.943/4: LMA, WCS/P41/1329.
28. *B*, 8 April 1843, p.112.
29. WCA, Acc.943/2: LMA, WCS/P45/1496: MDR 1845/6/167: BAL, Drawings Collection, U12/14/1–2; U12/16/1–2.
30. WCA, Acc.1004/7; Acc.943/4c: MDR 1845/6/167.
31. PRO, WORK16/36/2.
32. LMA, WCS/P41/1329; WCS/P45/1496; MBO/plans/61–2: MDR 1845/6/167: PRO, WORK16/441.
33. *PP* 1852 (1453), XXVI.275, *Report of the Commissioners Appointed to Inquire into the Cost and Applicability of the Exhibition Building in Hyde Park*, 12 Feb 1852, p.31.
34. DSR 1846/175; 1847/24.
35. RB: *POD*.
36. Account based on – PRO, CRES38/1535; WORK16/36/2; WORK 16/441: *B*, 25 July 1846, p.353: Davis, p.163.
37. PRO, WORK16/36/2.
38. DSR: MDR 1848/5/940, etc.
39. DSR 1848/226–9; 1849/36–42: MDR 1849/10/889–99.
40. *B*, 15 Feb 1851, p.93.
41. *The Times*, 18 July 1851, p.8d.
42. *PP* 1852 (1453), XXVI.275, *Report . . . into the Cost and Applicability of the Exhibition Building in Hyde Park*, 12 Feb 1852, pp.31–3.
43. RB: MDR 1852/10/848; 1852/11/381, 639; 1852/16/478.
44. BAL, Drawings Collection, U12/16(1): MDR 1847/11/494.
45. MDR 1847/11/494.
46. MDR.
47. *Ibid*: RB: *POD*: Census (1851).
48. DSR: MDR: RB: *POD*.
49. WCA, Acc.943/4.
50. WCA, Acc.943/2.
51. *Survey of London*, vol.XLI, 1983, p.45: *B*, 21 Jan 1854, p.30.
52. Censuses (1841–51): RB.
53. BAL, Drawings Collection, U12/14–16.
54. *B*, 8 Jan 1848, p.24.
55. Leigh Hunt, *The Old Court Suburb*, 3rd edn [*c*.1860], pp.14–15.
56. *Civil Engineer and Architect's Journal*, 26 July 1851, pp.402–3.
57. *Ibid.*, 26 July 1851, p.402; 9 Aug 1851, p.426: postcard in Brian Girling collection (116D): NMR, photo BB46/02330.
58. BAL, Drawings Collection, U12/14(3–4); U12/15(3–13).
59. *PP* 1852 (1453), XXVI.275, *Report . . . into the Cost and Applicability of the Exhibition Building in Hyde Park*, 12 Feb 1852, p.32.
60. *Ibid.*, p.33.
61. WBC: PRO, IR58/91020/164–90.
62. WBC: PRO, IR58/91020, 91040.
63. *The Gentlewoman*, 29 July 1893, pp.137–8: *DNB*.
64. DSR: RB: MDR 1848/5/940, etc.
65. LMA, GLC/AR/BR/06/058950: WCA, Acc.1004/4.
66. DSR: MDR 1847/5/939: BAL, Drawings Collection, U12/16(6): NMR, photos BL 26048–9: WBC.
67. LMA, GLC/AR/BR/06/45725: DSR 1920/95: *Survey of London*, vol.XLI, 1983, p.46.
68. Unless otherwise indicated this section is based on information in the General Records of the Department of State (Record Group 59, 1910–1929) in the US National Archives and Records Administration (accession no.124.411), provided by Louis P.Nelson: J.P.Morgan Jr Papers in the Pierpont Morgan Library, New York: John Horder and Stephen Pasmore, *14 Prince's Gate: Home of the Royal College of General Practitioners*, 1987: PRO, IR58/91040/1133–4: RB: *POD*.
69. DSR 1846/175: MDR 1848/3/268; 1855/11/323; 1858/14/623.
70. MDR 1870/21/559.
71. Edward Fowles, *Memories of Duveen Brothers*, 1976, pp.7, 26: S.N.Behrman, *Duveen*, 1972 edn, p.53.
72. e.g. *New York Journal*, 27 May 1920.
73. *AR*, Jan 1927, pp.16–24.
74. DSR 1925/265.
75. Hastings' original design is reproduced in *Apollo*, June 1999, p.33.
76. Information provided by Simon Bradley of the Buildings of England.
77. *The Times*, 24 April 1925, p.12e; 13 May 1927, p.19c; 14 May 1927 p.15c.
78. Brian N.Morton, *Americans in London*, 1988 edn, p.210.
79. *Evening Standard*, 22 June 1993, p.15: *The Independent*, 7 Dec 1993, p.11: WBC.
80. DSR 1848/253; 1849/43.
81. DSR 1853/7.
82. MDR 1854/2/85; 1855/11/501; 1857/13/317; 1866/6/218; 1884/26/586: RB: *POD*.
83. WBC: *POD*: KLS, K64/216.
84. *Survey of London*, vol.XXXVIII, 1975, p.304.
85. MDR 1851/1/427; 1855/11/501.
86. WCA, Acc.943/2.
87. *POD*: MBW *Mins*, 22 March 1861, p.230: *The Times*, 15 Dec 1886, p.4f: Principal Probate Registry, will of Peter Thorn.
88. Principal Probate Registry, will of Peter Thorn: *The Times*, 15 Dec 1886, p.4f: *POD*.
89. MDR 1867/8/232: WCA, Acc.943/2, 4.
90. WCA, Acc.1004/7.
91. WCA, Acc.943/2.
92. WCA, Acc.943/4.
93. WCA, Acc.943/4c.
94. WCA, Acc.943/2, 4: MDR 1868/28/1063: LMA, MBW/BA/11220.
95. MBW *Mins*, 1 May 1868, p.638; 22 May 1868, p.713.
96. *The Architect*, 20 May 1871, pp.265–6: RB: *POD*: MDR.
97. *The Architect*, 20 May 1871, pp.265–6: WCA, Acc.1004/1, 6: RB: *POD*.
98. DSR: MDR: WCA, Acc.1004/1, 6.
99. RB: *POD*.
100. *The Architect*, 20 May 1871, p.266.
101. *B*, 12 May 1877, p.483.
102. *The Architect*, 3 Dec 1870, p.323; 20 May 1871, p.266: Corporation of London Records Office, Comptrollers Deed Box 326, no.6.
103. Henry-Russell Hitchcock, *Early Victorian Architecture in Britain*, vol.I, 1972, p.482.
104. *The Architect*, 20 May 1871, p.266.

105. *B*, 31 June 1858, p.514: *Survey of London*, vol.XL, 1980, pp.278–9.

106. *The Architect*, 20 May 1871, pp.265–6: WCA, Acc.1004/1.

107. *The Architect*, 20 May 1871, p.265: C.Cunningham and P.Waterhouse, *Alfred Waterhouse 1830–1905*, 1992, p.237: MBW *Mins*, 21 Oct 1870, p.498; 3 Feb 1871, p.215.

108. WCA, Acc.1004/4.

109. WCA, Acc.1004/2.

110. WCA, Acc.943, Box 2, bundle 1.

111. *Ibid.*

112. WCA, Acc.1004, Box 2: MDR 1874/27/797.

113. *B*, 11 May 1872, p.358.

114. Lincolnshire Archives, BNLW 2/1/2/22.

115. Plans, elevations, and correspondence for Alford House are in Lincolnshire Archives (ref.BNLW).

116. Lincolnshire Archives, BNLW 2/1/2/25.

117. *Ibid.*, BNLW 2/1/2/22 (enclosure).

118. *Ibid.*, BNLW 2/1/2/22.

119. *Ibid.*, BNLW 2/1/2/19, 20, 22.

120. Schlesinger Library, Radcliffe College, Cambridge, Mass., microfilm reel 5, folder 114, Hosmer to Cornelia Crow, 17 June 1861.

121. Royal Archives, Queen Victoria's Journal, 23 March 1867.

122. Schlesinger Library, microfilm reel 5, folder 120, Hosmer to Cornelia Crow, n.d.

123. Lincolnshire Archives, BNLW 2/1/2/20, 24, 25.

124. MDR 1888/2/21–22: sale particulars in WCA, Acc.943/2: *The Estate Exchange Year Book*, 1931, p.127.

125. WCA, Acc.1004/1.

126. WCA, Acc.943/4: DSR 1878/4: MDR 1880/22/63.

127. Anderson's contract drawings and a perspective are in the BAL, Drawings Collection, Arc3/377.

128. MDR 1886/24/556: *ILN*, 30 Oct 1886, p.473: Raymond Cazelles, *Le Duc D'Aumale: Prince Aux Dix Visages*, (Paris) 1984, pp.430–1.

129. WCA, Acc.943/4, Instructions of 22 June 1887: DSR 1887/21.

130. Cazelles, *op.cit.*, pp.431, 432.

131. MDR 1890/17/244.

132. Charles Lines, *Stapleford Park*, n.d., pp.9–10.

133. *POD*: National Archives of Canada, Coll.DND–WW1, Box 9.

134. *Who Was Who in America*, vol.3, 1960, p.328: WCA, Acc.943/4, draft lease of 1922: *POD*.

135. Ethel M. Richardson, *The Story of All Saints Ennismore Gardens (Knightsbridge)*, nd. [*c*.1935], p.100.

136. DSR 1883/86: *Survey of London*, vol.XLII, 1986, pp.23–4.

137. WCA, Acc.943/4, draft lease of 27 Feb 1886; Andrew Saint, *Richard Norman Shaw*, 1976, p.453: Royal Academy of Arts, Shaw Bequest, RP4/3A.

138. Information provided by Andrew Saint.

139. PRO, IR58/91020/195.

140. LMA, GLC/AR/BR/23/160469(1): DSR 1903/76.

141. LMA, GLC/AR/BR/23/160469(1).

142. Except where otherwise indicated this account is based on – WCA, Acc.943/2; Acc.1004/3: DSR: PRO, IR58/91020/193–6.

143. MBW *Mins*, 22 March 1878, p.498.

144. MBW *Mins*, 14 Nov 1879, p.642.

145. *Survey of London*, vol.XXXVII, 1973, pp.122–5, 261–6: *Dictionary of Business Biography*, ed. D.J.Jeremy, vol.2, 1984, pp.800–2.

146. WCA, Acc.943/2/1.

147. WCA, Acc.1004/5.

148. MBW *Mins*, 19 Jan 1883, p.141; 26 Jan 1883, p.170.

149. WCA, Acc.1004/5: PRO, IR58/91020/193.

150. Scottish RO, GD.112/20/6/11–12.

151. *POD*: LMA, GLC/AR/BR/23/160469.

152. *The Observer*, 5 May 1963, p.13: *POD*.

153. Unless otherwise indicated this and the succeeding paragraphs are based on – *BN*, 23 July 1886, p.126: Giles Walkley, *Artists' Houses in London 1764–1914*, 1994, pp.75–7.

154. David Watkin, *The Architecture of Basil Champneys*, 1989, pp.5, 7, 27: *B*, 28 June 1912, p.754.

155. DSR 1884/46, 90.

156. NMR, photo BL 5955.

157. *B*, 11 July 1892, p.52 and illus.

158. PRO, IR58/91021/202.

159. *POD*: PRO, IR58/91021/202: sale particulars in WCA, Acc.943/2, bundle 4.

160. LMA, GLC/AR/BR/06/05891; GLC/AR/BR/06/057997: DSR: WCA, Acc.1004/4; Acc.943/4b.

161. *POD*: Electoral Registers: *The Sunday Times Magazine*, 30 Jan 2000, pp.34–43: WBC.

162. BAL, Drawings Collection, RAN 74/L/5(1–4, 14): WCA, WDP2/710: *B*, 16 Dec 1938, pp.1161–2.

163. DSR: *Architecture Illustrated*, July 1938, pp.3–5: WBC.

164. *Architecture Illustrated*, July 1938, pp.6–10: BAL, Drawings Collection, RAN 74/J/6(1–49); RAN 74/L/5(102): WBC.

165. *B*, 16 Dec 1938, pp.1161–2.

166. *B*, 12 Aug 1949, pp.203–4.

167. WBC.

168. *Ibid*: WCA, WDP2/710.

169. *Modern Buildings in London: A Guide*, ed. Charles McKean and Tom Jestico, 1976, p.28.

170. WBC.

171. Except where otherwise indicated this and the succeeding paragraphs are based on LMA, GLC/AR/BR/76249; GLC/AR/ BR/23/125862; GLC/AR/BR/23/160468–9.

172. WCA, Acc.943/2; Acc.1004/6: *Financial Times*, 25 Sept 1935, p.10.

173. *Architect & Building News*, 31 Jan 1936, p.149.

174. DSR 1937/112: WCA, WDP2/480.

175. LMA, GLC/AR/BR/23/160469(2).

176. WBC.

177. CERC, Church Commissioners' file 15834/2.

178. *Ibid.*, file 33082/1.

179. WCA, Acc.943/4.

180. *B*, 8 April 1843, p.112.

181. PRO, CRES2/650: CERC, Church Commissioners' file 15834/1.

182. PRO, CRES2/650.

183. *Ibid*: *Ecclesiologist*, Aug 1849, p.64: CERC, Church Commissioners' file 33082: BAL, Drawings Collection, V7/19.

184. CERC, Church Commissioners' file 15834/1.

185. *Ibid.*, file 15834/2.

186. DSR 1848/193: Richardson, *op.cit.*, p.45.

187. CERC, Church Building Districts, Orders in Council, vol.6 (1848–52), p.96; Church Commissioners' file 15834/2.

188. PRO, CRES2/650.

189. LMA, MBO 73 (case 402), pp.16–17: *Ecclesiologist*, *loc.cit.*

190. Richardson, *op.cit.*, p.44.

191. Gwent RO, D361 F/P10–6.

192. CERC, Church Commissioners' file 15834/2.

193. BAL, Drawings Collection, R. L. Roumieu drawings [5] 1–2.

194. Alistair Service, 'Charles Harrison Townsend', in *Edwardian Architecture and its Origins*, ed. A.Service, 1975, p.163.

195. *BN*, 5 April 1872, p.283.

196. GL, MSS 18319/8, 39: DSR 1885/171.

197. MBW *Mins*, 25 Sept, 2 Oct 1885, pp.376–7, 409: GL, MS 9531/39, p.134.

198. *BN*, 5 April 1889, p.472.

199. *Ibid*.

200. GL, MS 18319/8; *The Studio*, vol.12, 1897, p.118.

201. GL, MS 18319/39.

202. DSR 1892/1.

203. *B*, 21 Nov 1891, p.381.

204. *Ibid*: F.Hamilton Jackson, 'The work of T. R. Spence, Designer, Decorator, and Architect', in *The Magazine of Art*, 1903, pp.81, 83.

205. Richardson, *op.cit.*, pp.62, 71.

206. GL, MS 18319/135.

207. Richardson, *op.cit.*, pp.75–6, 126, 140.

208. GL, MS 18319/75: Richardson, *op.cit.*, p.147.

209. BAL, Drawings Collection, V6/29.

210. Richardson, *op.cit.*, pp.135–6, 138: PRO, IR58/91020/190.

211. CERC, Church Commissioners' file 33082/5: GL, MS 19224/21.

212. Cathedral web site.

213. Information provided by M.P.Mandrigin.

214. Information provided by Sarah Brown.

215. Richardson, *op.cit.*, p.44.
216. *B*, 17 Jan 1903, p.8: *The Studio*, vol.28, Feb 1903, pp.118, 123.
217. Richardson, *op.cit.*, p.121.

CHAPTER X (pp.191–210)

The Freake Estate

1. For details of Freake's career, see *Survey of London*, vol.XXXVIII, 1975, pp.288–9; vol.XLI, 1983, pp.103–4: *Dictionary of Business Biography*, vol.2, 1984, pp.427–30.
2. *Survey of London*, vol.XXXVIII, 1975, p.4.
3. RB: GL, MS 8674/81, p.237.
4. *Ibid*: MDR 1856/9/175.
5. *BN*, 2 Jan 1857, p.21; 17 April 1857, p.383.
6. MDR 1852/7/372, 783: *Survey of London*, vol.XXXVIII, 1975, p.57.
7. *Survey of London*, vol.XXXVIII, 1975, p.54.
8. *Ibid.*, p.57.
9. MDR 1856/9/202.
10. MDR 1881/36/934.
11. *Survey of London*, vol.XXXVIII, 1975, p.59.
12. MDR 1857/5/83–88: *BN*, 2 Jan 1857, p.21; 17 April 1857, p.388; 26 June 1857, p.665; 4 Sept 1857, p.931.
13. *The Times*, 9 April 1857, p.9e: *BN*, 18 April 1857, p.224: *Dictionary of Business Biography*, vol.2, 1984, p.428.
14. MDR 1858–61.
15. RB.
16. LMA, MBW/BA/01574.
17. RB: MDR 1859/11/433.
18. *BN*, 30 Sept 1859, pp.879–80.
19. MDR 1860/13/582–3, 983–4, 1001–2: *BN*, 19 Oct 1860, p.810.
20. RB: *POD*: PRO, WORK33/1248.
21. *B*, 3 May 1862, p.318: MBW *Mins*, 7 March 1862, p.198; 28 March 1862, p.251.
22. RB: MDR 1875/2/697.
23. *Survey of London*, vol.XXXVIII, 1975, pp.294, 303–4.
24. *BN*, 17 June 1859, p.334: *Survey of London*, vol.XXXVIII, 1975, p.304, Pl.2b: MDR 1859–75.
25. Census (1891).
26. *BN*, 19 Oct 1860, p.810.
27. *The Architect*, 1 May 1891, p.264.
28. BAL, FRIBA Nomination Papers.
29. Archives of the Commissioners for the Exhibition of 1851, file no.106.
30. *BN*, 17 June 1859, p.554; 19 Oct 1860, p.810.
31. WBC.
32. *BN*, 19 Oct 1860, p.810.
33. Julian Hawthorne, *Shapes that Pass: Memories of Old Days*, 1928, p.134.
34. Lady Mount Temple, *Memorials*, 1890, p.65: Margaret Leicester Warren, *Diaries*, vol.II, 1924, p.245.
35. *The Architect*, 18 May 1872, p.262.
36. NMR, Bedford Lemere day-books.
37. PRO, IR58/91040/1178.
38. PRO, IR58/91038/1075–1100; IR58/91040/1101–19.
39. The most recent study, laid under heavy contribution here, is Linda Merrill's exhaustive investigation *The Peacock Room: A Cultural Biography*, 1998.
40. Theodore Child, 'A Pre-Raphaelite Mansion', in *Harper's New Monthly Magazine* (New York), Dec 1890, p.86.
41. MDR 1870/5/518–19: RB.
42. MDR 1874/24/955: RB.
43. *Murray Marks and His Friends. A Tribute of Regard by Dr G. C. Williamson*, 1919, p.85.
44. Child, *op.cit.*, p.84.
45. NAL, Cole Diary, 30 June 1876.
46. *The Times*, 9 Sept 1874, p.8f.
47. Alnwick Castle, Estates Office, William Collins's bill for Northumberland House, 1822–4: *The Times*, 26 May 1823, p.3f.

48. Merrill, *op.cit.*, pp.178–9.
49. *Ibid.*, pp.182–3.
50. Child, *op.cit.*, p.82.
51. Merrill, *op.cit.*, p.195.
52. *Ibid.*, p.206.
53. Williamson, *op.cit.*, p.85.
54. Norman Shaw to Murray Marks, 2 June 1904. Quoted by permission of the syndics of the Fitzwilliam Museum.
55. *The Architect*, 24 Feb 1877, p.118.
56. Andrew Saint, *Richard Norman Shaw*, 1976, p.188: DSR 1876/291.
57. WCA, E3355/(2)/15.
58. Merrill, *op.cit.*, p.157.
59. Information provided by Andrew Saint.
60. *No. 49 Princes Gate*, sale particulars, 1892 (copy in NMRC, no. 697).
61. MDR 1894/26/987; 1894/31/458.
62. *Thorney House Estate*, sale particulars, 1894 (copy in possession of Survey of London): *POD*.
63. Information provided by Andrew Saint.
64. LMA, GLC/AR/BR/22/007483: LCC *Mins*, 15 Jan 1895, p.39: *The Architect*, 14 May 1897, p.318.
65. *49, Princes' Gate, S.W.7.*, sale particulars, 1919 (copy in LMA).
66. Merrill, *op.cit.*, p.312.
67. Information provided by Linda Merrill.
68. Merrill, *op.cit.*, p.315.
69. *Ibid*.
70. *Builders' Journal*, 28 Dec 1904 (*Supplement*), p.10: *The Peacock Room: . . . Removed in its entirety from the late owners' residence and exhibited at Messrs Obach's galleries at 168 New Bond St. London*, catalogue, June 1904.
71. Merrill, *op.cit.*, pp.5–6.
72. *BN*, 6 Jan 1905, p.9.
73. Information provided by the late Clive Wainwright.
74. PRO, IR58/91040/1169.
75. LMA, GLC/AR/BR/22/007482: DSR 1921/86: *POD*.
76. *The Times*, 26 May 1823, p.3f.
77. RB.
78. MDR 1875/19/248.
79. Merrill, *op.cit.*, p.222.
80. Hawthorne, *op.cit.*, pp.135–8: BAL, Drawings Collection, Z25/11(4): *Thomas Armstrong, C.B., A Memoir*, ed. L.M.Lamont, 1912, pp.15–6.
81. PRO, IR58/91040/1172.
82. *Thomas Armstrong . . .*, ed. L.M.Lamont, 1912, p.16: Dianne Sachko Macleod, *Art and the Victorian middle class: Money and the making of cultural identity*, 1996, p.293.
83. BAL, Drawings Collection, Z25/11(1–3): *B*, 19 May 1877, p.497: Walter Crane, *An Artist's Reminiscences*, 1907, p.166: 'George Aitchison, Lord Leighton's Architect', notes for BAL Drawings Collection Exhibition, Jan/Feb 1980, p.6.
84. *B*, 6 May 1876, p.425: Hawthorne, *op.cit.*, p.134.
85. Joanna Banham, Sally MacDonald, Julia Porter, *Victorian Interior Design*, 1991, p.145.
86. Macleod, *op.cit.*, 1996, p.475.
87. This account is largely based on the following sources – *AJ*, 17 Feb 1938, pp.299–301: *B*, 11 March 1938, pp.499–501: *Architect & Building News*, 18 March 1938, pp.327–31: *Country Life*, 12 Feb 1938, pp.xxii, xxiv: LMA, GLC/AR/BR/7/64977.
88. *Country Life*, 12 Feb 1938, p.xxiv.
89. *Ibid.*, p.xxii.
90. NMR, photo AA56/00405.
91. Account based on WBC and WCA, WDP2/710.
92. LMA, GLC/AR/BR/TP/31646.
93. ICST Archive, 2/1: WCA, WDP2/709.
94. Sherban Cantacuzino, *Wells Coates, a monograph*, 1978, pp.71–2.
95. *Imperial College 1953–1963: Report on a Decade of Expansion*, p.1.
96. ICST Archive, 2/1, memos of 27 Jan 1956, 22 March 1956.
97. *Ibid.*, memos of 17 Aug–18 Dec 1956.
98. *Architect & Building News*, 20 April 1961, p.503.
99. *AJ*, 5 Dec 1957, p.834: *The Spectator*, 10 May 1963, p.60: *B*, 16 May 1958, p.895.

100. ICST, *Annual Reports*, 1957, p.12; 1960, p.5.
101. Account based on – *Architect & Building News*, 20 April 1960, pp.501–10: *AJ*, 10 Nov 1960, pp.687–96: *AR*, June 1960, pp.417–18: *B*, 29 April 1960, pp.816–20: *Interbuild*, April 1960, pp.12–15.
102. *Architectural Design*, Dec 1963, pp.566–74: *Architect & Building News*, 8 Jan 1964, pp.51–8.
103. WBC: LMA, GLC/AR/BR/17/100475: WCA, WDP2/708: ICST, *Annual Reports*, 1960, p.16; 1963, p.4.
104. WBC.
105. WCA, WDP2/708: WBC.
106. *AJ*, 20 Nov 1997, p.xi: *36th Annual Report of The Knightsbridge Association*, Dec 1997, p.25: information provided by Nicholas Black.

Index

Where individual streets, buildings and other subjects have more than one page reference, the substantive references are those in bold type. Symbols in the left-hand margin indicate individuals and firms known to have worked on the fabric of the area, including the authors of unexecuted designs:

[a]architects, surveyors and designers
[b]builders, contractors and allied tradesmen
[c]craftsmen, artists and decorators
[e]engineers (civil, structural, etc)
[f]suppliers of building materials, plant and fittings

PLATES

Knightsbridge *c*.1905. Looking east from Park Mansions to Albert Gate and Holy Trinity Church: Hyde Park Hotel and Nos 68–70 left, Strathnairn statue in foreground, Harvey Nichols right

a. Mansions and gardens on the south side of the Kensington road in 1766, from Park House (left) to Powis House

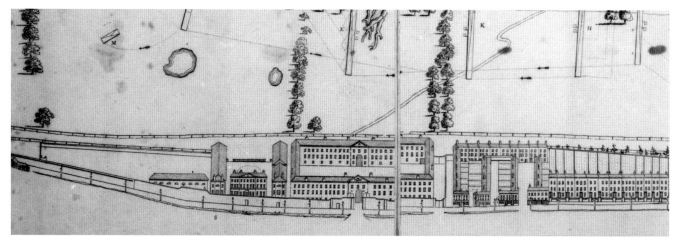

b. Knightsbridge, north side in 1799, from the cavalry barracks (left) to High Row

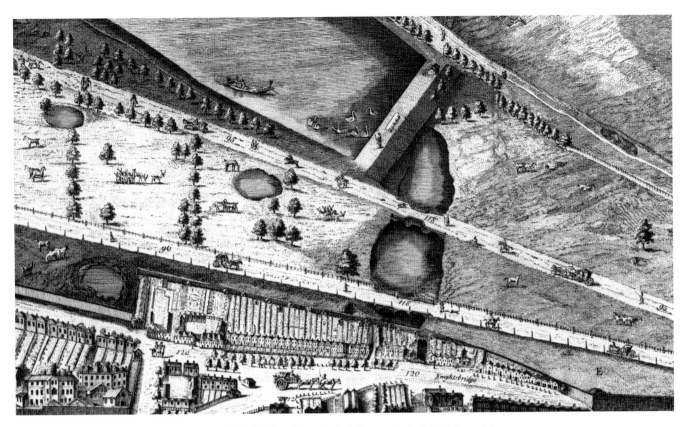

a. Knightsbridge Green, High Row and Park Side in 1766

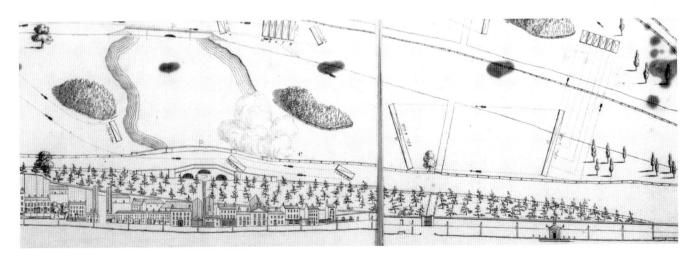

b. Knightsbridge, north side in 1799, from High Row (left) and Park Side towards Hyde Park Corner

EIGHTEENTH CENTURY

4

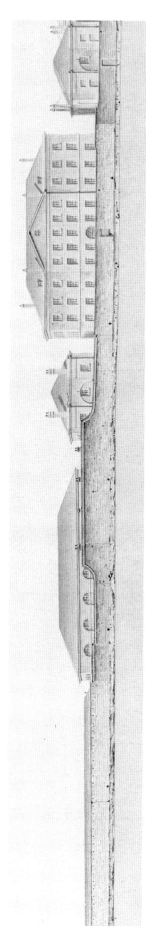
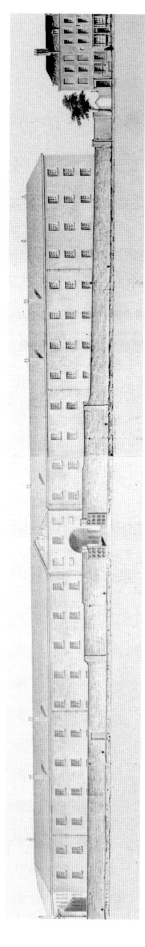

KNIGHTSBRIDGE: NORTH SIDE IN 1811

a. Knightsbridge Barracks: Riding-school (centre left), Horse Infirmary, Officers' Quarters and Hospital

b. Barrack Block, Park Place and houses in High Row

c. High Row: entrances to Jobbins Court (left) and Mills's Buildings (under lantern)

a. High Row: Cannon Brewhouse (centre), Fox alehouse and culverts for the Westbourne (right)

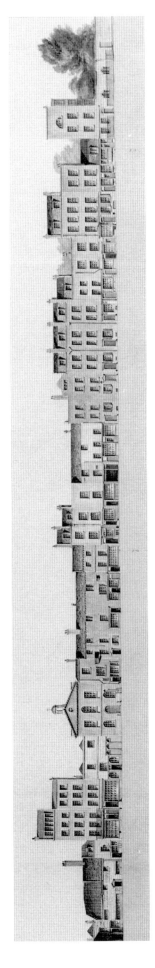

b. Park Side: White Hart (left), Trinity chapel (with cupola)

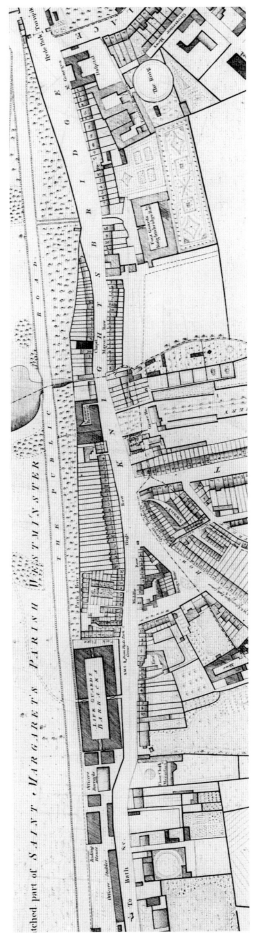

c (below). Knightsbridge area in 1813

a. Knightsbridge, *c.*1846. View looking east from the roof of No. 1 Albert Gate, showing the pagoda entrance to the Chinese Collection (p. 24)

b. Elevated view from above the Crystal Palace in 1851, showing Knightsbridge from the High Road to Princes Gate

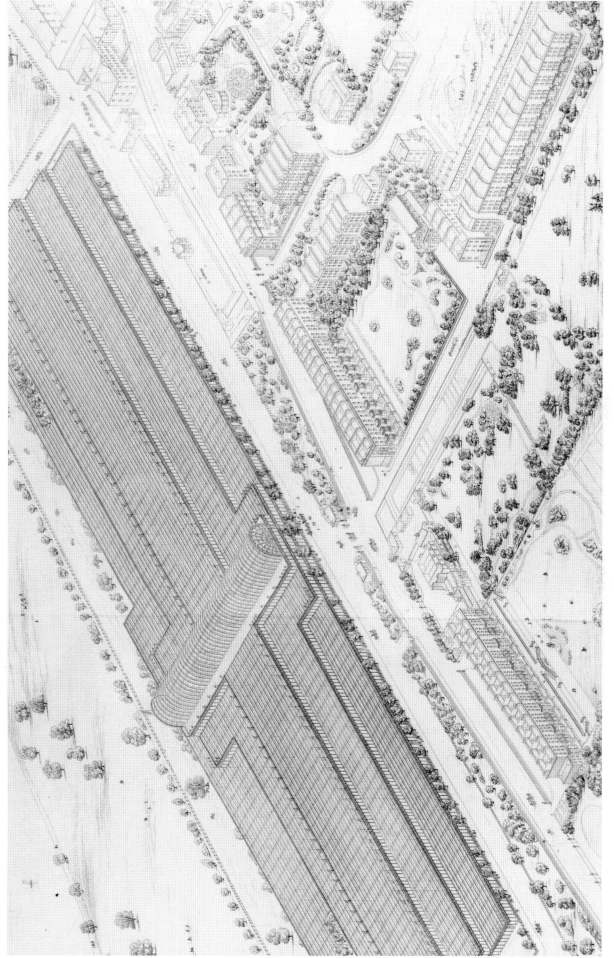

7

Princes Gate and Rutland Gate area in 1851. Bird's-eye view of developments opposite the Crystal Palace

Knightsbridge in 1963. Aerial view looking north-east from above Princes Gardens and Ennismore Gardens (foreground) towards the post-war developments around Knightsbridge Green

a. St George's Place immediately east of Old Barrack Yard prior to redevelopment in 1856–8 (p. 22)

b. St George's Hospital (left) and Nos 1–8 St George's Place in the 1830s. *All demolished*

c. St George's Hospital (left) and Nos 1–11 Knightsbridge in 1939. *Nos 1–9 demolished*

KNIGHTSBRIDGE: SOUTH SIDE

a. Looking west from near the Alexandra Hotel (p. 23) in *c*.1910

b. Nos 11–13 Knightsbridge in *c*.1914 (p. 26)

c. Agriculture House (far left) and Nos 33–45 Knightsbridge in 1963 (pp. 22, 27). *Mostly demolished*

KNIGHTSBRIDGE: SOUTH SIDE

b. Nos 19–23 Knightsbridge, *c.*1946 (p. 22). *Demolished*

a (left). Entrance to the Chinese Collection exhibition hall, St George's Place, *c.*1842 (p. 24). *Demolished*

c. Interior of the Chinese Collection exhibition hall, *c.*1842. *Demolished*

a. Nos 13–19 Knightsbridge. Nos 15 and 17 built 1870–1, George Legg, architect. *Nos 13 and 19 demolished*

b. Front drawing-room

NO. 15 KNIGHTSBRIDGE, DURING RESIDENCE

a. Inner hall, with chimneypiece designed by Frank Baden-Powell

b. Rear drawing-room and organ

OF MRS BADEN-POWELL, *c*.1897 (p. 27)

14

a. Architect's perspective, 1900

b. First-floor showrooms in 1899

WOOLLANDS. Henry L. Florence, architect, 1896–1901 (p. 33). *Demolished*

a. Knightsbridge front in 1996. C. W. Stephens, architect, 1889–94

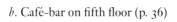

b. Café-bar on fifth floor (p. 36)

c. Sloane Street front (p. 36)

HARVEY NICHOLS (p. 34)

c (above). No. 27. Hunter and Partners, architects, 1993–5 (p. 27)

b. No. 1. Fitzroy Robinson Partnership, architects, 1991 (p. 26)

a (top). South side, looking west from No. 21 in 1996

POST-WAR KNIGHTSBRIDGE

a (left). Berkeley Hotel, north front. Brian O'Rorke, architect, 1966–72 (pp. 27–8)

b (below). No. 60. Guy Morgan and Partners, architects, 1961–4 (p. 53)

c. Sheraton Park Tower Hotel. Richard Seifert and Partners, architects, 1970–3 (p. 33). Harvey Nichols bottom right

POST-WAR KNIGHTSBRIDGE

a, b. Bowater House and Edinburgh Gate. Guy Morgan and Partners, architects, 1956–8; sculptural group by Jacob Epstein (p. 59)

c, d. Mercury House. Guy Morgan and Partners, architects, 1956–9; *The Seer* by Gilbert Ledward (p. 94)

POST-WAR KNIGHTSBRIDGE

a, b. Trinity Chapel in 1767 (left) and after refronting in 1789

c, d. Holy Trinity Church. Raphael Brandon and Henry M. Eyton, architects, 1860–1

TRINITY CHAPEL AND HOLY TRINITY CHURCH (p. 41). *Demolished*

b (right). Queen's Arms in 1902 (p. 46). *Demolished*

a (below). Park Row and Mills's Buildings in 1913 (p. 45).
Demolished

d. Nos 20–26 in *c.*1910 (pp. 38,39). *Demolished*

c. Nos 62–64, London and County Bank, in 1890. Frederick W. Porter,
architect, 1884–5 (p. 54)

KNIGHTSBRIDGE: NORTH SIDE

a. Nos 84–98 (right to left)

b. Nos 68–84 (right to left)

c. Nos 68–84 (left to right) from Hyde Park

KNIGHTSBRIDGE: NORTH SIDE. Nos 68–98 in 1931 (pp. 42–4). *Site of Bowater House*

Knightsbridge about 1910, looking west from the Alexandra Hotel (left) to the Hyde Park Hotel

a. Perspective view looking north, *c*.1846

b. Hyde Park House in 1942. *Demolished*

c. No. 1 and (right) No. 58 Knightsbridge in 1946

ALBERT GATE. Thomas Cubitt, developer, 1841–55 (p. 46)

a. Salon in 1902

b, c. Staircase and arcaded gallery before alteration in the early 1930s

NO. 1 ALBERT GATE: FRENCH EMBASSY (p. 49)

a. Ballroom looking east in 1902

b. Banqueting-room looking north-west in 1902

NO. 58 KNIGHTSBRIDGE: FRENCH EMBASSY EXTENSION. Olivier Carré, architect, 1899–1902 (p. 50)

b. Detail of staircase balustrade

a (left). Staircase in 1888

c. Ballroom in 1888

No. 2 Albert Gate: Interiors (p. 51)

a (above). Drawing-room

b (below). Morning room

No. 2 Albert Gate: Interiors in 1888

28

a

b

c

HYDE PARK HOUSE: INTERIORS (p. 52). *Demolished*

a (right). Main staircase in 1961

Opposite page
a. Outer hall and main staircase in 1961
b. Staircase compartment and first-floor landing in 1961
c. Picture gallery in 1902

b (below). Ballroom in 1902

HYDE PARK HOUSE: INTERIORS. *Demolished*

a, b. Hyde Park Hotel site: unexecuted designs for a residence for the Earl of Rosebery. Henri Parent, architect, 1881 (p. 54). Elevations to Hyde Park (top) and Knightsbridge

c. Knightsbridge looking east *c.*1884. Nos 62–64 under construction; Hyde Park Hotel site behind hoardings. Lowndes Terrace on right

b. Detail of the front railings

a (left). Knightsbridge front in 1993

c. Hyde Park front in 1968

HYDE PARK HOTEL, now Mandarin Oriental Hyde Park. Archer and Green, architects, 1888–92 (p. 54)

a. Palm Court, *c*.1927. Mewès & Davis, architects, 1925 (p. 58)

b. Smoking-room in 1925 (p. 58)

HYDE PARK HOTEL: INTERIORS

a. Ballroom, enlarged and redecorated by C. Mewès in 1911–12 (p. 58)

b. Restaurant, redecorated by Mewès & Davis in 1925 (p. 58)

HYDE PARK HOTEL: INTERIORS in 1965

a (above). Kensington Road front in 1912: No. 1 Rutland Gate on right

b, c. Details of carved stonework

RUTLAND COURT. Delissa Joseph, architect, 1901–3 (p. 141)

a. Perspective view, *c*.1909

b–e. Details of Knightsbridge entrance, carved brick panels and window mouldings

PARKSIDE. A. H. Hart and Leslie Waterhouse, architects, 1906–7 (p. 42)

36

b (right). Park Mansions in 1902. G. D.
Martin, architect, 1897–1902 (p. 81)

a (below). Albert Gate Court in 1992.
H. C. Newmarch, architect, 1887 (p. 63)

c. Wellington Court (left) and Park Lodge in 1993

d. Park Lodge, perspective view. G. D. Martin
and E. K. Purchase, architects, 1890–2 (p. 61)

MANSION FLATS

a. Park Mansions, *c*.1920 (p. 81)

b. Wellington Court in 1992. M. E. Collins, architect, 1892–5 (p. 61)

c. Albert Gate Mansions, perspective view. Romaine-Walker and Tanner, architects, 1883–4 (p. 83). *Demolished*

MANSION FLATS

a. Strathnairn statue in 1910. E. Onslow Ford, sculptor, 1895 (p. 81). *Removed*

b–i. Nos 55–91 Knightsbridge, W. D. Carö̈e, architect, 1902: decorative details (above) and portrait busts of Edward VII, Queen Alexandra, Lord Kitchener, Lord Roberts, Archbishop Temple and Lord Salisbury (p. 29)

a. Horse Infirmary (right), Officers' Quarters and Forage Barn

b. Barrack Block and (right) Forage Barn

c. Looking east from the old Horse Infirmary (right) *c*.1860

KNIGHTSBRIDGE BARRACKS OF 1792–3: HYDE PARK FRONT. James Johnson, architect (pp. 64–8). *Demolished*

40

a, b. Barrack Blocks, elevations to the park (top) and Knightsbridge

c. South Barrack Block, Knightsbridge front, looking west in 1964

KNIGHTSBRIDGE BARRACKS OF 1878–80. T. H. WYATT, architect (pp. 68–71). *Demolished*

a. Hyde Park front *c*.1895, looking east from the Officers' Mess to the Riding-school and north Barrack Block

b, c. Officers' Mess in 1964; detail of entrance and dining-room chimneypiece

KNIGHTSBRIDGE BARRACKS OF 1878–80 (pp. 68–71). *Demolished*

42

a. Looking north-east in 1964 over the Riding-school to the Barrack Blocks

b, c. Main entrances to the Barrack Blocks in 1964, from Knightsbridge (left) and the park

KNIGHTSBRIDGE BARRACKS OF 1878–80 (pp. 68–71). *Demolished*

a. Parade-ground in 1895, looking west to the Riding-school

b. Riding-school, north front in 1964

Knightsbridge Barracks of 1878–80 (pp. 68–71). *Demolished*

44

a. Knightsbridge front, looking east in 1992

b. Knightsbridge front, looking west in 1970

KNIGHTSBRIDGE BARRACKS OF 1967–70. Sir Basil Spence, architect (pp. 71–6)

a. Entrance to Officers' Mess, *c*.1971

b. Parade-ground in 1995; Barrack Block on left

c. Stone busts from the Victorian barracks
outside Officers' Mess

KNIGHTSBRIDGE BARRACKS OF 1967–70 (pp. 71–6)

46

a. Horse ramp between the Stables and the Forge in 1970

b. Stables in 1970

KNIGHTSBRIDGE BARRACKS OF 1967–70 (pp. 71–6)

a. Horse ramp, looking east towards Stables in 1970

b. Smithy in 1995

KNIGHTSBRIDGE BARRACKS OF 1967–70 (pp. 71–6)

a. Rose and Crown Yard, High Road, Knightsbridge, in 1857 (p. 79). *Demolished*

b. Tattersalls, Knightsbridge Green front in 1869. Charles Freeman, architect, 1863–5 (p. 89). *Demolished*

a. Auction yard in 1865

b. Subscription room in 1865

c (right). Entrance archway in 1902

TATTERSALLS (p. 89). *Demolished*

a, b. All Saints' School: plans and perspective view, and west front in 1902. Robert Hesketh, architect, 1875 (p. 91)

c. Looking north in 1963

d. Normandie Hotel in 1992. Paul Hoffman, architect, 1910–11 (p. 83)

KNIGHTSBRIDGE GREEN

a (above). Lounge

b (below). Dining-room

NORMANDIE HOTEL: INTERIORS IN 1912 (p. 83)

a (above). North side, Nos 2–11 (right to left), in the early 1900s

b. South side, corner with Knightsbridge Green in 1902

c. Pakenham Tavern in *c*.1875 (p. 91)

RAPHAEL STREET BEFORE REDEVELOPMENT (p. 91)

a, b. Japanese Native Village, Humphreys' Hall, 1885. Buddhist temple and houses (left) and a tea-house (p. 85). *Demolished*

c. Prince's Club, converted from Humphreys' Hall. E. H Bourchier, architect, 1888–9 (p. 86). *Demolished*

54

a (top). Perspective view of the new factory, *c.*1824. W. F. Pocock, architect

b (above left). Drying-room, *c.*1843

c (above right). Exterior in 1973

d (left). Previous factory, as rebuilt after a fire in 1794

FLOORCLOTH MANUFACTORY, TREVOR PLACE (p. 105). *Demolished*

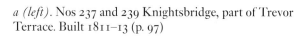

a (left). Nos 237 and 239 Knightsbridge, part of Trevor Terrace. Built 1811–13 (p. 97)

b (below). Trevor Square, east side. Developed *c.*1819–21 (p. 99)

d. No. 38 Trevor Square. Built *c.*1824 (p. 99)

c (left). Trevor Square, west side. Developed *c.*1820–7 (p. 99)

TREVOR SQUARE AREA IN 1992

a. No. 1 Trevor Square (right) and the east side of Trevor Street. Developed *c.*1823 (p. 99)

b. Trevor Street, west side. Developed *c.*1819–23 (p. 99)

c. Trevor Place, south-western side. Developed *c.*1847–52 (p. 101)

TREVOR SQUARE AREA IN 1992

b. Footpath between Raphael Street and Trevor Square in 1939. Prince's Club tennis-court building (p. 86) and back of No. 1 Trevor Square on right

a. Nos 2–8 Trevor Place in 1993. No. 2 (left) built *c*. 1828, Nos 3–8 built 1844–5 (p. 101)

c (left). Former Harrods depot from Trevor Place in 1993. C. W. Stephens and E. J. Munt, architects, 1913–*c*.1920 (p. 103)

58

a. Trevor Estate, unexecuted redevelopment
scheme, 1911 (p. 102)

b. Nos 3–7 Lancelot Place in 1993. Jack E. Dalling,
architect, 1953 (p. 100)

c, d. South Lodge redevelopment in 1992:
houses in Trevor Place (below) and view looking
east from Kent House (p. 134)

a. Bird's-eye view from the barracks tower in 1995

b. South side, built 1826–*c*.1830: looking west in 1993

MONTPELIER SQUARE: developed *c*.1825–53 (pp. 109–16)

a. Nos 6–7 Montpelier Terrace, built 1851–2 (p. 116)

c (below). No. 35 Montpelier Square, built *c*.1849 (p. 114)

b. No. 17A Montpelier Square (right) and Nos 5 and 6 Sterling Street (p. 118)

d (below). The King George IV public house, built *c*.1827, in 1991 (p. 111). *Demolished*

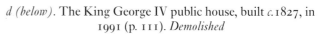

a. No. 17A Montpelier Square, detail of balcony

b (right). Montpelier Place, developed *c*.1828–31, south side in the early 1900s (p. 121)

c (below). Montpelier Street, west side looking north in 1992 (p. 117)

MONTPELIER SQUARE AREA

a, b. No. 1 Montpelier Walk in 1964 (left) and after remodelling by C. Bernard Brown (p. 117)

c (left). No. 30 Montpelier Place in 1995 (p. 122)

d (below). Nos 3–4 Montpelier Terrace in 1992 (p. 117)

MONTPELIER SQUARE AREA

a. No. 1 Montpelier Walk, drawing-room in 1965 (p. 117)

b. No. 23 Montpelier Square, conservatory in 1996 (p. 114)

c. No. 8 Montpelier Square, entrance hall in 1996 (p. 111)

MONTPELIER SQUARE AREA: INTERIORS

a. Architects' perspective view, 1904

b. Exterior in 1991

c. Nave and sanctuary in 1991

DEUTSCHE EVANGELISCHE CHRISTUSKIRCHE, MONTPELIER PLACE. Charles G. F. Rees and
Edward Boehmer, architects, 1904 (p. 124)

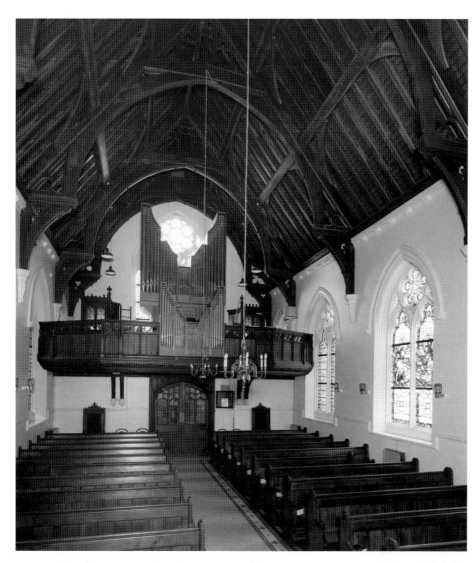

b. Font

a (left). Nave, looking south

c (below left). Ambassador's pew and door to vestry

d (below). View from Meeting Room into Deacon's room

DEUTSCHE EVANGELISCHE CHRISTUSKIRCHE, MONTPELIER PLACE: INTERIORS IN 1991 (pp. 126–7)

a. Exterior in 1908

b. Staircase and landing in 1908

c (above). Dining-room chimneypiece in 1908

d (right). Outer hall in *c*.1913, after remodelling by
Reginald Blomfield

KENT HOUSE, RUTLAND GARDENS. Henry Clutton, architect, 1872–3 (pp. 135–9)

a. Staircase compartment in 1991

b. Hall in 1913

c. Music-room in 1913

KENT HOUSE, RUTLAND GARDENS: INTERIORS. Reginald Blomfield, architect (p. 138)

a. Rutland House and Nos 1 and 2 Rutland Gardens in 1993.
Walker & Elsam, architects, 1872–3 (p. 139)

b. Rutland Lodge in 1993. Frederick Sang, architect, 1872–3
(pp. 139–40)

c. Hall and staircase at Rutland House *c*.1906 (p. 139)

RUTLAND GARDENS

a. South Lodge, gate-keeper's lodge and entrance gates in 1896. Boulnois & Warner, architects, *c*.1893 (p. 131).
Lodge demolished

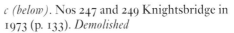

b (left). South Lodge in 1967 (p. 130). *Demolished*

c (below). Nos 247 and 249 Knightsbridge in 1973 (p. 133). *Demolished*

SOUTH LODGE AREA

a. Salon (p. 132)

b. Eastern Room. H. & J. Cooper, decorators, 1883 (pp. 132–3)

SOUTH LODGE: INTERIORS IN 1902. *Demolished*

SOUTH LODGE. Drawing-room in 1902 (p. 132). *Demolished*

72

a. North front in 1833

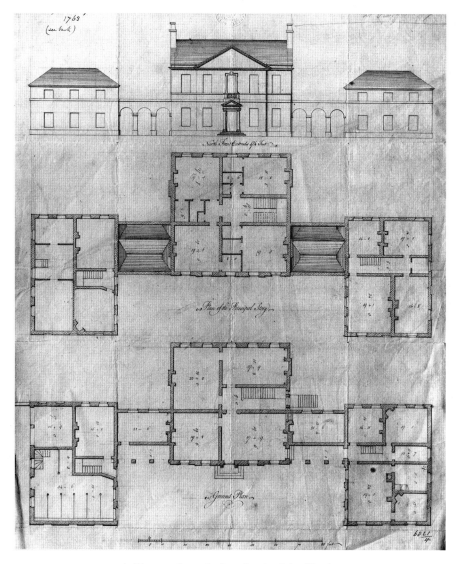

b. Plans and north elevation by John Vardy

RUTLAND HOUSE. John Vardy, architect, 1752–3 (pp. 143–4). *Demolished*

a. Nos 1–7 (odd) Rutland Gate and gate-keeper's lodge in 1946. *Lodge demolished*

b. Bird's-eye view looking south-west in 1995

RUTLAND GATE (pp. 141–56)

a. Nos 3–7 (odd), built 1837

b. Nos 10–20 (even), built 1838

c. No. 24, Park House, built 1841 for John Sheepshanks (pp. 149–51)

UPPER RUTLAND GATE in 1992–3 (pp. 144–9)

75

a. West side, looking north in the early 1900s

c. Clock House in 1992. Remodelled by A. Blomfield, architect, in early 1960s (p. 156)

b (left). Nos 45–47 in 1998

LOWER RUTLAND GATE. Developed by John Elger, 1853–9 (pp. 151–2)

The former roof garden at No. 64 Rutland Gate, looking north (top) and south in 1913 (p. 153)

a. Nos 4–8A. Francis Lorne, architect, 1936–7 (p. 154). Original No. 2 on right. *All demolished*

b. Nos 43–44. Walter and Eva Segal, architects, 1955–8 (p. 153)

c. No. 15. Leslie Sacks and Partners, architects, 1968–70 (p. 153)

RUTLAND GATE: REDEVELOPMENTS

78

b. Princes Gate Mews in 1998 (p. 194)

c (left). Montpelier Mews in 1996 (p. 118)

d (right). Ennismore Mews in 1993 (p. 166)

Mews

a. Rutland Gardens Mews in 1993 (p. 133)

a. No. 1 Ennismore Street in 1922 (p. 167)

b. Kent Yard in 1993 (p. 140)

c. Gate Mews in 1992 (p. 153)

d, e. Ennismore Gardens Mews in the early 1900s (left) and east entrance in 1993 (p. 173)

MEWS

79

80

b. Conservatory

a (above left). Kensington Road front

c (left). Garden front: on the left is the Regency saloon built over the west service wing

KINGSTON HOUSE IN 1937. Built for Elizabeth Chudleigh in 1757–8 (pp. 159–60). *Demolished*

b. Saloon

a (above left). Staircase

c (left). Kitchen

d (right). Chimneypiece in saloon

KINGSTON HOUSE: INTERIORS IN 1937. *Demolished*

82

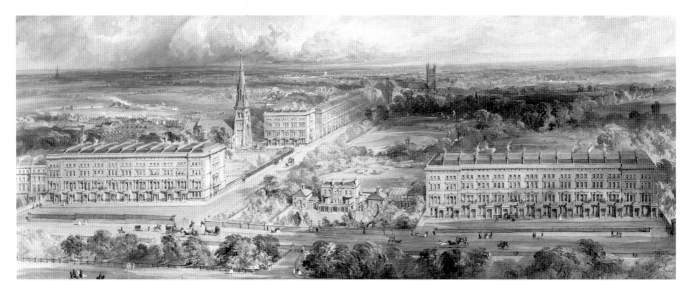

a. Kingston House Estate: panoramic view by Thomas Allom of proposed development, *c*.1845 (p. 160)

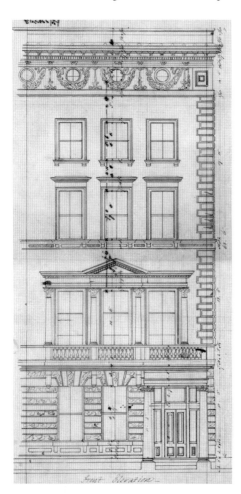

c (above). Nos 18–24 in 1993. John Elger, builder, 1848–51

b (above left). Design by H. L. Elmes for No. 14, *c*.1845–6

d (left). Detail of frieze at No. 14

PRINCES GATE (pp. 162–6)

a. Garden front, design by H. L. Elmes, *c*.1845–6

b. Nos 10 (right) and 11, rear view in the early 1900s. John Kelk, builder, 1849–51. *Demolished*

c. Garden fronts of Nos 14–16 (formerly Nos 13–16) in 1998. John Elger, builder, 1846–9

PRINCES GATE (pp. 162–6)

a. Nos 61–64 in 1998. G. W. Mayhew, builder, 1847–9 (p. 163)

b. Nos 45–50 in 1938. John Elger, builder, 1849–54 (p. 163)

c. Aerial view in 1947, looking north-west to Princes Gardens

ENNISMORE GARDENS

a. Nos 1–9, built 1868–71. Garden front in 1992

b. West side, built 1871–4. Looking north in the early 1900s, to Nos 70 and 69 (pp. 180–2)

ENNISMORE GARDENS. Peter and Alexander Thorn, developers, 1868–74 (pp. 171–4)

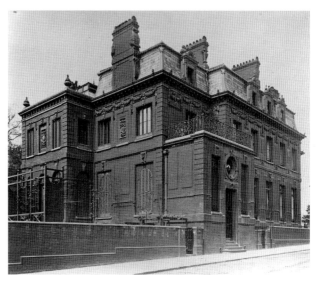

b. Looking north-west in the 1870s

a (left). Preliminary design, *c*.1868

c. Perspective view from north-east, exhibited 1872

ALFORD HOUSE. Sir Matthew Digby Wyatt, architect, 1869–72 (pp. 175–7). *Demolished*

b. Alford House, inner hall in 1931 (p. 177)

a. Alford House, fountain room in 1931. Harriet Hosmer, sculptress (p. 177)

c (right). Bolney House in 1946. Richard Norman Shaw, architect, 1883–5 (p. 179)

d (left). Bolney House, front (west) elevation, 1883

ALFORD HOUSE INTERIORS AND BOLNEY HOUSE. *Demolished*

88

a. Moncorvo House, perspective view. J. Macvicar Anderson, architect, 1878–80 (pp. 177–9)

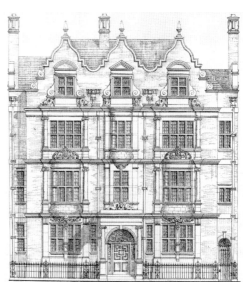

c. No. 70 Ennismore Gardens, Basil Champneys, architect, 1884–5 (p. 181)

b. Moncorvo House in 1888. On the left the 'ornamental' flank wall of No. 67 Ennismore Gardens (p. 180)

MONCORVO HOUSE AND NO. 70 ENNISMORE GARDENS. *Both demolished*

a. Saloon in *c*.1914–18

b (right). Reception room in 1933

c. Drawing-room in 1933

Moncorvo House: Interiors (p. 178). *Demolished*

a, b. Exterior *c.*1904 (below) and (right) after refronting in 1925–6

c. Ambassador's Ballroom in 1938

NO. 14 PRINCES GATE (pp. 167–9)

a. French Drawing Room in 1938

b, c. Circular Hall: looking east to the staircase in 1938
(above), and west in 1998

No. 14 Princes Gate: Interiors

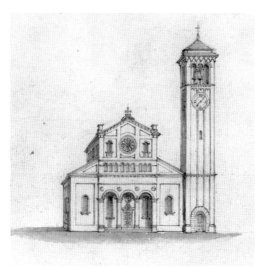

a, b, d. West front: original drawing by Vulliamy
(above), perspective of the remodelling by
C. Harrison Townsend, 1891 (right), and view
in 1928 (below right)

c. Elevated view from the south-east in 1950s

FORMER ALL SAINTS' CHURCH, ENNISMORE GARDENS, now Russian Orthodox Cathedral. Lewis Vulliamy, architect,
1846–9 (pp. 186–90)

a. Nave, looking east in 1956

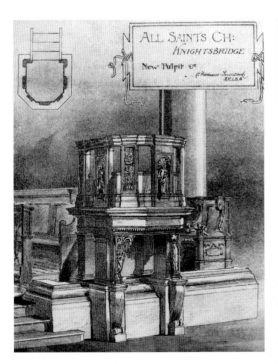

b. Pulpit, drawing of 1889 (p. 188)

c (right). Nave, looking west in 1956

FORMER ALL SAINTS' CHURCH, ENNISMORE GARDENS

a. Chancel arch and east end in 1956

b. Monument to William Wilson; F. Derwent Wood, sculptor, *c*.1910 (p. 190)

FORMER ALL SAINTS' CHURCH, ENNISMORE GARDENS

a. Nos 26–31, built 1856–7, in 1993

b. Nos 30–31, Exhibition Road corner, in 1993

c. Looking south along Exhibition Road from No. 32 in *c*.1900. *Nos 32–43 demolished*

PRINCES GATE: HOUSES BUILT BY C. J. FREAKE (pp. 191–6)

a. Nos 49–58, built *c*.1868–75. Exhibition Road front in 1968

b. Nos 49–50, Princes Gardens front in 1992

c. No. 48, built *c*.1860. Princes Gardens front in 1992

PRINCES GATE: HOUSES BUILT BY C. J. FREAKE

a. North side, built 1859–61. Looking west in 1938 (p. 192). *All except Nos 8–15 demolished*

b. Nos 8–15, garden front in 1998 (p. 196)

c (right). No. 15 and (right) Weeks Hall (p. 208)

PRINCES GARDENS. C. J. FREAKE, builder, 1859–66

a. Hall, looking south-west in 1892 (p. 199)

b. Hall, looking south-west in 1919 (p. 203)

No. 49 Princes Gate

No. 49 Princes Gate in 1892. Enfilade through drawing-rooms looking west (p. 202)

a. East drawing-room looking south-west (p. 202)

b. Morning room (Tapestry room) looking south-east (p. 202)

No. 49 Princes Gate in 1892

b (above). After remodelling in 1905 (p. 203)

a (above left). Looking south in 1892

c (left). In 1992 (p. 204)

No. 49 Princes Gate: The Peacock Room (pp. 199–202)

a, *b*. Hall (above) and staircase

c. Library

No. 26 Princes Gate: Interiors in 1894 (p. 197)

a. No. 19, drawing-room in the 1860s, during the occupancy of Lord Dinevor (p. 197). *Demolished*

b. No. 6, drawing-room in the 1920s (p. 198). *Demolished*

PRINCES GARDENS: INTERIORS

a. No. 52, dining-room chimneypiece designed by G. Aitchison (p. 205)

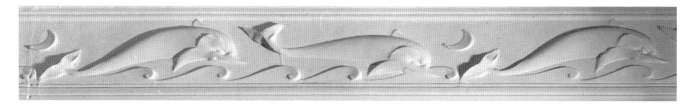

b. No. 52, frieze in front drawing-room (p. 205)

d. No. 53, boudoir chimneypiece

c (left). No. 52, boudoir chimneypiece (p. 205)

Nos 52 and 53 Princes Gate: Details

a (right). No. 53, brackets to first-floor landing (p. 197)

b, c (below). No. 58, staircase balustrade and over-door mouldings in hall (p. 198)

d. No. 49, the Northumberland House staircase balustrade (p. 199)

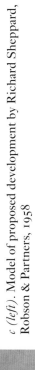

b. Southside in 1963

c (left). Model of proposed development by Richard Sheppard,
Robson & Partners, 1958

PRINCES GARDENS: IMPERIAL COLLEGE (pp. 207–9)

a (above). Linstead
Hall (left) and
Southside in 1968

a. Linstead Hall, extension building. Norman & Dawbarn, architects, 1978–80

b (*above right*). Southside, refectory in 1963

c (*right*). Weeks Hall, assembly room in 1959

PRINCES GARDENS: IMPERIAL COLLEGE

108

ERESBY HOUSE, RUTLAND GATE. T. P. Bennett & Son, architects, 1933–4 (p. 153). Exterior from the south-west in 1936: main entrance, carved panel (by E. Aumonier), and entrance hall in 1992

a. North front looking south–east in 1992

b, c. No. 7, lift and entrance hall in 1998

NOS 1–7 PRINCES GATE. Septimus Warwick, architect, 1937–49; No. 6 by Turner Lansdown Holt & Partners, 1972–4 (pp. 182–4)

b. Kingston House North, garden front in 1993. Michael Rosenauer, architect, 1937
(p. 185)

1930s FLATS

a. Nos 59–63 Princes Gate in 1938. Adie, Button and Partners, architects, 1937–8
(p. 206)

a, b. Nos 59–63 Princes Gate in 1937–8. View into living-room from hallway, and (top right) main entrance hall (p. 207)

c (right). Cecil Beaton's flat at No. 12 Rutland Court, 1936 (p. 142)

1930s INTERIORS

Knightsbridge, bird's-eye view looking east from the barracks tower in 1995. Bowater House, centre left, Harvey Nichols, centre right, Sheraton Park Tower Hotel, behind

COLOUR PLATES

114

a. Albert Gate as intended in 1841: perspective view prepared for submission to the Queen (p. 48)

b. Nos 14–24 Princes Gate, garden front in 1998 (p. 165)

c. Nos 1–7 Princes Gate, garden front in 1998 (pp. 182–4)

a, b. Knightsbridge Barracks: Peninsular Tower in 1992 (p. 75) and main gate in 1982 (p. 75)

c (above). Mandarin Oriental Hyde Park, part of Knightsbridge front in 1998 (p. 57)

d (right). Parkside, Hyde Park front in 1996 (p. 42)

116

a. Entrance Hall and Staircase (p. 57)

MANDARIN ORIENTAL HYDE
PARK: INTERIORS IN 1998

c (below). Restaurant (p. 58)

b (left). Upper lobby (p. 57)

a, b. No. 14 Rutland Gate, staircase and first floor looking west in 1992. Eva Jiricna, architect (p. 153)

c, d. Knightsbridge Barracks, ante-room (left) and dining-room in Officers' Mess in 1995 (pp. 75–6)

a *(above)*. No. 14 Princes Gate, chimneypiece in former French Drawing Room (p. 168)

c, d. Kent House (Westminster Synagogue): chimneypiece in old library, and (right) the Ark of the Covenant (pp. 137, 138)

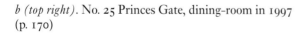

b *(top right)*. No. 25 Princes Gate, dining-room in 1997 (p. 170)

b. Reception Hall at No. 14 in 1998 (p. 169)

a (left). Drawing-room at No. 25 in 1997 (p. 170)

c. Entrance hall at No. 58 in 1991 (p. 198)

PRINCES GATE INTERIORS

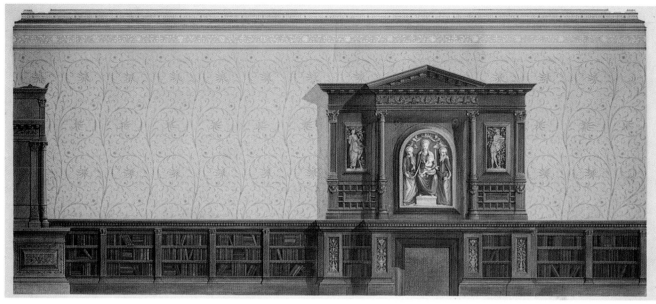

a. Dining-room, drawing exhibited in 1878

No. 52 Princes Gate. Interior decoration by G. Aitchison, 1876–8 (pp. 204–5)

a. No. 52, dado in rear drawing-room

b (right). No. 52, sliding doors between drawing-rooms

c (below). No. 52, De Morgan tiles, boudoir chimneypiece

Opposite page
b, c. Boudoir, drawings exhibited in 1877
d, e. Boudoir in 1998, and detail of dado

d. No. 53, Minton tiling in hall (p. 197)

Nos 52 and 53 Princes Gate: Interiors

a, b. Interior in 1991, looking east towards the iconostasis, and (top) the sgraffito decoration over the chancel arch (pp. 189, 190)

RUSSIAN ORTHODOX CATHEDRAL, ENNISMORE GARDENS, formerly All Saints' Church

RUSSIAN ORTHODOX CATHEDRAL, ENNISMORE GARDENS. Sgraffito decoration by Heywood Sumner (p. 189)

a (above).
Wheel window

c (below). Apse

b. Clerestory (top) and west front

RUSSIAN ORTHODOX CATHEDRAL, ENNISMORE GARDENS. Stained glass (p. 189)

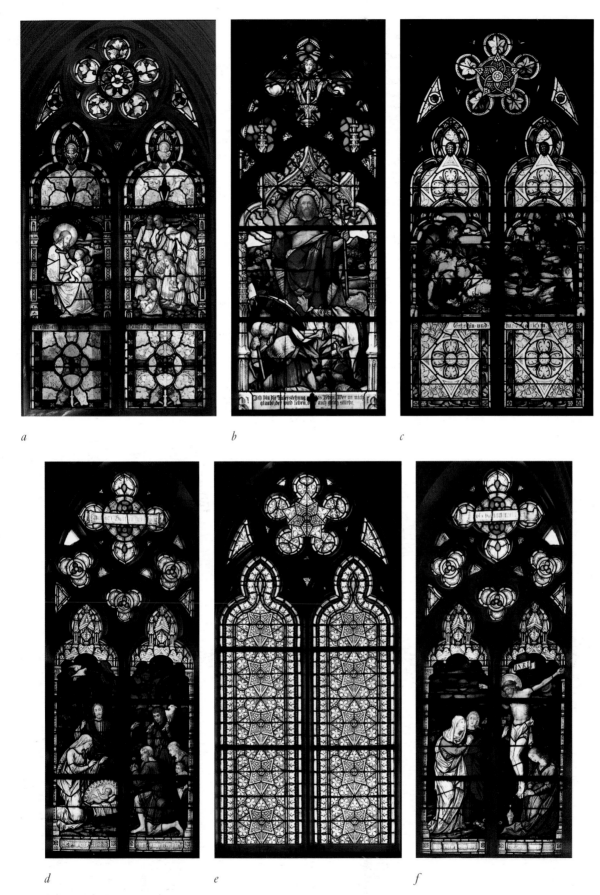

a   *b*   *c*

d   *e*   *f*

DEUTSCHE EVANGELISCHE CHRISTUSKIRCHE, Montpelier Place. Stained and painted glass (p. 126)

a. The Chinese Collection at the Celestial Palace in Albert Gate, 1851 (p. 52). *Demolished*

b. The Peacock Room from No. 49 Princes Gate as reassembled in the Freer Gallery, Washington, DC.
Thomas Jeckyll, designer, J. M. Whistler, decorator (pp. 199–202)